Connected Mathematics™

UNIT	STRAND
Thinking with Mathematical Models *Representing Relationships*	Algebra
Looking for Pythagoras *The Pythagorean Theorem*	Geometry
Growing, Growing, Growing *Exponential Relationships*	Algebra
Frogs, Fleas, and Painted Cubes *Quadratic Relationships*	Algebra
Say It with Symbols *Algebraic Reasoning*	Algebra
Kaleidoscopes, Hubcaps, and Mirrors *Symmetry and Transformations*	Geometry
Samples and Populations *Data and Statistics*	Data Analysis and Probability
Clever Counting *Combinatorics*	Number and Operations

Glenda Lappan James T. Fey
William M. Fitzgerald Susan N. Friel
Elizabeth Difanis Phillips

PEARSON
Prentice Hall

Glenview, Illinois
Needham, Massachusetts
Upper Saddle River, New Jersey

Connected Mathematics™ was developed at Michigan State University with the support of National Science Foundation Grant No. MDR 9150217.

This project was supported, in part, by the
National Science Foundation
Opinions expressed are those of the authors and not necessarily those of the Foundation

The Michigan State University authors and administration have agreed that all MSU royalties arising from this publication will be devoted to purposes supported by the Department of Mathematics and the MSU Mathematics Education Enrichment Fund.

PEARSON
Prentice Hall

ISBN 0-13-180835-4
1 2 3 4 5 6 7 8 9 10 07 06 05 04 03

The Connected Mathematics Project Staff

Project Directors

James T. Fey
University of Maryland

William M. Fitzgerald
Michigan State University

Susan N. Friel
University of North Carolina at Chapel Hill

Glenda Lappan
Michigan State University

Elizabeth Difanis Phillips
Michigan State University

Project Manager

Kathy Burgis
Michigan State University

Technical Coordinator

Judith Martus Miller
Michigan State University

Curriculum Development Consultants

David Ben-Chaim
Weizmann Institute

Alex Friedlander
Weizmann Institute

Eleanor Geiger
University of Maryland

Jane Mitchell
University of North Carolina at Chapel Hill

Anthony D. Rickard
Alma College

Collaborating Teachers/Writers

Mary K. Bouck
Portland, Michigan

Jacqueline Stewart
Okemos, Michigan

Graduate Assistants

Scott J. Baldridge
Michigan State University

Angie S. Eshelman
Michigan State University

M. Faaiz Gierdien
Michigan State University

Jane M. Keiser
Indiana University

Angela S. Krebs
Michigan State University

James M. Larson
Michigan State University

Ronald Preston
Indiana University

Tat Ming Sze
Michigan State University

Sarah Theule-Lubienski
Michigan State University

Jeffrey J. Wanko
Michigan State University

Evaluation Team

Mark Hoover
Michigan State University

Diane V. Lambdin
Indiana University

Sandra K. Wilcox
Michigan State University

Judith S. Zawojewski
National-Louis University

Teacher/Assessment Team

Kathy Booth
Waverly, Michigan

Anita Clark
Marshall, Michigan

Julie Faulkner
Traverse City, Michigan

Theodore Gardella
Bloomfield Hills, Michigan

Yvonne Grant
Portland, Michigan

Linda R. Lobue
Vista, California

Suzanne McGrath
Chula Vista, California

Nancy McIntyre
Troy, Michigan

Mary Beth Schmitt
Traverse City, Michigan

Linda Walker
Tallahassee, Florida

Software Developer

Richard Burgis
East Lansing, Michigan

Development Center Directors

Nicholas Branca
San Diego State University

Dianne Briars
Pittsburgh Public Schools

Frances R. Curcio
New York University

Perry Lanier
Michigan State University

J. Michael Shaughnessy
Portland State University

Charles Vonder Embse
Central Michigan University

Special thanks to the students and teachers at these pilot schools!

Baker Demonstration School
Evanston, Illinois
Bertha Vos Elementary School
Traverse City, Michigan
Blair Elementary School
Traverse City, Michigan
Bloomfield Hills Middle School
Bloomfield Hills, Michigan
Brownell Elementary School
Flint, Michigan
Catlin Gabel School
Portland, Oregon
Cherry Knoll Elementary School
Traverse City, Michigan
Cobb Middle School
Tallahassee, Florida
Courtade Elementary School
Traverse City, Michigan
Duke School for Children
Durham, North Carolina
DeVeaux Junior High School
Toledo, Ohio
East Junior High School
Traverse City, Michigan
Eastern Elementary School
Traverse City, Michigan
Eastlake Elementary School
Chula Vista, California
Eastwood Elementary School
Sturgis, Michigan
Elizabeth City Middle School
Elizabeth City, North Carolina
Franklinton Elementary School
Franklinton, North Carolina
Frick International Studies Academy
Pittsburgh, Pennsylvania
Gundry Elementary School
Flint, Michigan
Hawkins Elementary School
Toledo, Ohio
Hilltop Middle School
Chula Vista, California
Holmes Middle School
Flint, Michigan
Interlochen Elementary School
Traverse City, Michigan
Los Altos Elementary School
San Diego, California
Louis Armstrong Middle School
East Elmhurst, New York
McTigue Junior High School
Toledo, Ohio
National City Middle School
National City, California
Norris Elementary School
Traverse City, Michigan
Northeast Middle School
Minneapolis, Minnesota
Oak Park Elementary School
Traverse City, Michigan
Old Mission Elementary School
Traverse City, Michigan
Old Orchard Elementary School
Toledo, Ohio
Portland Middle School
Portland, Michigan
Reizenstein Middle School
Pittsburgh, Pennsylvania
Sabin Elementary School
Traverse City, Michigan
Shepherd Middle School
Shepherd, Michigan
Sturgis Middle School
Sturgis, Michigan
Terrell Lane Middle School
Louisburg, North Carolina
Tierra del Sol Middle School
Lakeside, California
Traverse Heights Elementary School
Traverse City, Michigan
University Preparatory Academy
Seattle, Washington
Washington Middle School
Vista, California
Waverly East Intermediate School
Lansing, Michigan
Waverly Middle School
Lansing, Michigan
West Junior High School
Traverse City, Michigan
Willow Hill Elementary School
Traverse City, Michigan

Thinking with Mathematical Models

Representing Relationships

Looking for Pythagoras

The Pythagorean Theorem

Growing Growing, Growing

Exponential Relationships

Frogs, Fleas, and Painted Cubes

Quadratic Relationships

Say It with Symbols

Algebraic Reasoning

Kaleidoscopes, Hubcaps, and Mirrors

Symmetry and Transformations

Samples and Populations

Data and Statistics

Clever Counting

Combinatorics

Connected Mathematics™

Thinking with Mathematical Models

Representing Relationships

Student Edition

Glenda Lappan
James T. Fey
William M. Fitzgerald
Susan N. Friel
Elizabeth Difanis Phillips

PEARSON
Prentice Hall

Glenview, Illinois
Needham, Massachusetts
Upper Saddle River, New Jersey

Thinking with Mathematical Models

Connected Mathematics™ was developed at Michigan State University with the support of National Science Foundation Grant No. MDR 9150217.

This project was supported, in part, by the
National Science Foundation
Opinions expressed are those of the authors and not necessarily those of the Foundation

The Michigan State University authors and administration have agreed that all MSU royalties arising from this publication will be devoted to purposes supported by the Department of Mathematics and the MSU Mathematics Education Enrichment Fund.

Photo Acknowledgements: 5 © Ron Sanford/Tony Stone Images; 23 © Owen Franken/Stock, Boston; 27 © Frank Siteman/Stock, Boston; 41 © Joseph Schuyler/Stock, Boston; 45 © Lionel Delevingne/Stock, Boston; 47 © Bert Sagara/Tony Stone Images; 54 (Big Ben) © George Hunter/Tony Stone Images; 54 (Eiffel Tower) © John Lawrence/Tony Stone Images

Contents

Thinking with Mathematical Models

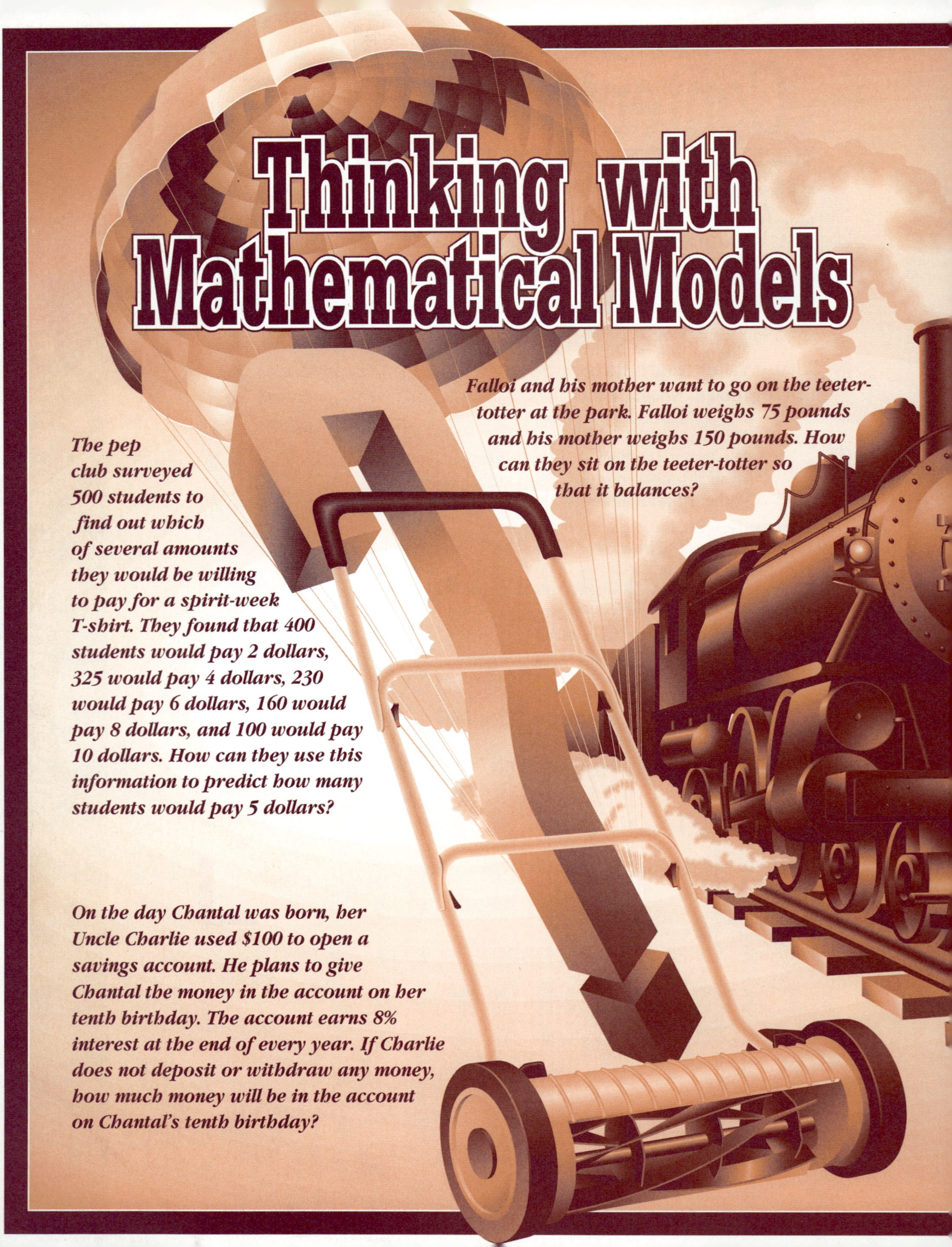

Falloi and his mother want to go on the teeter-totter at the park. Falloi weighs 75 pounds and his mother weighs 150 pounds. How can they sit on the teeter-totter so that it balances?

The pep club surveyed 500 students to find out which of several amounts they would be willing to pay for a spirit-week T-shirt. They found that 400 students would pay 2 dollars, 325 would pay 4 dollars, 230 would pay 6 dollars, 160 would pay 8 dollars, and 100 would pay 10 dollars. How can they use this information to predict how many students would pay 5 dollars?

On the day Chantal was born, her Uncle Charlie used $100 to open a savings account. He plans to give Chantal the money in the account on her tenth birthday. The account earns 8% interest at the end of every year. If Charlie does not deposit or withdraw any money, how much money will be in the account on Chantal's tenth birthday?

People in many professions make important predictions every day. Sometimes millions of dollars, and often people's lives, depend on the accuracy of these predictions. A company may develop a wonderful new product, but without accurate predictions about the number and location of potential customers and the price they would be willing to pay, the company could lose a great deal of money. When designing a bridge, a civil engineer must make accurate predictions about how much weight the bridge can hold and about how it will stand up to strong winds and earthquakes. People often use mathematical models to help them make such predictions. People construct mathematical models by gathering data about a situation and then finding a graph or equation that fits the data.

In this unit, you will find mathematical models for many situations, and you will use your models to answer interesting questions like those on the previous page.

Mathematical Highlights

In *Thinking with Mathematical Models* you will extend your work with linear relations and begin exploring some important non-linear relationships. The unit should help you to

- Collect data from experiments and display that data in tables and coordinate graphs;
- Construct equations in the form $y = mx + b$ to express linear patterns that appear in data tables and graphs;
- Recognize non-linear patterns in tables and graphs and describe those patterns using ideas about rate of change, slope, and intercepts;
- Identify variables that are inversely related to each other; and
- Interpret the shapes of graphs that model various problem situations and use graph sketches to express relationships among variables.

As you work on the problems of this unit, make it a habit to ask questions about problem situations that involve related quantities: *How could I collect data from an experiment to learn how the variables are related? How could I express given data in graphic form to display and detect patterns? Is the relation between given variables linear, inverse, or some other type of non-linear pattern? If a relation between variables looks linear, what equation would express that relation in symbolic form? What does the pattern of the given graph tell about the relationship between variables of interest in this situation?*

INVESTIGATION 1

Linear Models

Most bridges are built with frames of steel beams. Steel is very strong, but if you put enough weight on any beam, it will bend or break. The amount of weight a beam can support is related to its thickness and design. To design a bridge, engineers need to understand these relationships thoroughly. Engineers often use scale models to test the strength of their bridge designs.

1.1 Testing Paper Bridges

In this problem, you will do an experiment to test some of the principles involved in building bridges.

Equipment: several 11-inch-by-4-inch strips of paper, two books of the same thickness, a small paper cup, and about 50 pennies

Directions:

- Make a paper "bridge" by folding up 1 inch on each long side of one of the paper strips.

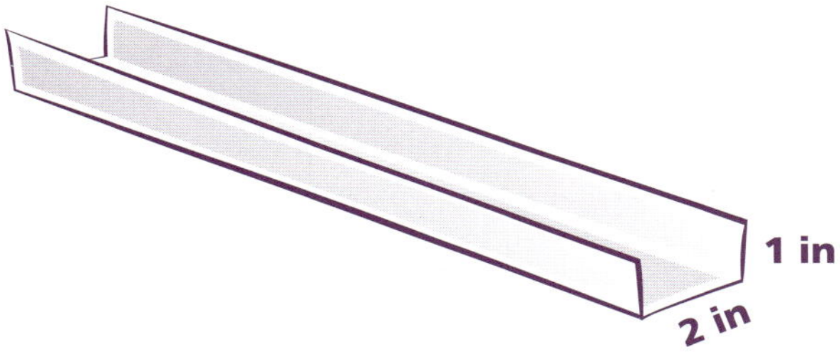

- Suspend the bridge between the two books. The bridge should overlap each book by about 1 inch. Place the paper cup in the center of the bridge.
- Put pennies into the cup, one at a time, until the bridge crumples. Record the number of pennies you added to the cup. This number is the *breaking weight* of the bridge.

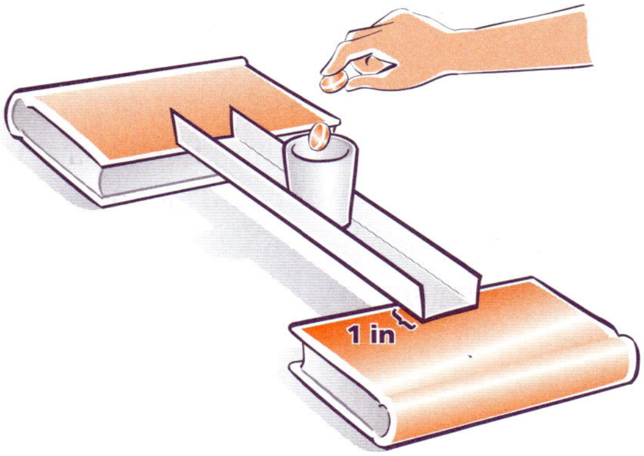

- Put two strips together to make a bridge of double thickness. Find the breaking weight for this bridge. Repeat this experiment to find breaking weights for bridges made from three, four, and five strips of paper.

Problem 1.1

A. Do the experiment described above to find breaking weights for bridges 1, 2, 3, 4, and 5 layers thick.

B. Make a table and a graph of your data.

C. Describe the pattern of change in the data. Then, use the pattern to predict the breaking weights for bridges 6 and 7 layers thick.

D. Suppose you could use half-layers of paper to build the bridges. What breaking weights would you predict for bridges 2.5 layers thick and 3.5 layers thick?

Problem 1.1 Follow-Up

How would you expect your results to change if you used a stronger material, such as poster board or balsa wood, to make your bridges?

1.2 Drawing Graph Models

A class in Maryland did the bridge-thickness experiment. They combined the results from all the groups and found the average breaking weight for each bridge. They organized their data in a table.

Thickness (layers)	1	2	3	4	5
Breaking weight (pennies)	10	14	23	37	42

The class then made a graph of the data. They thought the pattern looked somewhat linear, so they drew a line to show this trend. This line is a good *model* for the relationship because, for the thicknesses the class tested, the points on the line are close to points from the experiment.

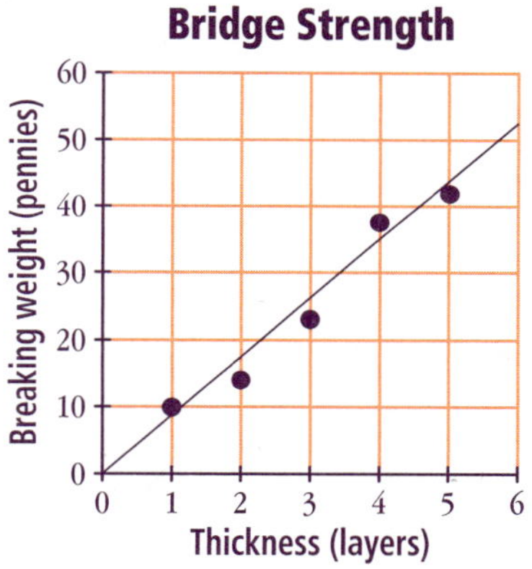

The line that the Maryland class drew is a graph model for their data. A **graph model** is a straight line or a curve that shows a trend in a set of data. Once you fit a graph model to a set of data, you can use it to make predictions about values between and beyond the values in your data.

Did you know?

When designing a bridge, engineers need to consider the *load,* or the amount of weight the bridge must support. The *dead load* is the permanent weight of the bridge and fixed objects on the bridge. The *live load* is the weight of moving objects on the bridge. On many metropolitan bridges in Europe—such as the famous Ponte Vecchio in Florence, Italy—dead load can become extremely high as tollbooths, apartments, and even miniature shopping districts are built right onto the surface of the bridge. Live load can usually be controlled by limiting the amount of rail or automobile traffic on the bridge at one time.

Problem 1.2

A. Draw a straight line that seems to fit the pattern in the (thickness, breaking weight) data you graphed in Problem 1.1.

B. Based on your graph model, what breaking weights would you predict for bridges 6 layers thick and 7 layers thick?

C. Suppose you could use half-layers of paper to build the bridges. What breaking weights would you predict for bridges 2.5 layers thick and 3.5 layers thick?

Problem 1.2 Follow-Up

1. It is unlikely that your (thickness, breaking weight) data fit a linear pattern exactly. Below are two students' attempts to draw lines to model their group's data.

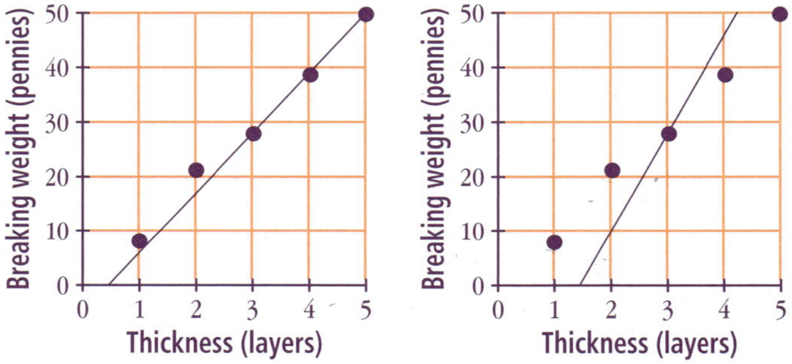

a. Which graph model would allow the students to make better predictions about breaking weights for bridges of different thicknesses? Why?

b. Do you have any suggestions for how the students could change the graph model you chose in part a to help them make even better predictions?

2. For each graph on Labsheet 1.2, try to find a graph model that fits the experimental data as closely as possible. Compare your graph models with those drawn by others in your group. What strategies did you use to help you draw an appropriate graph model?

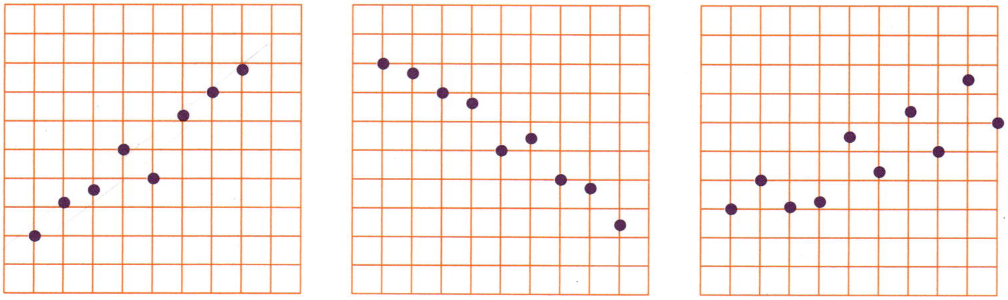

1.3 Finding Equation Models

In your earlier work, you saw that linear relationships can be described by equations of the form $y = mx + b$, where m is the slope, and b is the y-intercept. The line drawn to model the data in the Maryland students' bridge-thickness experiment is shown below. By looking at the graph and comparing vertical change to horizontal change, the students found that the slope of the line is about 8.7. Since the line passes through the origin, its y-intercept is 0. They wrote the equation $y = 8.7x$ to represent the line.

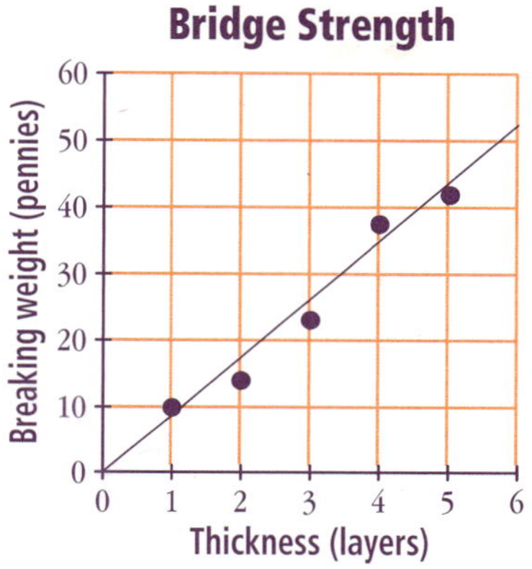

Because the equation and the line represent the same information, the equation is also a model of the pattern in the data. This means that you can show the trend in the bridge-thickness data by using a *graph model* or an *equation model.*

Problem 1.3

Use a graphing calculator to explore the equation $y = 8.7x$.

A. Make a table of (x, y) data for $y = 8.7x$, using the x values 0, 1, 2, 3, . . . , 10. Explain how the entries in your table relate to the fact that $m = 8.7$ and $b = 0$.

B. Make a graph of $y = 8.7x$ for $x = 0$ to $x = 10$. Explain how the slope and the y-intercept of the graph are related to the equation.

C. What do the facts that $m = 8.7$ and $b = 0$ mean in terms of bridge thickness and breaking weight?

D. Solve the equation $60 = 8.7x$. What does the solution tell you about bridge thickness and breaking weight?

■ **Problem 1.3 Follow-Up**

1. Find a linear equation for the graph model from your bridge-thickness experiment. What do the values of m and b in your equation tell you about the graph and about the relationship between bridge thickness and breaking weight for the paper you used?

2. A group in Ms. Hollister's class finds that the equation model $y = 5.5x$ fits their bridge-thickness data. The group conjectures that if they repeat the experiment with cardboard, the relationship will be modeled by $y = 4(5.5x)$.
   a. What is this group's conjecture about the strength of cardboard?
   b. Is $y = 5.5(4x)$ equivalent to $y = 4(5.5x)$? Is $y = 22x$ equivalent to $y = 4(5.5x)$? Give evidence to support your answers.

1.4 Setting the Right Price

To raise money for a local charity, the Student Government Association (SGA) at Kennedy High decides to sell spirit-week baseball caps embroidered with the school mascot. The caps are being donated by a local merchant. The SGA must figure out how many caps to order and how much to charge for each cap.

Think about this!

What advice would you give the SGA to help them decide how many caps to order and how much to charge for each cap?

To help with their project, the SGA conducts a market-research study. They ask 500 students in their school which of the following amounts they would be willing to pay for a baseball cap: \$2, \$4, \$6, \$8, \$10, \$12. The results are shown in the table below.

Price (dollars)	2	4	6	8	10	12
Number of buyers	400	325	230	160	100	25

The SGA can use the pattern in the (price, buyers) data to make some predictions.

Problem 1.4

A. Graph the (price, buyers) data, and draw a straight line that models the trend in the data.

B. Write a linear equation of the form $y = mx + b$ for your graph model.

C. What do the patterns of change in the (price, buyers) data and the graph model tell you about the relationship between the price and the number of buyers?

D. What do the values of m and b in the equation model tell you about the relationship between the price and the number of buyers?

E. Which data pair from the survey data is farthest from your graph model? Why do you think this point is so far from the graph?

Problem 1.4 Follow-Up

The SGA wrote the equation $y = {}^{-}40x + 480$ to fit their (price, buyers) data. In this equation, x represents the price, and y represents the number of buyers.

1. What do the numbers $^{-}40$ and 480 in the equation tell you about the relationship between the price and the number of buyers? What do they tell you about the graph of the relationship?

2. Although the SGA gathered data for only a few prices, they can use their equation model to make a table with information for many more prices.

a. Make a table like the one below. In the second column, enter the number of buyers the equation model $y = {}^{-}40x + 480$ predicts for each whole-number price from \$2 to \$15.

Price	Number of buyers	Income
\$2	400	
3	360	
4		
.		
.		
.		

b. Which data pair from the survey is most different from the prediction made by the equation model? Are any predictions the same as the survey data?

c. In the third column, enter the income the SGA would earn from each combination of price and buyers.

3. How much should the SGA charge for each cap if they want the maximum possible income? Explain your answer.

4. Make a graph of the (price, income) data. Describe the shape of your graph. How is your answer to question 3 shown on your graph?

1.5 Writing Equations for Lines

Linear equations will not model every relationship you explore. However, you can use them to model relationships in many different situations. For example, Denise and Jonah earn allowances for mowing their lawns each week.

- Denise's father pays her $5 each week.
- Jonah's mother paid him $20 at the beginning of the summer and now pays him $3 each week.

The graphs of the relationships between the number of weeks and the dollars earned are shown below. The graphs were made by plotting points for several values and then fitting lines. Why do you think the lines fit the data points exactly?

Problem 1.5

A. Which graph model shows Jonah's earnings as a function of the number of weeks? In other words, which shows how Jonah's earnings relate to the number of weeks? Which graph model shows Denise's earnings? Explain how you know which graph is which.

B. Write linear equations of the form $y = mx + b$ to show the relationships between Denise's and Jonah's earnings and the number of weeks.

C. What do the values of m and b in each equation tell you about the relationship between the number of weeks and the dollars earned? What do the values of m and b tell you about each graph model?

Problem 1.5 Follow-Up

Many problems require you to find a linear equation that matches a pattern in a graph or a table. You know that in a linear equation of the form $y = mx + b$, m is the slope of the line and b is the y-intercept. If you are given the slope and the y-intercept, or if you can read them from a graph or a table, finding an equation is easy. However, finding the slope and the y-intercept often requires a bit of work.

1. How would you find an equation for the line with slope 1.5 that passes through the point (5, 9.5)? Because the slope is the value of m in $y = mx + b$, you know that the equation is of the form $y = 1.5x + b$. But how can you find b?

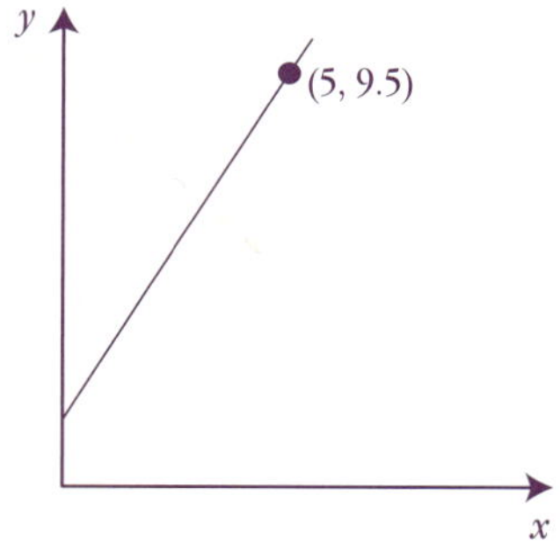

a. Substitute 5 for x and 9.5 for y in the equation $y = 1.5x + b$. Solve for b, and explain what the result tells you about the line. Use your result to help you write an equation for the line.

b. Use your reasoning from part a to find the equation of the line with slope 3 that passes through the point (2, 5).

2. a. Modify the reasoning you used in question 1 to find an equation for the line that passes through the points (2, 1) and (7, 11).

b. Use the reasoning you used in part a to find an equation for the line that passes through the points (1, 8) and (4, 2).

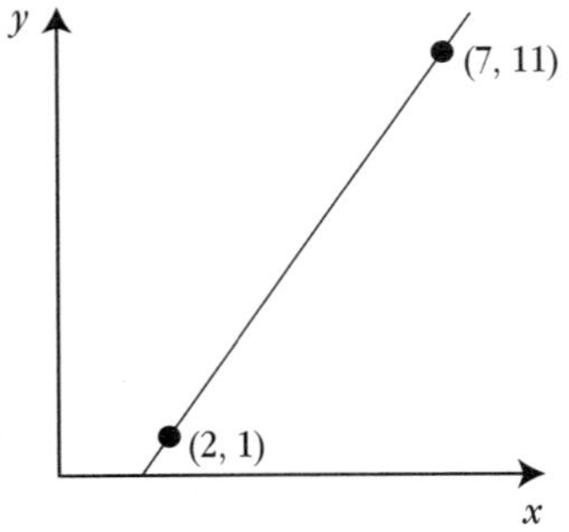

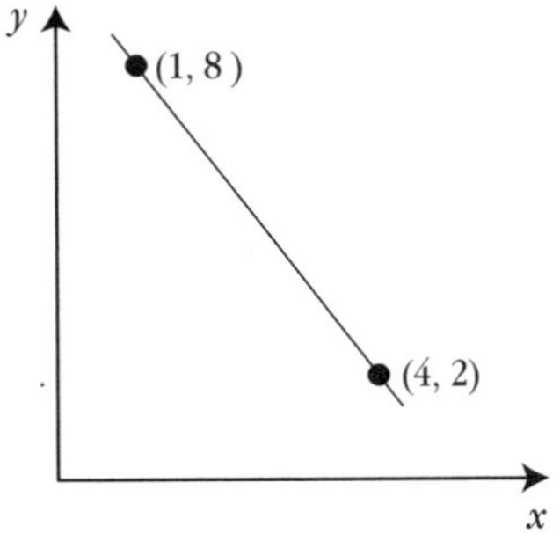

c. Compare the equations you wrote for parts a and b. How are they alike? How are they different?

3. Match each equation with its line in the diagram. Give reasons for your choices.

a. $y = 0.5x + 3$

b. $y = ^{-}0.5x + 6$

c. $y = 0.5x + 6$

d. $y = ^{-}0.5x + 3$

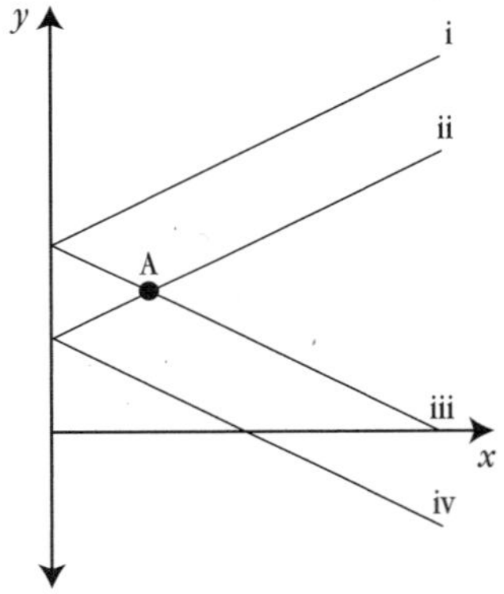

4. a. Point *A* is on lines ii and iii. Its *x*-coordinate is 3. Calculate its *y*-coordinate by substituting 3 for *x* in the equation for line ii. Then, calculate its *y*-coordinate by substituting 3 for *x* in the equation for line iii. What do you observe? Why does this happen?

b. Abdul and Wendy did some calculations to find the *y*-coordinate of point *A*. Which student did the calculations correctly? What error did the other student make?

Abdul's work

$y = 0.5 \times 3 + 3$

$y = 0.5 \times 6$

$y = 3$

Wendy's work

$y = 0.5 \times 3 + 3$

$y = 1.5 + 3$

$y = 4.5$

As you work on these ACE questions, use your calculator whenever you need it.

Applications

1. A class in Oregon did the bridge-thickness experiment with construction paper. Their results are shown in this table.

Thickness (layers)	1	2	3	4	5	6
Breaking weight (pennies)	12	20	29	42	52	61

a. Make a graph of the (thickness, breaking weight) data, and draw a straight line that models the trend in the data.

b. Use your graph model to estimate the breaking weight for a bridge 7 layers thick.

c. Find an equation for your graph model, and use it to check your answer for part b.

2. The astronomy club at King Middle School is planning a field trip to the science center to see a new 3-D science film. Renting a bus for the trip will cost \$125. Admission to the film is \$2.50 per person.

a. Write an equation to show the relationship between the number of students who go on the trip, n, and the cost of the trip, c.

b. Make a table showing the cost of the trip for 0 students, 5 students, 10 students, and so on, up to 50 students.

c. Make a graph of the equation on grid paper or by using a graphing calculator.

d. What do the slope and the y-intercept of the graph tell you about the cost and the number of students?

3. The student government at Waverly Middle School conducted a survey to find out how much students would be willing to pay to attend a concert by a popular music group. The graph below shows the results of the survey.

a. Make a table showing the approximate (price, customers) data given in the graph.

b. Copy the graph, and draw a straight line that models the trend in the data. Use your model to estimate the number of students who would pay prices of \$7.50, \$12.50, \$17.50, and \$22.50.

c. Write an equation for your graph model, and use it to check your estimates from part b.

In 4–8, write an equation for the pattern of change shown in the table.

4.

x	0	1	2	3	4	5	6	7	8
y	0	4	8	12	16	20	24	28	32

5.

x	0	1	2	3	4	5	6	7	8
y	3	8	13	18	23	28	33	38	43

6.

x	1	2	3	4	5	6	7	8	9
y	5	11	17	23	29	35	41	47	53

7.

x	1	3	5	7	9	11	13	15	17
y	2.5	7.5	12.5	17.5	22.5	27.5	32.5	37.5	42.5

8.

x	0	1	2	3	4	5	6	7	8
y	3	2.5	2	1.5	1	0.5	0	−0.5	−1

In 9–13, find the equation for the line.

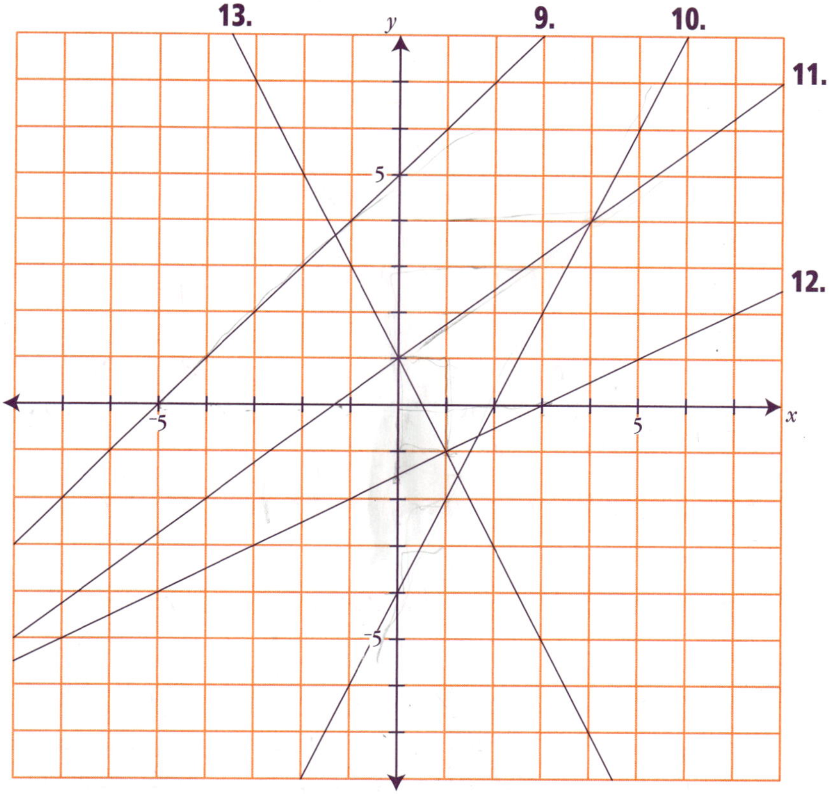

14. Write an equation for the line with slope 4.2 and y-intercept (0, 3.4).

15. Write an equation for the line with slope $\frac{2}{3}$ and y-intercept (0, 5).

16. Write an equation for the line with slope 2 that passes through the point (4, 12).

17. Write an equation for the line that passes through the points (1, 3) and (7, 6).

18. Write an equation for the line that passes through the points (0, 15) and (5, 3).

19. Write an equation for the line that passes through the points (2, 7) and (5, 4).

In 20–23, the coordinates of two points on a line are given. Find an equation for the line, and give the slope and *y*-intercept of the line.

20.

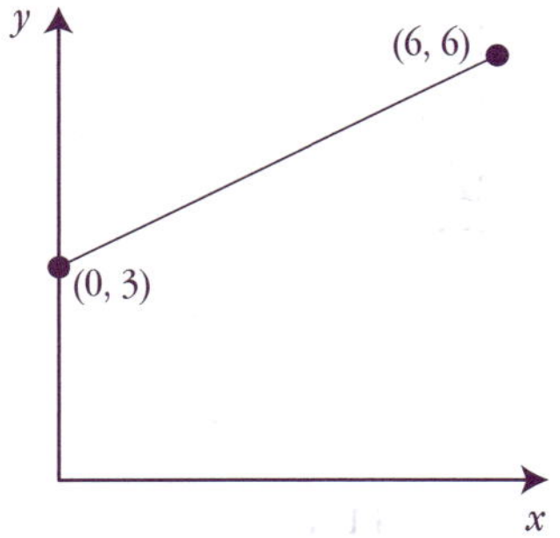

21.

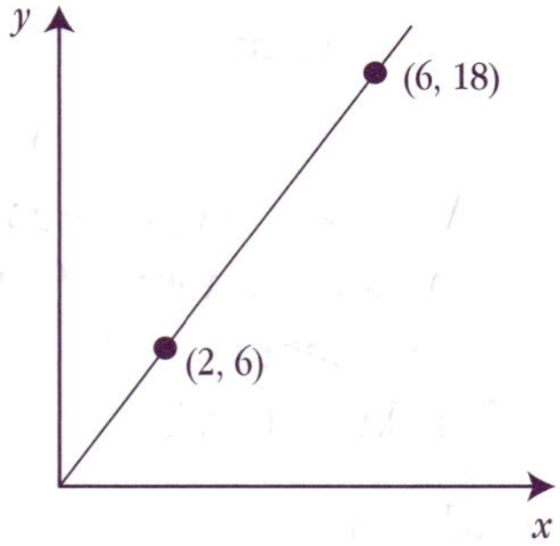

22.

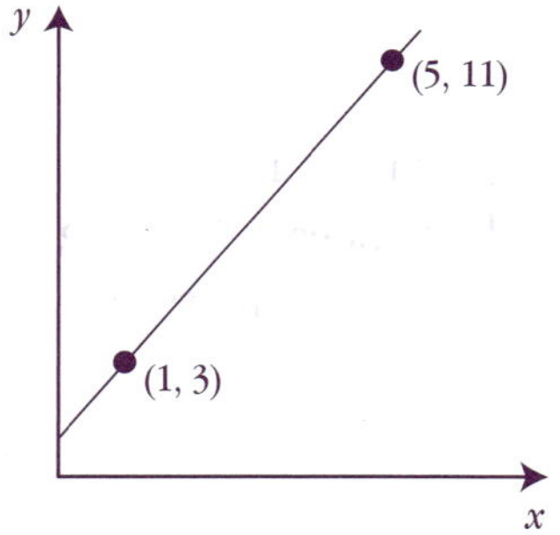

23.

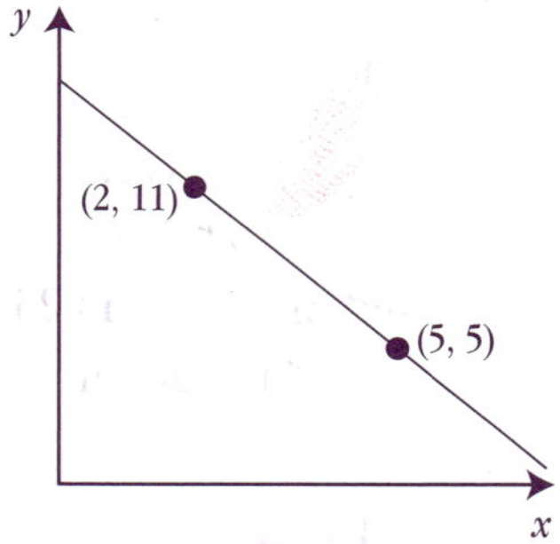

24. Spartan Publishing Company's delivery truck has a broken fuel gauge. Luckily, the driver always keeps track of mileage and gas consumption. She uses her data to write the equation $G = 25 - \frac{1}{15}M$ for the relationship between the number of gallons of gasoline in the tank, G, and the number of miles driven since the last fill-up, M.

a. The driver has just filled the tank and is about to start the engine. What is the value of M for this situation? Use the equation to figure out the value of G for this situation. What does the result tell you about the gas tank?

b. If the driver travels 50 miles after filling the tank, how much gas will be left?

c. After filling the tank, how many miles can the driver travel before 5 gallons remain?

d. Solve the equation $10 = 25 - \frac{1}{15}M$. What does the solution tell you about the amount of gas left and the number of miles driven since the last fill-up?

e. Use the equation to figure out how many miles the driver would have to travel to use 1 gallon of gas. Explain how you got your answer.

f. In the equation $G = 25 - \frac{1}{15}M$, what do the numbers 25 and $\frac{1}{15}$ tell you about the situation?

g. What patterns would you expect to see in the table and the graph of the relationship between miles driven and gallons of gas remaining? How would the numbers 25 and $\frac{1}{15}$ from the equation be represented in the table and the graph?

Connections

25. A survey of one homeroom class at Pioneer Middle School finds that 20 out of 30 students in the class would be willing to spend $8 for a school-spirit T-shirt.

a. If there are 600 students in the school, how many do you predict would be willing to spend $8 for a school-spirit T-shirt?

b. If there are 450 students in the school, how many do you predict would be willing to spend $8 for a school-spirit T-shirt?

26. The table below gives name lengths, heights, and foot lengths for a group of middle school students.

Student	Name length (letters)	Height (cm)	Foot length (cm)
Thomas Petes	11	126	23
Michelle Hughes	14	117	21
Shoshana White	13	112	17
Deborah Locke	12	127	21
Tonya Stewart	12	172	32
Richard Mudd	11	135	22
Tony Tung	8	130	20
Janice Vick	10	134	21
Bobby King	9	156	29
Kathleen Boylan	14	164	28

a. Make a graph of the (name length, height) data, a graph of the (name length, foot length) data, and a graph of the (height, foot length) data.

b. Of the graphs you made in part a, which could be modeled with a straight line? Explain your answer.

c. For each graph you think can be modeled with a straight line, explain what the line would tell you about the relationship between the variables.

27. You can produce odd and even numbers by substituting integers for n in the linear equations $O = 2n + 1$ and $E = 2n$.

a. Copy and complete the table below to show the odd and even numbers produced by these equations for the given values of n.

n	0	1	2	5	10
O					
E					

b. Compare the equations for O and E to the general linear form $y = mx + b$. What are the values of m and b in each equation? What do these values tell you about the patterns you would see in the table and the graphs of the equations?

28. The equations below express the relationship between a person's height, H, and femur (thigh bone) length, F. Both measurements are in inches.

$$\text{Males: } H = 27.5 + 2.24F$$
$$\text{Females: } H = 24 + 2.32F$$

a. If a man's femur is 20 inches long, about how tall is he?

b. If a woman's femur is 15 inches long, about how tall is she?

c. If a man is 65 inches tall, about how long is his femur?

d. If a woman is 68 inches tall, about how long is her femur?

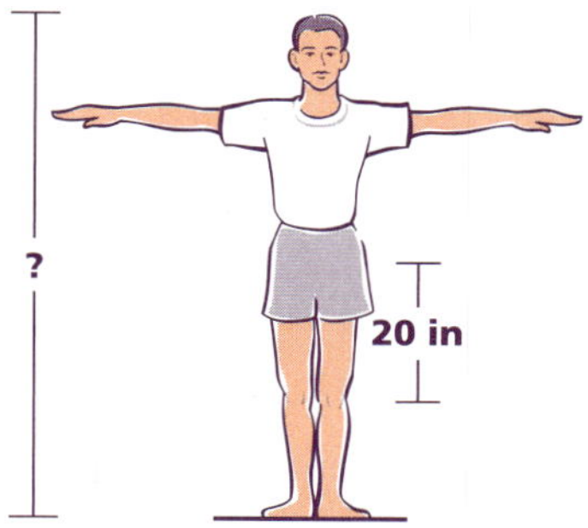

e. What do the numbers 2.24 and 2.32 tell you about the relationship between femur length and height for males and females?

f. What do the numbers 2.24 and 2.32 tell you about the patterns you would see in the tables and the graphs of (femur length, height) data?

In 29–31, tell whether the data in the table represent a linear relationship, and explain your answer.

29.

x	2	4	6	8	10	12	14
y	0	1	2	3	4	5	6

30.

x	1	2	3	4	5	6	7
y	0	3	8	15	24	35	48

31.

x	1	4	6	7	10	12	16
y	2	−1	−3	−4	−7	−9	−13

In 32–38, tell whether the equation represents a linear relationship, and explain how you arrived at your conclusion. If the equation is linear, give the slope and the y-intercept of the graph.

32. Renting a bus for a school trip costs \$240, and food and accomodations cost \$25 per person. If n people go on the trip, the cost per person, C, in dollars is

$$C = \frac{240 + 25n}{n}$$

33. At Josie's Buffet, lunch costs \$6.50 per person. The total cost, T, in dollars for n people to eat lunch is $T = 6.5n$.

34. If the cost for car insurance is d dollars per year, then the cost, C, in dollars for a three-month policy is $C = \frac{d}{4}$.

35. $y = \frac{20}{x}$ **36.** $y = 20x$ **37.** $y = \frac{x}{20}$ **38.** $y = 0.05x$

Extensions

39. The 24 students in Mr. McKeever's homeroom were asked which of several prices they would be willing to pay for a ticket to the school play. The results are shown in this table.

Ticket price (dollars)	1.00	1.50	2.00	2.50	3.00	3.50	4.00	4.50
Probable ticket sales	20	20	18	15	12	10	8	7

a. There are 480 students in the school. Use the data from Mr. McKeever's class to predict ticket sales for the entire school for each price in the table.

b. Use your results from part a to predict the income the school could expect if tickets were sold at each price in the table.

c. What ticket price should the school charge if they want the maximum income?

40. This table gives the numbers of stories and the heights for 15 U.S. buildings.

Building	Location	Number of stories	Height (feet)
National City Center	Akron, Ohio	23	301
IBM Tower	Atlanta, Georgia	50	813
U.S.F. & G. Building	Baltimore, Maryland	40	529
John Hancock Tower	Boston, Massachusetts	60	800
NCNB Plaza	Charlotte, North Carolina	40	503
Sears Tower	Chicago, Illinois	110	1454
Sohio Tower	Cleveland, Ohio	46	650
Interfirst Plaza	Dallas, Texas	73	939
Westin Hotel	Detroit, Michigan	71	720
Pacific Tower	Honolulu, Hawaii	30	350
Texas Commerce Tower	Houston, Texas	75	1002
Indiana Bell Telephone Bldg.	Indianapolis, Indiana	20	320
Los Angeles City Hall	Los Angeles, California	28	454
Empire State Building	New York, New York	102	1250
United Nations Building	New York, New York	39	505

a. Graph the (stories, height) data for these buildings, and draw a straight line that models the trend in the data.

b. Write an equation of the form $y = mx + b$ for your graph model, and explain what the value of m tells you about this situation.

c. The Mellon Bank Center in Philadelphia, Pennsylvania, has 56 stories and is 880 feet tall. How does this data pair compare to the data pair predicted by your equation model from part b?

41. This table gives the average heights of boys of even-numbered ages from birth to age 16.

Age (years)	0	2	4	6	8	10	12	14	16
Height (cm)	52	87	103	116	127	138	150	163	174

a. Graph the (age, height) data, and draw a straight line that models the trend in the data.

b. Write an equation of the form $y = mx + b$ for your graph model. What do the values of m and b tell you about age and height in this situation?

c. Use your model to estimate the average heights of boys of odd-numbered ages from 1 to 15. Then, compare your estimates to the actual data given in the table below.

Age (years)	1	3	5	7	9	11	13	15
Height (cm)	74	91	107	119	132	142	152	163

Mathematical Reflections

In this investigation, you used graph models and equation models to represent linear relationships between variables. These questions will help you summarize what you have learned:

1. In Problem 1.2, you drew a straight line to model the trend in the (thickness, breaking weight) data. For data that can be modeled with a straight line, how do the y values change as the x values increase or decrease?

2. Write the general form of the equation for a linear relationship. Explain what each part of the equation means.

3. If you know the coordinates of two points on a line, how can you find an equation for the line? Use an example if it helps you to explain your thinking.

4. **a.** Describe the graph of a line that has a negative slope.

   b. What part of the linear equation $y = mx + b$ tells you whether the graph has a negative slope?

   c. For a line with a negative slope, how do the y values change as the x values increase?

5. **a.** Explain how you would check whether the point (2, 7.5) is on the line with equation $y = 3x + 0.5$.

   b. After you substitute a number for x in the equation $y = 10x + 2.8$, in what order should you do the calculations to find the value of y? What does the result of your calculations tell you?

Think about your answers to these questions, discuss your ideas with other students and your teacher, and then write a summary of your findings in your journal.

INVESTIGATION 2

Nonlinear Models

In the last investigation, you tested paper bridges of various thicknesses. You found that thicker bridges are stronger than thinner bridges, and you discovered that the relationship between thickness and breaking weight is approximately linear. In this investigation, you will explore relationships with different types of models.

2.1 Testing Bridge Lengths

In this problem, you will experiment with paper bridges of various lengths. What relationship do you expect to find between the length of a bridge and its breaking weight? Do you think longer bridges will be stronger or weaker than shorter bridges?

Equipment: eight 4-inch-wide strips of paper with lengths 4, 5, 6, 7, 8, 9, 10, and 11 inches, two books of the same thickness, a small paper cup, and about 50 pennies

Directions:

- Make paper bridges by folding up 1 inch on each long side of the paper strips.

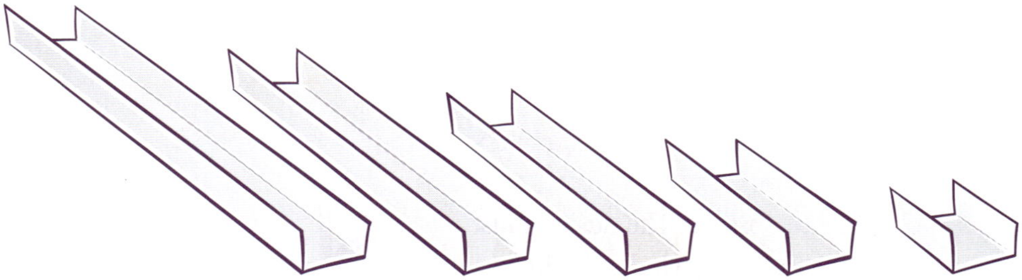

- Suspend one of the bridges between the two books. The bridge should overlap each book by about 1 inch. Place the paper cup in the center of the bridge.
- Put pennies into the cup, one at a time, until the bridge crumples. Record the length and breaking weight of the bridge.
- Repeat this experiment to find the breaking weights of the remaining bridges.

Problem 2.1

A. Do the experiment described to find the breaking weights of paper bridges of lengths 4, 5, 6, 7, 8, 9, 10, and 11 inches. Organize your data in a table. Study the table, and look for a pattern. Do you think the relationship between bridge length and breaking weight is linear?

B. Make a graph of the (length, breaking weight) data from your experiment, and describe the pattern you see. Do the data appear to be linear?

C. Draw a straight line or a curve that seems to model the trend in the data. Do you think your graph fits the data satisfactorily? Explain.

D. Use your graph model to predict breaking weights for bridges of lengths 4.5, 5.5, and 6.5 inches. Make bridges of these lengths, and test your predictions.

E. How is the relationship between bridge length and breaking weight in this problem similar to and different from the linear relationships you studied in the last investigation?

Problem 2.1 Follow-Up

1. If you were to do the bridge-length experiment using strips of paper 12, 13, 14, and 15 inches long, what pattern would you expect to see in the results? Explain your reasoning.
2. What breaking weight would you expect for a bridge 3 inches long? Explain your reasoning.

Did you know?

When designing bridges, engineers must think about *impact*, or the effect of outside forces on the bridge. The design must account for gusting winds, shifting water, and the possibility of seismic activity. In addition, engineers must consider changes in air temperature that may cause the materials in the bridge to expand or contract. Typically, the milder temperature ranges of coastal regions create less of a change in size than the more extreme temperature ranges of desert and mountain areas.

2.2 Keeping Things Balanced

The pattern you saw in the (length, breaking weight) data shows up in many other important and familiar problems. For example, you may have thought about this problem when you were a child:

How do people of different weights balance on a teeter-totter?

You probably discovered that the lighter person has to sit farther from the balance point (called the *fulcrum*) than the heavier person does.

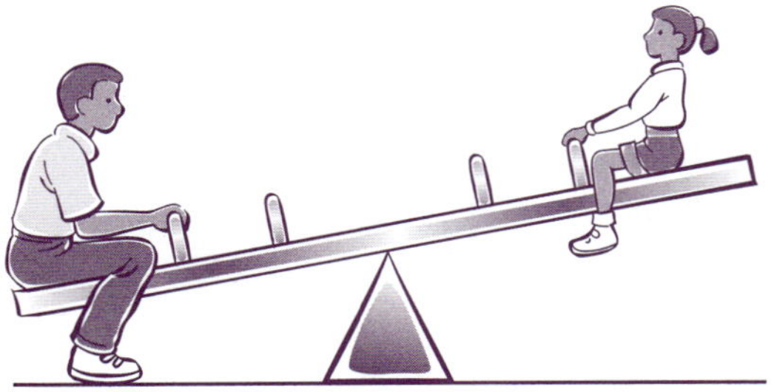

You might have found the balance point by trial and error, but there is a mathematical relationship between weight and distance. The following experiment will help you discover this relationship.

Equipment: a meterstick, several identical small weights (heavy washers work well), and a block of wood to use as a fulcrum (a triangular prism works best)

Directions:

- Balance the meterstick on the fulcrum. The 50-centimeter mark should be directly over the fulcrum.
- Place 3 weights 40 centimeters to the left of the fulcrum. Leave these weights in this position for the entire experiment.
- Place 4 weights to the right of the fulcrum so that the meterstick balances. Record the distance of the 4 weights from the fulcrum.

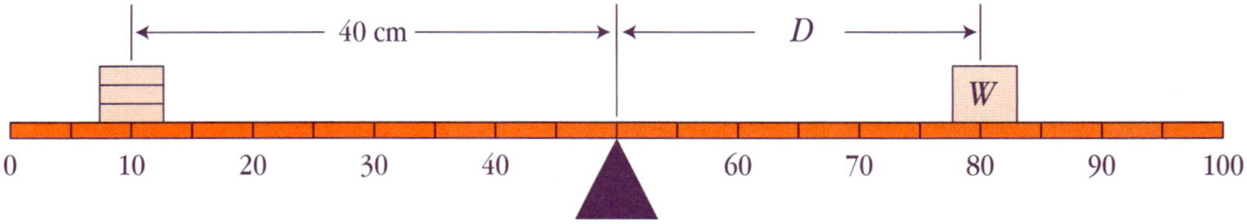

- Find several other (distance, weight) combinations that balance the meterstick. For example, where would you have to place 6 weights? 10 weights? How many weights would you have to place 10 centimeters from the fulcrum? How many weights would you have to place 20 centimeters from the fulcrum?

Problem 2.2

A. Do the experiment described above, and make a table of the (distance, weight) combinations you find. What does your table suggest about the relationship between distance and weight?

B. Make a graph of your data, and draw a straight line or a curve that models the trend. What does your graph suggest about the relationship between distance and weight?

C. How is the pattern of change in the (distance, weight) data similar to and different from the pattern of change in the (bridge length, breaking weight) data from Problem 2.1?

D. How is the pattern of change in the (distance, weight) data similar to and different from the pattern of change in the (bridge thickness, breaking weight) data from Problems 1.1 and 1.2?

Problem 2.2 Follow-Up

1. How would the results of this experiment have been different if you had started with 2 weights placed 30 centimeters to the left of the fulcrum? With 4 weights placed 30 centimeters to the left of the fulcrum? With 2 weights placed 50 centimeters to the left of the fulcrum?

2. Some (distance, weight) combinations that balance 3 weights 40 centimeters from the fulcrum are (30, 4), (24, 5), and (20, 6). Which of the following equations do these three data pairs satisfy? Explain.

a. $W = 120D$

b. $W = \frac{120}{D}$

c. $D = \frac{120}{W}$

d. $W = \frac{D}{120}$

e. $WD = 120$

f. $DW = 120$

2.3 Testing Whether Driving Fast Pays

Riders on the Ocean and History Bicycle Tour cycle from Philadelphia, Pennsylvania, along the Atlantic Coast to Norfolk, Virginia, and then to Williamsburg, Virginia. When the tour is over, the riders take a bus from Williamsburg back to Philadelphia—a distance of about 300 miles. Everyone is anxious to get home, so the bus driver is tempted to drive fast.

In this problem, you will study the relationship between the average speed of the bus and the time it takes to reach Philadelphia. You will see how much difference in travel time driving fast really makes.

Problem 2.3

A. Copy and complete the table below to show the time it would take for the 300-mile trip at various average speeds.

Average speed (miles per hour)	30	40	50	60	70
Trip time (hours)					

B. Make a graph of the relationship between the average speed, *S*, and the time, *T*.

C. Find an equation for the relationship between *S* and *T*.

D. Is the relationship between *S* and *T* linear or nonlinear? Explain how the table, the graph, and the equation support your answer.

Problem 2.3 Follow-Up

1. The bus driver figured out that if he increased his average speed from 40 to 45 miles per hour, the time for the trip would be shortened from $7\frac{1}{2}$ hours to $6\frac{2}{3}$ hours, a savings of 50 minutes. He then reasoned that increasing his average speed from 45 to 50 miles per hour would cut another 50 minutes off the trip, and increasing his average speed from 50 to 55 miles per hour would cut another 50 minutes off the trip.

   a. Do you agree with the bus driver's conclusions about the time he would save by driving faster? Explain your reasoning.

   b. How is your answer for part a illustrated in your graph of the (speed, time) data?

2. How would the table, the graph, and the equation change if the trip were 500 miles instead of 300 miles?

3. Look back at your work from Problem 2.2. Find an equation for the relationship you explored in that problem.

Applications • Connections • Extensions

As you work on these ACE questions, use your calculator whenever you need it.

Applications

1. These data are from an ad for a construction crane. They show the maximum weight the crane arm can lift at various distances from the cab out along the arm.

Distance (ft)	12	24	36	48	60
Weight (lbs)	7500	3750	2500	1875	1500

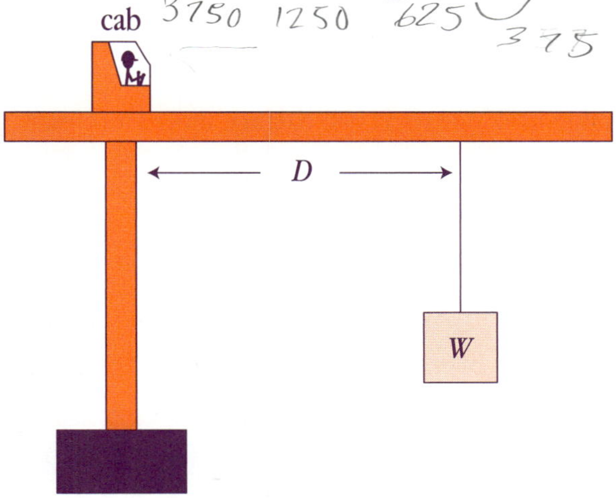

a. Describe the relationship between distance and weight for the crane.

b. Write an equation for the weight, *W*, as a function of the distance, *D*.

c. Use your equation to estimate the weight the crane can lift at these distances from the cab.

i. 18 ft **ii.** 30 ft **iii.** 72 ft

d. Make a graph of the relationship between *D* and *W*, and explain how the graph's shape illustrates the relationship you described in part a.

e. How, if at all, is this situation related to the bridge-length and teeter-totter experiments?

2. Suppose you and some friends are planning a 20-mile bike trip to a park campsite.

a. At what average speed would you have to ride to complete the trip in 4 hours? In 2 hours? In 1.5 hours? In 1 hour?

b. Write an equation for the relationship between riding time, t, in hours and average speed, s, in miles per hour for a 20-mile trip.

c. Is the relationship between t and s linear? Use a table and a graph to support your answer.

d. Which of the following causes the greater change in required average speed: increasing the riding time from 1 hour to 2 hours or increasing the riding time from 2 hours to 3 hours?

In 3–6, find the value of W or D that will balance the teeter-totter.

3.

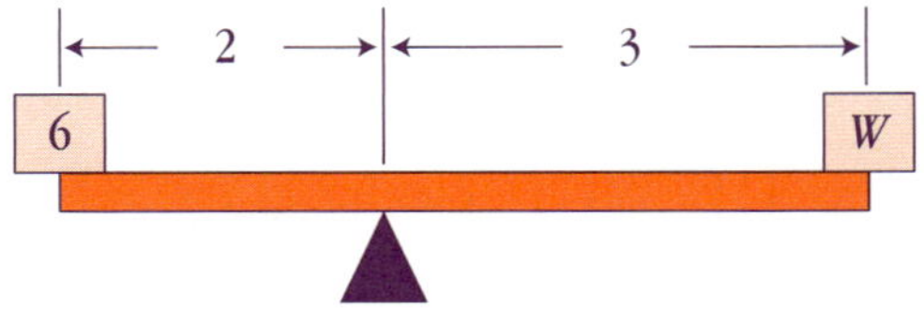

4.

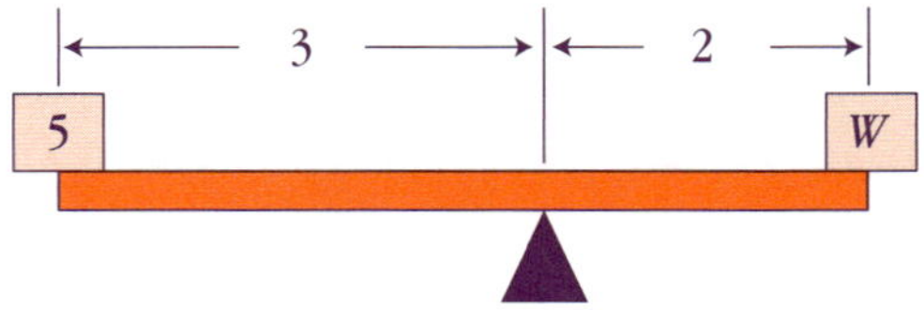

5.

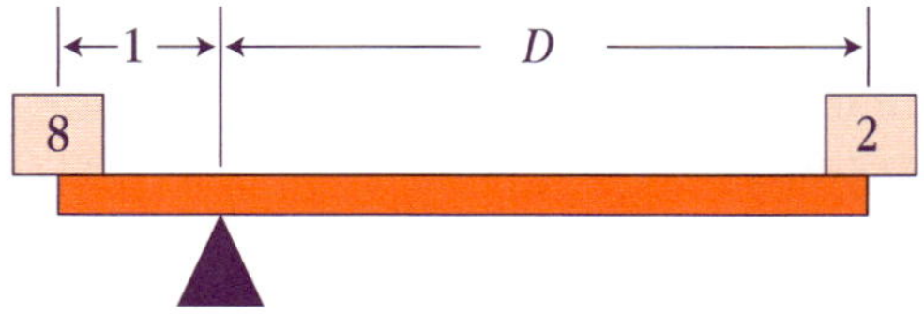

6.

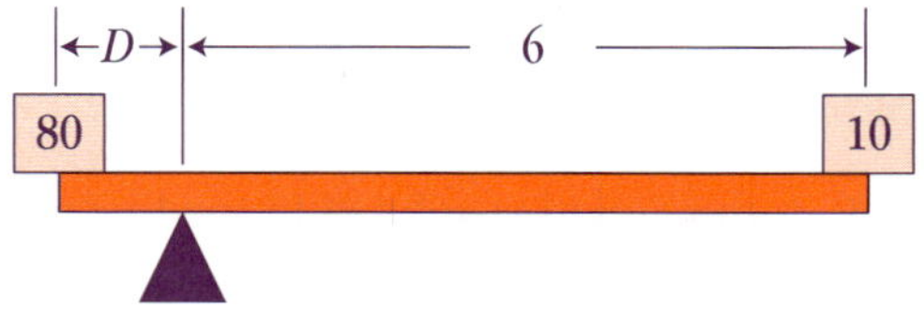

Connections

7. Find all combinations of whole-number values for D and W that will make this teeter-totter balance.

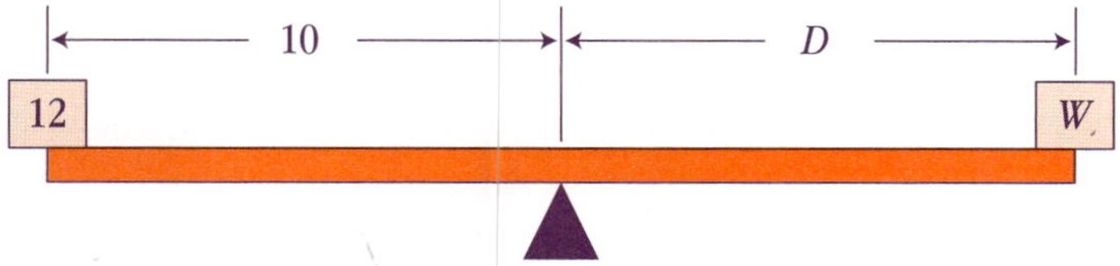

8. **a.** At right is a scale drawing of a rectangle with an area of 300 ft^2. Make scale drawings of some other rectangles with areas of 300 ft^2.

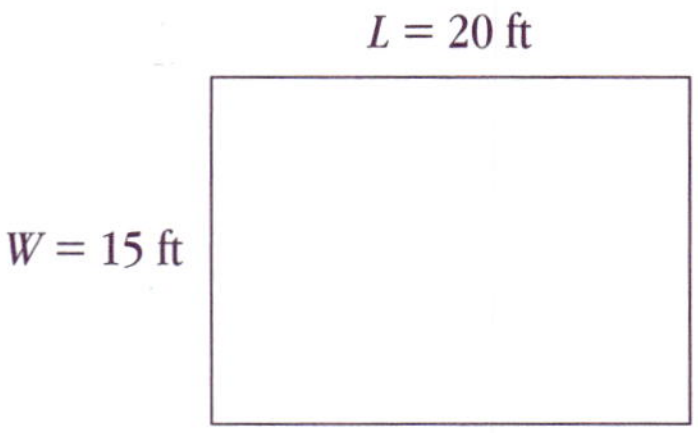

b. What width must a rectangle with an area of 300 ft^2 have if its length is 1 ft? 2 ft? 3 ft? L ft?

c. How does the width change as the length increases?

d. Make a graph of (W, L) pairs that give an area of 300 ft^2. Explain how your graph illustrates your answer for part c.

e. Is the relationship between W and L linear or nonlinear? Explain how the pattern in your graph can help you answer this question.

9. **a.** The rectangle pictured in question 8 has a perimenter of 70 ft. Make scale drawings of some other rectangles with perimeters of 70 ft.

b. What width must a rectangle with a perimeter of 70 ft have if its length is 1 ft? 2 ft? L ft?

c. How does the width change as the length increases?

d. Make a graph of (W, L) pairs that give a perimeter of 70 ft. Explain how your graph illustrates your answer for part c.

e. Is the relationship between W and L linear or nonlinear? Explain how the pattern in your graph can help you answer this question.

10. On the Ocean and History Bicycle Tour, there are some free mornings when participants can choose from several side trips.

a. The time allowed for a side trip is 4 hours. What (distance, average speed) combinations are possible for a side trip? Record some of the possible combinations in a table.

Distance (miles)	20				
Average speed (miles per hour)	5				

b. Write an equation showing the relationship between the average speed and the distance.

c. Use your table or equation to find the average speed required for a 60-mile trip.

d. Use your table or equation to find the distance a helicopter traveling at an average speed of 80 miles per hour could cover in 4 hours.

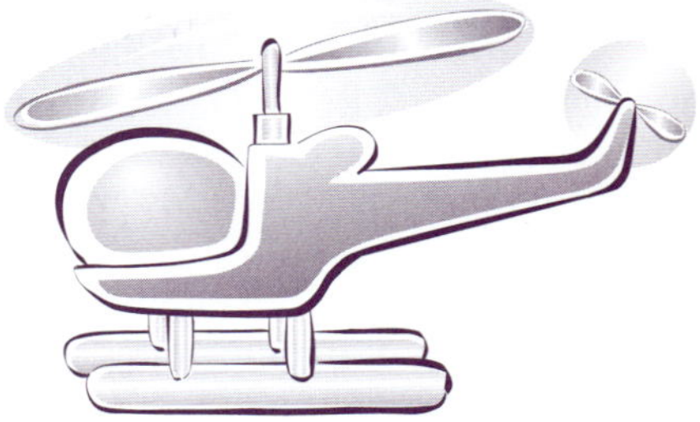

e. Is the relationship between distance and average speed linear? Explain how you found your answer.

11. In this problem, you will use a graphing calculator to explore graphs of $y = a + \frac{2}{x}$ for different positive values of a.

a. Set the window on your calculator to display x and y values from $^{-}8$ to 8. Graph $y = \frac{2}{x}$. Make a sketch of the graph.

b. Graph each of these equations, and watch what happens to the graphs as different positive numbers are added to the value of y:

$y = 1 + \frac{2}{x}$ $\quad$ $y = 2 + \frac{2}{x}$ $\quad$ $y = 3 + \frac{2}{x}$ $\quad$ $y = 4 + \frac{2}{x}$

c. Describe what happens to the graph of $y = \frac{2}{x}$ when a positive number is added to the value of y.

d. Describe what the graph of $y = 100 + \frac{2}{x}$ would look like.

Extensions

12. In this problem, you will use a graphing calculator to explore graphs of $y = a + \frac{2}{x}$ for different negative values of a.

a. Set the window on your calculator to display x and y values from $^-8$ to 8. Graph $y = \frac{2}{x}$. Make a sketch of the graph.

b. Graph each of these equations, and watch what happens to the graphs as different negative numbers are added to the value of y:

$y = {}^-1 + \frac{2}{x}$ $\quad y = {}^-2 + \frac{2}{x}$ $\quad y = {}^-3 + \frac{2}{x}$ $\quad y = {}^-4 + \frac{2}{x}$

c. Describe what happens to the graph of $y = \frac{2}{x}$ when a negative number is added to the value of y.

d. Describe what the graph of $y = {}^-100 + \frac{2}{x}$ would look like.

Mathematical Reflections

In this investigation, you explored nonlinear relationships.

- In Problem 2.1, you investigated the relationship between length and breaking weight for a bridge.
- In Problem 2.2, you investigated the relationship between weight and distance from the fulcrum for a teeter-totter.
- In Problem 2.3, you investigated the relationship between speed and time for a trip.

These questions will help you summarize what you have learned:

1. What common patterns of change did you find in the tables and the graphs of these relationships? Did all three relationships fit the same pattern?
2. How are the patterns in the tables and the graphs of these relationships different from the patterns in the tables and the graphs of the linear relationships you explored in Investigation 1?
3. There are many types of nonlinear relationships, some of which you will explore later this year. The type of relationship you studied in this investigation is called an *inverse* relationship. Can you think of some reasons this name is appropriate?

Think about your answers to these questions, discuss your ideas with other students and your teacher, and then write a summary of your findings in your journal.

INVESTIGATION 3

More Nonlinear Models

In previous investigations, you found graph models and equation models to fit trends in data. You saw that finding models for data can help you make predictions. In Investigation 1, you worked with data that showed linear trends. You drew straight lines to model the data and then wrote equations for the lines. The data in Investigation 2 showed nonlinear trends. You may have found it difficult to find graph and equation models for these data.

In this investigation, you will continue to explore nonlinear situations. You will begin to see familiar patterns in tables and graphs of data. For example, you saw that the data pattern for the teeter-totter experiment was similar to the data pattern for the bridge-length experiment. Recognizing a familiar pattern can give you hints about what type of model might fit a set of data.

As you work through the remaining problems in this book, think about how the data patterns you find compare with patterns you have seen before.

3.1 Earning Interest

On the day Chantal was born, her Uncle Charlie used $100 to open a savings account. He planned to use the money in the account to buy Chantal a gift on her tenth birthday. Charlie forgot about the money until last week when he received an invitation to Chantal's fourteenth birthday party.

Charlie called Chantal and told her about the account. He said, "I'm sorry I forgot about your tenth birthday. Would you like me to give you the money that's in the account now, or would you like me to leave it in the bank and give it to you on your eighteenth birthday?"

The savings account that Charlie opened earns 8% interest each year. This means that at the end of each year, the bank calculates 8% of the balance and adds this amount to the account. At the end of the first year, the interest earned was

$$I = 8\% \text{ of } \$100$$
$$I = 0.08 \times \$100$$
$$I = \$8$$

The interest was added to the account, giving a new balance of $108. So, on Chantal's first birthday there was $108 in the account.

At the end of the second year, the bank again calculated 8% interest and added it to the account. Since there was $108 in the account, the interest earned was

$$I = 8\% \text{ of } \$108$$
$$I = 0.08 \times \$108$$
$$I = \$8.64$$

This amount was added to the account, giving a new balance of $108 + $8.64 = $116.64. So, on Chantal's second birthday there was $116.64 in the account.

Problem 3.1

Charlie's account has been earning 8% interest at the end of every year since Chantal was born. Charlie has not deposited or withdrawn any money since he opened the account. How much money is in the account on Chantal's fourteenth birthday?

Problem 3.1 Follow-Up

1. Copy and complete the table to show the birthday year, the balance at the beginning of that year, and the interest earned at the end of that year. Your table should include data up through Chantal's fourteenth birthday.

Birthday	Balance	Interest earned
0 (birth)	$100.00	$8.00
1	108.00	8.64
2	116.64	
3		
.		
.		
.		

2. Make a graph of the (birthday, balance) data from your table, and draw a straight line or curve to model the trend. Is the graph linear? Explain how you know.

3. About how much money will be in the account on Chantal's eighteenth birthday? Explain how you found your answer.

4. Do you think Chantal should take the money in the account now or wait until her eighteenth birthday? Explain your answer.

5. Is the pattern of change for these data similar to the pattern in the bridge-thickness data, the bridge-length data, or the teeter-totter data? Explain.

3.2 Pouring Water

When you describe a relationship between two variables, you might say that as the x values increase, the y values also increase or that as the x values increase, the y values decrease. However, such a description does not tell the whole story.

In both the graph of the (thickness, breaking weight) data and the graph of the (birthday, balance) data, an increase in the x values produces an increase in the y values. However, the shapes of these graphs are very different. In the (thickness, breaking weight) graph, the y values increase at a constant rate. In the (birthday, balance) graph, the rate at which the y values increase is not constant.

In this problem, you will experiment with another relationship. Think about how the graph of this relationship compares with other graphs you have seen.

As a class, conduct the following experiment:

Equipment: 8 identical clear drinking glasses, stick-on notes or masking tape, a pen or marker, and water

Directions:

- Line up the glasses. Use stick-on notes or masking tape to label the glasses 1, 2, 3, 4, and so on.
- Fill glass 1 with water.
- Pour half the water from glass 1 into glass 2, and return glass 1 to its place.
- Pour half the water from glass 2 into glass 3, and return glass 2 to its place.
- Continue this process until you have poured half the water from glass 7 into glass 8.

Look at the water levels in the glasses. How is the glass number related to the amount of water in the glass?

Problem 3.2

A. If you started the experiment with 32 ounces of water in glass 1, how much water would be in each glass when you were done pouring? Arrange these (glass number, amount of water) data into a table. Describe the relationship between the glass number and the amount of water in the glass.

B. Make a graph of the data, and draw a straight line or a curve to model the trend.

C. Describe the pattern you see in your graph.

D. If you continued to add glasses and pour half the water from the last glass into the new glass, how much water would be in glass 20?

Problem 3.2 Follow-Up

1. Does it make sense to connect the data points on your graph? Why or why not?

2. Compare the graph you made in Problem 3.2 with the other graphs you have made in this unit. Describe how it is similar to and different from the other graphs.

3. If you continued to add glasses and pour half the water from the last glass into the new glass, would you ever run out of water? Explain your answer.

Applications • Connections • Extensions

As you work on these ACE questions, use your calculator whenever you need it.

Applications

1. Betty's Bakery sells giant cookies for $1.00 each. This price is no longer high enough to create a profit, so Betty decides to raise the price. She doesn't want to shock her customers by raising the price too suddenly or too dramatically. She considers these three plans:

- Plan 1: Raise the price by $0.05 each week until the price reaches $1.80.
- Plan 2: Raise the price by 5% each week until the price reaches $1.80.
- Plan 3: Raise the price by the same amount each week for 8 weeks, so that in the eighth week the price reaches $1.80.

a. Make a table for each plan. How many weeks will it take the price to reach $1.80 under each plan?

b. On the same set of axes, graph the data for each plan. Compare the shapes of the graphs and what they mean in terms of the changing cookie price paid by customers.

c. Are any of the graphs you drew linear? Explain.

d. Which plan do you think Betty should implement? Give reasons for your choice.

2. Betty, the owner of Betty's Bakery, suspects that someone is stealing her chocolate chips.

   a. There are 1 million chips in a new canister of chocolate chips. Betty uses about 40,000 chips each day. How many days should the canister last?

   b. **i.** Make a graph that shows the relationship between the number of days after Betty opens a new canister and the approximate number of chips that should be in the canister at the end of each day.

   ii. Write an equation for this relationship.

   c. A gauge on the side of the chip canister allows Betty to estimate the number of chips remaining. On a day when she opens a new canister, Betty begins keeping track of the approximate number of chips left at the end of each day.

Day	1	2	3	4	5	6	7	8
Chips left	800,000	640,000	512,000	410,000	330,000	260,000	210,000	170,000

   Make a graph of these data. Compare this graph with your graph from part b. Are Betty's suspicions about the chocolate chip thefts justified? Explain.

Connections

3. Since Betty raised her prices, cookie sales have fallen. Betty calls in a business consultant to help. The consultant suggests that Betty conduct a customer survey. Betty's customers are asked which of several amounts they would be willing to pay for a cookie. Here are the results:

Price	$1.75	$1.50	$1.25	$1.00
Customers willing to pay this price	100	117	140	175

   a. Make a graph of these data, and draw a straight line or a curve that models the trend.

   b. Use your graph model to predict the number of customers who would be willing to pay $1.35 and the number who would be willing to pay $2.00.

   c. Do you think predictions based on your graph model are accurate? Explain.

d. The shape of this graph resembles the shape of another graph you have drawn. Look back at your work in this unit. Which situation has a graph similar to this one?

4. When you see a trend in plotted data, you can usually draw a graph model that you can use to make predictions. Labsheet 3.ACE contains the data graphs shown below. For each graph, decide whether there is a trend in the data. If there is a trend, do the following:

- Draw a straight line or a curve that models the trend. If the graph model is a line, give its slope.
- Identify a situation you studied in this unit that has a similar graph model.

a.

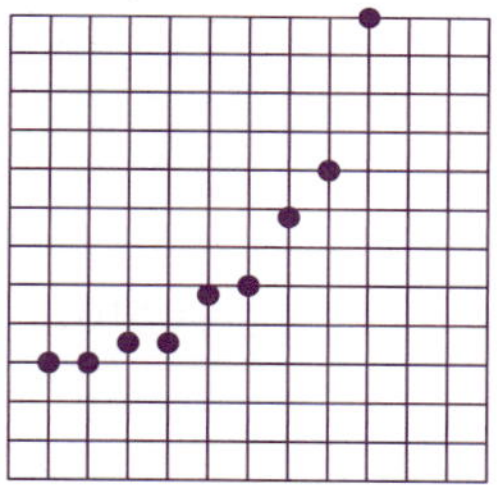

b.

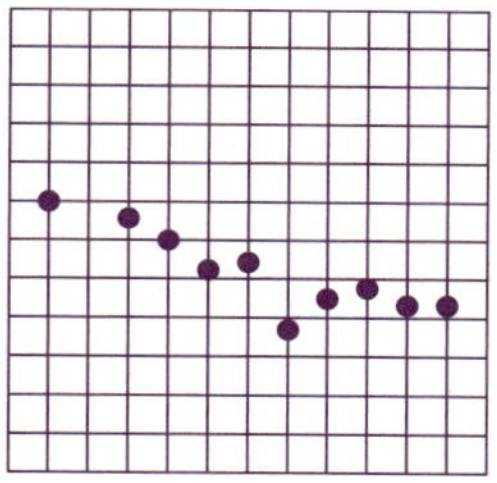

c.

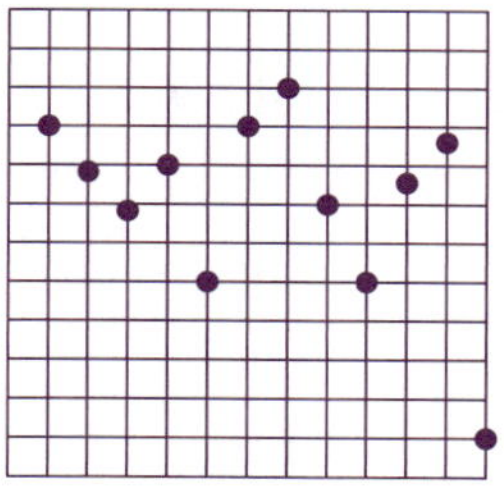

d.

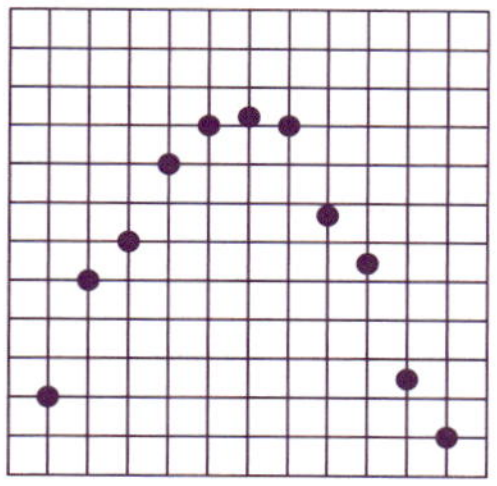

e.

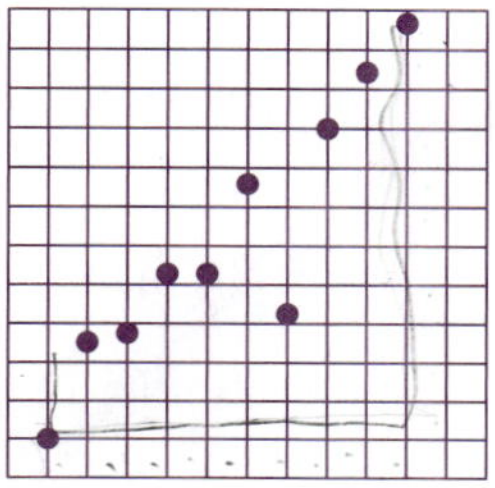

f.

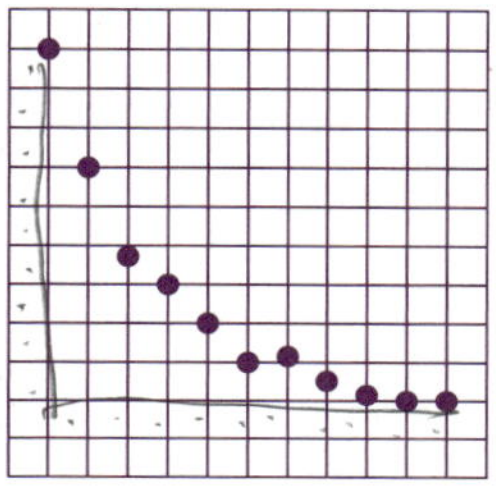

5. Betty's Bakery has a phone system for which the monthly bill depends on the amount of time the phones are in use. The billing formula is $c = 50 + 6h$, where c is the cost in dollars and h is the number of hours of use.

   a. In June, the phone was used for 70 hours. What was the phone bill for June?

   b. What do the numbers 50 and 6 in the billing formula tell you about the relationship between the hours of use and the monthly bill?

   c. Is the relationship between cost and hours of use linear or nonlinear?

   d. What do the numbers 50 and 6 tell you about the pattern you would see in a table and a graph of the (hours, cost) data?

   e. Solve the equation $230 = 50 + 6h$, and explain what the answer tells you about the phone bill for Betty's Bakery.

Extensions

6. Kareem's youth group is going on an outing. They will rent a dormitory for $600 and charter a bus for $250. In addition, each person will pay $20 for food and supplies.

   a. In general, how will the cost per person change as the number of people increases?

   b. Copy and complete this table to show the cost per person for various numbers of people.

Number of people	5	10	15	20	25	30
Cost per person (dollars)						

   c. Make a graph of the data, and draw a straight line or a curve that models the trend. Describe the pattern of change.

   d. Use your graph to predict the cost per person if 37 people go on the trip.

   e. Write an equation for the relationship between the number of people, n, and the cost per person, c.

f. Use your equation to predict the cost per person if 37 people go on the trip.

g. Compare the predictions given by the graph and equation models. Which prediction do you think is most accurate? Explain your choice.

h. Which problems from this unit have graphs with similar patterns of change?

7. Four biologists are studying the caribou and wolf populations in a particular area of Alaska. The caribou are prey to the wolves, and keeping the two populations in balance is important to the survival of both species. The biologists are trying to predict what will happen if no measures are taken to control the populations. After studying the situation, each biologist makes a graph of his or her prediction. Describe what each graph represents in terms of the animal populations.

Biologist A

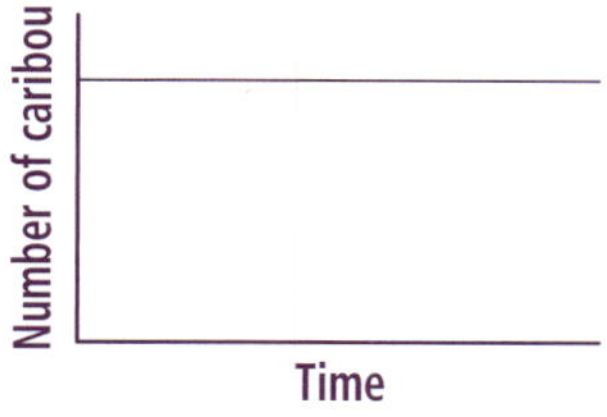

Biologist B

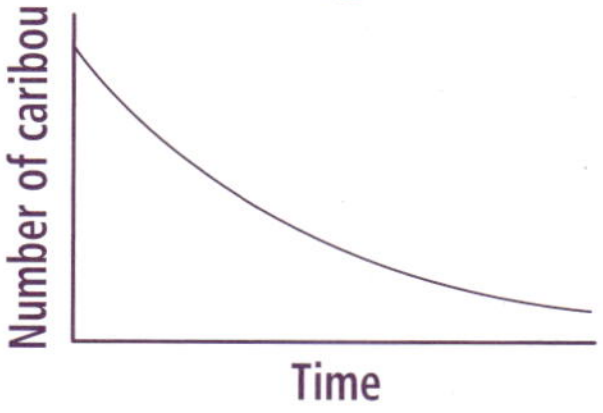

Biologist C

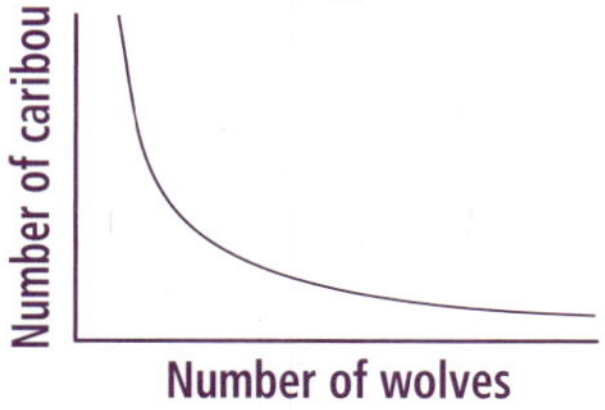

Biologist D

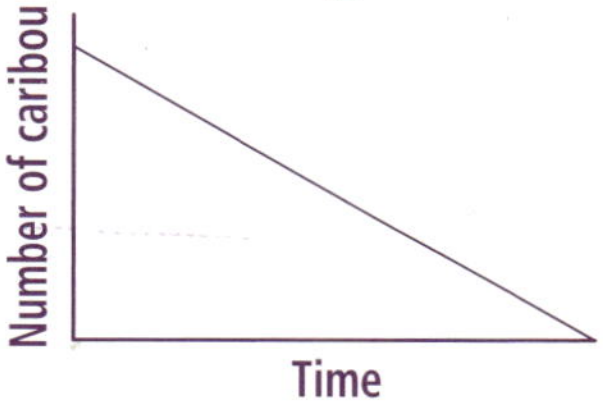

Mathematical Reflections

In this investigation, you explored more nonlinear relationships.

- In Problem 3.1, you investigated the relationship between the number of years money is invested and the amount of money in the bank account.
- In Problem 3.2, you investigated the relationship between the glass number and the amount of water in the glass.

These questions will help you summarize what you have learned:

1. How are the graph models for these two relationships similar?
2. How are the graph models for these two relationships different?
3. How can you tell that a relationship is linear without making a graph?
4. Describe the different kinds of graph models you have discovered in your work so far in this unit.

Think about your answers to these questions, discuss your ideas with other students and your teacher, and then write a summary of your findings in your journal.

INVESTIGATION 4

A World of Patterns

In this Investigation, you will sketch graphs that fit written descriptions, and you will make up stories about what a given graph might represent.

4.1 Modeling Real-Life Events

The East Coast bus tour is just entering Charleston, South Carolina. The tour group plans to see a warship from the Civil War era and then have lunch. When they arrive at the ship, the tide is low and the ship is nearly aground in the harbor. They are told that no more tours may board the ship until the tide rises and the ship is afloat. The tour cannot agree on what to do while they wait, so they divide into smaller groups.

One group goes for an early lunch. Unfortunately, the furnace at the restaurant breaks just as they arrive. It's a cold day, and the restaurant cools down very quickly until it reaches the outside temperature. The manager apologizes and asks the group to come back later for a free meal.

A second group goes parasailing. It's cold outside, so they wear wet suits. Paige goes first. She is pulled along briefly by the boat. Then her parachute opens, and she soars into the air. After taking her once around the harbor, the boat operator adjusts the speed, and Paige descends gradually and lands gently on a platform at the back of the boat. The others take their turns, and they all agree that the experience is thrilling.

A third group decides to get some exercise after sitting so long on the bus. They rent bicycles and ride at a steady pace along some quiet, winding streets. By the time they finish their ride, the tide has risen, and they meet the rest of the group for the boat tour. After the boat tour, everyone goes out to dinner and then walks along the beach as the tide goes out.

Many of the events in the story of the group's day can be modeled with graphs. In this problem, you will explore some of these graph models.

Problem 4.1

A. The graphs below model events described in the story. Tell which event each graph represents, and explain why you think the graph is a good model for the event. Copy each graph, and label the axes with the variable names.

1.

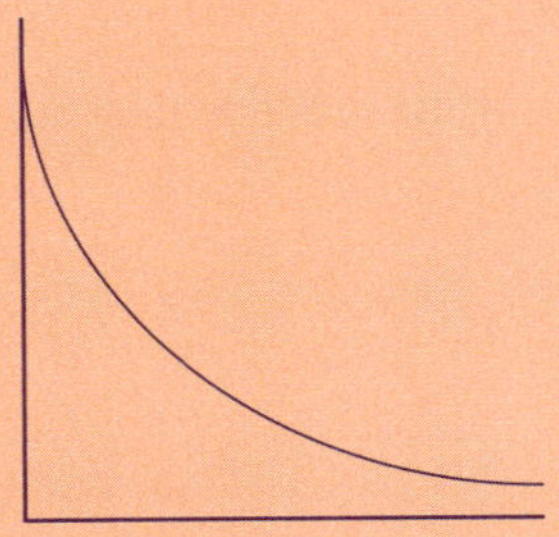

2.

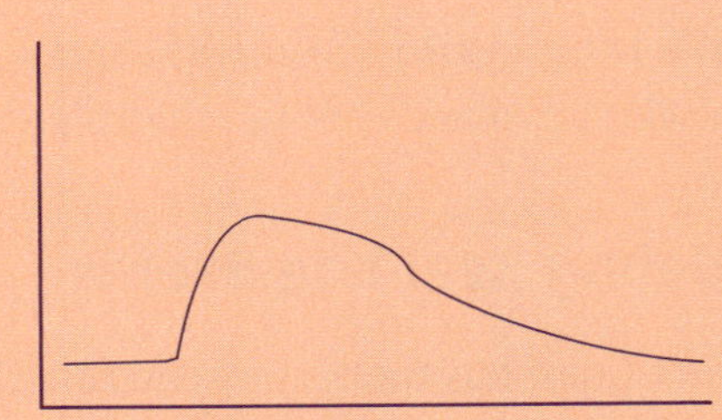

B. Identify other events in the story that involve relationships between two variables. For each event, sketch a graph that models the relationship between the variables. Carefully label the axes so it is easy to see what the graph represents.

C. For each graph you sketched in part B, write a sentence or two explaining what the graph shows and how it fits the description in the story.

D. Write a paragraph about the experiences a fourth group had while waiting for the tide to rise. Sketch a graph or graphs that show how the variables in your story are related.

Problem 4.1 Follow-Up

The following graphs show the relationship between time and distance traveled by a cyclist.

1. a. Describe the relationship shown in this graph. Make up a story about the cyclist that could be modeled by the graph.

b. Over what interval in the graph is the cyclist traveling the fastest? Explain how you know.

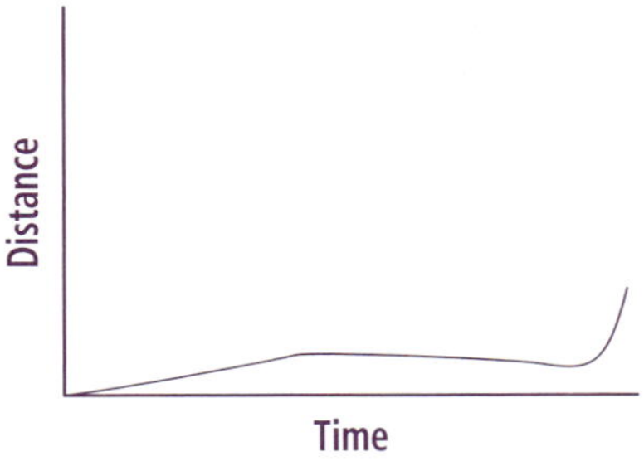

2. a. Describe the relationship shown in this graph. Make up a story about the cyclist that could be modeled by the graph.

b. Over what interval in the graph is the cyclist traveling the fastest? Explain how you know.

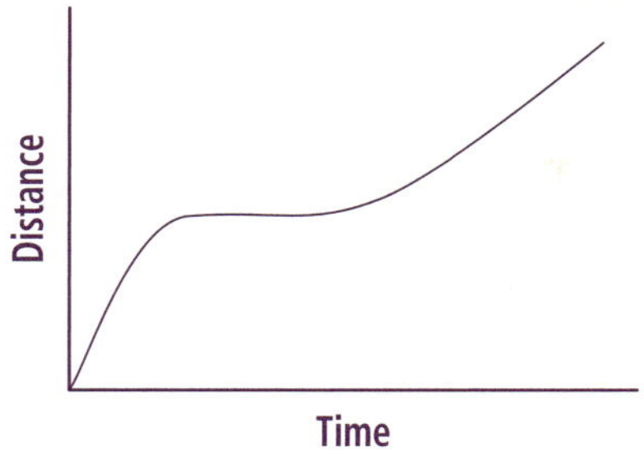

3. a. Describe the relationship shown in this graph. Make up a story about the cyclist that could be modeled by the graph.

b. Speculate about what will happen next, and explain how the graph would change.

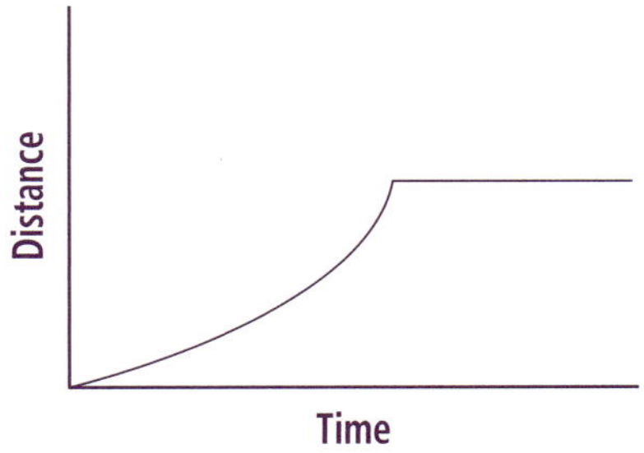

4.2 Writing Stories to Match Graphs

In the last problem, you matched graphs with real-life events described in a story, and you sketched graphs to match written descriptions. In the follow-up, you made up stories about what given graphs might represent. In this problem, you will continue to work with graphs of real-life events.

A car and a bus are traveling in the same direction on the same road. The bus has just stopped to pick up a passenger, and the car has stopped directly behind it. In this problem, you will look at several graphs that show what might happen next, and you will make up stories that the graphs could represent.

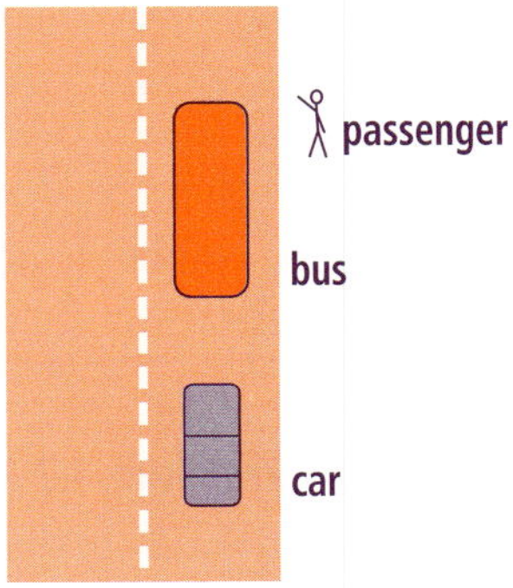

Problem 4.2

Graphs A–F show six possibilities for what might happen at some point after the passenger boards the bus. Each graph shows the relationship between time and distance from the bus station for the bus and the car. For each graph, make up a story about the bus and the car that matches the information in the graph.

A.

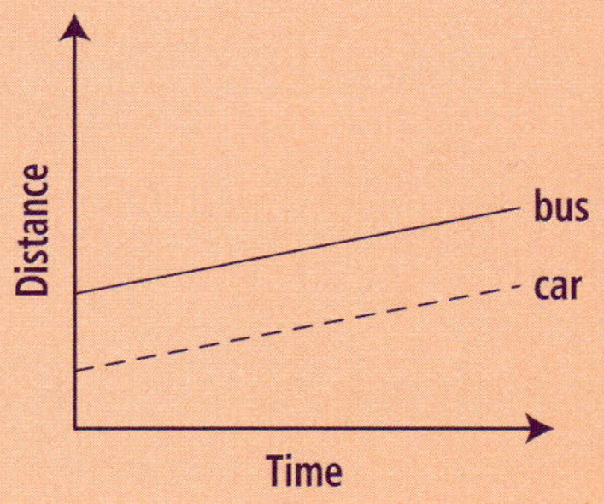

B.

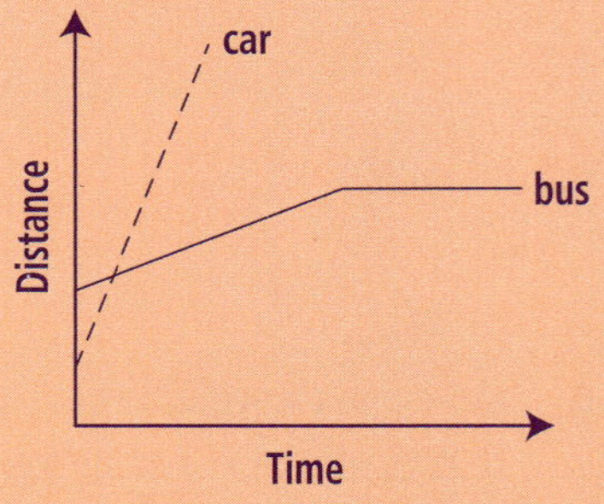

C.

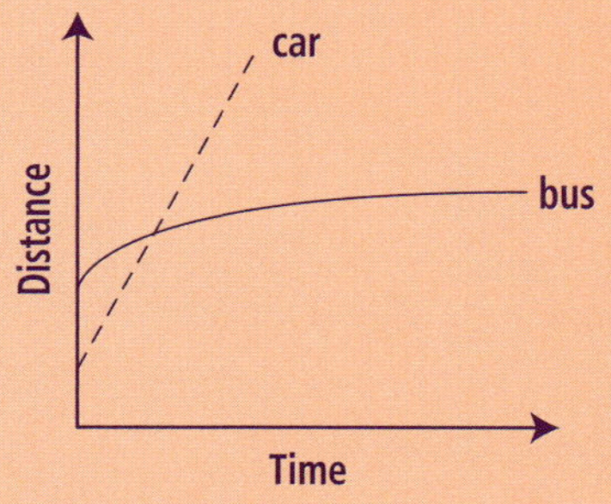

D.

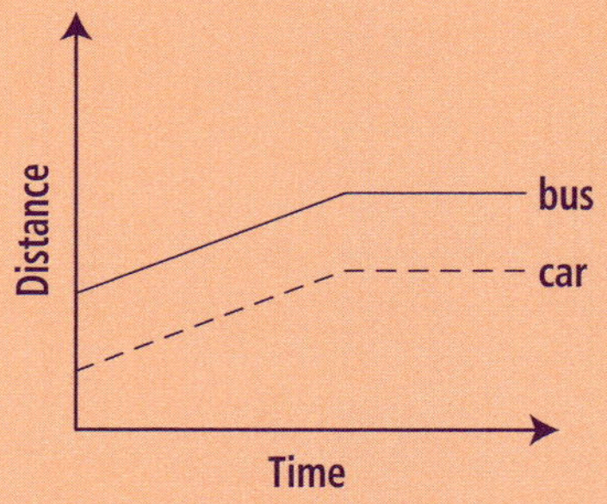

E.

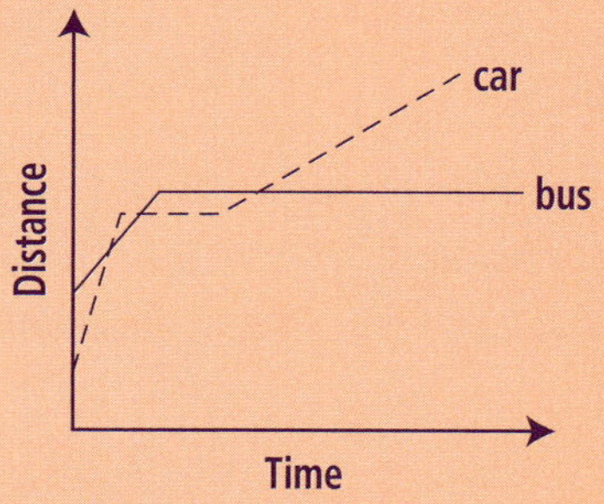

F.

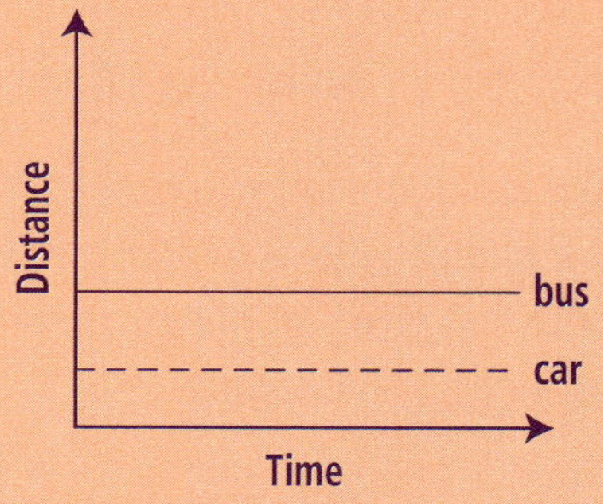

Which graph do you think best represents what might really happen? If none of the graphs seem correct, sketch a graph of what you think is likely to happen.

Problem 4.2 Follow-Up

1. In which graph does the car reach its greatest speed? Explain how you know.
2. In which graph does the bus reach its greatest speed? Explain.

4.3 Exploring Graphs

A graphing calculator is a useful tool for exploring graphs of interesting equations. Making graphs of equations by hand can take a lot of time. With a graphing calculator, you can enter an equation and see its graph almost instantly.

Problem 4.3

A. Use your graphing calculator to graph each equation below. Adjust the window settings until you think you have a good view of the graph. Copy the graph onto your paper.

1. $y = \frac{1}{x}$

2. $y = (x - 1)(5 - x)$

3. $y = 2.7x$

4. $y = 2^x$

B. Choose two of the graphs from part a, and make up stories that could be modeled by them. For each graph you choose, be sure to tell which variable in your story is on the horizontal axis and which variable is on the vertical axis.

Problem 4.3 Follow-Up

1. a. Do you think every real-life situation can be modeled by a graph?

b. Do you think every graph can be represented by an equation?

2. Look back at the graph models you have made in this unit. For each graph you made in part A of Problem 4.3, find a graph model from your earlier work with a similar shape. Make a sketch of the graph model you find, and give its equation if you know it.

As you work on these ACE questions, use your calculator whenever you need it.

Applications

In 1–3, do parts a and b.

1. 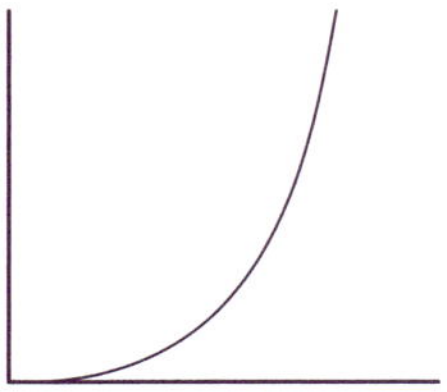

2. 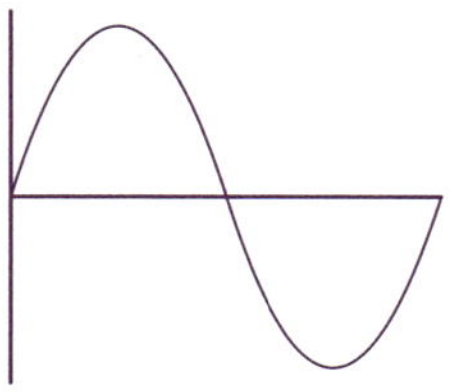

3. 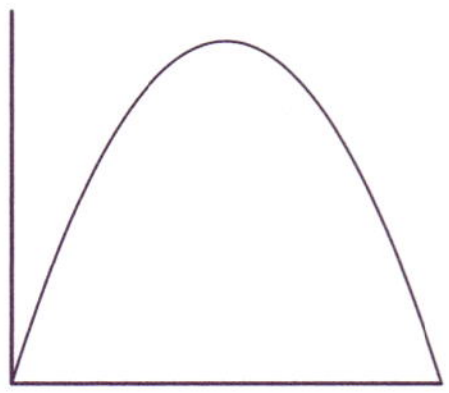

a. Describe a situation you think could be modeled by the graph. Be sure to tell which variable each axis represents.

b. Explain why the graph is a good model for the situation you described.

4. The table below shows Jamie's height from age 5 to age 18.

Age	5	6	7	8	9	10	11
Height (cm)	110	116	121	127	132	137	143

Age	12	13	14	15	16	17	18
Height (cm)	149	157	165	173	176	178	180

a. Graph the (age, height) data. Draw a straight line or curve to model the data.

b. What was Jamie's average rate of growth from age 5 to age 12? If this rate of growth had continued, how tall would Jamie have been at age 18? How tall would he have been at age 25?

c. During what time period did Jamie grow the fastest? How can you see this in the graph?

5. The drawings below show the progress of a tour bus over a 35-second period.

a. Describe what is happening in the drawings.

b. Sketch a graph of the relationship between time and distance from the starting point for this series of drawings.

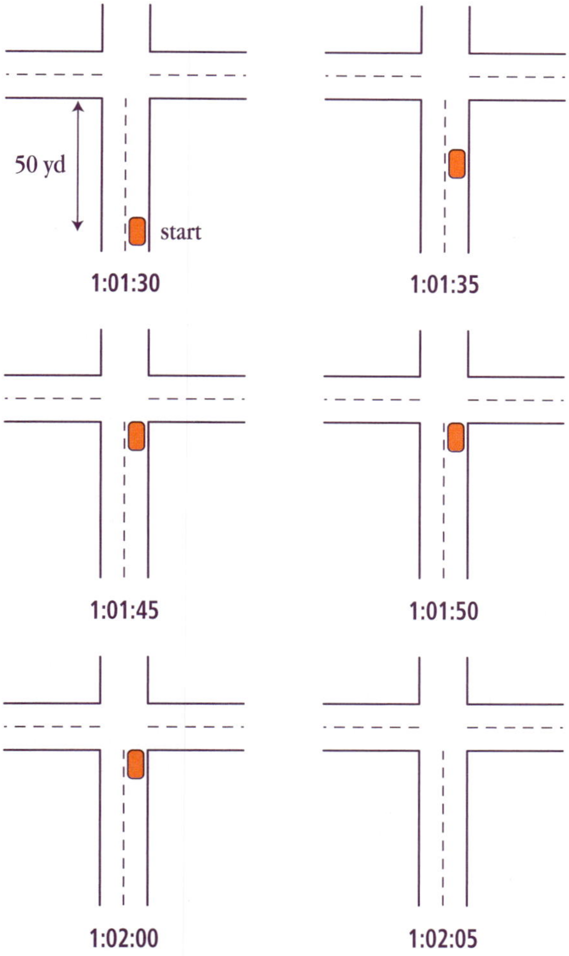

Connections

6. The graph below shows the progress of the Orient Express on a trip from London to Paris.

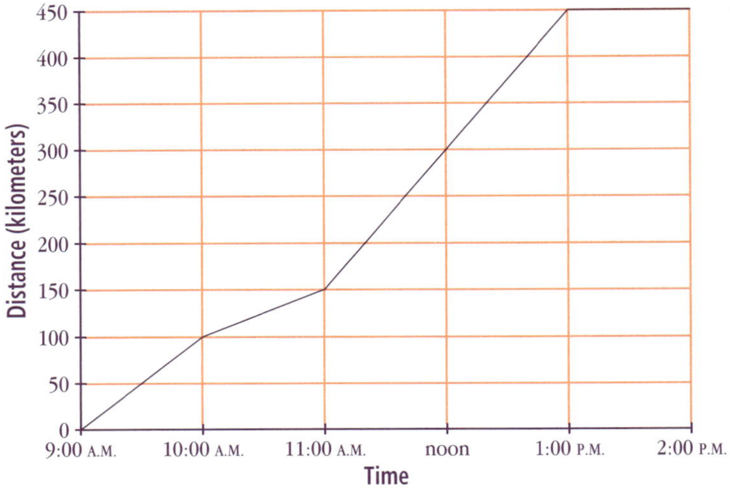

a. Describe in words what the graph shows.

b. Write an equation for the part of the graph between 9 A.M. and 10 A.M.

c. Write an equation for the part of the graph between 10 A.M. and 11 A.M.

d. Write an equation for the part of the graph between 11 A.M. and 1 P.M.

Big Ben in London

The Eiffel Tower in Paris

7. In your previous math work, you investigated the relationships among the radius, height, base area, and volume of a cylinder. You found that the volume of a cylinder is equal to its base area multiplied by its height.

a. Suppose you are in charge of designing a cylindrical can to hold 250 ml of juice. Investigate some possible (base area, height) combinations for the can. Try radii of 2.5 cm, 3 cm, 3.5 cm, and any other measurements you think are reasonable. Record your findings in a table like the one below. (Recall that 1 ml = 1 cm^3.)

Radius (cm)	Base area (cm^2)	Height (cm)	Volume (ml)
			250

b. Make a graph of your (base area, height) data.

c. Draw a straight line or curve to model the data. What other situations in this unit have similar graph models?

d. Write an equation that fits your graph model.

e. Which (base area, height) combination would you choose for the can? Give reasons for your answer.

Did you know?

Designing a can is a complex process. Manufacturers must consider the cost of the sterilization process, the strength of the can, the amount of waste metal left after cutting the base and side, and the packing and shipping space the cans require. Here are three important relationships they must think about:

- There is an *inverse relationship* between the amount of material used and the sterilization time. In other words, for a given volume, cans with less surface area take more time to sterilize than cans with greater surface area.
- Cans with wider bases must be made of thicker metal so they will be strong enough to withstand the pressures of the sterilization process.
- Cans with smaller diameters waste less space in packing and shipping.

8. Terri is designing a can. She has collected the following data about diameters and sterilization times.

Diameter (cm)	1	1.2	1.8	2.4	2.8	3	3.2	3.5	3.8
Time (seconds)	6.2	5.2	3.5	2.6	2.2	2.1	1.9	1.8	1.6

a. Make a graph of the data by hand or by using a graphing calculator. Draw a straight line or curve that models the data. Which other problems in this unit have similar graph models?

b. Find an equation that fits your graph model. If you are using a graphing calculator, enter your equation and check the fit.

c. Use your graph or equation model to predict the sterilization times for a can with a diameter of 1.5 centimeters and a can with a diameter of 4.5 centimeters. Explain how you made your predictions.

Extensions

9. The diagrams below document the growth of a pea root at regular intervals. Use these diagrams to answer parts a and b on the next page.

Diagram 1

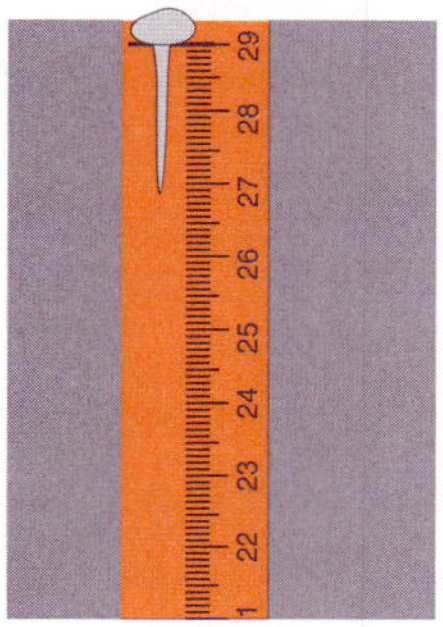

Diagram 2

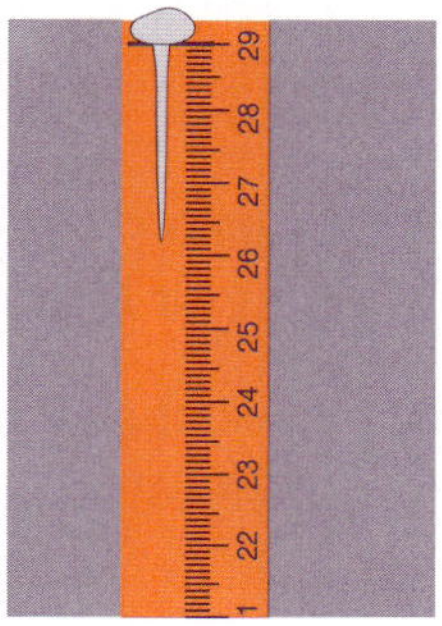

Diagram 3

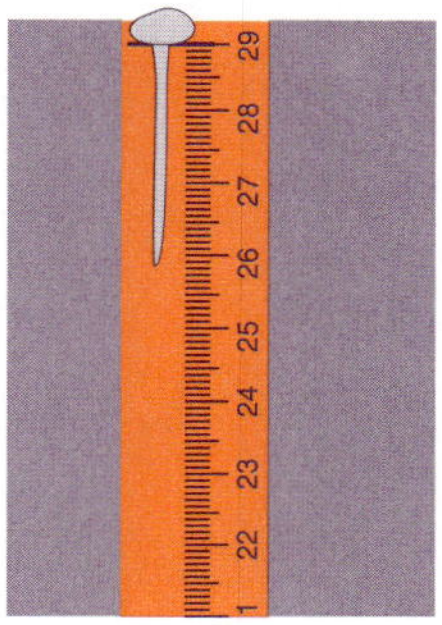

Diagram 4

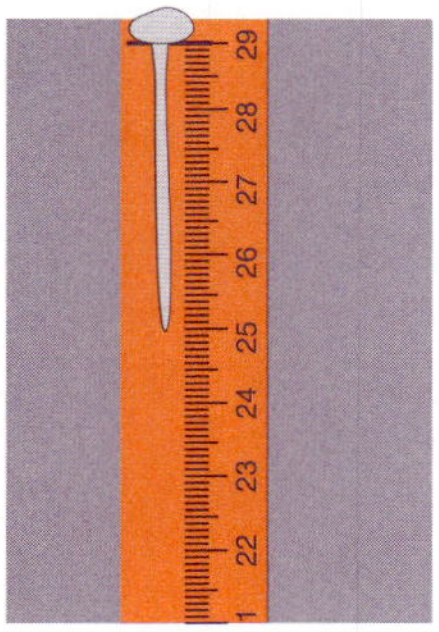

Diagram 5

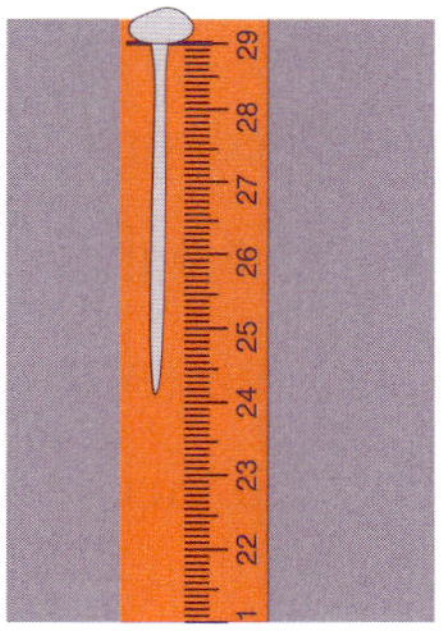

Diagram 6

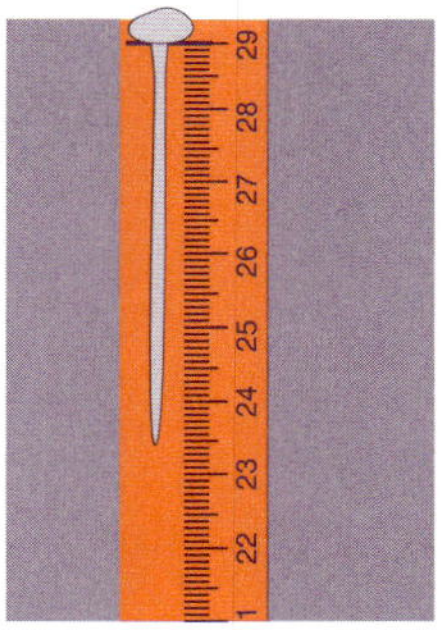

Diagram 7

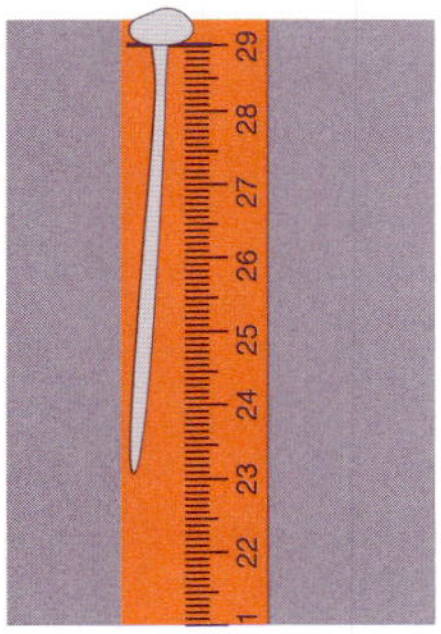

Diagram 8

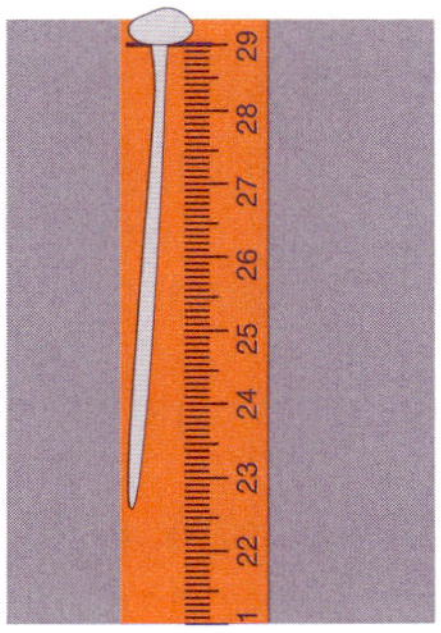

Diagram 9

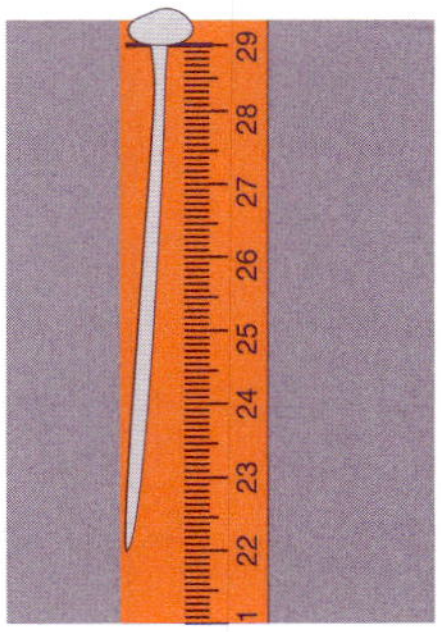

a. Make a graph of the relationship between the diagram number and the length of the pea root.

b. Draw a straight line or a curve that models the data. Is your graph model linear? Explain.

10. Some of the equations below have appeared in problems you worked on in this unit. The other equations have graphs with the same general shapes as graphs you have investigated.

a. Without graphing the equations, organize them into three groups according to the shapes you predict for their graphs.

b. Use your graphing calculator to graph the equations. (Suggested window settings are given for each equation.) Make any adjustments necessary in your groupings.

i. $y = 8.7x$ (suggested window: $x = 0$ to 10, $y = 0$ to 100)

ii. $y = {}^{-}40x + 480$ (suggested window: $x = 0$ to 14, $y = {}^{-}50$ to 500)

iii. $y = \frac{120}{x}$ (suggested window: $x = 0$ to 100, $y = 0$ to 100)

iv. $y = \frac{8.7}{x}$ (suggested window: $x = 0$ to 20, $y = 0$ to 20)

v. $y = 100(1.08^x)$ (suggested window: $x = 0$ to 20, $y = 0$ to 500)

vi. $y = \frac{40}{x}$ (suggested window: $x = 0$ to 50, $y = 0$ to 50)

vii. $y = 1.08x$ (suggested window: $x = 0$ to 10, $y = 0$ to 10)

viii. $y = 100(0.5^x)$ (suggested window: $x = 0$ to 10, $y = 0$ to 100)

ix. $y = 100 - 1.08x$ (suggested window: $x = 0$ to 100, $y = 0$ to 100)

x. $y = 2^x$ (suggested window: $x = 0$ to 10, $y = 0$ to 100)

xi. $y = 2x$ (suggested window: $x = 0$ to 10, $y = 0$ to 10)

xii. $y = \frac{2}{x}$ (suggested window: $x = 0$ to 10, $y = 0$ to 10)

c. For each group of equations, make up a different equation that you think belongs in the group. Use your calculator to check your equations.

Mathematical Reflections

In this investigation and throughout this unit, you looked at relationships associated with real-life situations. You found that many of these relationships can be represented by graph models and equation models. These questions will help you summarize what you have learned:

1. Look back at the graphs you have made in this unit. Find several graphs that show relationships in which y increases as x increases. Try to find graphs with as many different shapes as you can. Sketch each graph, and describe it in words.

2. Look back at the graphs you have made in this unit. Find several graphs that show relationships in which y decreases as x increases. Describe each graph in words.

3. Look back at the graphs you have made in this unit. Find several graphs that show relationships in which y both increases and decreases as x increases. Describe each graph in words.

Think about your answers to these questions, discuss your ideas with other students and your teacher, and then write a summary of your findings in your journal.

Looking Back and Looking Ahead

Unit Reflections

Working on the problems of this unit expanded your skill in building and using *mathematical models* for relationships among variables. You had experience *collecting data* from experiments, *graphing* the data, *finding equations* that express the patterns in those graphs, and using equations to *make predictions*. You worked again with *linear relations* and their equations in the form $y = mx + b$, but you also explored several important kinds of *nonlinear relations*.

Using Your Algebraic Reasoning—To test your understanding and skill in finding and applying mathematical models, consider the following problems suggested by visits to a large recreation area that has a playground, hiking trails, amusement rides, and a small farm.

1 *The farm has animals varying in size from small rabbits to goats and pigs. The farm staff keep records of how the animals grow and what they eat.*

a. The following table shows the weight of one pig that grew up on the farm.

Age (months)	0	1	2	3	4	5	6
Weight (pounds)	3	15	28	40	54	66	80

i. Plot these (age, weight) data on a coordinate graph, draw a linear graph that seems to fit the data pattern well, and find a linear equation in the form $y = mx + b$ for your graph.

ii. What do the values of m and b tell about the growth of the young pig?

iii. Use the linear model to estimate the pig's weight at age 3.5 months and 7 months.

b. One group of student visitors suspected that farm animals would eat less food in warm weather than in cold weather. They asked the farmers to keep records of what one adult goat ate on days with different high temperatures over a six-month period.

Temperature (°F)	30	40	45	55	60	75	85	90
Food (kilograms)	2.5	2.1	2.0	1.8	1.5	1.2	0.8	0.6

i. Plot these (temperature, food) data on a coordinate graph, draw a linear graph that seems to fit the data pattern well, and find a linear equation in the form $y = mx + b$ for the graph you draw.

ii. What do the values of m and b tell about the relation between temperature and the goat's food consumption?

iii. Use the linear equation to estimate the goat's appetite on a day when the high temperature is predicted to be 50°F and when it is predicted to be 70°F.

2 *A small train gives rides around the park on a 5000-meter track. Drivers complete the trip in different times. When many people are waiting in line they go faster, and when there are fewer customers they take a slower trip.*

a. Sketch a graph showing how *average speed, s,* (in meters per minute) is related to trip *time, t,* (in minutes) and find an equation relating s and t.

b. Write several sentences explaining as accurately as possible how speed changes as trip time changes. In particular, describe the kind of variation involved in this relationship between time and average speed.

3 *A pond in the park has a surface area of about 8000 square meters. Every summer, as the weather gets warm, lily pads cover part of the surface of the pond. By June 1, the lily pads cover about 200 square meters. Each week until the end of August, the area covered by lily pads increases by about 10%.*

a. Calculate the surface area of the pond covered by lily pads at the end of each week during June, July, and August.

b. Plot a graph of the data from part a and write several sentences describing how the area covered by the lily pads grows throughout the summer.

c. Explain how the growth of 10% per week can be calculated rapidly using a calculator.

4 *One of the most popular features on the playground is a 50-meter-long slide. A side view of the slide is shown in the sketch.*

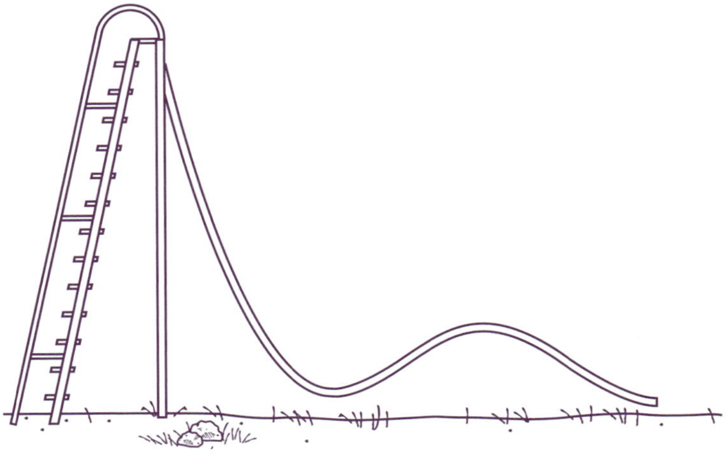

a. Sketch a graph showing how a slider's speed will vary along the path of the slide.

b. Write an explanation of your graph that tells in words what will happen and why.

Explaining Your Reasoning—To answer the questions about operations in the recreation area you had to use algebraic knowledge about number patterns, graphs, and equations or formulas. You had to recognize linear and nonlinear patterns and find matching equations.

1. How do you decide when a data pattern can be modeled well by a linear equation in the form $y = mx + b$? How will the values of m and b relate to the data pattern?
2. How are the data patterns, graphs, and symbolic equations in the nonlinear relations you studied similar to and different from those modeled by linear equations?
3. How can a graph or equation model for some relationship between variables be used in solving practical problems?
4. What limitations do algebraic models have as problem-solving tools?

The algebra ideas and techniques you've used in this unit will be applied and extended in many future units of *Connected Mathematics* such as *Growing, Growing, Growing* and *Frogs, Fleas, and Painted Cubes* and in problems of science and business. You'll study several important families of algebraic models and strategies for finding and using those models to solve problems.

Glossary

equation model An equation that describes the relationship between two variables. In this unit, you fit graph models to data points, and then, when possible, you used your graph models to find equation models. An equation model allows you to make predictions about values between and beyond the values in a set of data.

fulcrum The balance point of a teeter-totter or balance. In the teeter-totter experiment, you measured distances from the fulcrum to the weights on both sides. You found that for a teeter-totter to balance, the product of the weight and distance on one side of the fulcrum must equal the product of the weight and distance on the other side of the fulcrum.

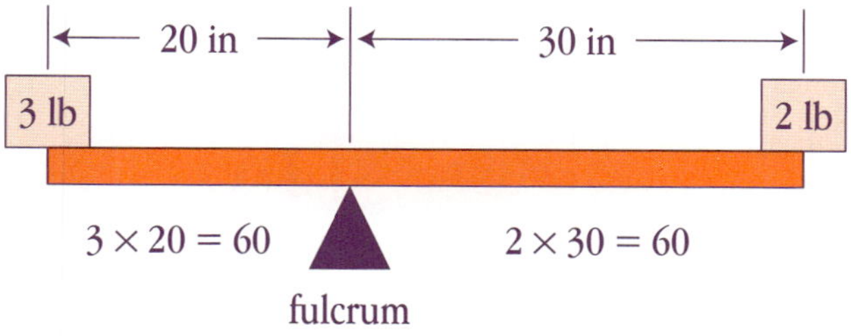

graph model A straight line or a curve that represents a mathematical relationship. If the data you plot show a trend, you can draw a graph model that fits the pattern of change in the data. A graph model allows you to make predictions about values between and beyond the values in a set of data.

inverse relationship A nonlinear relationship in which the product of two variables is constant. In an inverse relationship, the values of one variable decrease as the values of the other variable increase. In the bridge-length experiment, you found an inverse relationship between length and breaking weight. In the teeter-totter experiment, you found an inverse relationship between distance and weight.

linear relationship A relationship in which there is a constant rate of change between two variables. A linear relationship can be represented by a straight-line graph and by an equation of the form $y = mx + b$. In the equation, m is the slope of the line, and b is the y-intercept.

mathematical model A mathematical representation, such as a graph or an equation, of the relationship in a set of data.

relationship An association between two variables. A relationship can be represented in a graph, in a table, or with an equation.

Glosario

fulcro El punto de equilibrio de un subibaja o de una balanza. En el experimento del subibaja los estudiantes miden la distancia desde el fulcro a los pesos de ambos lados. Descubriste que para que un subibaja esté en equilibrio, el producto del peso y la distancia de un lado del fulcro debe ser igual al producto del peso y la distancia del otro lado del fulcro.

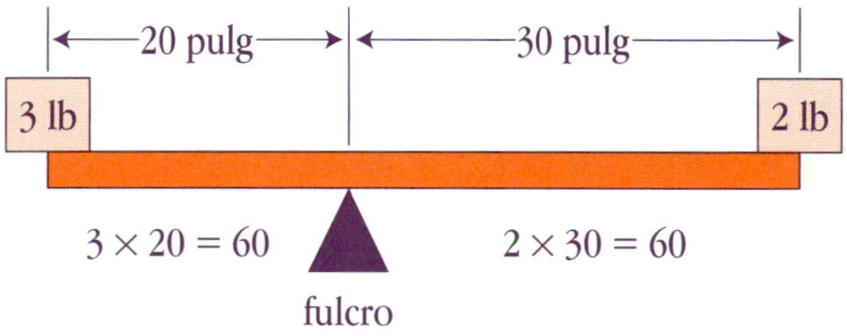

modelo de ecuación Una ecuación que describe la relación entre dos variables. En esta unidad, relacionaste modelos de gráficas con puntos de datos. Luego, cuando fue posible, usaste los modelos de gráficas para hallar modelos de ecuaciones. Un modelo de ecuación te permite hacer predicciones sobre valores, entre los valores de un conjunto de datos y más allá de ellos.

modelo de gráfica Una recta o una curva que representa una relación matemática. Si los datos marcados representan una tendencia, puedes dibujar un modelo de gráfica que represente el patrón de cambio en los datos. Un modelo de gráfica te permite hacer predicciones sobre valores, entre los valores de un conjunto de datos y más allá de ellos.

modelo matemático Una representación matemática, como una gráfica o una ecuación, de la relación de un conjunto de datos.

relación Una asociación entre dos variables. Una relación puede representarse con una gráfica, una tabla o una ecuación.

relación inversa Una relación no lineal en la que el producto de dos variables es constante. En una relación inversa, los valores de una variable disminuyen medida que los valores de la otra variable aumentan. En el experimento sobre la longitud de los puentes, hallaste una relación inversa entre la longitud y el peso de colapso. En el experimento sobre el subibaja, descubriste una relación inversa entre la distancia y el peso.

relación líneal Una relación en la que hay una tasa de cambio constante entre dos variables. Una relación lineal puede estar representada por una gráfica de línea recta y por una ecuación con la forma $y = mx + b$. En la ecuación, m es la pendiente de la recta y b es el punto de intersección de y.

Index

Connected Mathematics™

Looking for Pythagoras

The Pythagorean Theorem

Student Edition

Glenda Lappan
James T. Fey
William M. Fitzgerald
Susan N. Friel
Elizabeth Difanis Phillips

PEARSON
Prentice Hall

Glenview, Illinois
Needham, Massachusetts
Upper Saddle River, New Jersey

Looking for Pythagoras

Connected Mathematics™ was developed at Michigan State University with the support of National Science Foundation Grant No. MDR 9150217.

This project was supported, in part,
by the
National Science Foundation
Opinions expressed are those of the authors
and not necessarily those of the Foundation

The Michigan State University authors and administration have agreed that all MSU royalties arising from this publication will be devoted to purposes supported by the Department of Mathematics and the MSU Mathematics Education Enrichment Fund.

Photo Acknowledgements: 5 © Margot Granitsas/The Image Works; 10 © Robert Llewellyn/Superstock, Inc.; 13 © Bob Daemmrich/The Image Works; 14 © Laima Druskis/Stock, Boston; 30 © ET Archive/Superstock, Inc.; 41 © Lambert/Archive Photos

Contents

Looking for Pythagoras

In ancient Egypt, the Nile River overflowed annually, destroying property boundaries. As a result, the Egyptians had to remeasure their land every year. Their tool to mark right angles was a rope divided by knots into 12 segments. How do you think they used it?

A carpenter wants to check that the wall he is building is perpendicular to the ground. He makes a mark 8 feet high on the wall and then places one end of a 10-foot pole on the mark and the other end on the ground. If the wall is perpendicular to the ground, how far from the base of the wall will the pole touch the ground?

Horace is the catcher for the Humbolt Bees baseball team. Sally, the star of the Canfield Cats, is on first base. The pitcher throws a fastball, and the batter swings and misses. Horace catches the pitch as Sally takes off for second base. How far must Horace throw the baseball to get Sally out at second base

In this unit, you will explore side lengths and areas of right triangles and squares. Your explorations will lead you to discover one of the most important relationships in all of mathematics: the *Pythagorean Theorem*. The Pythagorean Theorem is so important that much of geometry, trigonometry, and calculus would be impossible without it.

In your previous math work, you used whole numbers and fractions to describe lengths. In this unit, you will work with lengths that are impossible to describe with whole numbers or fractions. To talk about such lengths, you need to use another type of number, called an *irrational number*.

As you work on this unit, you will use what you are learning to solve interesting problems like those on the previous page.

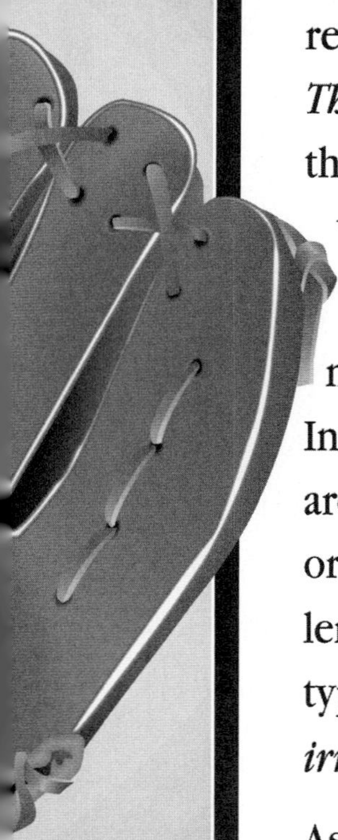

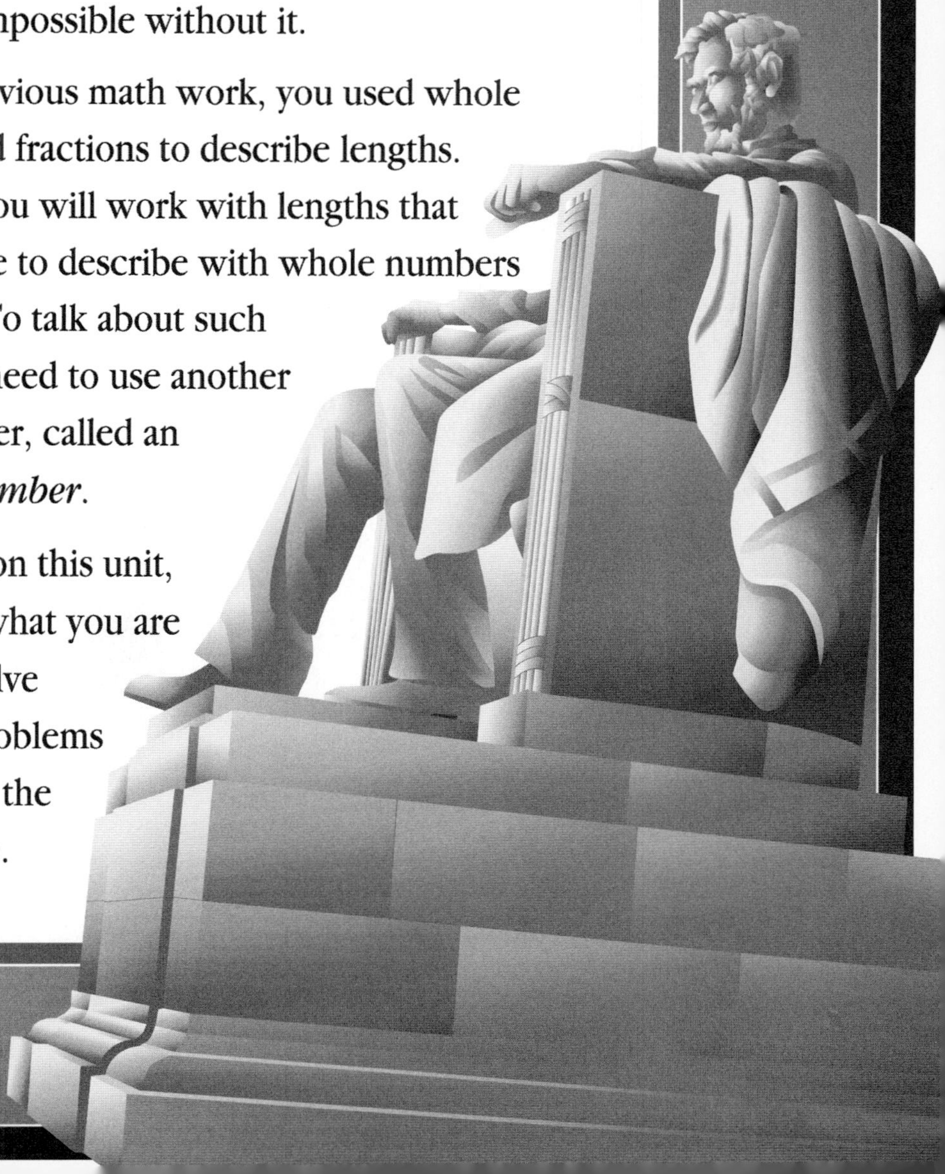

Mathematical Highlights

In *Looking For Pythagoras* you will explore an important relationship among the side lengths of a right triangle and learn about a new kind of number. The unit should help you to

- Relate the area of a square to the length of a side of the square;
- Develop strategies for finding the distance between two points on a coordinate grid;
- Understand and apply the Pythagorean Theorem;
- Extend understanding of number systems to include irrational numbers;
- Locate irrational numbers on a number line;
- Represent fractions as decimals and decimals as fractions;
- Determine whether the decimal representation for a fraction terminates or repeats; and
- Use the Pythagorean Theorem to solve everyday problems.

As you work problems in this unit, make it a habit to ask questions about problem situations involving the Pythagorean Theorem and rational and irrational numbers. *Is this a situation where it is appropriate to use the Pythagorean Theorem? Do I need to find the distance between two points? What quantities are in the problems? What patterns among fractions are useful to predict which fractions can be represented by terminating or repeating decimals? How can I estimate the square root of a number?*

INVESTIGATION 1

Locating Points

The map on the next page shows the central part of Washington, D.C. The streets form a grid of north-south and east-west lines. The city is divided into four sections, or *quadrants*, by the north-south line formed by North and South Capitol Streets and the east-west line stretching from the Lincoln Memorial, through the Mall, and down East Capitol Street.

U.S. Supreme Court Building

Think about this!

- How would you describe the locations of George Washington University, Dupont Circle, the White House, Union Station, and Benjamin Banneker Park?
- How would you describe the directions of Massachusetts Avenue, New York Avenue, and Vermont Avenue?
- How would you find the distance from Union Station to Dupont Circle?
- How do the locations of the intersection of G Street and 8th Street SE and the intersection of G Street and 8th Street NW relate to the location of the Capitol Building?

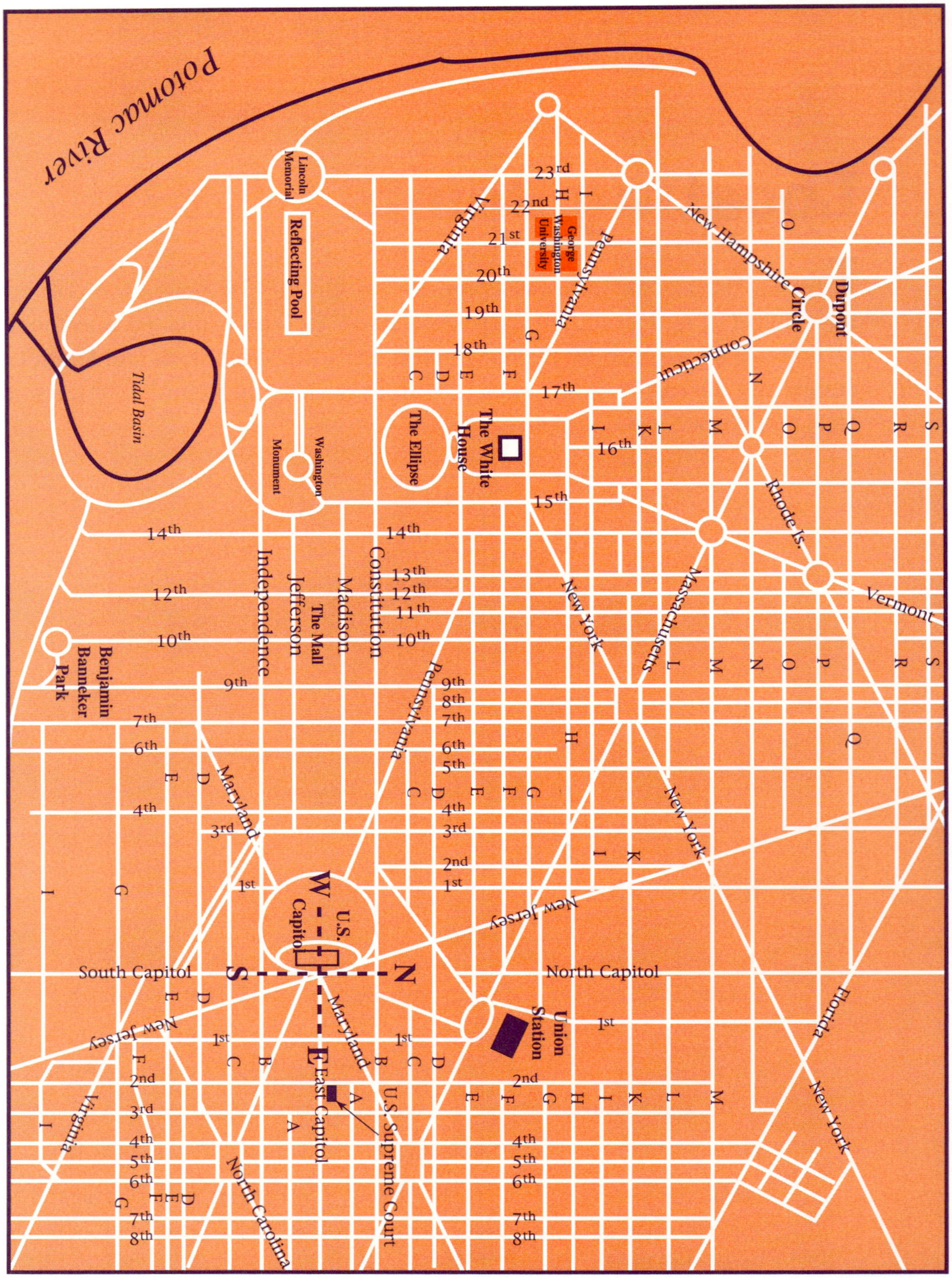

The street system of Washington, D.C., was designed 200 years ago by Pierre L'Enfant. L'Enfant's design is based on a *coordinate system,* with the origin at the Capitol and north-south and east-west streets forming grid lines.

In mathematics, we use a *coordinate system* to describe the locations of points. Recall that horizontal and vertical number lines, called the x- and y-axes, divide the plane into four quadrants. You describe the location of a point by giving its coordinates as an ordered pair of the form (x, y). On the coordinate grid below, four points are labeled with their coordinates.

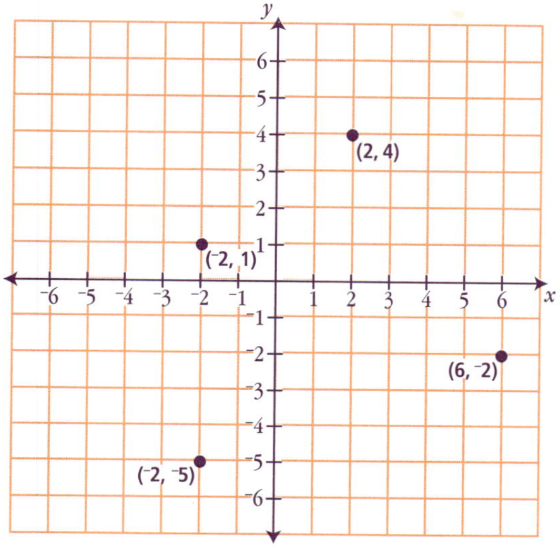

Did you know?

The coordinate system described above is called the *rectangular coordinate system.* You can also locate points in a plane by using the *polar coordinate system.* The polar coordinates of a point consist of a distance and an angle. Below is a polar grid with four points labeled with their coordinates. Can you figure out how to locate points on a polar grid?

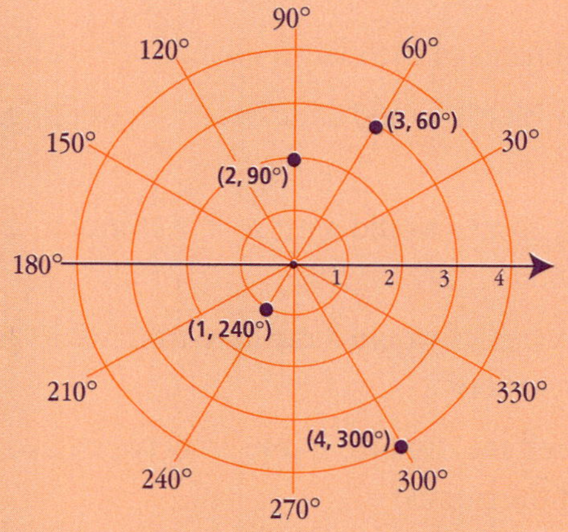

1.1 Driving Around Euclid

The founders of the city of Euclid liked math so much that they named their city after a famous mathematician and designed their street system to look like a coordinate grid. A map of the city is shown below. The Euclideans describe the locations of buildings and other landmarks by giving coordinates. For example, the animal shelter is located at (6, $^-2$).

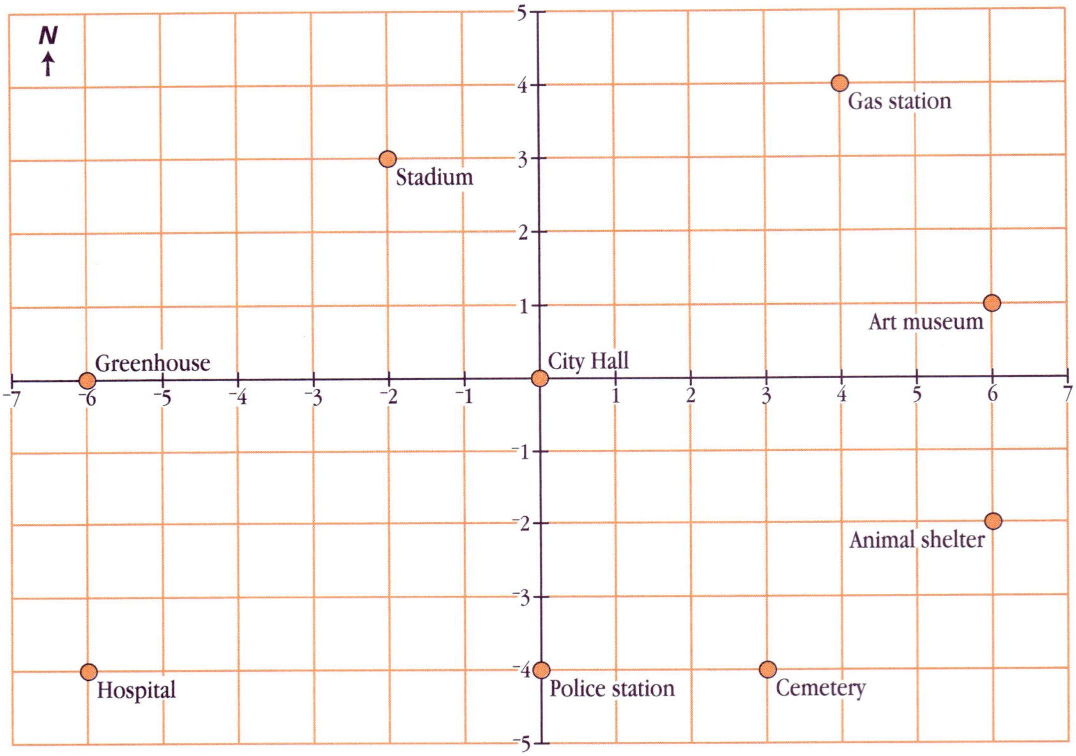

Problem 1.1

A. Give the coordinates of each labeled landmark on the map.

B. 1. How many blocks would a car have to travel to get from the hospital to the cemetery?

2. How many blocks would a car have to travel to get from City Hall to the police station?

3. How many blocks would a car have to travel to get from the art museum to the gas station?

C. How can you tell the distance in blocks between two points if you know the coordinates of the points?

Problem 1.1 Follow-Up

1. Chloe is at City Hall. She asks a police officer where the Corner Ice-Cream Shop is, and he replies, "It's three blocks from here." Can Chloe find the ice-cream shop based on these directions? Where might the ice-cream shop be located?

2. The library is located at an intersection that is the same number of blocks from the stadium as the animal shelter is from the art museum. Where might the library be located?

3. Each street in Euclid is named with its equation. For example, the animal shelter is located on the corner of X = 6 Street and Y = ⁻2 Street. For each labeled landmark on the map, give the names of the two streets that intersect at that location.

1.2 Planning Emergency Routes

Euclid's chief of police has hired you to map out emergency routes that will allow paramedics and police officers to arrive at the scene of an accident as quickly as possible. She wants the plan to include routes for automobiles and helicopters.

Problem 1.2

The chief of police tells you that your plan must include the shortest routes between the following pairs of locations. Answer parts A and B for each pair of locations.

Pair 1: the police station to City Hall
Pair 2: the hospital to City Hall
Pair 3: the hospital to the art museum
Pair 4: the police station to the stadium

A. **1.** Give the coordinates of each location, and give precise directions for an emergency car route from the starting location to the ending location.

2. Find the total distance, in blocks, a police car would have to travel to get from the starting location to the ending location along your route.

B. A helicopter can travel directly from one point to another. Find the total distance, in blocks, a helicopter would have to travel to get from the starting location to the ending location. You may find it helpful to use a centimeter ruler (1 centimeter = 1 block).

■ **Problem 1.2 Follow-Up**

1. How much farther is it from the greenhouse to the stadium by car than by helicopter?
2. How much farther is it from the hospital to the art museum by car than by helicopter?
3. Will the helicopter distance between two locations always be shorter than the car distance? Explain your reasoning.

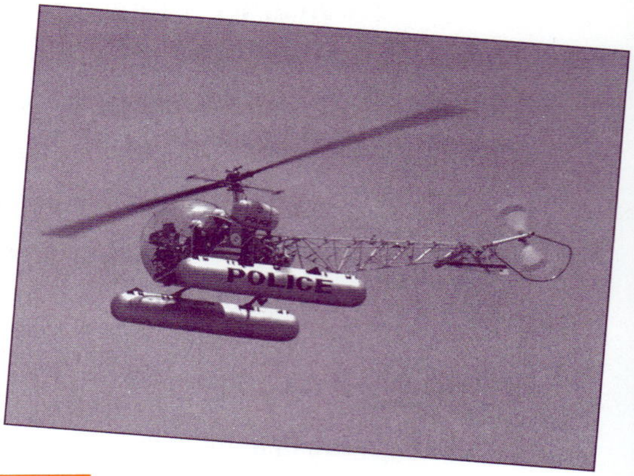

1.3 Planning Parks

The Euclid city council is planning to develop parks with geometric shapes. For some of the parks, the city council has given constraints to the park designers. For example, one of the parks must have a border that includes the vertices (1, 1) and (4, 2).

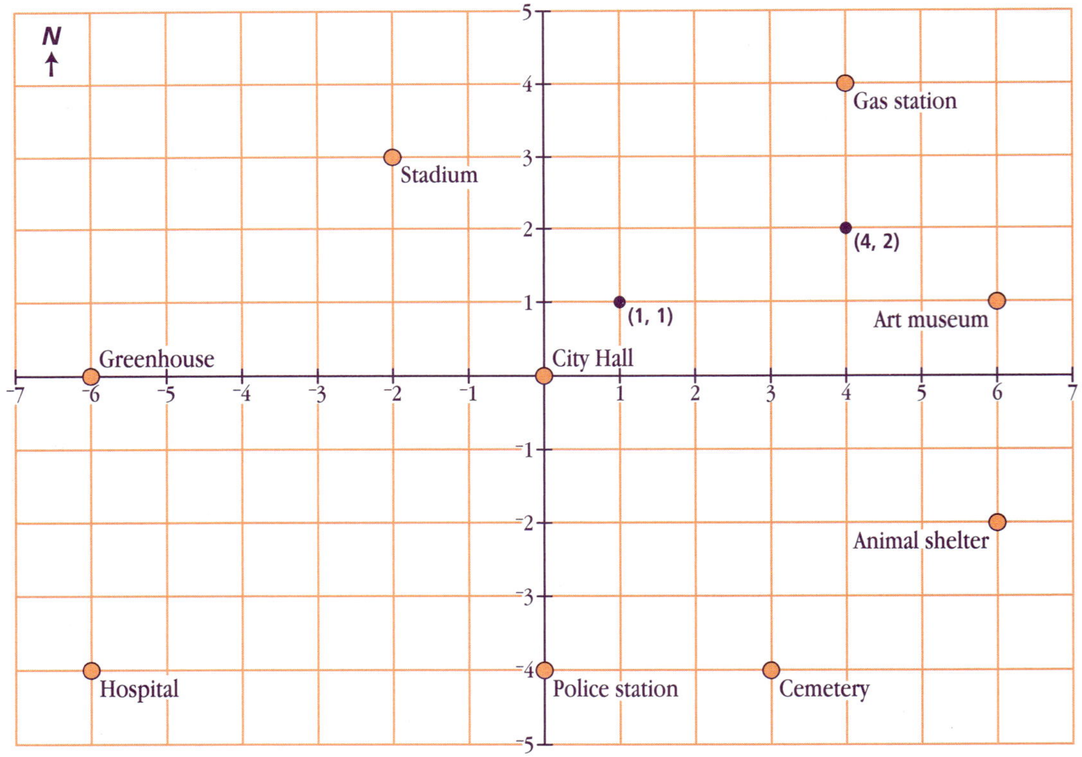

Problem 1.3

A. If the park with the given vertices is to be a square, what could the coordinates of the other two vertices be? Give two answers.

B. If this park is to be a nonsquare rectangle, what could the coordinates of the other two vertices be? Give two answers.

C. If this park is to be a right triangle, what could the coordinates of the other vertex be? Give two answers.

D. If this park is to be a parallelogram that is *not* a rectangle, what could the coordinates of the other two vertices be? Give two answers.

Problem 1.3 Follow-Up

Draw the diagonals of the quadrilaterals you found in Problem 1.3. For each quadrilateral, look at the lengths of the diagonals and the angles at which the diagonals intersect. Use your observations to make a conjecture about the diagonals of a square, a nonsquare rectangle, and a nonrectangular parallelogram. Test your conjecture on three different quadrilaterals.

As you work on these ACE questions, use your calculator whenever you need it.

Applications

In 1–4, use the map of Euclid on page 8.

1. What are the coordinates of a point halfway from City Hall to the hospital if you are traveling by taxi? Is there more than one answer to this question? Explain.

2. What are the coordinates of a point halfway from City Hall to the hospital if you are traveling by helicopter? Is there more than one answer to this question? Explain.

3. **a.** Which landmarks on the map are seven blocks from City Hall by car?

b. For each landmark you listed in part a, what information could you give someone so he or she would know exactly how to drive from City Hall to the landmark?

4. Euclid Middle School is located at an intersection on the map that is the same distance by car from the gas station as the hospital is from the greenhouse. List the coordinates of each place where the school might be located.

5. The points (0, 0) and (3, 2) are two vertices of a polygon.

a. If the polygon is a square, what might the other two vertices be? Give two answers.

b. If the polygon is a nonrectangular parallelogram, what might the other two vertices be? Give two answers.

c. If the polygon is a right triangle, what might the other vertex be? Give two answers.

6. The points (3, 3) and (2, 6) are two vertices of a right triangle.

a. List at least three points that could be the third vertex.

b. How many right triangles with vertices (3, 3) and (2, 6) can you draw? Explain.

Connections

In 7 and 8, use the map of Euclid on page 8.

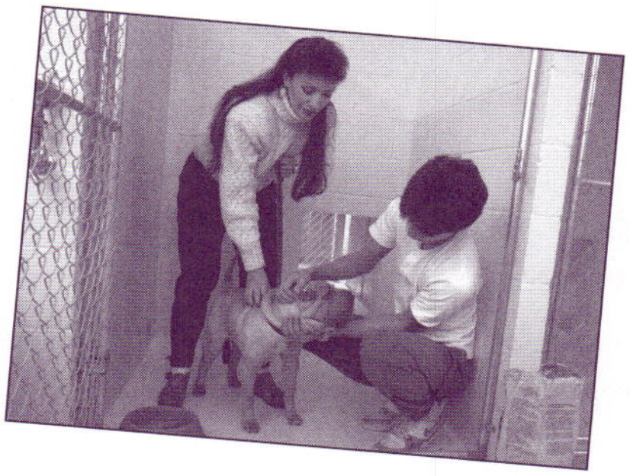

7. In the city of Euclid, a block is 150 meters long.

a. How many meters is it from City Hall to the animal shelter if you travel by car?

b. How many meters is it from the police station to the gas station if you travel by car?

8. **a.** Ki-Cho walked two blocks west from the Euclid police station and then walked three blocks north. Give the coordinates of the place where he stopped.

b. Plimpton left the Euclid stadium and walked three blocks east, three blocks south, two blocks west, and four blocks north. Give the coordinates of the place where he stopped.

c. Ki-Cho's friend Cassandra just left her job at City Hall. She is supposed to meet Ki-Cho at his ending location from part a. If she walks along city streets, what is the shortest route she could take? Is there more than one possible route?

d. Plimpton's sister Aida wants to meet him at his ending location from part b. She is now at City Hall. If she walks along city streets, what is the shortest route she could take? Is there more than one possible route?

e. In general, how can you find the shortest route from City Hall to any point in Euclid?

9. Look at the map of Washington, D.C., on page 6. You can think of the map as a coordinate grid with the origin at the Capitol Building. The coordinates of an intersection on the map would be in the form (vertical street name, horizontal street name). For example, the coordinates of George Washington University would be (21, H).

a. Give the coordinates of each landmark.

i. Union Station **ii.** White House **iii.** Benjamin Banneker Park

b. Does a coordinate pair determine a unique point on the map? If not, what additional information could you give to describe a unique point?

10. Find a road map of your state. Figure out how to use the map's index to locate a city, street, or other landmark. How is finding a landmark on a road map by using its index description similar to and different from finding a landmark in Euclid by using its coordinates?

11. Use a map of your state to plan an airplane trip from your city or town to four other locations in your state. Write a set of directions for your trip that you could give to the pilot.

Extensions

12. *Perpendicular lines* intersect at right angles. On grid paper, draw several parallelograms with diagonals that are perpendicular. What do you observe about these parallelograms?

13. In the LOGO programming language, the computer screen is considered to be a coordinate grid with the point (0, 0) at the starting, or home, location of the turtle. The turtle starts facing straight up. Write a set of LOGO commands for this delivery route in the city of Euclid: from City Hall to the greenhouse, to the cemetery, to the gas station, to the stadium, and back to City Hall. Assume that each block is 25 turtle steps.

Review of LOGO commands

`fd` The *forward* command tells the turtle to move forward. The `fd` command must be followed by a space and a number telling the turtle how many steps to take. For example, `fd 50` tells the turtle to move forward 50 steps.

`lt` The *left turn* command tells the turtle to turn to its left. The `lt` command must be followed by a space and a number telling the turtle how many degrees to turn. For example, `lt 90` tells the turtle to turn left 90°.

`rt` The *right turn* command tells the turtle to turn to its right. The `rt` command must be followed by a space and a number telling the turtle how many degrees to turn. For example, `rt 45` tells the turtle to turn right 45°.

Mathematical Reflections

In this investigation, you reviewed how to locate points and find distances on a coordinate grid. You also reviewed the geometric properties of some common polygons. These questions will help you summarize what you have learned:

1. In the city of Euclid, how does the distance a car needs to travel to get from one place to another compare to the distance a helicopter needs to travel?
2. If you know the coordinates of two landmarks in Euclid, how can you find the distance in blocks between them?
3. Can the following points be connected to form a parallelogram? Explain your answer.

   (1, 1) (2, $^-2$) (4, 2) (3, 5)

Think about your answers to these questions, discuss your ideas with other students and your teacher, and then write a summary of your findings in your journal.

INVESTIGATION 2

Finding Areas and Lengths

In the last investigation, you solved problems involving coordinate grids. You located points, calculated distances, and found coordinates of polygons that satisfied given conditions. In this investigation, you will find areas of figures and lengths of line segments drawn on a dot grid.

2.1 Finding Areas

In this problem, you will find areas of figures drawn on a dot grid. Consider the horizontal or vertical distance between two adjacent dots to be 1 unit. The area of a square with side lengths of 1 unit is 1 square unit.

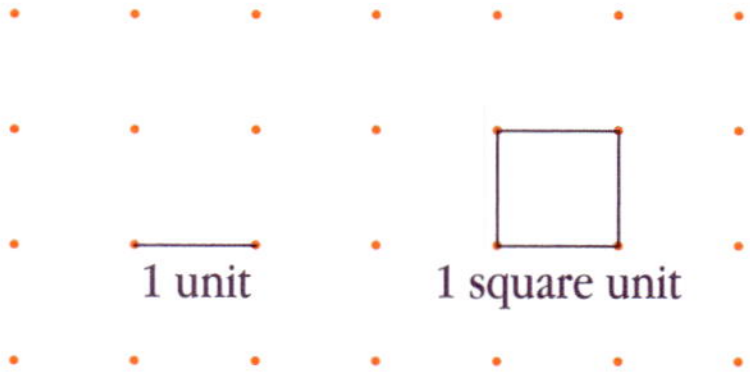

Problem 2.1

A. The figures below appear on Labsheet 2.1. Find the area of each figure below.

B. Describe the strategies you used to find the areas.

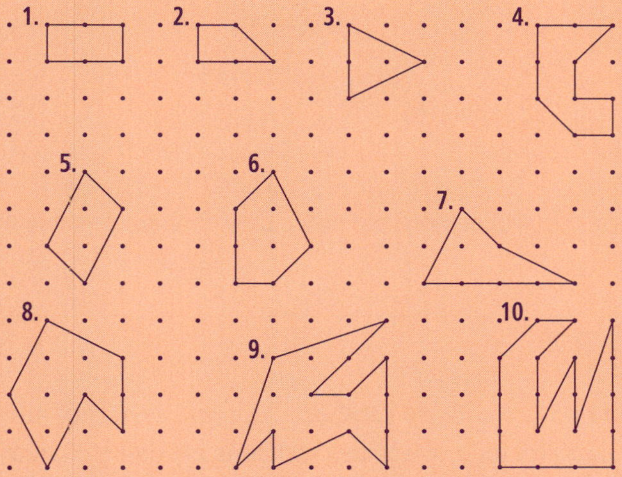

Problem 2.1 Follow-Up

1. Find the area of each triangle below.
2. Describe the strategies you used to find the areas.

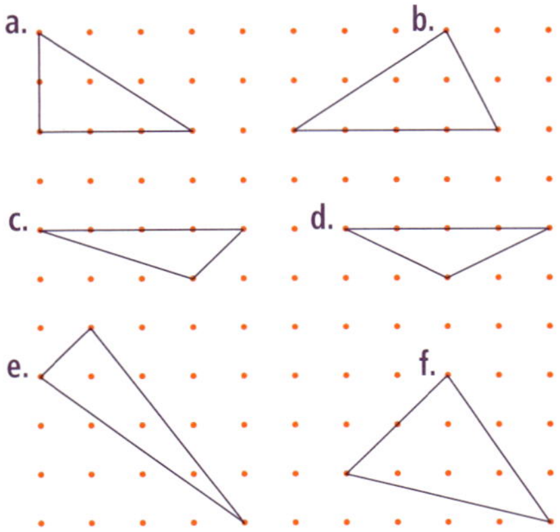

2.2 Looking for Squares

The smallest square you can draw by connecting the dots on a 5-dot-by-5-dot grid is a unit square, which has an area of 1 square unit. You can draw a 2-by-2 square by connecting the dots as shown. Since a 2-by-2 square contains 4 unit squares, it has an area of 4 square units.

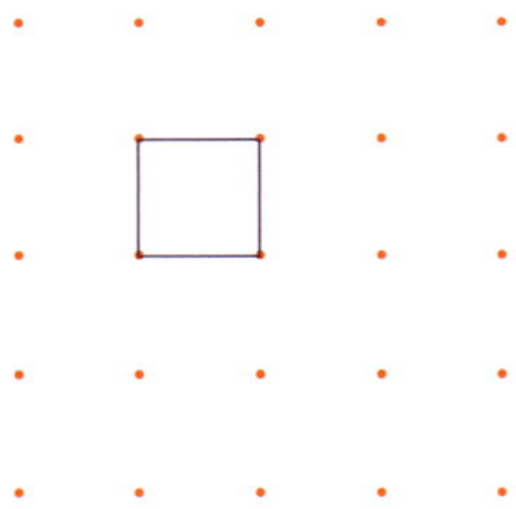

A unit square has an area of 1 square unit.

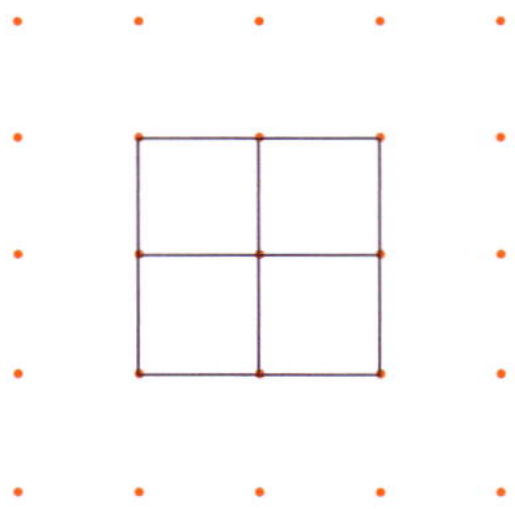

A 2-by-2 square has an area of 4 square units.

In this problem, you will explore the other areas that are possible for squares drawn on a 5-dot-by-5-dot grid.

Problem 2.2

On the 5-dot-by-5-dot grids on Labsheet 2.2, draw squares of various sizes by connecting dots. Try to draw squares with as many different areas as possible. Label each square with its area.

Problem 2.2 Follow-Up

1. We will call squares with vertical and horizontal sides "upright" squares. Which of the squares you drew are upright squares? Identify each square by giving its area.

2. We will call squares with sides that are not vertical and horizontal "tilted" squares. Which of the squares you drew are tilted squares? Identify each square by giving its area.

3. For which kind of square—upright or tilted—is it easier to find the length of a side? Why?

The area of a square is the length of a side multiplied by itself. This can be expressed by the formula $A = s \times s$, or $A = s^2$. If you know the area of a square, you can work backward to find the length of a side. For example, suppose a square has an area of 4 square units. To find the length of a side, you need to figure out what positive number multiplied by itself equals 4. Since $2 \times 2 = 4$, the side length is 2 units. We call 2 a *square root* of 4.

In general, if $A = s^2$, then s is called a **square root** of A. Since $2 \times 2 = 4$ and $^-2 \times {}^-2 = 4$, 2 and $^-2$ are both square roots of 4. Every positive number has two square roots. The symbol for the positive square root is $\sqrt{\ }$. We write $\sqrt{4} = 2$. The negative square root of 4 is $^-\sqrt{4} = {}^-2$.

4. a. What is the value of $\sqrt{1}$?
   b. What is the value of $\sqrt{9}$?
   c. What is the value of $\sqrt{16}$?
   d. What is the value of $\sqrt{25}$?

5. a. Is $\sqrt{2}$ greater than 1? Is $\sqrt{2}$ greater than 2? Explain your reasoning.
   b. The side length of a square with an area of 2 square units is $\sqrt{2}$ units. In Problem 2.2, you drew a square with an area of 2 square units. Use a centimeter ruler to find the side length of this square. You made your drawings on centimeter dot grids, so 1 centimeter = 1 unit.
   c. Use the square root button on your calculator to find $\sqrt{2}$. How does the answer compare to your answer to part b?

2.3 Finding Lengths

In Problem 2.2, you drew squares on 5-dot-by-5-dot grids. Some of the squares were upright and others were tilted. You learned that the positive square root of a number is the side length of a square with that number as its area. For example, $\sqrt{4} = 2$ because the square with an area of 4 square units has sides of length 2.

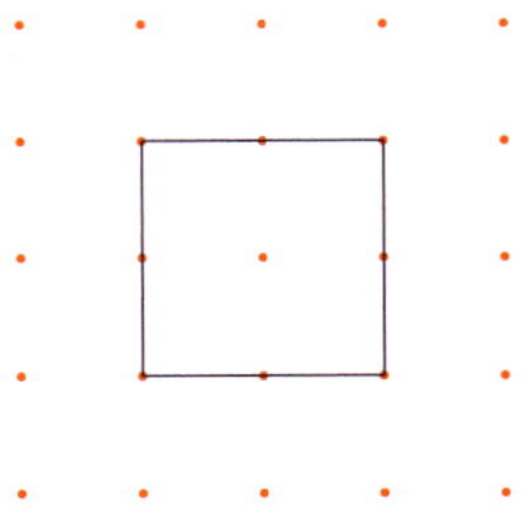

This square has an area of 4 square units. The length of a side is $\sqrt{4}$, or 2.

Sometimes a square root is not a whole number. For example, $\sqrt{2}$ is approximately 1.414. When a square root is not a whole number, we sometimes write it by using the $\sqrt{\ }$ symbol rather than finding a decimal approximation.

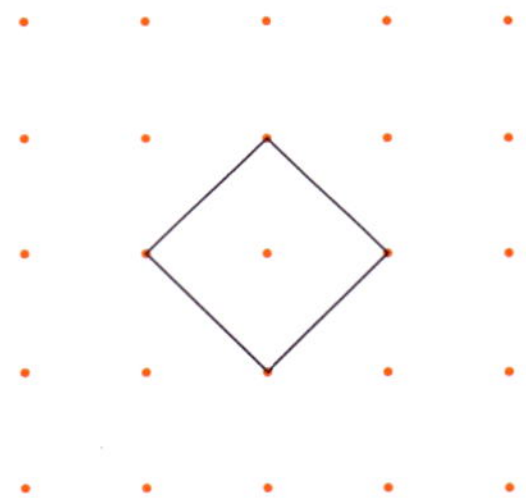

This square has an area of 2 square units. The length of a side is $\sqrt{2}$.

You can use a square to find the length of a line segment connecting dots on a grid. Just draw a square with the line segment as one side. The length of the segment is the square root of the square's area.

For example, to find the length of the line segment below, draw a square with the segment as one side. The square has an area of 5 square units, so the segment has a length of $\sqrt{5}$.

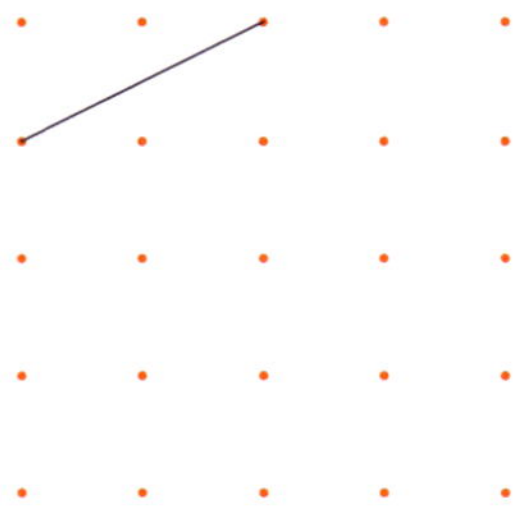

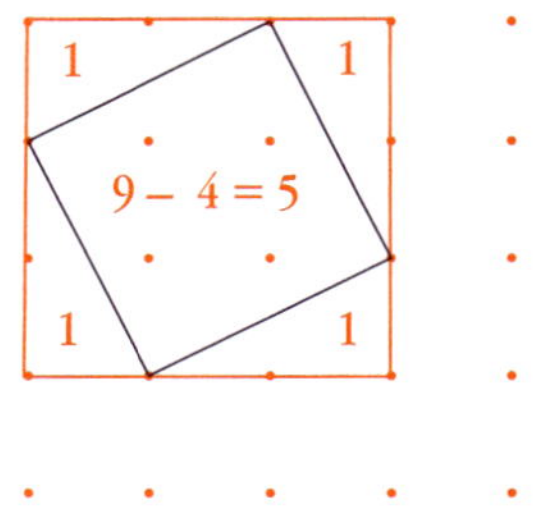

Problem 2.3

On the 5-dot-by-5-dot grids on Labsheet 2.3, draw line segments of various lengths by connecting dots. Try to draw segments with as many different lengths as possible. Use the method described on the previous page to find the length of each segment. To find some of the lengths, you will need to draw squares that extend beyond the 5-dot-by-5-dot grids. Label each segment with its length. Use the $\sqrt{\ }$ symbol to express lengths that are not whole numbers.

Problem 2.3 Follow-Up

1. a. Estimate each length that is not a whole number by measuring the segment with a centimeter ruler.

b. Use your calculator to express each length that is not a whole number as a decimal to the thousandths place.

2. Express the length of the line segment below by using the $\sqrt{\ }$ symbol.

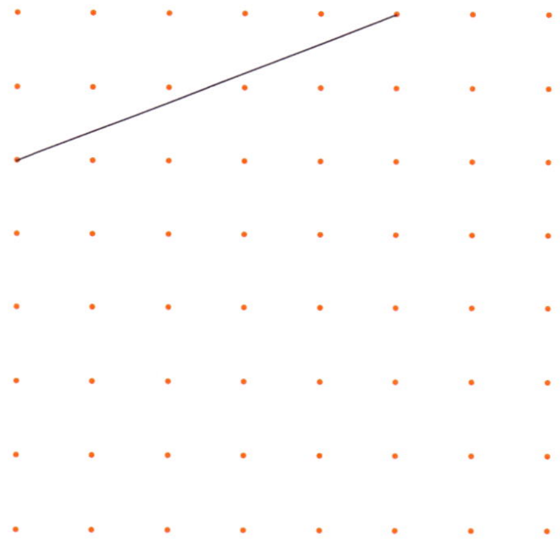

3. Between what two consecutive whole numbers is the length of the line segment in question 2?

As you work on these ACE questions, use your calculator whenever you need it.

Applications

In 1 and 2, refer to the figures below.

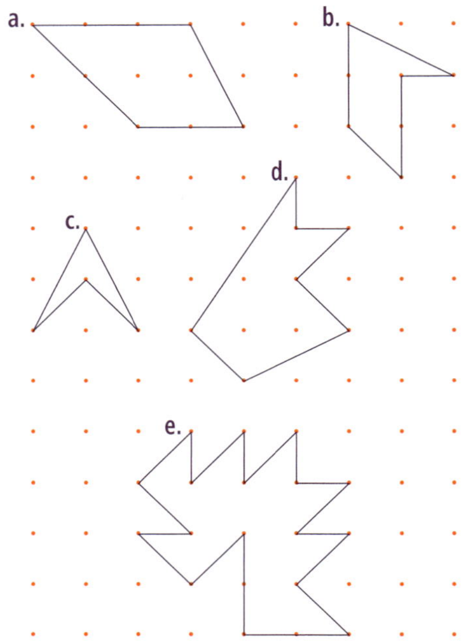

1. Find the area of each figure. Copy the figure onto dot paper if you need to. Describe the methods you use to find the areas.

2. For figures c and d, find the length of each side.

3. On dot paper, draw a hexagon with an area of 16 square units.

4. Find every possible area for a square drawn by connecting dots on a 3-dot-by-3-dot grid.

5. Find every possible length for a line segment drawn by connecting dots on a 3-dot-by-3-dot grid.

In 6 and 7, refer to the diagram below.

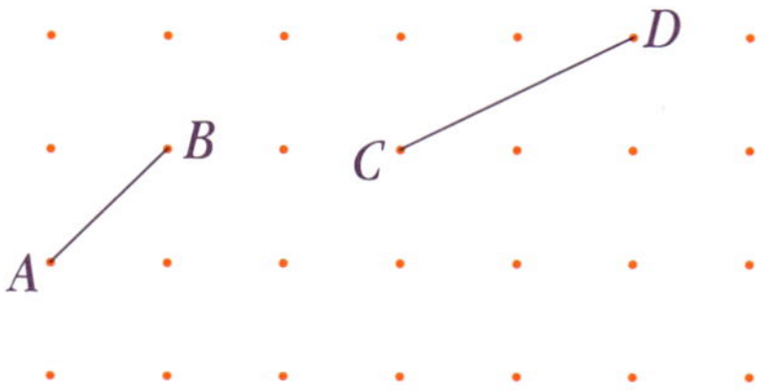

6. a. On dot paper, draw a square with segment *AB* as a side. What is the area of the square?

b. Use a calculator to estimate the length of segment *AB*.

7. a. On dot paper, draw a square with segment *CD* as a side. What is the area of the square?

b. Use a calculator to estimate the length of segment *CD*.

Connections

8. a. Find the areas of triangles *AST, BST, CST,* and *DST.* How do the areas compare? Why do you think this is true?

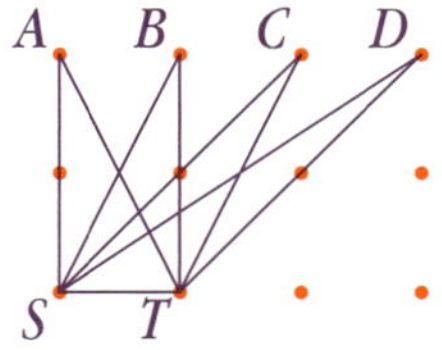

b. Find the areas of triangles *VMN, WMN, XMN, YMN,* and *ZMN.* How do the areas compare? Why do you think this is true?

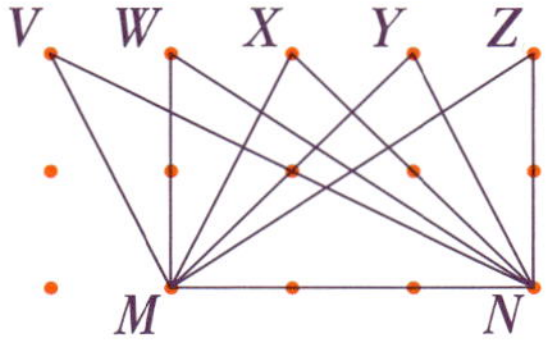

9. **a.** On dot paper, draw a square with an area of 2 square units. Write an argument to convince a friend that the area of the square is 2 square units.

b. Now, draw your square from part a inside an upright square with an area of 4 square units. There will be four triangles around your square. Find the area of each of these triangles. How can you use the upright square to find the area of the smaller square?

10. **a.** What rule can you use to calculate the perimeter of a square if you know the length of a side?

b. Give the perimeter of each square you drew in Problem 2.2 to the nearest hundredth.

11. **a.** Which of the triangles below are right triangles? Use the corner of a piece of paper to help you find right angles. Copy the right triangles onto dot paper, and mark the right angles.

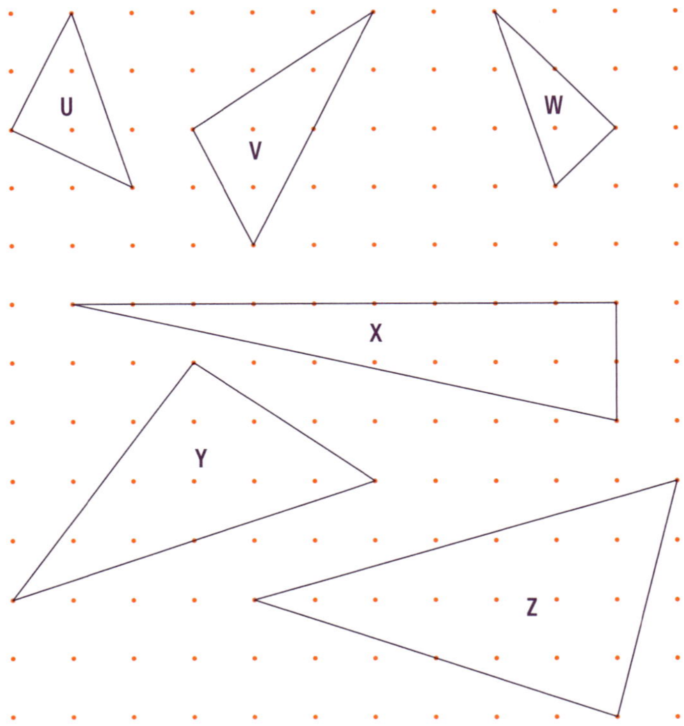

b. Find the area of each right triangle. Explain how you found the areas.

c. For each right triangle, find the sum of the measures of the two non–right angles. What do you notice? If you drew a different right triangle, what would be the sum of its non–right angles? How do you know?

Extensions

12. a. Three right triangles with a common side are drawn on the dot grid below. Find the length of the common side.

b. Do the three right triangles have the same area? Explain. Copy the figures onto dot paper if you need to.

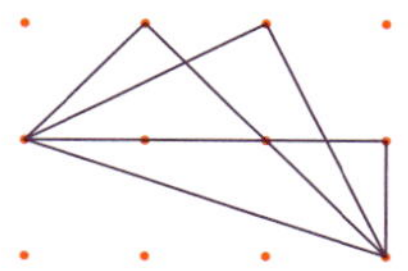

13. On dot paper, draw a parallelogram with an area of 6 square units.

14. On dot paper, draw a triangle with an area of 5 square units.

15. Give both square roots of each number.

a. 1 **b.** 4 **c.** 9

d. 16 **e.** 25 **f.** 2

Mathematical Reflections

In this investigation, you explored areas of figures and lengths of segments drawn on dot paper. You learned that the side length of a square is the positive *square root* of the area. You discovered that, in many cases, a square root is not a whole number. These questions will help you summarize what you have learned:

1. Describe the strategies you used to find areas of figures drawn on dot paper. Give examples if it helps you to explain your thinking.
2. Describe how you would find the side length of a square drawn on dot paper without using a ruler. Consider both upright and tilted squares.
3. Describe how you would find the length of a line segment drawn on dot paper without using a ruler. Be sure to consider horizontal, vertical, and tilted segments.

Think about your answers to these questions, discuss your ideas with other students and your teacher, and then write a summary of your findings in your journal.

INVESTIGATION 3

The Pythagorean Theorem

In the last investigation, you found areas of figures drawn on dot paper. To find these areas, you may have used a method that involved right triangles. Recall that a right triangle is a triangle with a right, or 90°, angle. The right angle of a right triangle is often marked with a square.

The longest side of a right triangle is the side opposite the right angle. We call this side the **hypotenuse** of the triangle. The other two sides are called the **legs.**

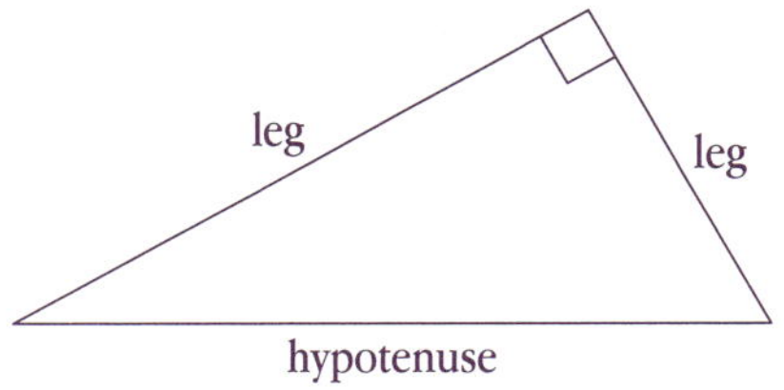

In this investigation, you will discover an interesting relationship among the side lengths of a right triangle.

3.1 Discovering the Pythagorean Theorem

Consider a right triangle with legs that each have a length of 1. Suppose you draw squares on the hypotenuse and legs of the triangle. How are the areas of these three squares related?

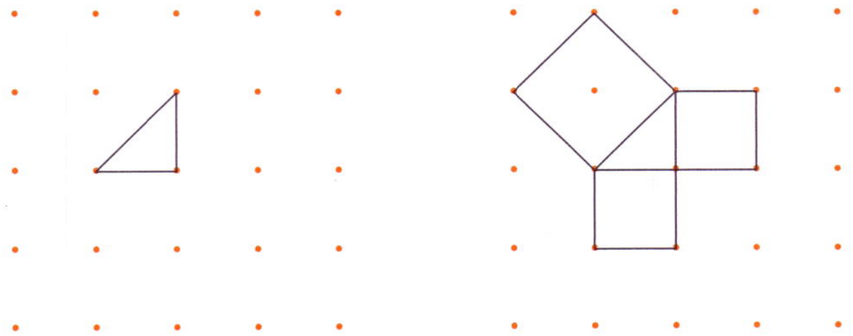

In this problem, you will look for a relationship among the areas of squares drawn on the sides of right triangles.

Problem 3.1

A. Copy the table below. For each row, draw a right triangle with the given leg lengths on dot paper. Then, draw a square on each side of the triangle.

Length of leg 1	Length of leg 2	Area of square on leg 1	Area of square on leg 2	Area of square on hypotenuse
1	1	1	1	2
1	2			
2	2			
1	3			
2	3			
3	3			
3	4			

B. For each triangle, find the areas of the squares on the legs and on the hypotenuse. Record your results in the table.

C. Look for a pattern in the relationship among the areas of the three squares drawn for each triangle. Use the pattern you discover to make a conjecture about the relationship among the areas.

D. Draw a right triangle with side lengths that are different from those given in the table. Use your triangle to test your conjecture from part C.

Problem 3.1 Follow-Up

1. Add another column to your table. In the column, record the hypotenuse length of each triangle using the $\sqrt{\ }$ symbol.

2. Approximate each hypotenuse length to the hundredths place.

3.2 Puzzling Through a Proof

The pattern you discovered in Problem 3.1 is a famous theorem named after the Greek mathematician Pythagoras. A *theorem* is a general mathematical statement that has been proven true. The Pythagorean Theorem is one of the most famous and important theorems in mathematics. Over 300 different proofs have been written for this theorem. One of these proofs is based on the geometric argument that you will explore in this problem.

Problem 3.2

Labsheet 3.2 contains two square puzzle frames and 11 puzzle pieces.

A. Cut out the puzzle pieces. Examine a triangular piece and the three square pieces. How do the side lengths of the squares compare to side lengths of the triangle?

B. Arrange the 11 puzzle pieces to fit exactly into the two puzzle frames. Use four triangles in each frame.

C. Carefully study the arrangements in the two frames. What conclusion can you draw about the relationship among the areas of the three square puzzle pieces?

D. What does the conclusion you reached in part C mean in terms of the side lengths of the triangles?

Compare your completed puzzles and your answers to parts C and D with those of another group.

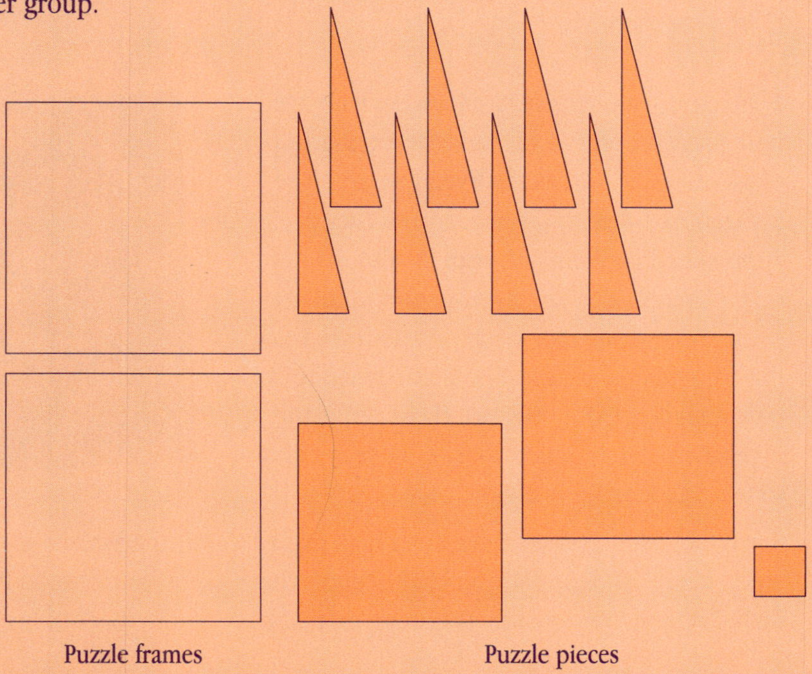

Problem 3.2 Follow-Up

1. In Problems 3.1 and 3.2, you explored the Pythagorean Theorem. State this relationship as a general rule for any right triangle with legs of lengths a and b and a hypotenuse of length c.

2. A right triangle has legs of lengths 3 centimeters and 5 centimeters.
   a. Use the Pythagorean Theorem to find the area of a square drawn on the hypotenuse of the triangle.
   b. What is the length of the hypotenuse?

3. A right triangle has legs of lengths 5 inches and 12 inches.
   a. Find the area of a square drawn on the hypotenuse of the triangle.
   b. What is the length of the hypotenuse?

4. Use the Pythagorean Theorem to find the length of the hypotenuse of this triangle.

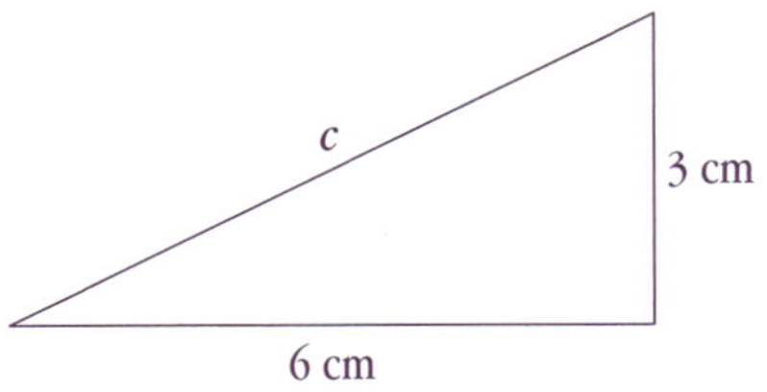

5. The hypotenuse of a right triangle is 15 centimeters long, and one leg is 9 centimeters long. How long is the other leg?

Did you know?

Pythagoras, a Greek mathematician who lived in the sixth century B.C., had a devoted group of followers known as the Pythagoreans. The Pythagoreans had many rituals, and they approached mathematics with an almost religious intensity. Their power and influence became so strong that some people feared that they threatened the local political structure, so they were forced to disband. However, many Pythagoreans continued to meet in secret and to teach Pythagoras's ideas.

Since they held Pythagoras in such high regard, the Pythagoreans gave him credit for all of their discoveries. Much of what we now attribute to Pythagoras, including the Pythagorean Theorem, may actually be the work of his followers.

3.3 Finding Distances

In Problem 2.3, you used squares to help you find the lengths of line segments connecting dots on a grid. The Pythagorean Theorem can also help you find these lengths.

Problem 3.3

A. 1. On the grid on Labsheet 3.3, draw a line segment connecting points *A* and *B*. Draw a right triangle with segment *AB* as its hypotenuse.

2. Find the lengths of the legs of the triangle.

3. Use the Pythagorean Theorem to find the length of the hypotenuse of the triangle.

B. Use the method described in part A to find the distance between points *C* and *D*.

C. Use the method described in part A to find the distance between points *E* and *F*.

Problem 3.3 Follow-Up

On a sheet of dot paper, find two points that are $\sqrt{13}$ units apart. Label the points *X* and *Y*. Explain how you know that the distance between the points is $\sqrt{13}$.

3.4 Measuring the Egyptian Way

In this investigation, you have discovered the Pythagorean Theorem, which describes a special relationship among the side lengths of a right triangle. The theorem states that if a right triangle has legs of lengths a and b and a hypotenuse of length c, then $a^2 + b^2 = c^2$. In this problem, you will explore these questions:

- Is any triangle whose side lengths satisfy the relationship $a^2 + b^2 = c^2$ a right triangle?
- If the side lengths of a triangle do not satisfy the relationship $a^2 + b^2 = c^2$, does this mean the triangle is not a right triangle?

Problem 3.4

A. 1. Do the whole-number lengths 3, 4, and 5 satisfy the relationship $a^2 + b^2 = c^2$?

2. Form a triangle using string or straws cut to these lengths.

3. Is the triangle you formed a right triangle?

4. Repeat parts 1–3 with the lengths 5, 12, and 13.

5. Make a conjecture about triangles whose side lengths satisfy the relationship $a^2 + b^2 = c^2$.

B. 1. Form a triangle with side lengths a, b, and c that do not satisfy the relationship $a^2 + b^2 = c^2$.

2. Is the triangle a right triangle?

3. Repeat parts 1 and 2 with a different triangle.

4. Make a conjecture about triangles whose side lengths do not satisfy the relationship $a^2 + b^2 = c^2$.

Problem 3.4 Follow-Up

1. Determine whether the triangle with the given side lengths is a right triangle.

a. 12, 16, 20

b. 8, 15, 17

c. 12, 9, 16

In ancient Egypt, the Nile River overflowed every year, flooding the surrounding lands and destroying property boundaries. As a result, the Egyptians had to remeasure their land every year. Since many plots of lands were rectangular, the Egyptians needed a reliable way to mark right angles. They devised a clever method involving a rope with equally spaced knots.

2. Mark off 12 segments of the same length on a piece of rope or string. Tape the ends of the string together to form a closed loop. Try to form a right triangle with side lengths that are whole numbers of segments. You may need to have a classmate hold the string in place while you check that your triangle is a right triangle. What are the side lengths of the triangle you formed? Do these side lengths satisfy the relationship $a^2 + b^2 = c^2$?

3. How do you think the Egyptians used the knotted rope?

Applications • Connections • Extensions

As you work on these ACE questions, use your calculator whenever you need it.

Applications

1. On dot paper, find two points that are $\sqrt{17}$ units apart. Label the points W and X. Explain how you know that the distance between the points is $\sqrt{17}$.

2. On dot paper, find two points that are $\sqrt{20}$ units apart. Label the points Y and Z. Explain how you know that the distance between the points is $\sqrt{20}$.

In 3–7, find the missing length or lengths.

3.

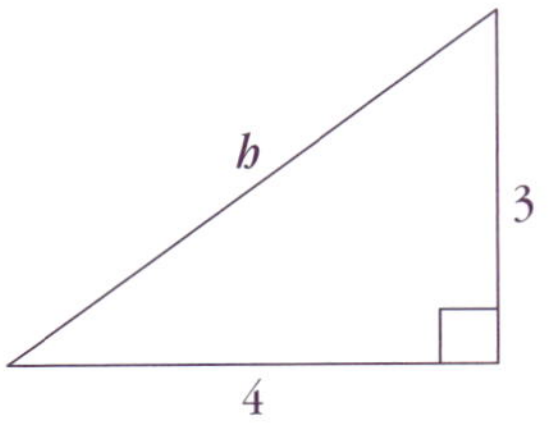

4.

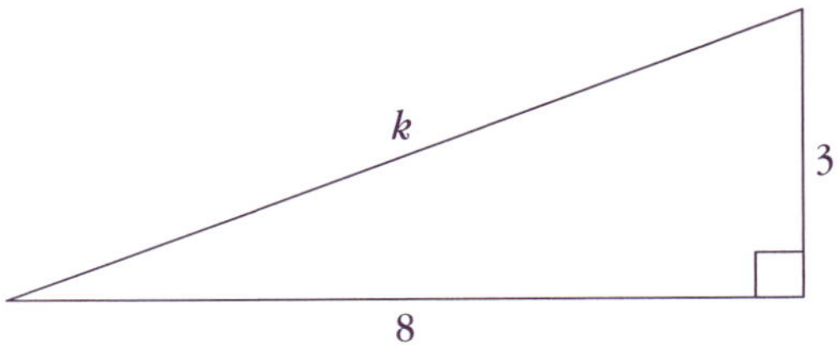

5.

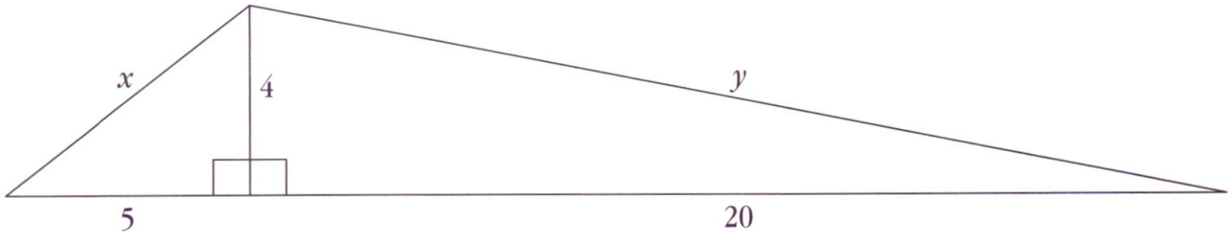

6.

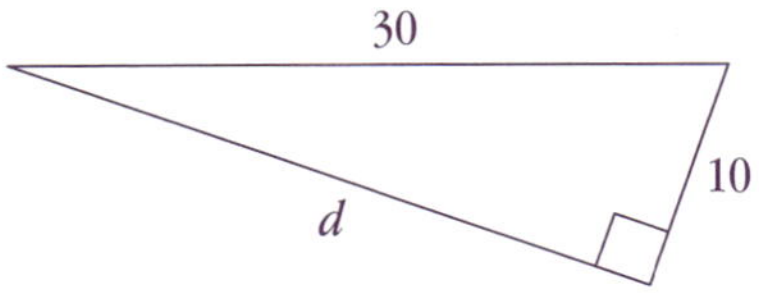

7.

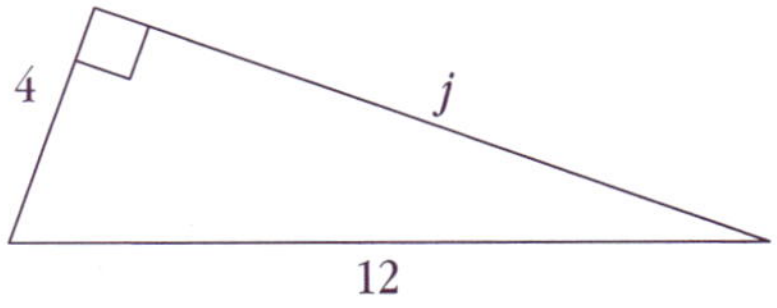

In 8–11, find the helicopter distance between the two locations in blocks without using a ruler, and explain how you found your answer.

8. the greenhouse and the stadium

9. the police station and the animal shelter

10. the greenhouse and the hospital

11. City Hall and the gas station

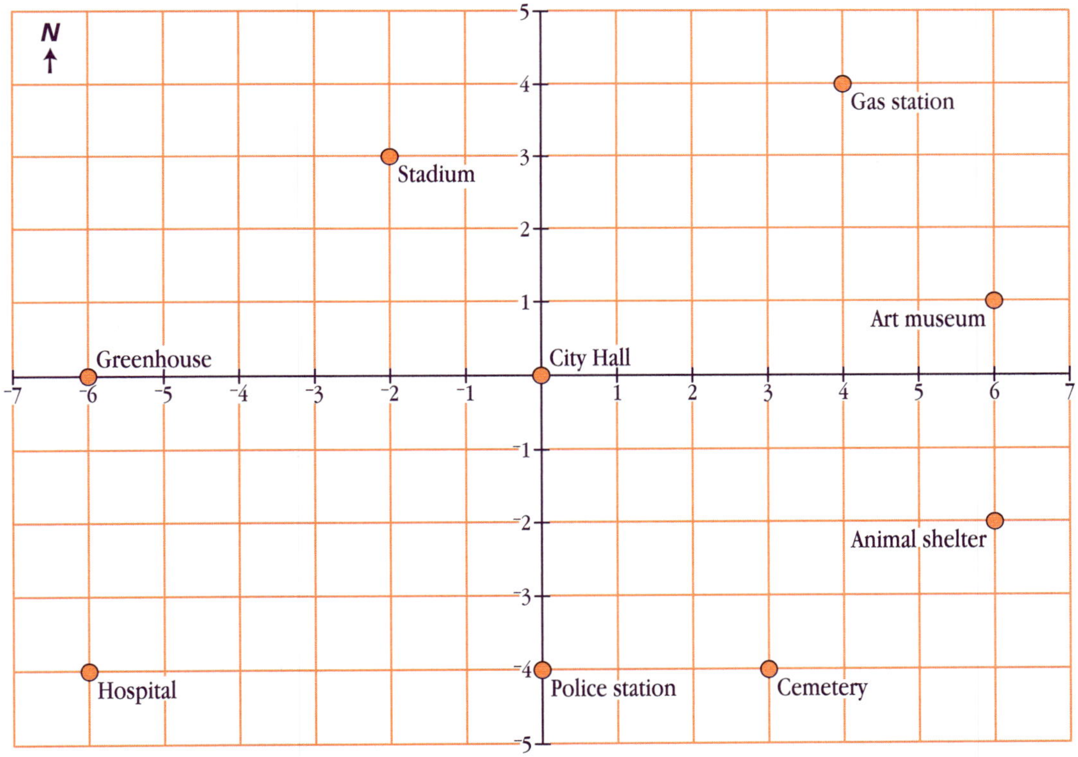

12. In this diagram, the squares on the legs of the right triangle are tilted, and the square on the hypotenuse is upright. Show that this triangle satisfies the Pythagorean Theorem. Copy the diagram onto dot paper if you need to.

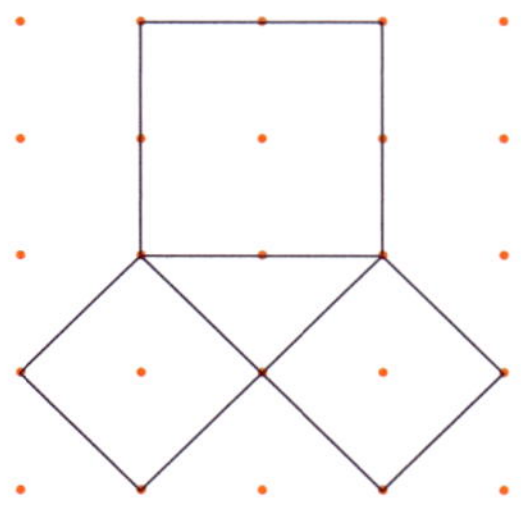

13. If you drew squares on the sides of this right triangle, they would all be tilted. Show that this triangle satisfies the Pythagorean Theorem. Copy the diagram onto dot paper if you need to.

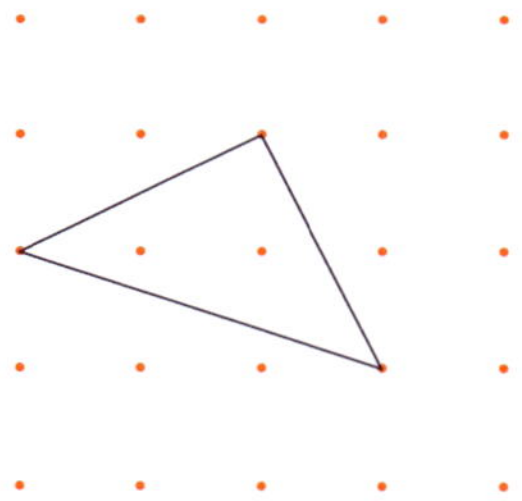

In 14–16, tell whether the triangle with the given side lengths is a right triangle.

14. 10, 24, 26

15. 10, 10, $\sqrt{200}$

16. 9, 16, 25

Connections

In 17 and 18, draw a square with the given area on dot paper.

17. 13 square units

18. 29 square units

19. Which labeled point is the same distance from point *A* as point *B* is from point *A*? Explain.

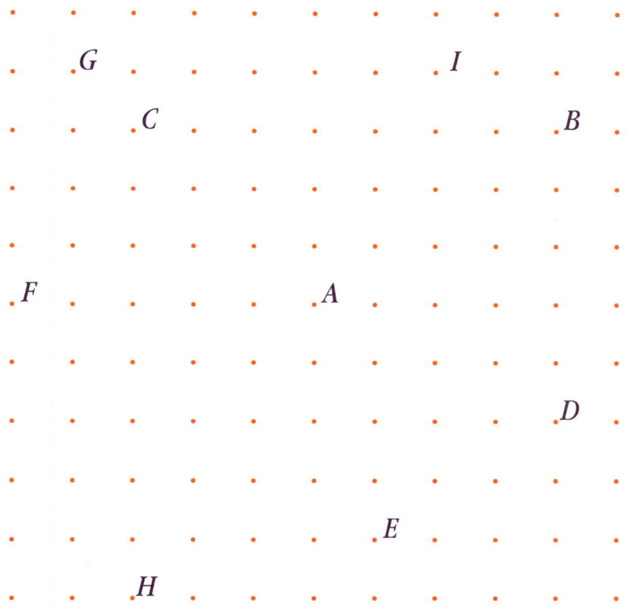

Extensions

20. Any tilted segment that connects two dots on a sheet of dot paper can be the hypotenuse of a right triangle. You can use this idea to draw segments of a given length. The key is finding two square numbers with a sum equal to the square of the length you want to draw.

For example, to draw a line segment with length $\sqrt{5}$, you can draw a right triangle in which the sum of the areas of the squares on the legs is 5. Since the area of the square on the hypotenuse will then be 5, the length of the hypotenuse will be $\sqrt{5}$.

Since 1 and 4 are square numbers, and 1 + 4 = 5, you can draw a right triangle with legs of lengths 1 and 2.

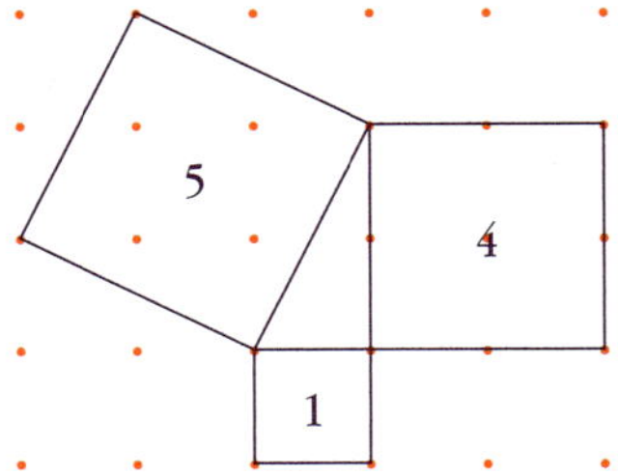

a. To use this technique, it helps to be familiar with sums of square numbers. Copy and complete this table to show the sums of pairs of square numbers.

+	1	4	9	16	25	36	49	64
1	2	5						
4	5							
9								
16								
25								
36								
49								
64								

b. Find two square numbers with the given sum.

i. 10 **ii.** 25 **iii.** 89

c. Use your table to help you draw segments on dot paper with the given length. Explain your work.

i. $\sqrt{26}$ **ii.** 10 **iii.** $\sqrt{50}$

In 21–26, tell whether it is possible to draw a *tilted* segment of the given length by connecting points on dot paper. Explain your reasoning.

21. 2 **22.** 3 **23.** 4

24. 5 **25.** 6 **26.** 7

27. When building a barn, a farmer must make sure the sides of the barn are *perpendicular* to the ground. This means that the sides of the barn form right angles with the ground.

a. One method for checking whether a wall is perpendicular to the ground involves a 10-foot pole. The farmer makes a mark exactly 8 feet high on the wall and then makes a triangle by placing one end of the 10-foot pole on the mark and the other end on the ground.

If the wall is perpendicular to the ground, how far from the base of the wall will the pole touch the ground? Explain how you found your answer.

b. You may have heard the saying, "I wouldn't touch that with a 10-foot pole!" What would this saying mean to a farmer who had just built a barn?

c. Suppose a farmer used a 15-foot pole and made a mark 12 feet high on the wall. If the wall is perpendicular to the ground, how far from the base of the wall will the pole touch the ground?

Mathematical Reflections

In this investigation, you worked with a very important mathematical relationship called the Pythagorean Theorem. These questions will help you summarize what you have learned:

1. **a.** Suppose you are given the lengths of the legs of a right triangle. Describe how you can find the length of the hypotenuse.

   b. Suppose you are given the lengths of one leg and the hypotenuse of a right triangle. Describe how you can find the length of the other leg.

2. Describe how you can use the Pythagorean Theorem to find the distance between two dots on a sheet of dot paper without measuring.

3. How can you determine whether a triangle is a right triangle if you know only the lengths of its three sides?

Think about your answers to these questions, discuss your ideas with other students and your teacher, and then write a summary of your findings in your journal.

INVESTIGATION 4

Using the Pythagorean Theorem

The Pythagorean Theorem is an important and useful mathematical idea. In this investigation, you will use the theorem to solve some interesting problems.

The Pythagorean Theorem

If a right triangle has legs of lengths a and b and a hypotenuse of length c, then $a^2 + b^2 = c^2$.

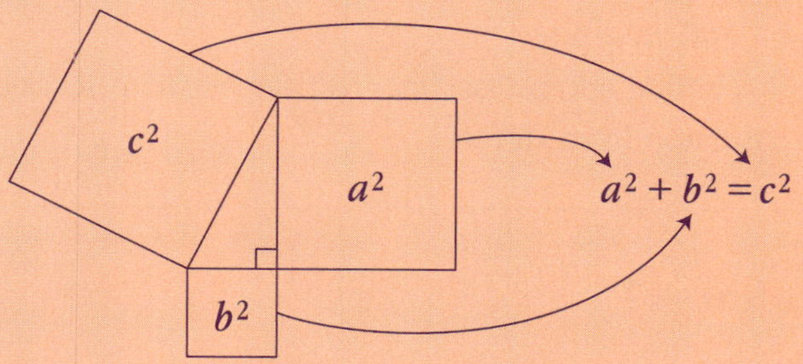

4.1 Stopping Sneaky Sally

The Pythagorean Theorem can be used in situations like the following, in which you need to find a missing length in a right triangle.

Horace Hanson is the catcher for the Humbolt Bees baseball team. Sneaky Sally Smith, the star of the Canfield Cats, is on first base. Sally is known for stealing bases, so Horace is keeping a sharp eye on her.

The pitcher throws a fastball, and the batter swings and misses. Horace catches the pitch. Out of the corner of his eye, he sees Sally take off for second base.

Problem 4.1

How far must Horace throw the baseball to get Sally out at second base? Explain how you found your answer.

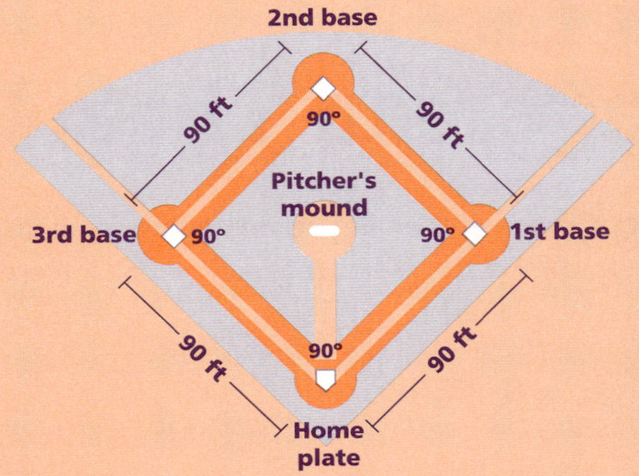

Problem 4.1 Follow-Up

The shortstop is standing on the baseline, halfway between second base and third base. How far is the shortstop from Horace?

Did you know?

Although most people consider baseball an American invention, a similar game, called *rounders,* was played in England as early as the 1600s. Like baseball, rounders involved hitting a ball and running around bases. However, in rounders, the fielders actually threw the ball at the base runners. If a ball hit a runner while he was off base, the runner was out.

Alexander Cartwright is considered the father of organized baseball. He started the Knickerbockers Base Ball Club of New York in 1845 and wrote an official set of rules. According to Cartwright's rules, a batter was out if a fielder caught the ball either on the fly or on the first bounce. Today, balls caught on the first bounce are not outs. Cartwright's rules also stated that the first team to have a total of 21 runs at the end of an inning was the winner. Today, the team with the highest score after nine innings wins the game.

4.2 Analyzing Triangles

In this problem, you will work with an equilateral triangle. An *equilateral triangle* is a triangle in which all three sides are the same length. What is true about the angle measures in an equilateral triangle?

Problem 4.2

Each side of equilateral triangle *ABC* has a length of 2.

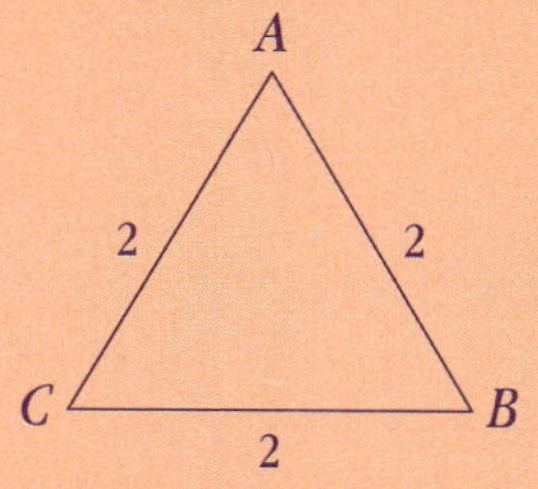

On Labsheet 4.2, find the point halfway between vertices *B* and *C*. Label this point *P*. Point *P* is the *midpoint* of segment *BC*. Draw a segment from vertex *A* to point *P*. This divides triangle *ABC* into two triangles. Cut out triangle *ABC* and fold it along line *AP*.

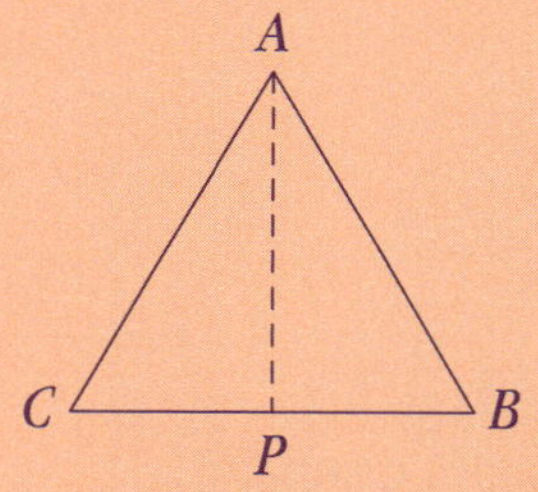

A. How does triangle *ABP* compare with triangle *ACP*?

B. Find the measure of each angle in triangle *ABP*. Explain how you found each measure.

C. Find the length of each side of triangle *ABP*. Explain how you found each length.

D. Two line segments that meet at right angles are called **perpendicular** line segments. Find a pair of perpendicular line segments in the drawing above.

E. What relationships do you observe among the side lengths of triangle *ABP*? Are these relationships also true for triangle *ACP*? Explain.

Problem 4.2 Follow-Up

1. A right triangle with a 60° angle is sometimes called a *30-60-90 triangle.* This 30-60-90 triangle has a hypotenuse of length 6. What are the lengths of the other two sides? Explain how you found your answers.

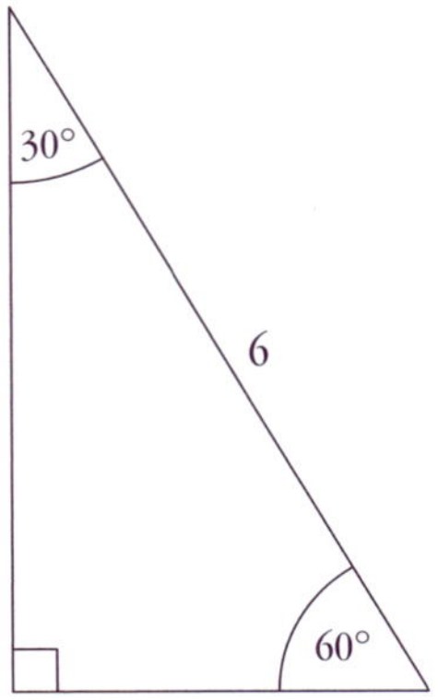

2. Square *ABCD* has sides of length 1. On Labsheet 4.2, draw a diagonal, dividing the square into two triangles. Cut out the square and fold it along the diagonal.

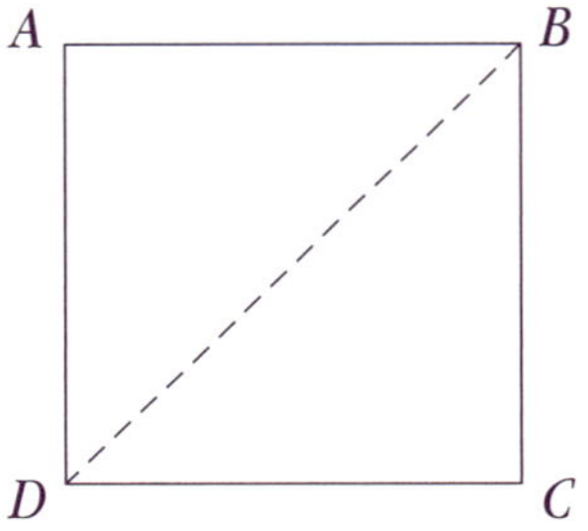

a. How do the two triangles compare?

b. What are the measures of the angles of one of the triangles? Explain how you found each measure.

c. What is the length of the diagonal? Explain how you found the length.

d. Suppose square *ABCD* had sides of length 5. How would this change your answers to parts b and c?

4.3 Finding the Perimeter

In this problem, you will apply many of the strategies you have developed in this unit.

Problem 4.3

In the diagram below, some lengths and angle measures are given. Use this information and what you have learned in this unit to help you find the perimeter of triangle *ABC*. Explain your work.

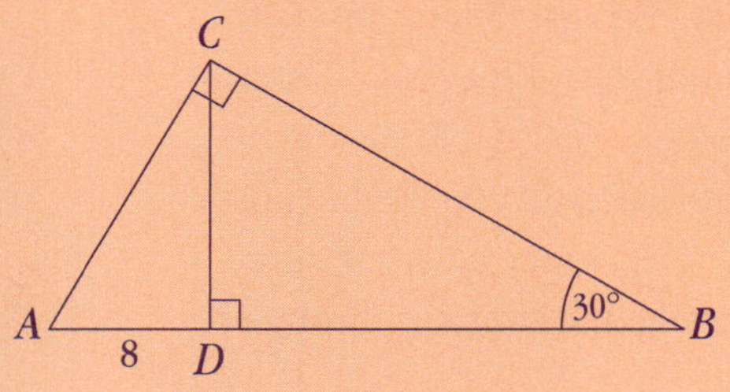

Problem 4.3 Follow-Up

1. Find the area of triangle *ABC*. Explain your reasoning.

2. Find the areas of triangle *ACD* and triangle *BCD*.

Applications • Connections • Extensions

As you work on these ACE questions, use your calculator whenever you need it.

Applications

1. Scott, a freshman at Michigan State University, needs to walk from his dorm room in Wilson Hall to his math class in Wells Hall. Normally, he walks 500 meters east and 600 meters north along the sidewalks, but today he is running late. He decides to take the shortcut through the Tundra.

a. How many meters long is Scott's shortcut?

b. How much shorter is the shortcut than Scott's usual route?

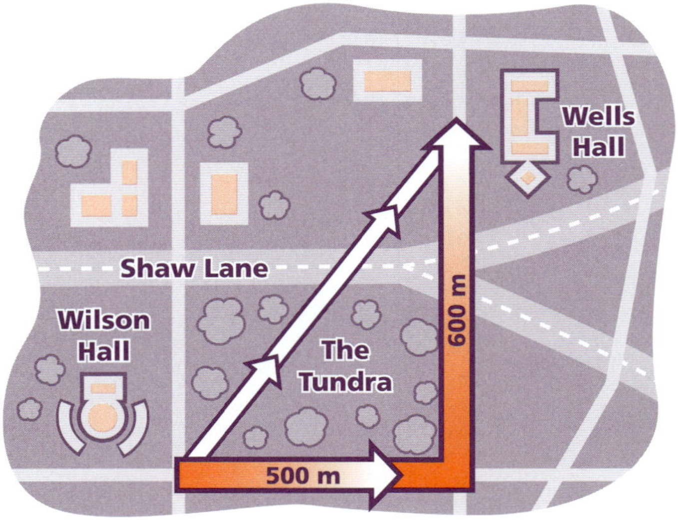

2. Lotsafun Amusement Park has a new ride, the Sky Breaker. The starting and ending points of the ride are separated by 1000 meters. The tram cars glide along a cable that rises at a 45° angle from the ground until it reaches a height of 15 meters. The cable runs parallel to the ground for most of the ride, eventually sloping down again at a 45° angle with the ground. How long, to the nearest tenth of a meter, is the cable for the Sky Breaker ride?

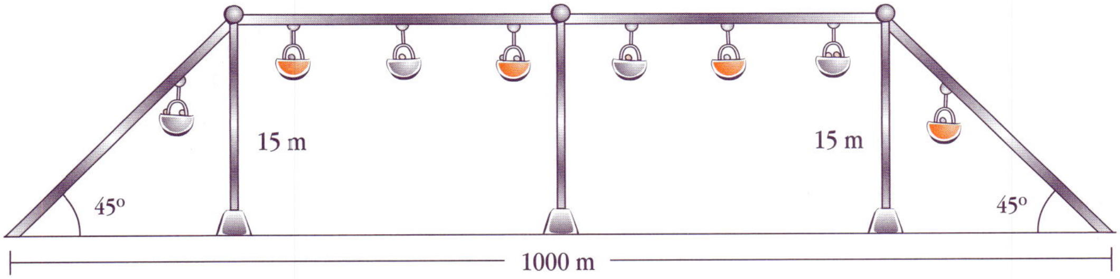

3. At Errol's Evergreen Farm, the taller trees are braced by a wire extending from 2 feet below the top of the tree to a stake in the ground. What is the tallest tree that can be braced with a 25-foot wire staked 15 feet from the base of the tree?

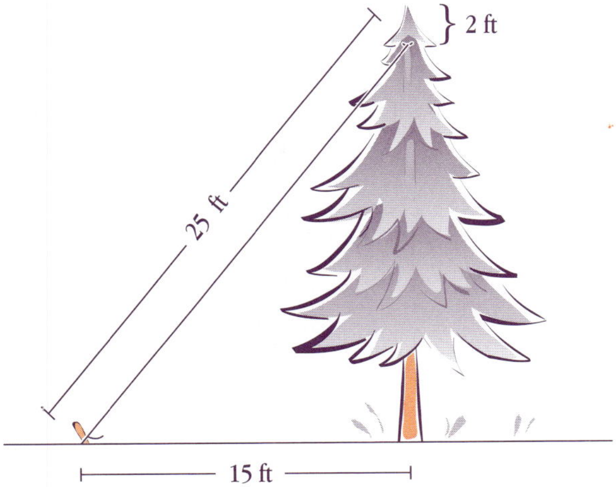

4. As part of his math assignment, Jeff has to estimate the height of Beaumont Tower without measuring it. His class has just studied 30-60-90 triangles, and Jeff decides to use what he learned to help him estimate the height of the tower.

Jeff uses an angle ruler to sight the top of the tower at 60°. Then, he marks the spot where he is standing and measures the distance from the tower to his mark. The distance is about 58 feet. When Jeff stands, his eyes are 5 feet from the ground. About how tall is Beaumont Tower? Explain how you found your answer.

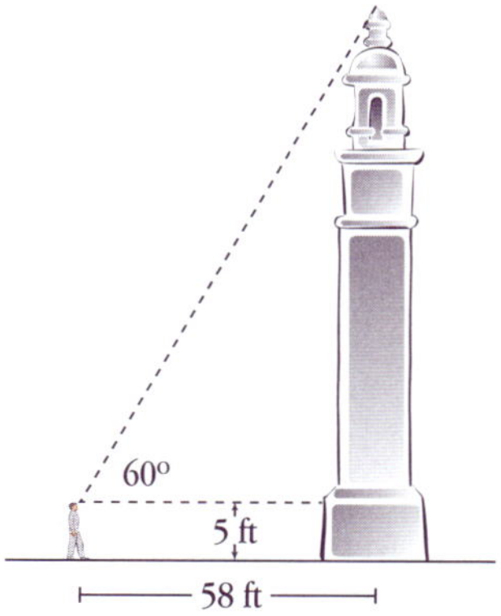

Connections

5. Find the length of the diagonal, d, of the box.

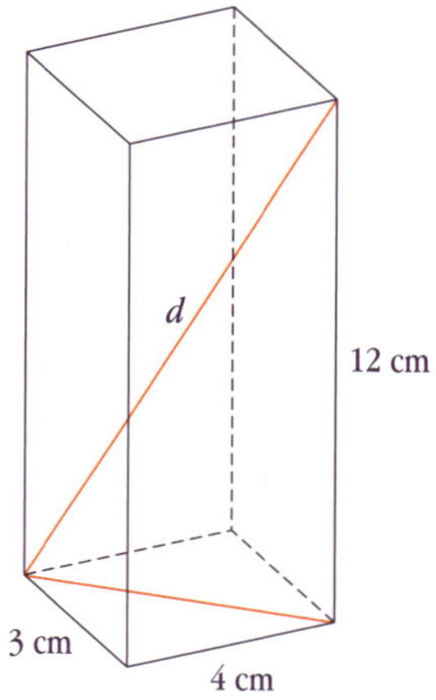

6. Find the length of the diagonal, d, of the box.

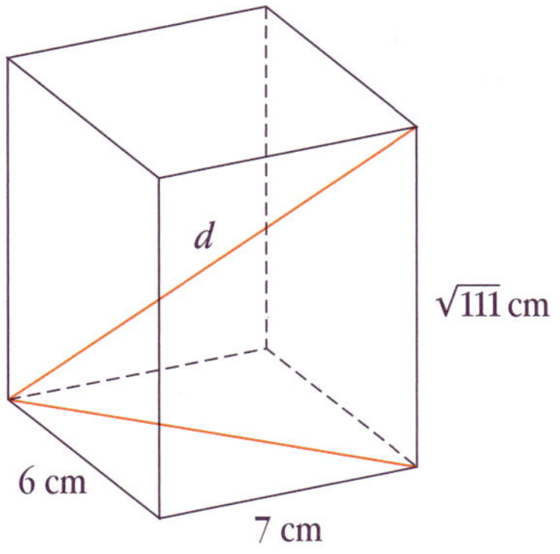

In 7 and 8, use this information: Two cars leave the city of Walleroo at noon. One car travels north and the other travels east.

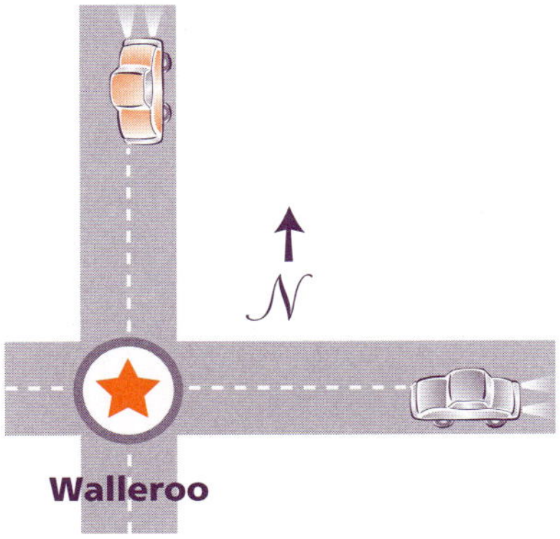

7. Suppose the northbound car is traveling at 60 miles per hour and the eastbound car is traveling at 50 miles per hour. Make a table that shows the distance each car has traveled and the distance between the two cars after 1 hour, 2 hours, 3 hours, and so on. Describe how the distances are changing.

8. Suppose the northbound car is traveling at 40 miles per hour, and after two hours, the two cars are 100 miles apart. How fast is the other car going? Explain how you found your answer.

Extensions

9. Find the perimeter of triangle *ABC.* (Hint: Look for similar triangles.)

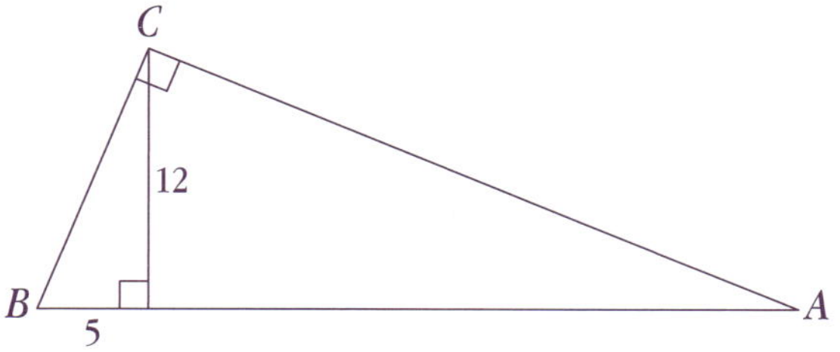

The Pythagorean Theorem describes the relationship among the areas of squares drawn on the sides of a right triangle. In questions 10–12, you will look for relationships among the areas of other shapes drawn on the sides of a right triangle.

10. Half-circles are drawn on the sides of this right triangle.

a. Find the area of each half-circle.

b. How are the areas of the half-circles related?

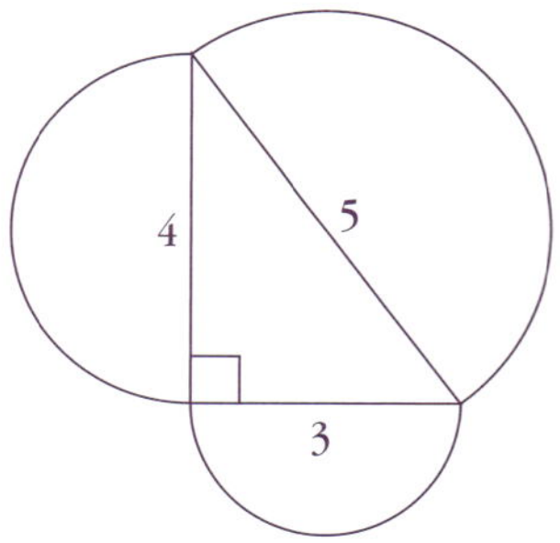

11. Equilateral triangles are drawn on the sides of this right triangle.

a. Find the area of each equilateral triangle.

b. How are the areas of the equilateral triangles related?

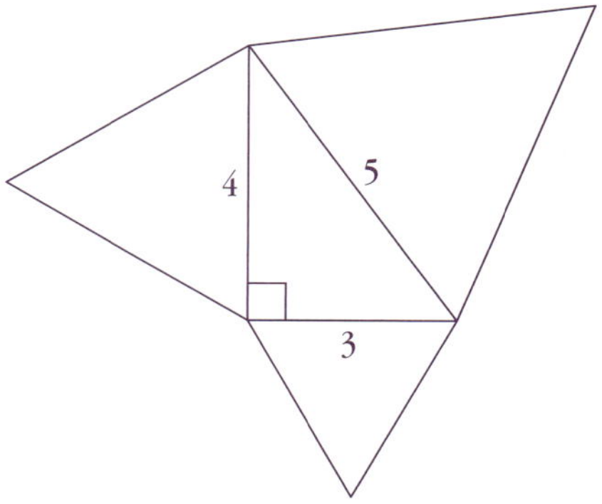

12. Regular hexagons are drawn on the sides of this right triangle.

a. Find the area of each hexagon.

b. How are the areas of the hexagons related?

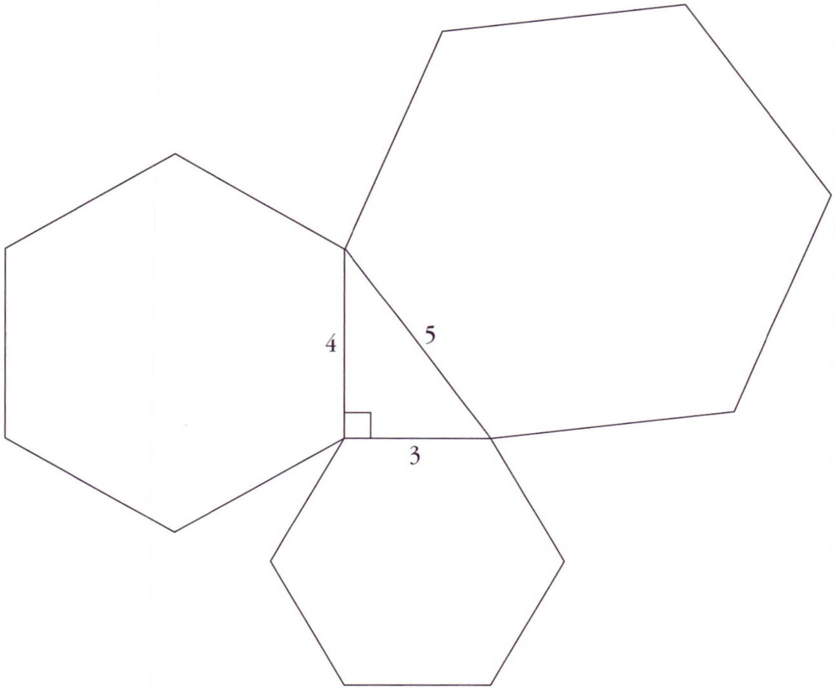

Mathematical Reflections

In this investigation, you applied the ideas from the first three investigations. The following questions will help you summarize what you have learned:

1. In what ways is the Pythagorean Theorem useful? Give at least two examples.
2. Describe the special properties of a 30-60-90 triangle.

Think about your answers to these questions, discuss your ideas with other students and your teacher, and then write a summary of your findings in your journal.

INVESTIGATION 5

Irrational Numbers

In Investigations 2 and 3, you learned methods for finding the lengths of segments connecting dots on a grid. Sometimes you could express the lengths as whole numbers; other times, you had to use $\sqrt{\ }$ symbols or decimal approximations.

The square below has an area of 2 square units. The length of a side of this square can be expressed as $\sqrt{2}$. Just how long is $\sqrt{2}$? If we draw a number line and mark off a segment with the same length as a side of the square, we can see that the length of the segment is about 1.4.

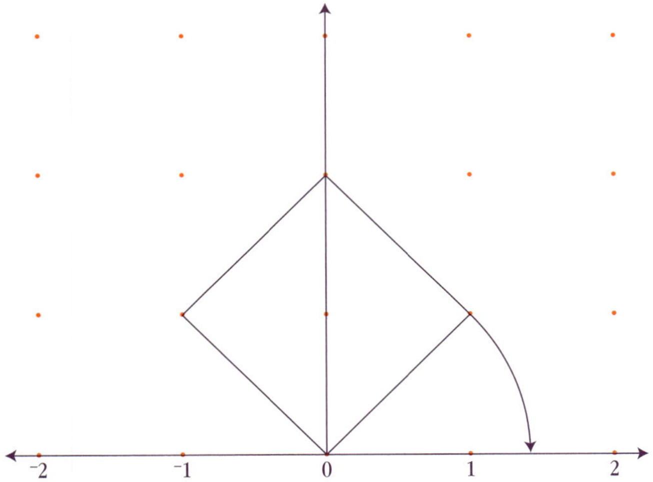

But $\sqrt{2} \times \sqrt{2} = 2$, while $1.4 \times 1.4 = 1.96$. So, 1.4 is too small. If we increase our estimate to 1.42, we get $1.42 \times 1.42 = 2.0164$. So, 1.42 is too large. Try squaring some other decimal numbers to see if you can get a square closer to 2.

If you use your calculator to find $\sqrt{2}$, you get something like 1.414213562, but if you multiply 1.414213562 by 1.414213562 by hand, you get 1.999999998944727844. It seems that even a calculator can't find the exact value of $\sqrt{2}$! So, although you can draw a line segment with a length of $\sqrt{2}$ and locate $\sqrt{2}$ precisely on a number line, it seems extremely difficult to find an exact decimal value for $\sqrt{2}$.

5.1 Analyzing the Wheel of Theodorus

In earlier investigations, you drew segments with lengths of $\sqrt{2}$, $\sqrt{3}$, $\sqrt{4}$, and so on by drawing squares with whole-number areas. In this problem, you will investigate an interesting pattern of right triangles called the Wheel of Theodorus. The pattern will suggest another way to draw segments with lengths that are positive square roots of whole numbers.

The Wheel of Theodorus begins with a triangle with legs of length 1 and winds around counterclockwise. Each triangle is drawn using the hypotenuse of the previous triangle as one leg and a segment of length 1 as the other leg. To make the Wheel of Theodorus, you only need to know how to draw right angles and segments of length 1.

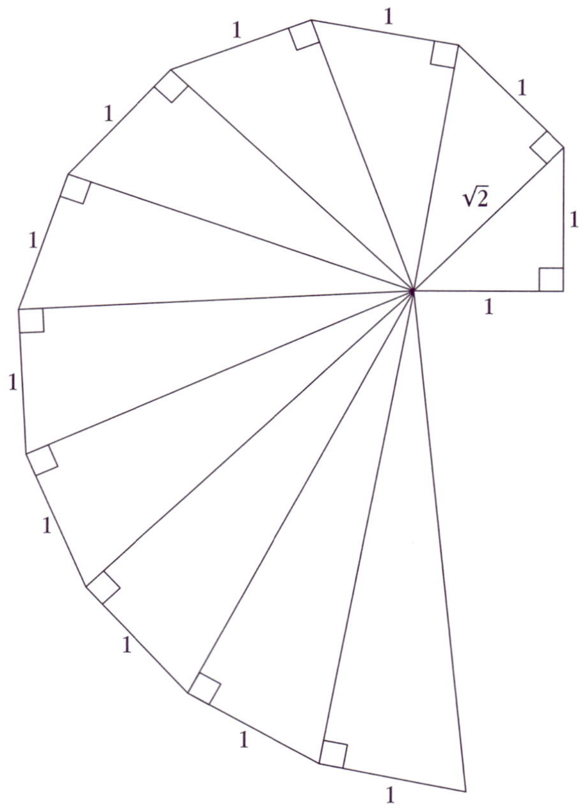

The Wheel of Theodorus is named for its creator, Theodorus of Cyrene. Theodorus was a Pythagorean and one of Plato's teachers.

Problem 5.1

A. Use the Pythagorean Theorem to find the length of each hypotenuse in the Wheel of Theodorus on Labsheet 5.1. Label each hypotenuse with its length. Use the $\sqrt{\ }$ symbol to express lengths that are not whole numbers.

B. Cut out the ruler from Labsheet 5.1. Measure each hypotenuse on the Wheel of Theodorus, and label the point on the ruler that represents its length. For example, the first hypotenuse length would be marked like this:

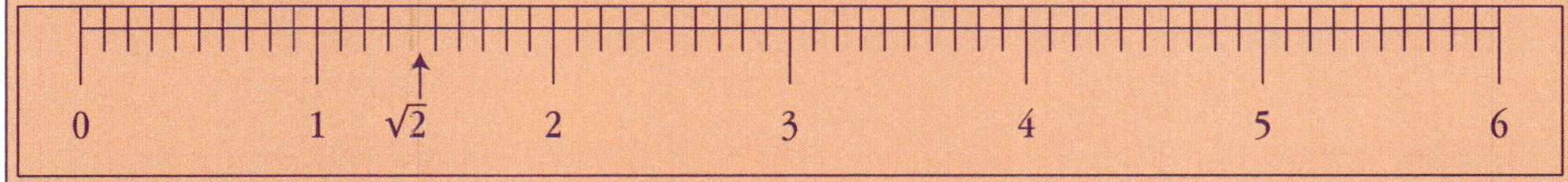

C. For each hypotenuse length that is not a whole number, give the two consecutive whole numbers between which the length is located. For example, $\sqrt{2}$ is between 1 and 2.

D. For each hypotenuse length that is not a whole number, use your completed ruler to find a decimal number that is slightly less than the length and a decimal number that is slightly greater than the length. Try to be accurate to the tenths place.

Problem 5.1 Follow-Up

1. In Problem 5.1, you used a $\sqrt{\ }$ symbol to express the hypotenuse lengths that were not whole numbers. Use your calculator to find the value of each square root, and compare the result to the approximations you found in part D.

2. When Joey used his calculator to find $\sqrt{3}$, he got 1.732050808. Geeta says that Joey's answer must be wrong because when she multiplies 1.732050808 by 1.732050808, she gets 3.000000001. Why do these students disagree?

```
√3
        1.732050808
```

```
1.732050808*1.73
2050808
        3.000000001
```

5.2 Representing Fractions as Decimals

Is it possible to find the exact value of $\sqrt{2}$? Earlier, you found decimal approximations for $\sqrt{2}$. When you multiply such an approximation by itself, you always get a number slightly greater than 2 or slightly less than 2. Even your calculator can't find the exact value of $\sqrt{2}$.

You will get similar results if you try to find an exact value for $\sqrt{3}$ or $\sqrt{5}$. In fact, the decimal representations of these numbers go on forever, and never show any pattern of repeating digits. To better understand these numbers, it helps to compare them to numbers with which you are more familiar: fractions.

In your earlier math work, you learned that any fraction whose numerator and denominator are integers can be expressed as a decimal. The decimal is found by dividing the numerator by the denominator. For example:

$\frac{1}{2} = 0.5$ $\quad \frac{1}{4} = 0.25$ $\quad \frac{1}{3} = 0.333333333333\ldots$ $\quad \frac{1}{11} = 0.090909090909\ldots$

The fractions $\frac{1}{2}$ and $\frac{1}{4}$ have decimal representations that end, or *terminate.* Decimals like these are called **terminating decimals.** The fractions $\frac{1}{3}$ and $\frac{1}{11}$ have decimal representations with groups of digits that repeat forever. Decimals like these are called **repeating decimals.**

Problem 5.2

Write each fraction as a decimal, and tell whether the decimal is terminating or repeating. If the decimal is repeating, tell which digits repeat.

A. $\frac{2}{5}$ **B.** $\frac{3}{8}$ **C.** $\frac{5}{6}$ **D.** $\frac{35}{10}$ **E.** $\frac{8}{99}$

Problem 5.2 Follow-Up

1. Find three fractions with the same decimal representation as the given fraction.

a. $\frac{2}{5}$ **b.** $\frac{5}{6}$

2. Find a fraction that is equivalent to the given terminating decimal.

a. 0.35 **b.** 2.1456 **c.** 89.050

5.3 Exploring Repeating Decimals

In the last problem, you saw that any fraction with a numerator and a denominator that are integers can be expressed as a terminating or repeating decimal. It is also true that any terminating or repeating decimal can be expressed as a fraction with a numerator and a denominator that are integers.

Terminating decimals can be written as fractions with a power of 10—such as 10, 100, 1000, and 10,000—in the denominator. For example,

$$0.75 \text{ can be expressed as } \frac{75}{100}, \text{ or } \frac{3}{4}$$

$$1.414213562 \text{ can be expressed as } \frac{1{,}414{,}213{,}562}{1{,}000{,}000{,}000}$$

In this problem, you will explore an interesting pattern that may give you some clues about how to write repeating decimals as fractions.

Problem 5.3

A. Copy the table below, and write each fraction as a decimal.

Fraction	Decimal
$\frac{1}{9}$	
$\frac{2}{9}$	
$\frac{3}{9}$	
$\frac{4}{9}$	
$\frac{5}{9}$	
$\frac{6}{9}$	
$\frac{7}{9}$	
$\frac{8}{9}$	

B. Describe the pattern you see in your table.

C. Use the pattern to write a decimal representation for each fraction. Use your calculator to check your answers.

1. $\frac{9}{9}$ **2.** $\frac{10}{9}$ **3.** $\frac{15}{9}$

D. What fraction is equivalent to each decimal? (Hint: The number 1.222 . . . can be written as 1 + 0.222 . . . .)

1. 1.2222 . . . **2.** 2.7777 . . .

Problem 5.3 Follow-Up

1. Explore the decimal representations of fractions with a denominator of 99. Try $\frac{1}{99}$, $\frac{2}{99}$, $\frac{3}{99}$, and so on. What patterns do you see?

2. Explore the decimal representations of fractions with a denominator of 999. Try $\frac{1}{999}$, $\frac{2}{999}$, $\frac{3}{999}$, and so on. What patterns do you see?

3. Use the patterns you discovered in the decimal representations of fractions with denominators of 9, 99, and 999 to find fractions with these decimal representations.

a. 0.3333 . . . **b.** 0.05050505 . . . **c.** 0.45454545 . . .

d. 0.045045045 . . . **e.** 10.121212 . . . **f.** 3.999 . . .

Did you know?

Numbers that can be represented by terminating or repeating decimals are called **rational numbers** because they can be written as a *ratio* of integers. Numbers that can be represented by nonrepeating decimals are called **irrational numbers** because they cannot be written as a ratio of integers. The set of irrational and rational numbers is called the set of **real numbers.**

The number $\sqrt{2}$ is an irrational number. You had trouble finding an exact decimal representation for $\sqrt{2}$ because such a representation does not exist! Other examples of irrational numbers are $\sqrt{3}$, $\sqrt{5}$, and $\sqrt{11}$. In fact, $\sqrt{n}$ is an irrational number for any whole-number value of n that is not a square number.

An amazing fact about irrational numbers is that there is an infinite number of them between any two fractions.

Applications • Connections • Extensions

As you work on these ACE questions, use your calculator whenever you need it.

Applications

1. a. Find decimal representations of $\frac{1}{11}$, $\frac{2}{11}$, $\frac{3}{11}$, and so on. Describe the pattern you see.

b. Find three other fractions with the same decimal representations as $\frac{1}{11}$, as $\frac{2}{11}$, and as $\frac{3}{11}$.

In 2–4, write a decimal representation of the fraction.

2. $\frac{30}{9}$ **3.** $\frac{51}{99}$ **4.** $\frac{1000}{999}$

In 5–7, write a fraction representation of the decimal.

5. 0.12121212 . . . **6.** 0. 06060606 . . . **7.** 5.15151515 . . .

8. The decimal below is close to, but between, which two fractions? (Hint: There is more than one answer to this question.)

0.101001000100001 . . .

In 9–12, approximate each square root to four decimal places.

9. $\sqrt{144}$ **10.** $\sqrt{0.36}$

11. $\sqrt{15}$ **12.** $\sqrt{1000}$

In 13 and 14, find the two consecutive whole numbers between which the square root is located. Explain how you found your answer.

13. $\sqrt{27}$ **14.** $\sqrt{1000}$

In 15–17, tell whether the statement is true.

15. $6 = \sqrt{36}$ **16.** $1.5 = \sqrt{2.25}$ **17.** $11 = \sqrt{101}$

Connections

Think about this!

You can estimate the square root of a number without using the square root key on your calculator. Here's how one student thought about estimating $\sqrt{5}$:

- First, I need to find the whole numbers that $\sqrt{5}$ is between. Since $2 \times 2 = 4$ and $3 \times 3 = 9$, I know that $\sqrt{5}$ is between 2 and 3, but it's much closer to 2.
- Next, I need to look at numbers with one decimal place. When I square 2.1, I get 4.41, which is too small. When I square 2.2, I get 4.84, which is closer to 5 but still too small. Squaring 2.3 gives me 5.29, which is too big. Now I know that $\sqrt{5}$ is between 2.2 and 2.3, but it's closer to 2.2. I could use 2.2 as my estimate, but I want to get even closer.
- To get a better estimate, I want to try numbers with two decimal places: $2.21 \times 2.21 = 4.8841$; $2.22 \times 2.22 = 4.9284$; $2.23 \times 2.23 = 4.9729$; $2.24 \times 2.24 = 5.0176$. Now I know that $\sqrt{5}$ is between 2.23 and 2.24. Since 5.0176 is closer to 5 than 4.9284 is, I will use 2.24 as my estimate.

In 18–20, use a method similar to that described in the "Think about this!" box above to estimate the square root to the nearest hundredth. Show your work.

18. $\sqrt{11}$ **19.** $\sqrt{30}$ **20.** $\sqrt{172}$

In 21–24, find the area of the shaded region.

21.

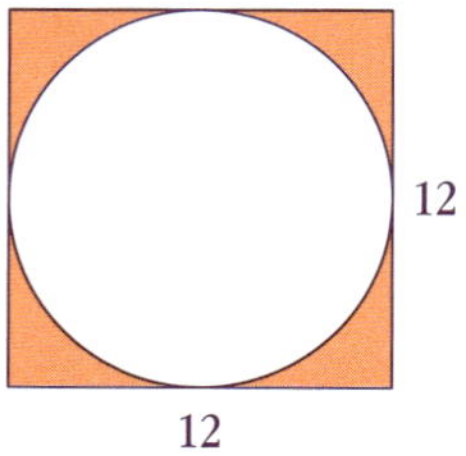

22.

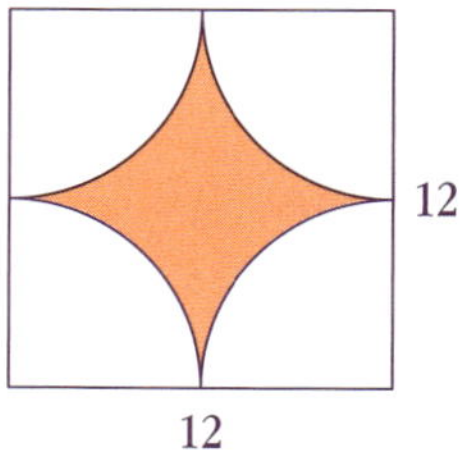

23. 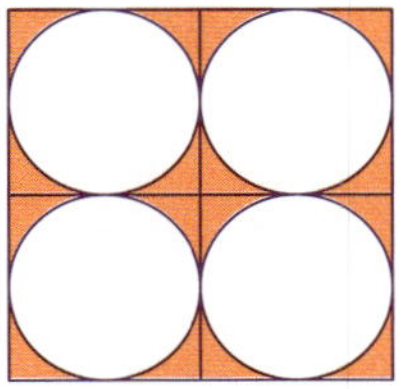

24. 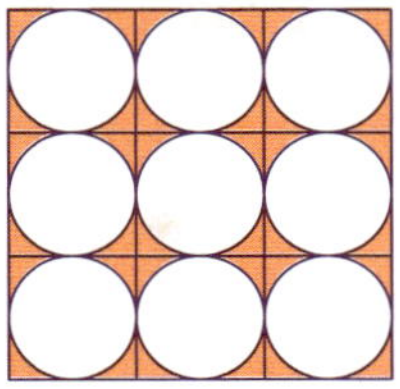

Extensions

25. You can use algebra to help you write a repeating decimal as a fraction. For example, suppose you want to write 0.12121212 . . . as a fraction.

Let $x = 0.12121212\ldots$. Multiply both sides of this equation by 100 to get $100x = 12.12121212\ldots$. Then, subtract the first equation from the second:

$$\begin{aligned} 100x &= 12.12121212\ldots \\ -\quad x &= 0.12121212\ldots \\ \hline 99x &= 12 \end{aligned}$$

Divide both sides of the resulting equation, $99x = 12$, by 99. This gives $x = \frac{12}{99}$. So, $0.12121212\ldots = \frac{12}{99}$.

The key to this method is to multiply each side of the original equation by a power of 10, such as 10, 100, or 1000. You need to use the power of 10 that will shift the decimal point so that one group of the repeating digits is to the left of the decimal point. In the example above, 100 was chosen because the repeating part consisted of two decimal places. Multiplying by 100 shifted the decimal point two places to the right.

Use this method to write each decimal as a fraction.

a. 0. 15151515 . . . **b.** 0. 7777 . . . **c.** 0.123123123123 . . .

In 26–29, tell whether the triangle with the given side lengths is a right triangle, and explain how you know.

26. 9, 12, 15

27. 5, 7, $\sqrt{74}$

28. $\sqrt{2}$, $\sqrt{7}$, 3

29. 6, 10, 12

30. Does $5^2 + 4^2 = (5 + 4)^2$? Explain.

31. Find an irrational number between $\frac{1}{7}$ and $\frac{1}{6}$.

Mathematical Reflections

In this investigation, you looked at decimal representations of fractions and fraction representations of decimals. You discovered that some decimals do not terminate or repeat and cannot be represented by fractions with numerators and denominators that are integers. These questions will help you summarize what you have learned:

1. How can you determine whether a given decimal can be written as a fraction?
2. Give three examples of fractions whose decimal representations terminate.
3. Give three examples of fractions whose decimal representations repeat.
4. Give three examples of irrational numbers greater than 5.
5. The positive square root of 10 is an irrational number.

   a. On dot paper, draw a square with sides of length $\sqrt{10}$. What is the area of the square?

   b. Find a fraction close to but less than $\sqrt{10}$. How can you tell that your fraction is less than $\sqrt{10}$?

   c. Find a fraction close to but greater than $\sqrt{10}$. How can you tell that your fraction is greater than $\sqrt{10}$?

Think about your answers to these questions, discuss your ideas with other students and your teacher, and then write a summary of your findings in your journal.

INVESTIGATION 6

Rational and Irrational Slopes

In this unit, you have used the Pythagorean Theorem to find lengths. In the process of finding lengths, you discovered irrational numbers—numbers that cannot be represented as fractions whose numerators and denominators are integers. In this investigation, you will explore an interesting application of irrational numbers.

Caitlin is playing a video game in which she directs a character named Oskar through a series of obstacles. At this point in the game, Oskar is trapped in the center of an immense forest made up of trees planted in rows and columns.

The trees are actually laser beams that are so narrow their widths cannot be measured. The beams are focused straight up. If Oskar hits a laser, he will be destroyed. To help him escape, Caitlin has used most of Oskar's power to reduce him to the width of a laser beam. Now he has only enough power to walk in a straight line. Can Oskar walk in a straight line out of the forest without running into a laser tree?

6.1 Revisiting Slopes

To help Oskar escape from the forest, Caitlin must find a straight-line path that does not hit any laser trees. In your earlier work, you used the idea of *slope*, or steepness, to help draw and describe lines. If you imagine a coordinate system with the origin where Oskar is now standing, you can think about the slopes of straight-line paths through the forest. For example, the line *OB* in the figure below has a slope of $\frac{1}{7}$ because it rises 1 unit for every 7 units it moves to the right.

Problem 6.1

The diagram below shows part of the forest. Some of the laser trees have been labeled with letters, and *x*- and *y*-axes have been added. Oskar's location is labeled with an *O*.

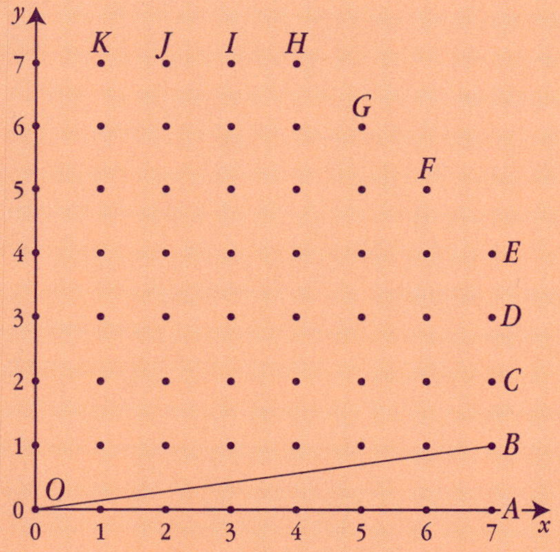

If Oskar had enough power, he could use a laser shield to walk right through the trees. Give the slope of the straight-line path he could follow to get from point *O* to each of the labeled trees.

Problem 6.1 Follow-Up

1. Suppose the forest continues for a great distance in all directions.

a. Give the coordinates of two more trees on line *OC*.

b. Give the coordinates of two more trees on line *OF*.

2. a. Give the coordinates of three trees on the line with slope 1 that passes through point *O*.
   b. What angle does the line described in part a make with the *x*-axis?
3. If a line contains two points on the grid, how can you find its slope?
4. If a line contains two points on the grid, will its slope be a rational number or an irrational number?

6.2 Escaping from the Forest

You have seen that irrational numbers, such as $\sqrt{2}$, $\sqrt{3}$, and $\sqrt{5}$, can represent lengths. Irrational numbers can also represent slopes of lines. Earlier in this unit, you found that $\sqrt{2}$ is between 1.4 and 1.5, or between $\frac{7}{5}$ and $\frac{3}{2}$. This means that the line through point *O* with slope $\sqrt{2}$ must lie between the line with slope $\frac{7}{5}$ and the line with slope $\frac{3}{2}$.

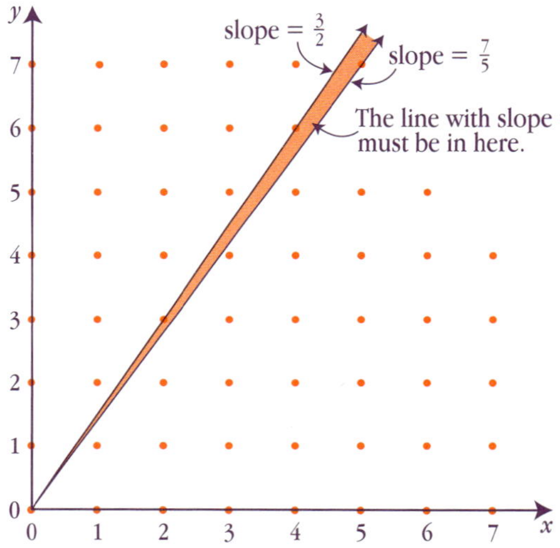

Problem 6.2

The laser forest extends beyond the screen, but Caitlin is not sure how far. She wants to be sure Oskar won't hit a tree anywhere along his escape path.

Study the drawing above. On Labsheet 6.2, draw a straight-line path that Oskar could follow to get out of the forest. Give the slope of the path you find. Explain why you think your path will work.

Problem 6.2 Follow-Up

1. a. On dot paper, draw a line with slope $\sqrt{5}$. Explain the steps you use to draw your line.

   b. On the same paper, draw a line with a slope that is a rational number slightly less than $\sqrt{5}$. Draw another line with a slope that is a rational number slightly greater than $\sqrt{5}$. Give the slopes of the lines you draw.

2. In addition to a path with slope $\sqrt{2}$, describe some other paths that Oskar could follow to get out the forest. What is true about the slope of any path he could follow?

Applications • Connections • Extensions

As you work on these ACE questions, use your calculator whenever you need it.

Applications

In 1–6, use this grid. Copy the points onto dot paper if you need to.

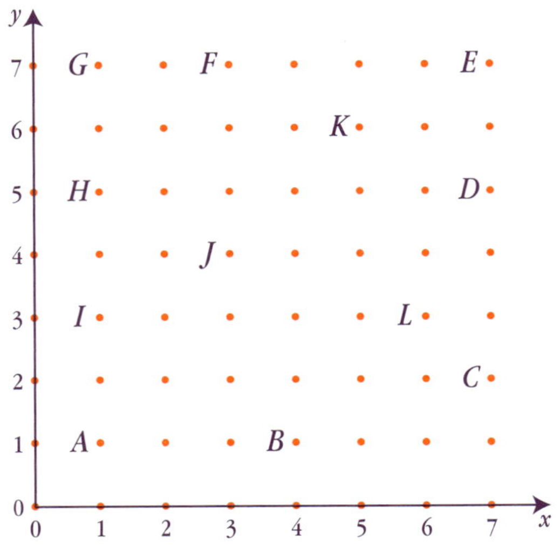

1. Find the slope of each line.

a. line *KE* **b.** line *GJ* **c.** line *LC*

d. line *AF* **e.** line *IF* **f.** line *IC*

g. line *CI* **h.** line *LE* **i.** line *JB*

2. a. How are lines *AE* and *JK* related? Find the slopes of these lines. What do you notice?

b. How are lines *FK* and *HJ* related? Find the slopes of these lines. What do you notice?

3. Find two other pairs of parallel lines. Find the slopes of the lines in each pair. What do you notice? Explain why this is true.

4. **a.** What kind of shape is quadrilateral *HFKJ*? Explain how you know.

   b. Points *J* and *K*, along with two other labeled points, are the vertices of another quadrilateral with the same kind of shape as quadrilateral *HFKJ*. Which points are the other two vertices of this quadrilateral?

5. **a.** If line segments *KL* and *BC* are extended until they meet, what will be true about the angle formed by their intersection?

   b. How are the slopes of lines *KL* and *BC* related?

6. **a.** Find a line perpendicular to line *AJ*. Give the slope of the line you found. How is the slope related to the slope of line *AJ*?

   b. Find a line perpendicular to line *BL*. Give the slope of the line you found. How is the slope related to the slope of line *BL*?

7. **a.** On dot paper, draw a line with slope $\sqrt{8}$. Explain the steps you use to draw your line.

   b. On the same paper, draw a line with a slope that is a rational number slightly less than $\sqrt{8}$, and a line with a slope that is a rational number slightly greater than $\sqrt{8}$. Give the slopes of the lines you draw.

Connections

8. **a.** What is the length of the hypotenuse of this triangle?

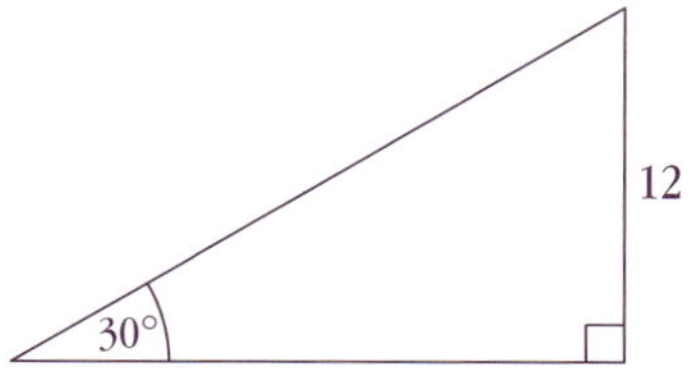

   b. What is the slope of the hypotenuse?

   c. What is the area of the triangle?

9. **a.** Draw line segments with as many different slopes as possible by connecting dots on 3-dot-by-3-dot grids. Label each segment with its slope. How many different slopes did you find? How do you know you have found every possible slope?

b. Draw line segments with as many different slopes as possible by connecting dots on 4-dot-by-4-dot grids. Label each segment with its slope. How many different slopes did you find?

c. Draw line segments with as many different slopes as possible by connecting dots on 5-dot-by-5-dot grids. Label each segment with its slope. How many different slopes did you find?

In 10–14, use the slopes of the sides to help you determine whether the figure is a right triangle, a rectangle, a nonrectangular parallelogram, or none of these. Copy the figures onto dot paper if you need to.

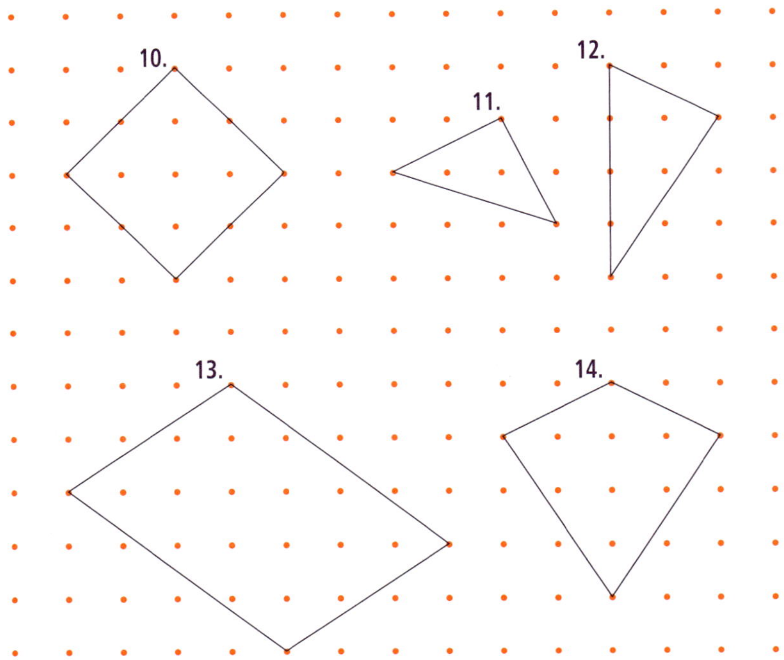

Extensions

15. In the diagram below, line segments connect point *P* on the circle to the endpoints of diameter *AB*.

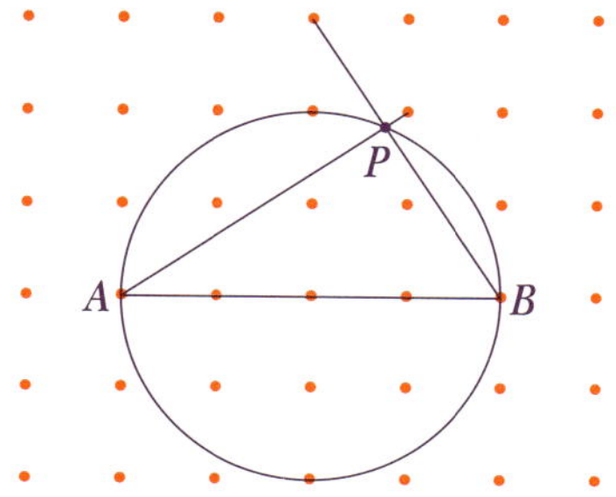

a. Segments *PA* and *PB* have each been extended to pass through a second dot. Find the slopes of lines *PA* and *PB*. How are the slopes of these lines related? When they intersect, what kind of angle do these lines form?

b. Copy this diagram onto dot paper. Choose another point on the circle, label it *Q*, and draw segments connecting it to points *A* and *B*. Find the slopes of lines *QA* and *QB*. How are the slopes of these lines related? What kind of angle do these lines form?

16. a. Find the following ratios of line segment lengths:

$\frac{\text{segment } PP'}{\text{segment } AP'}$ $\frac{\text{segment } QQ'}{\text{segment } AQ'}$ $\frac{\text{segment } RR'}{\text{segment } AR'}$ $\frac{\text{segment } CB}{\text{segment } AB}$

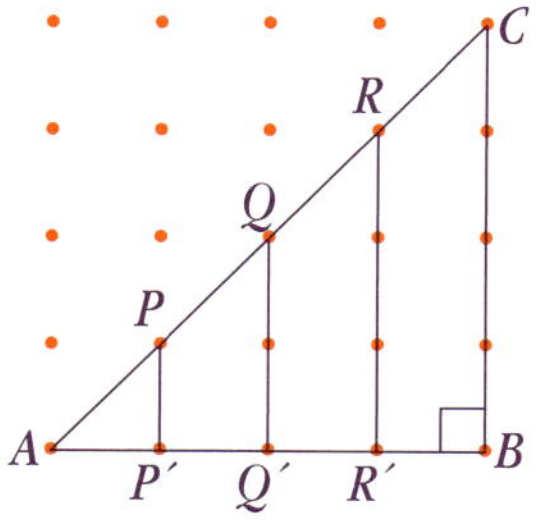

b. What do your answers tell you about the slope of the hypotenuse of triangle *ABC*?

Mathematical Reflections

In this investigation, you explored the slopes of lines, and you drew lines with slopes that are irrational numbers. These questions will help you summarize what you have learned:

1. How did you use slopes to help Oskar escape from the forest?
2. How can you use slopes to determine whether two lines are parallel?
3. How can you use slopes to determine whether two lines are perpendicular?
4. Explain how you would find the distance between two dots on a grid without measuring.
5. Explain how you would find the slope of a line passing through two dots on a grid.

Think about your answers to these questions, discuss your ideas with other students and your teacher, and then write a summary of your findings in your journal.

Looking Back and Looking Ahead

Unit Reflections

While working on problems in this unit you extended your skill in using *coordinate systems* to locate points and figures. Then, by studying patterns in the side lengths and areas of squares on coordinate grids, you learned the *Pythagorean Theorem* for right triangles. You used that property of right triangles to solve a variety of practical problems, some of which involved *irrational numbers*.

Using Your Understanding of the Pythagorean Theorem—Test your understanding of the Pythagorean Theorem and its relationship to area, lengths of line segments, and irrational numbers by solving the following problems.

1 *The diagram below shows a traditional Chinese tangram puzzle drawn on a 10-by-10 grid.*

a. What is the area of shape E?

b. What is the length of each side of shape E?

c. What are the lengths of the sides of triangle A?

d. Name all the triangles that are similar to triangle A. In each case, give a scale factor for the similarity relationship.

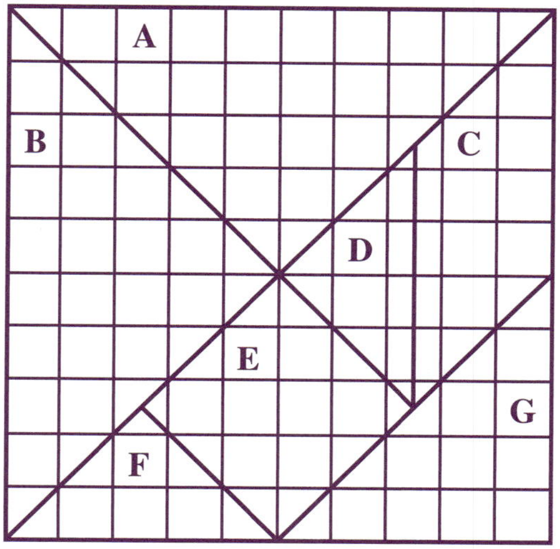

2 *Draw coordinate axes on graph paper or a dot grid to answer these questions.*

a. Sketch a line segment of length $\sqrt{17}$ with endpoints on the grid. Label the coordinates of the endpoints of the segment.

b. What is the slope of the line containing the line segment in part a?

c. Sketch three other segments with length $\sqrt{17}$ and find the slope of each of those segments.

d. Describe the relationship of the four segments you've drawn. Then describe the relationships among their slopes.

3 *Suppose that a 20-foot piece of wire is strung between a tower and the ground, making a 30-60-90 triangle as shown.*

a. How far out from the base of the tower is the wire attached to the ground?

b. How far up the tower is the wire attached?

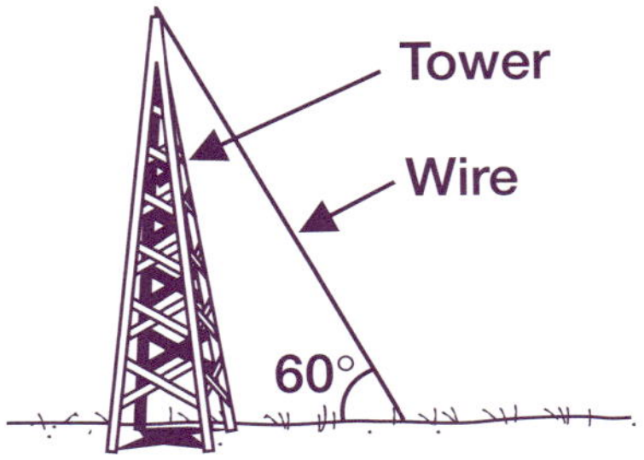

4 *For each of the following, decide whether the statement is true or false.*

a. $\sqrt{17}$ is between 16 and 18.

b. $\sqrt{3} + \sqrt{3}$ is greater than $\sqrt{6}$.

c. Each of the following numbers can be expressed as a repeating decimal.

$\frac{10}{9}$ $\frac{3}{7}$ $\sqrt{81}$ $\sqrt{13}$

5 *Locate these numbers on a number line.*

$\sqrt{5}$ 1.45 0.333... $-\frac{5}{4}$ $\sqrt{6.25}$ $-\sqrt{9}$ $\frac{9}{11}$

Explaining Your Reasoning—In this unit you learned how to use the Pythagorean Theorem to solve a variety of mathematical problems about lengths of sides and areas of triangles and other polygons. When you present work based on the Pythagorean Theorem, you should be able to justify your calculations and conclusions.

1. How can you find the length of each side of any square if you are given its area?

2. How can you find the length of the segment joining any two points on a coordinate grid?

3. The diagrams on page 75 show squares drawn on the sides of triangles. What is the relationship among the areas of those squares for the first triangle, but not the second? Explain why the relationship does not apply to the triangle in Case 2.

Case 1:

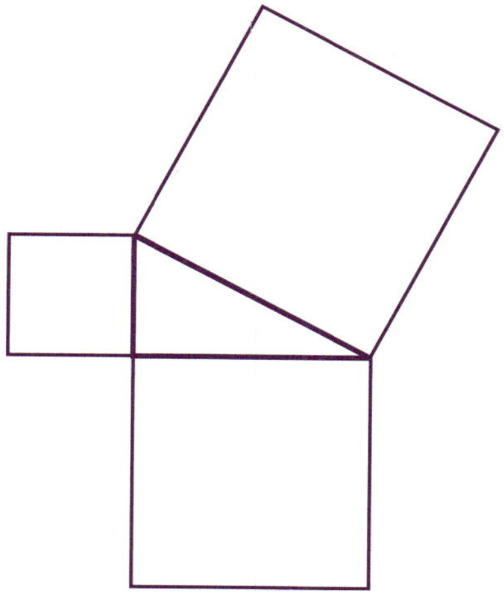

Case 2:

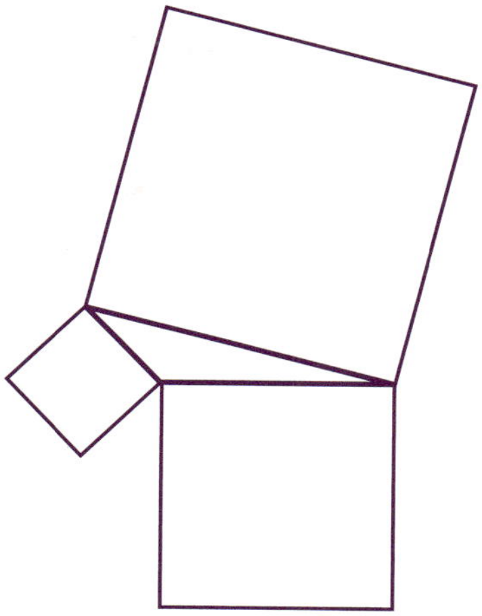

4. Explain with words and symbols how you can use the Pythagorean Theorem to find the length of the

a. diagonal of a square with side length *s*.

b. diagonal of a rectangle with side lengths *s* and *t*.

c. hypotenuse of a right triangle with legs of lengths *s* and *t*.

d. height of an equilateral triangle with side length *s*.

e. length of one side of a triangle when the lengths of the hypotenuse and the other side are *h* and *t* respectively.

5. What are rational and irrational numbers?

6. What are some of the ideas from prior *Connected Mathematics* units that were particularly useful in this unit on the Pythagorean Theorem and irrational numbers?

The set of rational and irrational numbers is called the set of *real numbers*. In the next several algebra units you will use real numbers to investigate important properties of linear, exponential, and quadratic functions. You will also find these numbers useful in solving equations. The Pythagorean Theorem has many applications—some of which you will see in the *Frogs, Fleas, and Painted Cubes* unit, as well as in your high school mathematics, science, and technology courses.

Glossary

hypotenuse The side of a right triangle that is opposite the right angle. The hypotenuse is the longest side of a right triangle. In the triangle below, the side labeled *c* is the hypotenuse.

irrational number A number that cannot be written as a fraction with a numerator and a denominator that are integers. The decimal representation of an irrational number never ends and never shows a repeating pattern of digits. The numbers $\sqrt{2}$, $\sqrt{3}$, $\sqrt{5}$, and π are examples of irrational numbers.

perpendicular Meeting at right angles. For example, the sides of a right triangle that form the right angle are perpendicular.

Pythagorean Theorem A statement about the relationship between the lengths of the sides of a right triangle. The theorem states that if *a* and *b* are the lengths of the legs of a right triangle and *c* is the length of the hypotenuse, then $a^2 + b^2 = c^2$.

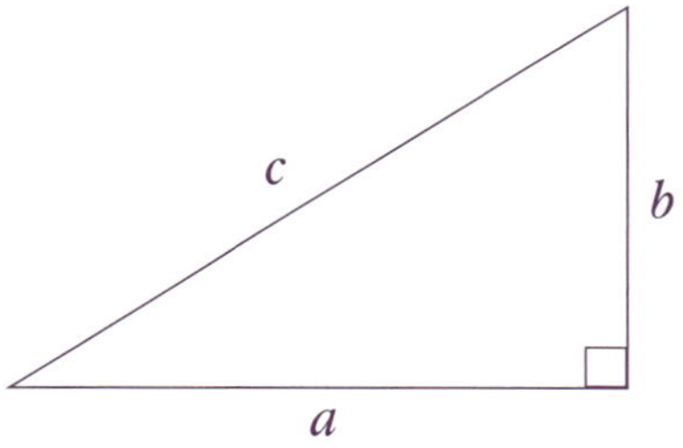

rational number A number that can be written as a fraction with a numerator and a denominator that are integers. The decimal representation of a rational number either ends or repeats. Examples of rational numbers are $\frac{1}{2}$, $\frac{79}{81}$, 7, 0.2, and .191919. . . .

real numbers The set of all rational numbers and all irrational numbers. The number line represents the set of real numbers.

repeating decimal A decimal with a pattern of digits that repeats forever, such as 0.3333333. . . and 0.73737373. . . . Repeating decimals are rational numbers.

square root If $A = s^2$, then s is the square root of A. For example, $^-3$ and 3 are square roots of 9 because $3 \times 3 = 9$ and $^-3 \times {}^-3 = 9$. The $\sqrt{\ }$ symbol is used to denote the positive square root. So, we write $\sqrt{9} = 3$. The positive square root of a number is the side length of a square that has that number as its area. So, you can draw a segment of length $\sqrt{5}$ by drawing a square with an area of 5; the side length of the square will have a length of $\sqrt{5}$.

terminating decimal A decimal that ends, or terminates, such as 0.5 or 0.125. Terminating decimals are rational numbers.

Glosario

decimal exacto Un decimal que se acaba o termina, como ser 0.5 ó 0.125. Los decimales exactos son números racionales.

decimal que se repite Un decimal con un patrón de dígitos que se repite indefinidamente, como ser 0.3333333... y 0.73737373... Los decimales que se repiten son números racionales.

hipotenusa El lado de un triángulo rectángulo que está opuesto al ángulo recto. La hipotenusa es el lado más largo de un triángulo rectángulo. En el triángulo que figura en la próxima página, el lado rotulado c es la hipotenusa.

número irracional Un número que no puede escribirse como una fracción con un numerador y un denominador que sean enteros. La representación decimal de un número irracional nunca termina y nunca muestra un patrón de dígitos que se repite. Los números $\sqrt{2}$, $\sqrt{3}$, $\sqrt{5}$ y π son ejemplos de números irracionales.

número racional Un número que puede escribirse como una fracción con un numerador y un denominador que sean enteros. La representación decimal de un número racional se termina o bien se repite. Ejemplos de números racionales son $\frac{1}{2}$, $\frac{79}{81}$, 7, 0.2, y 0.191919...

números reales El conjunto de todos los números racionales y todos los números irracionales. La recta numérica representa el conjunto de los números reales.

perpendicular Que se encuentran en ángulos rectos. Por ejemplo, los lados de un triángulo rectángulo que forman el ángulo recto son perpendiculares.

raíz cuadrada Si $A = s^2$, entonces s es la raíz cuadrada de A. Por ejemplo, $^-3$ y 3 son raíces cuadradas de 9 porque $3 \times 3 = 9$ y $^-3 \times {}^-3 = 9$. El símbolo $\sqrt{}$ se usa para indicar la raíz cuadrada positiva. Por eso, escribimos $\sqrt{9} = 3$. La raíz cuadrada positiva de un número es la longitud de lado de un cuadrado que tiene dicho número como su área. Entonces, puedes dibujar un segmento de longitud $\sqrt{5}$ dibujando un cuadrado con un área de 5; la longitud de lado del cuadrado tendrá una longitud de $\sqrt{5}$.

Teorema de Pitágoras Un enunciado acerca de la relación que existe entre las longitudes de los lados de un triángulo rectángulo. El teorema enuncia que si a y b son las longitudes de los catetos de un triángulo rectángulo y c es la longitud de la hipotenusa, entonces $a^2 + b^2 = c^2$.

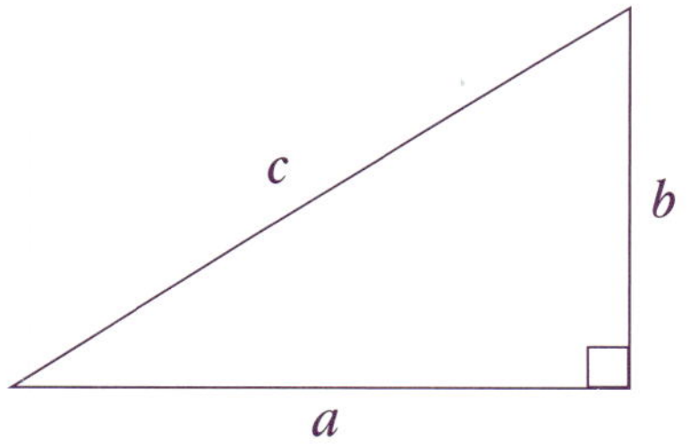

Index

Connected Mathematics™

Growing, Growing, Growing

Exponential Relationships

Student Edition

Glenda Lappan
James T. Fey
William M. Fitzgerald
Susan N. Friel
Elizabeth Difanis Phillips

PEARSON
Prentice Hall

Glenview, Illinois
Needham, Massachusetts
Upper Saddle River, New Jersey

Growing, Growing, Growing

Connected Mathematics™ was developed at Michigan State University with the support of National Science Foundation Grant No. MDR 9150217.

This project was supported, in part, by the
National Science Foundation
Opinions expressed are those of the authors and not necessarily those of the Foundation

The Michigan State University authors and administration have agreed that all MSU royalties arising from this publication will be devoted to purposes supported by the Department of Mathematics and the MSU Mathematics Education Enrichment Fund.

Photo Acknowledgements: 11 © Laima Druskis/Stock, Boston; 22 © Bill Bachmann/Photo Researchers, Inc.; 31 © Schuster/Superstock, Inc.; 38 (wolf) © D. Northcott/Superstock, Inc.; 38 (fly) Dr. Jeremy Burgess/SPL/Photo Researchers, Inc.; 43 © Charles Gupton/Tony Stone Images; 45 © Robert E. Daemmrich/Tony Stone Images; 48 © Lynn Lennon/Photo Researchers, Inc.

Contents

Growing, Growing, Growing

A veterinarian can give a pet medicine to relieve the discomfort of flea bites. The effects of such medicines wear off in a predictable pattern. Suppose that each day after an injection, the amount of medicine in a dog's blood is $\frac{3}{4}$ the amount of the previous day. After how many days will less than half of the original dose remain in the dog's blood?

Nicole is studying the growth of a beetle population. She begins her experiment with five beetles and finds that the population doubles each month. What would a graph of the number of beetles over a year's time look like?

When Ella was in sixth grade, she invested $500 in a low-risk stock. Ella has just graduated from high school and wants to sell her stock to help pay for a trip to Italy. If the value of the stock has increased by 5% each year since Ella bought it, how much is her stock now worth?

One of the most important uses of algebra is to model patterns of change. You are already familiar with linear patterns of change. Linear patterns are characterized by constant differences and straight-line graphs. In a table for a linear relationship, a constant amount is added to the y value each time the x value increases by 1.

In this unit, you will study exponential patterns of change. In a table for an exponential relationship, the y value is multiplied by a constant amount each time the x value increases by 1. Exponential patterns are fascinating because, although the values may change gradually at first, they eventually increase or decrease very rapidly.

Mathematical Highlights

In *Growing, Growing, Growing* you will explore one of the most important types of non-linear relations among variables—exponential functions. The unit should help you to

- Recognize situations where one variable is an exponential function of another variable;
- Recognize the connections between exponential equations and patterns in tables and graphs of those relations;
- Construct equations to express exponential patterns that appear in data tables, graphs, and problem conditions;
- Use tables, graphs, and equations of exponential relations to solve problems about exponential growth and decay in a variety of situations from science and business; and
- Compare exponential and linear relationships.

As you work on the problems of this unit, make it a habit to ask questions about problem situations that involve non-linear relations: *Is the relationship among variables in this situation an example of exponential growth or decay? What equation would model the data or the pattern in a graph relating the variables? How could I answer the questions of the situation by studying a table or graph of the exponential relation?*

INVESTIGATION 1

Exponential Growth

Repeated doubling, tripling, and quadrupling are types of exponential growth. In this investigation, you are introduced to exponential growth as you cut paper in half over and over and meet a very smart peasant from the ancient kingdom of Montarek. You will compare exponential growth with linear growth and explore exponential patterns in tables, graphs, and equations.

1.1 Making Ballots

Alejandro is making ballots for an election. He starts by cutting a sheet of paper in half. He then stacks the two pieces and cuts them in half. He stacks the resulting four pieces and cuts them in half. He repeats this process, creating smaller and smaller pieces of paper.

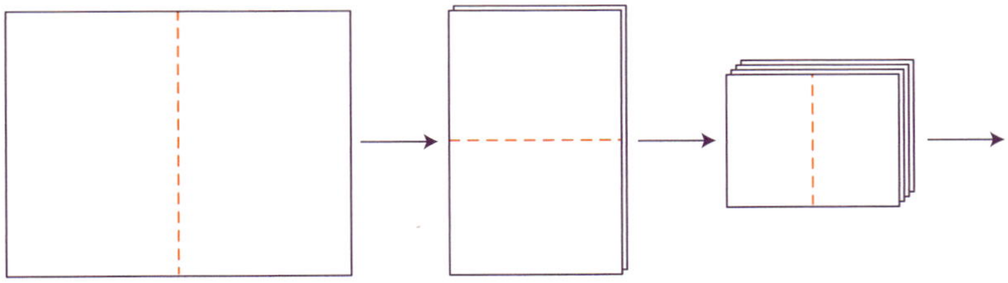

After each cut, Alejandro counts the ballots and records the results in a table.

Cuts	Ballots
1	2
2	4
3	
4	
5	

Alejandro wants to find a way to predict the number of ballots after any number of cuts.

Problem 1.1

A. Cut a sheet of paper as Alejandro did, and count the ballots after each cut. Make a table to show the number of ballots after 1 cut, 2 cuts, 3 cuts, and so on.

B. Look for a pattern in the way the number of ballots changes with each cut. Use your observations to extend your table to show the number of ballots for up to 10 cuts.

C. If Alejandro made 20 cuts, how many ballots would he have? How many ballots would he have if he made 30 cuts?

D. A stack of 250 sheets of the paper Alejandro is using is 1 inch high. How high would a stack of ballots be after 20 cuts? After 30 cuts?

E. How many cuts would Alejandro need to make to have a stack of ballots 1 foot high?

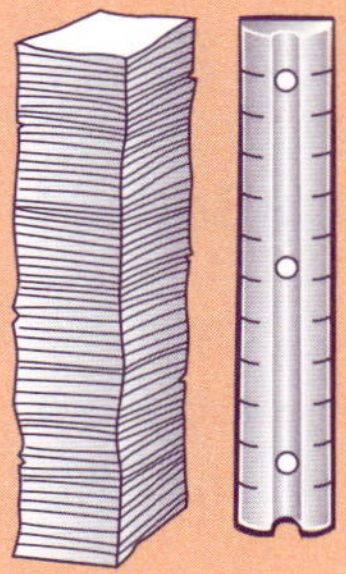

Problem 1.1 Follow-Up

When you found the number of ballots made by 10, 20, and 30 cuts, you probably found yourself multiplying long strings of 2s. Instead of writing out long product strings of the same factor, you can use **exponential form**. For example, you can write $2 \times 2 \times 2 \times 2 \times 2$ as 2^5, which is read "2 to the fifth power." In the expression 2^5, 2 is the **base** and 5 is the **exponent**. When you evaluate 2^5, you get $2^5 = 2 \times 2 \times 2 \times 2 \times 2 = 32$. We say that 32 is the **standard form** for 2^5.

1. Write each expression in exponential form.

a. $2 \times 2 \times 2$

b. $5 \times 5 \times 5 \times 5$

c. $1.5 \times 1.5 \times 1.5 \times 1.5 \times 1.5 \times 1.5 \times 1.5$

2. Write each expression in standard form.

a. 2^7 **b.** 3^3 **c.** 4.2^3

3. Most calculators have a $\boxed{\wedge}$ or $\boxed{y^x}$ key for evaluating exponents. Find out how to use your calculator to evaluate exponents, and then write each of these expressions in standard form.

a. 2^{15} **b.** 3^{10} **c.** 1.5^{20}

4. Explain how the expressions 5^2, 2^5, and 5×2 differ.

5. You know that $5^2 = 25$. How can you use this fact to evaluate 5^4?

6. The standard form for 5^{10} is 9,765,625. How can you use this fact to evaluate 5^{11}?

1.2 Requesting a Reward

One day in the ancient kingdom of Montarek, a peasant saved the life of the king's daughter. The king was so grateful that he told the peasant she could have any reward she desired. The peasant—who was also the kingdom's chess champion—made an unusual request:

"I would like you to place 1 ruba on the first square of a chessboard, 2 rubas on the second square, 4 on the third square, 8 on the fourth square, and so on, until you have covered all 64 squares. Each square should have twice as many rubas as the previous square."

The king replied, "Rubas are the least valuable coin in the kingdom. Surely you can think of a better reward." But the peasant insisted, so the king agreed to her request.

Problem 1.2

A. Make a table showing the number of rubas the king will place on squares 1 through 16 of the chessboard.

B. How does the number of rubas change from one square to the next?

C. How many rubas will be on square 20? On square 30? On square 64?

D. What is the first square on which the king will place at least 1 million rubas?

E. If a Montarek ruba had the value of a U.S. penny, what would be the dollar values of the rubas on squares 10, 20, 30, 40, 50, and 60?

Problem 1.2 Follow-Up

1. Graph the (number of the square, number of rubas) data for squares 1 to 10. As the number of the square increases, how does the number of rubas change? What does this pattern of change tell you about the peasant's reward?

2. Write an equation for the relationship between the number of the square, n, and the number of rubas, r.

3. If a chessboard had 100 squares, how many rubas would be on square 100?

4. The pattern of change in the number of ballots in Problem 1.1 and the pattern of change in the number of rubas in this problem show **exponential growth.**

  a. How are the patterns of change in these two situations similar?

  b. Write an equation for the relationship between the number of ballots, b, and the number of cuts, n, in Problem 1.1.

1.3 Making a New Offer

When the king told the queen about the reward he had promised the peasant, the queen said, "You have promised her more money than we have in the entire royal treasury! You must convince her to accept a different reward."

After much contemplation, the king thought of a plan. He would create a new board with only 16 squares. He would place 1 ruba on the first square, 3 on the next, 9 on the next, and so on. Each square would have three times as many rubas as the previous square.

Problem 1.3

A. In the table below, plan 1 is the reward requested by the peasant, and plan 2 is the king's new plan. Copy and complete the table to show the number of rubas on squares 1 to 16 for each plan.

Square	Number of rubas	
	Plan 1	Plan 2
1	1	1
2	2	3
3	4	9
4		

B. How is the pattern of change in the number of rubas under plan 2 similar to and different from the pattern of change in the number of rubas under plan 1?

C. Write an equation for the relationship between the number of the square, n, and the number of rubas, r, for plan 2.

D. Is the total reward under the king's plan greater than or less than the total reward under the peasant's plan? How did you decide?

Problem 1.3 Follow-Up

1. Make a graph of plan 2 for $n = 1$ to 10. How does your graph compare to the graph you made for plan 1?

The queen devised a third reward that the king could offer the peasant. Under plan 3, the king would make a board with 12 squares. He would start with 1 ruba in the first square and quadruple the number of rubas from one square to the next. So, the pattern of rubas would be 1, 4, 16, 64, and so on.

2. Make a graph of plan 3 for $n = 1$ to 10. How does this graph compare to the graphs of plans 1 and 2?

3. Write an equation for the relationship between the number of the square, n, and the number of rubas, r, for plan 3. How do the equations for the three plans compare?

4. Of the three plans, which is best for the peasant? Which is best for the king?

5. Design another reward plan with a pattern of change that you think shows exponential growth. Explain why you think the growth is exponential.

As you work on these ACE questions, use your calculator whenever you need it.

Applications

1. Cut a sheet of paper into thirds. Stack the three pieces, and cut the stack into thirds. Stack all the pieces, and cut that stack into thirds.

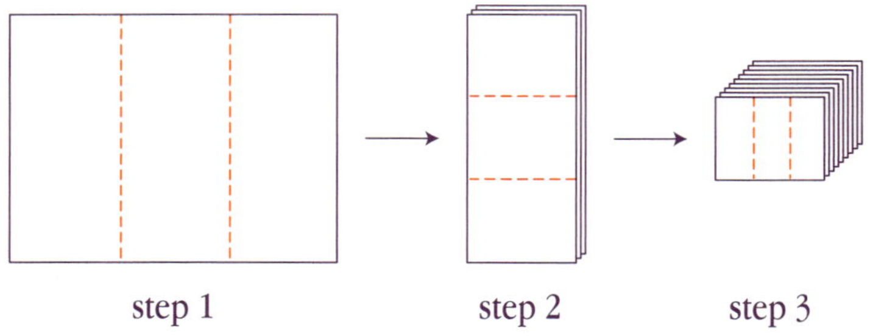

How many pieces of paper would you have at the end of

a. step 1 **b.** step 2 **c.** step 3

d. step 10 **e.** step *n*

2. While studying her family's history, Angie discovered records of ancestors 12 generations back. She wondered how many ancestors she had had in the past 12 generations. She decided to make a tree diagram to help her figure this out, but the diagram soon became very complex. Her diagram is shown on the next page.

a. Make a table and a graph showing the number of ancestors Angie would find in each of the 12 generations.

b. Write an equation for the number of ancestors, A, in a given generation, n.

c. What is the total number of ancestors in all 12 generations?

d. What similarities do you notice in the patterns of change for the number of ancestors, the number of ballots (Problem 1.1), and the number of rubas (Problems 1.2 and 1.3)? What differences do you notice?

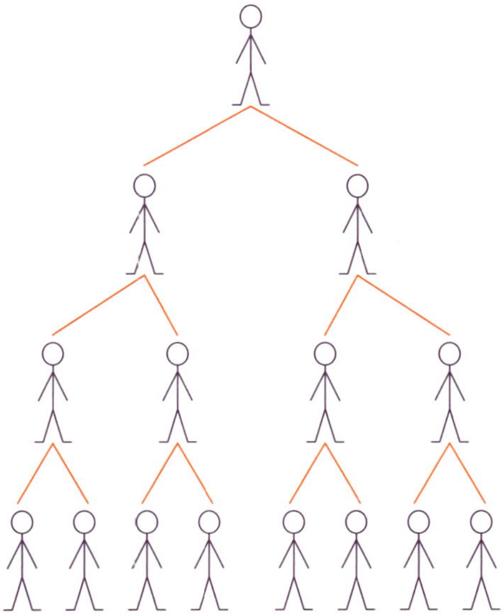

3. Many single-celled organisms reproduce by dividing into two identical cells. Suppose an amoeba divides into two amoebas every half hour.

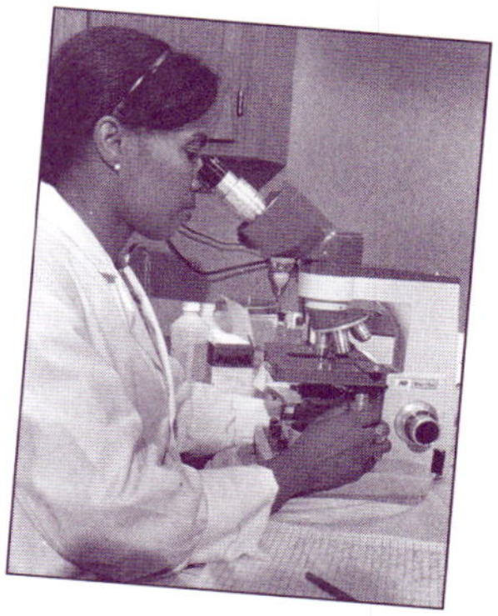

a. A biologist starts an experiment with one amoeba. Make a table showing the number of amoebas she would have at the end of each hour over an 8-hour period.

b. Write an equation for the number of amoebas, a, after t hours.

c. How many hours will it take for the number of amoebas to reach 1 million?

d. Make a graph of the (time, amoebas) data from part a.

e. What similarities do you notice in the patterns of change for the number of amoebas and the number of ancestors (ACE question 2)? What differences do you notice?

In 4–6, write the expression in exponential form.

4. $2 \times 2 \times 2 \times 2$

5. $10 \times 10 \times 10 \times 10 \times 10 \times 10 \times 10$

6. $2.5 \times 2.5 \times 2.5 \times 2.5 \times 2.5$

In 7–9, write the expression in standard form.

7. 2^{10} **8.** 10^2 **9.** 3^9

Connections

10. A ruba had the same thickness as a modern U.S. penny (about 0.06 inch). Suppose the king had been able to reward the peasant by using plan 1 (doubling the number of rubas on each square).

a. What would the height of the stack of rubas on square 64 have been?

b. The average distance from Earth to the moon is about 240,000 miles. Which (if any) of the stacks of rubas would have reached the moon?

11. Consider these two equations, which involve exponential expressions:

i. $R = 3^{n-1}$ **ii.** $R = 3^n - 1$

a. For each equation, find R when n is 2.

b. For each equation, find R when n is 10.

c. Explain why the equations give different values of R for the same value of n.

12. Cesar said that since he can group $2 \times 2 \times 2 \times 2 \times 2 \times 2 \times 2 \times 2 \times 2 \times 2$ as $(2 \times 2 \times 2 \times 2) \times (2 \times 2 \times 2 \times 2 \times 2 \times 2)$, it must be true that $2^{10} = 2^4 \times 2^6$.

a. Verify that Cesar is correct by evaluating both sides of the equation $2^{10} = 2^4 \times 2^6$.

b. Use Cesar's idea of grouping factors to write three other expressions that are equivalent to 2^{10}. Evaluate each expression you find to verify that it is equivalent to 2^{10}.

c. The standard form for 2^7 is 128, and the standard form for 2^5 is 32. Use these facts to evaluate 2^{12}. Show your work.

d. Test Cesar's idea to see if it works for exponential expressions with other bases, such as 3^8 or 1.5^{11}. Test several cases. Give an argument supporting your conclusion.

e. Find a general way to express Cesar's idea in words and with symbols.

Extensions

13. Molly figured out that $2^6 = 64$ and $4^3 = 64$. Then, since $2^2 = 4$, she substituted 2^2 for 4 in the expression 4^3 and got $(2^2)^3 = 64$. She said that since $2^6 = 64$ and $(2^2)^3 = 64$, it must be true that $(2^2)^3 = 2^6$.

a. Verify that Molly is correct by evaluating both sides of the equation $(2^2)^3 = 2^6$.

b. Use Molly's idea to find an exponential expression equivalent to the given expression.

i. $(3^2)^4$ **ii.** $(4^3)^2$

c. Find a general way to express Molly's idea in words and with symbols. Check your idea by testing it on three more examples.

14. Juan wrote out the first 12 powers of 2. He wrote $2^1 = 2$, $2^2 = 4$, $2^3 = 8$, and so on. He noticed a pattern in the digits in the units places of the results. He said he could use this pattern to predict the digit in the units place of 2^{100}.

a. What pattern did Juan observe?

b. What digit is in the units place of 2^{100}? Explain how you found your answer.

15. Here is a table like the one you made in Problem 1.1 with a row for 0 cuts added.

Cuts	Ballots
0	1
1	2
2	4
3	8
4	16

a. Write an equation for the pattern in the table.

b. Use your equation and the table to determine the value of 2^0.

c. What do you think b^0 should equal for any number b, such as 3^0, 6^0, and 23^0? Check your idea with a calculator.

16. When the king of Montarek tried to figure out the total number of rubas he would have to reward the peasant under plan 1, he made a table like the one on the next page.

Square	Number of rubas on square	Total number of rubas
1	1	1
2	2	3
3	4	7
4		

a. Copy and complete the table for $n = 1$ to 10.

b. The king noticed an interesting pattern of growth in the total number of rubas on the chessboard as the number of the square increases. Describe the pattern.

c. Write an equation for the relationship between the number of the square, n, and the total number of rubas on the board, t.

d. When the total number of rubas reaches 1,000,000, how many squares will have been covered?

e. If the king had been able to give the peasant the reward she requested, how many rubas would she have received?

Mathematical Reflections

In this investigation, you looked at several situations involving exponential growth. You learned how to recognize patterns of exponential growth in tables, graphs, and equations. These questions will help you summarize what you have learned:

1. Based on your work in this investigation, what do you think are the key properties of exponential growth patterns? How are exponential growth patterns different from the linear patterns you have worked with in earlier units?
2. Consider the exponential equation $y = 2^x$.
   - **a.** How can you calculate the value of y for a given value of x?
   - **b.** Describe the graph of $y = 2^x$.
3. Consider the exponential equation $y = 3^x$.
   - **a.** How is the method of calculating a y value for a given x value for $y = 3^x$ similar to calculating a y value for a given x value for $y = 2^x$? How is it different?
   - **b.** How is a table of values for $y = 3^x$ similar to a table of values for $y = 2^x$? How is it different?
   - **c.** How is the graph of $y = 3^x$ similar to the graph of $y = 2^x$? How is it different?

Think about your answers to these questions, discuss your ideas with other students and your teacher, and then write a summary of your findings in your journal.

INVESTIGATION 2

Growth Patterns

Now that you have learned to recognize exponential growth, you are ready to take a closer look at the tables, graphs, and equations of exponential relationships. In this investigation, you will explore these questions:

- If the values of a variable grow exponentially, how do they change from one stage to the next?
- How are the starting values and the size of the growth reflected in the table, the graph, and the equation for an exponential relationship?

2.1 Getting Costs in Line

Before presenting plans 2 and 3 to the peasant, the king consulted with his financial advisors. They told the king that either plan would devastate the royal treasury, and they proposed a fourth plan. Under plan 4, the king would put 20 rubas on the first square of a chessboard, 25 on the second, 30 on the third, and so on, increasing the number of rubas by 5 for each square, until all 64 squares were covered.

To help convince the peasant to accept their plan, the advisors prepared the table and graph below comparing the new offer to the original plan. The king presented the plan to the peasant and gave her a day to consider the offer.

	Number of rubas	
Square	Plan 1	Plan 4
1	1	20
2	2	25
3	4	30
4	8	35
5	16	40
6	32	45

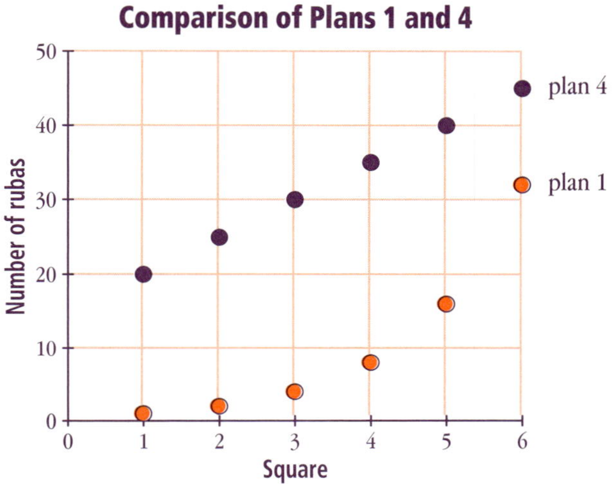

Problem 2.1

A. Make a table showing the number of rubas on squares 7, 8, 9, and 10 for plans 1 and 4.

B. For plan 4, write an equation for the relationship between the number of the square, *n,* and the number of rubas, *r.* How is this equation similar to the equation for plan 1? How is it different?

C. For plans 1 and 4, how many rubas would be on square 20? How many rubas would be on square 30?

D. Write a paragraph explaining why the peasant should or should not accept the king's new offer.

Problem 2.1 Follow-Up

As you compared the reward plans, you probably discovered at least two methods for calculating the number of rubas on a given square: you can use an equation, or you can figure out how the number of rubas changes from one square to the next.

1. For plan 1, there would be 16,384 rubas on square 15. How many rubas would there be on square 16?

2. For plan 4, there would be 90 rubas on square 15. How many rubas would there be on square 16?

3. **a.** How does the number of rubas change from one square to the next for plan 1?
b. How does the number of rubas change from one square to the next for plan 4?

4. How are your answers to question 3 represented in the equations for the plans?

2.2 Listening to the Queen

After considering plan 4, the peasant was convinced that the reward under plan 4 was not nearly as large as the original reward she had requested. She went to see the king and queen and politely refused the new offer.

The queen quickly devised yet another plan:

"The king will use a board with 16 squares. He will place 500 rubas on the first square, 1000 on the second, 2000 on the third, 4000 on the fourth, and so on, doubling the number of rubas on each square. As you can see, this plan starts with 500 rubas on the first square and your plan starts with only 1. Surely, you will accept this new offer."

Problem 2.2

A. Make a table showing the number of rubas on squares 5 to 16 for the queen's new plan.

B. Write an equation for the relationship between the number of the square, n, and the number of rubas, r, for the queen's new plan.

C. Write a paragraph explaining why the peasant should or should not accept the queen's offer.

Problem 2.2 Follow-Up

1. The king thinks the peasant will be more likely to accept a plan if there are many rubas on the first square. He proposes placing 5 million rubas on the first square of a 16-square board, 6 million on the second square, 7 million on the third, and so on, increasing the number of rubas by 1 million for each square.
   a. Write an equation for the relationship between the number of the square, n, and the number of rubas, r, for this plan.
   b. Is the relationship between the number of the square and the number of rubas linear or exponential? Explain.
   c. Would you advise the peasant to accept this offer? Why or why not?
2. Make up two reward plans that you think would be hard to choose between. Describe how you designed your plans so that choosing would be difficult. Show your plans to someone and ask which plan he or she would choose.
3. Write an ending to the story of the king and the peasant.

2.3 Growing Mold

Some living organisms grow or reproduce exponentially. Mold, for example, can spread rapidly. The area covered by mold on a loaf of bread left out in warm weather might grow in a pattern like the one shown in the table.

Day	Mold area (cm^2)
0 (start)	1
1	3
2	9
3	27
4	81

Problem 2.3

Look at the pattern in the (day, mold area) data.

A. Describe how the mold area changes from one day to the next.

B. Write an equation for the mold area, A, after d days.

C. How is your answer to part A reflected in your equation?

Problem 2.3 Follow-Up

Suppose that on day 0, a patch of bread mold has an area of 25 mm^2 (one fourth of a square centimeter) and that the mold grows in the same exponential way it did in Problem 2.3.

1. Copy and complete the table to show the growth of the mold area.

Day	Mold area (mm^2)
0 (start)	25
1	
2	
3	
4	

2. Write an equation for the mold area, A, after d days.

3. Which part of your equation indicates the starting value? Which part indicates the change from one day to the next?

You have looked at several examples of exponential growth patterns. You explored the growth in

- the area of a patch of mold with each day
- the number of rubas with each square
- the number of ballots with each cut

In each case, you found that the value for any stage—day, square, or cut—could be determined by multiplying the value for the previous stage by a fixed number. This fixed number is called the **growth factor.**

4. Give the growth factor for each situation.

a. making ballots by repeatedly cutting stacks of paper in half

b. reward plan 1 (Problem 1.2)

c. reward plan 2 (Problem 1.3)

d. the growth of bread mold (Problem 2.3)

5. Ilan's biology class did an experiment with bread mold. They wrote the equation $A = 50(3^d)$ to represent the area in mm^2 of the mold after d days.

a. What was the area of the patch of mold at the start of the experiment?

b. What was the growth factor?

c. What was the area of the mold after 5 days?

d. On which day did the area of the mold reach 10 cm^2?

As you work on these ACE questions, use your calculator whenever you need it.

Applications

1. If you don't brush your teeth regularly, it won't take long for large colonies of bacteria to grow in your mouth. Suppose that a single bacterium lands on one of your teeth and starts reproducing by a factor of 4 every hour.

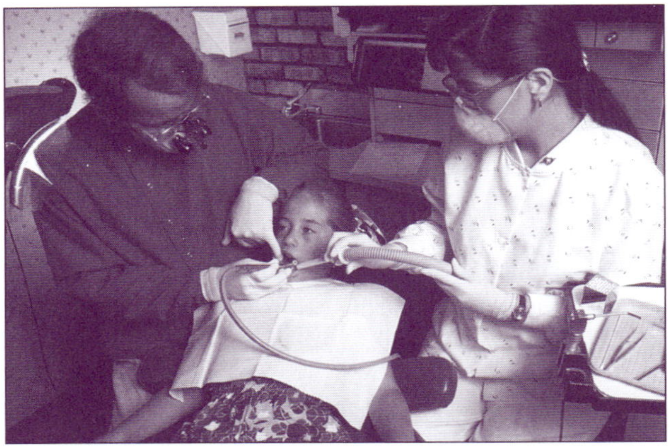

a. Write an equation that describes the number of bacteria, b, in the new colony after n hours.

b. How many bacteria will be in the new colony after 7 hours?

c. How many bacteria will be in the new colony after 8 hours? Explain how you can find this answer by using the answer from part b rather than the equation.

d. After how many hours will there be at least 1 million bacteria in the colony?

e. Suppose that 50 bacteria, not just 1 bacterium, land in your mouth. Write an equation that describes the number of bacteria, b, in this colony after n hours.

f. Under the conditions of part e, there will be 3,276,800 bacteria in this new colony after 8 hours. How many bacteria will there be after 9 hours? After 10 hours? Explain how you can find these answers without using the equation from part e.

2. As a biology project, Nicole is investigating how fast a particular beetle population will grow under controlled conditions. She started her experiment with 5 beetles. The next month she counted 15 beetles.

a. If the beetle population is growing linearly, how many beetles can Nicole expect to find after 2, 3, and 4 months?

b. If the beetle population is growing exponentially, how many beetles can Nicole expect to find after 2, 3, and 4 months?

c. Write an equation for the relationship between the number of beetles and the number of months if the beetle population is growing linearly.

d. Write an equation for the relationship between the number of beetles and the number of months if the beetle population is growing exponentially.

e. If the beetle population is growing linearly, how long will it take the population to reach 200?

f. If the beetle population is growing exponentially, how long will it take the population to reach 200?

3. One of the plans considered by the king's financial advisors involved putting 100 rubas on the first square of a chessboard, 125 on the second square, 150 on the third square, and so on, increasing the number of rubas by 25 for each square until all 64 squares were filled.

a. Write an equation for the numbers of rubas, r, on square n for this plan.

b. How would you expect the graph of this plan to look?

c. What would be the total number of rubas on the first 10 squares? On the first 20 squares?

4. Leaping Leonard just signed a contract with the Peoria Panthers basketball team. The contract guarantees him \$20,000 the first year, \$40,000 the second year, \$80,000 the third year, \$160,000 the fourth year, and so on, for 10 years.

   a. Make a table showing Leonard's salary each year of this contract.

   b. What is the total amount of money Leonard will earn in 10 years?

   c. Write an equation relating Leonard's salary, S, and the year, n, of his contract.

Connections

In 5–8, study the pattern in the table. Tell whether the relationship between x and y is linear, exponential, or neither, and explain your answer. If the relationship is linear or exponential, write an equation for the relationship.

5.

x	0	1	2	3	4	5
y	1	4	7	10	13	16

6.

x	0	1	2	3	4
y	1	6	36	216	1296

7.

x	0	1	2	3	4	5	6	7	8
y	1	5	3	7	5	8	6	10	8

8.

x	0	1	2	3	4	5	6	7	8
y	7	14	28	56	112	224	448	896	1792

9. Fido did not have fleas when his owners took him to the kennel. The number of fleas on Fido after he returned from the kennel grew according to the equation $f = 8(3^n)$, where f is the number of fleas and n is the number of weeks since he returned from the kennel.

a. How many fleas did Fido pick up from the dog kennel?

b. What is the growth factor for the number of fleas?

c. If this growth continues, how many fleas will Fido have after 10 weeks?

10. Copy the table below, and complete it according to these rules:

- In column *A*, find each value by adding 10 to the previous value.
- In column *B*, find each value by multiplying the previous value by 10.

N	*A*	*B*
1	7	7
2		
3		
4		
5		

a. Is the pattern of change in column *A* linear, exponential, or neither?

b. Is the pattern of change in column *B* linear, exponential, or neither?

c. Write an equation for the relationship between *A* and *N*.

d. Write an equation for the relationship between *B* and *N*.

11. Calculators use *scientific notation* to display very large results. For each expression, find the largest whole-number value of n for which your calculator will display the result in standard notation.

a. 3^n

b. π^n

c. 12^n

d. 237^n

12. The graph on the next page shows the exponential growth of a garter-snake population for 4 years after the population was introduced to a new area.

a. What is the population in year 2? In year 3? In year 4?

b. How does the population change from one year to the next?

c. Use the pattern in your answers from part a to estimate the population in year 1. Explain how you found your answer.

d. When is the population likely to be greater than 1500?

e. Assume the population started with one pregnant female. Write an equation relating time, t, in years, and population, P.

Growth of Garter Snake Population

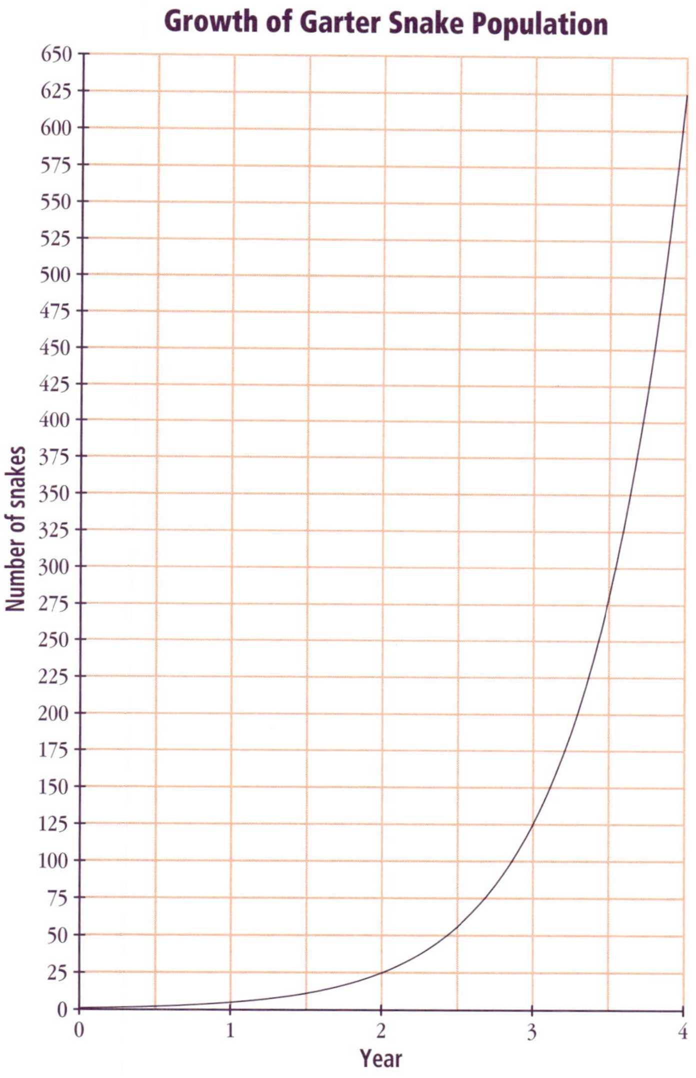

13. Shahla used a copy machine to enlarge a 2 cm by 3 cm rectangle by a factor of 2 to get a 4 cm by 6 cm rectangle. She then enlarged the 4 cm by 6 cm rectangle by a factor of 2. She continued this process, enlarging each new rectangle by a factor of 2.

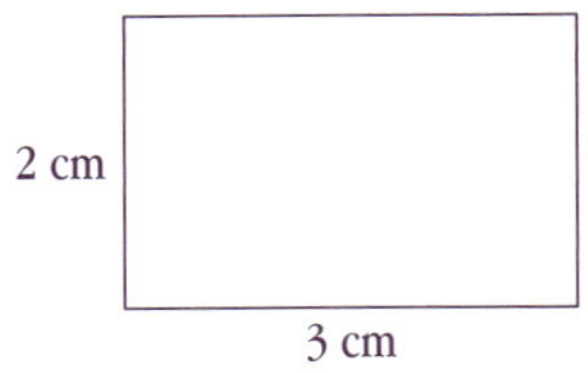

a. Copy and complete the table to show the area and the perimeter of the rectangle after each enlargement.

Enlargement	Dimensions (cm)	Perimeter (cm)	Area (cm^2)
0 (original)	2 by 3		
1	4 by 6		
2			
3			
4			
5			

b. Is the pattern of growth for the perimeter linear, exponential, or neither? Explain your answer.

c. Is the pattern of growth for the area linear, exponential, or neither? Explain your answer.

d. Write an equation for the perimeter, P, after n enlargements.

e. Write an equation for the area, A, after n enlargements.

f. How would your answers to parts a–e change if the copier were set to enlarge by a factor of 3?

14. On the next page are graphs of $y = 2^x$ and $y = 2x + 1$.

a. Which graph is the graph of $y = 2^x$ and which is the graph of $y = 2x + 1$? Explain your answer.

b. The dashed lines show the vertical and horizontal change between points spaced at equal x intervals. For each graph, compare the vertical and horizontal change between each pair of points. What do you notice?

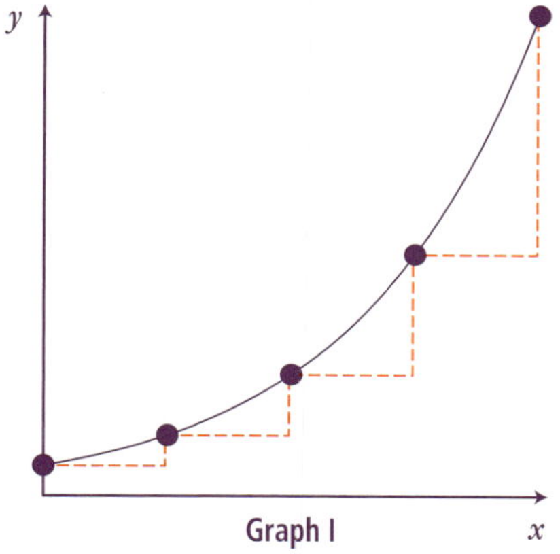

Graph I

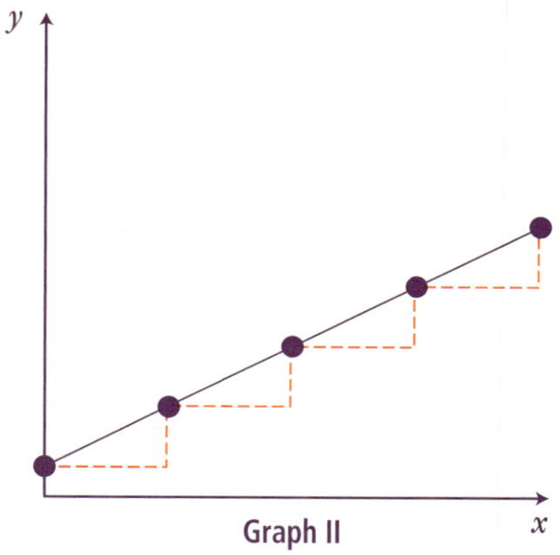

Graph II

Extensions

15. **a.** Copy and complete these tables.

x	2^x
1	
2	
3	
4	
5	

x	4^x
1	
2	
3	
4	
5	

x	8^x
1	
2	
3	
4	
5	

x	2^x
	4096
	16,777,216

x	4^x
	4096
	16,777,216

x	8^x
	4096
	16,777,216

b. What patterns do you see across the tables?

c. Is $2(2^x) = 4^x$? Why or why not?

d. Is $2(4^x) = 8^x$? Why or why not?

16. **a.** Make a table and a graph for the exponential equation $y = 1^x$.

b. How are the patterns in the table and the graph of $y = 1^x$ similar to patterns you have observed for other exponential relationships? How are they different?

Mathematical Reflections

In this investigation, you studied variables with values that grew exponentially. You looked at how the values changed from one stage to the next, and you wrote equations to find the value at any stage. You also compared exponential patterns of change to linear patterns of change. These questions will help you summarize what you have learned:

1. In the equation $y = 5^x$, how does the value of y change each time x increases by 1?
2. How do exponential relationships such as $y = 5^x$ differ from linear relationships such as $y = 5x$ in the way the y value changes as the x value increases?
3. How are graphs and tables of exponential relationships different from those of linear relationships?
4. In the equation $y = a(b^x)$, how does the value of a affect the relationship? For example, how are the table and the graph of $y = 12(5^x)$ different from the table and the graph of $y = 5^x$?
5. Suppose a table for an exponential relationship shows the x value increasing by 1. How can you find the growth factor for the relationship? For example, what is the growth factor for the relationship shown in this table?

x	y
1	343
2	2401
3	16,807
4	117,649

Think about your answers to these questions, discuss your ideas with other students and your teacher, and then write a summary of your findings in your journal.

INVESTIGATION 3

Growth Factors

In the previous investigations, you studied exponential growth of amoeba, bacterium, snake, and beetle populations. In each case, once you knew the growth factor and the starting population, you could make population predictions. The growth factors in these examples were small whole numbers. In this investigation, you will study examples of exponential growth with fractional growth factors.

3.1 Reproducing Rabbits

In 1859, rabbits were introduced to the island continent of Australia by English settlers who wanted animals they could hunt for sport. The rabbits had no natural predators in Australia, so they reproduced rapidly and became a serious problem, eating grasses intended for sheep and cattle.

Did you know?

A female rabbit can have up to seven litters with five or more rabbits each per year. In 1995, there were over 300 million rabbits in Australia. The damage caused by rabbits costs Australian agriculture $500 million per year. Although there have been many attempts to curb Australia's rabbit population, no method has proven inexpensive or reliable enough to have a significant impact.

If biologists had counted the rabbits in Australia in the years after the rabbits were introduced, they might have collected data like these:

Time (years)	Rabbit population
0	100
1	180
2	325
3	580
4	1050

Problem 3.1

A. The table above shows that the rabbit population grows exponentially. What is the growth factor for this rabbit population? The growth factor from one year to the next is the fraction:

$$\frac{\text{population for year } n}{\text{population for year } n-1}$$

To find an approximate overall growth factor, compute the growth factors between several pairs of consecutive years and average your results.

B. If this growth pattern had continued, how many rabbits would there have been after 10 years? After 25 years? After 50 years?

C. How many years would it have taken the rabbit population to exceed 1 million?

D. Assume this growth pattern continued. Write an equation you could use to predict the rabbit population, P, for any year, n, after the rabbits were first counted.

Problem 3.1 Follow-Up

After some time, the dangers of the rapid rabbit reproduction became clear to the Australian government, and officials began programs to control the population growth.

1. Suppose that when the rabbit population reached 1 million, the government began control programs that reduced the growth factor to 1.5.
   a. With this growth factor, how many years would it have taken the population to grow from 1 million to 2 million?
   b. How many years would it have taken the population to grow from 1 million to 5 million?
   c. How many years would it have taken the population to grow from 1 million to 10 million?
   d. How many years would it have taken the population to grow from 1 million to 20 million?

2. a. With a growth factor of 1.2, how many years would it have taken the population to double from any starting population?
   b. With a growth factor of 1.5, how many years would it have taken the population to double from any starting population?
   c. With a growth factor of 1.8, how long would it have taken the population to double from any starting population?
   d. What observations can you make about the time it would take the population to double with growth factors of 1.2, 1.5, and 1.8?

3. Suppose that during one time period, the rabbit population could be predicted by the equation $P = 15(1.2^t)$, where P is the population in millions, and t is the number of years.
   a. What does this equation assume about the population growth factor?
   b. What does this equation assume about the initial population?

4. You can think of a growth factor in terms of a percent change. For example, suppose the yearly growth factor for a rabbit population is 1.8.
   - If the initial population is 100 rabbits, there will be 180 rabbits at the end of 1 year.
   - A change from 100 to 180 is an increase of 80 rabbits.
   - Since 80 rabbits is $\frac{80}{100}$, or 80%, of the original population, the rabbit population will increase by 80% each year.

   Find the percent change associated with each growth factor.

   a. 1.5 b. 1.25 c. 1.1

3.2 Investing for the Future

Many people invest their money in land, art, antiques, or other items that will increase in value. Changes in the value of investments are often expressed as percents.

When Sam was in seventh grade, his uncle gave him a coin collection worth \$2500. Sam considered selling the collection, but his uncle told him that if he saved it, it would increase in value. Sam saved the collection, and its value increased by 6% each year for several years in a row.

One year after Sam received the coins, their value had increased to \$2650.

$$\begin{aligned}\$2500 + (6\% \text{ of } \$2500) &= \$2500 + 0.06(\$2500)\\ &= \$2500 + \$150\\ &= \$2650\end{aligned}$$

Two years after Sam received the coins, their value had increased to \$2809.

$$\begin{aligned}\$2650 + (6\% \text{ of } \$2650) &= \$2650 + 0.06(2650)\\ &= \$2650 + \$159\\ &= \$2809\end{aligned}$$

Sam got very excited when he realized that not only was the value of the coins increasing, but it was increasing by a greater amount each year!

Although the value of the coins increased by the same percent each year, the percent was applied to the current increased value. So, in the second year, the value increased by 6% of \$2650, not 6% of the original \$2500. This pattern of change is called **compound growth**.

Think about this!

Think about the examples of exponential growth you saw in the last two investigations. Did these situations show compound growth? Explain why or why not.

Problem 3.2

Assume that the value of Sam's coin collection increased by 6% each year for 10 years.

A. Make a table showing the value of the collection each year for the 10 years after Sam's uncle gave it to him.

B. For each year, find the ratio of the value of the coins to the value for the previous year. That is, find

$$\frac{\text{value in year } n}{\text{value in year } n - 1}$$

This ratio is the growth factor.

C. Suppose the value of the coins increased by 4% each year instead of 6%.

1. Make a table showing the value of the collection each year for the 10 years after Sam's uncle gave it to him.
2. Find the growth factor by examining successive values in the table.

D. What would the growth factor be if the value increased by 5% each year? Explain your answer.

Problem 3.2 Follow-Up

1. How does the reasoning below help explain the growth factor you found for a growth rate of 6%?

$$\begin{aligned}\text{next year's value} &= 100\% \text{ of this year's value} + 6\% \text{ of this year's value}\\ &= 106\% \text{ of this year's value}\\ &= 1.06 \times \text{this year's value}\end{aligned}$$

2. Use the reasoning from question 1 to find the growth factor if the value increased by 4% each year. Then, find the growth factor if the value increased by 5% each year. Are the growth factors you found the same as those you found in parts C and D?

3. Sam wrote this formula for calculating the value of the coins t years after he first received them:

$$V = 2500(1.06^t) \qquad \text{for } t = 1, 2, 3, \ldots, 10$$

Does Sam's formula give the same results that are in your table for part A?

3.3 Making a Difference

Suppose the value of Sam's coin collection increased by 6% each year for 30 years. To find the value of the collection after 30 years, you could make a very long table. A better plan would be to write and solve an equation. In earlier investigations, you used the growth factor and the starting value to help you write equations for exponential growth situations.

Think about this!

Think about how the starting value and the growth factor are used to write the equation in each example below.

- In the reward plan suggested by the peasant in Problem 1.2, 1 ruba would be placed on the first square of a chessboard, and the number of rubas would increase by a factor of 2 with each successive square. The equation for this situation is $r = 1(2^{n-1})$, or simply $r = 2^{n-1}$.
- An experiment began with 25 mm^2 of mold. The area covered by the mold grew by a factor of 3 each day. The equation for this situation is $A = 25(3)^n$.

Problem 3.3

Sam gave some of his coins to his sister to help her pay college expenses. The value of the remaining collection was $1250.

A. Suppose the value of the remaining coins increased by 4% each year. Make a table showing the value of the collection each year for the next 10 years.

B. Sam's friend Maya has a baseball card collection worth $2500. Add a column to your table showing the value of Maya's collection each year for a 10-year period if its value increases by 4% each year.

C. Compare the values of the collections over the 10-year period. How does the initial value of the collection affect the yearly increase in value?

D. How does the initial value of each collection affect the growth factor?

E. Write an equation for the value, V, of Sam's $1250 coin collection after t years.

F. Solve your equation to find the value of Sam's collection after 30 years.

Problem 3.3 Follow-Up

1. Sam made the following calculation to predict the value of his aunt's stamp collection several years from now:

$$\text{value} = \$2400 \times 1.05 \times 1.05 \times 1.05 \times 1.05$$

   a. What initial value, rate of increase in value, and number of years is Sam assuming?
   b. The result of Sam's calculation is $2917.22. If the value continued to increase at this rate, how much would the collection be worth in one more year?

2. Find the growth factor associated with each percent increase.
   a. 30% b. 15% c. 5% d. 75%

Applications • Connections • Extensions

As you work on these ACE questions, use your calculator whenever you need it.

Applications

1. In parts of the United States, wolves are being reintroduced to wilderness areas where they have become extinct. Suppose 20 wolves are released in northern Michigan, and the yearly growth factor for this population is expected to be 1.2.

a. Make a table showing the projected number of wolves at the end of each of the first 6 years.

b. Write an equation that models the growth pattern of the wolf population.

c. How long will it take for the new wolf population to exceed 100?

2. Fruit flies *(Drosophila melanogaster)* are often used in genetic experiments because they reproduce at a phenomenal rate. In 12 days, a pair of *Drosophila* can mature and produce a new generation of fruit flies. The table below shows the number of fruit flies in three generations of a laboratory colony.

Generation	0	1	2	3
Number of fruit flies	2	120	7200	432,000

a. What is the growth factor for this fruit-fly population? Explain how you found your answer.

b. If this pattern continues, how many fruit flies will there be in the fifth generation?

c. Write an equation for the population, P, of this fruit-fly colony as a function of the generation, g.

d. If the pattern in the table continues, after how many generations will the population exceed 1 million?

3. Currently, 1000 students attend Greenville Day School. The school can accommodate 1300 students. The directors of the school estimate that the student population will grow by 5% per year for the next several years.

a. In how many years will the population outgrow the present building?

b. Suppose the school limits its growth to 50 students per year. How many years will it take for the population to outgrow the present building?

4. Suppose that for several years the number of radios sold in the United States increased by 3% each year.

a. If 1 million radios were sold in the first year of this time period, about how many radios were sold in each of the next 6 years?

b. If 100,000 radios were sold in the first year, about how many radios were sold in each of the next 6 years?

5. Suppose a movie ticket costs about \$7, and inflation causes ticket prices to increase by 4% a year.

a. At this rate, how much will a ticket cost 5 years from now?

b. At this rate, how much will a ticket cost 10 years from now?

c. At this rate, how much will a ticket cost 30 years from now?

6. In Russia, shortly after the breakup of the Soviet Union, the growth factor for inflation was 1.5. What percent increase is associated with this growth factor? We call this percent increase the *inflation rate.*

7. If the price of a product increases by 25% per year, what is the growth factor from year to year?

Connections

8. Government workers often get cost-of-living pay raises. Suppose a government worker has an annual salary of $20,000.

a. What would be the dollar value of a 3% raise for this worker? Of a 4% raise? Of a 6% raise?

b. What would the worker's new annual salary be for each raise in part a?

c. You can find the new salary after a 3% raise in two ways:

$20,000 + (3% of $20,000)   or   103% of $20,000

Why do these two methods give the same result?

9. After graduating from high school, Kwan accepted a job with a package delivery service, earning $5.15 per hour.

a. How much will Kwan earn in a year if she works 40 hours per week for 50 weeks and gets 2 weeks of paid vacation time?

b. Suppose Kwan works for the company for 10 years, receiving a 3% raise each year. Make a table showing how her annual income grows over this time period.

c. When Kwan was hired, her manager told her that instead of a 3% annual raise, she could choose to receive a $350 raise each year. How do the two raise plans compare over a 10-year period? Which plan do you think is better? Explain your answer.

10. You can evaluate exponential expressions such as 1.25^{10} and 1.5^7 in several ways.

a. Determine which expressions below are equivalent to 1.25^{10}. Explain why each expression is or is not equivalent.

i. $1.25^5 \times 1.25^5$ **ii.** $1.25^3 \times 1.25^7$

iii. 1.25×10 **iv.** $1.25 + 10$

b. Determine which expressions below are equivalent to 1.5^7. Explain why each expression is or is not equivalent.

i. $1.5^5 \times 1.5^2$ **ii.** $1.5^3 \times 1.5^4$

iii. 1.5×7 **iv.** $1.5 + 7$

11. Katrina used a copy machine to enlarge this drawing of a flag to 110% of this size.

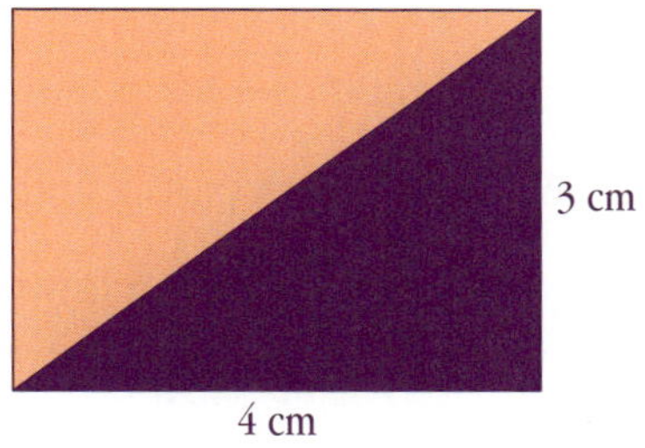

a. What are the length of the diagonal and the area of the shaded region of the original drawing?

b. What are the length of the diagonal and the area of the shaded region of the enlarged drawing?

c. Katrina enlarged the enlargement to 110% of its size. She continued this process, enlarging each new drawing to 110% of its size. After five enlargements, what were the length of the diagonal and the area of the shaded region?

d. Is each enlargement similar to the original figure? Explain. (Hint: Compare the ratio of the length to the width for each enlargement to the ratio of the length to the width for the original.)

In 12–14, tell whether the pattern represents exponential growth. Explain your answer.

12. 1   1.1   1.21   1.331   1.4641   1.61051   1.771561

13. 0   3   6   9   12   15   18

14. 2   8   18   32   50   72   98

Extensions

15. In 1990, the population of the United States was about 250 million and was growing exponentially at a rate of about 0.7% per year. (Remember, 0.7% = 0.007.)

a. At this growth rate, what will the population of the United States be in the year 2000?

b. At this rate, how long will it take the population to double?

c. Do you think the predictions in parts a and b are accurate? Explain.

16. The table below gives the world population from 1955 to 1990 in 5-year intervals.

Year	1955	1960	1965	1970	1975	1980	1985	1990
Population (billions)	2.70	2.98	3.29	3.63	4.01	4.43	4.84	5.29

a. One model of world population growth assumes that the population grows exponentially. Based on the data in this table, what would be a reasonable growth factor for this model?

b. Use your growth factor to write an equation for the growth of the population at 5-year intervals beginning in 1955.

c. Use your equation to predict the 5-year interval in which the population will be double the 1955 population.

d. Use your equation to predict when the population will be double the 1990 population.

17. If your calculator did not have an exponent key (^ or y^x), you could evaluate 1.5^{12} by entering $1.5 \times 1.5 \times 1.5 \times 1.5 \times 1.5 \times 1.5 \times 1.5 \times 1.5 \times 1.5 \times 1.5 \times 1.5 \times 1.5$.

a. How could you evaluate 1.5^{12} with fewer keystrokes?

b. What is the least number of times you could press $\times$ to evaluate 1.5^{12}?

18. The following graph shows the growth in the number of cellular-phone subscribers from 1986 to 1994.

a. What do the bars in the graph represent?

b. What does the curve represent?

c. Describe the pattern of change in the total number of subscribers. Is the pattern exponential? Explain.

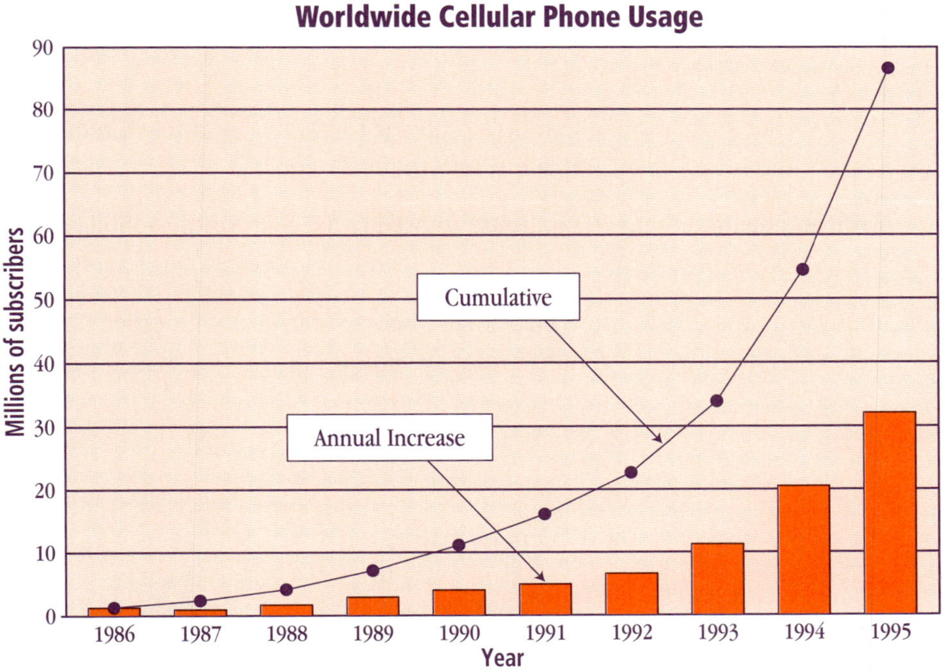

Source: *World Cellular Markets* published by MTA-EMCI

Mathematical Reflections

In this investigation, you explored exponential growth situations in which the growth factor was not a whole number. These questions will help you summarize what you have learned:

1. Suppose you had data about the growth of a fish population in a lake over several years.
   - **a.** How would you decide whether the population was growing exponentially?
   - **b.** If the population growth appeared to be exponential, how would you use the data to write an equation for the growth?
2. How is a growth rate of 20% related to an exponential growth factor of 1.2?
3. Suppose rents in a particular area are increasing by 20% per year.
   - **a.** Predict what an apartment that now rents for $1500 per month will rent for 1 year from now. Explain your work.
   - **b.** Predict what an apartment that now rents for $1500 per month will rent for each year for the next 5 years. Explain your work.
   - **c.** Write an equation that you could use to predict the rent for the $1500 apartment t years from now.

Think about your answers to these questions, discuss your ideas with other students and your teacher, and then write a summary of your findings in your journal.

INVESTIGATION 4

Exponential Decay

The exponential patterns you have studied so far in this unit have all involved variables with increasing values. In this investigation, you will explore variables with values that decrease, or *decay*, exponentially as time passes.

4.1 Making Smaller Ballots

In Problem 1.1, you read about the ballots that Alejandro was making for an election. Recall that Alejandro cut a sheet of paper in half, stacked the two pieces and cut them in half, and then stacked the resulting four pieces and cut them in half.

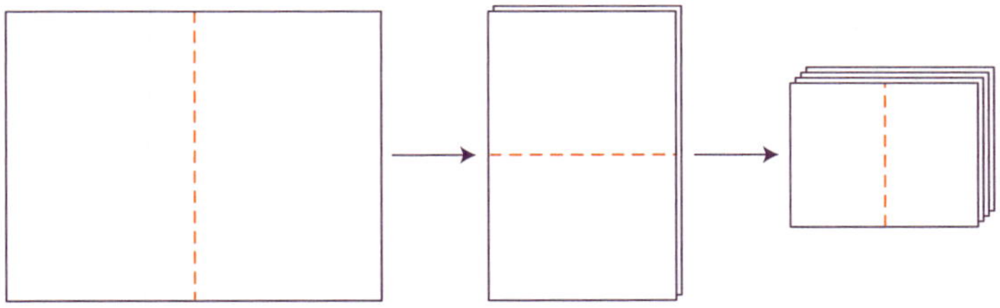

In Problem 1.1, you investigated the pattern in the number of ballots created by each cut. In this problem, you will look at the pattern in the areas of the ballots.

Problem 4.1

Cut a sheet of paper as Alejandro did, and look for a pattern in the area of the ballots after each cut. Use what you discover to help you complete this problem.

A. The sheet of paper Alejandro started with had an area of 64 in^2. Copy and complete the table below to show the area of a ballot after each of the first 10 cuts.

Cuts	Area (in^2)
0	64
1	32
2	16
3	
4	
5	
6	
7	
8	
9	
10	

B. How does the area of a ballot change with each cut?

C. How is the pattern of change in the area different from the exponential growth patterns you have seen in this unit? How is it similar?

Problem 4.1 Follow-Up

You may have described the pattern of change in the area of a ballot by saying it is "cut in half" or "divided in two" with each cut. This means that with each cut the area is multiplied by $\frac{1}{2}$, or divided by 2.

The area of the original sheet of paper was 64 in^2. The first cut multiplies this area by $\frac{1}{2}$, or 0.5:

$$\text{area after 1 cut} = 64 \times 0.5$$

The second cut multiplies the new area by 0.5:

$$\text{area after 2 cuts} = 64 \times 0.5 \times 0.5 = 64(0.5^2)$$

This pattern of multiplying by 0.5 continues with each cut:

$$\text{area after 3 cuts} = 64 \times 0.5 \times 0.5 \times 0.5 = 64(0.5^3)$$
$$\text{area after 4 cuts} = 64 \times 0.5 \times 0.5 \times 0.5 \times 0.5 = 64(0.5^4)$$

.
.
.

The area, A, of a ballot after n cuts can be represented by the equation $A = 64(0.5^n)$. Notice that this is an exponential equation similar to the equations you have worked with in previous investigations.

We say that exponential patterns like this, in which the quantity *decreases* with each stage, show **exponential decay**. We call the factor we multiply by at each stage the **decay factor.** In the example above, the decay factor is 0.5. While a growth factor is always greater than 1, a decay factor is always less than 1.

Suppose you start with a sheet of paper with an area of 27 in^2. Instead of cutting the stack of paper in half at each stage, you cut it into thirds:

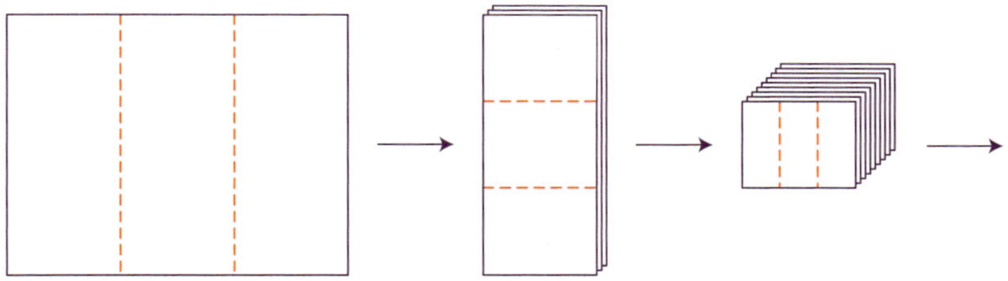

1. Copy and complete the table below to show the area of a ballot at each stage.

Stage	Area (cm^2)
0	27
1	9
2	
3	
4	
5	
6	

2. How does the area of a ballot change at each stage?

3. Write an equation for the area, A, of a ballot at any stage, n.

4. Make a graph of the (stage, area) data from your table.

4.2 Fighting Fleas

After a dog or cat is given a preventive flea medicine, the medicine begins to break down in the animal's bloodstream. With each passing hour, there is less active medicine in the blood. The table and the graph below show the amount of active medicine in a dog's bloodstream each hour for 6 hours after a 20-milligram dose.

Time since dose (hours)	Active medicine in blood (milligrams)
0	20
1	10
2	5
3	2.5
4	1.25
5	0.625
6	0.3125

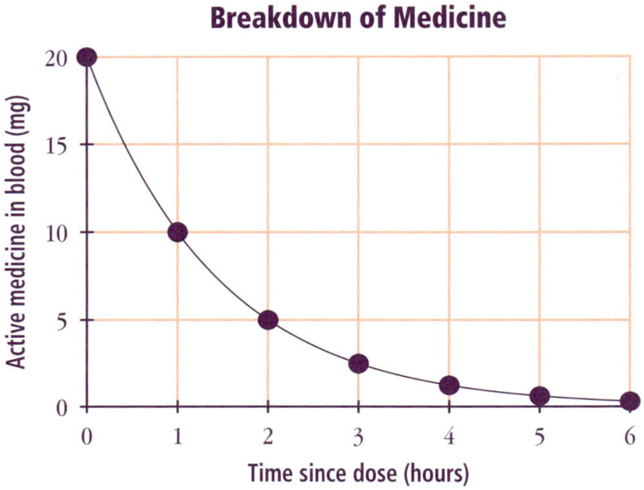

Problem 4.2

Study the pattern of change in the graph and the table.

A. How does the amount of active medicine in the dog's blood change from one hour to the next?

B. Write an equation to model the relationship between the number of hours since the dose was administered, h, and the milligrams of active medicine, m.

C. Based on your knowledge of exponential relationships, what pattern would you expect to see in the data if 40 milligrams of the medicine were given to the dog?

Problem 4.2 Follow-Up

1. Suppose that, after an initial dose of 60 milligrams, a flea medicine breaks down at a rate of 20% per hour in an animal's bloodstream. This means that as each hour passes, 20% of the active medicine is used. Copy and complete the table to show the amount of active medicine in an animal's blood at the end of each hour for 6 hours.

Time since dose (hours)	Active medicine in blood (milligrams)
0	60
1	
2	
3	
4	
5	
6	

2. For the medicine described in question 1, Janelle wrote the equation $m = 60(0.8^h)$ to model the relationship between the amount of medicine in the blood and the number of hours since it was administered. Compare the quantities of active medicine in your table to the quantities given by Janelle's equation for several time values. Explain any similarities or differences you find.

3. Janelle's friend Habib was confused by the terms *rate of decay* and *decay factor*. He said that since the rate of decay in question 1 is 20%, the decay factor should be 0.2 and the equation should be $m = 60(0.2^h)$. How would you explain to Habib why a rate of decay of 20% is equivalent to a decay factor of 0.8?

4.3 Exploring Exponential Equations

In this unit, you have studied situations that show patterns of exponential growth or exponential decay. All of these situations are modeled by equations of the form $y = a(b^x)$, where a is the starting value and b is the growth or decay factor. You can use your graphing calculator to explore how the values of a and b affect the graph of $y = a(b^x)$.

Problem 4.3

In this problem, you will let $a = 1$ and explore how the value of b affects the graph of $y = b^x$.

A. Use your calculator to investigate the equation $y = b^x$ for $b = 1.25, 1.5, 1.75$, and 2. That is, investigate these equations:

$y = 1.25^x$ $\quad y = 1.5^x$ $\quad y = 1.75^x$ $\quad y = 2^x$

Graph all four equations in the same window. Use window settings that show x values from 0 to 5 and y values from 0 to 20. Record your observations.

B. Use your calculator to investigate the equation $y = b^x$ for $b = 0.25, 0.5$, and 0.75. That is, investigate these equations:

$y = 0.25^x$ $\quad y = 0.5^x$ $\quad y = 0.75^x$

Use window settings that show $0 \leq x \leq 5$ and $0 \leq y \leq 1$. Record your observations.

C. Based on your explorations in parts A and B, describe how you could predict the general shape of the graph of $y = b^x$ for a specific value of b.

Problem 4.3 Follow-Up

In parts A and B, you explored how the value of b affects the graph of $y = b^x$. Now, you will look at how the value of a affects the graph of $y = a(b^x)$. You will need to adjust the window settings as you work.

1. Use your calculator to explore the equation $y = a(2^x)$ for $a = 2, 3$, and 4. That is, investigate these equations:

$y = 2(2^x)$ $\quad y = 3(2^x)$ $\quad y = 4(2^x)$

2. Use your calculator to explore the equation $y = a(1.5^x)$ for $a = 2$, 3, and 4. That is, investigate these equations:

$y = 2(1.5^x)$ $\quad\quad$ $y = 3(1.5^x)$ $\quad\quad$ $y = 4(1.5^x)$

Record your observations.

3. Use your calculator to explore the equation $y = a(0.5^x)$ for $a = 2$, 3, and 4. That is, investigate these equations:

$y = 2(0.5^x)$ $\quad\quad$ $y = 3(0.5^x)$ $\quad\quad$ $y = 4(0.5^x)$

Record your observations.

4. Describe how the value of a affects the graph of an equation of the form $y = a(b^x)$.

4.4 Cooling Water

Have you ever sipped from a cup of hot cocoa or tea and found that it was too hot to drink? What pattern of change would you expect to find in the temperature of a hot drink as time passes? What shape would you expect for a graph of (time, drink temperature) data? This experiment will help you explore these questions.

Equipment:

- very hot water, a thermometer, a cup or mug for hot drinks, and a watch or clock

Directions:

- Record the air temperature.
- Fill the cup with hot water.
- In a table, record the water temperature and the room temperature in 5-minute intervals throughout your class period.

Time (minutes)	Water temperature	Room temperature
0		
5		
10		

Problem 4.4

A. Make a graph of your (time, water temperature) data.

B. Describe the pattern of change in the (time, water temperature) data. When did the water temperature change most rapidly? When did it change most slowly?

C. Add a column to your table. In this column, record the difference between the water temperature and the room temperature for each time value.

D. Make a graph of the (time, temperature difference) data.

E. Compare the shapes of the graphs.

F. Describe the pattern of change in the (time, temperature difference) data. When did the temperature difference change most rapidly? When did it change most slowly?

G. Assume that the relationship between temperature difference and time in this experiment is exponential. Estimate the decay factor for this relationship. Explain how you made your estimate.

H. Find an equation for the (time, temperature difference) data. Your equation should allow you to predict the temperature difference at the end of any 5-minute interval.

Problem 4.4 Follow-Up

1. What do you think the graph of the (time, temperature difference) data would look like if you had continued the experiment for several more hours?

2. What factors might affect the rate at which a cup of hot liquid cools?

3. What factors might introduce errors in the data you collect?

As you work on these ACE questions, use your calculator whenever you need it.

Applications

1. Rosemary often shares her snacks with her friends. One day she had a 24-inch string of licorice. As each friend asked her for a piece, Rosemary gave him or her half of what she had left.

a. Make a table showing the amount of licorice Rosemary had left each time she gave a piece away.

b. Make a graph of the data from part a.

c. Suppose that, instead of half the licorice, Rosemary gave each friend 4 inches of licorice. Make a table and a graph for this situation.

d. Compare the tables and the graphs for the two situations. Explain the similarities and the differences.

2. Penicillin decays exponentially in the human body. If you receive a 300-milligram dose of penicillin to combat strep throat, about 180 milligrams will still be active in your blood after one day.

a. Assume the amount of active penicillin in your blood decreases exponentially. Make a table showing the amount of penicillin remaining active in your blood each day for 7 days after a 300-milligram dose.

b. Write an equation for the relationship between the number of days, d, since you took the penicillin and the amount of the medicine, m, remaining active in your body.

c. How would the equation change if you had taken a 400-milligram dose?

3. In a class experiment, hot coffee was poured into a cup and allowed to cool. The difference between coffee temperature and room temperature was recorded every minute for 10 minutes.

Time (minutes)	0	1	2	3	4	5	6	7	8	9	10
Temperature difference (°C)	80	72	65	58	52	47	43	38	34	31	28

a. Plot the (time, temperature difference) data. Explain what the patterns in the table and the graph tell you about the rate at which the coffee cooled.

b. Approximate the decay factor for this relationship.

c. Write an equation for the relationship between time and temperature difference.

d. About how long would it have taken the coffee to cool to room temperature? Explain how you found your answer.

Connections

4. a. The pizza in the ad for Mr. Costa's restaurant has a diameter of 5 inches. What are the circumference and the area of the pizza in the ad?

b. On most copy machines, reduction settings are given as percents. A setting of 90% reduces a drawing to 90% of its original size. Mr. Costa reduces his ad to 90% of its original size. He then reduces the reduced ad to 90% of its size. He continues this process, performing a total of five reductions. Copy and complete the table to show the diameter, circumference, and area of the pizza after each reduction.

Reduction	Diameter (in)	Circumference (in)	Area (in^2)
0			
1			
2			
3			
4			
5			

c. Write equations for the diameter, the circumference, and the area of the pizza after n reductions.

d. How would your equations change if Mr. Costa had used a reduction setting of 75%?

e. Mr. Costa claims that when he uses the 90% reduction setting, he is actually reducing the size of the drawing by 10%. Is Mr. Costa correct? Explain.

5. Consider these three equations:

$$y = 0.75^x \qquad y = 0.25^x \qquad y = {}^{-}0.5x + 1$$

a. Sketch the graphs of all three equations on one set of axes.

b. What points, if any, do the three graphs have in common?

c. In which graph does the y value decrease at the greatest rate as the x value increases?

d. How can you use your graphs to determine which of the equations is *not* an example of exponential decay?

e. How can you use the equations to determine which one is *not* an example of exponential decay?

6. A cricket is on the 0 point of a number line, hopping toward 1. She covers half the distance from her current location to 1 with each hop. So, she will be at $\frac{1}{2}$ after one hop, $\frac{3}{4}$ after two hops, and so on.

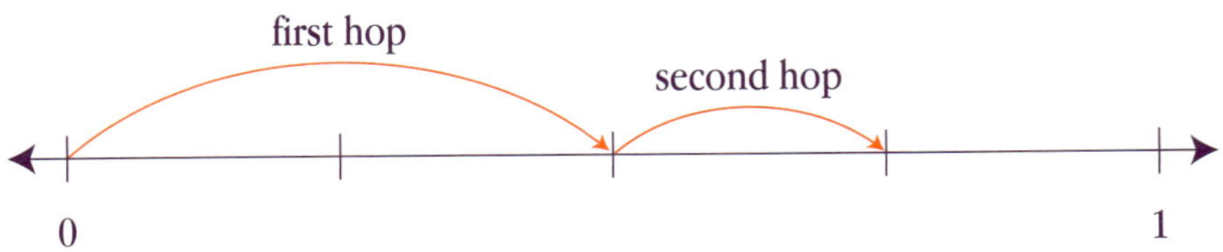

a. Make a table showing the cricket's location for the first 10 hops.

b. Where will the cricket be after n hops?

c. Will the cricket ever get to 1? Explain.

Extensions

7. Negative numbers can be used as exponents. This question will help you to understand negative exponents.

a. Consider the equation $y = 2^x$. Use your calculator to find the value of y for x values $^-1$, $^-2$, and $^-3$.

b. Consider the equation $y = (\frac{1}{2})^x$. Compute the value of y for x values 1, 2, and 3.

c. What observation can you make from your computations in parts a and b?

8. Freshly-cut lumber, known as *green lumber,* contains water. If green lumber is used to build a house, it may crack, shrink, and warp as it dries. To avoid these problems, green lumber is typically dried in a kiln that circulates dry air to remove moisture from the wood. Suppose that in one week a kiln removes $\frac{1}{3}$ of the moisture from a stack of lumber.

a. What fraction of the moisture *remains* in the lumber after 5 weeks?

b. What fraction of the moisture has been *removed* from the lumber after 5 weeks?

c. Write an equation for the fraction of moisture remaining in the lumber after w weeks.

d. Write an equation for the fraction of moisture that has been removed from the lumber after w weeks.

e. Graph your equations from parts c and d on the same set of axes. Describe how the graphs are related.

f. A different kiln removes $\frac{1}{4}$ of the moisture from a stack of lumber each week. Write equations for the fraction of moisture remaining and the fraction of moisture removed after w weeks.

g. Graph your two equations from part f on the same set of axes. Describe how the graphs are related. How do they compare to the graphs from part e?

h. Suppose a batch of green lumber is 40% water by weight and a builder wants its moisture content to be 10%. For each of the two kilns described above, how long should the lumber be dried before it is used to build the house?

9. Study this pattern:

row 1: $\frac{1}{2} =$

row 2: $\frac{1}{2} + (\frac{1}{2})^2 =$

row 3: $\frac{1}{2} + (\frac{1}{2})^2 + (\frac{1}{2})^3 =$

row 4: $\frac{1}{2} + (\frac{1}{2})^2 + (\frac{1}{2})^3 + (\frac{1}{2})^4 =$

a. Find the sum for each row.

b. Suppose the pattern continued. Write the expression that would be in row 5, and find its sum.

c. What would be the sum of the expression in row 10? In row 20?

d. Describe the pattern of sums in words and with an equation.

e. For which row does the sum first exceed 0.9?

f. As the row number increases, the sum gets closer and closer to what number?

g. Celeste claims that the pattern is related to the pattern of the areas of the ballots cut in Problem 4.1. She drew this picture to explain her thinking.

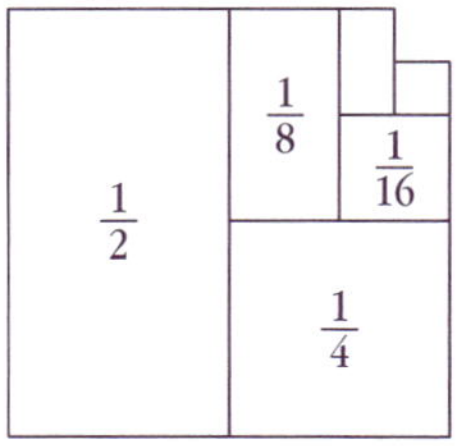

row 6 = $\frac{1}{2} + \left(\frac{1}{2}\right)^2 + \left(\frac{1}{2}\right)^3 + \left(\frac{1}{2}\right)^4 + \left(\frac{1}{2}\right)^5 + \left(\frac{1}{2}\right)^6$

What relationship do you think Celeste has observed?

10. Study this pattern:

row 1: $\frac{1}{3} =$

row 2: $\frac{1}{3} + (\frac{1}{3})^2 =$

row 3: $\frac{1}{3} + (\frac{1}{3})^2 + (\frac{1}{3})^3 =$

row 4: $\frac{1}{3} + (\frac{1}{3})^2 + (\frac{1}{3})^3 + (\frac{1}{3})^4 =$

a. Find the sum for each row.

b. Suppose the pattern continued. Write the expression that would be in row 5, and find its sum.

c. What would be the sum of the expression in row 10? In row 20?

d. Describe the pattern of sums in words and with an equation.

e. For which row does the sum first exceed 0.9?

f. As the row number increases, the sum gets closer and closer to what number?

Mathematical Reflections

In this investigation, you explored situations that showed patterns of exponential decay. These questions will help you summarize what you have learned:

1. How can you recognize an exponential decay pattern from a table of data? From a graph? From an equation?
2. How is a table for an exponential decay situation different from a table for an exponential growth situation? How is the graph different? How is the equation different?
3. How are patterns in tables, graphs, and equations for exponential decay situations similar to and different from tables, graphs, and equations for decreasing linear relationships?

Think about your answers to these questions, discuss your ideas with other students and your teacher, and then write a summary of your findings in your journal.

The Unit Project

Half-Life

Most of the objects and substances around you are composed of atoms that are stable. However, the atoms that make up *radioactive* substances are unstable—they tend to break down in a process known as *radioactive decay*. As these substances decay, they emit radiation. At high levels, radiation can be dangerous to humans and other living creatures.

The rate of decay varies from substance to substance. Scientists use the term *half-life* to describe the time it takes for half of the atoms in a radioactive sample to decay. For example, the half-life of carbon-11 is 20 minutes. This means that 2000 carbon-11 atoms will be reduced to 1000 carbon-11 atoms in 20 minutes and to 500 carbon-11 atoms in 40 minutes.

Half-lives vary from a fraction of a second to billions of years. For example, the half-life of polonium-214 is 0.00016 seconds, and the half-life of rubidium-87 is 49 billion years.

In this experiment, you will model the decay of a radioactive substance known as iodine-124. About $\frac{1}{6}$ of the atoms in a sample of iodine-124 decay each day. This experiment will help you determine the half-life of this substance.

Follow these steps to conduct your experiment:

- Use 100 cubes to represent 100 iodine-124 atoms. Mark one face of each cube.
- Place all 100 cubes in a container, shake the container, and pour the cubes onto the table.
- The cubes for which the mark is facing up represent atoms that have decayed on the first day. Remove these cubes, and record the number of cubes that remain. Place the remaining cubes in the container.

- Repeat this process to find the number of atoms that remain after the second day.
- Repeat this process until one cube or no cubes remain.

When you complete your experiment, answer these questions:

1 **a.** In your experiment, how many days did it take to reduce the 100 iodine-124 atoms to 50 atoms? In other words, how many times did you have to roll the cubes until about 50 cubes remained?

b. How many days did it take to reduce 50 iodine-124 atoms to 25 atoms?

c. Based on your answers to parts a and b, what do you think the half life of iodine-124 is?

2 **a.** In a sample of real iodine-124, $\frac{1}{6}$ of the atoms decay after 1 day. What fraction of the atoms remain after 1 day?

b. Suppose a sample contains 100 iodine-124 atoms. Use your answer from part a to write an equation for the number of atoms, n, remaining in the sample after d days.

c. Use your equation to find the half-life of iodine-124.

d. How does the half-life you found based on your equation compare to the half-life you found from your experiment?

3 **a.** Make up a problem about a radioactive substance with a different rate of decay that can be modeled by an experiment involving cubes or other common objects. Describe the situation and your experiment.

b. Conduct your experiment, and record your results.

c. Use the results of your experiment to predict the half-life of your substance.

d. Use what you know about the rate of decay to write an equation that models the decay of your substance.

e. Use your equation to find the half-life of your substance.

Write a report summarizing your findings about decay rates and half-lives. Your report should include tables and graphs justifying your answers to the questions above.

Looking Back and Looking Ahead

Unit Reflections

Working on the problems of this unit expanded your skill in recognizing and using *exponential* relationships among variables. You used equations in the form $y = a(b^x)$ to describe exponential *growth* of various populations and investments and *decay* of medicines and radioactive materials. You used those equations to produce tables and graphs of the relations. Then the tables and graphs were used to make predictions and solve equations.

Using Your Algebraic Reasoning—To test your understanding and skill in finding and applying exponential models, consider the following questions that arose when the Student Council at Spartan Middle School planned some entertainment for a fund-raising event. One popular idea was to sponsor a quiz show called "Who Wants To Be Rich?" The general idea was that as questions increased in difficulty, the prize package increased as well.

1. *One proposal was to have the first question worth \$5 and to have the total prize increase by \$10 for each additional question answered correctly.*
   a. What equation gives the prize, P, for correctly answering questions 1 to n?
   b. How many questions will a contestant need to answer correctly in order to win \$50? \$75? \$100?
   c. Sketch a graph of the proposal data for $0 \le n \le 10$.
2. *A second proposal was to have the first question worth \$5 and to have the contestant's total winnings double for each additional question answered correctly.*
   a. What equation gives the prize, P, for correctly answering questions 1 to n?
   b. How many questions will a contestant need to answer correctly in order to win \$50? \$75? \$100?
   c. Sketch a graph of this proposal data for $0 \le n \le 10$.

3 *Contestants for "Who Wants to Be Rich?" would be chosen by a drawing. Students and guests at the fund-raiser would buy tickets like the one shown below. The purchaser would keep one half of the ticket and add the other half to the entries for the drawing.*

a. To make the tickets, the event's planners took a large piece of paper and folded it in half many times to make a grid of small rectangles. How many such rectangles were there after n folds?

b. If the original piece of paper for tickets was a 60-cm square, what is the area for each ticket rectangle after n folds?

Explaining Your Reasoning—To answer the questions about the game plans, you had to use algebraic knowledge about number patterns, graphs, and equations or formulas. You had to recognize linear and exponential patterns and find matching equations and graphs.

1. How do you decide when a data pattern can be modeled well by an exponential equation in the form $y = a(b^x)$? How will the values of a and b relate to the data pattern?

2. What are the possible shapes of graphs for exponential relations and how can they be predicted from values of a and b in the corresponding equations?

3. How are the data patterns, graphs, and symbolic equations in exponential relations you studied similar to and different from those modeled by linear equations?

The algebra ideas and techniques you've used in this unit will be applied and extended in future units of *Connected Mathematics* and in problems of science and business. You'll study several other important families of algebraic models and strategies for finding and using those models to solve problems.

Glossary

base The number that is raised to a power in an exponential expression. In the expression 3^5, read "3 to the fifth power," 3 is the base and 5 is the exponent.

compound growth Another term for exponential growth, usually used when talking about the monetary value of an investment. The change in the balance of a savings account shows compound growth because the bank pays interest not only on the original investment, but on the interest earned.

decay factor The constant factor that each value in an exponential decay pattern is multiplied by to get the next value. The decay factor is the base in an exponential decay equation. For example, in the equation $A = 64(0.5^n)$, where A is the area of a ballot and n is the number of cuts, the decay factor is 0.5. It indicates that the area of a ballot after any number of cuts is 0.5 times the area after the previous number of cuts. In a table of (x, y) values for an exponential decay relationship (with the x value increasing by 1), the decay factor is the ratio of any y value to the previous y value.

exponent A number that indicates how many times another number (the base) is to be used as a factor. Exponents are written as raised numbers to the right of the base. In the expression 3^5, read "3 to the fifth power," 5 is the exponent and 3 is the base. So, 3^5 means $3 \times 3 \times 3 \times 3 \times 3$. In the formula for the area of a square, $A = s^2$, the 2 is an exponent. This formula can also be written as $A = s \times s$.

exponential decay A pattern of decrease in which each value is found by multiplying the previous value by a constant factor greater than 0 and less than 1. For example, the pattern 27, 9, 3, 1, $\frac{1}{3}$, $\frac{1}{9}$, . . . shows exponential decay in which each value is $\frac{1}{3}$ times the previous value.

exponential form A quantity expressed as a number raised to a power. In exponential form, 32 can be written as 2^5.

exponential growth A pattern of increase in which each value is found by multiplying the previous value by a constant factor greater than 1. For example, the pattern 1, 2, 4, 8, 16, 32, . . . shows exponential growth in which each value is 2 times the previous value.

growth factor The constant factor that each value in an exponential growth pattern is multiplied by to get the next value. The growth factor is the base in an exponential growth equation. For example, in the equation $A = 25(3^d)$, where A is the area of a patch of mold and d is the number of days, the growth factor is 3. It indicates that the area of the mold for any day is 3 times the area for the previous day. In a table of (x, y) values for an exponential growth relationship (with x the value increasing by 1), the growth factor is the ratio of any y value to the previous y value.

standard form The most common way to express a quantity. For example, 27 is the standard form of 3^3.

Glosario

base El número que se eleva a una potencia en una expresión exponencial. En la expresión 3^5, que se lee "3 elevado a la quinta potencia", 3 es la base y 5 es el exponente.

crecimiento compuesto Otro término para crecimiento exponencial, normalmente usado para referirse al valor monetario de una inversión. El cambio en el saldo de una cuenta de ahorros muestra un crecimiento compuesto, ya que el banco paga intereses no sólo sobre la inversión original, sino sobre los intereses ganados.

crecimiento exponencial Un patrón de crecimiento en el cual cada valor se calcula multiplicando el valor anterior por un factor constante mayor que 1. Por ejemplo, el patrón 1, 2, 4, 8, 16, 32… muestra un crecimiento exponencial en el que cada valor es el doble del valor anterior.

disminución exponencial Un patrón de disminución en el cual cada valor se calcula multiplicando el valor anterior por un factor constante mayor que 0 y menor que 1. Por ejemplo, el patrón 27, 9, 3, 1, $\frac{1}{3}$, $\frac{1}{9}$,… muestra una disminución exponencial en la que cada valor es $\frac{1}{3}$ del valor anterior.

exponente Es un número que indica la cantidad de veces que otro número (la base) se va a usar como factor. Los exponentes se escriben como números elevados a la derecha de la base. En la expresión 3^5, que se lee como "3 elevado a la quinta potencia", 5 es el exponente y 3 es la base. Así, 3^5 significa $3 \times 3 \times 3 \times 3 \times 3$. En la fórmula para calcular el área de un cuadrado, $A = l^2$, el 2 es un exponente. Esta fórmula también se puede escribir como $A = l \times l$.

factor de crecimiento El factor constante por el cual se multiplica cada valor en un patrón de crecimiento exponencial para obtener el valor siguiente. El factor de crecimiento es la base en una ecuación de crecimiento exponencial. Por ejemplo, en la ecuación $A = 25(3^d)$, donde A es el área enmohecida y d es el número de días, el factor de crecimiento es 3. Esto indica que el área enmohecida en un día cualquiera es 3 veces el área del día anterior. En una tabla de valores (x, y) para una relación de crecimiento exponencial (donde el valor de x aumenta de a 1), el factor exponencial es la razón entre cualquier valor de y y su valor anterior.

factor de disminución El factor constante por el cual se multiplica cada valor en un patrón de disminución exponencial para obtener el valor siguiente. El factor de disminución es la base en una ecuación de disminución exponencial. Por ejemplo, en la ecuación $A = 64(0.5^n)$, donde A es el área de una papeleta y n es el número de cortes, el factor de disminución es 0.5. Esto indica que el área de una papeleta después de un número cualquiera de cortes es 0.5 veces el área después del número anterior de cortes. En la tabla de valores (x, y) para una relación de disminución exponencial (donde el valor x crece de a 1), el factor de disminución es la razón entre cualquier valor de y y su valor anterior.

forma exponencial Una cantidad que se expresa como un número elevado a una potencia. En forma exponencial, 32 puede escribirse como 2^5.

forma normal La manera más común de expresar una cantidad. Por ejemplo, 27 es la forma normal de 3^3.

Index

Connected Mathematics™

Frogs, Fleas, and Painted Cubes

Quadratic Relationships

Student Edition

Glenda Lappan
James T. Fey
William M. Fitzgerald
Susan N. Friel
Elizabeth Difanis Phillips

PEARSON
Prentice Hall

Glenview, Illinois
Needham, Massachusetts
Upper Saddle River, New Jersey

Frogs, Fleas, and Painted Cubes

Connected Mathematics™ was developed at Michigan State University with the support of National Science Foundation Grant No. MDR 9150217.

This project was supported, in part, by the
National Science Foundation
Opinions expressed are those of the authors and not necessarily those of the Foundation

The Michigan State University authors and administration have agreed that all MSU royalties arising from this publication will be devoted to purposes supported by the Department of Mathematics and the MSU Mathematics Education Enrichment Fund.

Photo Acknowledgements: 5 © The Bettman Archives; 7 © Gene Ahrens/FPG International; 21 © Mali Apple; 28 © Jean Morman Unsworth; 41 © Dean Abramson/Stock, Boston; 54 © Jeffrey Sylvester/FPG International; 55 © Corbis Bettmann Archives; 56 © Blake Sell/Rueters/Bettmann; 61 © Bob Daemmrich/Stock, Boston; 65 © Michael Mauney/Tony Stone Images; 71 © Bryce Flynn/Stock, Boston

Contents

Frogs, Fleas, and Painted Cubes

A ball is thrown into the air. The height of the ball in feet after t seconds can be described by the equation $h = -16t^2 + 64t$. What is the maximum height reached by the ball? When does the ball reach this maximum height?

Imagine that you are prospecting diamonds in the barren outback of western Australia. You are told that you can claim any rectangular piece of land that can be surrounded by 60 meters of fencing. How should you arrange your fencing in order to enclose the maximum area possible?

After a victory, members of a winning team may congratulate each other with a round of high fives. How many high fives would be exchanged among a team with 5 players? Among a team with 6 players? Among a team with n players?

Mathematics is useful for solving practical problems in science, business, engineering, and economics. In earlier units, you studied problems that could be modeled with linear or exponential relationships. In this unit, you will explore quadratic relationships. Quadratic relationships are found in many interesting situations including those on the opposite page.

Mathematical Highlights

In *Frogs, Fleas, and Painted Cubes* you will explore an important type of non-linear relationship, quadratic functions. The unit should help you to

- Recognize situations where one variable is a quadratic function of another;
- Construct equations to express quadratic patterns that appear in data tables, graphs, and problem conditions;
- Recognize the connections between quadratic equations and patterns in tables and graphs of those relations;
- Use quadratic equations to locate maximum and minimum values of a dependent variable and the x- and y-intercepts of graphs;
- Recognize and construct equivalent symbolic expressions for quadratic relations;
- Use tables, graphs, and equations of quadratic relations to solve problems in a variety of situtations from geometry, science, and business; and
- Compare properties of quadratic, linear, and exponential relationships.

As you work on the problems in this unit, ask yourself questions about problem situations that involve non-linear relations: *Is the relationship among variables in this situation a quadratic function? What equation would model the data or graph pattern relating the variables? How could I answer the questions of the situation by studying a table or graph of the quadratic relation?*

INVESTIGATION 1

Introduction to Quadratic Relationships

When Mexico ceded California to the United States in 1848, California was a relatively unexplored territory with only a few thousand people. Then, in January of 1848, gold was discovered at Sutter's mill near Sacramento. By 1849, a great gold rush had begun. The gold rush brought 500,000 new residents to California. By 1850, California had enough people to be admitted to the Union as a state. Today, California has the greatest population of any U.S. state.

Throughout history, people have traveled to particular areas of the world with hopes of getting rich.

- In 1871, prospectors headed to South Africa in search of diamonds.
- From 1860 to 1900, farmers moved to the American prairie where land was free to homesteaders.
- The 1901 Spindletop oil gusher brought drillers by the thousands to eastern Texas.

The prospectors and farmers had to stake claims on the land they wanted to work. Those who made smart claims knew the land . . . and some mathematics. Surveying, determining acreage, buying fencing, and analyzing costs all required the tools of mathematics.

1.1 Staking a Claim

Imagine that it is the year 2100 and a rare and precious metal has just been discovered on the planet Mars. You and hundreds of other adventurers are traveling to the planet to stake your claim. Each new prospector is allowed to claim any piece of land that can be surrounded by 20 meters of laser fencing. You want to arrange your fencing to enclose the maximum area possible.

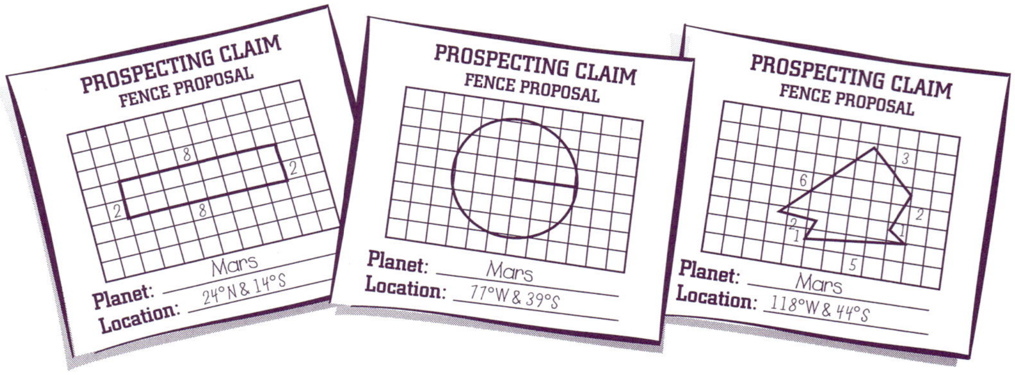

Problem 1.1

Suppose the Mars colony adds the restriction that each claim must be rectangular.

A. Sketch several rectangles with a perimeter of 20 meters. Include some with small areas and some with large areas. Label the dimensions of each rectangle.

B. Make a table showing the length of a side and the area for each rectangle with a perimeter of 20 meters and whole-number side lengths.

C. Make a graph of your (length of a side, area) data. Describe the shape of the graph.

D. If you want to enclose the greatest area possible with your fencing, what should the dimensions of your fence be? How can you use your graph to justify your answer?

Problem 1.1 Follow-Up

1. Suppose the dimensions of the rectangle were not restricted to whole numbers. Would this change your answer to part D? Explain.

2. Suppose the shape of a claim were not restricted to a rectangle. How could you arrange your 20 meters of fencing to enclose a greater area?

1.2 Reading a Graph

The relationship between length and area in Problem 1.1 is an example of a **quadratic relationship**. Quadratic relationships are characterized by their U-shaped graphs, which are called **parabolas**. In this relationship, the area depends on, or is a *function* of, the length. We refer to a relationship in which one variable depends on another as a **function.**

Many of the linear and exponential relationships you studied in earlier units are functions. For example, if a van travels at a steady rate, the distance it covers is a function of the travel time. The relationship between travel time and distance is a linear function. The value of an investment that grows by 4% per year is a function of the number of years. The relationship between the number of years and the value is an exponential function.

As you explore quadratic functions in this unit, look for common patterns in tables, graphs, and equations.

The Gateway Arch in St. Louis, Missouri, resembles a parabola.

Problem 1.2

The graph below shows length and area data for rectangles with a fixed perimeter.

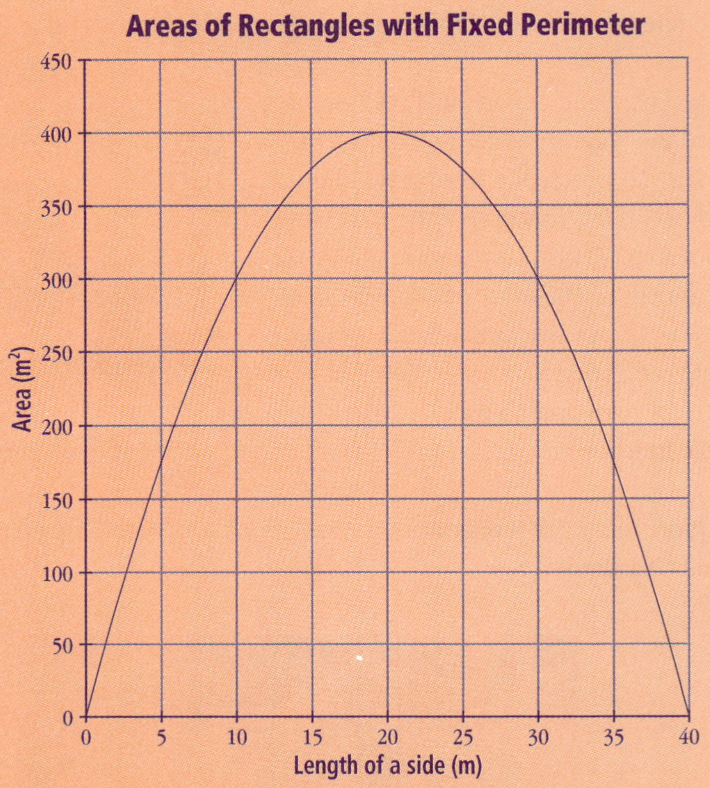

A. Describe the shape of the graph and any special features you observe.

B. What is the greatest area possible for a rectangle with this perimeter? What are the dimensions of this rectangle?

C. What is the area of the rectangle with a side of length 12 meters? What is the area of the rectangle with a side of length 28 meters? Explain how these two rectangles are related.

D. What are the dimensions of the rectangle with an area of 300 square meters?

E. What is the fixed perimeter for the rectangles represented by the graph? Explain how you found the perimeter.

Problem 1.2 Follow-Up

The table below shows length and area data for rectangles with a fixed perimeter.

Length of a side (m)	Area (m^2)
0	0
1	11
2	20
3	27
4	32
5	35
6	36
7	35
8	32
9	27
10	20
11	11
12	0

1. How do the shape and the special features you observed for the graph in Problem 1.2 appear in the table?
2. What is the fixed perimeter for the rectangles represented in this table? Explain how you found the perimeter.
3. What is the greatest area possible for a rectangle with this perimeter? What are the dimensions of this rectangle?
4. Approximate the dimensions of a rectangle with this fixed perimeter and an area of 16 square meters.

1.3 Writing an Equation

In Problems 1.1 and 1.2, you looked at tables and graphs of relationships between length and area for rectangles with fixed perimeters. In this problem, you will write equations for these relationships.

Problem 1.3

The rectangle below has a perimeter of 20 meters and a side of length l meters.

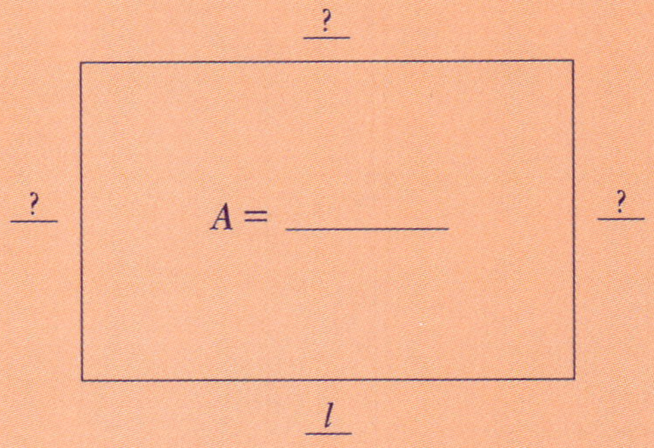

A. Express the length of each side of the rectangle in terms of l. That is, write an expression that contains the variable l to represent the length of each side.

B. Write an equation for the area, A, of the rectangle in terms of l.

C. If the length of a side of the rectangle is 6 meters, what is the area?

D. Use a calculator to make a table and a graph for your equation. Show x values from 1 to 10 and y values from 0 to 30. Compare your table and graph to those you made in Problem 1.1.

Problem 1.3 Follow-Up

1. Consider rectangles with a perimeter of 60 meters.

   a. As in Problem 1.3, draw a rectangle to represent this situation. Label one side l, and label the other sides in terms of l.

   b. Write an equation for the area, A, in terms of l.

   c. Make a table for your equation. Then, use your table to estimate the greatest area possible for a rectangle with a perimeter of 60 meters. Give the side lengths of this rectangle.

   d. Use a calculator or data from your table to help you sketch a graph of the relationship between the length of a side and the area.

   e. How can you use your graph to find the maximum area? How does your graph show the side length that corresponds to the maximum area?

2. An equation for the area of rectangles with a certain fixed perimeter is $A = l(35 - l)$.

a. Draw a rectangle to represent this situation. Label one side l, and label the other sides in terms of l.

b. If the length of a side of a rectangle with this fixed perimeter is 20 meters, what is the area?

c. Describe two ways you could find the perimeter for the rectangles represented by this equation. What is the perimeter?

d. Describe the graph of this equation.

e. What is the maximum area for this family of rectangles? What dimensions correspond to this maximum area? Explain how you found your answers.

3. If you know the perimeter of a rectangle, how can you write an equation for the area in terms of the length of a side?

4. Graphs of quadratic functions are called *parabolas.* Describe the characteristics of the parabolas you have seen so far.

5. Study the graphs, tables, and equations for areas of rectangles with fixed perimeters. Which representation is most useful for predicting the maximum area?

Applications • Connections • Extensions

As you work on these ACE questions, use your calculator whenever you need it.

Applications

1. This rectangle has a perimeter of 30 meters and a side of length l meters.

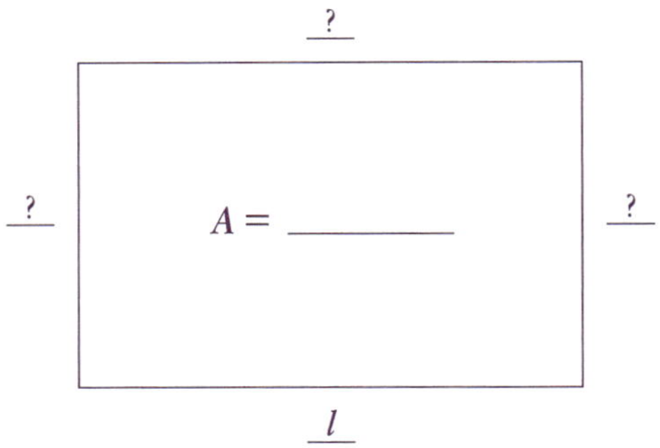

a. Express the lengths of the other sides in terms of l.

b. Write an equation for the area, A, in terms of l.

c. Make a graph of your equation, and describe its shape.

d. **i.** Use your equation to find the area of the rectangle if the length of one side is 10 meters.

ii. Describe how you could use your graph to find the area of the rectangle if the length of one side is 10 meters.

iii. Describe how you could use a table to find the area of the rectangle if the length of one side is 10 meters.

e. What is the maximum area possible for a rectangle with a perimeter of 30 meters? What are the dimensions of the rectangle with the maximum area?

2. This rectangle has a perimeter of 50 meters and a side of length l meters.

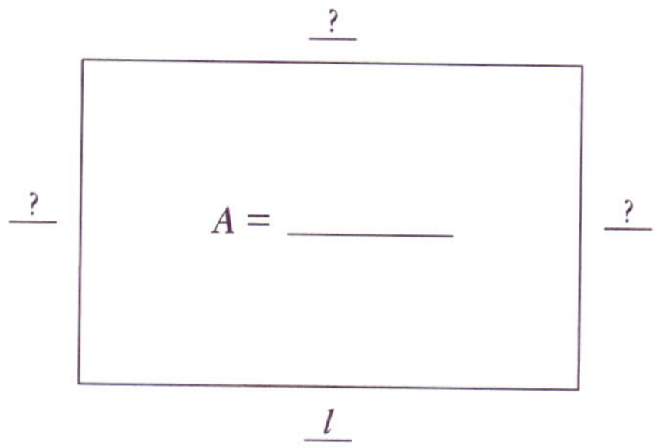

a. Express the lengths of the other sides in terms of l.

b. Write an equation for the area, A, in terms of l.

c. Make a graph of your equation, and describe its shape.

d. **i.** Use your equation to find the area of the rectangle if the length of one side is 10 meters.

ii. Describe how you could use your graph to find the area of the rectangle if the length of one side is 10 meters.

iii. Describe how you could use a table to find the area of the rectangle if the length of one side is 10 meters.

e. What is the maximum area for a rectangle with a perimeter of 50 meters? What are the dimensions of this rectangle?

3. Find the maximum area for a rectangle with a perimeter of 120 meters. Make your answer convincing by including these things:

- Sketches of rectangles with a perimeter of 120 meters that do not have the maximum area and a sketch of the rectangle you think does have the maximum area
- A table of lengths and areas for rectangles with a perimeter of 120 meters, using increments of 5 meters for the lengths
- A graph of the relationship between length and area

Explain how each piece of evidence supports your answer.

4. What is the maximum area for a rectangle with a perimeter of 130 meters? As in ACE question 3, support your answer with sketches of rectangles, a table, and a graph. In your table, use increments of 2.5 for the lengths.

5. The graph below shows lengths and areas for rectangles with a fixed perimeter.

Areas of Rectangles with a Fixed Perimeter

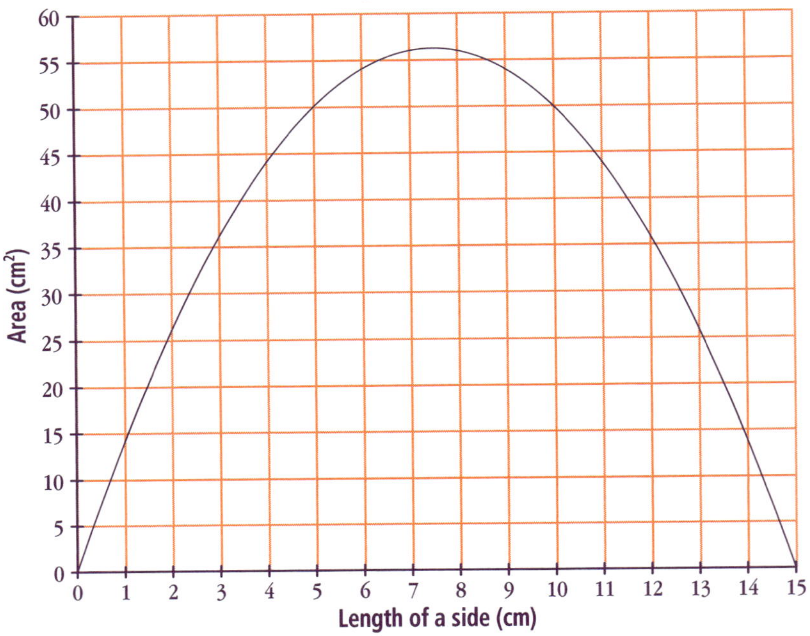

   a. Describe the shape of the graph and any special features you observe.

   b. What is the maximum area for a rectangle with this fixed perimeter? What are the dimensions of this rectangle?

   c. As the length of a side gets very close to 15 centimeters, what happens to the area?

   d. What is the area of a rectangle with this fixed perimeter and a side of length 3 centimeters?

   e. Describe two ways you could find the fixed perimeter for the rectangles represented by the graph.

6. An equation for the area in square meters of rectangles with a fixed perimeter is $A = l(25 - l)$.

a. Describe the graph of this equation.

b. What is the maximum area for a rectangle with this perimeter? What dimensions correspond to this area? Explain how you found your answers.

c. What is the area of a rectangle with this fixed perimeter and a side of length 20 meters?

d. Describe two ways to find the fixed perimeter for rectangles represented by this equation.

7. This incomplete graph shows data for rectangles with a fixed perimeter.

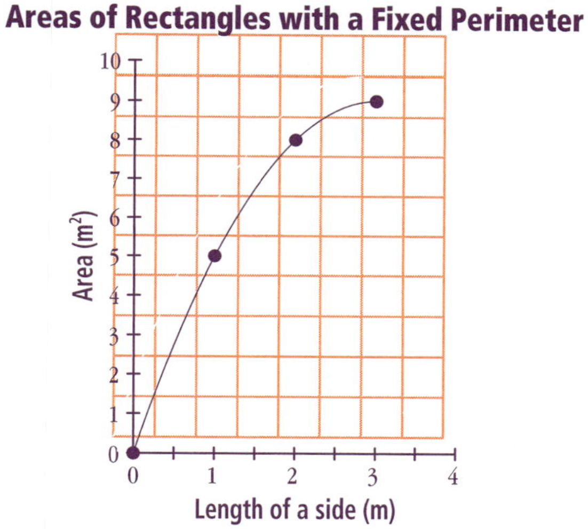

a. Copy and complete the graph to show areas for rectangles with side lengths greater than 3 meters. Explain why your graph is correct.

b. Make a table of data for this situation.

c. What is the maximum area for a rectangle with this perimeter? What are the dimensions of this rectangle? Explain how you found your answers.

d. Which of these equations describes the graph?

$A = l(l - 6)$ $\quad$ $A = l(12 - l)$ $\quad$ $A = l(6 - l)$ $\quad$ $A = l(3 - l)$

8. This table contains data for rectangles with a fixed perimeter.

Length of a side (m)	Area (m^2)
0	0
1	7
2	12
3	15
4	16
5	
6	
7	
8	

a. Copy and complete the table. Explain why you think your table is correct.

b. Make a graph of the relationship between length and area for rectangles with this perimeter.

c. What are the dimensions of the rectangle with maximum area?

d. Which of these equations describes the graph?

$A = l(8 - l)$ $A = l(16 - l)$ $A = l(4 - l)$ $A = l(l - 8)$

Connections

9. a. Suppose a rectangular field has a perimeter of 300 yards. The relationship between the length and the width of the field can be represented by the equation $l = 150 - w$. Is the relationship between the length and the width quadratic? How do you know?

b. Suppose a field is a nonrectangular parallelogram with a perimeter of 300 yards. Is the relationship between the side lengths the same as it is for the rectangular field in part a? How do you know?

c. Suppose a field is a quadrilateral that is not a parallelogram. The perimeter of the field is 300 yards. Is the relationship between the side lengths the same as it is for the rectangular field in part a? How do you know?

10. Ms. Carillo, a photographer, sells prints of her photographs. She would like to increase her profit by raising the price of the prints. However, she knows if the price is too high, she won't sell as many prints and her profit will decrease. Assume the following equation gives the monthly profit, P, she would earn if she charges d dollars for each print:

$$P = d(100 - d)$$

a. Make a table and a graph for this equation. Use increments of 10 dollars for the price.

b. Estimate the price that will produce the maximum profit. Explain how you found your answer.

c. How are the table and the graph for this situation similar to the table and graph you made in Problem 1.3? How are they different?

d. How is the equation similar to and different from the equation you wrote in Problem 1.3?

Extensions

11. Of all rectangles with whole-number side lengths and an area of 20 square centimeters, which has the smallest perimeter? Give evidence for your answer.

12. Mr. DeAngelo is designing a school building. The floor of the music room will be a rectangle with an area of 1200 square feet.

a. Make a table with about ten rows showing a range of possible lengths and widths for the music room floor.

b. Add a column to your table for the perimeter of each rectangle.

c. What pattern do you see in the perimeter column? What kinds of rectangles have large perimeters and what kinds of rectangles have small perimeters?

d. Write an equation you could use to calculate the length of the floor for any given width.

Mathematical Reflections

In this investigation, you found the maximum area for rectangles with a fixed perimeter. The relationship between length and area for rectangles with a fixed perimeter is an example of a quadratic function. These questions will help you summarize what you have learned:

1. In a function relating two variables, one variable *depends* on the other variable. For a function relating length and area for rectangles with a fixed perimeter, which variable is the dependent variable? Which variable is the independent variable?
2. The graph of a quadratic function is a parabola.

   a. What patterns did you observe in the parabolas in this investigation?

   b. How do the patterns in a parabola appear in the table of values for a quadratic function?
3. Describe two ways to find the maximum area for rectangles with a fixed perimeter.
4. How are tables, graphs, and equations for quadratic functions different from those for linear and exponential functions?

Think about your answers to these questions, discuss your ideas with other students and your teacher, and then write a summary of your findings in your journal.

INVESTIGATION 2

Quadratic Expressions

If you gave a friend two $1 bills, and your friend gave you eight quarters, you would consider it a fair trade. If you left your job an hour early one day and worked an hour later the next day, your boss would probably consider it a fair trade. Sometimes it is not as easy to determine whether a trade is fair.

Think about this!

U.S. Malls Incorporated wants to build a new shopping center. The mall developer has bought all the land on the proposed site except for one square lot that measures 125 meters on each side. The family that owns the lot is reluctant to sell it. In exchange for the lot, the developer has offered to give the family a rectangular lot that is 100 meters longer on one side and 100 meters shorter on another side than the square lot. Do you think this is a fair trade?

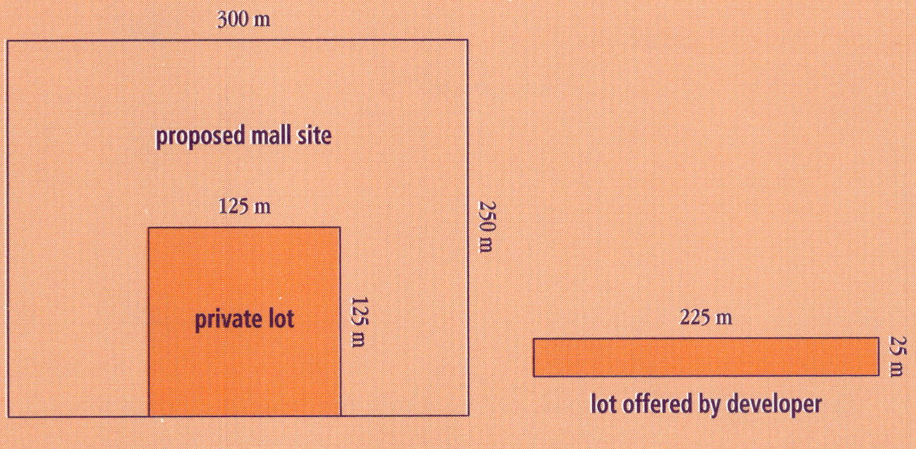

2.1 Trading Land

In this problem, you will explore whether a trade like the one offered by U.S. Malls Incorporated will always be fair, sometimes be fair, or never be fair. You will look at a simple trade situation to see if you can discover a pattern that will help you make predictions about more complex situations.

Problem 2.1

Suppose you own a square piece of land with sides n meters long. You trade your land for a rectangular lot. The length of your new lot is 2 meters longer than the side length of your original lot, and the width of your new lot is 2 meters shorter than the side length of the original lot.

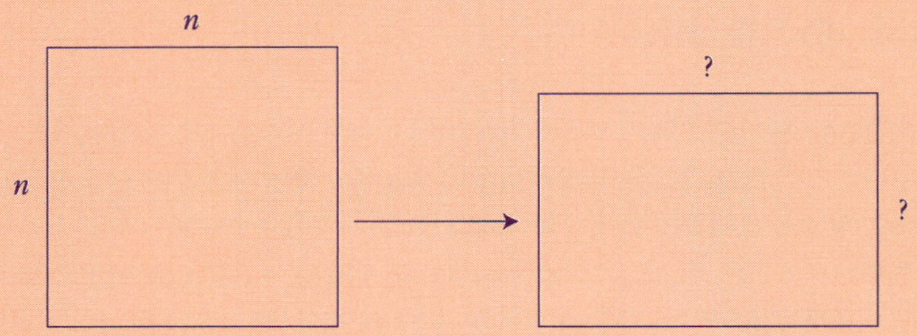

A. Copy and complete the table below.

Original square		New rectangle			Difference in areas (m^2)
Side length (m)	Area (m^2)	Length (m)	Width (m)	Area (m^2)	
3	9	5	1	5	4
4					
5					
6					
7					

B. For each side length in the table, tell how the area of your new lot compares with the area of the original lot. For which side lengths, if any, is this a fair trade?

C. The side length of the original square lot was n meters. For each column in the table, write an expression for the values in the column in terms of n. For example, the expression for the area of the original square is n^2.

Problem 2.1 Follow-Up

Symbolic rules such as n^2 are often called *symbolic expressions,* or simply *expressions.* When you use symbols to show what an expression represents, you get an *equation.* If we let A be the area of the original lot, we can write the equation $A = n^2$.

1. a. Graph the equation for the relationship between the side length and the area of the original lot. Use n values from $^{-}10$ to 10 and A values from $^{-}20$ to 100.

b. Write an equation for the relationship between the side length of the original lot and the area of the new lot. Graph the equation using the same window settings as before.

c. Describe the shapes of your graphs.

d. Do all the values for area and side length on your graph make sense? Why or why not?

2. a. Compare the table of side lengths and areas for the lots of land with the tables of lengths and areas for rectangles with fixed perimeters from Investigation 1. How are the tables similar? How are they different?

b. Compare the graphs of side lengths and areas for the lots of land with the graphs of lengths and areas for rectangles with fixed perimeters from Investigation 1. How are the graphs similar? How are they different?

c. Compare the equations for the areas of the lots of land with the equations for the areas of rectangles with fixed perimeters from Investigation 1. How are the equations similar? How are they different?

3. Look back at the situation discussed in the "Think about this!" box on page 19. Is the trade offered by U.S. Malls Incorporated a good idea for the family that owns the private lot? Explain your answer.

2.2 Changing One Dimension

In mathematics, there is often more than one way to express a quantity. For example, $2 + 5$, $3 + 4$, and 7 are equivalent expressions. In this problem, you will use diagrams to help you write equivalent expressions for the area of a rectangle.

Problem 2.2

A. A square has sides of length x centimeters. A new rectangle is created by increasing one dimension of the square by 2 centimeters.

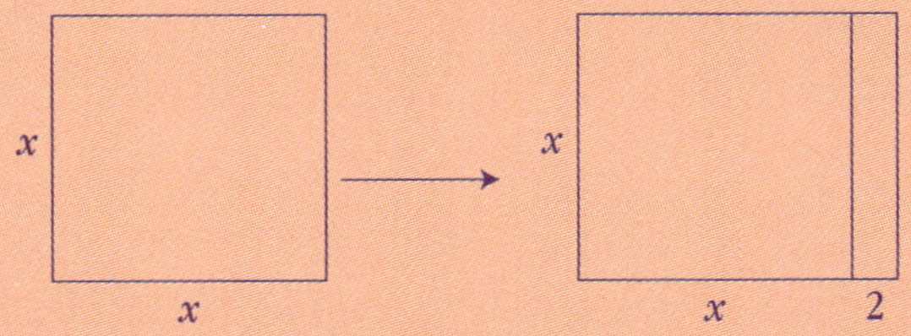

1. The new rectangle is made up of the original square and an added rectangle. What are the dimensions of the added rectangle? What is its area?
2. Write an equation for the area of the new rectangle as the sum of the area of the original square and the area of the added rectangle.
3. What are the length and the width of the new rectangle? Write an equation for the area of the new rectangle as its length times its width.
4. Graph your equations from parts 2 and 3 on your calculator, and copy the graphs onto your paper. Describe the shapes of the graphs. How do the graphs compare? What does this tell you about the two equations?

B. A square has sides of length x centimeters. One dimension of the square is increased by 3 centimeters to create a new rectangle.

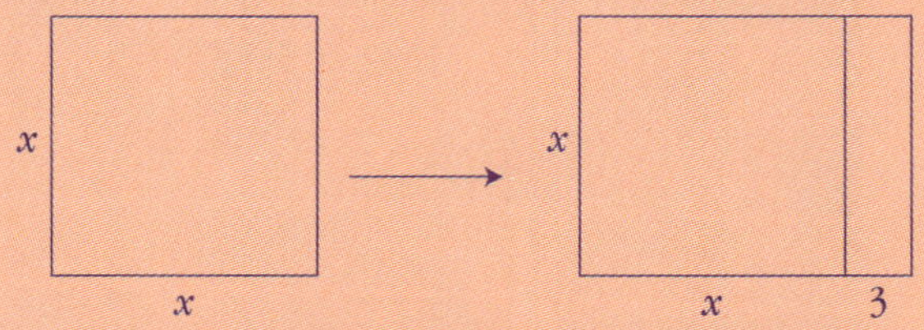

1. How much greater is the area of the new rectangle than the area of the square?
2. Write two equations for the area of the new rectangle.
3. Graph both equations on your calculator, and copy the graphs onto your paper. Describe the shapes of the graphs. How do the graphs compare?

Problem 2.2 Follow-Up

You can express the area of the rectangular lot in Problem 2.1 in two ways. You can write $(n-2)(n+2)$ to express the area as the product of the length and the width, or you can write $n^2 - 4$ to express the fact that the area of the rectangular lot is 4 square meters less than the area of the square lot.

The expression $(n-2)(n+2)$ is said to be in **factored form** because it is written as the product of two linear factors. An expression that is written as the sum or difference of terms is said to be in *term form,* or **expanded form**. A **term** is an expression that consists of variables and/or numbers multiplied together. The expression $n^2 - 4$ is in expanded form because it is written as the difference of the terms n^2 and 4. Since $(n-2)(n+2)$ and $n^2 - 4$ are equivalent, you can write $(n-2)(n+2) = n^2 - 4$.

In part A of Problem 2.2, you expressed the area of a rectangle in two equivalent ways. The factored form, $x(x+2)$, is the product of the two linear factors x and $x+2$. The equivalent expanded form is $x^2 + 2x$.

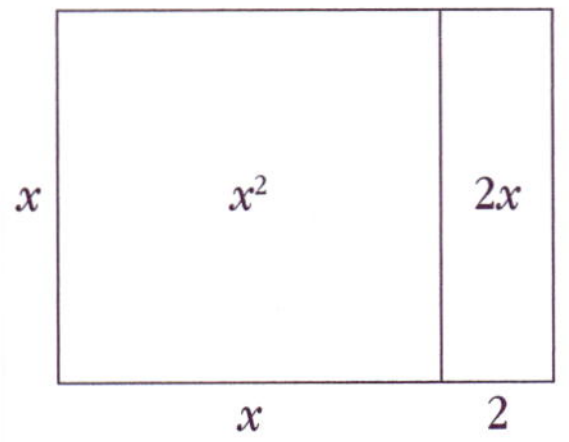

$x(x+2) = x^2 + 2x$

1. The diagram below shows a rectangle divided into two smaller rectangles. Write two expressions, one in factored form and one in expanded form, for the area of the large rectangle.

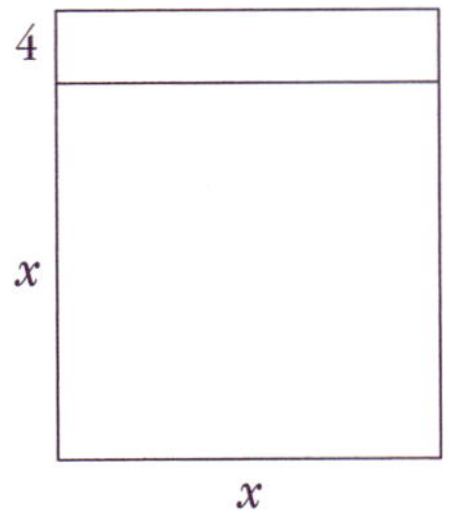

2. Write two expressions, one in factored form and one in expanded form, for the area of the unshaded region.

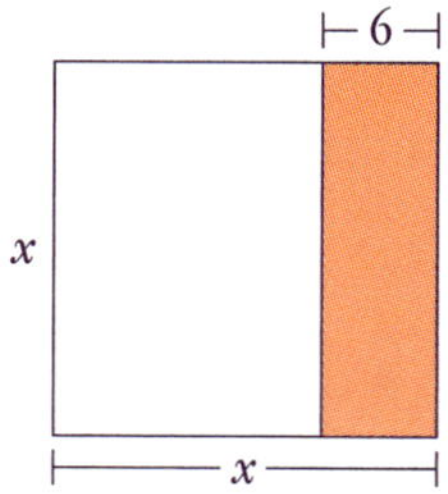

3. Each expression below represents the area of a rectangle. Do parts a and b for each expression.

$x(x + 4)$ $x(x - 4)$ $x(5 + 2)$

a. Draw a rectangle divided to show that its area is represented by the expression. Label the lengths and areas on your drawing.

b. Write an equivalent expression in expanded form.

4. Each expression below represents the area of a rectangle. Do parts a and b for each expression.

$x^2 + 5x$ $x^2 - 5x$ $5x + 4x$

a. Draw a rectangle divided to show that its area is represented by the expression. Label the lengths and areas on your drawing.

b. Write an equivalent expression in factored form.

5. An equation that describes a quadratic function is called a *quadratic equation.* If one side of an equation is not written in factored form, how can you tell whether it is a quadratic equation?

2.3 Changing Both Dimensions

In Problem 2.2, you looked at how the area changes when one dimension of a square is increased or decreased to form a new rectangle. You will now explore what happens to the area when *both* dimensions of a square are increased to form a new rectangle.

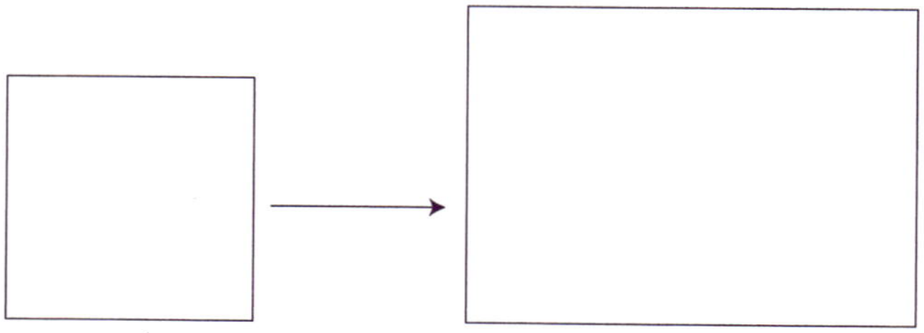

Problem 2.3

A. A square has sides of length x centimeters. A new rectangle is created by increasing one dimension of the square by 2 centimeters and increasing the other dimension by 3 centimeters.

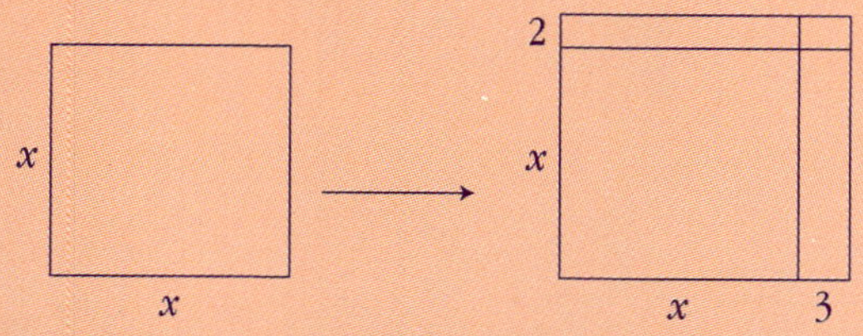

1. Copy the new rectangle. Label the area of each of the four sections.

2. Write two expressions, one in factored form and one in expanded form, for the area of the new rectangle.

3. Use your expressions from part 2 to write two equations for the area, A, of the rectangle. Graph both equations on your calculator. Compare these graphs with the graphs you made in Problem 2.2.

B. A square has sides of length x centimeters. One dimension of the square is doubled and then increased by 2 centimeters, and the other dimension is increased by 3 centimeters.

1. Make a sketch to show how the square is transformed into the new rectangle. Label the area of each section of the new rectangle.

2. Write two expressions, one in factored form and one in expanded form, for the area of the new rectangle.

3. Use your expressions from part 2 to write two equations for the area, A, of the rectangle. Graph both equations on your calculator. Compare these graphs with the graphs you made in Problem 2.2.

C. The rectangle below is divided into four smaller rectangles. Write two expressions, one in factored form and one in expanded form, for the area of the large rectangle.

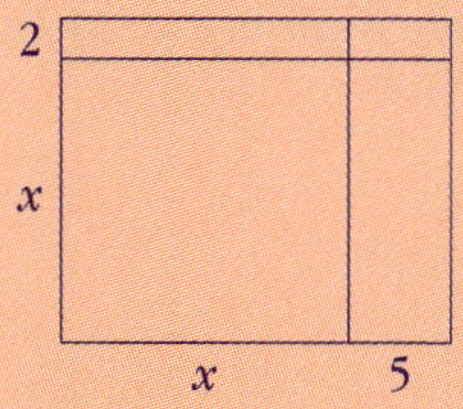

Problem 2.3 Follow-Up

1. In a–c, write two expressions, one in factored form and one in expanded form, for the area of the entire figure.

a.

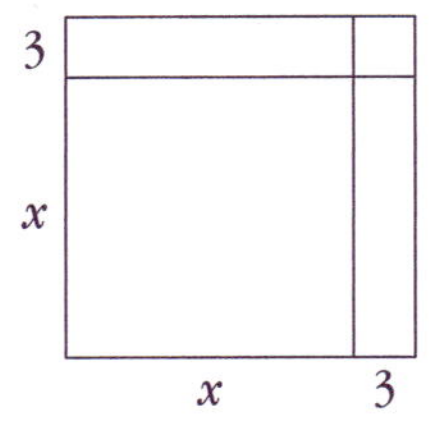

b.

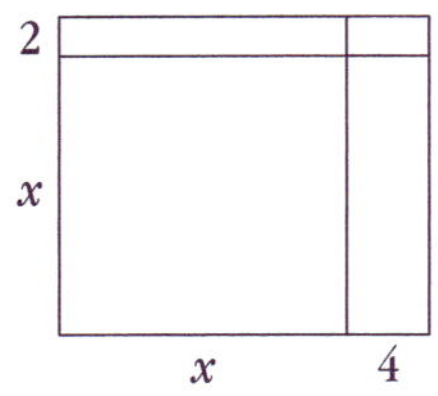

c.

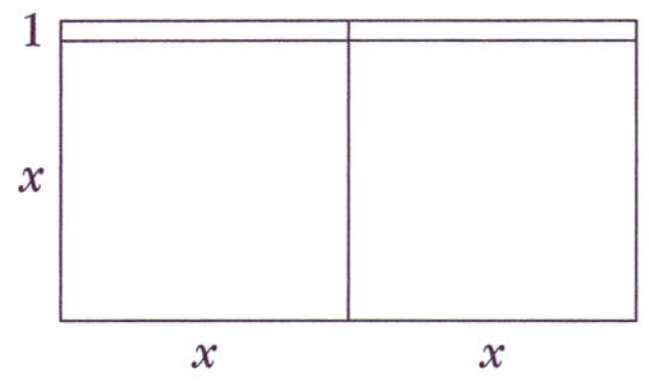

2. One dimension of a square is increased by 1 centimeter, and the other dimension is increased by 3 centimeters. Write two expressions, one in factored form and one in expanded form, for the area of the new rectangle.

3. One dimension of a square is doubled, and the other dimension is increased by 4 centimeters. Write two expressions, one in factored form and one in expanded form, for the area of the new rectangle.

4. Do parts a and b for each expression.

$(x + 3)(x + 4)$ $(x + 5)(x + 5)$ $2x(x + 2)$

a. Draw and label a rectangle whose area is represented by the expression.

b. Write an equivalent expression in expanded form.

The area of the rectangle below can be written in expanded form as $x^2 + 2x + 3x + 6$. Since $2x$ and $3x$ have the same variable with the same exponent (in this case the exponent is 1), they are called **like terms.** You can combine like terms to get a single term. In the expression $x^2 + 2x + 3x + 6$, you can combine $2x$ and $3x$ to get $5x$. The expression then becomes $x^2 + 5x + 6$.

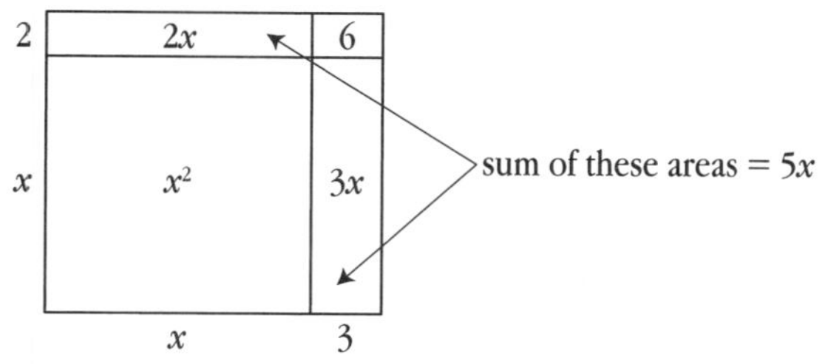

Sometimes it is helpful to combine like terms; other times it is helpful to break a term into two terms. For example, you can write $8x$ as $7x + x$, $6x + 2x$, $5x + 3x$, and so on.

5. a. Copy the diagram below, replacing each question mark with the correct length or area.

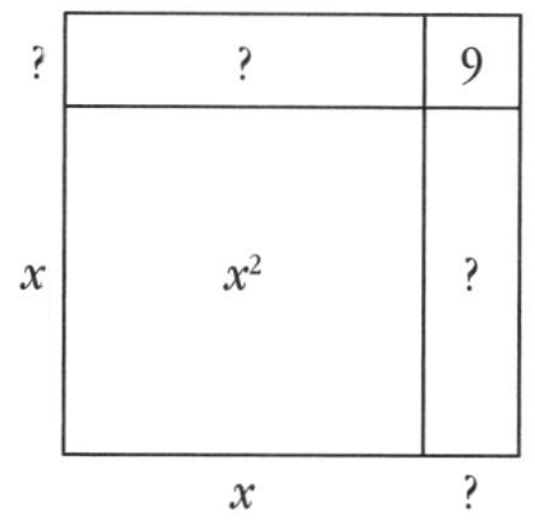

b. Write two expressions for the area of the large rectangle.

6. a. Draw a rectangle made up of four smaller rectangles similar to the one in question 5. Make the area of the square in the lower left corner x^2, and make the area of the rectangle in the upper right corner 8. What might the areas of the other two small rectangles be? Find one solution, and use it to label the lengths and areas in your diagram.

b. Write two expressions for the area of the large rectangle.

7. Do parts a and b for each expression below.

$x^2 + x + 5x + 5$ $\qquad$ $x^2 + 7x + 6$ $\qquad$ $x^2 + 8x + 16$

a. Draw and label a rectangle whose area is represented by the expression.

b. Write an equivalent expression in factored form.

2.4 Looking Back at Parabolas

All the functions you have studied in Investigations 1 and 2 are quadratic functions. The graphs of these functions are parabolas. The parabolas in Investigation 1 are upside-down U-shapes, and the parabolas in Investigation 2 are right-side-up U-shapes.

If you draw a vertical line through the maximum point or minimum point of a parabola and then fold along this line, the two halves of the parabola will exactly match. This vertical line is called the **line of symmetry** for the graph.

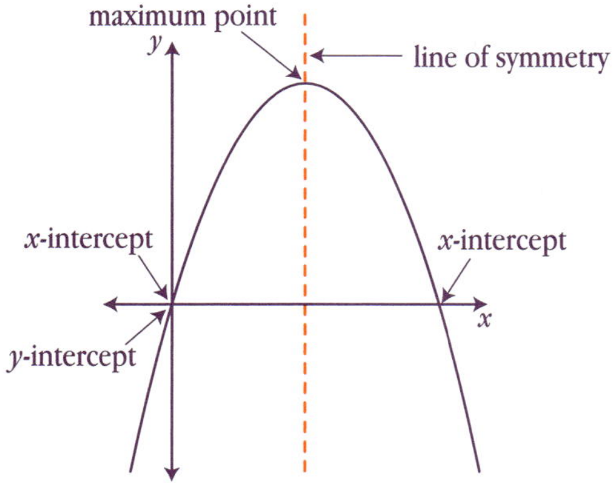

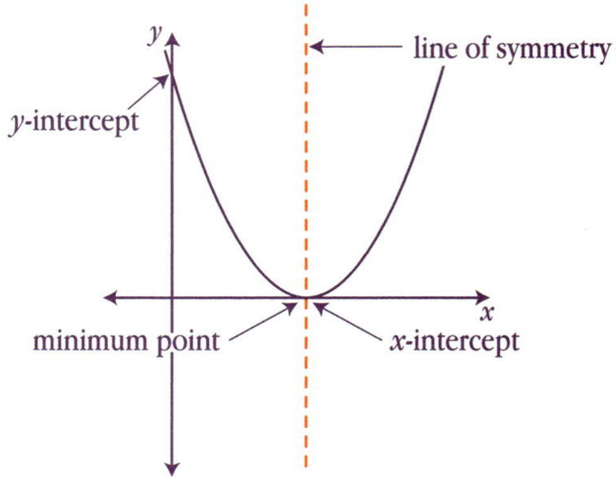

Many important patterns occur in graphs, tables, and equations of quadratic functions. In this problem, you will explore these questions:

What can you learn about a quadratic function from its graph?

How are the features of a parabola related to its equation?

The St. Louis Priori Chapel has windows shaped like parabolas.

Problem 2.4

The eight equations below were graphed on a calculator using the window settings shown. The graphs shown below and on the next page are reproduced on Labsheet 2.4.

$y = x^2$	$y = x(x + 4)$
$y = x(4 - x)$	$y = (x + 3)(x - 3)$
$y = (x + 3)(x + 3)$	$y = (x + 2)(x + 3)$
$y = x(x - 4)$	$y = 2x(x + 4)$

```
WINDOW
 XMIN=⁻5
 XMAX=5
 XSCL=1
 YMIN=⁻10
 YMAX=10
 YSCL=1
```

Do parts A–F for each equation.

A. Match the equation to its graph.

B. Label the coordinates of the x-intercepts on the graph. Describe how you can predict the x-intercepts from the equation.

C. Draw the line of symmetry on the graph.

D. Describe the shape of the graph, and label the coordinates of the maximum or minimum point.

E. Tell what features of the graph you can predict from the equation.

F. Draw and label a rectangle whose area is represented by the equation. Then, express the area of the rectangle in expanded form.

Graph 1

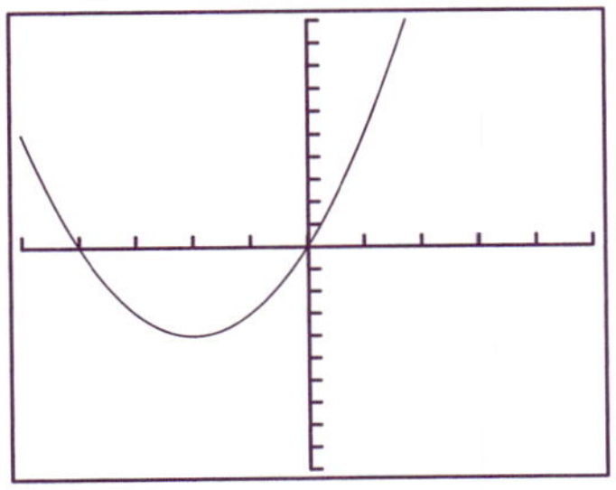

Graph 2

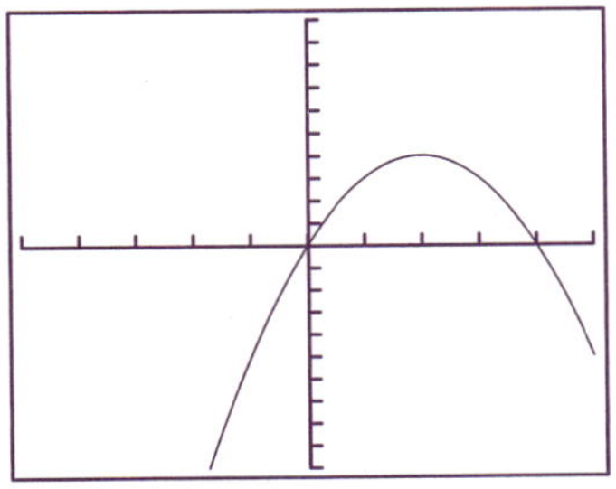

Graph 3

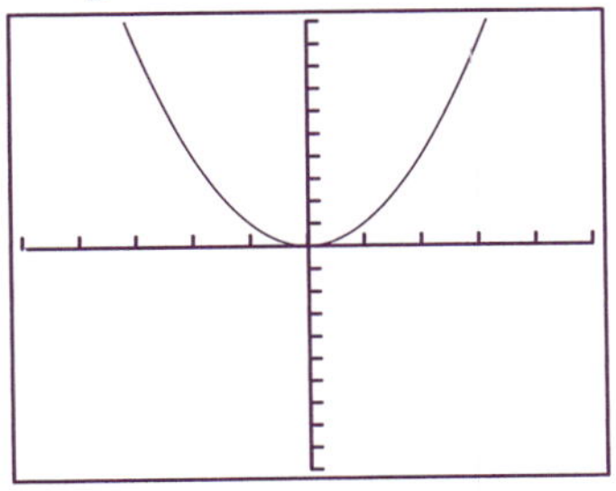

Graph 4

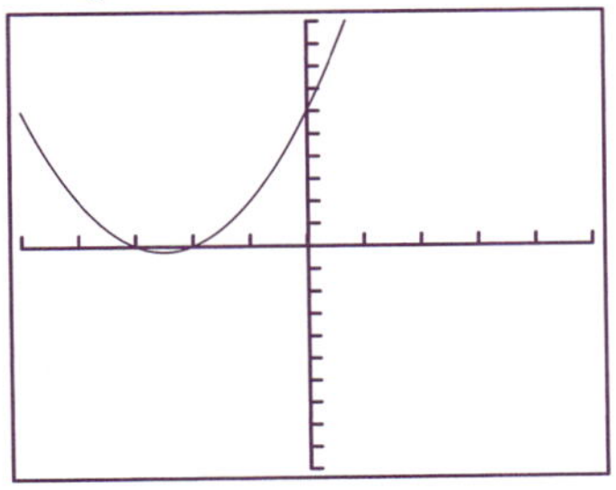

Graph 5

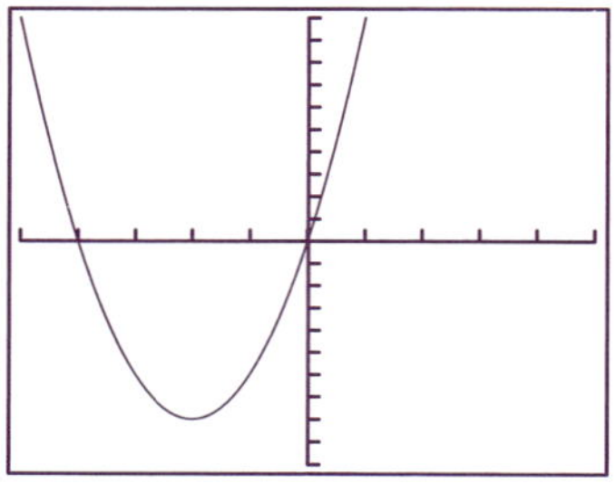

Graph 6

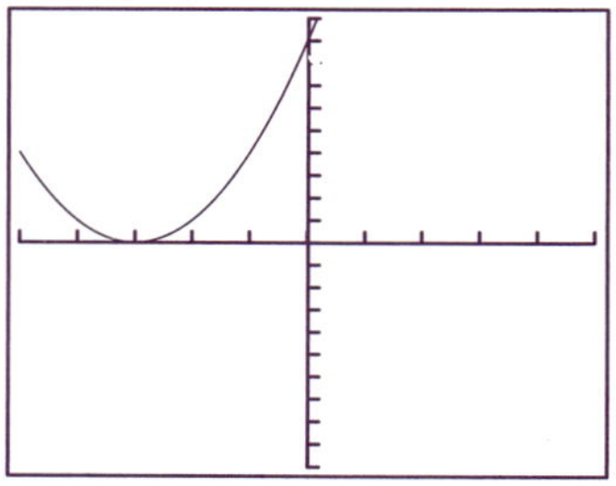

Graph 7

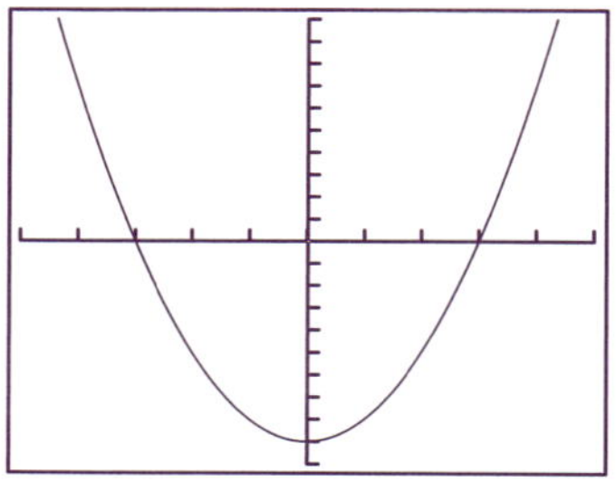

Graph 8

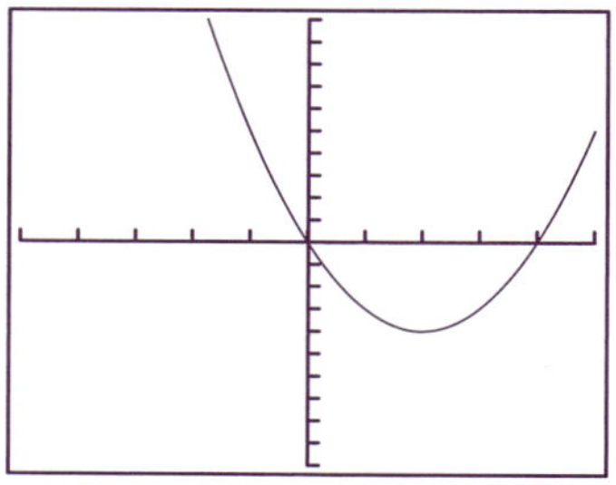

Problem 2.4 Follow-Up

1. If an equation is written in factored form, how can you tell whether it represents a quadratic function?

2. If an equation is written in expanded form, how can you tell whether it represents a quadratic function?

Applications • Connections • Extensions

As you work on these ACE questions, use your calculator whenever you need it.

Applications

1. A square has sides of length x centimeters. A new rectangle is created by increasing one dimension by 4 centimeters and decreasing the other dimension by 4 centimeters.

a. Make a table showing the area of the square and the area of the new rectangle for whole-number x values from 4 to 16.

b. On the same set of axes, graph the (x, area) data for both the square and the rectangle.

c. For which representation—the table or the graph—is it easier to compare the area of a square with the area of the new rectangle?

d. Write an equation for the area of the square and an equation for the area of the new rectangle.

e. Use your calculator to graph both equations for x values from $^{-}10$ to 10. Copy the graphs onto your paper.

2. A square has sides of length x centimeters. A new rectangle is created by increasing one dimension by 5 centimeters.

a. Make a sketch to show how the square is transformed into the new rectangle.

b. Write two expressions, one in factored form and one in expanded form, for the area of the new rectangle.

c. Write an equation for the area, A, of the rectangle, and graph the equation.

3. A square has sides of length x centimeters. A new square is created by increasing both dimensions by 5 centimeters.

a. Make a sketch to show how the original square is transformed into the new square.

b. Write two expressions, one in factored form and one in expanded form, for the area of the new square.

c. Write an equation for the area, A, of the new square, and graph the equation.

4. A square has sides of length x centimeters. A new rectangle is created by increasing one dimension by 4 centimeters and increasing the other dimension by 5 centimeters.

a. Make a sketch to show how the square is transformed into the new rectangle.

b. Write two expressions, one in factored form and one in expanded form, for the area of the new rectangle.

c. Write an equation for the area, A, of the new rectangle, and graph the equation.

In 5–9, write two expressions, one in factored form and one in expanded form, for the area of the unshaded region.

5.

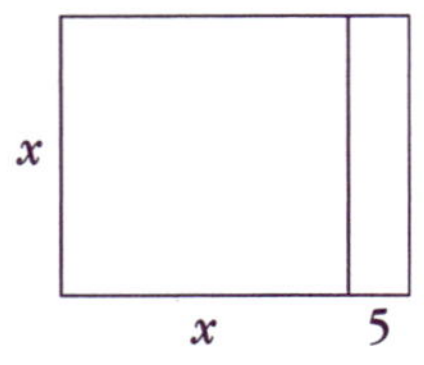

6.

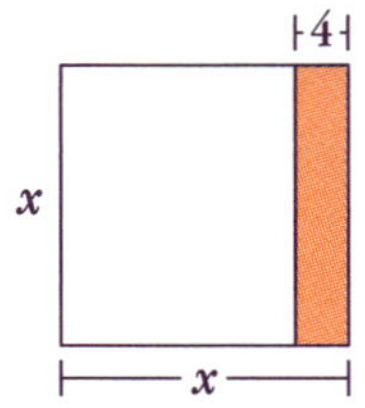

7.

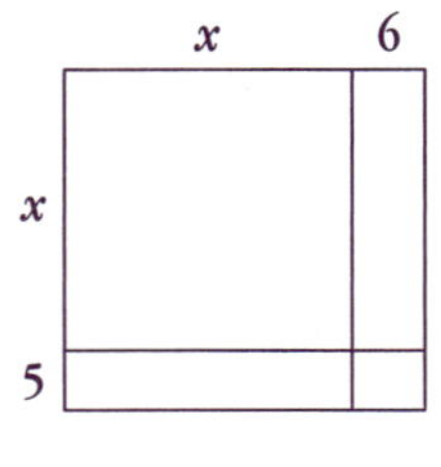

8.

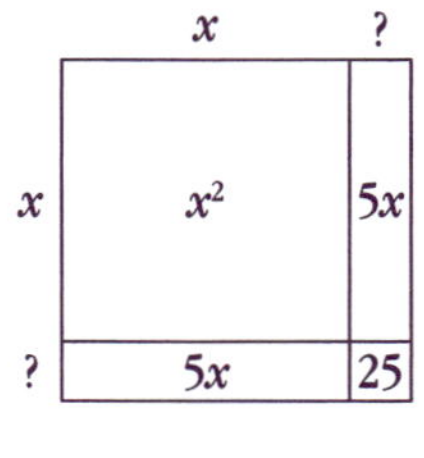

9.

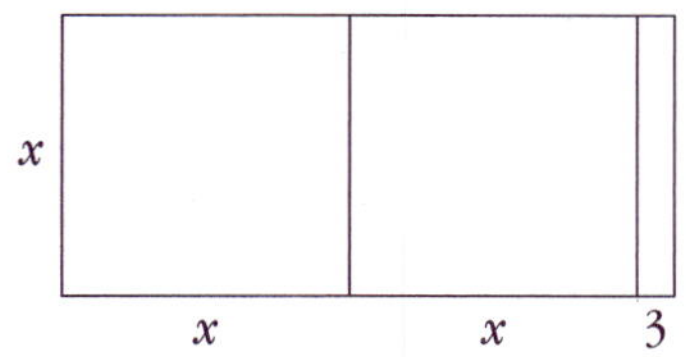

In 10–14, the expression represents the area of a rectangle made by changing the dimensions of a square with sides of length x centimeters. Match the expression with the correct instructions.

	Area		**Instructions for changing a square into a rectangle**
10.	$(x - 3)(x + 3)$	**a.**	Increase one dimension by 3 centimeters, and increase the other dimension by 5 centimeters.
11.	$x(x + 5)$	**b.**	Increase one dimension by 3 centimeters, and decrease the other dimension by 3 centimeters.
12.	$(x + 3)(x + 5)$	**c.**	Decrease one dimension by 5 centimeters, and increase the other dimension by 3 centimeters.
13.	$(x - 3)(x + 5)$	**d.**	Increase one dimension by 5 centimeters, and do not change the other dimension.
14.	$(x + 3)(x - 5)$	**e.**	Increase one dimension by 5 centimeters, and decrease the other dimension by 3 centimeters.

15. For each expression in ACE questions 10–14, write an equivalent expression in expanded form.

16. In ACE questions 10–14, which of the areas is always greater than the area of the original square? Explain how you found your answers.

17. For each expression in ACE questions 10–14, tell where the line of symmetry for the corresponding graph crosses the x-axis. For example, for question 10, tell where the line of symmetry for the graph of $A = (x - 3)(x + 3)$ crosses the x-axis.

In 18–21, the equation represents the area of a rectangle made by changing the dimensions of a square with side lengths of x centimeters. Answer parts a–c.

18. $A = (x + 5)(x + 5)$

19. $A = x(x + 3)$

20. $A = (x + 1)(x + 3)$

21. $A = x(2x + 2)$

a. Make a sketch to show how the rectangle was created from the square.

b. Write an expression for the area in expanded form.

c. What are the x-intercepts of the graph of the equation? How can you determine the x-intercepts from the graph? How can you determine the x-intercepts from the equation?

In 22–26, based on what you have learned so far, tell whether the equation represents a quadratic relationship, a linear relationship, or an exponential relationship. Explain your answer.

22. $y = 5x + x^2$

23. $y = 2x + 8$

24. $y = (9 - x)x$

25. $y = 4x(x + 3)$

26. $y = 3^x$

27. Oletha made a rectangle from a square by doubling one dimension and then adding 3. She left the other dimension unchanged.

a. Write an equation for the area, A, of the new rectangle in terms of the side length, x, of the original square.

b. Graph your area equation. What are the x-intercepts of the graph? How can you find the x-intercepts from the graph? How can you find them from the equation?

In 28–31, do parts a–c.

28. $y = (x + 7)(x + 2)$

29. $y = x(x + 3)$

30. $y = (x - 4)(x + 6)$

31. $y = (x - 5)(x + 5)$

a. Match the equation with its graph.

i.

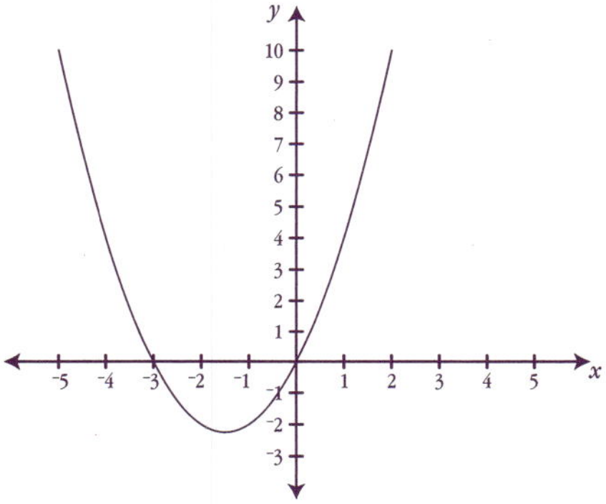

ii.

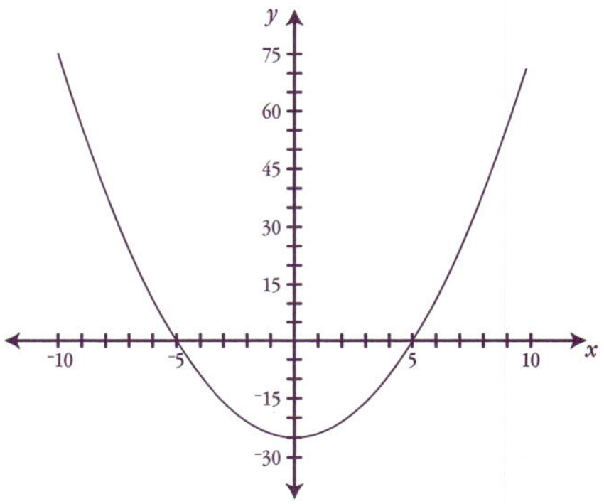

iii.

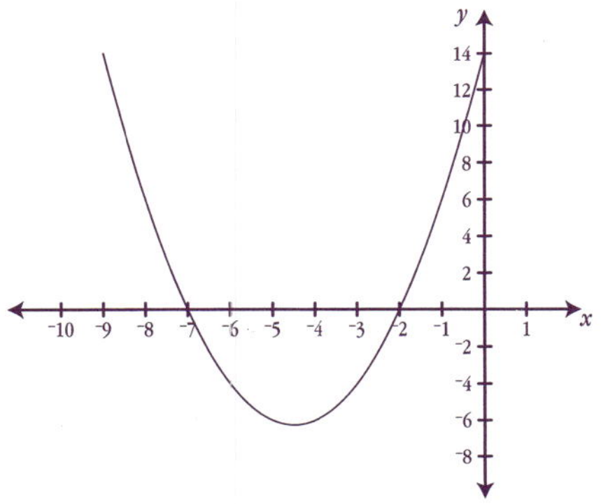

iv.

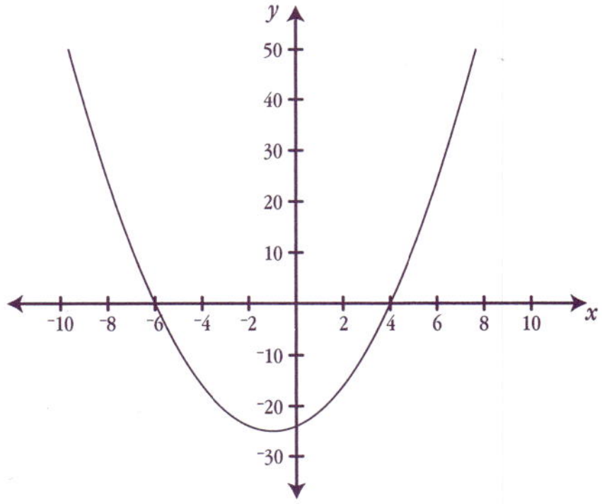

b. Tell where the line of symmetry for the graph crosses the x-axis.

c. Draw and label the rectangle whose area is represented by the equation.

Connections

32. The Stellar Cellular long-distance company charges $13.95 per month plus $0.39 per minute of calling time. The Call Anytime company has no monthly service fee but charges $0.95 per minute of calling time.

a. When deciding which company to use, what factors should a potential customer consider?

b. Describe each charge plan with an equation, a table, and a graph.

c. For each plan, tell whether the relationship between calling time and monthly cost is quadratic. How do your equation, table, and graph support your answer?

33. The winner of the Jammin' Jelly jingle contest will receive $500. Antonia and her friends are writing a jingle for the contest. They plan to divide the prize money equally if they win.

a. If n friends write the winning jingle, how much prize money will each person receive?

b. Describe the relationship between the number of friends and the amount of prize money each friend receives.

c. What kinds of questions about this relationship would be easiest to answer by making a graph? What kinds of questions would be easiest to answer by making a table? What kinds of questions would be easiest to answer by writing an equation?

d. Is this relationship quadratic? Explain why or why not.

34. Suppose the circumference of a tree is x feet.

a. What is the diameter of the tree in terms of x?

b. What is the radius of the tree in terms of x?

c. What is the area of a cross section of the tree in terms of x? Is the relationship between the circumference and the area of the cross section linear, quadratic, exponential, or none of these?

d. If the circumference of the tree is 10 feet, what are the diameter, the radius, and the area of a cross section?

35. A square has sides of length x centimeters.

a. The square is enlarged by a scale factor of 2. What is the area of the enlarged square?

b. How does the area of the original square compare with the area of the enlarged square?

36. A rectangle has dimensions x centimeters and $x + 1$ centimeters.

a. The rectangle is enlarged by a scale factor of 2. What is the area of the enlarged rectangle?

b. How does the area of the original rectangle compare with the area of the enlarged rectangle?

Extensions

37. A square has sides of length x centimeters. A new rectangle is created by increasing one dimension by 5 centimeters and decreasing the other dimension by 4 centimeters.

a. Make a sketch to show how the square is transformed into the new rectangle.

b. Write an expression for the area of the original square and an expression for the area of the new rectangle.

c. For what x values is the area of the new rectangle greater than the area of the square? For what x values is the area of the new rectangle less than the area of the square? For what x values are the areas equal? Explain how you found your answers.

38. A square has sides of length x centimeters. A new rectangle is created by increasing one dimension by 2 centimeters and decreasing the other dimension by 3 centimeters.

a. Make a sketch to show how the square is transformed into the new rectangle.

b. Write two expressions, one in factored form and one in expanded form, for the area of the new rectangle.

c. Write an equation for the area, A, of the new rectangle. Graph the equation, and describe the graph.

39. A square has sides of length x centimeters. A new rectangle is created by increasing one dimension by 2 centimeters and doubling the other dimension and then adding 2 centimeters.

a. Make a sketch to show how the original square is transformed into the new rectangle.

b. Write two expressions, one in factored form and one in expanded form, for the area of the new rectangle.

c. Write an equation for the area, A, of the new rectangle. Graph the equation, and describe the graph.

In 40–43, the equation represents the area of a rectangle made by changing the dimensions of a square with sides of length x centimeters. Answer parts a and b.

40. $A = x^2 - 6x$

41. $A = x^2 - 9$

42. $A = x^2 + 8x + 16$

43. $A = x^2 + 10x + 16$

a. Write an expression for the area in factored form.

b. Sketch a graph of the equation, and describe the shape of the graph.

In 44–46, do parts a and b.

44. $y = x^2 - 2x - 8$

45. $y = x^2 - 5x$

46. $y = x^2 + 8x + 16$

a. Match the equation with its graph.

i.

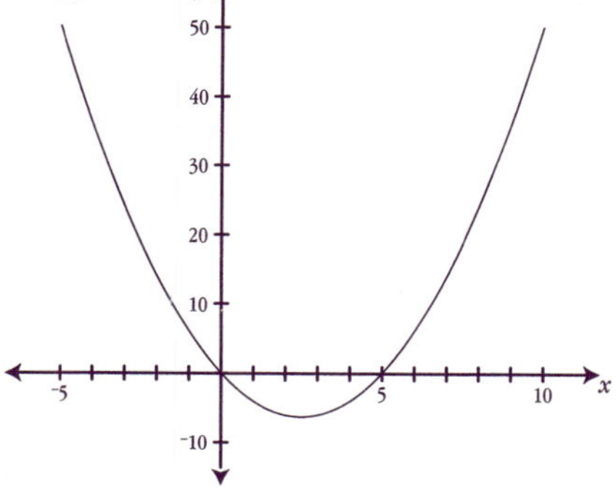

ii.

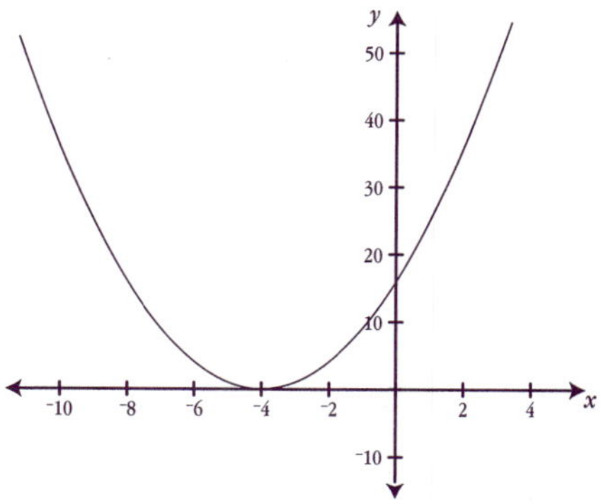

iii.

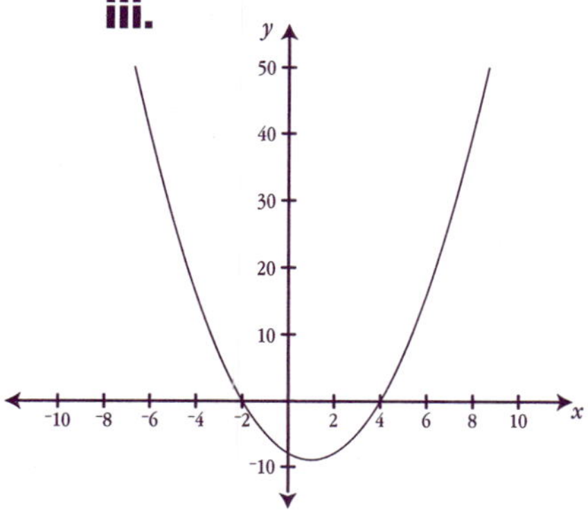

b. Write each equation in factored form. Describe how you found the factored form.

Mathematical Reflections

In this investigation, you explored quadratic equations representing the areas of rectangles formed by transforming a square. These questions will help you summarize what you have learned:

1. The quadratic expression $x(x + 7)$ is in factored form. How can you find an equivalent expression in expanded form? Write the expanded form for the expression, and sketch a rectangle to show that the two expressions are equivalent.
2. The quadratic expression $x^2 + 7x + 12$ is in expanded form. How can you find an equivalent expression in factored form? Write the factored form for the expression, and sketch a rectangle to show that the two expressions are equivalent.
3. In the graphs you made of the areas of the rectangles in this investigation, what information did the x-intercepts give you? How can you predict the x-intercepts for a quadratic function by looking at its equation?
4. How can you recognize a quadratic function from its equation?
5. Describe what you know about the shape of the graph of a quadratic function. Include the line of symmetry and any other important features you have observed.

Think about your answers to these questions, discuss your ideas with other students and your teacher, and then write a summary of your findings in your journal.

INVESTIGATION 3

Quadratic Patterns of Change

In earlier units, you studied linear relationships. In a linear relationship, the *y* value changes at a constant rate. This means that in a table of values, the difference in successive *y* values is constant. In this investigation, you will explore the patterns of change for quadratic relationships as you solve some interesting counting problems.

3.1 Counting Handshakes

After a sporting event, the opposing teams often line up and shake hands. To celebrate their victory, members of the winning team may congratulate each other with a round of high fives. In this problem, you will explore the total number of handshakes or high fives that take place in several situations. You will consider three cases.

Case 1
Two teams with the same number of players shake hands.

Case 2
Two teams with different numbers of players shake hands. For example, although 5 players from each basketball team participate at one time, one team may have a total of 8 players and the other may have a total of 10 players.

Case 3
Members of the same team exchange high fives.

Problem 3.1

A. Consider case 1, in which two teams have the same number of players. Each player on one team shakes hands with each player on the other team.

1. How many handshakes will take place between two basketball teams with 10 players each?
2. How many handshakes will take place between two soccer teams with 15 players each?
3. Write an equation for the number of handshakes, h, between two teams with n players each.

B. Consider a restricted form of case 2, in which the numbers of players on the two teams differ by 1. Each player on one team shakes hands with each player on the other team.

1. How many handshakes will take place between a water polo team with 10 players and a water polo team with 9 players?
2. How many handshakes will take place between a field hockey team with 15 players and a field hockey team with 14 players?
3. Write an equation for the number of handshakes, h, between a team with n players and a team with $n - 1$ players.

C. Consider case 3, in which each member of a team gives a high five to each teammate.

1. How many high fives will take place among an academic quiz team with 4 members?
2. How many high fives will take place among a golf team with 12 members?
3. Write an equation for the number of high fives, h, that will take place among a team with n members.

Problem 3.1 Follow-Up

1. a. For cases 1, 2, and 3 in Problem 3.1, make a table showing the number of players on each team and the number of handshakes or high fives. Include data for teams with from 1 to 10 members. For case 2, consider only the case when the numbers of players on the two teams differ by 1.

b. For each table, describe a pattern that would help you predict the number of handshakes or high fives for larger teams.

c. Compare the patterns for the three tables. How are the patterns similar? How are they different?

2. a. Graph your three equations from Problem 3.1. Show n values from 1 to 10.

b. How do your three graphs compare?

3. Look at the tables, graphs, and equations for the three cases. Are any of the relationships quadratic? Explain.

4. Tyler expressed the number of handshakes between a team with n members and a team with $n - 1$ members as $n(n - 1)$. Asuko wrote $n^2 - n$ to represent the same situation.

a. Describe how Tyler might have thought about the situation in order to formulate his expression. Describe how Asuko might have thought about the situation.

b. Draw and label a rectangle whose area can be represented by these expressions.

3.2 Exploring Triangular Numbers

Study the pattern below.

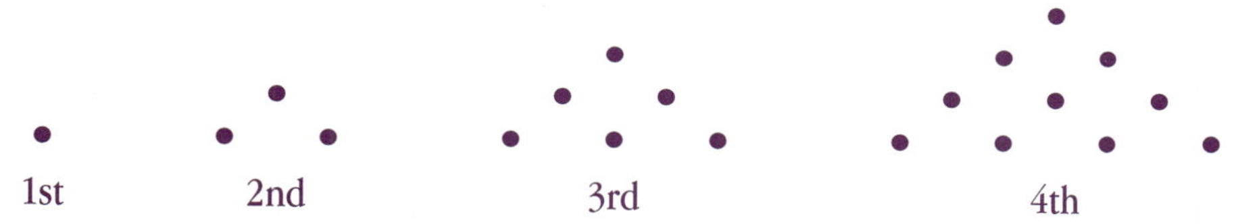

How many dots do you predict will be in the 5th figure? In the nth figure?

Problem 3.2

The numbers of dots in the figures above are called **triangular numbers.** The first triangular number is 1, the second triangular number is 3, the third is 6, the fourth is 10, and so on.

A. What two variables are important in this situation? Which is the independent variable, and which is the dependent variable?

B. Look for a pattern in the figures above. Use the pattern to help you make a table of the first ten triangular numbers.

C. Describe the pattern of change from one triangular number to the next.

D. How can you use this pattern of change to predict the 15th triangular number without making a drawing?

E. Write an equation that can be used to determine the nth triangular number.

F. Does your equation represent a quadratic relationship? Explain your answer.

Problem 3.2 Follow-Up

The pattern below represents the triangular numbers as collections of squares.

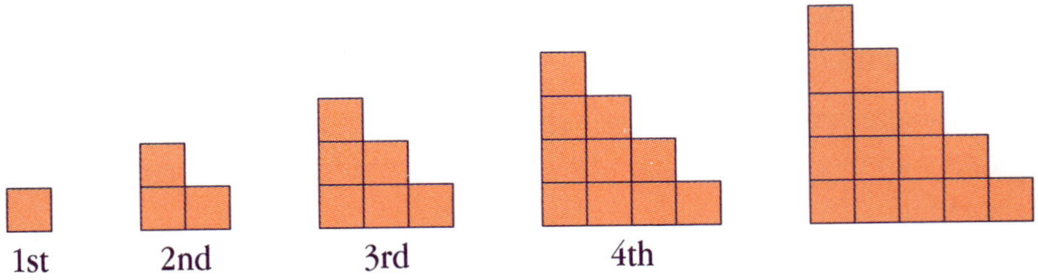

You can combine two copies of each figure to form a rectangle.

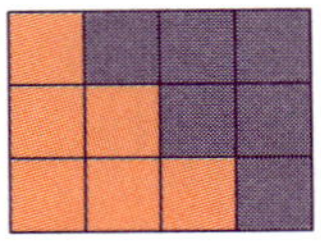

1. Give the dimensions and the area of the rectangle formed by combining two copies of the given figure.
   a. the 4th figure
   b. the 5th figure
   c. the 10th figure
   d. the *n*th figure
2. For each part of question 1, how does the number of squares in the rectangle compare with the number of squares in the original figure?
3. Use your answers from questions 1 and 2 to help you write an equation for calculating the *n*th triangular number. How does your equation compare with the equation you wrote in Problem 3.2?
4. What is the 18th triangular number?
5. Is 210 a triangular number? Explain your answer.

Applications • Connections • Extensions

As you work on these ACE questions, use your calculator whenever you need it.

Applications

1. In a school math league, each team has six student members and two coaches.

a. At the start of a match, the coaches and student members of one team exchange handshakes with the coaches and student members of the other team. How many handshakes will be exchanged?

b. At the end of the match, the members and coaches of the winning team exchange high fives to celebrate their victory. How many high fives will be exchanged?

2. The dot patterns below represent the first four *square numbers,* 1, 4, 9, and 16.

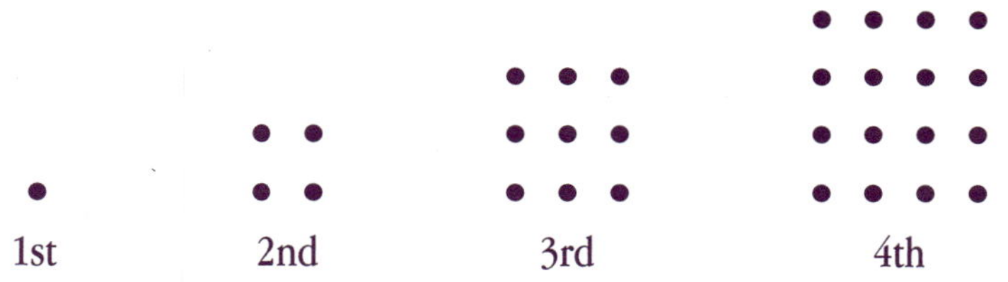

a. What are the next two square numbers?

b. Write an equation for calculating the nth square number.

c. Make a table and a graph of the first ten square numbers. Describe the pattern of change from one square number to the next.

3. The dots below are arranged in rectangular patterns. The numbers of dots in the figures are called the *rectangular numbers.*

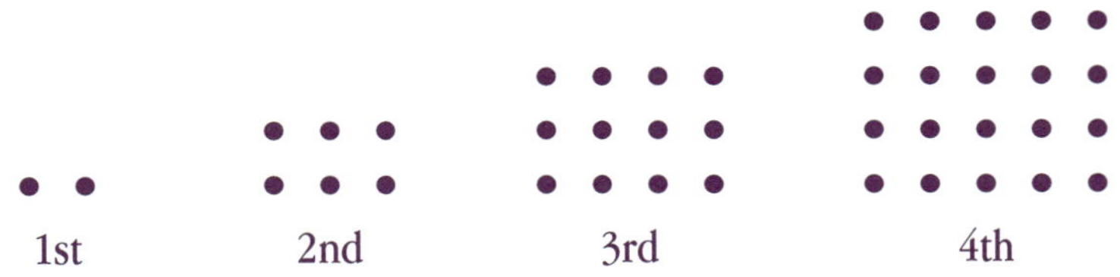

a. What are the first four rectangular numbers?

b. Find the next two rectangular numbers.

c. Describe the pattern of change from one rectangular number to the next.

d. Use the pattern of change to predict the 7th and 8th rectangular numbers.

e. Write an equation for calculating the *n*th rectangular number.

4. In what ways are triangular numbers, square numbers, and rectangular numbers similar to the cases given in Problem 3.1?

In 5–8, tell whether the number is a triangular number, a square number, a rectangular number, or none of these, and explain how you know you are correct.

5. 110 6. 66 7. 121 8. 60

9. Graphs i–iv on the next page represent situations you have looked at in this unit. Study the graphs and then answer the following questions.

a. Which graph might represent the number of high fives exchanged among a team with *n* players? Justify your choice.

b. Which graph might represent areas of rectangles with a fixed perimeter? Justify your choice.

c. Which graph might represent the area of a rectangle formed by increasing one dimension of a square by 2 centimeters and decreasing the other dimension by 3 centimeters? Justify your choice.

i.

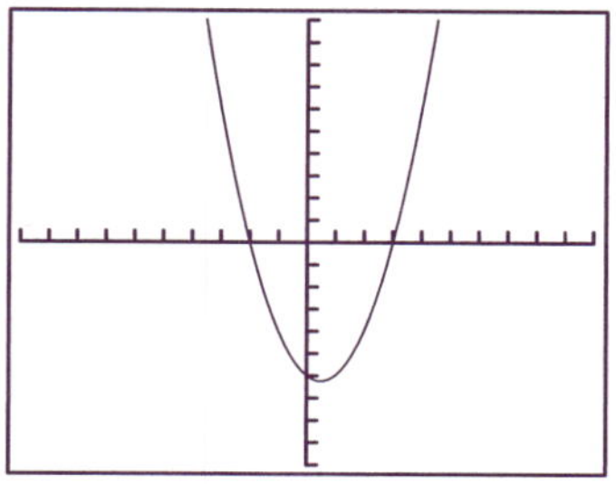

ii.

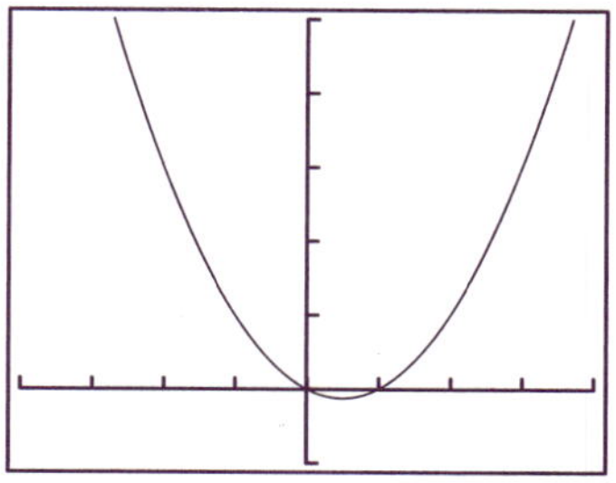

iii.

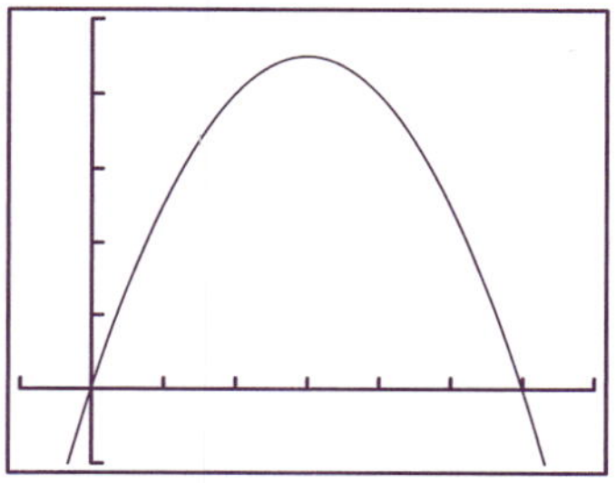

iv.

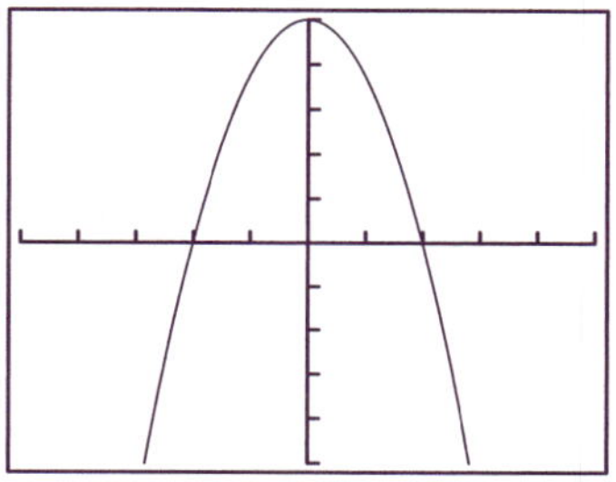

In 10–12, describe a situation that can be represented by the given equation, and tell what the variables P and n represent in that situation.

10. $P = n(n - 1)$ **11.** $P = n^2$ **12.** $P = n(n - 2)$

Connections

13. A *diagonal* is a line segment connecting any two nonadjacent vertices of a polygon. A quadrilateral has two diagonals.

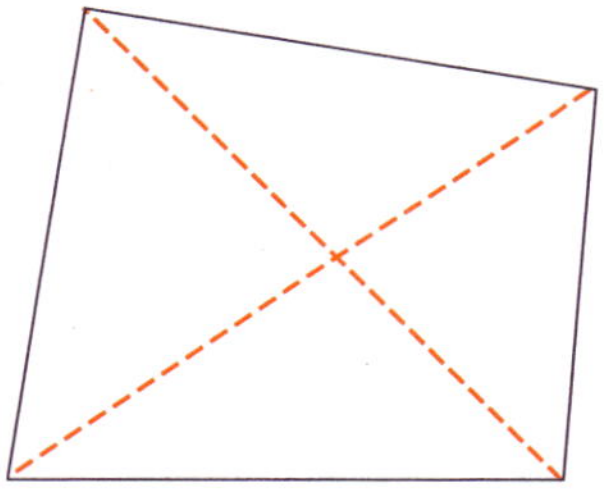

a. How many diagonals does a pentagon have? A hexagon? A heptagon? An octagon?

b. How many diagonals does an n-sided polygon have?

14. These "trains" were formed by joining identical squares.

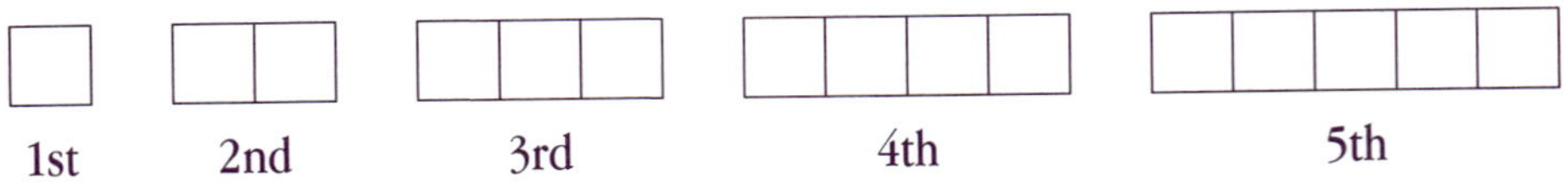

a. How many rectangles can be found in each of the first five trains? For example, the shading below shows that there are 6 rectangles in the 3rd train. (Remember, a square is a special kind of rectangle.)

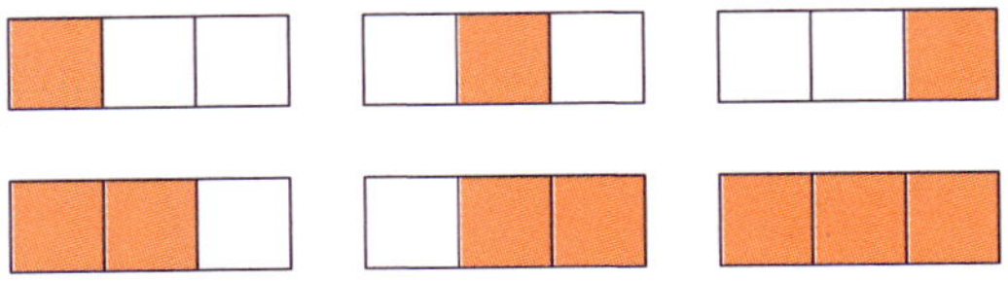

b. Make a table showing the number of rectangles in each of the first ten trains.

c. Describe how you could use the pattern of change in your table to find the number of rectangles in the 15th train.

d. Write an equation for calculating the number of rectangles in the nth train.

e. Use your equation to find the number of rectangles in the 15th train.

Extensions

15. You can quickly find the sum of the whole numbers from 1 to 10 by grouping them as shown below:

$$\begin{aligned}(1 + 10) + (2 + 9) + (3 + 8) + (4 + 7) + (5 + 6) &= 11 + 11 + 11 + 11 + 11 \\ &= 5 \times 11 \\ &= 55\end{aligned}$$

a. How could you use this idea to calculate $1 + 2 + 3 + \ldots + 99 + 100$?

b. How could you use this idea to calculate $1 + 2 + 3 + \ldots + n$ for any whole number n?

16. The dots below are arranged in patterns that represent the first three *star numbers.*

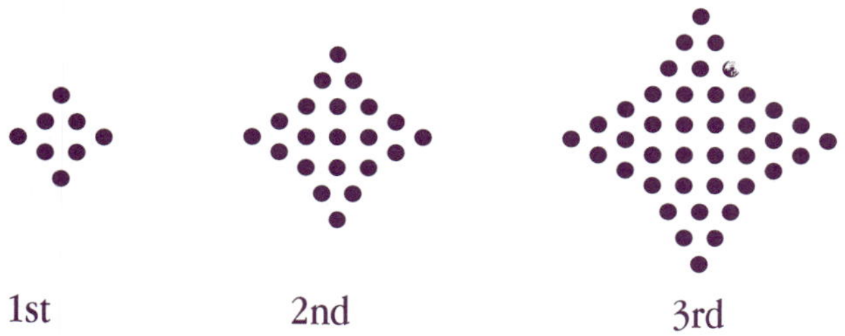

a. What are the first three star numbers?

b. Use the dot patterns and your answers for part a to find the next three star numbers.

c. Write an equation you could use to calculate the *n*th star number.

17. **a.** Ten former classmates attend their class reunion. They all shake hands with each other. How many handshakes are exchanged? Explain your answer by drawing a picture or writing a convincing argument.

b. A little later, two more classmates arrive. If these two people shake hands with each other and the ten other classmates, how many new handshakes are exchanged? Explain your answer by drawing a picture or writing a convincing argument.

18. The dots below are arranged in hexagonal patterns. The numbers of dots in the patterns represent the *hexagonal numbers.*

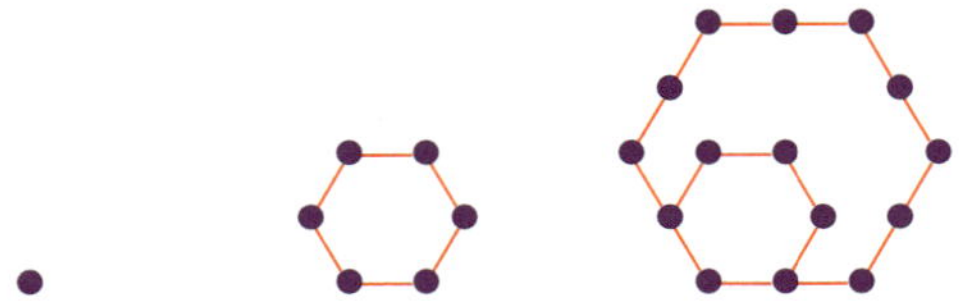

1st 2nd 3rd

a. What are the first three hexagonal numbers?

b. Use the dot patterns and your answers from part a to find the next two hexagonal numbers.

c. Which equation below could you use to calculate the *n*th hexagonal number?

$h = \frac{n}{2}(n + 1)$ $h = n(3n - 2)$ $h = n(2n - 1)$

19. If you look carefully, you can find 30 squares of various sizes in this 4-by-4 grid.

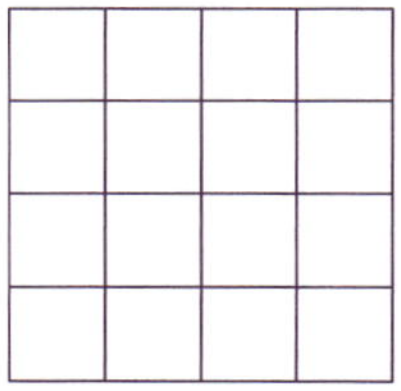

a. Sixteen of the 30 squares are the identical small squares that make up the grid. Find the other 14 squares. Draw pictures or give a description that would help someone else see all 30 squares.

b. How many squares can you find in an *n*-by-*n* grid? (Hint: Start with some simple cases and search for a pattern.)

Mathematical Reflections

In this investigation, you counted handshakes and studied geometric patterns. You found that these situations could be represented by quadratic functions. These questions will help you summarize what you have learned:

1. In what ways are the relationships in the handshake problems similar to the relationships in the dot-pattern problems? In what ways are these relationships different?
2. In what ways are the quadratic functions in this investigation similar to the quadratic functions in Investigations 1 and 2? In what ways are they different?
3. **a.** Describe the patterns of change for the quadratic functions in this investigation.

   b. In a table of values for a quadratic function, how can you use the pattern of change to predict the next entry?

Think about your answers to these questions, discuss your ideas with other students and your teacher, and then write a summary of your findings in your journal.

INVESTIGATION 4

What Is a Quadratic Function?

If you jump from a diving board or a bungee tower, gravity pulls you toward Earth. If you throw or kick a ball into the air, gravity brings it back down. For several hundred years, scientists have used mathematical models to describe and predict the effect of gravity on the position, velocity, and acceleration of falling and thrown objects.

In the first two problems of this investigation, you will look at how the height of a ball changes after it is thrown and how the distance from the ground of a person, a frog, and a flea change after they jump. You will look at tables, graphs, and equations for these situations and explore how changing the starting position affects the representations. In the last problem, you will review all you have learned so far about tables, graphs, and equations of quadratic functions, concentrating on the patterns of change in tables.

4.1 Tracking a Ball

No matter how hard you throw or kick a ball into the air, gravity always returns it to Earth. In this problem, you will explore how the height of a ball changes over time.

Problem 4.1

Suppose you throw a ball straight up into the air. This table describes how the height of the ball might change as it travels through the air.

Time (s)	Height (ft)
0.00	0
0.25	15
0.50	28
0.75	39
1.00	48
1.25	55
1.50	60
1.75	63
2.00	64
2.25	63
2.50	60
2.75	55
3.00	48
3.25	39
3.50	28
3.75	15
4.00	0

A. Describe how the height of the ball changes over this 4-second time period.

B. Without making the graph, describe what the graph of these data would look like. Include as many important features as you can.

C. Do you think these data represent a quadratic function? Explain why or why not.

Problem 4.1 Follow-Up

1. The height, h, of the ball after t seconds can be described by the equation

$$h = {}^{-}16t^2 + 64t.$$

a. Graph this equation on your calculator.

b. Does the graph match your description from part B of Problem 4.1? Explain.

c. Use the equation or the graph to figure out when the ball reaches a height of about 58 feet.

d. Use the equation to find the height of the ball after 1.6 seconds.

2. In Problem 4.1, the initial height of the ball is 0 feet. This is not very realistic because it means that you would have to lie on the ground and release the ball without extending your arm. A more realistic equation for the height of the ball after t seconds is

$$h = {}^{-}16t^2 + 64t + 6.$$

a. Make a table and a graph for this quadratic function.

b. The 6 in the equation above is called a constant term. A **constant term** is a term that does not contain a variable. How does the constant term affect the table and the graph? What information does the constant term in this equation give?

c. Compare the graphs of the equations in questions 1 and 2. Discuss the similarities and differences in the following:

- **i.** the maximum height reached by the ball
- **ii.** the x-intercepts
- **iii.** the pattern of change in the height of the ball over time

Did you know?

Aristotle, the ancient Greek philosopher and scientist, believed that heavier objects fall faster than lighter objects. This idea was widely accepted until the late 1500s when it was challenged by the great Italian scientist Galileo Galilei. Galileo is highly regarded for his work in astronomy, mathematics, and physics, but is perhaps best known for his devotion to the scientific method. The scientific method involves observing, developing a hypothesis based on observations, and then designing an experiment to test that hypothesis.

Galileo began to doubt Aristotle's idea when he observed a hailstorm. He noticed that large and small hailstones hit the ground at the same time. If Aristotle's idea were correct, this would happen only if the larger stones dropped from a greater altitude than the smaller stones, or if the smaller stones started falling before the larger stones. Galileo didn't think either of these explanations was probable.

To prove his theory that heavy and light objects fall at the same rate, Galileo performed an experiment. He reportedly climbed to the highest point he could find—the top of the Tower of Pisa—and dropped two objects simultaneously. Although they had different weights, the objects hit the ground at the same time.

4.2 Measuring Jumps

Many animals are known for their jumping abilities. Most frogs can jump several times their body length. Fleas are tiny, but they can easily leap onto a dog or a cat. Some humans have amazing jumping ability as well. Many professional basketball players have vertical leaps of more than 3 feet.

Suppose you filmed a frog, a flea, and a basketball player as they jumped straight up as high as possible. If you studied the films frame by frame, you would find that the time, t, in seconds and the height, H, in feet are related by equations similar to these:

$$\text{frog: } H = -16t^2 + 12t + 0.2$$
$$\text{flea: } H = -16t^2 + 8t$$
$$\text{basketball player: } H = -16t^2 + 16t + 6.5$$

Problem 4.2

A. Use your calculator to make tables and graphs of these three equations. Since a jump doesn't take much time, look at heights for time values between 0 seconds and 1 second. In your tables, use intervals of 0.1 second.

B. What is the maximum height reached by each jumper, and when is the maximum height reached?

C. How long does each jump last? Explain how you found your answer.

D. What do the constant terms 0.2 and 6.5 tell you about the frog and the basketball player?

Problem 4.2 Follow-Up

1. For each jumper, describe the pattern of change in the height over time, and explain how the pattern is reflected in the table and the graph.

2. Mr. Jain is a jewelry maker. He would like to increase his profit by raising the price of his jade earrings. However, he knows that if he raises the price too high, he won't sell as many earrings and his profit will decrease. Using records of past sales, a business consultant developed the equation $P = 50s - s^2$ to predict the monthly profit, P, for a given sales price, s.

a. Make a table and a graph for this equation.

b. What do the equation, the table, and the graph suggest about the relationship between price and profit?

c. What price will bring the greatest profit?

d. How does this equation compare with the equations in Problem 4.2?

Did you know?

- The average flea weighs 0.000001 pound and is 2 to 3 millimeters long. It can pull 160,000 times its own weight and can jump 150 times its own length. This is equivalent to a human being pulling 24 million pounds and jumping 1000 feet!
- There are 2375 known species and subspecies of fleas, and fleas are found on all land masses, including Antarctica.
- Most fleas make their homes on bats, rats, squirrels, and mice.
- The bubonic plague, which killed a quarter of Europe's population in the fourteenth century, was spread by rat fleas.
- Flea circuses originated about 300 years ago and were popular in the United States a century ago.

Source: *New York Times Magazine,* 22 October 1995, p. 18.

4.3 Putting It All Together

In this unit, you have used algebraic equations to model a variety of quadratic functions. You may have noticed some common characteristics of these equations. Below are some familiar equations.

square numbers: $s = n^2$

rectangular numbers: $r = n(n + 1)$

area of a rectangle with a perimeter of 20: $A = (10 - l)l$

number of high fives: $h = \frac{n}{2}(n - 1)$

a flea jump: $H = {}^-16t^2 + 8t$

You have also observed patterns in the graphs of quadratic functions. These graphs, called *parabolas,* are symmetric U-shapes with a maximum point or a minimum point.

In the previous investigation, you began to explore patterns in the tables of quadratic functions. In this problem, you will look more closely at these patterns.

To understand a relationship between two variables, it helps to look at how the value of one variable changes each time the value of the other variable increases by a fixed amount. You have seen that for a linear relationship, the y value increases by a constant amount each time the x value increases by 1. For example, look at this table for the linear relationship $y = 3x + 1$. The calculations under "First differences" are the differences between consecutive y values.

$y = 3x + 1$

x	y
0	1
1	4
2	7
3	10
4	13
5	16

First differences

$4 - 1 = 3$

$7 - 4 = 3$

$10 - 7 = 3$

$13 - 10 = 3$

$16 - 13 = 3$

Since the y value increases by 3 each time the x value increases by 1, the first differences for $y = 3x + 1$ are all 3.

Now, let's look at a quadratic relationship. The simplest quadratic relationship is $y = x^2$, the rule for generating square numbers. In fact, the word *quadratic* is derived from the Latin word for "square." The table below shows that the first differences for $y = x^2$ are not constant.

$y = x^2$

x	y
0	0
1	1
2	4
3	9
4	16
5	25

First differences

$1 - 0 = 1$

$4 - 1 = 3$

$9 - 4 = 5$

$16 - 9 = 7$

$25 - 16 = 9$

However, look at what happens when we find the *second* differences.

$y = x^2$

x	y
0	0
1	1
2	4
3	9
4	16
5	25

First differences	Second differences
$1 - 0 = 1$	
	$3 - 1 = 2$
$4 - 1 = 3$	
	$5 - 3 = 2$
$9 - 4 = 5$	
	$7 - 5 = 2$
$16 - 9 = 7$	
	$9 - 7 = 2$
$25 - 16 = 9$	

Do you think the tables for other quadratic functions will show a similar pattern?

Problem 4.3

A. Make a table for each quadratic equation below. Use integer values of x from $^-5$ to 5. Add columns to your tables showing first and second differences.

$y = 2x(x + 3)$ $\quad y = 3x - x^2$ $\quad y = (x - 2)^2$ $\quad y = x^2 + 5x + 6$

B. Consider the patterns of change in the y values and in the first and second differences for the four equations. In what ways are the patterns similar for the four equations? In what ways are they different?

Problem 4.3 Follow-Up

1. The patterns of differences for quadratic functions are not like the patterns of differences for the linear and exponential functions you studied in other units.

a. Make a table of (x, y) values for each equation below. Include columns for the first and second differences.

$y = x + 2$ $\quad y = 2x$ $\quad y = 2^x$ $\quad y = x^2$

b. For each table, look at the pattern of change in the y value as the x value increases by 1. How are the patterns similar in the four tables? How are they different?

c. How are the patterns of change in the tables reflected in the equations?

2. You have seen that a parabola is a symmetric shape with either a maximum point or a minimum point. Describe the graph of each equation in Problem 4.3 and question 1 above. Be sure to consider maximum or minimum points, x-intercepts, and lines of symmetry. Use a calculator to check your descriptions.

Applications • Connections • Extensions

As you work on these ACE questions, use your calculator whenever you need it.

Applications

1. A basketball player takes a shot. The graph below shows the height of the ball, starting from when it leaves the player's hands.

a. Estimate the height of the ball when it is released by the player.

b. When does the ball reach its maximum height? What is the maximum height?

c. How long does it take the ball to reach the basket, which is set at a height of 10 feet?

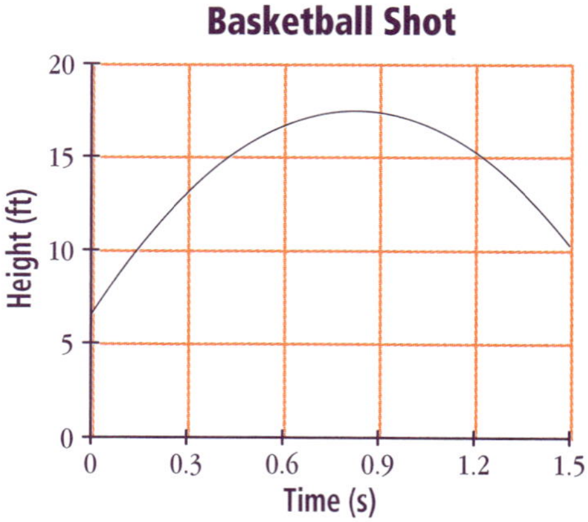

2. The highest dive in the Olympic Games is from a 10-meter platform. The height in meters of a diver t seconds after leaving the platform can be estimated by the equation $h = 10 - 4.9t^2$.

a. Make a table of the relationship between time and height.

b. Sketch a graph of the relationship between time and height.

c. When will the diver hit the water's surface? How can you find this answer by using your graph? How can you find this answer by using your table?

d. When will the diver be 5 meters above the water?

e. When is the diver falling fastest? How is this shown in the table and graph?

3. Kelsey jumps from a diving board, springing up into the air and then dropping feet-first toward the pool. The distance from her toes to the water's surface in feet t seconds after she leaves the board is $d = {}^{-}16t^2 + 18t + 10$.

a. What is the maximum height of Kelsey's toes during this jump? When does the maximum height occur?

b. When do Kelsey's toes hit the water?

c. What does the constant term 10 in the equation tell you about Kelsey's jump?

In 4–8, tell whether the table represents a quadratic relationship. If the relationship is quadratic, tell whether it has a maximum value or a minimum value.

4.

x	$^{-}3$	$^{-}2$	$^{-}1$	0	1	2	3	4	5
y	$^{-}4$	1	4	5	4	1	$^{-}4$	$^{-}11$	$^{-}18$

5.

x	0	1	2	3	4	5	6	7	8
y	2	3	6	11	18	27	38	51	66

6.

x	0	1	2	3	4	5	6	7	8
y	0	$^-4$	$^-6$	$^-6$	$^-4$	0	6	14	24

7.

x	$^-4$	$^-3$	$^-2$	$^-1$	0	1	2	3	4
y	5	4	3	2	1	2	3	4	5

8.

x	$^-4$	$^-3$	$^-2$	$^-1$	0	1	2	3	4
y	18	10	4	0	$^-2$	$^-2$	0	4	10

9. The distance from the ground of a ball in feet after t seconds can be described by the equation $h = {}^-16t^2 + 48t + 8$.

a. What is the maximum height attained by the ball? Explain how you could use a table and a graph of this relationship to find the answer.

b. When does the ball hit the ground? Explain how you could use a table and a graph to find the answer.

c. Describe the pattern of change in the height of the ball over time. Explain how this pattern would appear in a table and a graph.

d. What does the constant term 8 mean in this context?

10. a. For each equation below, describe the pattern of change in the y value as the x value increases or decreases at a constant rate.

$y = 2x^2$ $\quad$ $y = 3x^2$ $\quad$ $y = \frac{1}{2}x^2$ $\quad$ $y = {}^-2x^2$

b. What relationship do you see between the second difference and the number multiplied by the x^2 term in each equation in part a?

c. Use what you discovered in parts a and b to predict the pattern of change for each of these equations.

$y = 5x^2$ $\quad$ $y = {}^-4x^2$ $\quad$ $y = \frac{1}{4}x^2$ $\quad$ $y = ax^2$

11. A signal flare is fired into the air from a boat. The height of the flare in feet t seconds after it is fired is $h = {}^{-}16t^2 + 160t$.

a. How high will the flare travel? When will it reach this maximum height?

b. When will the flare hit the water?

c. Explain how your answers to parts a and b could be found in a table and a graph of the equation.

In 12–15, do parts a–d.

12. $y = 9 - x^2$

13. $y = 2x^2 - 4x$

14. $y = 6x - x^2$

15. $y = x^2 + 6x + 8$

a. Sketch a graph of the equation.

b. Find the coordinates of the points where the graph crosses the x- and y-axes, and label these points on your graph.

c. Draw and label the line of symmetry.

d. Find the coordinates of the maximum or minimum point, and label this point on your graph.

16. A quadratic relationship between x and y is shown in the graph below.

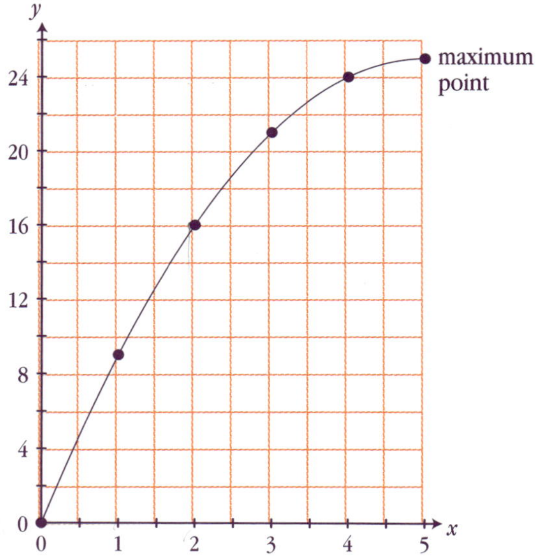

a. Make a table of (x, y) values for the six points shown.

b. Copy the graph, and extend it to show x values from 5 to 10. Explain how you know your graph is correct.

17. A quadratic relationship between x and y is shown in the graph below. Extend the x-axis to show values from $^-5$ to 0. Explain how you know your graph is correct.

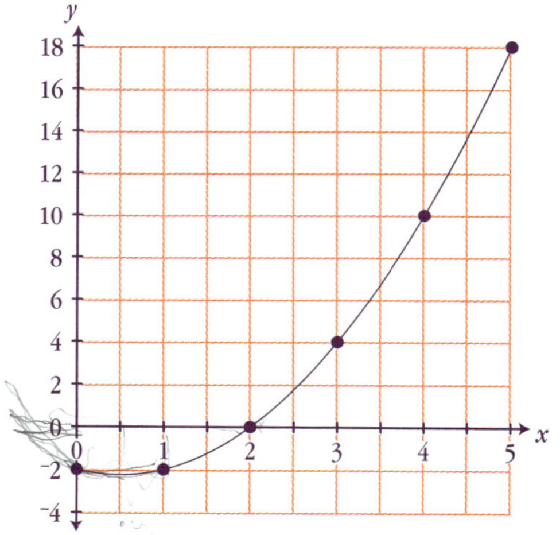

18. **a.** For each equation below, predict the shape of the graph. Give the maximum or minimum point, the x-intercepts, the y-intercepts, and the line of symmetry for each graph. Use a graphing calculator to check your predictions.

$y = x^2$ $\quad$ $y = {}^-x^2$ $\quad$ $y = x^2 + 1$

$y = x^2 - 2$ $\quad$ $y = x(4 - x)$ $\quad$ $y = (x + 2)^2$

b. How can you tell from a quadratic equation whether the graph will have a maximum point or a minimum point?

c. How are the x- and y-intercepts of the graph of a quadratic function related to the equation?

Connections

19. A jeweler has tried to increase her profit by raising and lowering the price of her necklaces. Using past sales data, she has generated two equations relating income, i, to selling price, p:

$i = (100 - p)p$ and $i = 100p - p^2$

a. Are the two equations equivalent? How do you know?

b. Show that $i = 100 - p^2$ is not equivalent to the two original equations.

c. It costs $350 to rent a booth at a local art fair. Assume that the jeweler's profit for the fair will be her income from necklaces minus the cost of the booth. Write an equation for profit, M, as a function of selling price, p.

d. What price would give the maximum profit? What will the profit be for this price?

e. For what prices will there be a profit rather than a loss?

20. Use the table below to answer parts a and b.

x	−1	0	1	2	3	4	5
y	3	5	7	9	11		

a. Describe the pattern in the table, and use the pattern to predict the missing y values.

b. Tell whether the relationship between x and y is linear, exponential, quadratic, or none of these. Explain how you know.

21. Use the table below to answer parts a and b.

x	−1	0	1	2	3	4	5
y	−10	0	8	14	18		

a. Describe the pattern in the table, and use the pattern to predict the missing y values.

b. Tell whether the relationship between x and y is linear, exponential, quadratic, or none of these. Explain how you know.

22. Use the table below to answer parts a and b.

x	0	1	2	3	4	5	6
y	1	3	9	27	81		

a. Describe the pattern in the table, and use the pattern to predict the missing y values.

b. Tell whether the relationship between x and y is linear, exponential, quadratic, or none of these. Explain how you know.

23. Use the table below to answer parts a and b.

x	2	3	4	5	6	7	8
y	$\frac{1}{2}$	$\frac{1}{3}$	$\frac{1}{4}$	$\frac{1}{5}$	$\frac{1}{6}$		

a. Describe the pattern in the table, and use the pattern to predict the missing y values.

b. Tell whether the relationship between x and y is linear, exponential, quadratic, or none of these. Explain how you know.

24. Use the table below to answer parts a and b.

x	-1	0	1	2	3	4	5
y	-5	0	3	4	3		

a. Describe the pattern in the table, and use the pattern to predict the missing y values.

b. Tell whether the relationship between x and y is linear, exponential, quadratic, or none of these. Explain how you know.

Extensions

25. A puzzle involves a strip of seven squares, three pennies, and three nickels. To start, the pennies are placed on the left three squares and the nickels are placed on the right three squares.

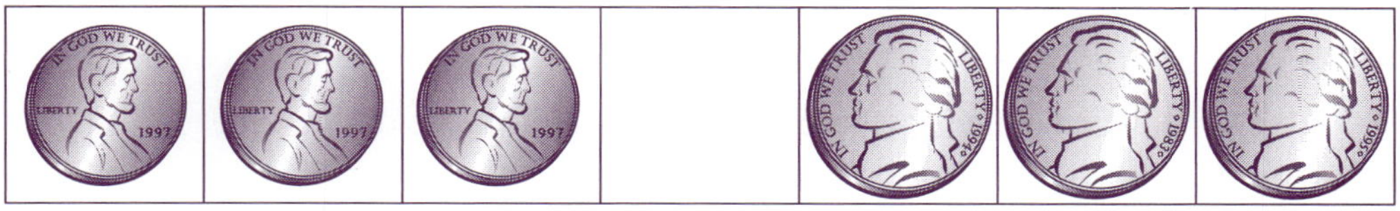

The object of the puzzle is to switch the positions of the coins so that the nickels are on the left and the pennies are on the right. You can move a coin to an empty square by sliding it or by jumping it over one coin. You can move pennies only to the right and nickels only to the left.

You can make variations of this puzzle by using more or fewer coins and longer or shorter strips of squares. Each puzzle should have the same number of each type of coin and one empty square. You will explore these puzzles in parts a and b on the next page.

a. Make drawings that show each move (slide or jump) required to solve puzzles with 1, 2, and 3 coins of each type. How many moves does it take to solve each puzzle?

b. A puzzle with n nickels and n pennies can be solved with $n^2 + 2n$ moves. Use this quadratic expression to calculate the number of moves required to solve puzzles with 1, 2, 3, 4, 5, 6, 7, 8, 9, and 10 of each type of coin. Do the numbers of moves you found for 1, 2, and 3 coins of each type agree with the numbers you found in part a?

c. By calculating first and second differences in the data from part b, verify that the relationship between the number of moves and the number of each type of coin is quadratic.

In 26–28, use the following information: The soccer coach wants to take her team of 20 students to the state capital for a tournament. The travel agent says the trip will cost $125 per student, but the coach thinks this is too expensive. The travel agent suggests that the coach persuade other students to go with the team. For each extra student, the cost per student would be reduced by $1.

26. The trip actually costs the travel agent $75 per student. The remaining money is profit.

a. What will the agent's profit be if only the 20 soccer team members go on the trip?

b. What will the agent's profit be if 25 students go on the trip?

c. What will the agent's profit be if 60 students go?

d. What will the agent's profit be if 80 students go?

27. Let n represent the number of students who go on the trip. In a–d, write an equation for the relationship described. It may help to make a table like the one shown here and look for patterns in the columns.

Number of students	Price per student	Travel agent's income	Travel agent's expenses	Travel agent's profit
20	\$125	$20 \times \$125 = \$2500$	$20 \times \$75 = \$1500$	$\$2500 - \$1500 = \$1000$
21	124			

a. the relationship between the price per student and n

b. the relationship between the travel agent's income and n

c. the relationship between the travel agent's expenses and n

d. the relationship between the travel agent's profit and n

28. Make a table and a graph of the equation for the travel agent's profit. Study the pattern of change in the profit as the number of students increases from 25 to 75.

a. What number of students gives the travel agent the maximum profit?

b. What numbers of students will guarantee that the travel agent will earn a profit?

c. What numbers of students will give the travel agent a profit of at least \$1200?

Mathematical Reflections

In this investigation, you analyzed the relationship between height and time for several situations. You also looked for common features in the tables, graphs, and equations for quadratic relationships. These questions will help you summarize what you have learned:

1. Quadratic functions can be used to model many real-world situations. Describe three situations for which quadratic functions are appropriate models. For each situation, give examples of questions that quadratic representations help to answer.
2. What patterns of change occur in tables of (x, y) values for quadratic functions?
3. What patterns of change occur in graphs of quadratic functions?
4. How can you recognize a quadratic function from its equation?

Think about your answers to these questions, discuss your ideas with other students and your teacher, and then write a summary of your findings in your journal.

INVESTIGATION 5

Painted Cubes

Rubik's® Cube is a puzzle made of smaller cubes joined in the center by a special connector. When you first purchase a Rubik's Cube, each face is a different color: red, orange, green, white, blue, or yellow. The connector in the center allows you to twist the faces of the cube, mixing up the colors. Once you rearrange the colors, returning the puzzle to its original state can be very challenging.

Think about this!

The small cubes that make up Rubik's Cube are colored only on their exposed faces.

How many of the small cubes are colored on only one face? How many are colored on two faces? On three faces? On four faces? On five faces? On six faces?

5.1 Analyzing Cube Puzzles

As his midterm math project, Leon invented a puzzle. He made a large cube from 1000 centimeter cubes and then painted the faces of the large cube. When the paint dried, he separated the puzzle into the original centimeter cubes. The object of Leon's puzzle is to reassemble the cubes so that no unpainted faces are showing.

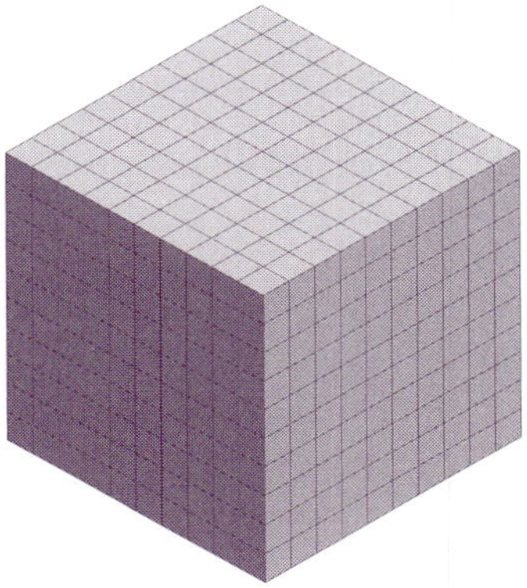

When Leon examined the centimeter cubes, he noticed that some were painted on only one face, some on two faces, and some on three faces. Many of the cubes weren't painted at all.

Problem 5.1

In this problem, you will investigate puzzles similar to Leon's.

A. 1. A cube with edges of length 2 centimeters is built from centimeter cubes. If you paint the faces of this cube and then break it into centimeter cubes, how many cubes will be painted on three faces? How many will be painted on two faces? On one face? How many will be unpainted?

2. Answer the questions from part 1 for cubes with edges of lengths 3, 4, 5, and 6 centimeters.

Organize your data into a table like the one below.

Edge length of large cube	Number of cm cubes	Number of centimeter cubes painted on 3 faces	2 faces	1 face	0 faces
2					
3					
4					
5					
6					

B. Study the patterns in the table. Look for a relationship between the edge length of the large cube and the number of centimeter cubes. Tell whether the pattern of change is linear, quadratic, exponential, or none of these.

C. Look for relationships between the edge length of the large cube and the number of centimeter cubes painted on three faces, two faces, one face, and zero faces. Describe each relationship you find, and tell whether the pattern of change is linear, quadratic, exponential, or none of these.

Problem 5.1 Follow-Up

1. a. Use the patterns you discovered in the problem to extend your table to include data for cubes with edges of lengths 7, 8, and 9 centimeters.

b. Make a graph of the data for each of the five relationships in the table.

2. What strategy would you use to reassemble the centimeter cubes to form the large cube so that no unpainted faces are showing?

5.2 Exploring Painted-Cube Patterns

In Problem 5.1, you discovered interesting relationships between the edge length of the large cube and the number of centimeter cubes painted on zero, one, two, or three faces. In this problem, you will write equations to generalize these relationships.

Problem 5.2

A large cube with edges of length n centimeters is built from centimeter cubes. The faces of the large cube are painted.

A. Write an equation for the number of centimeter cubes in the large cube.

B. Write an equation for the number of centimeter cubes painted on

1. three faces
2. two faces
3. one face
4. no faces

Problem 5.2 Follow-Up

1. a. Graph each of the five equations you wrote in Problem 5.2 on your calculator. Use the window settings shown. Make one graph at a time, and copy each onto your paper.

```
WINDOW
 XMIN=⁻10
 XMAX=10
 XSCL=1
 YMIN=⁻220
 YMAX=220
 YSCL=20
```

b. How do the graphs you made in part a compare to those you made in Problem 5.1 Follow-Up?

2. a. What is the relationship between the surface area, S, and the edge length, n, of the large cube? Write an equation for this relationship.

b. For a cube with edge length n, use the equations you wrote in parts 1–3 of part B to help you write an equation for the relationship between the total number of painted faces, T, and n.

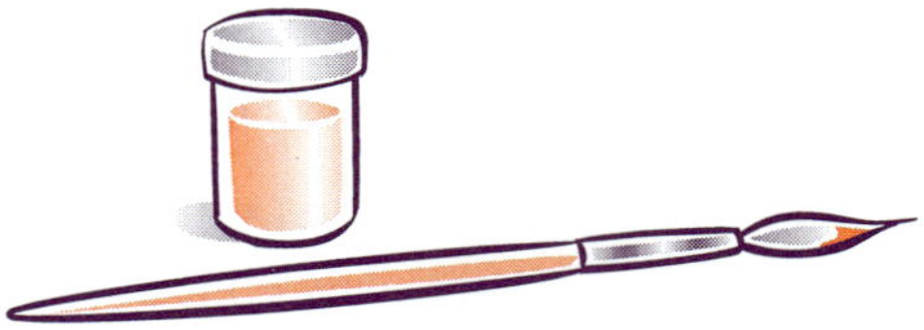

c. What is the relationship between the surface area, S, and the total number of painted faces, T? Write an equation for this relationship.

3. a. Copy and complete the tables below.

x	x
1	1
2	
3	
4	
5	

x	x^2
1	1
2	
3	
4	
5	

x	x^3
1	1
2	
3	
4	
5	

b. For each table, describe the pattern of change in the second column.

c. Compare the patterns in these tables to the patterns in your table for the painted cubes. Match each table above with a column of the painted-cube table that shows a similar pattern of change, and explain how the two patterns are similar.

4. Compare the functions below with the functions represented by the tables in question 3. Match each equation with the table that shows a similar pattern of change, and explain how the two patterns are similar.

$$y = 2x \qquad y = x^3 - 2 \qquad y = (x - 1)^2$$

As you work on these ACE questions, use your calculator whenever you need it.

Applications

1. A large cube with edges of length 12 centimeters is built from centimeter cubes. The faces of the large cube are painted.

a. How many of the centimeter cubes are painted on three faces?

b. How many of the centimeter cubes are painted on two faces?

c. How many of the centimeter cubes are painted on one face?

d. How many of the centimeter cubes are unpainted?

2. A large cube is built from centimeter cubes. The faces of the large cube are painted. Of the centimeter cubes, 1000 are unpainted.

a. What is the length of an edge of the large cube?

b. How many of the centimeter cubes are painted on one face?

c. How many of the centimeter cubes are painted on two faces?

d. How many of the centimeter cubes are painted on three faces?

3. A large cube is built from centimeter cubes. The faces of the large cube are painted. Of the centimeter cubes, 864 are painted on one face.

a. What is the length of an edge of the large cube?

b. How many of the centimeter cubes are unpainted?

c. How many of the centimeter cubes are painted on two faces?

d. How many of the centimeter cubes are painted on three faces?

4. A large cube is built from centimeter cubes. The faces of the large cube are painted. Of the centimeter cubes, 132 are painted on two faces.

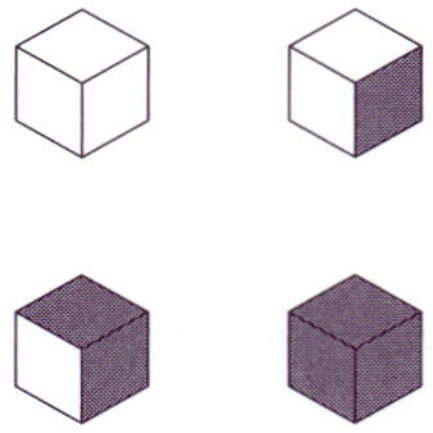

a. What is the length of an edge of the large cube?

b. How many of the centimeter cubes are unpainted?

c. How many of the centimeter cubes are painted on one face?

d. How many of the centimeter cubes are painted on three faces?

5. A large cube is built from centimeter cubes. The faces of the large cube are painted. Of the centimeter cubes, 8 are painted on three faces.

a. What is the length of an edge of the large cube?

b. How many of the centimeter cubes are unpainted?

c. How many of the centimeter cubes are painted on one face?

d. How many of the centimeter cubes are painted on two faces?

6. A large cube with edges of length n centimeters is built from centimeter cubes. The faces of the large cube are painted.

a. How many centimeter cubes were used to build the large cube?

b. If 125 centimeter cubes were used, what is the value of n?

c. If 343 of the centimeter cubes are unpainted, what is the value of n?

d. If 120 of the centimeter cubes are painted on two faces, what is the value of n?

e. If 486 of the centimeter cubes are painted on one face, what is the value of n?

7. The Tarheel Tile Company manufactures floor tiles with grid patterns based on this rule: corner squares are purple, edge squares that are not corners are gold, and inside squares are white. The illustration shows this pattern for a 4-by-4 grid.

a. If the same design rule is applied to a 5-by-5 grid, how many small squares will be purple? How many will be gold? How many will be white?

b. If the same design rule is applied to a 10-by-10 grid, how many small squares will be purple? How many will be gold? How many will be white?

c. If the same design rule is applied to a n-by-n grid, how many small squares will be purple? How many will be gold? How many will be white?

d. Tell whether each relationship described in part c is linear, quadratic, exponential, or none of these.

8. The block pictured is made from centimeter cubes and then painted.

a. How many of the centimeter cubes are painted on three faces?

b. How many of the centimeter cubes are painted on two faces?

c. How many of the centimeter cubes are painted on one face?

d. How many of the centimeter cubes are unpainted?

e. How many centimeter cubes does the block contain?

9. A cube has edges of length x centimeters.

a. Write an equation for the volume, V, of the cube in terms of x.

b. If the length of each edge were doubled, how would the volume change?

c. If the length of each edge were tripled, how would the volume change?

10. a. Copy and complete the table below.

Cube Data

Edge length (cm)	Surface area (cm^2)	Volume (cm^3)
0		
1		
2		
3		
4		
5		
6		
7		
8		
9		
10		
11		
12		

b. Sketch a graph of the relationship between edge length and surface area.

c. Sketch a graph of the relationship between edge length and volume.

d. Does the relationship between edge length and surface area appear to be linear, quadratic, exponential, or none of these? Explain your answer.

e. Does the relationship between edge length and volume appear to be linear, quadratic, exponential, or none of these? Explain your answer.

Connections

11. Some egg producers send eggs to supermarkets in 12-by-12-by-12 blocks.

a. How many eggs are in one layer of a block?

b. What is the total number of eggs in a block?

c. What is the total number of eggs in a truckload 4 blocks wide, 4 blocks high, and 10 blocks long?

d. Write an expression for the total number of eggs in a truckload n blocks long, m blocks wide, and 4 blocks high.

12. A square has sides of length x meters.

a. Write equations for the area, A, and perimeter, P, of the square in terms of x.

b. If the length of each side were doubled, how would the area change? How would the perimeter change?

c. If the length of each side were tripled, how would the area change? How would the perimeter change?

d. If the area of a square is 36 square meters, what is its perimeter?

13. **a.** Make a table showing the side length, perimeter, and area for squares with integer side lengths from 0 centimeters to 12 centimeters.

b. Make a graph of the relationship between side length and perimeter for squares with side lengths from 0 centimeters to 12 centimeters.

c. Make a graph of the relationship between side length and area for squares with side lengths from 0 centimeters to 12 centimeters.

d. Does the relationship between side length and perimeter appear to be linear, quadratic, exponential, or none of these? Explain your answer.

e. Does the relationship between side length and area appear to be linear, quadratic, exponential, or none of these? Explain your answer.

In 14–17, do parts a–e.

14.

x	y
0	25
1	50
2	100
3	200
4	400
5	

15.

x	y
$^-3$	3
$^-2$	6
$^-1$	9
0	12
1	15
2	

16.

x	y
2	6
3	12
4	20
5	30
6	42
7	

17.

x	y
$^-2$	21
$^-1$	24
0	25
1	24
2	21
3	

a. Describe the pattern of change in the table, and use the pattern to predict the missing entry.

b. Match the table with one of these equations.

$y = x^2 - 12$ $\quad$ $y = 3x$ $\quad$ $y = x(x + 1)$

$y = 25 - x^2$ $\quad$ $y = (x)(x)(x)$ $\quad$ $y = 3(x + 4)$

$y = 25(2^x)$

c. Does the table represent a quadratic relationship? How did you decide?

d. Does the relationship represented in the table have a maximum value?

e. Does the relationship have a minimum value?

In 18–21, tell whether the graph represents a quadratic relationship, and explain your reasoning. For those graphs that represent quadratic relationships, use a calculator to find an equation that matches the graph reasonably well. Record your equation and the window settings you used.

18.

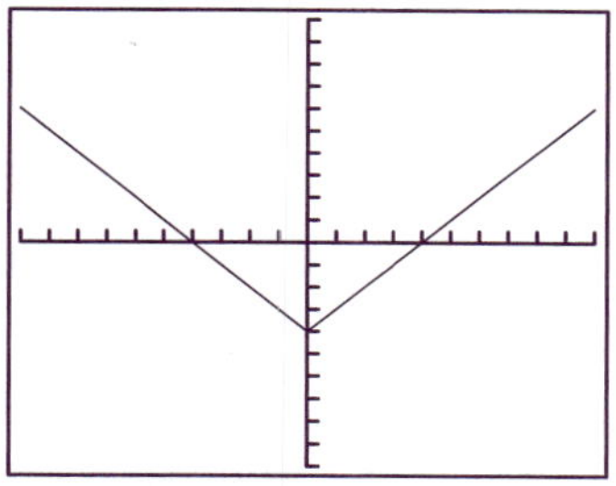

19.

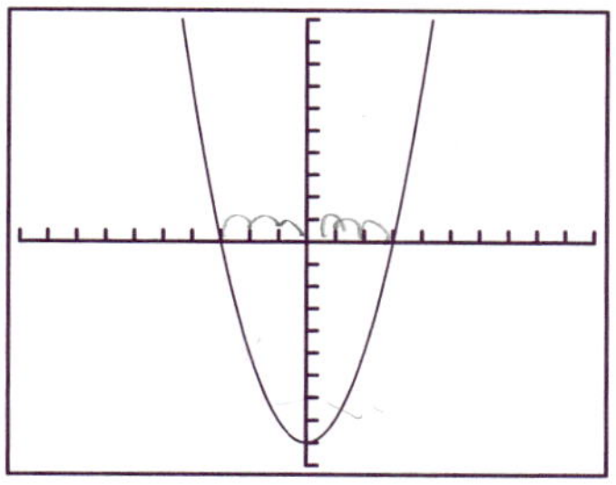

20.

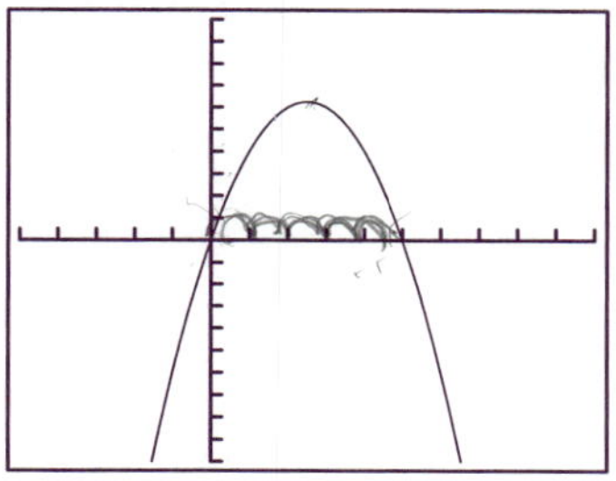

21.

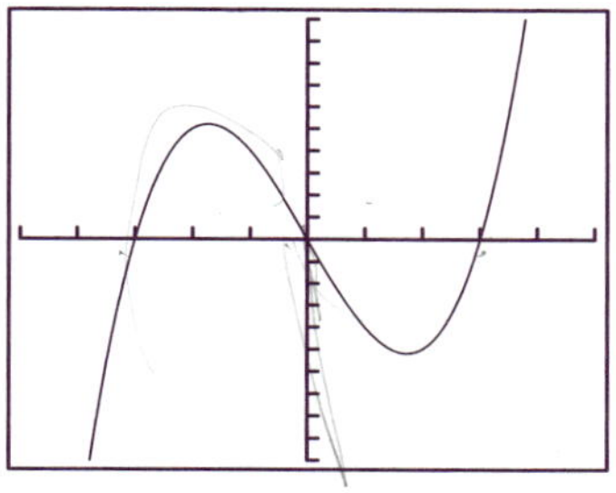

Extensions

22. Make a table of values and a graph for each function below. Include x values from $^-10$ to 10. Describe the patterns you observe.

$y = x$ $\quad$ $y = x^2$ $\quad$ $y = x^3$

$y = x^4$ $\quad$ $y = x^5$ $\quad$ $y = x^6$

23. Do parts a and b for each equation below.

$y = x + 1$ $\qquad$ $y = (x + 1)(x + 2)$

$y = (x + 1)(x + 2)(x + 3)$ $\qquad$ $y = (x + 1)(x + 2)(x + 3)(x + 4)$

a. Make a graph of the equation. Describe the shape of the graph, including important features.

b. Make a table of (x, y) values for the equation. Describe the pattern of change in the table.

24. A shell of white centimeter cubes is built around a large purple cube.

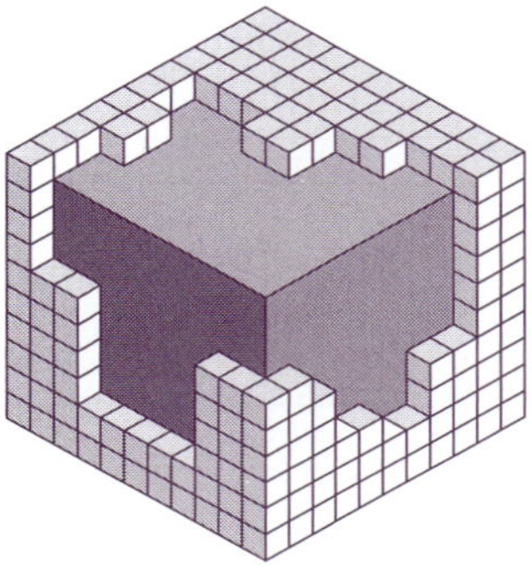

a. How many white cubes are needed if the purple cube has edges of length 2 centimeters? Explain.

b. How many white cubes are needed if the purple cube has edges of length 7 centimeters? Explain.

c. Write an equation for calculating the number of white cubes, W, needed to cover a purple cube with edges of length n centimeters.

d. Make a table and a graph of your equation for n values from 0 to 12.

e. If the white shell contains 218 cubes, what is the edge length of the purple cube?

f. If the white shell contains 602 cubes, what is the edge length of the purple cube?

25. Centimeter cubes are stacked in the following pattern.

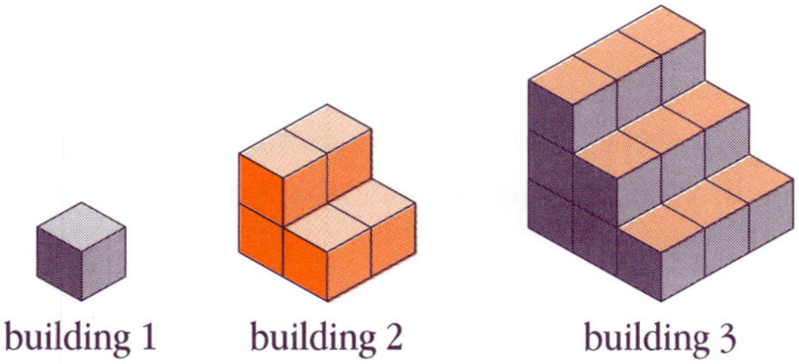

a. How many cubes will be in building 4? How many cubes will be in building 5?

b. Write an equation for the relationship between the building number and the number of cubes in the building.

c. Is the relationship between the building number and the number of cubes quadratic? Explain.

Mathematical Reflections

In this investigation, you explored the relationships involved in cube puzzles. These questions will help you summarize what you have learned:

1. **a.** Which of the relationships involved in the cube puzzles are linear?

   b. What common patterns occur in tables, graphs, and equations for linear relationships?

2. **a.** Which of the relationships involved in the cube puzzles are quadratic?

   b. What common patterns occur in tables, graphs, and equations for quadratic relationships?

3. **a.** Which of the relationships involved in the cube puzzles are neither linear nor quadratic?

   b. What are some patterns you observed in tables, graphs, and equations for these relationships?

Think about your answers to these questions, discuss your ideas with other students and your teacher, and then write a summary of your findings in your journal.

Looking Back and Looking Ahead

Unit Reflections

The problems of this unit focused on quadratic relationships between variables. You learned how to recognize *quadratic patterns* in graphs and tables and how to write *equations* and *formulas* to represent those patterns. You learned how to use quadratic relations to answer questions by *solving equations* and by finding *maximum points* and *minimum points* of quadratic tables and graphs. You also reviewed properties of linear relationships and began exploring *cubic relationships*.

Using Your Algebraic Reasoning—Test your understanding and skill in work with quadratic relationships by considering the following questions about events at a traveling carnival.

1. *Chris decided to try the "Show Your Strength" game at the carnival. The object of the game is to hit the end of a lever as hard as possible with a sledgehammer. The hammer blow propels a weight upward in a tall shaft. If the weight reaches the top of the shaft, a bell sounds and lights flash to show that there is a winner.*

   The "Show Your Strength" game is designed so that when the lever is hit, the height of the weight (in feet) after t *seconds is given by a quadratic equation in form* $h = -16t^2 + bt$. *The value of* b *in the equation depends on how hard the hammer hits the lever.*

   a. Sketch the general shape of graphs that can be expected for the relation between time and height for any attempt at the "Show Your Strength" game.

   b. Would Table 1 or Table 2 be the better match for the (time, height) data from an attempt at the "Show Your

Strength" game when the weight rose to a height of 9 feet and fell back to the ground in 1.5 seconds?

Table 1

Time in seconds	0.0	0.25	0.5	0.75	1.0	1.25	1.5
Height in feet	0	5	8	9	8	5	0

Table 2

Time in seconds	0.0	0.25	0.5	0.75	1.0	1.25	1.5
Height in feet	0	3	6	9	6	3	0

2 *Chris's hit was hard enough for the weight to reach the top of the shaft and win him a prize. The force gauge on the lever showed that the (time, height) equation for Chris's hit was* $h = -16t^2 + 32t$.

a. How high did the weight go as a result of Chris's hit?

b. How long did it take the weight to rise to the top of the shaft and then fall to its starting position?

c. When was the weight 12 feet above the ground?

3 *The carnival has pony rides for young children. The rides are inside a rectangular fenced region with a perimeter of 180 feet. At different sites, the fence for the pony rides is arranged in different length-and-width patterns.*

a. If the length of the pony corral at a carnival site is x feet, what expression represents the width in terms of x?

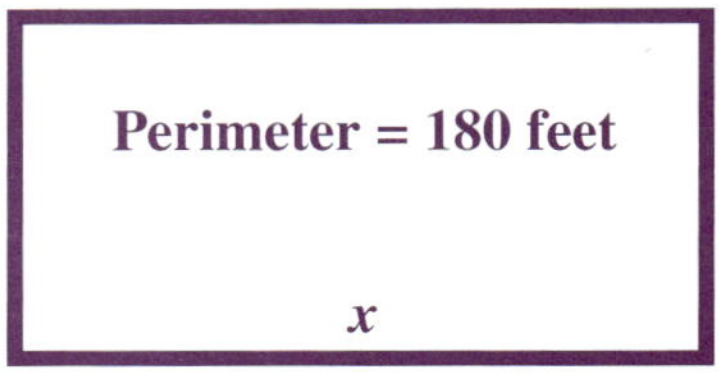

b. Write an equation that shows how the corral area, A, is related to length x.

c. What length and width measurements will give a corral area of 2000 square feet? Write and solve an equation in x whose solution gives the needed length.

d. What length and width measurements will give maximum corral area? Justify your answer by explaining how you could study a table or graph of the area function to find this maximum value.

Explaining Your Reasoning—To answer the questions in Problems 1–3, you had to use your knowledge of quadratic functions and of the table patterns, graphs, and formulas that arise in different quadratic situations.

1. What patterns would you expect for a quadratic function

a. in tables of (x, y) value pairs?

b. in graphs of (x, y) value pairs?

c. in equations relating x and y?

2. How are the equations, tables, and graphs for quadratic relations different from those for

a. linear relations?

b. exponential relations?

3. For a quadratic relation in the form $y = ax^2 + bx + c$, how can you tell whether the graph will have a maximum or minimum point?

4. What strategies can be used to solve quadratic equations such as $3x^2 - 5x + 3 = 0$ and $x^2 + 4x = 7$ using

a. tables of values of a quadratic function?

b. graphs of a quadratic function?

Quadratic functions are models for several important relationships between variables. They are also among the simpler examples of nonlinear patterns. You will encounter quadratic functions in future *Connected Mathematics* units and mathematics and science courses.

Glossary

constant term A number in an algebraic expression that is not multiplied by a variable. In the expanded form of a quadratic expression, the constant term is the number that is added. The constant term in the expression $^-16t^2 + 64t + 7$ is 7, and the constant term in the expression $x^2 - 4$ is $^-4$.

expanded form The form of an expression composed of sums or differences of terms rather than products of factors. The expressions $x^2 + 7x + 12$ and $x^2 + 2x$ are in expanded form.

factored form The form of an expression composed of products of factors rather than sums or differences of terms. The expressions $(x + 3)(x + 4)$ and $x(x - 2)$ are in factored form.

function A relationship between two variables in which the value of one variable depends on the value of the other variable. The relationship between length and area for rectangles with a fixed perimeter can be thought of as a function, where the area of the rectangle depends on, or is a *function of,* the length. If the variable y is a function of the variable x, then there is exactly one y value for every x value.

like terms Terms with the same variable raised to the same exponent. In the expression $4x^2 + 3x - 2x^2 - 2x + 1$, $3x$ and ^-2x are like terms and $4x^2$ and $^-2x^2$ are like terms.

line of symmetry A line that divides a graph or drawing into two halves that are mirror images of each other.

linear term A part of an algebraic expression in which the variable is raised to the first power, especially in the expanded form of an expression. In the expression $4x^2 + 3x - 2x^2 - 2x + 1$, $3x$ and ^-2x are linear terms.

maximum value The greatest y value of a function. If y is the height of a thrown object, then the maximum value of the height, or simply the maximum height, is the greatest height the object reaches. If you throw a ball into the air, its height increases until it reaches the maximum height, and then its height decreases as it falls back to the ground. If y is the area of a rectangle with a fixed perimeter, then the maximum value of the area, or simply the maximum area, is the greatest area possible for a rectangle with that perimeter. In this unit, you found that the maximum area for a rectangle with a perimeter of 20 meters is 25 square meters.

minimum value The smallest y value of a function. If y is the cost of an item, then the minimum value of the cost, or simply the minimum cost, is the least cost possible for that item.

parabola The graph of a quadratic function. A parabola has a line of symmetry that passes through the maximum point if the graph opens downward or through the minimum point if the graph opens upward.

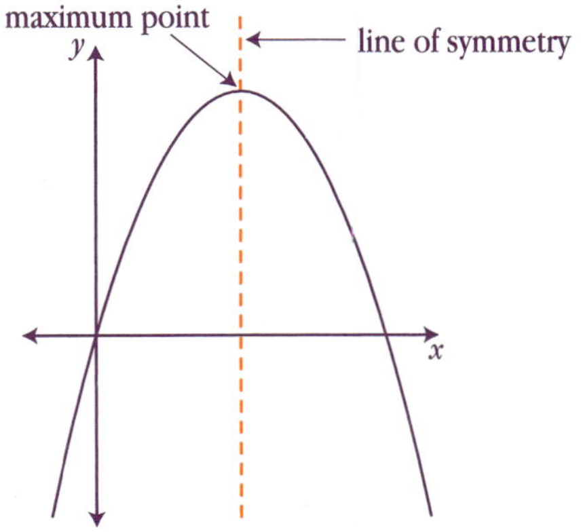

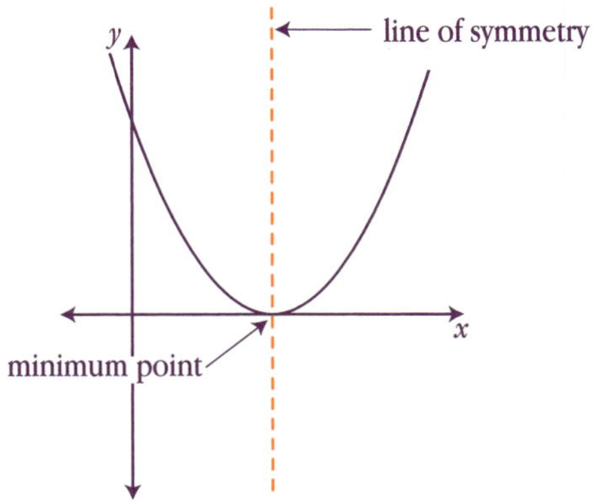

quadratic expression In expanded form, an expression with quadratic terms and possibly constant or linear terms as well. In factored form, a quadratic expression has two linear factors. The quadratic expression $x^2 - 2x$ is in expanded form. The equivalent expression in factored form is $x(x - 2)$. Quadratic expressions are often used to describe situations in two dimensions, such as area.

quadratic term A part of an algebraic expression in which the variable is raised to the second power, especially in the expanded form of an expression. In the expression $4x^2 + 3x - 2x^2 - 2x + 1$, $4x^2$ and $^-2x^2$ are quadratic terms.

term An expression with numbers and/or variables multiplied together. In the expression $3x^2 - 2x + 10$, $3x^2$, ^-2x, and 10 are terms.

triangular number A quantity that can be arranged in a triangular pattern. The first four triangular numbers are 1, 3, 6, and 10.

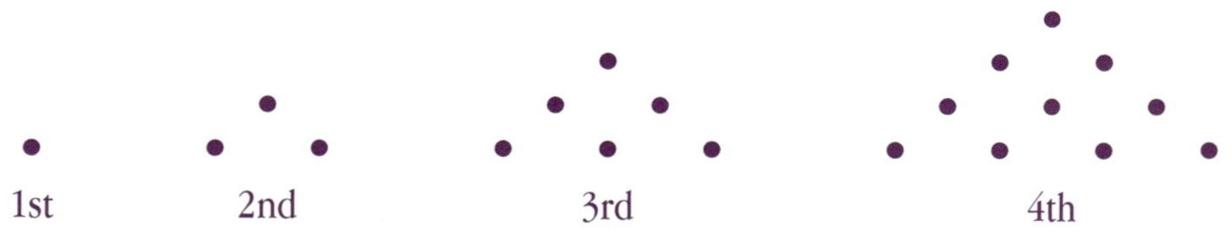

Glosario

eje de simetría Una línea que divide una gráfica o un dibujo en dos mitades que son imágenes especulares entre sí.

expresión cuadrática En la forma desarrollada, una expresión con términos cuadráticos y también posibles términos constantes o lineales. En la forma de factores, una expresión cuadrática tiene dos factores lineales. La expresión cuadrática $x^2 - 2x$ está representada en forma desarrollada. La expresión equivalente expresada en forma de factores es $x(x - 2)$. Las expresiones cuadráticas a menudo se usan para describir situaciones en dos dimensiones, como el área.

forma desarrollada La forma de una expresión compuesta de sumas o diferencias de términos en vez de productos de factores. Las expresiones $x^2 + 7x + 12$ y $x^2 + 2x$ están representadas en forma desarrollada.

forma de factores La forma de una expresión compuesta de productos de factores en vez de sumas o diferencias de términos. Las expresiones $(x + 3)(x + 4)$ y $x(x - 2)$ están representadas en forma de factores.

función Una relación entre dos variables en la cual el valor de un variable depende del valor de la otra variable. La relación entre la longitud y el área para rectángulos con un perímetro fijo puede considerarse como una función, donde el área del rectángulo depende de la longitud, o es una *función de* ésta. Si la variable y es una función de la variable x, entonces hay exactamente un valor de y para cada valor de x.

número triangular Una cantidad que puede disponerse en un patrón triangular. Los cuatro primeros números triangulares son 1, 3, 6 y 10.

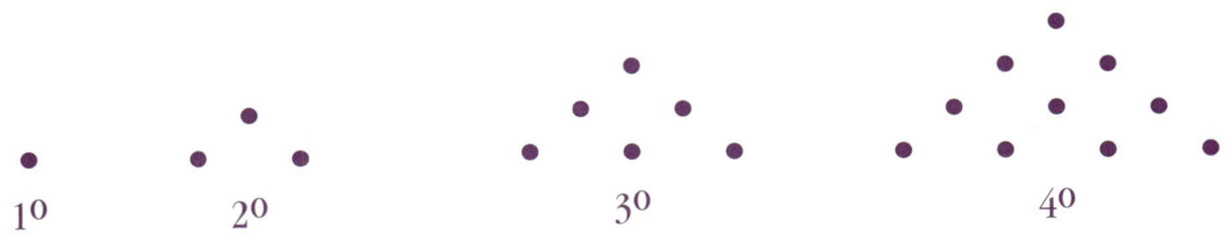

parábola La gráfica de una función cuadrática. Una parábola tiene un eje de simetría que pasa por el punto máximo si la gráfica se abre hacia abajo o por el punto mínimo si la gráfica se abre hacia arriba.

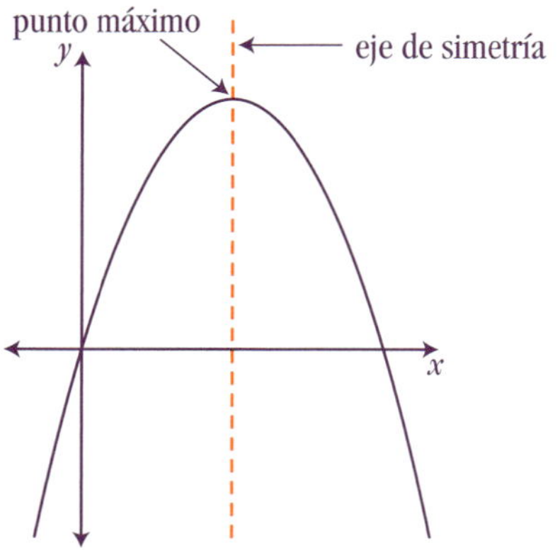

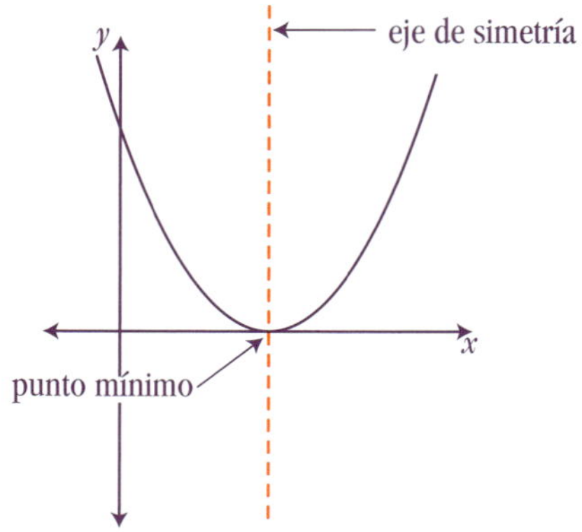

término Una expresión con números y/o variables multiplicados entre sí. En la expresión $3x^2 - 2x + 10$, $3x^2$, ^-2x y 10 son términos.

término constante Un número en una expresión algebraica que no está multiplicado por una variable. En la forma desarrollada de una expresión cuadrática, el término constante es el número que se agrega. El término constante en la expresión $^-16t^2 + 64t + 7$ es 7, y el término constante en la expresión $x^2 - 4$ es $^-4$.

término cuadrático Una parte de una expresión algebraica en la que la variable está elevada a la segunda potencia, especialmente en la forma desarrollada de una expresión. En la expresión $4x^2 + 3x - 2x^2 - 2x + 1$, $4x^2$ y $^-2x^2$ son términos cuadráticos.

término lineal Una parte de una expresión algebraica en la que la variable está elevada a la primera potencia, especialmente en la forma desarrollada de una expresión. En la expresión $4x^2 + 3x - 2x^2 - 2x + 1$, $3x$ y $^{-}2x$ son términos lineales.

términos semejantes Términos con la misma variable elevada al mismo exponente. En la expresión $4x^2 + 3x - 2x^2 - 2x + 1$, $3x$ y $^{-}2x$ son términos semejantes y $4x^2$ y $^{-}2x^2$ son términos semejantes.

valor máximo El mayor valor de y en una función. Si y es la altura de un objeto lanzado, entonces el valor máximo de la altura, o simplemente la altura máxima, es la altura mayor que alcanza el objeto. Si lanzas una pelota al aire, su altura aumenta hasta que alcanza la altura máxima, y luego su altura disminuye a medida que vuelve a caer hacia la tierra. Si y es el área de un rectángulo con un perímetro fijo, entonces el valor máximo del área, o simplemente el área máxima, es la mayor área posible para un rectángulo con ese perímetro. En esta unidad, encontraste que el área máxima para un rectángulo con un perímetro de 20 metros es 25 metros cuadrados.

valor mínimo El valor más pequeño de y en una función. Si y es el costo de un artículo, entonces el valor mínimo del costo, o simplemente el costo mínimo, es el menor costo posible para ese artículo.

Index

Connected Mathematics™

Say It with Symbols

Algebraic Reasoning

Student Edition

Glenda Lappan
James T. Fey
William M. Fitzgerald
Susan N. Friel
Elizabeth Difanis Phillips

PEARSON
Prentice Hall

Glenview, Illinois
Needham, Massachusetts
Upper Saddle River, New Jersey

Say It with Symbols

Connected Mathematics™ was developed at Michigan State University with the support of National Science Foundation Grant No. MDR 9150217.

This project was supported, in part,
by the
National Science Foundation
Opinions expressed are those of the authors
and not necessarily those of the Foundation

The Michigan State University authors and administration have agreed that all MSU royalties arising from this publication will be devoted to purposes supported by the Department of Mathematics and the MSU Mathematics Education Enrichment Fund.

Photo Acknowledgements: 6 © Mike Valeri/FPG International; 7 © Jeff Greenberg/Peter Arnold, Inc.; 11 © Medford Taylor/Superstock, Inc.; 14 © Mike Greenlar/The Image Works; 17 © Superstock; 24 © Gale Zucker/Stock, Boston; 29 © Cathlyn Melloan/Tony Stone Images; 41 © Elizabeth Crews/The Image Works; 48 © Peter Menzel/Stock, Boston

Contents

Say It with Symbols

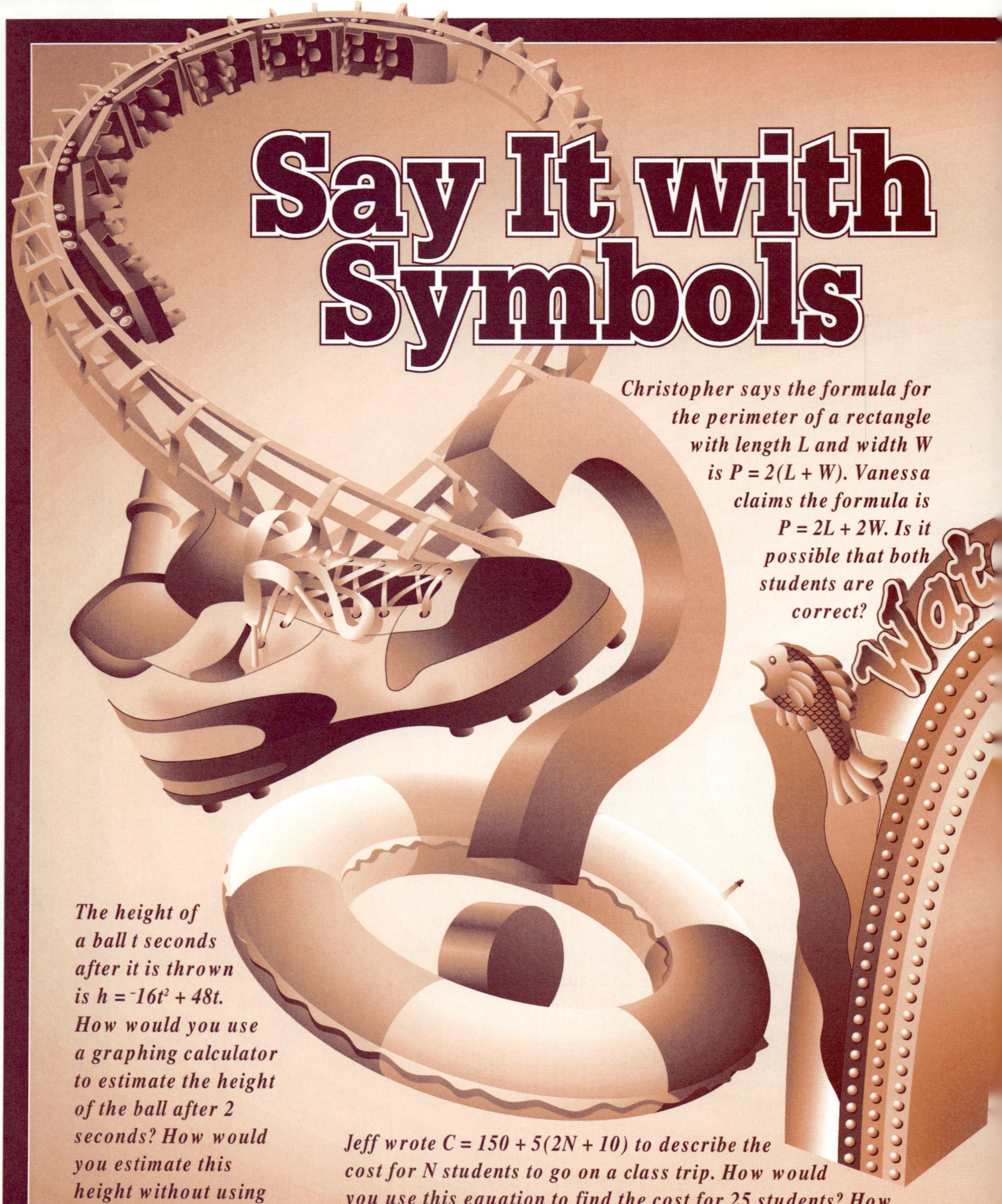

Christopher says the formula for the perimeter of a rectangle with length L and width W is $P = 2(L + W)$. Vanessa claims the formula is $P = 2L + 2W$. Is it possible that both students are correct?

The height of a ball t seconds after it is thrown is $h = ^{-}16t^2 + 48t$. How would you use a graphing calculator to estimate the height of the ball after 2 seconds? How would you estimate this height without using a calculator?

Jeff wrote $C = 150 + 5(2N + 10)$ to describe the cost for N students to go on a class trip. How would you use this equation to find the cost for 25 students? How would you write an equation for the average cost per student?

You have used many powerful tools, including graphs, tables, and equations, to represent relationships among variables. Graphs allow you to see the shape of a relationship and help you identify intercepts and maximum and minimum points. Tables help you to observe patterns of change in the values of the variables. Equations offer an efficient way to generalize relationships.

In this unit, you will concentrate on symbolic expressions and equations. You will learn about the rules mathematicians have established for evaluating expressions. You will see that different ways of reasoning about a situation can lead to different, but equivalent, expressions. You will use mathematical properties to rewrite expressions, and you may discover that an equivalent expression gives you an entirely new way of thinking about a problem. And, you will learn new ways to solve equations. As you work through the investigations, you will solve problems like those on the previous page.

Mathematical Highlights

In *Say It With Symbols* you will extend your ability to use symbolic expressions to describe and reason about relations between variables. The unit should help you to

- Use *order of operations* rules to write and evaluate algebraic expressions and equations that model quantitative patterns and relationships;
- Interpret given symbolic expressions to discover the relations between variables that are implied by those expressions;
- Understand and apply properties of numbers and operations to write algebraic expressions and equations in equivalent forms; and
- Solve linear and quadratic equations by symbolic reasoning.

As you work on the problems of this unit, make it a habit to ask questions about problem situations that involve symbolic expressions and equations: *What symbolic expression or equation correctly expresses the sequence of calculations required by given conditions? Is there a way that a given expression or equation can be written in equivalent form to provide new information about a relationship? What operations would transform a given equation into an equivalent form from which the solution will be clear?*

INVESTIGATION 1

Order of Operations

Equations are an efficient way to communicate information about relationships among variables. To help us communicate clearly, mathematicians have established rules for writing and interpreting algebraic expressions. In this investigation, you will explore these rules.

Think about this!

The rugby club wants to order new jerseys. The jersey manufacturer tells the club members that they can figure out the total cost by using the equation

$$C = 100 + 15N$$

where C is the cost in dollars and N is the number of jerseys ordered. The team wants 20 jerseys. Pedro and David both calculate the amount the club will owe.

Pedro's calculation

$$\begin{aligned} C &= 100 + 15 \times 20 \\ &= 100 + 300 \\ &= 400 \end{aligned}$$

David's calculation

$$\begin{aligned} C &= 100 + 15 \times 20 \\ &= 115 \times 20 \\ &= 2300 \end{aligned}$$

Who did the calculation correctly? What mistake did the other boy make?

1.1 Adding and Multiplying

The Water Works amusement park features exciting water rides and slides. The park discounts admission prices for large groups. Group prices are determined by using the equation $p = 100 + 10a + 8c$, where p is the price in dollars, a is the number of adults, and c is the number of children.

Problem 1.1

As part of an advertising brochure, the Water Works marketing manager wants to include a table showing admission prices for groups with certain numbers of adults and children.

Group Admission Prices

		Number of children				
		20	40	60	80	100
Number of adults	10					
	20					
	30					
	40					

A. Copy and complete the table to show admission prices for groups with various numbers of adults and children. Do your calculations without using a calculator.

B. Look for patterns in the rows and columns of the table. Describe each pattern you find, and tell which part of the equation creates the pattern.

C. In the equation $p = 100 + 10a + 8c$, what do the numbers 100, 10, and 8 tell you about calculating the group price?

D. What mathematical operations do you need to perform to calculate the group price for a particular number of adults and children? In what order must you perform the operations?

Problem 1.1 Follow-Up

The Water Works business manager used data collected over the past several years to write equations that help him make predictions about the daily operations of the park.

1. The daily profit in dollars, P, from the park concession stands depends on the number of visitors, V. The business manager wrote the equation $P = 2.50V - 500$ to model this relationship.

a. If 300 people visit the park, about how much concession profit will be made? Do your calculations without using a calculator.

b. If 600 people visit the park, about how much concession profit will be made? Do your calculations without using a calculator.

c. What mathematical operations did you perform to calculate your answers in parts a and b? In what order did you perform the operations?

d. Check your answer from part a by entering $2.5 \times 300 - 500$ on a graphing calculator and pressing ENTER. Check your answer for part b by entering $2.5 \times 600 - 500$ and pressing ENTER. Do the results agree with the results you found by doing the calculations by hand?

2. The manager uses the equation $V = 600 - 500R$ to predict the number of visitors based on the probability of rain, R.

a. If the probability of rain is 25%, about how many people will visit the park? Do your calculations without using a calculator.

b. If the probability of rain is 75%, about how many people will visit the park? Do your calculations without using a calculator.

c. What mathematical operations did you perform to calculate your answers in parts a and b? In what order did you perform the operations?

d. Use a graphing calculator to check your answers from parts a and b. Do the results agree with the results you found by doing the calculations by hand?

3. Use the equations from questions 1 and 2 to answer these questions.

a. If the probability of rain is 50%, about how much profit will be made from the concession stands?

b. If the probability of rain is 10%, about how much profit will be made from the concession stands?

c. What mathematical operations did you perform to calculate your answers in parts a and b? In what order did you perform the operations?

4. You can combine the equations from questions 1 and 2 into a single equation. Since $V = 600 - 500R$, you can substitute the expression $600 - 500R$ for V in the equation $P = 2.50V - 500$. This gives the equation $P = 2.50(600 - 500R) - 500$, which tells you the expected concession profit in terms of the probability of rain. The parentheses indicate that you should evaluate $600 - 500R$ *before* multiplying by 2.50.

a. Use this equation to find the expected concession profit if the probability of rain is 50% and if the probability of rain is 10%. Check both results with your calculator.

b. How do your answers compare with the results you found in parts a and b of question 3?

5. The equations used by the Water Works business manager involve addition, subtraction, and multiplication. When you evaluate expressions with these operations, in what order should you perform the operations? For example, what steps would you follow to evaluate $40 - 5x + 7y$ when $x = 3$ and $y = 5$?

1.2 Dividing

As with division of numbers, division of algebraic expressions is often shown as a fraction. In the last problem, you saw that the daily concession profit at Water Works can be predicted by the equation $P = 2.50V - 500$. The business manager used this profit equation to derive the following equation for the average daily concession profit per visitor:

$$A = \frac{2.50V - 500}{V}$$

Problem 1.2

A. **1.** If 300 people visit the park, about how much concession profit will be made?

2. About how much concession profit will be made per visitor?

B. Copy and complete the table below to show the average per-visitor concession profit for various numbers of visitors. Do your calculations without using your calculator.

Visitors	100	200	300	400	500	600	700	800
Average profit								

C. Find the average per-visitor concession profit for 250, 350, and 425 visitors.

D. What mathematical operations do you need to perform to calculate the average per-visitor profit for a given number of visitors? In what order must you perform the operations?

E. The Water Works business manager claims that the average concession profit per visitor can also be calculated with either of these equations:

$$A = \frac{1}{V}(2.50V - 500) \qquad A = (2.50V - 500) \div V$$

Do you agree? Explain.

Problem 1.2 Follow-Up

1. **a.** Use the example of calculating the average per-visitor concession profit as a guide to help you evaluate $\frac{100 + 3x}{x}$ when $x = 25$.

b. Check your answer by entering an expression into your graphing calculator and pressing ENTER. What expression did you enter?

2. **a.** Use the example of calculating the average per-visitor concession profit as a guide to help you evaluate $\frac{3x}{4x + 3}$ when $x = 10$.

b. Check your answer by entering an expression into your graphing calculator and pressing ENTER. What expression did you enter?

3. When evaluating an expression that is in fraction form, in what order should you perform the operations?

1.3 Working with Exponents

The president of Water Works wants a large arch built at the entrance to the park. He gave the architect the sketch and equation below. The equation gives the height, y, of the arch above a point x feet from one of the bases of the arch. This means that if you are standing under the arch x feet from one base, the point of the arch directly over your head will be $5x - 0.1x^2$ feet above the ground.

$y = 5x - 0.1x^2$

Problem 1.3

A. Use the equation to find the height of the arch at these distances from the left base. Do your calculations without using a calculator.

1. 10 feet
2. 30 feet
3. 50 feet

B. What operations did you perform to calculate your answers for part A? In what order did you perform these operations?

C. Check your answers for part A by using a graphing calculator to help you make a table.

D. **1.** The expression $5x - 0.1x^2$ is equivalent to the expression $0.1x(50 - x)$. Use this second expression to calculate the heights for the x values given in part A.

2. In what order did you perform the operations?

Problem 1.3 Follow-Up

When a giant roller coaster was built at Water Works, attendance began to increase. The business manager wrote the equation $V = 1000(1.2^m)$ to estimate the daily number of visitors m months after the roller-coaster ride opened.

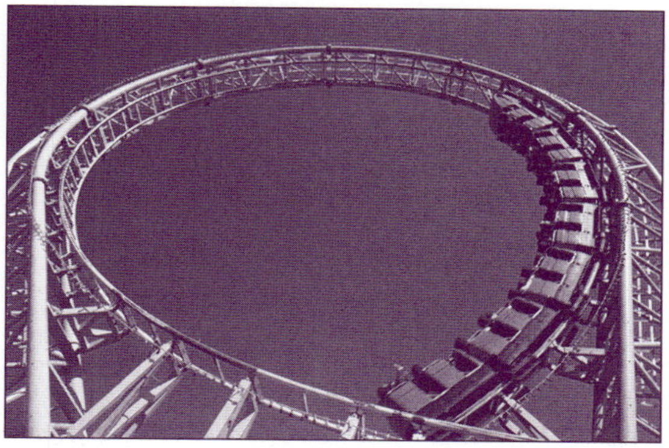

1. **a.** Estimate the number of visitors 1 month after the roller-coaster ride opened.
   b. Estimate the number of visitors 5 months after the roller-coaster ride opened.
   c. Estimate the number of visitors 12 months after the roller-coaster ride opened.
2. What operations did you perform to find your answers in question 1? In what order did you perform the operations?
3. Check your answer to part c of question 1 by entering an expression into your calculator and pressing ENTER. What expression did you enter?

Did you know?

Americans have been splashing at water-slide parks for more than 100 years! The first water park was opened in 1894 in Chicago's South Side by Captain Paul Boynton. The popular and successful "Captain Boynton's Water Chutes" was the first modernized amusement park in the world. The parked served as a model for amusement parks built during the recreation boom of the early 1900s.

Applications • Connections • Extensions

As you work on these ACE questions, use your calculator whenever you need it.

Applications

In 1–5, evaluate the expression for the given x value, and describe the order in which you performed the operations.

1. $3x + 15$ when $x = 12$

2. $25 + 8x$ when $x = 2$

3. $10x - 12$ when $x = 4$

4. $^{-}3x + 10$ when $x = 7$

5. $40 - 5x$ when $x = 6$

In 6–9, evaluate the expression for the given x value, and describe the order in which you performed the operations.

6. $5x^2$ when $x = 4$

7. $5x^2$ when $x = {}^{-}3$

8. $^{-}3x^2$ when $x = 4$

9. $^{-}3x^2$ when $x = {}^{-}4$

In 10–17, evaluate the expression for the given x value, and describe the order in which you performed the operations.

10. $4x^2 + 3x$ when $x = 7$

11. $4x^2 + 3x$ when $x = {}^{-}7$

12. $4x^2 - 3x$ when $x = 7$

13. $4x^2 - 3x$ when $x = {}^-7$

14. $4x^2 + 3x + 5$ when $x = 2$

15. $4x^2 + 3x - 5$ when $x = 2$

16. $4x^2 - 3x - 5$ when $x = {}^-3$

17. ${}^-4x^2 - 3x - 5$ when $x = {}^-3$

In 18–22, evaluate the expression for the given x value, and describe the order in which you performed the operations.

18. $7(x + 8)$ when $x = {}^-3$

19. $7(5x + 8)$ when $x = 3$

20. $7(8 - 5x)$ when $x = 3$

21. $(8 - 5x)(3x + 2)$ when $x = 4$

22. $(x - 5)(x + 2)$ when $x = 10$

In 23–27, evaluate the expression for the given x value, and describe the order in which you performed the operations.

23. $\frac{36}{2x}$ when $x = 6$

24. $\frac{3x + 2}{5}$ when $x = 11$

25. $\frac{72}{2x + 1}$ when $x = 4$

26. $\frac{50x + 10}{x}$ when $x = 2$

27. $\frac{8 + 3x}{x + 1}$ when $x = 4$

28. **a.** Find the value of $2 + 3x \div 2$ when $x = 4$.

b. Write an expression that is equivalent to $2 + 3x \div 2$ and that includes a fraction.

c. Evaluate the expression you wrote in part b for $x = 4$. How does your result compare to the result you found in part a?

Connections

In 29 and 30, use this information: The ski club is planning a trip for winter break. They wrote the equation $C = 200 + 10N$ to estimate the cost in dollars of the trip if N students attend.

29. Duncan and Gish both used the equation to estimate the cost for 50 students. Duncan said the cost would be \$10,500, and Gish said it would be \$700.

a. Determine which estimate is correct. Show the calculations needed to find the estimate.

b. How do you think Duncan and Gish found such different estimates if they both used the same equation?

30. **a.** Write an equation for the cost per student, S, if N students go on the trip.

b. What will be the cost per student if 20 students go on the trip?

c. What will be the cost per student if 40 students go on the trip?

In 31–33, you will explore some relationships involved in the operation of Water Works.

31. The concession profit, in dollars, for V visitors can be estimated by the equation $P = 2.50V - 500$.

a. Make a table of data for five V values.

b. Graph the equation.

c. Identify the slope and the y-intercept of the graph. Explain what each of these values tells you about the relationship between the variables.

32. The number of visitors can be estimated from the probability of rain, R, by using the equation $V = 600 - 500R$.

a. Make a table of data for five R values.

b. Graph the equation.

c. Identify the slope and the y-intercept of the graph. Explain what each of these values tells you about the relationship between the variables.

33. The daily increase in the employee-bonus fund, in dollars, can be estimated from the number of visitors by using the equation $B = 100 + 0.50V$.

a. Make a table of data for five V values.

b. Graph the equation.

c. Identify the slope and the y-intercept of the graph. Explain what each of these values tells you about the relationship between the variables.

In 34–39, you will practice evaluating familiar geometric formulas. As you evaluate each formula, think carefully about the order of operations.

34. The formula for the area of a circle with radius r is $A = \pi r^2$. Find the area of a circle with a radius of 4 centimeters.

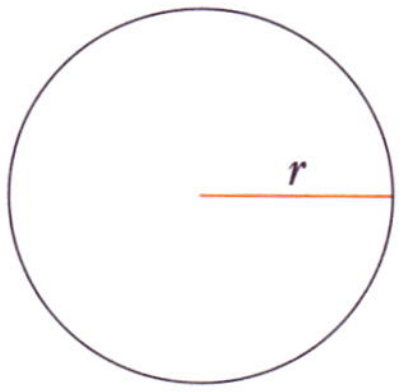

35. The formula for the surface area of a cube with edges of length e is $A = 6e^2$. Find the surface area of a cube with edges of length 5 centimeters.

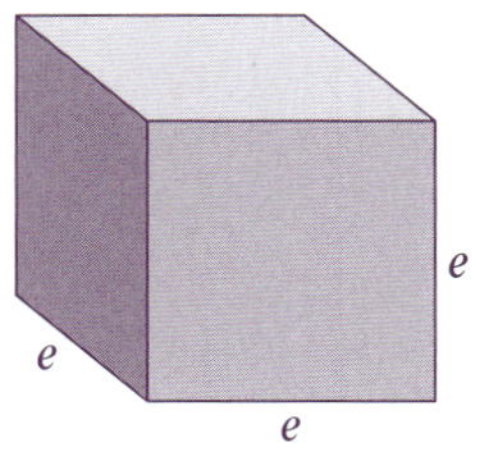

36. The formula for the volume of a cone with radius r and height h is $V = \frac{1}{3}\pi r^2 h$. Find the volume of a cone with a radius of 7 centimeters and a height of 10 centimeters.

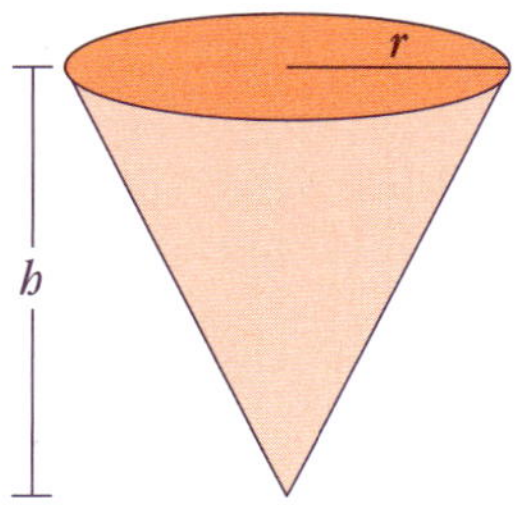

37. The formula for the surface area of a cylinder with radius r and height h is $A = 2\pi r^2 + 2\pi rh$. The $2\pi r^2$ part represents the area of the circular top and bottom, and the $2\pi rh$ part represents the "side" that can be unrolled to form a rectangle. Find the surface area of a cylinder with a radius of 3 centimeters and a height of 8 centimeters.

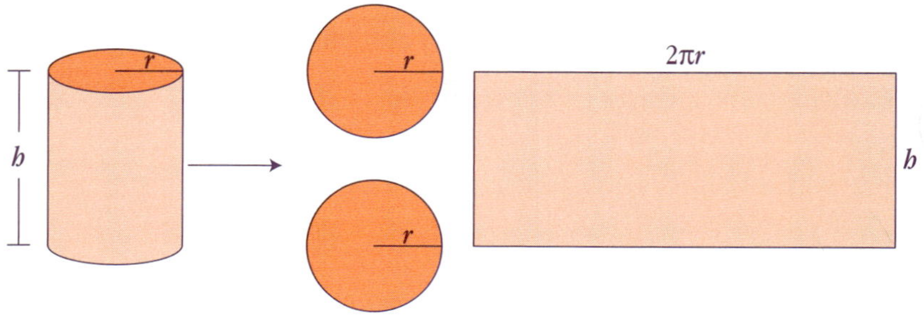

38. The formula for the area of a circle with radius r is $A = \pi r^2$. Tina, Hyung, and Jamal used this formula to estimate the area of a pizza with a diameter of 9 inches. They each found a different area. In a–c, decide whether the student's estimate is reasonable. If the estimate is not reasonable, figure out what mistake the student might have made in his or her calculation.

a. Tina estimated the area to be about 254 square inches.

b. Hyung estimated the area to be about 200 square inches.

c. Jamal estimated the area to be about 64 square inches.

39. The formula for the surface area of a sphere with radius r is $A = 4\pi r^2$.

a. Find the surface area of a globe with radius 1 foot.

b. The radius of Earth is about 4000 miles. Find the surface area of Earth.

c. The radius of the sun is about 430,000 miles. Find the surface area of the sun.

d. What is the ratio of Earth's radius to the sun's radius?

e. What is the ratio of Earth's surface area to the sun's surface area?

f. How does your ratio from part d compare to your ratio from part e?

40. A bacterium colony begins with 5000 bacteria. The population doubles every hour. This pattern of exponential growth can be modeled by the equation $b = 5000(2^t)$, where b is the number of bacteria and t is the number of hours.

a. What is the population of the colony after 3 hours? After 5 hours?

b. What mathematical operations did you perform to calculate your answers in part a? In what order did you perform these operations?

41. The equation $d = {}^-16t^2 + 16t + 6.5$ represents the distance in feet from the ground to the top of a basketball player's head t seconds after the player jumps.

a. Find the distance to the top of the player's head after 0.1 second.

b. Find the distance to the top of the player's head after 0.3 second.

c. Find the distance to the top of the player's head after 1 second.

d. What mathematical operations did you perform to calculate your answers in parts a–c? In what order did you perform these operations?

Extensions

42. The equation $y = 0.1x^2 - 2x + 25$ describes the height of a suspension cable above the bridge it supports as a function of the distance, x, from one end of the bridge. All measurements are in feet. Several students used this equation to estimate the height for different x values.

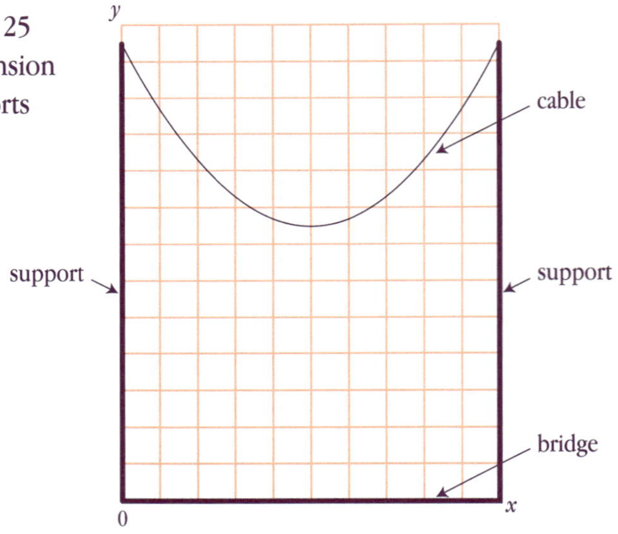

a. For $x = 10$, Santha calculated a height of 6 feet, and Julio calculated a height of 15 feet. Which student is correct? What error do you think the other student made?

b. For $x = 20$, Joyce calculated a height of $^-11$ feet, and Donny calculated a height of 25 feet. Which student is correct? What error do you think the other student made?

Mathematical Reflections

In this investigation, you evaluated algebraic expressions for given values of the variables. As you worked, you explored the rules for order of operations. These questions will help you summarize what you have learned:

1. **a.** When an expression involves addition, subtraction, and multiplication, in what order should you perform the operations?

   b. Illustrate your answer to part a by writing an appropriate expression and evaluating it for specific values of the variables.

2. **a.** When an expression involves division and other operations such as addition, subtraction, and multiplication, in what order should you perform the operations?

   b. Illustrate your answer to part a by writing an appropriate expression and evaluating it for specific values of the variables.

3. **a.** When an expression involves exponents and other operations such as addition, subtraction, and multiplication, in what order should you perform the operations?

   b. Illustrate your answer to part a by writing an appropriate expression and evaluating it for specific values of the variables.

Think about your answers to these questions, discuss your ideas with other students and your teacher, and then write a summary of your findings in your journal.

INVESTIGATION 2

Equivalent Expressions

Throughout your work in mathematics this year, you have written symbolic expressions and equations to represent situations involving variables. Because there is usually more than one way to think about a situation, there is often more than one way to express the situation in symbols. For example, consider the perimeter of a rectangle with length L and width W.

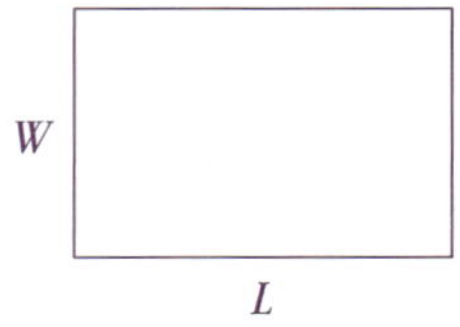

Think about this!

Jim says the perimeter of the rectangle above is $2(L + W)$. Lilia says the perimeter is $2L + 2W$. How could you convince the students that their expressions are equivalent?

Since $2(L + W)$ and $2L + 2W$ represent the same quantity, they are **equivalent expressions**. In this investigation, you will look at situations that can be described with several different, but equivalent, expressions, and you will see how each expression represents a unique way of interpreting a situation. You will also learn some methods for showing that two expressions are equivalent.

2.1 Tiling Pools

Hot tubs and in-ground swimming pools are sometimes surrounded by borders of tiles. This drawing shows a square hot tub with sides of length 5 feet surrounded by square border tiles. The border tiles measure 1 foot on each side. A total of 24 tiles are needed for the border.

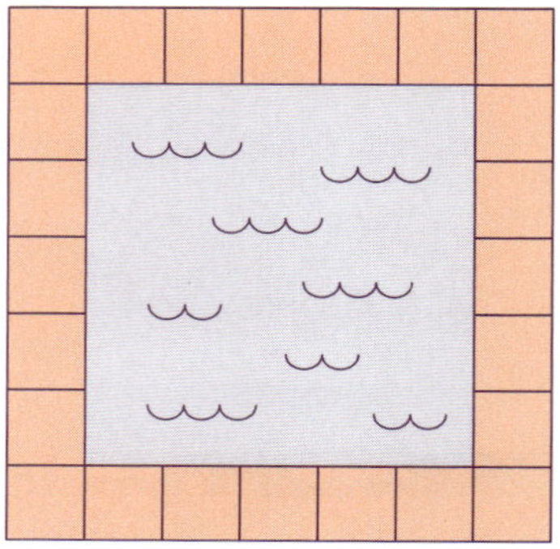

Problem 2.1

In this problem, you will explore this question: If a square pool has sides of length *s* feet, how many tiles are needed to form the border?

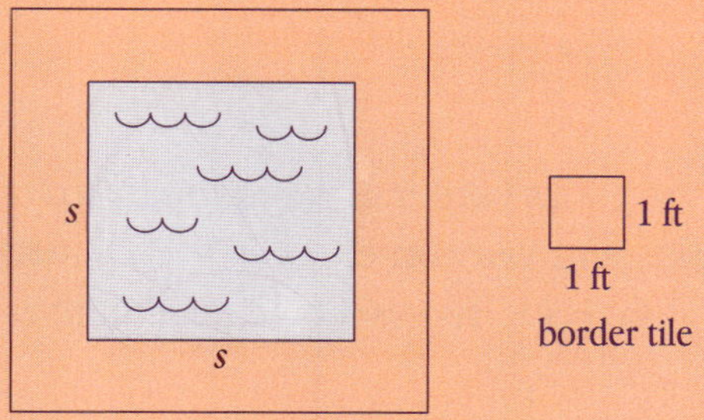

A. Make sketches on grid paper to help you figure out how many tiles are needed for the borders of square pools with sides of length 1, 2, 3, 4, 6, and 10 feet. Record your results in a table.

B. Write an equation for the number of tiles, N, needed to form a border for a square pool with sides of length s feet.

C. Try to write at least one more equation for the number of tiles needed for the border of the pool. How could you convince someone that your expressions for the number of tiles are equivalent?

Problem 2.1 Follow-Up

1. Make a table and a graph for each equation you wrote in part a of Problem 2.1. Do the table and the graph indicate that the equations are equivalent? Explain.

2. Is the relationship between the side length of the pool and the number of tiles linear, quadratic, exponential, or none of these? Explain your reasoning.

3. **a.** Write an equation for the area of the pool, A, in terms of the side length, s.

b. Is the equation you wrote linear, quadratic, exponential, or none of these? Explain.

4. **a.** Write an equation for the combined area of the pool and its border, C, in terms of the side length, s.

b. Is the equation you wrote linear, quadratic, exponential, or none of these? Explain.

2.2 Thinking in Different Ways

You and your classmates probably found more than one way to express the number of tiles needed for the border of a square pool. Now you will explore how different ways of thinking about this problem lead to different expressions.

Problem 2.2

Takashi thought of the pool's border as being composed of four 1-by-s rectangles, each made from s tiles, and four corner squares, each made from one tile. He wrote the expression $4s + 4$ to represent the total number of border tiles.

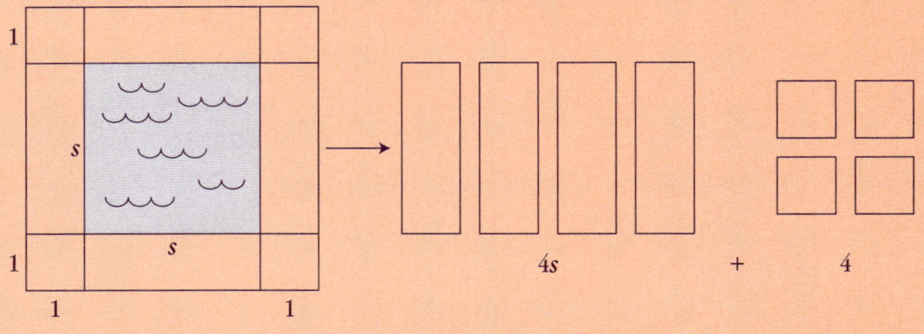

A. Stella wrote the expression $4(s + 1)$ to represent the number of border tiles. Draw a picture that illustrates how Stella might have been thinking about the border of the pool.

B. Jeri wrote the expression $s + s + s + s + 4$ to represent the number of border tiles. Draw a picture that illustrates how Jeri might have been thinking about the border of the pool.

C. Sal wrote the expression $2s + 2(s + 2)$ to represent the number of border tiles. Draw a picture that illustrates how Sal might have been thinking about the border of the pool.

D. Jackie wrote the expression $4(s + 2) - 4$ to represent the number of border tiles. Draw a picture that illustrates how Jackie might have been thinking about the border of the pool.

E. Explain why each expression in parts A–D is equivalent to Takashi's expression.

■ Problem 2.2 Follow-Up

1. Evaluate each of the five expressions given in the problem for $s = 10$. Can you conclude from your results that all the expressions are equivalent? Explain your reasoning.
2. Make a table and a graph for each of the five expressions. Do the tables and the graphs indicate that the expressions are equivalent? Explain.

2.3 Diving In

Swimming pools are sometimes divided into sections that are used for different purposes. For example, a pool may have a section for lap swimming and a section for diving, or a section for experienced swimmers and a section for small children.

In this problem, you will investigate ways to express the surface area of the water in several divided pools. The problem illustrates an important and useful mathematical property that you will use throughout the remainder of this unit.

Problem 2.3

Below are four designs for pools with swimming and diving sections. For each design, show two methods for calculating the total surface area of the water. Then tell which method is more efficient. That is, tell which method requires fewer mathematical operations.

A.

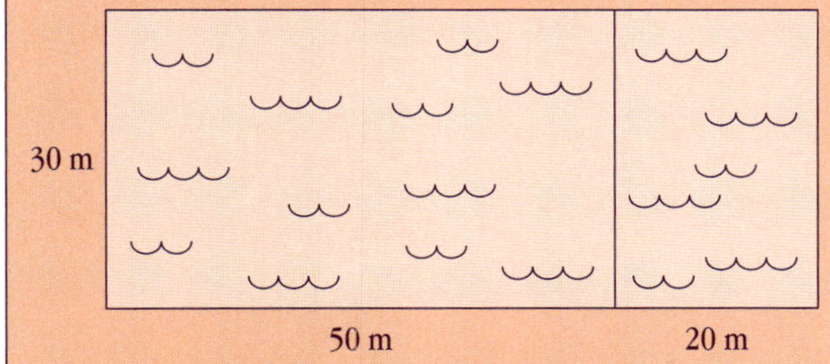

B.

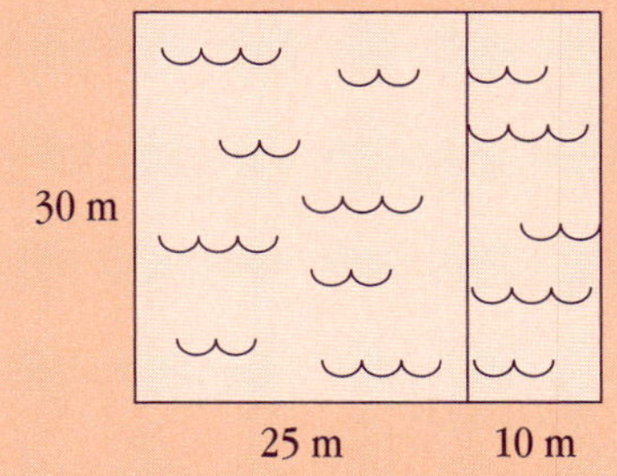

C.

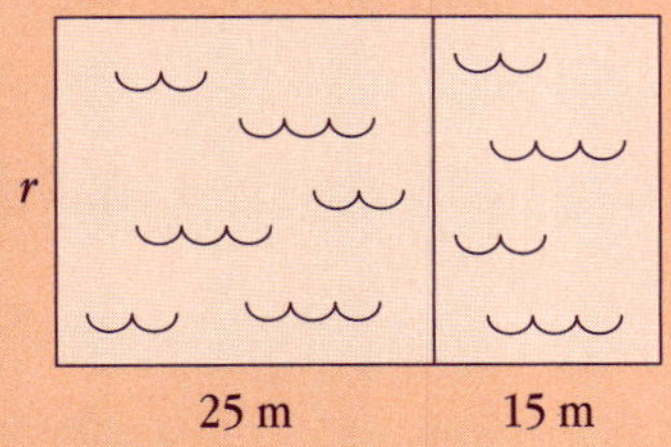

D.

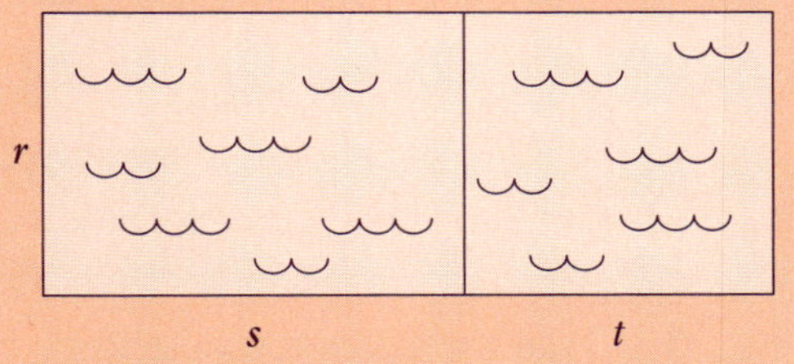

Problem 2.3 Follow-Up

As you worked on Problem 2.3, you found two equivalent expressions for the surface area of the water in each pool. For example, to find the surface area of the pool in part A, you might have multiplied the length of the entire pool by its width to get 30(50 + 20), and you might have added the areas of the two sections to get 30(50) + 30(20). The expressions 30(50 + 20) and 30(50) + 30(20) are equivalent. We say that 30(50 + 20) is in **factored form** and 30(50) + 30(20) is in **expanded form**.

1. Use the drawings below to answer parts a–d.

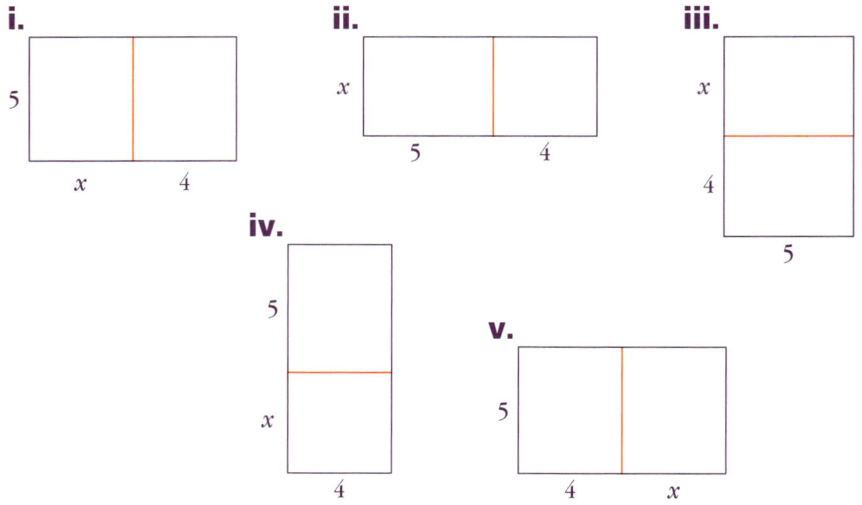

a. Which of the rectangles have an area of $5(4 + x)$?

b. Write an expression in expanded form that is equivalent to $5(4 + x)$. Explain how you know that your expression is equivalent to $5(4 + x)$.

c. Which of the rectangles have an area of $5x + 4x$?

d. Write an expression in factored form that is equivalent to $5x + 4x$. Explain how you know that your expression is equivalent to $5x + 4x$.

2. **a.** Draw a diagram that uses areas of rectangles to illustrate that $5x + 10$ and $5(x + 2)$ are equivalent.

b. Use tables or graphs to show that $5x + 10$ and $5(x + 2)$ are equivalent.

3. Write an expression in expanded form that is equivalent to the given expression. Draw a diagram to illustrate the equivalence.

a. $1.5(4 + x)$

b. $x(3 + 5)$

4. Write an expression in factored form that is equivalent to the given expression. Draw a diagram to illustrate the equivalence.

a. $27 + 36x$

b. $2x + 7x$

5. Express the area of the purple rectangle in both factored form and expanded form.

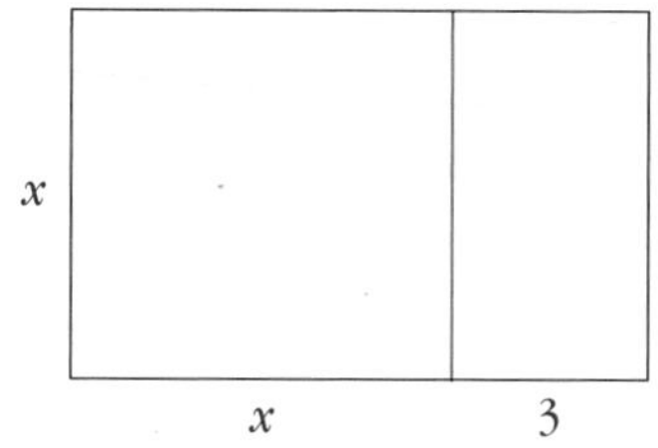

6. **a.** Draw a rectangle whose area can be represented by the expression $x(5 + x)$.

b. Write an expression in expanded form that is equivalent to $x(5 + x)$.

7. As you worked on the border-tile and pool-area problems in this investigation, you found equivalent ways to express a quantity.

a. Use what you have learned to write some expressions that are equivalent to $4x + 6$.

b. Use what you have learned to write some expressions that are equivalent to $x^2 + 4x$.

c. What general rules have you discovered that can help you write equivalent expressions?

Applications • Connections • Extensions

As you work on these ACE questions, use your calculator whenever you need it.

Applications

1. **a.** How many 1-foot-square tiles are needed to form a border for a pool that is 10 feet long and 5 feet wide?

b. Write an expression for the number of border tiles needed for a pool that is *L* feet long and *W* feet wide.

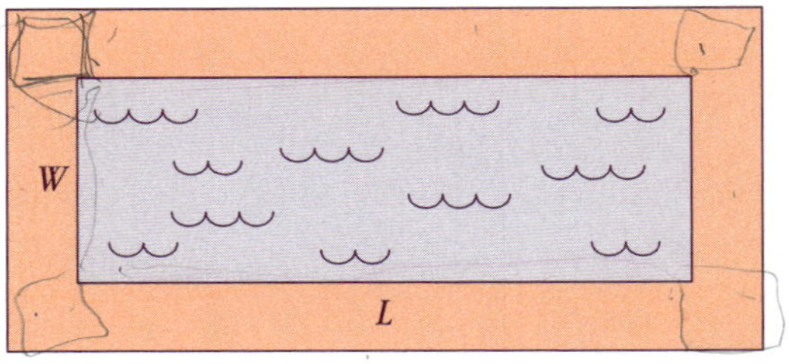

c. Write a different expression for the number of tiles needed. Explain why your expressions are equivalent.

2. A square hot tub has sides of length *s* feet. A border is created by placing square tiles measuring 1 foot on each side along the edges of the tub and triangular tiles in the corners. The triangular tiles were made by cutting square tiles in half.

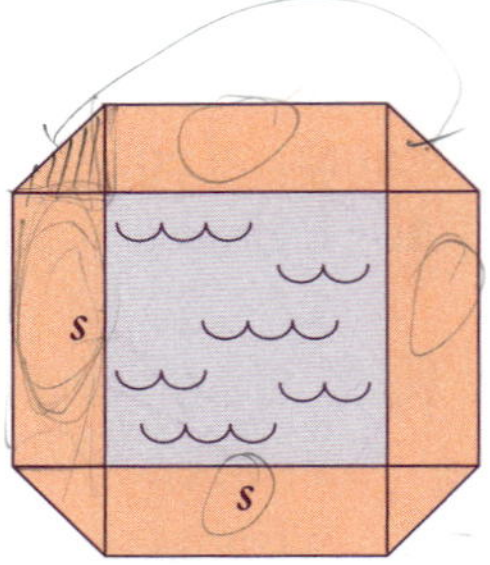

a. If the hot tub has sides of length 7 feet, how many square tiles are needed to make the border?

b. Write two equations for the number of square tiles, *N*, needed to build this type of border for a square tub with sides of length *s* feet.

3. A rectangular pool is L feet long and W feet wide. A border is created by placing square tiles measuring 1 foot on each side along the edges of the pool and triangular tiles in the corners. The triangular tiles were made by cutting square tiles in half.

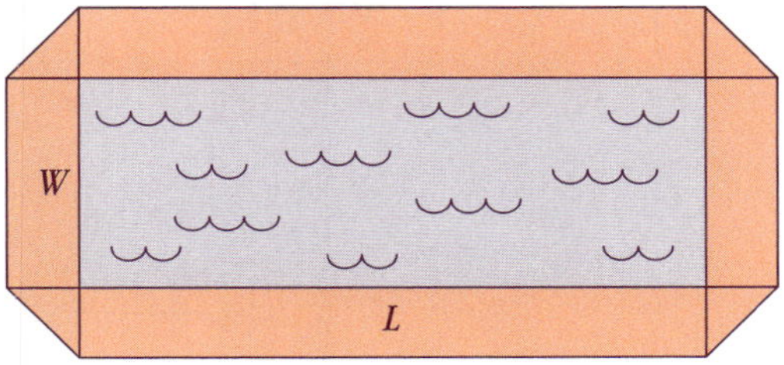

a. If the pool is 30 feet long and 20 feet wide, how many square tiles are needed to make the border?

b. Write two equations for the number of square tiles, N, needed to make this type of border for a pool L feet long and W feet wide.

In 4 and 5, write two expressions, one in factored form and one in expanded form, for the area of the purple rectangle.

4.

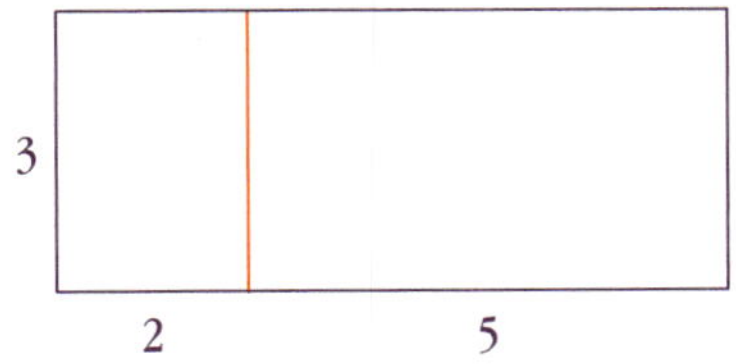

5.

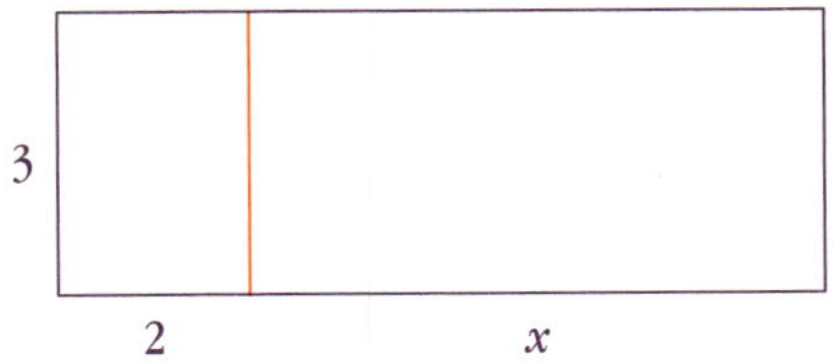

6. **a.** Which rectangles below have an area of $6(x + 1)$?

b. Write an expression in expanded form that is equivalent to $6(x + 1)$.

i.

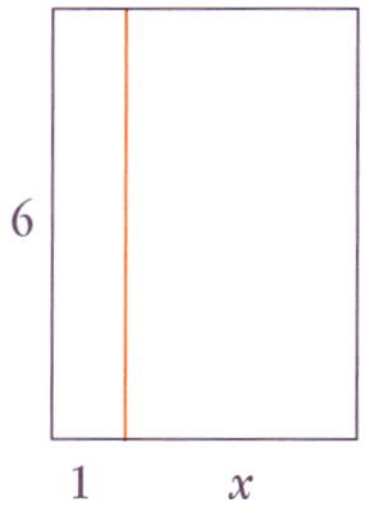

ii.

iii.

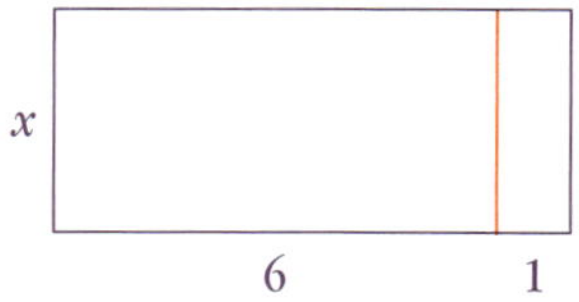

iv.

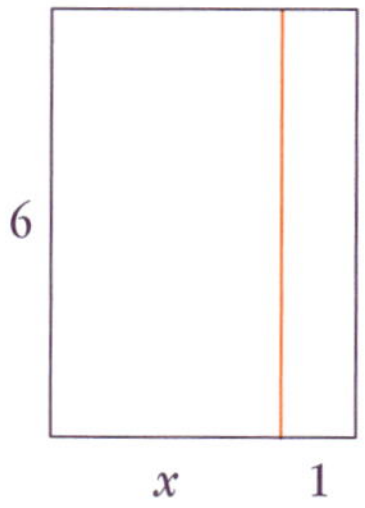

7. **a.** Which rectangles below have an area of $5(2x)$? Explain your answer.

b. Write an expression that is equivalent to $5(2x)$.

i.

ii.

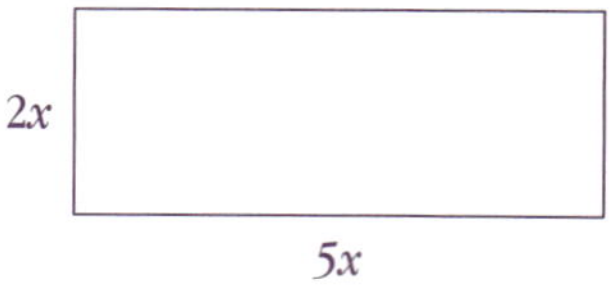

iii.

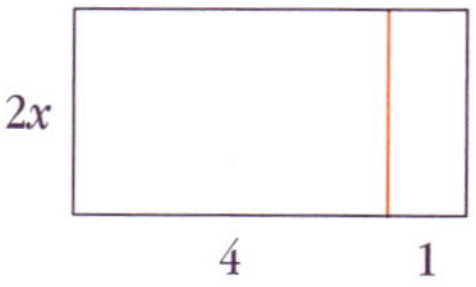

iv.

v.

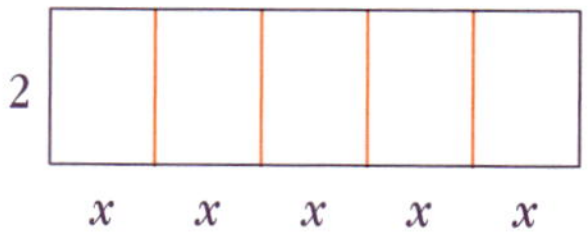

8. **a.** Is $3x + 8$ equivalent to $3(x + 8)$? Explain.

b. Is $3(x + 8)$ equivalent to $3(8 + x)$? Explain.

c. Is $3x + 8$ equivalent to $8 + 3x$? Explain.

In 9–12, write an expression that is equivalent to the given expression. If the given expression is in factored form, write an expression in expanded form. If the given expression is in expanded form, write an expression in factored form. Draw a diagram to illustrate the equivalence.

9. $4(x + 1)$

10. $16x + 8$

11. $3(2x + 5)$

12. $x^2 + 3x$

In 13–18, tell whether the expressions are equivalent, and explain how you know.

13. $2x + 11x$ and $13x$

14. $x + 3.5x$ and $3.5x$

15. $5(x + 12)$ and $5x + 12$

16. $7x$ and $6x + x$

17. $2L + 12$ and $2(1 + L + 5)$

18. $3R + 7 + 5R$ and $8R + 7$

19. Franklin's younger sister Taj and her friend Meredith are selling cookies for their girls' club. The cookies sell for $2.50 a box. For each case below, show two methods for calculating the girls' combined income.

a. Taj sells 76 boxes and Meredith sells 49 boxes.

b. Taj sells 43 boxes and Meredith sells 57 boxes.

c. Taj sells x boxes and Meredith sells y boxes.

20. Sanjay did the following calculation to compute the surface area of the water in his swimming pool:

$$\text{surface area} = 20(30 + 15) = 20(45) = 900 \text{ m}^2$$

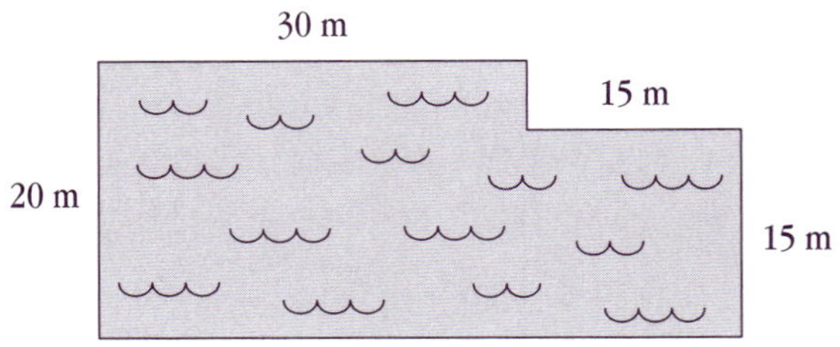

Is Sanjay's calculation correct? If so, explain his reasoning. If not, explain the mistake in his thinking.

Connections

21. A square has sides of length x centimeters. A new rectangle is created by increasing one dimension of the square by 2 centimeters and increasing the other dimension by 3 centimeters. Write two equivalent expressions, one in factored form and one in expanded form, for the area of the new rectangle. Draw a picture to illustrate the equivalence.

22. Write two expressions, one in factored form and one in expanded form, for the area of the purple rectangle below.

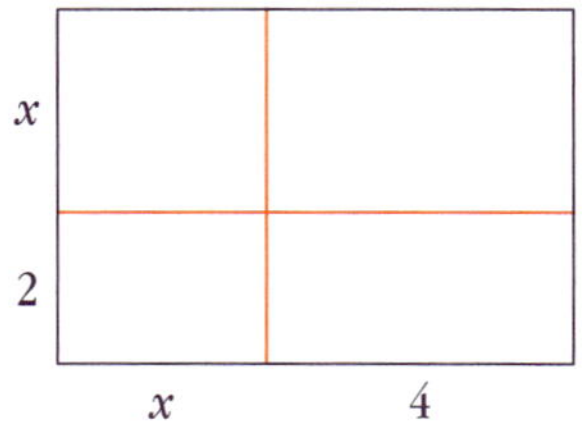

23. A circular hot tub with a radius of 4 feet is surrounded by a border 1 foot wide.

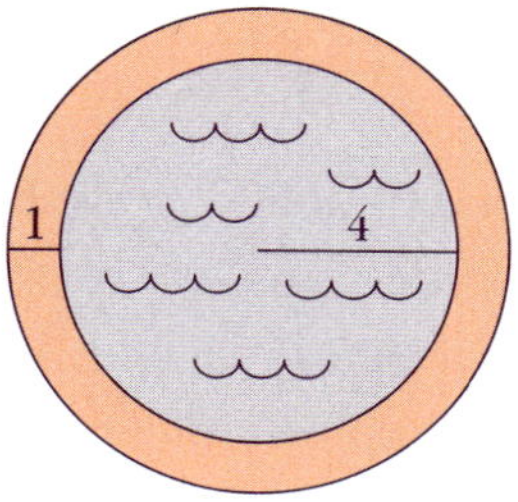

a. What is the surface area of the water?

b. What is the area of the border?

c. Write an expression for the surface area of the water in a circular pool with a radius of r feet.

d. Write an expression for the area of a 1-foot border around a circular pool with a radius of r feet.

24. The dimensions of the pool below are in feet.

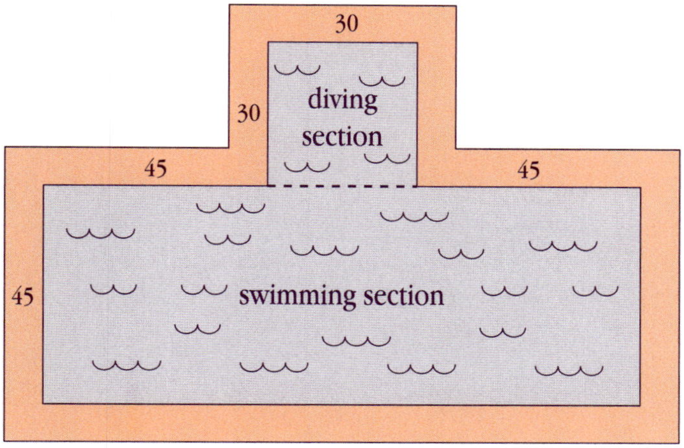

a. How many square tiles measuring 1 foot on a side are needed to create a border for the pool?

b. What is the surface area of the water?

c. The swimming section is 4 feet deep and the diving section is 10 feet deep. What is the volume of the pool?

d. The pool is filled at the rate of 600 cubic feet per hour. How long does it take to fill the pool?

Extensions

25. Susan wanted to write an expression for the number of tiles needed to make a border for a square pool with sides of length s feet. She made a table for pools with sides of length 1, 2, 3, 4, and 5 feet and used a pattern in her table to write the expression $8 + 4(s - 1)$.

Side length	1	2	3	4	5
Tiles needed	8	12	16	20	24

a. What pattern did Susan see in her table?

b. Is Susan's expression for the number of tiles equivalent to Takashi's expression in Problem 2.2? Explain why or why not.

Mathematical Reflections

In this investigation, you looked at situations that could be described by different, but equivalent, expressions. These questions will help you summarize what you have learned:

1. What do we mean when we say that the expressions $4n + 4$ and $4(n + 1)$ are *equivalent*? Make a diagram, a table, and a graph to illustrate that the expressions are equivalent.

2. **a.** Write $5x + 8x$ in factored form.

   b. Write $5(x + 7)$ in expanded form.

   c. How can you tell whether an expression is in expanded form or factored form?

3. **a.** Use drawings, graphs, tables, or some other method to show that $5(2x)$ is equivalent to $2x(5)$.

   b. Use drawings, graphs, tables, or some other method to show that $5 + 2x$ is equivalent to $2x + 5$.

   c. Make a drawing to show why $5(10) + 2$ is equivalent to $50 + 2$ but not equivalent to $5(10 + 2)$.

4. As you worked with equivalent expressions in this investigation, what patterns did you observe that you could use to show that other expressions are equivalent?

Think about your answers to these questions, discuss your ideas with other students and your teacher, and then write a summary of your findings in your journal.

INVESTIGATION 3

Some Important Properties

In the last investigation, you used areas of rectangles to help you find equivalent expressions. The rectangle below, for example, illustrates that $4(5 + x) = 20 + 4x$.

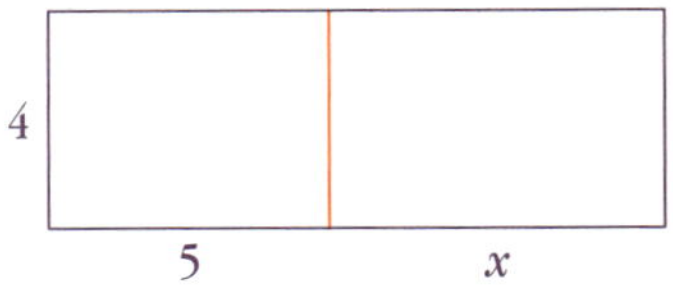

This example illustrates an important property of the real number system called the **distributive property**. You can use the distributive property in two ways:

1. If an expression is written as a factor multiplied by a sum, you can use the distributive property to *multiply* the factor by each term in the sum.

$$4(5 + x) = 4(5) + 4x = 20 + 4x$$

2. If an expression is written as a sum of terms and the terms have a common factor, you can use the distributive property to rewrite the expression as the common factor multiplied by a sum. This process is called *factoring*.

$$20 + 4x = 4(5) + 4x = 4(5 + x)$$

The diagram below illustrates the two ways of applying the distributive property.

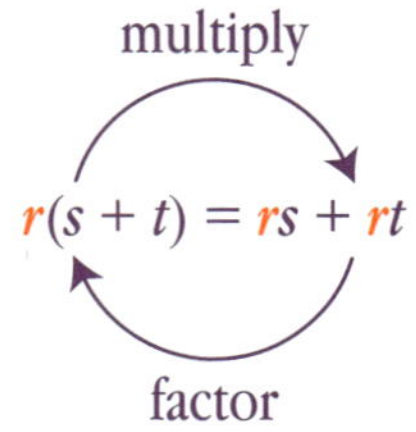

Think about this!

Brenda says that because subtracting a number is the same as adding its opposite, you can use the distributive property to rewrite expressions involving differences. She gave this example:

$$\begin{aligned} 5(x - 2) &= 5(x + {}^{-}2) \\ &= 5(x) + 5({}^{-}2) \\ &= 5x + {}^{-}10 \\ &= 5x - 10 \end{aligned}$$

Can you explain each step in Brenda's example?

The equations $2x + 10 = 10 + 2x$ and $2(x + 5) = (x + 5)2$ illustrate two other important properties. The **commutative property of addition** says that the order in which two quantities are added does not matter. The **commutative property of multiplication** says that the order in which two quantities are multiplied does not matter. These properties can be written using symbols as

$$a + b = b + a \quad \text{and} \quad ab = ba.$$

These properties are sometimes called the **rearrangement property of addition** and the **rearrangement property of multiplication**.

The distributive and commutative properties are useful for writing equivalent expressions. The distributive property allows you to rewrite expressions that involve combinations of multiplication and addition or subtraction. The commutative properties allow you to reorder the terms in an expression so you can group like terms. In this investigation, you will use these properties to solve some interesting problems.

3.1 Walking Together

Leanne, Gilberto, and Alana are participating in a walkathon to raise money for a local hospital. Each participant must find sponsors to pledge a certain amount of money per mile walked.

- Leanne asks her sponsors to pledge $1 for each mile she walks.
- Gilberto asks his sponsors to pledge $2 for each mile he walks.
- Alana asks her sponsors to pledge $5 plus $0.50 for each mile she walks.

The amount raised by each student will depend on the number of sponsors the student has and the number of miles the student walks.

Problem 3.1

The walkathon organizers have offered a prize to the three-person team that raises the most money. Leanne, Gilberto, and Alana will walk together and combine their earnings to compete for the prize. On the day of the walkathon, Leanne has pledges from 16 sponsors, Gilberto has pledges from 7 sponsors, and Alana has pledges from 11 sponsors.

A. For each student, write an equation for the amount of money the student will raise if he or she walks x miles. Then write an equation for the total amount the three-person team will raise if they walk x miles.

A_{Leanne} = ____________________

$A_{Gilberto}$ = ____________________

A_{Alana} = ____________________

A_{total} = ____________________

B. Alana asked each of her 11 sponsors to pledge $5 in addition to an amount per mile, so the team will raise $55 regardless of how far they walk.

1. Excluding the $55, how much will the team raise per mile?

2. Use your answer from part 1 to help you write a different equation for the total amount the team will raise if they walk x miles.

C. 1. Use the distributive and commutative properties to show that the two expressions you wrote for the total amount the team will raise are equivalent.

2. Verify that the expressions are equivalent by making and comparing tables or graphs.

Problem 3.1 Follow-Up

In Problem 3.1, you used the distributive and commutative properties to write equivalent expressions for the amount of money the team will raise. The context of the problem may have helped you understand why these properties make sense. Now you will practice applying the properties to algebraic expressions that are not in context.

In 1–12, tell whether the expressions are equivalent, and explain your reasoning.

1. $3x + 5x$ and $8x$
2. $3x + 5$ and $8x$
3. $4(x + 7)$ and $4x + 7$
4. $5(x + 2)$ and $5x + 10$
5. $12 + 8x$ and $4(3 + 2x)$
6. $4x + x + 2x$ and $8x$
7. $7 + 5x$ and $5x + 7$
8. $3x + 8$ and $8x + 3$
9. $5x + 3x + 4x$ and $4x + 5x + 3x$
10. $6 + 2t$ and $2(t + 3)$
11. $2(L + 2) + 2W$ and $2L + 2W + 4$
12. $2L + 2W + 4$ and $2(L + W + 2)$

3.2 Estimating Profit

At their planning meeting, the organizers of the hospital walkathon discussed expenses and income. They made the following estimates:

- Expense for posters and newspaper, radio, and TV ads: $500
- Expense for souvenir T-shirts for participants: $6 per child, $8.50 per adult
- Income from business sponsors whose logos will appear on T-shirts and signs: $1000
- Expense for paramedics and an ambulance in case of emergency: $250
- Income from registration fees: $5 per child, $15 per adult

Notice that some of the expenses are fixed, while others depend on the number of adults and children who participate. The difference between the total income and the total expenses is the profit. The organizers will donate any profit from the event to the hospital.

Problem 3.2

A. Estimate the total income, the total expenses, and the total profit if 40 children and 30 adults participate in the walkathon.

B. Write two equivalent expressions for the total income in terms of the number of adults, a, and the number of children, c, who participate.

C. Write two equivalent expressions for the total expenses in terms of the number of adults, a, and the number of children, c, who participate.

D. Use parentheses and your results from parts B and C to write an expression showing the profit as total income minus total expenses. That is, express the profit as (expression for income) – (expression for expenses).

E. Write an expression for profit that is equivalent to your expression from part D but that is as short as possible. Use the distributive and commutative properties to show that the two profit expressions are equivalent.

F. Evaluate your profit expressions from parts D and E for $a = 100$ and $c = 75$. Can you conclude from your results that the expressions are equivalent? Explain.

G. Compare the profit expressions you wrote in parts D and E. What are the advantages and disadvantages of writing the profit expression in a shorter form?

Problem 3.2 Follow-Up

In Problem 3.2, you might have written this expression for profit:

$$(1000 + 5c + 15a) - (500 + 6c + 8.50a + 250)$$

The first pair of parentheses in this expression can be deleted, but to remove the second pair, you must *distribute* the minus sign to each term within the parentheses.

$$(1000 + 5c + 15a) - (500 + 6c + 8.50a + 250) = 1000 + 5c + 15a - 500 - 6c - 8.50a - 250$$

Distributing the minus sign to each term is a special case of the distributive property.

$$^{-}(s + t) = {}^{-}1(s + t) = {}^{-}1(s) + {}^{-}1(t) = {}^{-}s + {}^{-}t = {}^{-}s - t$$

1. Benjamin's math test consisted of 10 questions, each worth 5 points. Benjamin answered two questions incorrectly. Show at least two ways to calculate his score.

2. **a.** Describe a situation that can be represented by the expression $100 - (x + y)$. Explain what x and y represent in your situation.

   b. Use the distributive property to help you write an expression that is equivalent to $100 - (x + y)$.

3. **a.** Describe a situation that can be represented by the expression $50 - 2x - 2y$. Explain what x and y represent in your situation.

   b. Use the distributive property to help you write an expression that is equivalent to $50 - 2x - 2y$.

4. The expression $3 + 2x$ is equivalent to $2x + 3$. Is $3 - 2x$ equivalent to $2x - 3$? Explain why or why not.

5. Apply the properties you have learned in this investigation to simplify each expression.

   a. $(9x + 15) - (8 + 2x)$

   b. $(7x - 12) - (9x + 15)$

   c. $(14r + 9t + 15) + (23 - 9r + 3t)$

   d. $19 - 12x + 20 + 9x$

3.3 Finding the Area of a Trapezoid

The figure below is a trapezoid. A *trapezoid* is a quadrilateral with one pair of parallel sides. The parallel sides, labeled *a* and *b,* are called the *bases* of the trapezoid. The distance from side *a* to side *b,* labeled *h,* is the *height*.

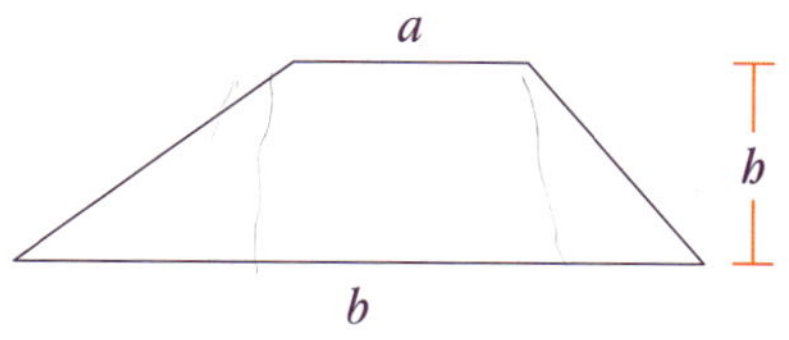

Ms. Ochoa's students have learned how to find areas of triangles, rectangles, and parallelograms. Now, Ms. Ochoa has challenged her students to find a method for calculating the area of a trapezoid.

Tua, Sam, and Carlos have found three methods for calculating the area. Each method involves dividing and rearranging the trapezoid into other shapes.

Problem 3.3

The students made drawings to illustrate their methods for calculating the area of a trapezoid. Try to figure out how each student thought about the problem.

Tua's method

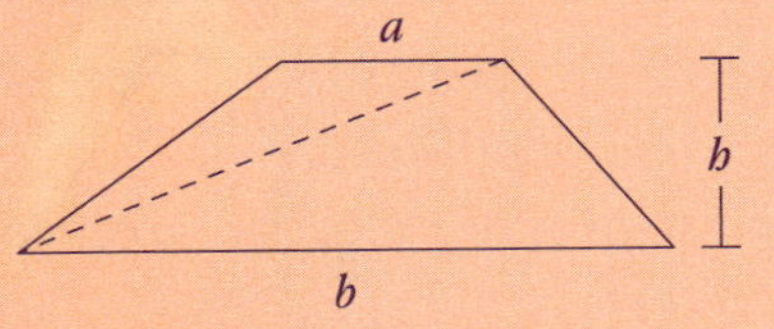

Sam's method

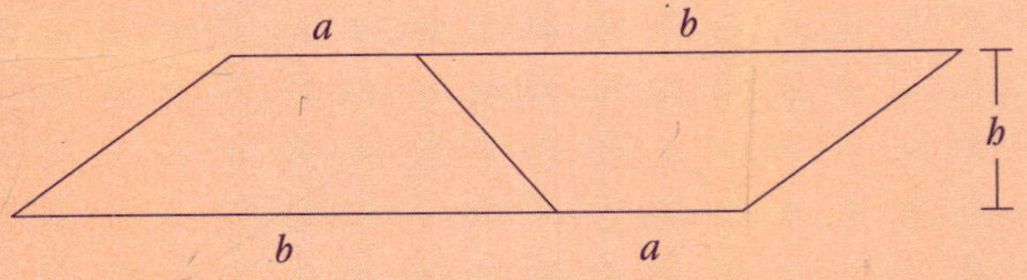

Carlos's method

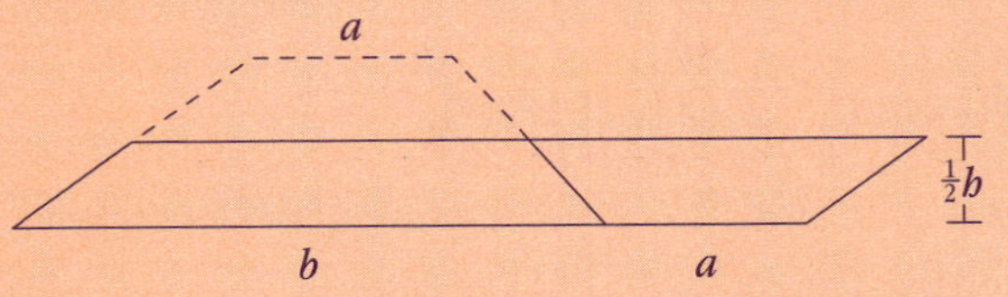

A. Explain each student's method for finding the area.

B. Write an algebraic expression to describe each method.

C. Show that the expressions you wrote in part B are equivalent.

Problem 3.3 Follow-Up

1. a. Natasha lost her drawing, but she had written this expression for finding the area of a trapezoid:

$$\frac{1}{2}h(b-a)+ha$$

Use this expression to decide what Natasha's drawing might have looked like. Make a drawing, and use it to help explain Natasha's method for finding the area.

b. Is Natasha's expression equivalent to the three expressions in part B? Explain.

2. A trapezoid has a height of 10 centimeters and bases of 9 centimeters and 15 centimeters. Find the area of the trapezoid using each of the four expressions.

3.4 Writing Quadratic Expressions

In your work in this unit, you have discovered that a situation can often be represented by different, but equivalent, algebraic expressions. Most of the expressions you have worked with have been linear expressions. In this problem, you will practice finding equivalent *quadratic* expressions.

The table below shows the results of the games played by a five-team soccer league. Each team played each of the other teams twice—once at home and once away. A *W* means the home team won the game; an *L* means the home team lost. For example, the Alligators won their home game against the Cats, but they lost when they played on the Cats' home field. What do the "—" symbols mean? How many games were played in all?

Visiting Team

Home Team		Alligators	Buzzards	Cats	Ducks	Elks
	Alligators	—	*W*	*W*	*L*	*W*
	Buzzards	*L*	—	*L*	*L*	*W*
	Cats	*W*	*W*	—	*L*	*L*
	Ducks	*W*	*W*	*W*	—	*W*
	Elks	*L*	*W*	*W*	*W*	—

Problem 3.4

In parts A–C, you will explore three ways of thinking about this question: If a league has n teams and each team plays each of the other teams twice, how many games are played in all?

A. Figure out how many games would be played for leagues with 2, 3, 4, 5, and 6 teams. Record your results in a table similar to the one below.

Number of teams	2	3	4	5	6
Number of games					

Look for a pattern in your table. Use the pattern to write an expression for the number of games played by a league with n teams.

B. Suppose a sports reporter wants to attend exactly one game in the schedule of an n-team league.

1. How many choices does the reporter have for the home team for the game she attends?
2. Once she has chosen a home team, how many choices does she have for the visiting team?
3. Use your answers from parts 1 and 2 to write an expression for the total number of games the reporter can choose from.

C. Suppose you made a table similar to the one on page 41 to record wins and losses for an n-team league.

Visiting Team

		T_1	T_2	T_3	...	T_n
Home Team	T_1					
	T_2					
	T_3					
	⋮					
	T_n					

1. How many cells would your table have?
2. How many cells in the table would not be used for W or L entries?
3. Use your answers from parts 1 and 2 to write an expression for the total number of games played.

D. In parts A–C, you wrote expressions for the number of games played by an n-team league. Show that these expressions are equivalent.

Problem 3.4 Follow-Up

Many quadratic expressions can be written in both factored form and expanded form. The area of the purple rectangle below can be written as $x^2 + 3x$ or as $x(x + 3)$.

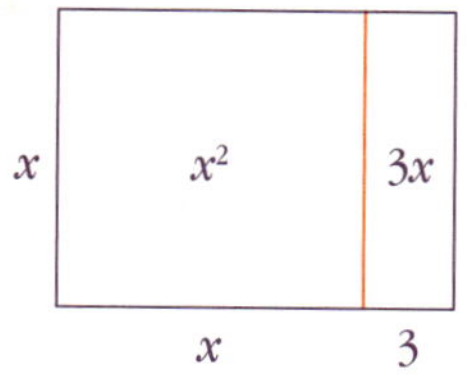

You can use the distributive property to show the equivalence of the factored and expanded forms of a quadratic expression. For example, you can change $x^2 + 3x$ to $x(x + 3)$ by factoring an x from each term. You can change $x(x + 3)$ to $x^2 + 3x$ by multiplying each term by x.

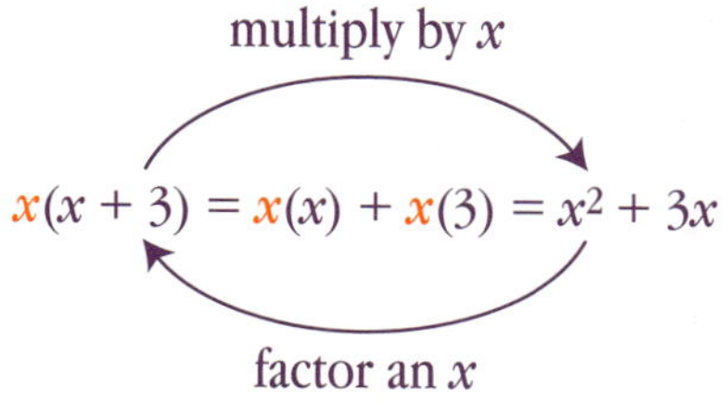

You can apply the distributive property to more complex factored expressions. This example shows how you can change the factored expression $(x + 2)(x + 3)$ to expanded form by applying the distributive property several times.

$(x + 2)(x + 3) =$	$(x + 2)x + (x + 2)3$	Multiply $(x + 2)$ by each term of $x + 3$.
	$= x^2 + 2x + (x + 2)3$	Multiply x by each term of $x + 2$.
	$= x^2 + 2x + 3x + 6$	Multiply 3 by each term of $x + 2$.
	$= x^2 + 5x + 6$	Combine like terms.

Writing an expanded quadratic expression in factored form often poses more difficult challenges. You will learn more about factoring quadratic expressions in future math classes.

In 1–6, use the distributive property to find an expression that is equivalent to the given expression. Check each answer by using your calculator to compare tables and graphs.

1. $x(^-4x + 3)$ **2.** $(4x + 3)(x + 7)$ **3.** $(x - 4.5)(x + 6.5)$

4. $(2x - 5)(5x - 2)$ **5.** $x^2 - 6x$ **6.** $12x - 3x^2$

7. Look at your reasoning and your results from questions 1–6.

a. Describe any general rules you discover for multiplying two linear factors.

b. Describe any general rules you discover for factoring a quadratic expression.

Applications • Connections • Extensions

As you work on these ACE questions, use your calculator whenever you need it.

Applications

1. **a.** Write an expression that is equivalent to $3x - (4 + 2x)$.

b. Evaluate $3x - (4 + 2x)$ and the expression you wrote for $x = 5$ and $x = {}^-1$.

2. **a.** Write an expression that is equivalent to $3(x + 2) + 2(x + 2)$.

b. Evaluate $3(x + 2) + 2(x + 2)$ and the expression you wrote for $x = 5$ and $x = {}^-1$.

3. **a.** Write an expression that is equivalent to $3(x + 2) - 2(x + 2)$.

b. Evaluate $3(x + 2) - 2(x + 2)$ and the expression you wrote for $x = 5$ and $x = {}^-1$.

In 4–9, use the distributive and commutative properties to write two expressions that are equivalent to the given expression. Then tell which of the three expressions is easiest to evaluate for a given x value.

4. $3x + 2 + 5x$

5. $12 - 8x + 15 + 10x$

6. $(3x^2 + 5x + 8) + (9x^2 + 2x - 7)$

7. $(5 - 7x) - 2(5x + 12)$

8. $7(4x - 2) + 3(5 + 2x)$

9. $(3x^2 + 5x + 8) - (9x^2 + 2x - 7)$

10. **a.** Evaluate the expression $5000 - 50(75 - T)$ for $T = 25$. Describe the order in which you performed the operations.

b. Write an expression that is equivalent to $5000 - 50(75 - T)$, and evaluate your expression for $T = 25$. Did the order in which you performed the operations change? Explain.

c. Which expression is easier to evaluate?

11. Describe a real-life situation you could use to convince someone that $2x + 5x$ and $7x$ are different ways of expressing the same information.

12. Describe a real-life situation you could use to convince someone that $3x + 5 + 4x$ and $7x + 5$ are different ways of expressing the same information.

In 13–18, copy the statement and insert parentheses, if needed, to make the statement true. For example, to make $3x + 1 - 2x = x + 3$ a true statement, you could write $3(x + 1) - 2x = x + 3$.

13. $6x - 4x - 3x = 5x$

14. $6x - 4x - 3x = {}^{-}x$

15. $7 + 5p - p = 11p$

16. $7 + 5p - p = 7$

17. $7 + 5p - p = 7 + 4p$

18. $7 + 5p - p = 0$

In 19 and 20, copy the statement, replacing the question mark with a number or an expression that makes the statement true.

19. $2(4 + ?) = 18$

20. $2(4 + ?) = 8 + 6x$

21. a. Write 12 as a product of two factors and as a product of three factors.

 b. Write 12 as a sum of two terms and as a sum of three terms.

 c. Write 12 as a product of two factors in which one of the factors is the sum of two terms.

Connections

In 22–24, write two expressions, one in factored form and one in expanded form, for the area of the purple rectangle. Show how the equivalence of the two expressions illustrates the distributive property.

22.

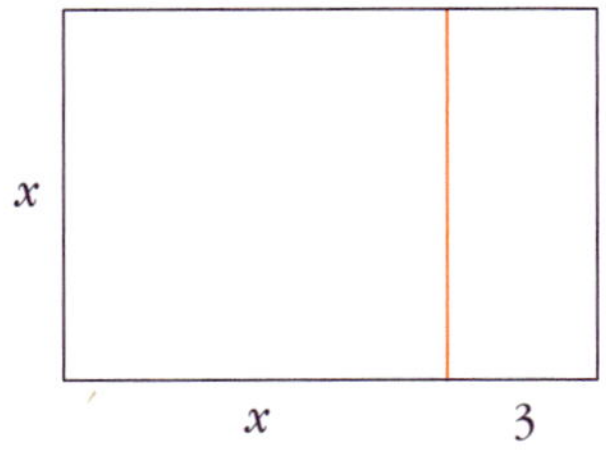

23.

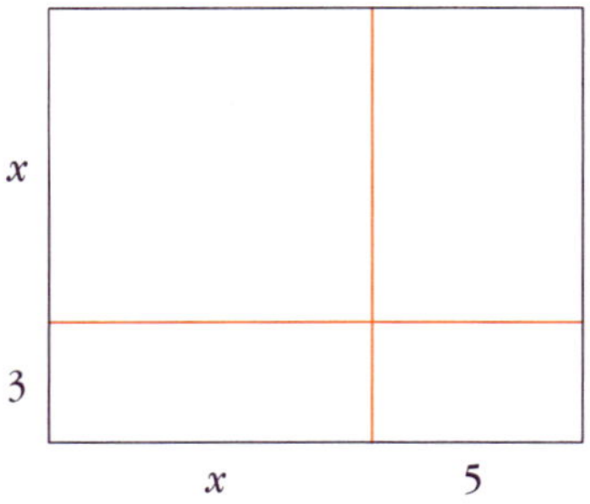

24.

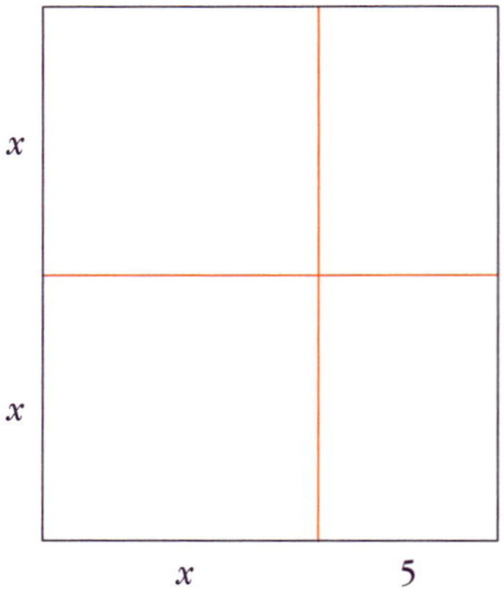

In 25–29, do parts a–c.

25. $^{-}3x + 6 + 5x$ and $6 + 2x$

26. $10 - 5x$ and $5x - 10$

27. $(3x + 4) + (2x - 3)$ and $5x + 1$

28. $9x - 5(x - 3) - 20$ and $5 - 4x$

29. $(10x - 5) - (4x + 2)$ and $10x - 5 - 4x + 2$

a. Make a table and a graph for the two expressions. Show x values from $^{-}5$ to 5 on the graph.

b. Based on your table and graph, tell whether you think the expressions are equivalent.

c. If you think the expressions are equivalent, use the commutative and distributive properties to verify their equivalence. If you think they are not equivalent, use the properties to show why.

In 30–32, use the distributive property to show that the expressions are equivalent. Draw a rectangle to illustrate their equivalence.

30. $x(x + 5)$ and $x^2 + 5x$

31. $(2 + x)(2 + 3x)$ and $4 + 8x + 3x^2$

32. $(x + 2)(2x + 3)$ and $2x^2 + 7x + 6$

33. You have seen that many quadratic expressions can be written in factored form and in expanded form.

a. Which form would you use to determine whether a quadratic relationship has a maximum point or a minimum point? Why?

b. Which form would you use to find the x- and y-intercepts of a quadratic relationship? Why?

c. Which form would you use to find the line of symmetry for a quadratic relationship? Why?

d. Which form would you use to find the coordinates of the maximum or minimum point for a quadratic relationship? Why?

34. For each pair of expressions in questions 30–32, there is an associated quadratic relationship. For example, the expressions in question 30 are associated with the relationship $y = x(x + 5)$, or $y = x^2 + 5x$. Do parts a–c for each pair of expressions in questions 30–32.

a. Find the x- and y-intercepts of the associated quadratic relationship.

b. Find the line of symmetry.

c. Find the coordinates of the maximum or minimum point.

d. Sketch the graph and indicate the information from parts a–c.

In 35–37, tell whether the expressions are equivalent. If they are, use the distributive and commutative properties to illustrate their equivalence. If they are not equivalent, explain why not.

35. $5x^2 + x$ and $x(5x + 1)$

36. $3x^2 + 15$ and $3x(x + 15)$

37. $^{-}4x + 12x^2$ and $^{-}4x(1 - 3x)$

38. Data from past seasons show that the number of people who visit Water Works park on a given day depends on the day's high temperature. The manager wrote the equation $V = 200 + 50(T - 70)$ to estimate the number of visitors based on the day's predicted high temperature, T, in degrees Fahrenheit.

a. What sequence of operations do you need to perform to find the expected number of visitors for a given temperature?

b. Use the commutative and distributive properties to find a different equation for the number of visitors as a function of the temperature.

c. Describe how the expected number of visitors changes as the temperature increases.

d. Without using the table feature of your calculator, estimate the number of visitors on a day when the predicted high temperature is 83°F.

e. Estimate the number of visitors on a day when the predicted high temperature is 68°F and on a day when the predicted high temperature is 65°F. What do your answers indicate about the limitations of this equation model?

f. In parts c–e, which equation did you use to calculate your answers? Explain why you chose this equation.

39. Suppose D dollars are invested in a money-market account that earns 10% interest per year. If no money is withdrawn, the amount of money in the account at the end of one year is $D + 0.10D$.

a. Write an equivalent expression in factored form.

b. If \$1500 is invested, how much money will be in the account at the end of the first year?

40. a. Write an expression for the total price of an item that costs P dollars plus 6% sales tax.

b. What is the total price of a jacket that costs \$47 plus 6% sales tax?

41. a. A store is offering a 30% discount on all purchases. Write an expression for the discounted price of an item that normally sells for P dollars.

b. What is the discounted price of a pair of hiking boots that normally sells for \$68.50?

42. A tour operator's total expense for a bus tour with N people is $200 + 10N$. The tour operator charges each person \$30.

a. Write two equivalent expressions for the profit the tour operator will earn if N people go on the tour.

b. What will the profit be if 10 people go on the tour? If 75 people go?

c. How many people must go on the tour for the tour operator to break even? Explain.

d. Write an expression for the average per-person profit the operator will earn.

Extensions

In 43–45, tell whether the expressions are equivalent. If they are, use the distributive and commutative properties to illustrate their equivalence.

43. $x^2 + 5x + 4$ and $(x + 1)(x + 4)$

44. $3x^2 + 15x$ and $3x(x + 15)$

45. $(x - 5)(x + 2)$ and $x^2 - 3x - 10$

In 46 and 47, use this information: In Problem 3.2, you may have written the following expression for the estimated profit from the walkathon:

$$(1000 + 5c + 15a) - (500 + 6c + 8.50a + 250)$$

An equivalent expression in simplified form is this:

$$250 - c + 6.50a$$

46. When Marcel simplified the profit expression, he found a different result. Study the steps in his reasoning, and find his mistake.

$$\begin{aligned}(1000 + 5c + 15a) - (500 + 6c + 8.50a + 250)\\ &= 1000 + 5c + 15a - 500 + 6c + 8.50a + 250\\ &= 1000 - 500 + 250 + 5c + 6c + 15a + 8.50a\\ &= 750 + 11c + 23.50a\end{aligned}$$

47. Kirtee found a different simplified expression. Study the steps in her reasoning, and find her mistake.

$$\begin{aligned}(1000 + 5c + 15a) - (500 + 6c + 8.50a + 250)\\ &= 1000 + 5c + 15a - 500 - 6c - 8.50a - 250\\ &= 1000 - 500 - 250 + 5c - 6c + 15a - 8.50a\\ &= 250 + c + 6.50a\end{aligned}$$

In 48–51, rewrite the expression so that the calculation is easy to do in your head. Then perform the calculation mentally, and check the result with your calculator.

48. 7(25) + 7(75)

49. 9(4) + 11(4)

50. 3(99) + 3(101)

51. 5(106)

In 52–57, use the distributive and commutative properties to simplify each expression as much as possible. Check that the original expression and your simplified expression are equivalent by testing several x values in both expressions.

52. $2(9x + 15) - (8 + 2x)$

53. $(7x - 12) - 2(3x + 10)$

54. $(19 - 12x) - ({}^{-}9x - 20)$

55. $2[3x + 5(x + 1)] - (10x + 2)$

56. $4 - 2(3x + 5) - ({}^{-}10 - 6x) - 4$

57. $(3x + 1)(2x - 3) - (1 - x)(1 - 6x)$

Mathematical Reflections

In this investigation, you used the distributive and commutative properties to write equivalent expressions. These questions will help you summarize what you have learned:

1. Explain how the distributive and commutative properties can be used to write equivalent expressions. Use examples to illustrate your explanations.

2. **a.** Give an example of a real-life situation that can be represented by at least two equivalent expressions. Explain how each expression represents the situation.

   b. Use the distributive and commutative properties to show that the expressions are equivalent.

Think about your answers to these questions, discuss your ideas with other students and your teacher, and then write a summary of your findings in your journal.

INVESTIGATION 4

Solving Equations

Solving mathematical problems often requires finding solutions to equations or inequalities. In this investigation, you will learn algebraic methods for solving linear and quadratic equations.

4.1 Comparing Costs

Imagine that you are a member of a creative-writing club. The club wants to publish a book of students' short stories, poems, and essays. You contact two local printers to obtain bids on the cost of printing the books.

bid 1: cost = \$100 + \$4 × the number of books printed
bid 2: cost = \$25 + \$7 × the number of books printed

In earlier units, you learned strategies for comparing the two bids. If you let x represent the number of books printed and y represent the cost in dollars, the equations become $y = 100 + 4x$ and $y = 25 + 7x$. You can use your graphing calculator to make and compare tables and graphs of these equations.

Problem 4.1

Use your graphing calculator to help answer parts A–C.

A. Make a table of x and y values for each bid. Use your table to find the number of books for which the two bids are equal. Explain your work.

B. Make a graph of the two equations. Use your graph to find the number of books for which the two bids are equal. Copy the graph onto your paper, and use it to help explain how you found your answer.

C. For what numbers of books is bid 1 less than bid 2? Explain how you found your answer.

Problem 4.1 Follow-Up

1. For each bid, find the cost of printing 75 books. Explain how you found your answers.
2. For each bid, find the greatest number of books that can be printed if the cost is not to exceed $300. Explain your answers.
3. The club decides to request bids from two more printers.

   bid 3: cost = $8 × the number of books printed
   bid 4: cost = $30 + $6 × the number of books printed

   For what number of books are these two bids equal? Explain how you found your answer.

4.2 Solving Linear Equations

You know how to solve equations by using your calculator to make and compare graphs and tables. However, you can solve many equations without using a calculator by operating on the symbols. In Problem 4.1, the equation for bid 1 is $y = 100 + 4x$, where y is the cost and x is the number of books printed. To find out how many books can be printed for $300, you can solve the equation $300 = 100 + 4x$ for the variable x.

In your earlier mathematics work, you learned that to solve linear equations such as $300 = 100 + 4x$, you need to *undo* the mathematical operations until x is alone on one side of the equation. To make sure the sides of the equation remain equal, you must apply any mathematical operation to *both* sides. This *symbolic method* of solution is illustrated in the example below.

$$300 = 100 + 4x$$

$$300 - 100 = 100 - 100 + 4x$$

$$200 = 4x$$

Since 100 is added to $4x$, subtract 100 from *both sides* of the equation.

$$\frac{200}{4} = \frac{4x}{4}$$

Since x is multiplied by 4, divide *both sides* by 4.

$$50 = x$$

Now x is alone on one side of the equation. It is easy to see that the solution is 50. This means that 50 books can be printed for $300.

In Problem 4.1, you found the number of books for which the two bids are equal. This is the same as solving the equation $100 + 4x = 25 + 7x$ for the variable x. Unlike the previous example, this equation has an x on both sides. However, the method for solving the equation is the same: *undo* the mathematical operations until the variable is alone on one side of the equation, making sure to apply all mathematical operations to *both sides* of the equation.

Problem 4.2

The example below shows one way to solve the equation $100 + 4x = 25 + 7x$.

$$100 + 4x = 25 + 7x$$
$$100 + 4x - 4x = 25 + 7x - 4x \quad 1.$$
$$100 = 25 + 3x$$
$$100 - 25 = 25 + 3x - 25 \quad 2.$$
$$75 = 3x$$
$$\frac{75}{3} = \frac{3x}{3} \quad 3.$$
$$25 = x$$

A. Supply an explanation for each numbered step in the above solution to $100 + 4x = 25 + 7x$.

B. The solution above begins by subtracting $4x$ from both sides of the equation. Show a solution that begins with a different step.

C. How can you check that $x = 25$ is the correct solution? Show that your method works.

Problem 4.2 Follow-Up

Solutions to linear equations are often given in fewer steps, with some of the details omitted. It is assumed that the reader can fill in the gaps. In this solution to $11x - 12 = 30 + 5x$, some of the details have been omitted.

$$11x - 12 = 30 + 5x$$
$$11x = 42 + 5x$$
$$6x = 42$$
$$x = 7$$

1. Copy the solution above, filling in the details that were omitted.

2. How can you check that $x = 7$ is the correct solution? Demonstrate your method.

3. Explain how you could use a graph and a table to solve the equation $11x - 12 = 30 + 5x$.

4.3 Reasoning with Symbols

Although you can solve equations by making tables or graphs, it is often more efficient to use the symbolic method described in Problem 4.2.

Problem 4.3

In A–D, use the symbolic method to solve the equation.

A. $7x + 15 = 12x + 5$

B. $14 - 3x = 1.5x + 5$

C. $^{-}3x + 5 = 2x - 10$

D. $3 + 5(x + 2) = 7x - 1$

E. Check your solutions to the equations in A–D.

F. Look over your work for A–D. Record any general strategies that seem to work well in solving linear equations.

Problem 4.3 Follow-Up

1. In a–c, the given equation is related to the equation $y = 7.5x - 23.5$. Explain what question the solution to the given equation answers. For example, the solution to $7.5x - 23.5 = 10$ answers the question "What is the value of x in the equation $y = 7.5x - 23.5$ when $y = 10$?" Then use a table or a graph to solve the equation, and explain how you found your solution.

a. $7.5x - 23.5 = 51.5$ **b.** $7.5x - 23.5 = 0$ **c.** $7.5x - 23.5 = {}^{-}30$

2. Write a linear equation with a solution of $x = 2$. Do you think everyone in your class wrote the same equation? Explain.

3. The school choir is selling boxes of greeting cards to raise money for a trip. The equation for the profit in dollars, P, in terms of the number of boxes sold, x, is

$$P = 3x - (100 + 2x).$$

a. How many boxes must the choir sell to make a \$200 profit? Explain how you found your answer.

b. How many boxes must the choir sell to break even? Explain how you found your answer.

4.4 Solving Quadratic Equations

Different ways of thinking about a problem can lead to different methods for solving it. For example, finding the x-intercepts of the graph of $y = x^2 + 5x$ is the same as solving the equation $x^2 + 5x = 0$.

In earlier units, you solved quadratic equations by using tables and graphs. For example, to solve $x^2 + 5x = 0$, you can trace a graph of $y = x^2 + 5x$ to find x values for which $y = 0$. Or you can make a table of values and look for the x values that correspond to a y value of 0.

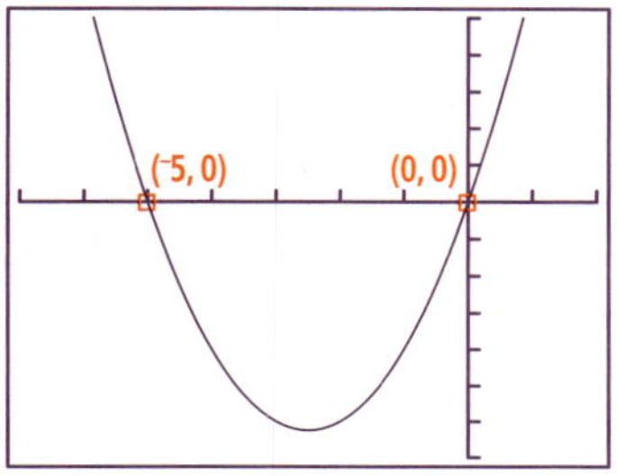

x	y
⁻7	14
⁻6	6
⁻5	0
⁻4	⁻4
⁻3	⁻6
⁻2	⁻6
⁻1	⁻4
0	0
1	6
2	14
3	24

The solutions to $x^2 + 5x = 0$ are called the **roots** of the equation $y = x^2 + 5x$. A quadratic equation may have zero, one, or two roots. If r is a root of an equation, then the point $(r, 0)$ is an x-intercept of the graph.

Algebra provides important tools that can help you solve quadratic equations such as $x^2 + 5x = 0$ without using tables or graphs. This problem illustrates a symbolic method for finding the roots of some quadratic equations.

Problem 4.4

A. The expression $x^2 + 3x$ is in expanded form. Write an equivalent expression in factored form.

B. Find all possible solutions to the equation $x^2 + 3x = 0$. Explain how you know you have found all the solutions.

C. What are the x-intercepts of $y = x^2 + 3x$? Explain how your answers to part B can help you answer this question.

D. Which form of the expression $x^2 + 3x$, the expanded form or the factored form, is more useful for finding the roots, or x-intercepts, of the equation $y = x^2 + 3x$? Explain your reasoning.

E. In 1 and 2, an equation is given for both the factored form and the expanded form of a quadratic expression. Find the roots, or x-intercepts, of the equation without making a table or a graph, and tell which form of the equation you used to find your answer.

1. $y = 4x^2 - 8x$ or $y = 4x(x - 2)$ **2.** $y = 6x(5 - 2x)$ or $y = 30x - 12x^2$

F. In 1–3, solve the equation by first factoring the quadratic expression.

1. $x^2 + 4.5x = 0$ **2.** $x^2 - 9x = 0$ **3.** $^-x^2 + 10x = 0$

Problem 4.4 Follow-Up

1. Check your answers to part F without using a table or a graph.

2. Check your answers to part F by making graphs and finding the x-intercepts.

3. **a.** For each expression below, find an equivalent expression in expanded form.

b. Which form of the expression would you use to predict the x-intercepts of the related graph? Find the x-intercepts and explain your reasoning.

i. $(2x + 1)(x + 5)$ **ii.** $(x + 2)(x - 2)$

4. Use the diagram below to find the linear factors of $x^2 + 8x + 12$. Use the factors to solve the equation $x^2 + 8x + 12 = 0$.

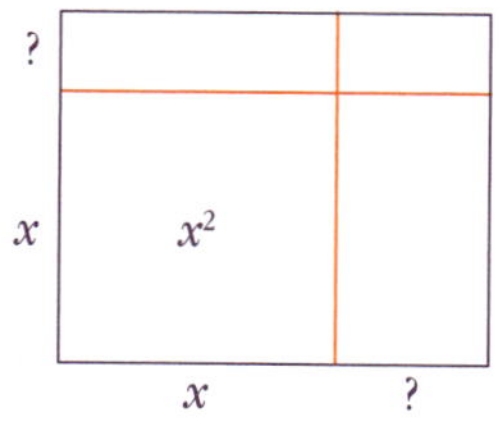

$$x^2 + 8x + 12 = (x + ?)(x + ?)$$

Applications • Connections • Extensions

As you work on these ACE questions, use your calculator whenever you need it.

Applications

In 1–10, solve the equation by using the symbolic method. Check your solution by making tables or graphs with your calculator.

1. $6x + 10 = 4x + 18$

2. $3x + 47 = 7x + 7$

3. $10 - 5x = 10x + 5(x - 6)$

4. $^{-}13x + 36 = 20x - 30$

5. $8.3x - 10.75 = 51.5$

6. $x(x - 7) = 0$

7. $x^2 + 1.5x = 0$

8. $x^2 + 6x + 8 = 0$

9. $x^2 + 2x + 1 = 0$

10. $8x - x^2 = 0$

11. The student council is sponsoring a T-shirt sale. They plan to take orders in advance so they know how many T-shirts to have printed. They made the following estimates of expenses and income for their sale:

- Expense of \$350 for advertising
- Expense of \$3.25 for each T-shirt
- Income of \$10 for each T-shirt
- Income of \$200 from a local business in exchange for printing the business's logo on the back of the T-shirts

a. Write an equation for the profit, P, the student council will make if they sell n T-shirts.

b. How many T-shirts must the student council sell to break even? Describe at least three ways you could find the answer to this question. Use one of the ways to find the solution.

Connections

12. The equations $N = 2s + 2(s + 2)$ and $N = 4(s + 2) - 4$ represent the number of square tiles, measuring 1 foot on each side, needed to make a border for a square pool with sides of length s feet.

a. Solve $N = 2s + 2(s + 2)$ for $N = 48$.

b. Solve $N = 4(s + 2) - 4$ for $N = 48$.

c. How do your answers for parts a and b compare? Why?

13. The number of visitors to a park depends on the day's high Fahrenheit temperature, T, according to the equation $V = 200 + 50(T - 70)$. If 1000 people visit the park one day, what would you predict was that day's high temperature?

14. The number of games played in a league with n teams if each team plays each of the other teams twice is $g = n^2 - n$. What are the x-intercepts of the graph of this equation? Explain what information they represent.

15. The height in feet of an arch above a point x feet from one of its bases is given by the equation $y = 0.2x(100 - x)$. What is the maximum height of the arch? Explain how you found your answer.

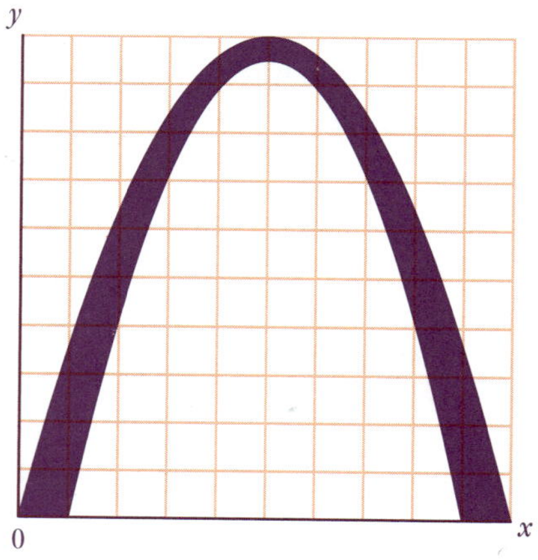

16. Below are the graphs of $y = 1.5x + 6$ and $y = {}^{-}2x + 15$. The scale on the x-axis is 1, and the scale on the y-axis is 3.

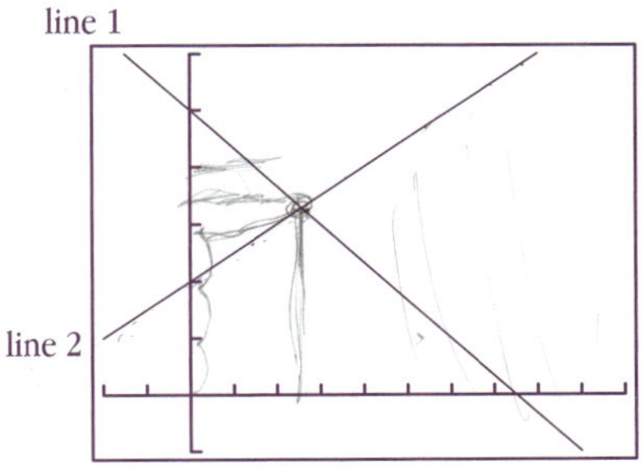

a. Match each equation, $y = 1.5x + 6$ and $y = {}^{-}2x + 15$, to line 1 or line 2.

b. What are the coordinates of the point of intersection of the two lines?

c. How could you find the answer to part b without using a graph or a table?

d. What values of x satisfy the inequality $1.5x + 6 < {}^{-}2x + 15$? How is your answer shown on the graph?

e. What values of x satisfy the inequality $1.5x + 6 > {}^{-}2x + 15$? How is your answer shown on the graph?

17. Below is the graph of $y = x^2 - 9x$. The scale on the x-axis is 1, and the scale on the y-axis is 2. Use the graph to answer parts a–e on the next page.

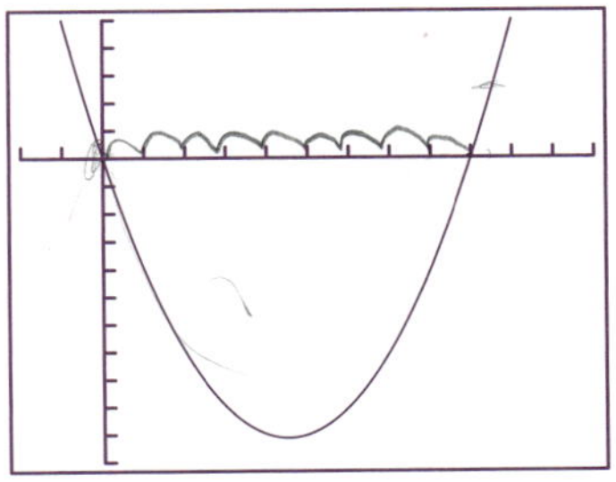

a. What are the coordinates of the x-intercepts?

b. How could you find the answer to part a without using a graph or a table?

c. What values of x satisfy the inequality $x^2 - 9x < 0$? How is your answer shown on the graph?

d. What values of x satisfy the inequality $x^2 - 9x > 0$? How is your answer shown on the graph?

e. What is the minimum y value? What x value corresponds to this minimum value?

Extensions

18. Below is the graph of $y = (x + 3)(x - 2)$. The scale on both axes is 1.

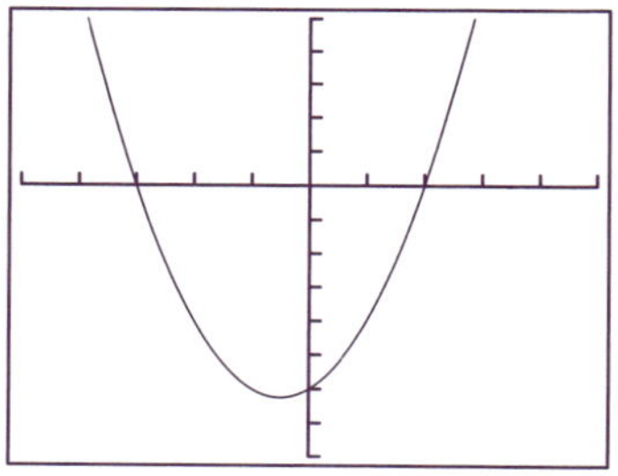

a. Solve $(x + 3)(x - 2) = 0$? How are the solutions shown on the graph?

b. What values of x satisfy the inequality $(x + 3)(x - 2) < 0$? How is your answer shown on the graph?

c. How can you find the answer to part b, without using the graph, by analyzing the inequality? (Hint: Use what you know about multiplying positive and negative numbers.)

19. Here is the graph of $y = (x + 2)(x - 1)(x - 5)$. The scale on the x-axis is 1, and the scale on the y-axis is 5.

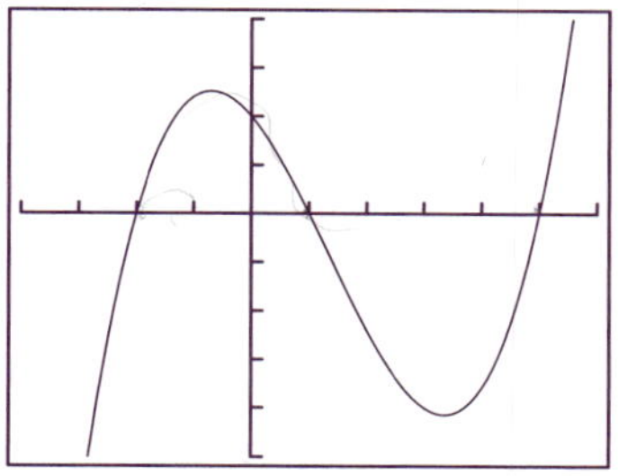

a. Solve $(x + 2)(x - 1)(x - 5) = 0$? How are the solutions shown on the graph?

b. What values of x satisfy the inequality $(x + 2)(x - 1)(x - 5) < 0$? How is your answer shown on the graph?

c. How can you find the answer to part b, without using the graph, by analyzing the inequality? (Hint: Use what you know about multiplying positive and negative numbers.)

In 20 and 21, solve the equation and check your answer.

20. $5 + 8(x + 2) = 6(1 + x) - 1$

21. $2x - 3(x + 4) - 10 = 9 - 3(2 + 2x)$

22. a. Use an area model to find the factored form of the expression $x^2 + 7x + 12$.

b. Use your answer to help you solve the equation $x^2 + 7x + 12 = 0$.

23. a. Use an area model to find the factored form of the expression $x^2 + 8x + 15$.

b. Use your answer to help you solve the equation $x^2 + 8x + 15 = 0$.

24. a. Use an area model to find the factored form of the expression $x^2 - 9$.

b. Use your answer to help you solve the equation $x^2 - 9 = 0$.

25. a. Use an area model to find the factored form of the expression $2x^2 + 5x + 3$.

b. Use your answer to help you solve the equation $2x^2 + 5x + 3 = 0$.

In 26 and 27, solve the equation. Explain your reasoning.

26. $x^2 + 5x + 7 = 1$

27. $x^2 + 6x + 15 = 6$

Mathematical Reflections

In this investigation, you learned methods for solving linear and quadratic equations. These questions will help you summarize what you have learned:

1. Describe some general strategies for solving linear equations. Give examples that illustrate your strategies.

2. **a.** What general strategies can you use to solve quadratic equations of the form $ax^2 + bx = 0$?

   b. Will the strategies you described in part a work for solving quadratic equations of the form $ax^2 + bx + c = 0$? Use an example to help explain your answer.

3. In a–c, illustrate your ideas with an example.

   a. How could you solve a linear equation of the form $mx + b = 0$ by using a graph?

   b. How could you solve a linear equation of the form $ax + b = cx + d$ by using a graph?

   c. How could you solve a quadratic equation of the form $ax^2 + bx = 0$ by using a graph?

Think about your answers to these questions, discuss your ideas with other students and your teacher, and then write a summary of your findings in your journal.

INVESTIGATION 5

Writing Expressions for Surface Area

In this unit, you have seen that many situations can be represented by several different, but equivalent, algebraic expressions, and you have learned methods for writing equivalent expressions. You have also developed algebraic strategies for solving linear and quadratic equations. In this investigation, you will apply all the ideas you have learned.

5.1 Stacking Rods

In this problem, you will find the surface area of stacks of staggered rods.

Problem 5.1

You will need four to six rods of the same length and several unit rods. In this problem, you will find the surface area of stacks of the longer rods. The rods in each stack should be staggered by 1 unit, as shown below.

stacked rods

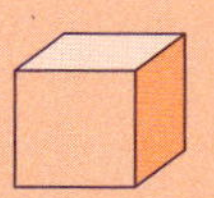
unit rod

A. Use the unit rods to determine the dimensions of one of the longer rods.

B. Find the surface area of a single rod, a stack of two rods, a stack of three rods, and so on.

C. Use your findings to help you write an equation for the relationship between the surface area, A, and the number of rods in the stack, N.

Problem 5.1 Follow-Up

1. Compare your expression for surface area with the expressions written by other groups who used rods of the same length.

a. Are all the expressions equivalent? Explain why or why not by using the rules you have learned for writing equivalent expressions.

b. Use your calculator to make a table and a graph of your equation. How could you use tables or graphs to check whether the expressions found by your group and the other groups are equivalent?

2. a. Use your equation to find the surface area of a stack of 12 rods.

b. Use your equation to find the surface area of a stack of 20 rods.

3. Will your equation work to calculate the surface area of stacks made from rods of a different length? If not, how could you change your equation so it would work? Check your idea by looking at the equations written by groups who used rods of a different length.

4. Is the relationship between the surface area and the number of rods linear, quadratic, exponential, or none of these? Explain your answer.

As you work on these ACE questions, use your calculator whenever you need it.

Applications

1. In their work in Problem 5.1, Kwang-Hee's group used rods that are 4 units long. They wrote this equation for the surface area of a stack of N rods:

$$A = 18 + 12(N - 1)$$

a. Is this equation correct? Explain how you know.

b. What is the surface area of a stack of 15 of these rods?

c. If the surface area of a stack of these rods is 246 square units, how many rods are in the stack? Explain how you found your answer.

2. In their work in Problem 5.1, two groups in Mr. Samartino's class used rods that are 4 units long. Each group wrote an equation for the surface area of a stack of N rods.

$$A = 18 + 12(N - 1)$$

$$A = 4(2N + 2) + 2(2N - 1)(1)$$

a. For each equation, describe how the group might have thought about the problem. Explain what each part of the equation represents.

b. Show that the expressions for the surface area are equivalent.

c. The surface area of a particular stack of these rods is 258 square units. Use one of the equations to find the number of rods in the stack. Check your answer by substituting the values for A and N into both equations.

3. In Problem 5.1, Brianna worked with rods that are 4 units long. To find the surface area of each stack, she slid the rods into a rectangular prism. She found the surface area of the prism and then added the extra area created by staggering the rods.

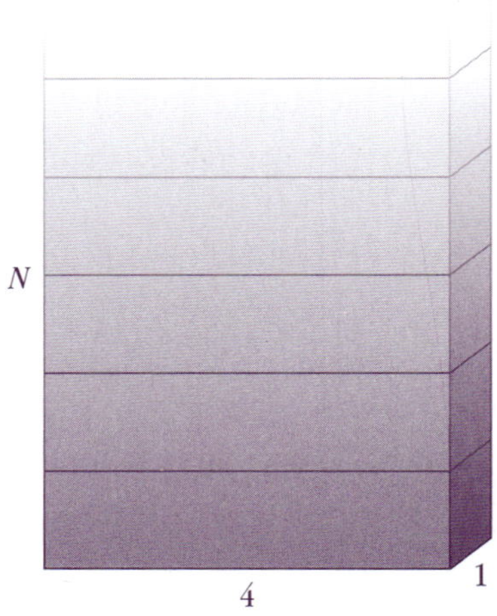

a. Write an expression for surface area that represents Brianna's method.

b. Show that your expression from part a is equivalent to the expressions in ACE question 2.

Connections

4. a. Write an equation for the surface area of a stack of N staggered rods if each rod is 12 units long.

b. If the surface area of a particular stack of these rods is 162 square units, how many rods are in the stack?

c. Write an equation for the volume of a stack of N of these rods.

Extensions

5. Consider rods of length 1, 2, 3, 4, 5, 6, 7, 8, 9, and 10 units.

a. Make a table showing the surface area of a stack of N staggered rods of each length.

Length of rod	Surface area of a stack of N rods
1	
2	
3	

b. Describe any patterns in your table.

c. Write an equation for the surface area, A, of a stack of N rods of length L.

6. Rods of length 4 units are stacked to form a rectangular prism.

a. What are the dimensions of the prism?

b. Write an equation for the surface area, A, of the prism.

c. What is the surface area of a prism 10 rods high and 10 rods wide?

d. Is the relationship between the surface area and the number of rods linear, quadratic, exponential, or none of these? Explain your answer.

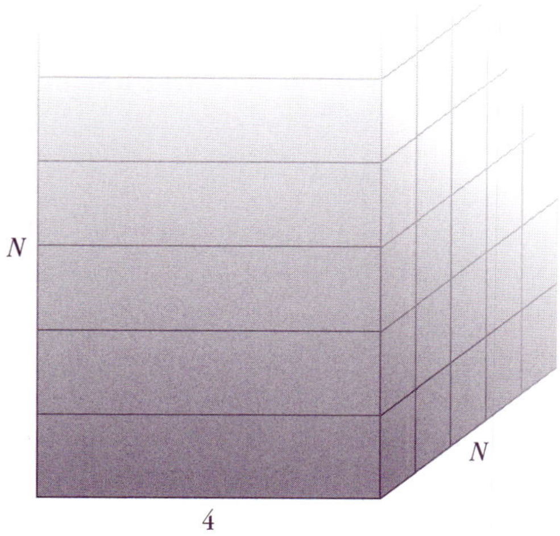

Mathematical Reflections

In this investigation, you wrote equations to represent the surface area of a stack of rods. You saw that different ways of thinking about the surface area led to different equations. These questions will help you summarize what you have learned:

1 **a.** Describe at least two of the strategies your class used to find the surface area of the stacks.

b. Choose two of the strategies you described in part a, and show how they can be represented symbolically.

2 **a.** Describe situations that can be represented by several different, but equivalent, expressions. Explain how each expression represents a different way of thinking about the situation.

b. For each situation you described in part a, use the distributive and commutative properties to show that the expressions are equivalent.

Think about your answers to these questions, discuss your ideas with other students and your teacher, and then write a summary of your findings in your journal.

The Unit Project

Counting Cubes

Study the sequence of cube buildings below. What pattern do you see? Use the pattern to build the next building in the sequence. Think about the steps you are taking as you construct your building. The labels below the drawing illustrate one way you might think about the pattern.

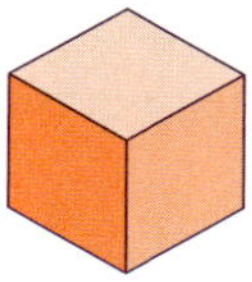

1 cube

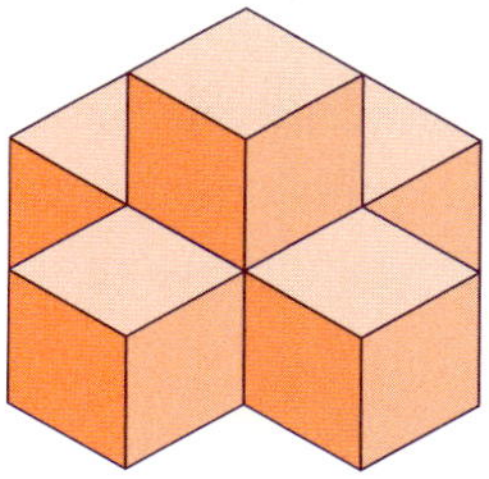

1 cube in the center and 5 arms with 1 cube each

1 cube in the center and 5 arms with 2 cubes each

1. Describe a pattern *you* see in the cube buildings.

2. Use your pattern to write an expression for the number of cubes in the nth building. You may find it helpful to make a table to organize your thinking.

3. Use your expression to find the number of cubes in the fifth building. Check your result by constructing the fifth building and counting the cubes.

4. Look for a different pattern in the buildings. Describe the pattern, and use it to write a different expression for the number of cubes in the nth building.

5. Start with one of the expressions you wrote, and use the distributive and commutative properties to write a third expression. Does the third expression suggest another pattern in the cube buildings? Explain.

6. Now make your own sequence of cube buildings by following a particular pattern.

a. Sketch the first few buildings in your sequence, and write an expression for the number of cubes in the nth building.

b. Challenge a classmate to describe the pattern in your buildings and to use the pattern to write an expression for the number of cubes in the nth building.

c. Compare the expression you wrote in part a to the expression written by your classmate. If the expressions are not identical, use the commutative and distributive properties to prove or disprove their equivalence.

Looking Back and Looking Ahead

Unit Reflections

Working on the problems of this unit you learned and practiced the standard rules for using symbolic expressions in algebra. You learned the *order of operations* rules for evaluating expressions when you were given values of the variables involved. You found properties of numbers and operations that can be used to write algebraic expressions in *equivalent forms* and to *solve linear* and *quadratic equations* with algebraic reasoning.

Using Your Algebraic Reasoning—To test your understanding and skill in use of algebraic notation and reasoning, consider several problems that arise in the business of managing a summer concert tour for a popular music group.

1 *The promoter pays appearance fees to each group on the concert program. Some groups also get a share of the ticket sale income. Suppose that*

- *the lead group will be paid $15,000, plus $5 for every ticket sold.*
- *one of the other groups will receive $1500, plus $1.50 for every ticket sold.*
- *the third group will receive a flat fee of $1250.*

a. Write three different but equivalent equations showing how the promoter's expenses for performers, E, depend on the number of tickets sold for the concert, t.

i. Write the first equation to show payments to each separate group.

ii. Write the second equation to show the payment to the lead group and the combined payments to the other groups.

iii. Write the third equation to show the simplest calculation of the total amount paid to the performers.

b. Suppose that tickets are priced at $25, $30, and $40.

i. Write an equation that shows how the promoter's income from ticket sales, I, depends on the number sold of each type of ticket, x, y, and z.

ii. Find the average income per ticket if there are sales of 5000 tickets at $25, 3000 tickets at $30, and 950 tickets sold at $40.

iii. Write an equation showing how the average income per ticket sold, V, depends on the variables x, y, z, and t.

2 *Suppose that the lead group has a new CD that will be sold only at concerts during the tour. Experience from other concert tours tells that the relation between the number of CDs sold,* s, *and price in dollars for the CD,* p, *can be modeled by the equation* $s = 10{,}000 - 200p$.

a. If the price is \$10, how many CDs will likely be sold?

b. What price(s) will yield sales of 3500 CDs?

c. What do the numbers 10,000 and −200 tell about the relation between CD price and the number that will be sold at a typical concert?

d. Write an equation expressing the income, I, from CD sales in terms of s and p. Then write another equation expressing I only in terms of p, the price of the CD.

e. What price(s) will yield total income of \$0?

f. What price(s) will yield maximum income?

3 *Suppose that concert seating is usually arranged in three sections as shown. Specific dimensions of the sections vary depending on the space available at each concert site.*

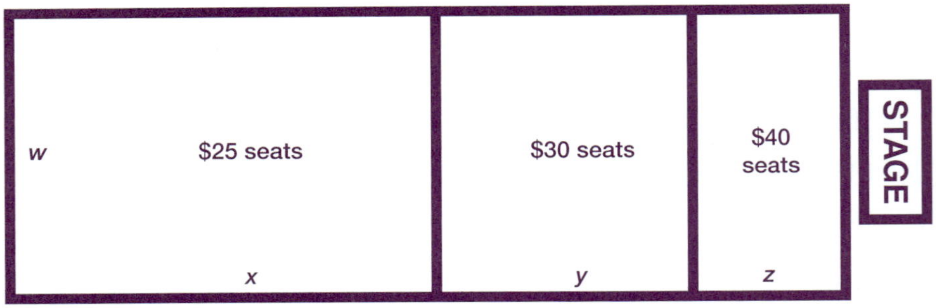

a. Write two equivalent equations showing the area of the entire seating area, A.

i. In one equation, show how A depends on the areas of the three seating sections.

ii. In the other equation, write an equivalent expression that requires fewer calculations to find A.

b. Seating is arranged to allow one square meter of space for every 2 people. Write two equivalent equations that show the number of seats, S, in terms of w, x, y, and z.

i. In one equation, show how S depends on the numbers of seats in the separate sections.

ii. In the other equation, write an expression that requires fewer calculations to find S.

c. When the concert is on a grassy field, aisles around and between the seating sections must be covered with boards that are 1.5 meters wide. How many square meters of board will be needed to cover the aisles for any given set of dimensions *w, x, y,* and *z*? Express your answer in at least two equivalent ways.

Explaining Your Reasoning—When you solve problems by writing and operating on symbolic expressions, you have to be careful to follow standard rules for use of such expressions and operations. When you present your conclusions to others, you should be able to explain your reasoning by application of those rules.

1. Evaluate the following expressions for the given values of x and y. Be prepared to explain the reasons for your answers.

   a. $5(x + 12y)$ when $x = {}^{-}7$ and $y = 0.5$

   b. $15 - 8x^2$ when $x = {}^{-}3$

   c. $\frac{5x^2 - 4x}{7 - 3x}$ when $x = {}^{-}2$

2. Write each of the following expressions in two different but equivalent forms. Be prepared to explain why the new forms are equivalent to those that are given.

   a. $7x(3 - 9x)$

   b. $15x + 8x^2$

   c. $(5x^2 - 9x + 7) + 4x(3 + 5x)$

   d. $(450 - 8a + 7b) - 3(5a - 2b)$

   e. $(2x + 3)(5x - 7)$

3. Solve the following equations by rewriting them in equivalent forms from which the roots are easy to find. Give the properties of numbers and operations that justify each step of your solution process.

   a. $9.5x + 12.5 = 50.5$

   b. $3x^2 + 12x = 0$

   c. $(x + 4)(3x - 6) = 0$

   d. $2(9x + 15) = 8 + 2x$

4. What does it mean to say that two algebraic expressions are *equivalent*?

The algebraic ideas and techniques you've used in this unit will be applied and extended in future mathematics courses and in science and business problems. The rules for expressing relationships among variables and for solving given equations are consistent around the world and in every discipline!

Glossary

commutative property of addition A mathematical property that states that the order in which quantities are added does not matter. For example, $5 + 7 = 7 + 5$ and $2x + 4 = 4 + 2x$. The commutative property of addition is sometimes called the *rearrangement property of addition.*

commutative property of multiplication A mathematical property that states that the order in which quantities are multiplied does not matter. For example, $5 \times 7 = 7 \times 5$ and $2x(4) = (4)2x$. The commutative property of multiplication is sometimes called the *rearrangement property of multiplication*.

distributive property A mathematical property used to rewrite expressions involving addition and multiplication. The distributive property states that for any three quantities *a, b,* and *c*, $a(b + c) = ab + ac$. If an expression is written as a factor multiplied by a sum, you can use the distributive property to *multiply* the factor by each term in the sum.

$$4(5 + x) = 4(5) + 4(x) = 20 + 4x$$

If an expression is written as a sum of terms and the terms have a common factor, you can use the distributive property to rewrite the expression as the common factor multiplied by a sum. This process is called *factoring*.

$$20 + 4x = 4(5) + 4(x) = 4(5 + x)$$

equivalent expressions Expressions that represent the same quantity. For example, $2 + 5$, $3 + 4$, and 7 are equivalent expressions. In this unit, you used the distributive and commutative properties to write equivalent expressions. For example, you can apply the distributive property to $2(x + 3)$ to write the equivalent expression $2x + 6$. By applying the commutative property to $2x + 6$, you can write the equivalent expression $6 + 2x$.

expanded form The form of an expression made up of sums or differences of terms rather than products of factors. The expressions $x^2 + 7x + 12$ and $x^2 + 2x$ are in expanded form.

factored form The form of an expression made up of products of factors rather than sums or differences of terms. The expressions $(x + 3)(x + 4)$ and $x(x - 2)$ are in factored form.

parabola The graph of a quadratic function. A parabola has a line of symmetry that passes through the maximum point if the graph opens downward or through the minimum point if the graph opens upward.

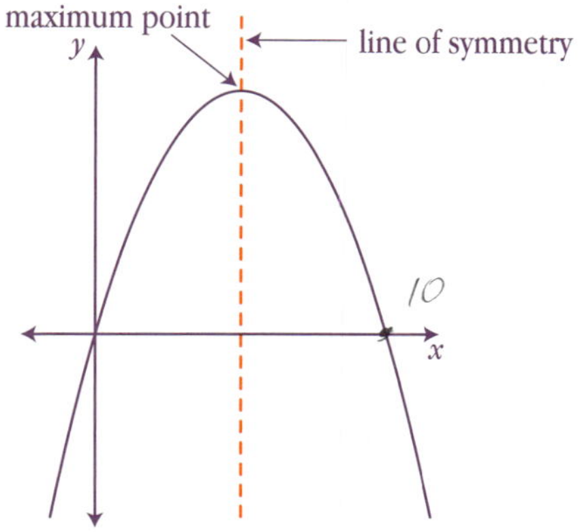

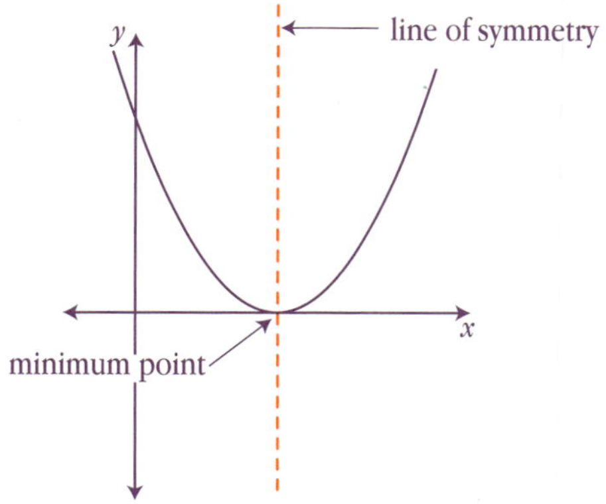

roots The roots of an equation are the values of x that make y equal 0. For example, the roots of $y = x^2 + 5x$ are $^{-}5$ and 0 because $(^{-}5)^2 + 5(^{-}5) = 0$ and $0^2 + 5(0) = 0$. The roots of $y = x^2 + 5x$ are the solutions to the equation $0 = x^2 + 5x$. The roots of an equation are the x-intercepts of its graph.

term An expression with numbers and/or variables multiplied together. In the expression $3x^2 - 2x + 10$, $3x^2$, $^{-}2x$, and 10 are terms.

Glosario

expresiones equivalentes Expresiones que representan la misma cantidad, como por ejemplo 2 + 5, 3 + 4 y 7. En esta unidad, usaste las propiedades distributiva y conmutativa para escribir expresiones equivalentes. Por ejemplo, puedes aplicar la propiedad distributiva a $2(x + 3)$ para escribir la expresión equivalente $2x + 6$. Mediante la aplicación de la propiedad conmutativa a $2x + 6$, puedes escribir la expresión equivalente $6 + 2x$.

forma de factores La forma de una expresión compuesta de productos de factores en vez de sumas o diferencias de términos. Las expresiones $(x + 3)(x + 4)$ y $x(x - 2)$ están representadas en forma de factores.

forma desarrollada La forma de una expresión compuesta de sumas o diferencias de términos en vez de productos de factores. Las expresiones $x^2 + 7x + 12$ y $x^2 + 2x$ están representadas en forma desarrollada.

parábola La gráfica de una función cuadrática. Una parábola tiene un eje de simetría que pasa por el punto máximo si la gráfica se abre hacia abajo o por el punto mínimo si la gráfica se abre hacia arriba.

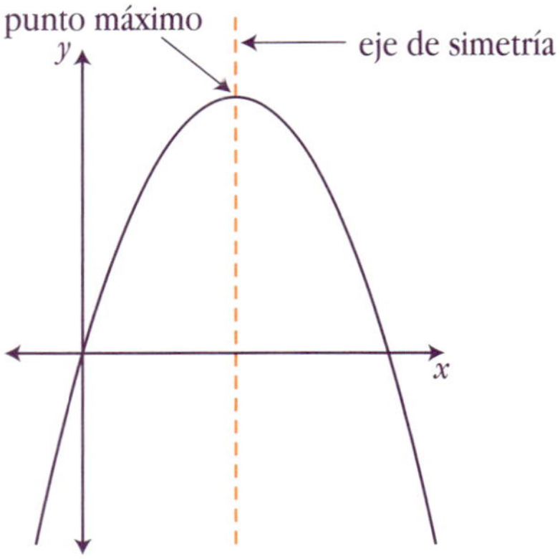

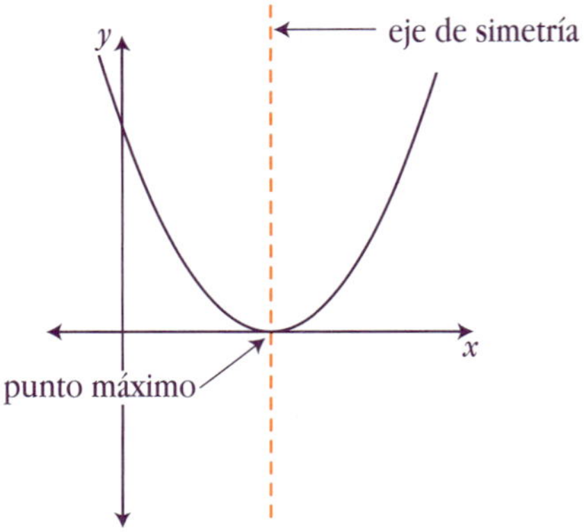

propiedad conmutativa de la multiplicación Una propiedad matemática que dice que el orden en que se multiplican los factores no tiene importancia. Por ejemplo, $5 \times 7 = 7 \times 5$ y $2x(4) = (4)2x$. A veces se la llama *propiedad de reordenamiento de la multiplicación*.

propiedad conmutativa de la suma Una propiedad matemática que dice que el orden en que se suman las cantidades no tiene importancia. Por ejemplo, $5 + 7 = 7 + 5$ y $2x + 4 = 4 + 2x$. A veces se la llama *propiedad de reordenamiento de la suma*.

propiedad distributiva Una propiedad matemática usada para reescribir expresiones que incluyen la suma y la multiplicación. La propiedad distributiva se establece para tres cantidades cualesquiera a, b y c, $a(b + c) = ab + ac$. Si una expresión se escribe como la multiplicación de un factor por una suma, la propiedad distributiva puede usarse para *multiplicar* el factor por cada término de la suma.

$$4(5 + x) = 4(5) + 4(x) = 20 + 4x$$

Si una expresión se escribe como la suma de los términos y los términos tienen un factor común, la propiedad distributiva puede usarse para reescribir o descomponer en factores la expresión como la multiplicación del factor común por una suma.

$$20 + 4x = 4(5) + 4(x) = 4(5 + x)$$

raíces Las raíces de una ecuación son los valores de x que hacen que y equivalga a 0. Por ejemplo, las raíces de $y = x^2 + 5x$ son $^-5$ y 0 porque $(^-5)^2 + 5(^-5) = 0$ y $0^2 + 5(0) = 0$. Las raíces de $y = x^2 + 5x$ son las soluciones de la ecuación $0 = x^2 + 5x$. Las raíces de una ecuación son los puntos de intersección del eje de las x de la gráfica de esa ecuación.

término Una expresión con números y/o variables multiplicados entre sí. En la expresión $3x^2 - 2x + 10$, $3x^2$, ^-2x y 10 son términos.

Index

Connected Mathematics™

Kaleidoscopes, Hubcaps, and Mirrors

Symmetry and Transformations

Student Edition

Glenda Lappan
James T. Fey
William M. Fitzgerald
Susan N. Friel
Elizabeth Difanis Phillips

PEARSON
Prentice Hall

Glenview, Illinois
Needham, Massachusetts
Upper Saddle River, New Jersey

Kaleidoscopes, Hubcaps, and Mirrors

Connected Mathematics™ was developed at Michigan State University with the support of National Science Foundation Grant No. MDR 9150217.

This project was supported, in part,
by the
National Science Foundation
Opinions expressed are those of the authors
and not necessarily those of the Foundation

The Michigan State University authors and administration have agreed that all MSU royalties arising from this publication will be devoted to purposes supported by the Department of Mathematics and the MSU Mathematics Education Enrichment Fund.

Photo Acknowledgements: 6 © Jeffry Myers/Stock, Boston; 7 (left) © Bob Kalman/The Image Works; 7 (center and right) © Mali Apple; 8 (left) © Photoworld/FPG International; 8 (center) © Science Source/Photo Researchers, Inc.; 8 (right) © Mali Apple; 9 © Charles Orrico/Superstock, Inc.; 11 © Bob Daemmrich/The Image Works; 14 (left) © Robert Frerck/Tony Stone Images; 14 (right) © Ira Kirschenbaum/Stock, Boston; 26 © Jean-Claude Lejeune/Stock, Boston; 38 © Richard B. Hoit/Photo Researchers, Inc.

Contents

Kaleidoscopes, Hubcaps, and Mirrors

Look at the drawing of the butterfly. The right half of the butterfly is the mirror image of the left half. You could fold the butterfly so that the two halves match exactly. Does anything else on these pages show this property? Can you think of other things that have this property?

Look at the hubcap. You could rotate the hubcap less than a full turn to a point at which it looks the same as the original. Does anything else on these pages show this property? Can you think of other things that have this property?

Now, look at the pattern on the quilt. You could slide one part of the pattern in a straight line so that it exactly matches another part. Does anything else on these pages show this property? Can you think of other things that have this property?

The butterfly, the hubcap, and the quilt pattern that you see here may look very different, but they share an important characteristic called *symmetry*. There is some part of each drawing that is repeated to create a balanced pattern. In each drawing, can you describe the part and how it is repeated to make the pattern?

In this unit, you will study the mathematical properties of different types of symmetry. You will also investigate the motions that are used to create symmetric designs.

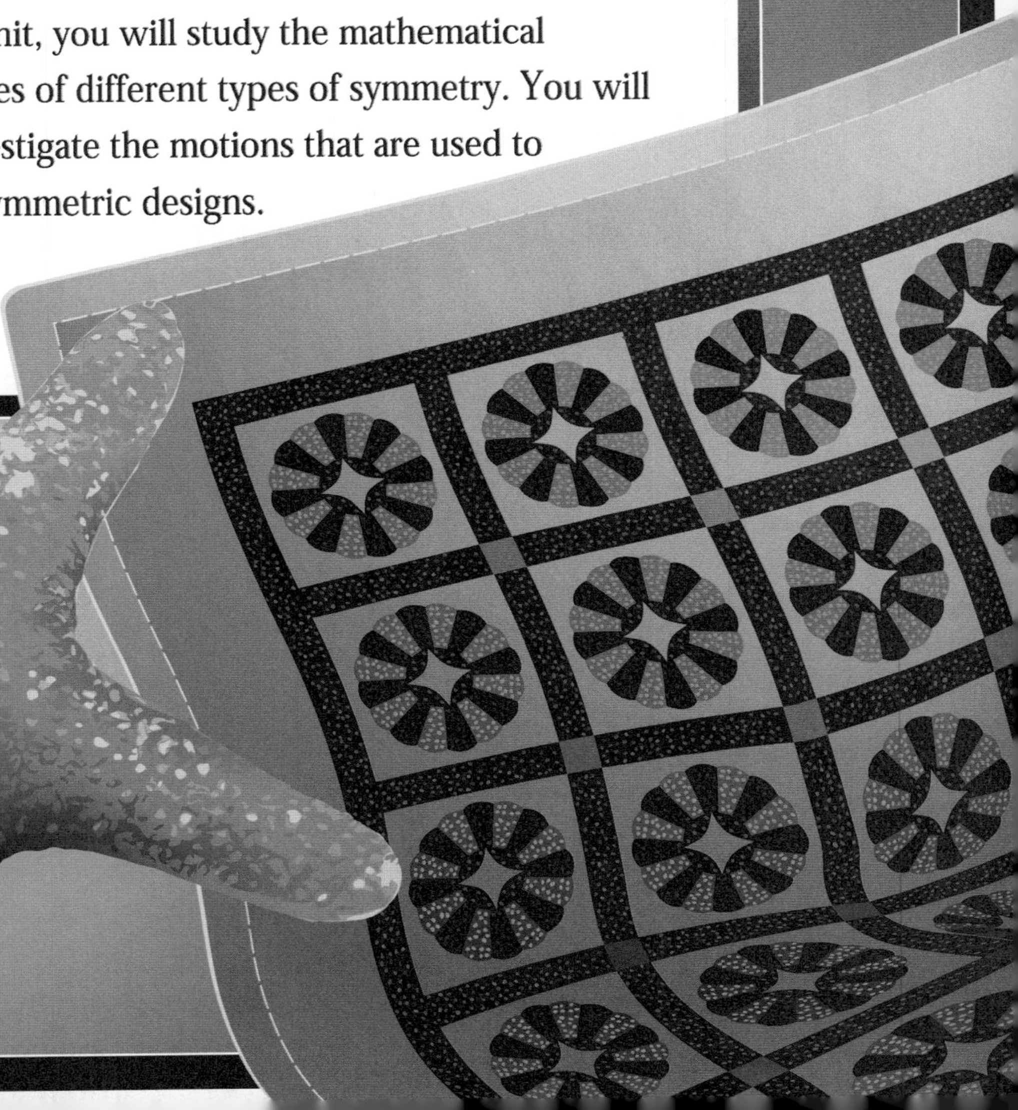

Mathematical Highlights

In *Kaleidoscopes, Hubcaps, and Mirrors* you will explore the geometric concept of symmetry and its uses in design of products and works of art. The unit should help you to

- Recognize and describe the basic forms of geometric symmetry;
- Construct figures and designs with various types of symmetry;
- Describe symmetry in terms of transformations—reflections, rotations, and translations;
- Use transformations to construct symmetric figures from simple elements;
- Analyze the algebraic properties of operations that combine symmetry transformations one after another; and
- Use symmetry concepts and properties to solve design problems.

As you work on the problems of this unit, make it a habit to ask questions about problem situations that involve shapes: *What kinds of symmetry are evident in the given figures? What does symmetry of the figure or pattern tell about its properties and applications? How can symmetry ideas be used to describe a figure so someone else could reproduce it? What figure will result from combining several symmetry transformations?*

INVESTIGATION 1

Three Types of Symmetry

When part of an object or design is repeated to create a balanced pattern, we say that the object or design has *symmetry.* Butterflies, the blades of a fan, and wallpaper designs often have symmetry.

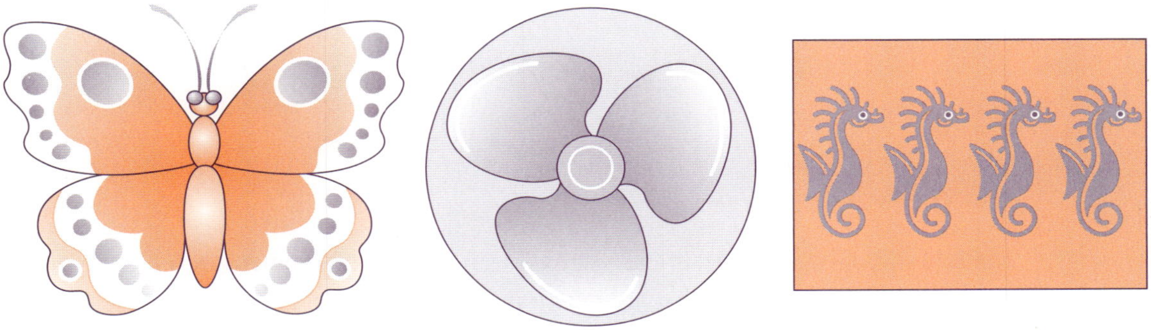

You can find examples of symmetry all around you. Artists use symmetry to make designs that are pleasing to the eye. Architects use symmetry to create a sense of balance in their buildings. And symmetry is found throughout the natural world.

There are several types of symmetry:

- The butterfly above has **reflectional symmetry,** which is also called *line symmetry* or *mirror symmetry*. If you drew a vertical line through the center of the butterfly, the two halves of the drawing would be mirror images.
- The fan blades have **rotational symmetry**. You could rotate the drawing less than a full turn about its centerpoint to a position in which it looks the same as the original drawing.
- The wallpaper design has **translational symmetry**. You could slide, or *translate,* any figure in the design in a regular straight-line pattern so that it exactly matches any other figure.

These three types of symmetry have unique mathematical properties. In this investigation, you will look for symmetry, and you will create designs with different types of symmetry.

1.1 Reflectional Symmetry

You may already have experience creating shapes and designs with *reflectional symmetry*. You can produce a symmetric design by folding a sheet of paper in half and making cuts.

The fold through the center of the heart above is the line of symmetry. A *line of symmetry* divides a design into halves that are mirror images. If you fold a design on a line of symmetry, the halves will exactly match. Mirrors and other reflecting devices are useful for checking for reflectional symmetry. When you place a mirror on a line of symmetry, the reflected image looks identical to the design behind the mirror.

Tracing paper can also be helpful in looking for reflectional symmetry. You can trace one half of a design and then flip your tracing over the line of symmetry to see whether it matches the other half of the design.

Think about this!

The objects below have reflectional symmetry. Can you identify the lines of symmetry?

Problem 1.1

The designs below are reproduced on Labsheet 1.1. Use mirrors, tracing paper, or other tools to help you find all the lines of symmetry in each design.

A.

B.

C.

D.

Problem 1.1 Follow-Up

Explain why these traditional quilt designs do *not* have reflectional symmetry.

1.

Next-door neighbor

2.

Nocturne

1.2 Rotational Symmetry

The pinwheel design at right has *rotational symmetry*. It can be rotated 45°, 90°, 135°, 180°, 225°, 270°, 315°, or 360° about its centerpoint to a position in which it looks the same as the original design. The *angle of rotation* is the smallest angle through which a design can be rotated to coincide with the original design. The angle of rotation for this pinwheel is 45°. Notice that the other rotation angles are multiples of 45°.

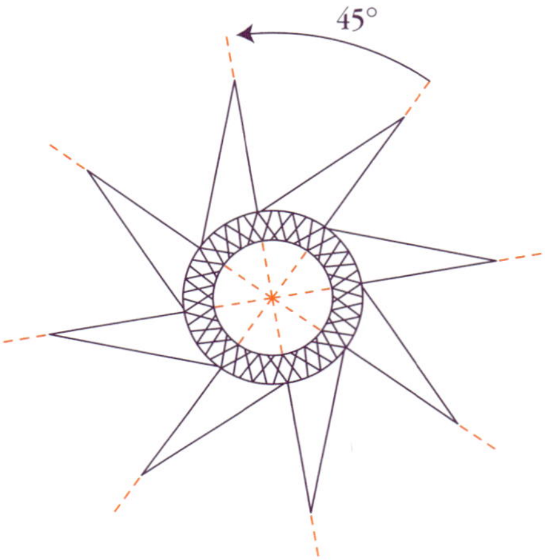

Think about this!

The objects below display rotational symmetry. Can you identify the angles of rotation?

Problem 1.2

Rotational symmetry can be found in many objects that rotate about a centerpoint. For example, the automobile hubcaps shown below have rotational symmetry. These hubcaps are reproduced on Labsheet 1.2.

A. Determine the angle of rotation for each hubcap. Explain how you found the angle.

B. Some of the hubcaps also have reflectional symmetry. Sketch all the lines of symmetry for each hubcap.

hubcap 1

hubcap 2

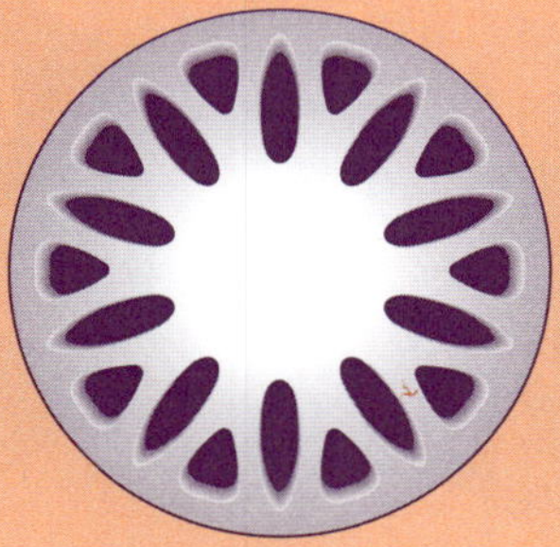

hubcap 3

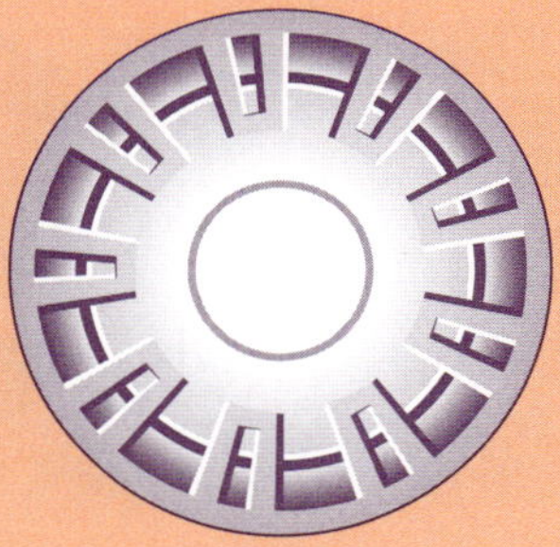

hubcap 4

Problem 1.2 Follow-Up

1. Create a hubcap design that has rotational symmetry with a 90° angle of rotation but no reflectional symmetry.

2. Create a hubcap design that has rotational symmetry with a 60° angle of rotation and at least one line of symmetry.

3. Why do you think many rotating objects are designed to have rotational symmetry?

1.3 Symmetry in Kaleidoscope Designs

A **kaleidoscope** is a tube containing colored beads or pieces of glass and carefully placed mirrors. When a kaleidoscope is held to the eye and rotated, the viewer sees colorful, symmetric patterns.

Kaleidoscopes were patented in 1817 by the Scottish scientist Sir David Brewster. Brewster was intrigued by the science of nature, and he developed kaleidoscopes in an effort to simulate the designs he saw in the world around him.

The designs below are called *kaleidoscope designs* because they are similar to designs you would see if you looked through a kaleidoscope. In this problem, you will explore the symmetries in these designs.

design 1

design 2

design 3

design 4

design 5

design 6

Source: Dale Seymour. *Kaleidoscope Symmetry* poster. Palo Alto, Calif.: Dale Seymour Publications, 1993.

Problem 1.3

The kaleidoscope designs are reproduced on Labsheet 1.3. Do parts A and B for each design.

A. Look for reflectional symmetry in each design. Sketch all the lines of symmetry you find.

B. Look for rotational symmetry in each design. Determine the angle of rotation for each design.

Problem 1.3 Follow-Up

1. For the kaleidoscope designs in Problem 1.3, describe the relationship between the number of lines of symmetry and the angle of rotation.

2. For each kaleidoscope design, sketch or outline the *basic design element*. That is, sketch or outline a part of the design from which the entire design could be created.

1.4 Translational Symmetry

A **translation** is a geometric motion that slides a figure from one position to another. A design has *translational symmetry* if it can be created by sliding a basic design element in a regular, straight-line pattern. Designs on ribbons, belts, and wallpaper often have translational symmetry.

To describe the translational symmetry in a design, you can draw the basic design element and an arrow indicating the direction and length of a slide that would move one part of the design to another.

Problem 1.4

The designs below are tessellations. A **tessellation** is a design made from copies of a single basic design element that cover a surface without gaps or overlaps. The tessellations are reproduced on Labsheet 1.4. Each tessellation has translational symmetry. Do parts A and B for each tessellation.

A. Outline a basic design element that could be used to create the tessellation using only translations.

B. Write directions or draw an arrow showing how the basic design element can be copied and slid to produce another part of the pattern.

tessellation 1

tessellation 2

tessellation 3

tessellation 4

Problem 1.4 Follow-Up

1. Describe the rotational and reflectional symmetries that appear in the tessellations in Problem 1.4. As you consider possible symmetries, imagine that the tessellations continue forever in all directions.

2. Cut a strip of paper about 1 inch wide. Make a design with translational symmetry on your strip by continuing the following pattern. This pattern appears in fabrics created by the Mayan people of Central America.

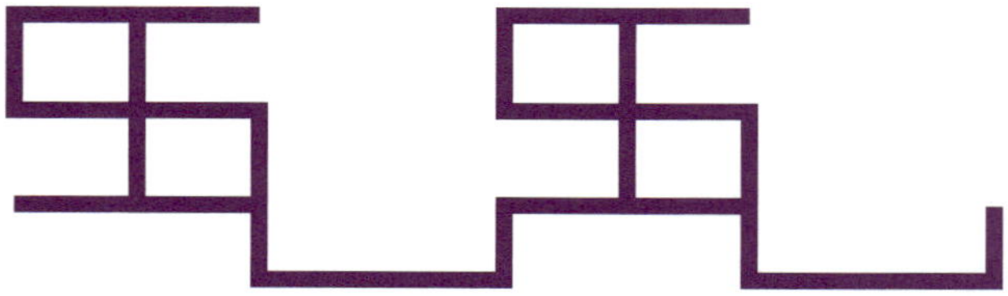

Think about this!

Can you identify the symmetries in the designs below?

As you work on these ACE questions, use your calculator whenever you need it.

Applications

In 1–3, a line design is given. A *line design* is a pattern that is formed entirely by straight lines but that appears to contain curves. On Labsheet 1.ACE1, indicate the lines of symmetry and the angle of rotation for the design.

1.

2.

3.

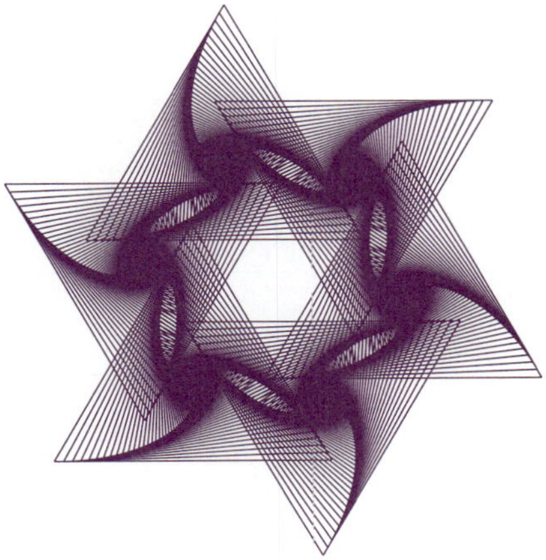

Source: Dale Seymour. *Introduction to Line Designs.* Palo Alto, Calif.: Dale Seymour Publications, 1992.

In 4–7, a basic design element and one or more lines are given. On Labsheet 1.ACE2, use the basic design element to create a design with the given lines as lines of symmetry.

4.

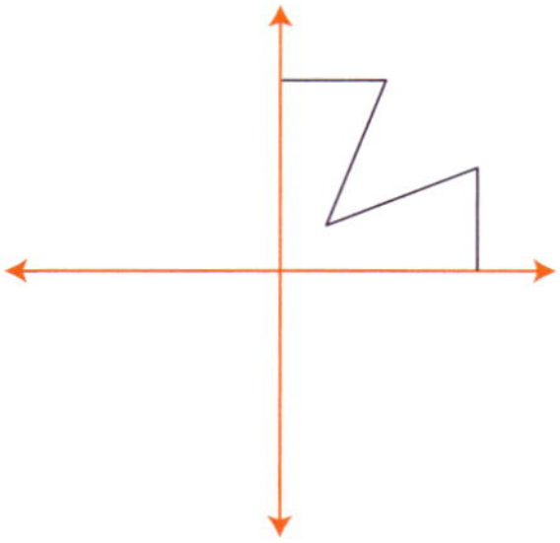

5.

6.

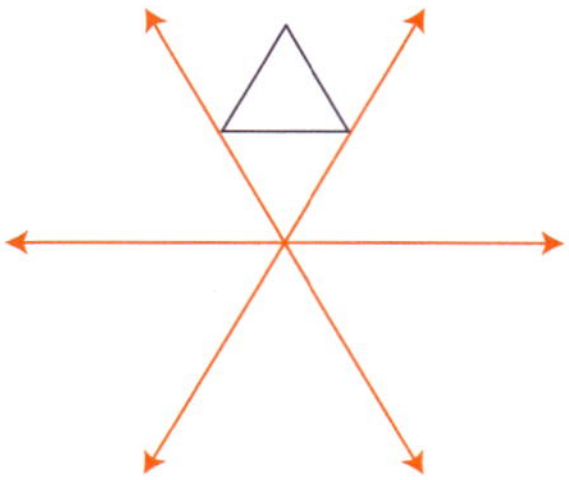

7.

8. A tessellation of stars and hexagons has been started on the triangular grid below. Labsheet 1.ACE2 contains a copy of this figure. Continue the pattern to completely fill the grid.

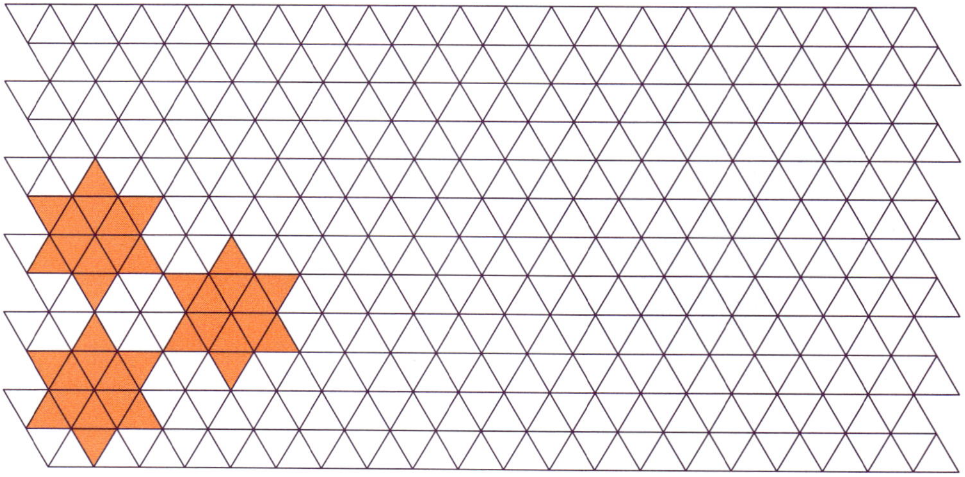

a. Describe all the types of symmetry in this tessellation, and give at least one example of each type. As you consider possible symmetries, imagine that the tessellation continues forever in all directions.

b. Describe how you could check each symmetry by using a mirror or tracing paper or by folding the labsheet.

In 9–12, do parts a–c. These tessellations are reproduced on Labsheet 1.ACE3.

9.

10.

11.

12.

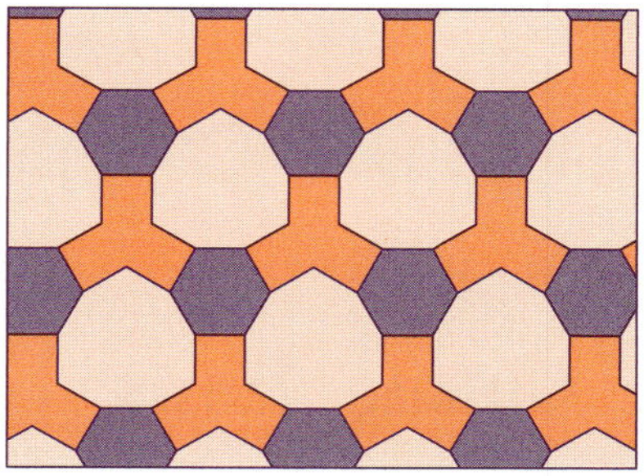

a. Sketch a basic design element that could be used to create the tessellation using only translations.

b. Tell what types of symmetry appear in the tessellation. Imagine that each tessellation continues forever in all directions.

c. Describe the lines of symmetry for the reflectional symmetries, the centers and angles of rotation for the rotational symmetries, and the directions and lengths of the translational symmetries.

In 13–17, describe the symmetry in the name.

13.

14.

15.

16.

17.

Connections

18. Many of the letters in our alphabet have symmetry.

A B C D E F G H I J K L M
N O P Q R S T U V W X Y Z

a. Identify the capital letters that have reflectional symmetry. Sketch each letter you find, and show all the lines of symmetry.

b. What state name has reflectional symmetry when written horizontally in capital letters?

c. What four state names have reflectional symmetry when written vertically in capital letters?

d. Write at least one word, name, or phrase that has reflectional symmetry when written horizontally.

e. Write at least one word, name, or phrase that has reflectional symmetry when written vertically.

f. Identify the capital letters that have rotational symmetry. Sketch each letter you find, and give its angle of rotation.

g. Write at least one word, name, or phrase that has rotational symmetry.

19. In this investigation, you studied designs with reflectional, rotational, and translational symmetry. The design below is a bit different from those you have seen.

a. Trace a basic design element from which the rest of the pattern could be created by using only translation.

b. Trace a smaller basic design element from which the rest of the pattern could be created by using reflection and translation. Indicate the line of symmetry and the length and direction of the translation.

c. In part b, the movement required to generate the pattern from the basic design element is called a *glide reflection*. What is the difference between a reflection and a glide reflection?

In 20–23, a *strip pattern* is given. Many traditional cultures use strip patterns to decorate pottery and weavings. The patterns below are reproduced on Labsheet 1.ACE4. For each pattern, identify a basic design element, and describe the lines of symmetry and the centers and angles of rotation in the strip pattern. Imagine that each design continues forever in both directions.

20.

21.

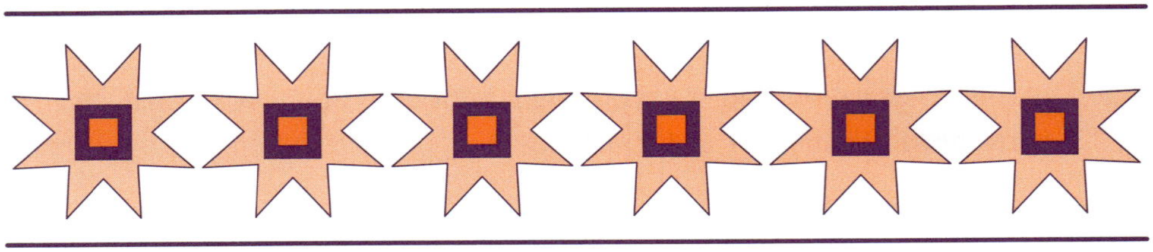

22.

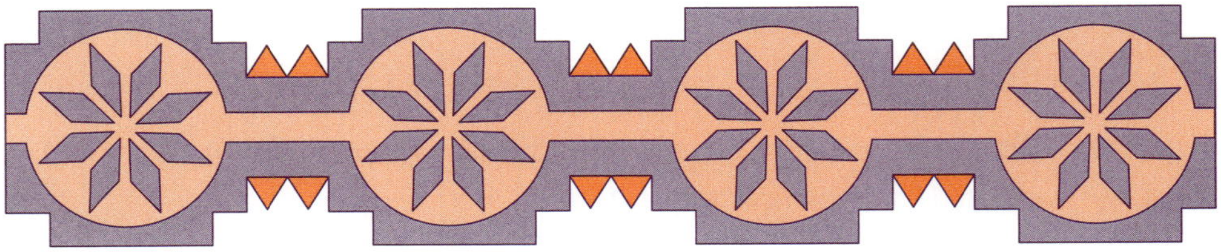

23.

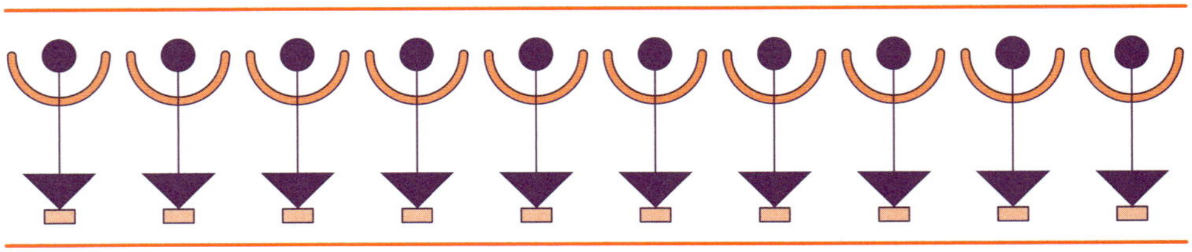

24. Look back at your answers to questions 21–23. What are the limitations on the possible angles of rotation for a strip pattern?

25. A regular hexagon can be enclosed by a circle.

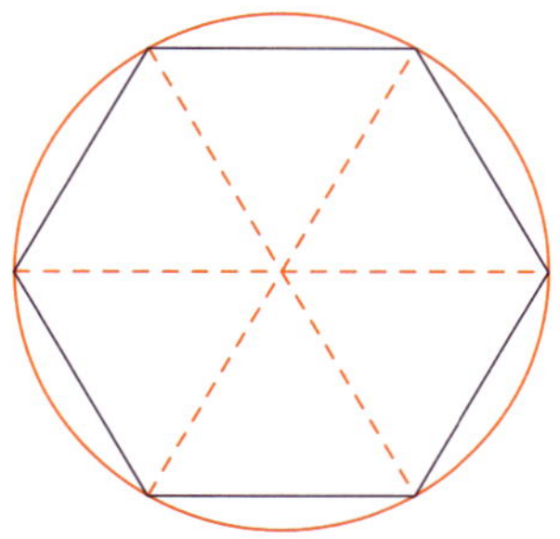

a. What are the angle measures of the triangles formed by the diagonals of the hexagon?

b. How are the side lengths of the hexagon related to the radius of the enclosing circle?

c. How are your answers to parts a and b related to the steps required to make a kaleidoscope design from a basic design element?

d. How are your answers to parts a and b related to the symmetries that occur in any kaleidoscope pattern?

26. Copy the design below. Then use tracing paper to help you sketch a full kaleidoscope design from this basic design element.

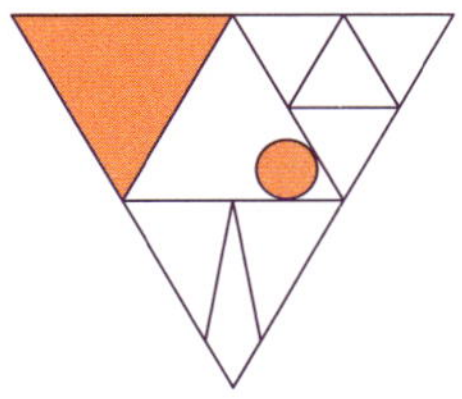

Extensions

27. How could you use the information about hexagons and enclosing circles in ACE question 25 to draw a regular hexagon by using only a straightedge and compass?

In 28–33, the given design can be re-created by outlining and shading parts of a regular hexagon drawn inside of a circle. Use a compass and a straightedge to re-create each design.

28.

29.

30.

31.

32.

33.

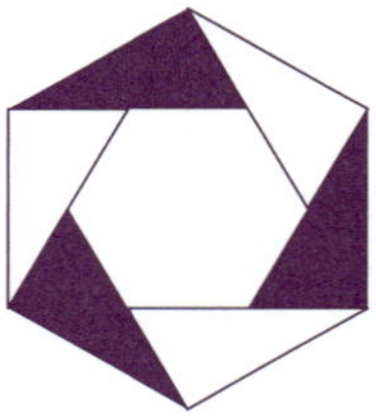

Mathematical Reflections

In this investigation, you looked at designs that have symmetry, and you explored some of the ways a basic design element can be used to generate a pattern with symmetry. These questions will help you summarize what you have learned:

1. **a.** How can you determine whether a design has reflectional symmetry?

   b. How can you determine whether a design has rotational symmetry? If a design has rotational symmetry, how can you find the angle of rotation?

   c. How can you determine whether a design has translational symmetry? If a design has translational symmetry, how can you describe the translation used to create the design?

2. **a.** Describe the tools and the process you would use to create a design with reflectional symmetry from a basic design element.

   b. Describe the tools and the process you would use to create a design with rotational symmetry from a basic design element.

   c. Describe the tools and the process you would use to create a design with translational symmetry from a basic design element.

Think about your answers to these questions, discuss your ideas with other students and your teacher, and then write a summary of your findings in your journal.

INVESTIGATION 2

Symmetry Transformations

You can draw a figure with reflectional symmetry by finding the mirror image of polygon *ABCDE* over the line. To help you draw your figure, you could set a mirror on the line to see what the image looks like.

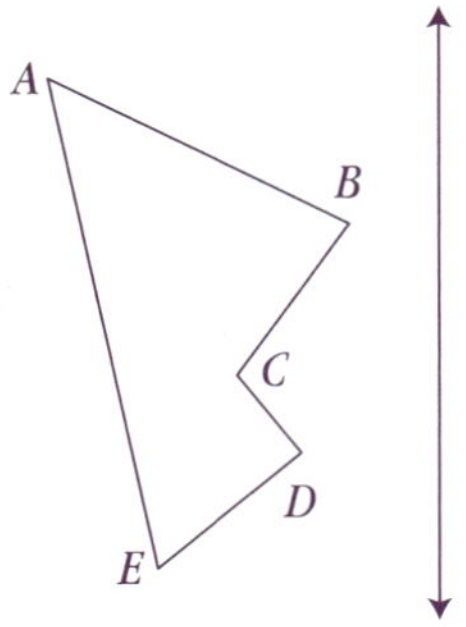

Reflect polygon *ABCDE* over the line.

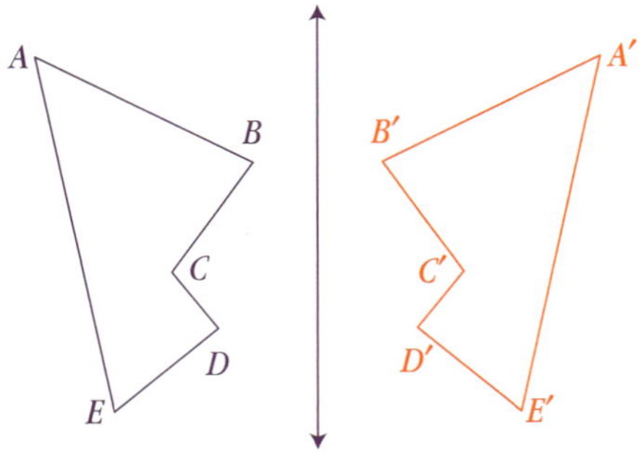

Polygon *A′B′C′D′E′* is the image of polygon *ABCDE*.

Drawing the mirror image of a figure is an example of a geometric operation called a *transformation*. **Transformations** produce a copy of a figure in a new position. The copy is called the *image* of the original figure.

In this investigation, you will explore transformations associated with different types of symmetry, and you will learn to give precise mathematical instructions for performing transformations.

2.1 Describing Line Reflections

Transformations that create figures with reflectional symmetry are called **line reflections**. When you make a design using a line reflection or any other transformation, it helps to know precisely how the transformation matches each point on a figure to a point on the image of the figure. In this problem, you will consider this question:

What is the relationship between a figure and its image under a line reflection?

Problem 2.1

A. In the figure on page 24, polygon $A'B'C'D'E'$ is the image of polygon *ABCDE* under a line reflection. This figure is reproduced on Labsheet 2.1A.

1. Draw a line segment from each vertex of polygon *ABCDE* to its image on polygon $A'B'C'D'E'$.
2. Measure the angles formed by each segment you drew and the line of reflection.
3. For each vertex of polygon *ABCDE*, measure the distance from the vertex to the line of reflection along the segment you drew and the distance from the line of reflection to the image of the vertex.
4. Describe the patterns in your measurements from parts 2 and 3.

B. The figure at right is reproduced on Labsheet 2.1A. Use what you discovered in part A to draw the image of polygon *JKLMN* under a reflection over the line. Use only a pencil, a ruler, and an angle ruler or protractor. Describe how you drew the image.

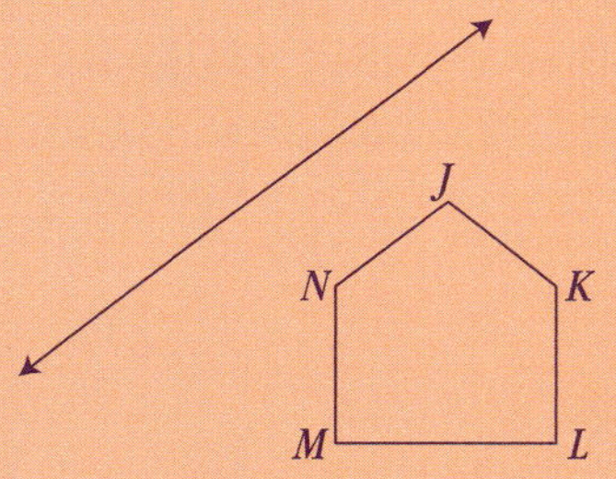

C. The reflection-symmetric design below is reproduced on Labsheet 2.1A. Use only a pencil, a ruler, and an angle ruler or protractor to find the line of symmetry for this design. Describe how you found the line of symmetry.

D. Complete this definition of a line reflection: A *line reflection* matches each point *X* on a figure to an image point X' so that . . .

Problem 2.1 Follow-Up

1. **a.** Draw a shape and a line. Then draw the image of your shape under a reflection over the line.
   b. What information would you need to give a classmate so that, starting with your original drawing, he or she could duplicate your line reflection?
   c. Explain how your shape and its image fit the definition of *line reflection* you wrote in part D of Problem 2.1.

2. The figures below appear on Labsheet 2.1B. Notice that in two of the figures, the shape crosses the line of reflection. Do parts a and b for each figure.
   a. Draw the image of the shape under a reflection over the line.
   b. Does the final drawing have reflectional symmetry? Explain.

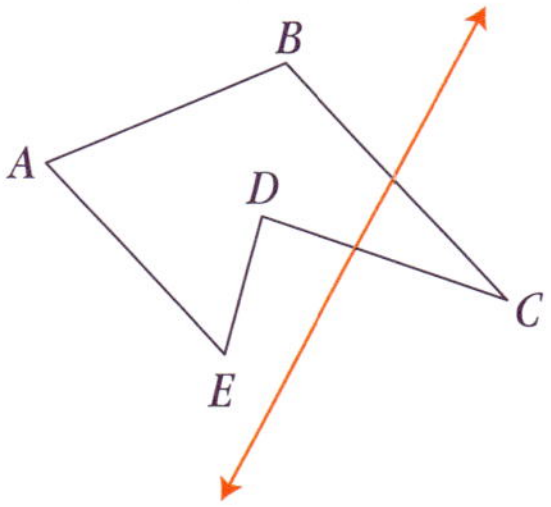

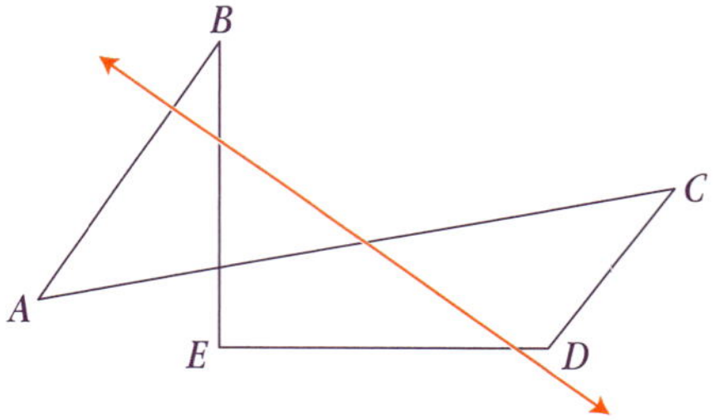

3. What tools are useful for performing a line reflection? Carefully describe how each tool is used.

The figures you have reflected in this unit are two-dimensional. Two-dimensional figures are drawn in a *plane*. You can picture a plane as a sheet of paper that extends infinitely in all directions. When you reflect a figure over a line, you can imagine that you are reflecting the entire plane over the line. The figure just goes along for the ride.

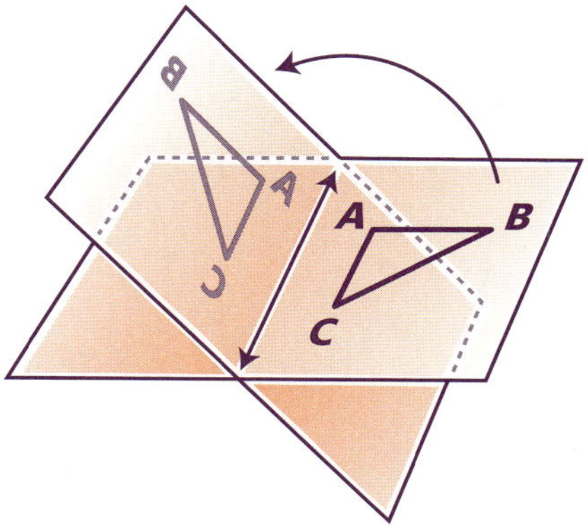

4. When you perform a line reflection, are any points in the plane in the same location *after* the reflection? Explain your answer.

Points that are in the same location after a transformation are called *fixed points*. Some transformations have fixed points; other transformations move every point in the plane to a new location. As you consider the transformations in the rest of this investigation, you will be asked to think about fixed points.

2.2 Describing Translations

You have seen how line reflections are related to reflectional symmetry. Other types of symmetry also have associated transformations. In Investigation 1, you saw how patterns with translational symmetry could be created by translating, or sliding, a basic pattern. A translation is a type of transformation. In this problem, you will look at examples of translations in search of an answer to this question:

What is the relationship between a figure and its image under a translation?

As you work on each example, think about the instructions you could give so that someone else could re-create the translation exactly.

Problem 2.2

A. Each diagram below shows polygon *ABCDE* and its image under a translation. These figures are reproduced on Labsheet 2.2. Do parts 1 and 2 for each diagram.

diagram 1

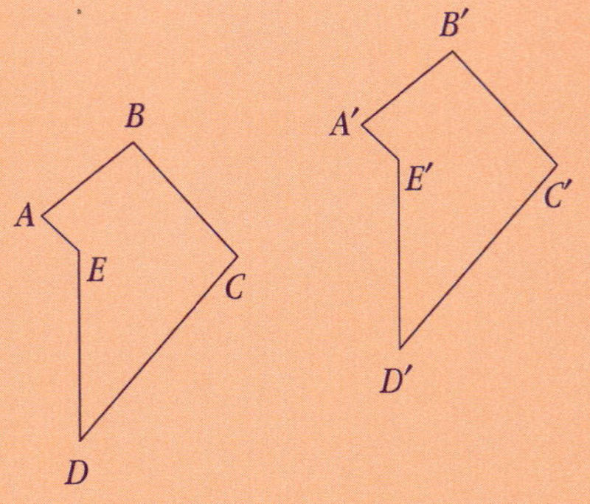

diagram 2

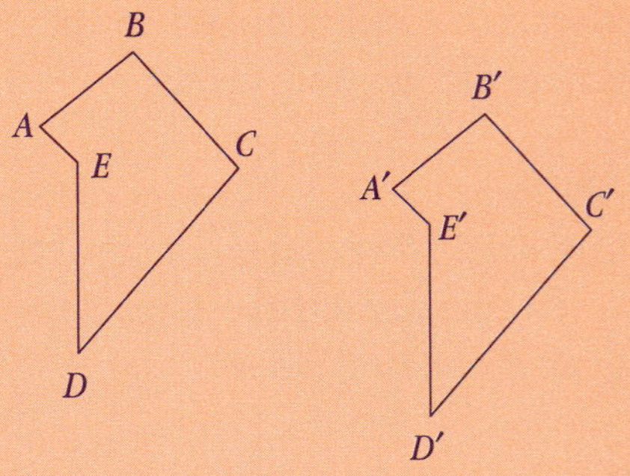

1. Draw a line segment from each vertex of polygon *ABCDE* to its image.

2. Describe the relationship among the line segments you drew.

B. The translations in part A slide polygon *ABCDE* onto its image, polygon $A'B'C'D'E'$. Do parts 1–3 for each diagram in part A.

1. By performing the same translation that was used to slide polygon *ABCDE* to polygon $A'B'C'D'E'$, slide polygon $A'B'C'D'E'$ to create a new image. Label the image $A''B''C''D''E''$.

2. Polygon $A''B''C''D''E''$ is the image of polygon *ABCDE* after two identical translations. How is polygon $A''B''C''D''E''$ related to polygon *ABCDE*?

3. Does your final drawing have translational symmetry? Explain.

C. Complete this definition of a translation: A *translation* matches any two points *X* and *Y* on a figure to image points X' and Y' so that . . .

Problem 2.2 Follow-Up

1. Ella specified a translation of a polygon by drawing an arrow.

a. How would you interpret Ella's drawing?

b. On Labsheet 2.2, perform the translation Ella specified.

2. a. Draw a shape. Then draw the image of your shape under a translation.

b. What information would you need to give a classmate so that, starting with your original drawing, he or she could duplicate your translation?

c. Explain how your shape and its image fit the definition of *translation* you wrote in part C of Problem 2.2.

3. What tools are useful for performing a translation? Carefully describe how each tool is used.

4. When you translate a figure, you can imagine that you are translating the entire plane and bringing the figure along for the ride. When you perform a translation, are any points in the plane in the same location *after* the translation? That is, are there any *fixed points*? Explain your answer.

2.3 Describing Rotations

In Investigation 1, you explored rotational symmetry, and you created symmetric designs by rotating figures about a point. A rotation is a type of transformation. The rotations in this unit are *counterclockwise* turns about a point.

In this problem, you will try to answer this question:

What is the relationship between a figure and its image under a rotation?

As you work on each example, think about the instructions you could give so that someone else could re-create the rotation exactly.

Problem 2.3

A. In the figure on the right, polygon $A'B'C'D'$ is the image of polygon $ABCD$ under a rotation of 60° about point P. This figure is reproduced on Labsheet 2.3A.

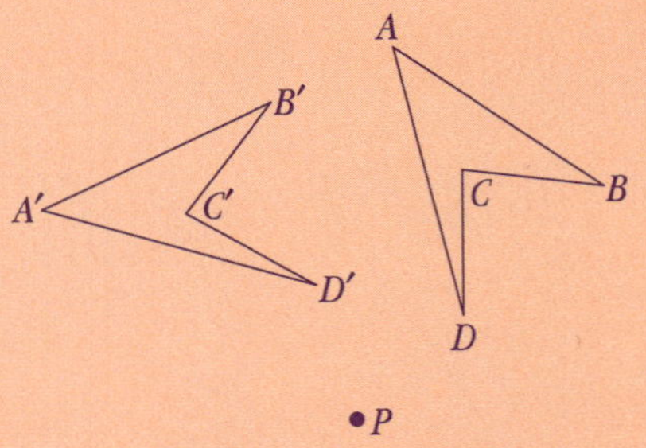

1. What relationship would you expect to find between each vertex, its image, and point P?

2. For each vertex of polygon $ABCD$, find the measure of the angle formed by the vertex, point P, and the image of the vertex. For example, find the measure of angle APA'.

3. For each vertex of polygon $ABCD$, find the distance from the vertex to point P and the distance from the image of the vertex to point P. For example, find AP and $A'P$.

4. What patterns do you see in your measurements? Do these patterns confirm the conjecture you made in part 1?

B. The figures below are reproduced on Labsheet 2.3A. Do parts 1 and 2 for each figure.

1. Perform the indicated rotation, and label the image vertices appropriately.

2. Describe the path each vertex follows under the rotation.

Rotate 90° about point P.

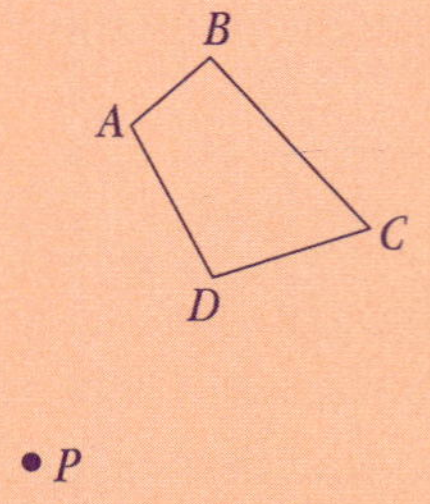

Rotate 45° about point Q.

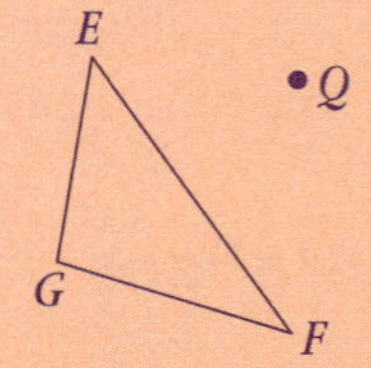

C. For the figures in part B, use the specified rotation to rotate the *image* of the original polygon. The result is the image of the original polygon after two identical rotations. How does the location of the final image compare with the location of the original polygon? Be very specific.

D. Complete this definition of a rotation: A *rotation* of d degrees about a point P matches any point X on a figure to an image point X' so that . . .

Problem 2.3 Follow-Up

1. **a.** Draw a shape and a point. Then draw the image of your shape under a rotation about the point.
   b. What information would you need to give a classmate so that, starting with your original drawing, he or she could duplicate your rotation?
   c. Explain how your figure and its image fit the definition of *rotation* you wrote in part D of Problem 2.3.

2. Polygon $A'B'C'D'E'F'$ is the image of polygon $ABCDEF$ after a rotation. This figure is reproduced on Labsheet 2.3B.

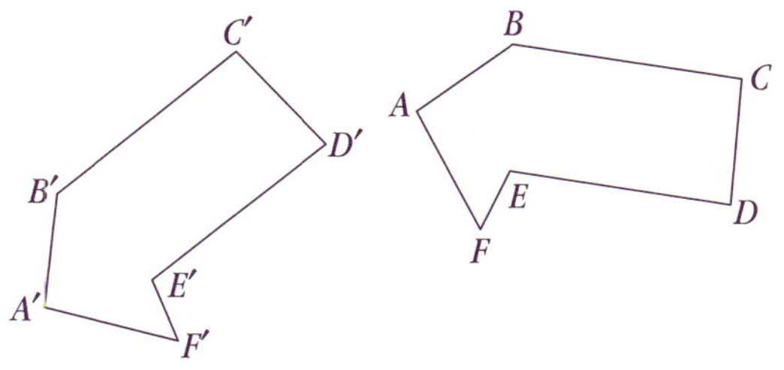

   a. Find the center of rotation, and describe how you found it.
   b. Find the angle of the rotation, and describe how you found it.

3. On Labsheet 2.3B, draw a line segment from a vertex of polygon $ABCDEF$ to its image. The midpoint of this segment is the same distance from the original vertex as it is from the image of that vertex. Find some other points that are the same distance from the vertex and the image of the vertex. What do all of these points have in common?

4. After a polygon is rotated, how does the distance from a vertex of the polygon to the center of rotation compare to the distance from the image of the vertex to the center of rotation?

5. Look back at the rotations you have seen in this problem. Do the final drawings after the rotations have rotational symmetry? Explain.

6. What tools are useful for performing a rotation? Carefully describe how each tool is used.

7. When you rotate a figure, you can imagine that you are rotating the entire plane and bringing the figure along for the ride. When you perform a rotation, are any points in the plane in the same location after the rotation? That is, are there any *fixed points*? Explain your answer.

2.4 Combining Transformations

Now you will explore what happens when you perform two transformations in a row, the first on the original figure and the second on the image of that figure.

Problem 2.4

A. **1.** The figure below is reproduced on Labsheet 2.4A. Reflect triangle *ABC* over line 1. Then reflect the image over line 2. Label the final image $A''B''C''$.

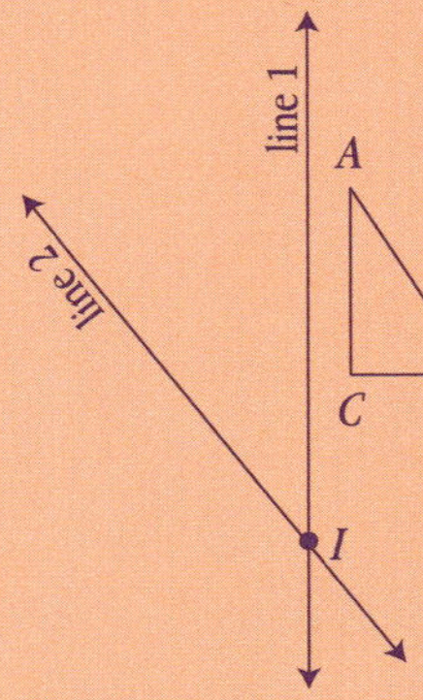

2. For each vertex of triangle *ABC,* measure the angle formed by the vertex, point *I,* and the image of the vertex. For example, measure angle AIA''. What do you observe?

3. For each vertex of triangle *ABC,* compare the distance from the vertex to point *I* with the distance from the image of the vertex to point *I*. What do you observe?

4. Could you move triangle *ABC* to triangle $A''B''C''$ with a single transformation? If so, describe the transformation.

5. Make a conjecture about the result of reflecting a figure over two intersecting lines. Test your conjecture with an example.

B. **1.** What will happen if you reflect a figure over a line and then reflect the image over a second line that is *parallel* to the first line? Would the combination of the two reflections be equivalent to a single transformation?

2. Test your conjecture from part 1 on several examples, including the one at right. Do the results support your conjecture? If so, explain why. If not, revise your conjecture to better explain your results.

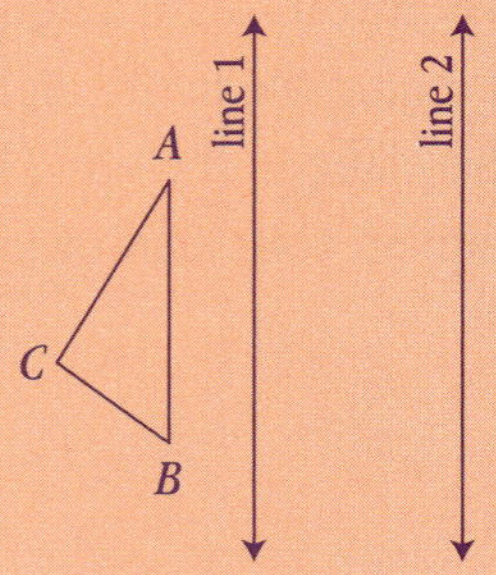

Problem 2.4 Follow-Up

1. **a.** What single transformation is equivalent to reflecting a figure over a line and then reflecting the image over an intersecting line?

   b. What single transformation is equivalent to reflecting a figure over a line and then reflecting the image over a parallel line?

2. The figure below is reproduced on Labsheet 2.4B. Draw two parallel lines so that if you reflect triangle *ABC* over one line and then reflect the image over the other line, the result will be triangle *A″B″C″*. Explain how you found the lines.

3. The figure below is reproduced on Labsheet 2.4B. Draw two intersecting lines so that if you reflect polygon *ABCD* over one line and then reflect the image over the other line, the result will be polygon *A″B″C″D″*. Explain how you found the lines.

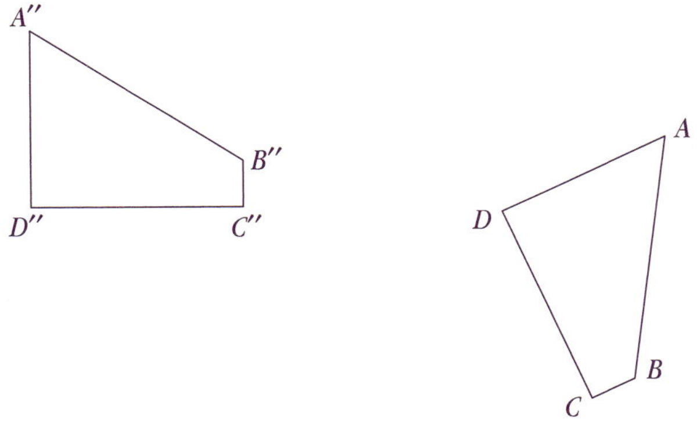

4. What would happen if you translated a figure and then translated the image? Would the combination of translations be equivalent to a single transformation? Make a conjecture about combining two translations. Test your conjecture on several examples.

5. What would happen if you rotated a figure about a point and then rotated the image about the same point? Would the combination of rotations be equivalent to a single transformation? Make a conjecture about combining two rotations. Test your conjecture on several examples.

As you work on these ACE questions, use your calculator whenever you need it.

Applications

In 1 and 2, draw the image of the polygon under a reflection over the line. Describe the image of each point of the original polygon under the reflection. These figures are reproduced on Labsheet 2.ACE1.

1.

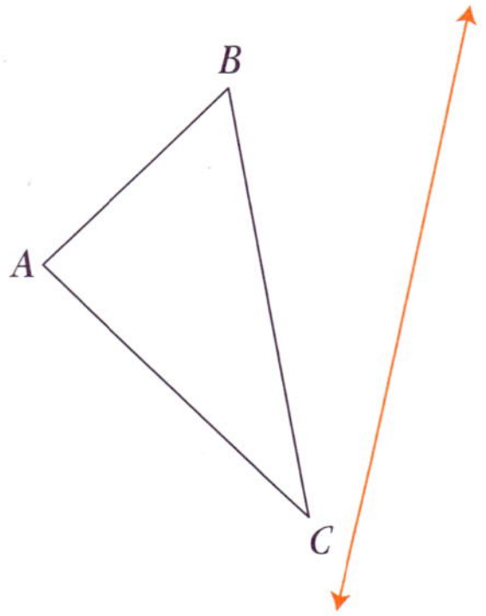

2.

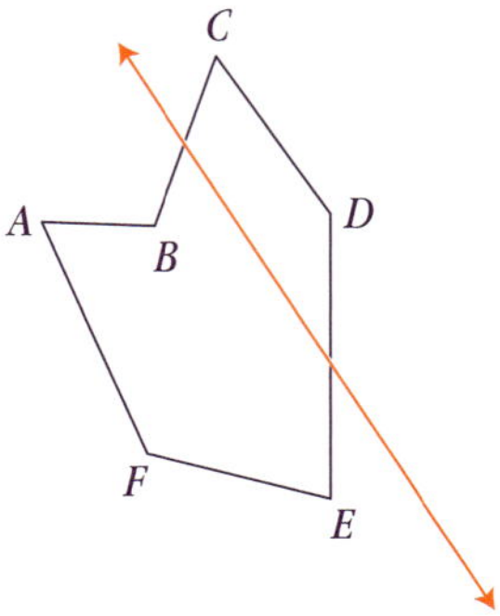

3. Shown below are a shape and its image under a line reflection. The figure is reproduced on Labsheet 2.ACE1.

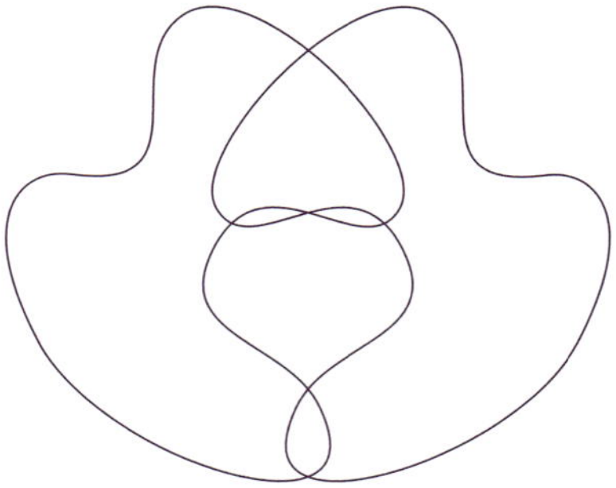

a. Draw the line of symmetry for the figure.

b. Label three points on the figure, and label the corresponding image points.

4. Shown at right are a shape and its image under a line reflection. The figure is reproduced on Labsheet 2.ACE1.

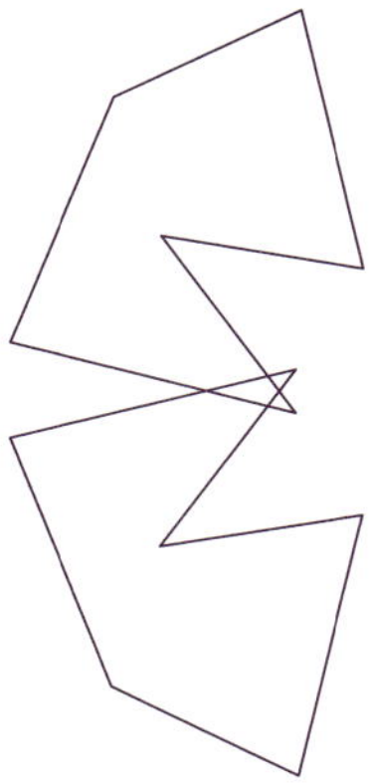

a. Draw the line of symmetry for the figure.

b. Label three points on the figure, and label the corresponding image point.

In 5 and 6, perform the translation indicated by the arrow. Describe the relationship between each point on the original polygon and its image point under the translation. These figures are reproduced on Labsheet 2.ACE2.

5.

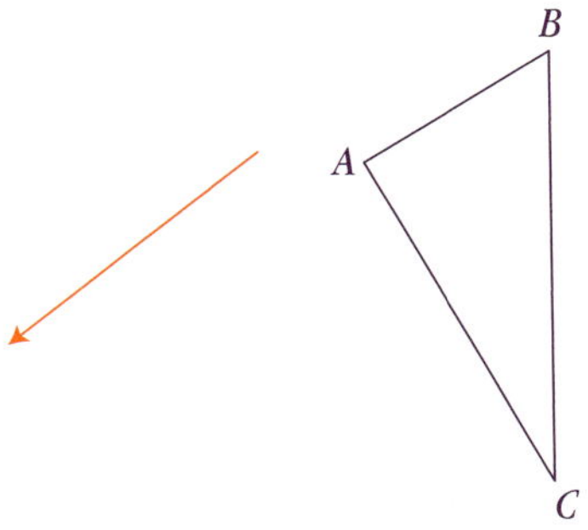

6.

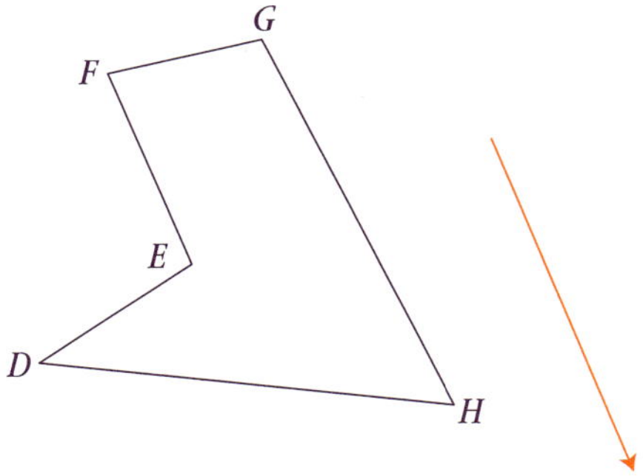

7. On Labsheet 2.ACE2, rotate triangle *ABC* 90° about point *R*. Describe the relationship between each point on the original polygon and its image point under the rotation.

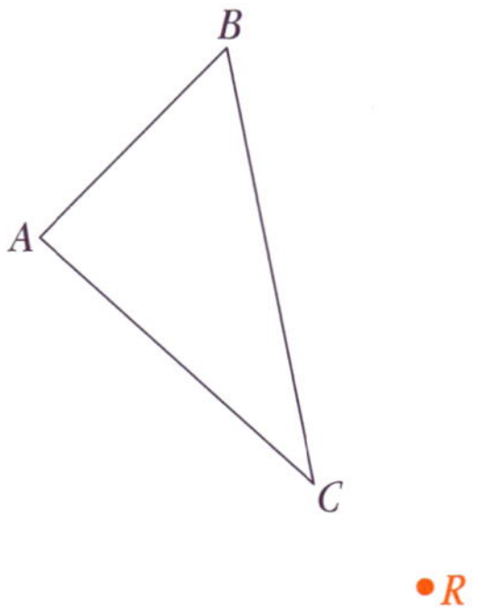

8. On Labsheet 2.ACE2, rotate polygon *ABCDEF* 180° about point *R*. Describe the relationship between each point on the original polygon and its image point under the rotation.

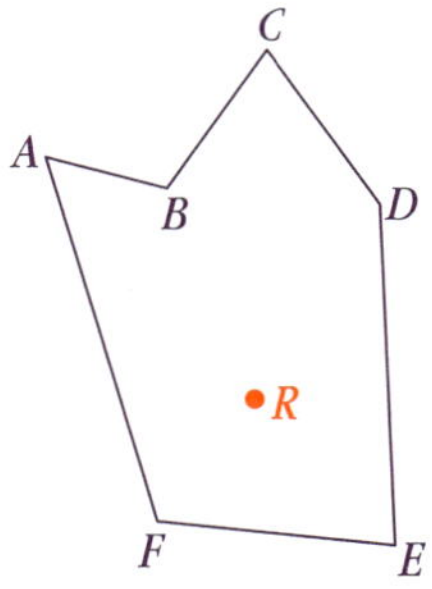

In 9–11, refer to this diagram, which is reproduced on Labsheet 2.ACE3.

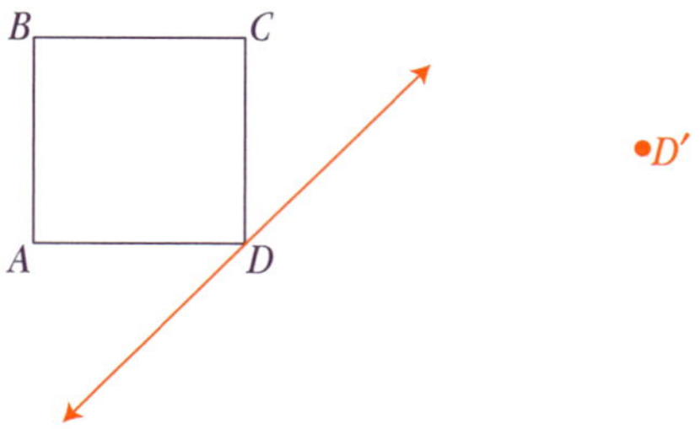

9. Draw the image of square *ABCD* under a reflection over the line.

10. Draw the image of square *ABCD* under a 45° rotation about point *A*.

11. Draw the image of square *ABCD* under the translation that slides point *D* to point *D′*.

In 12–15, a polygon and its image under a transformation are given. Decide whether the transformation was a *line reflection,* a *rotation,* or a *translation.* Then, on Labsheet 2.ACE4, indicate the line of reflection, the center and angle of rotation, or the direction and distance of translation.

12.

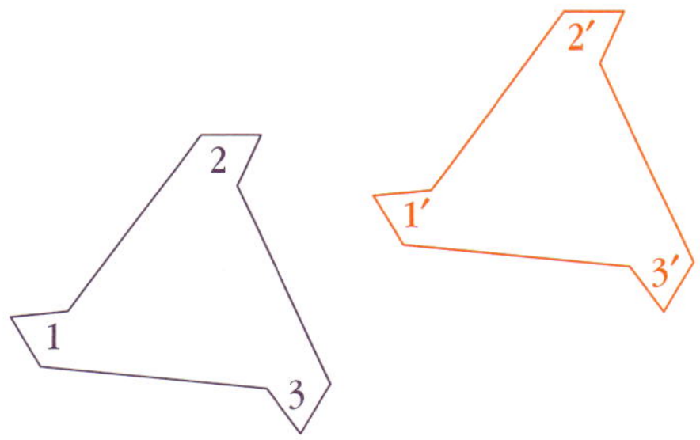

13.

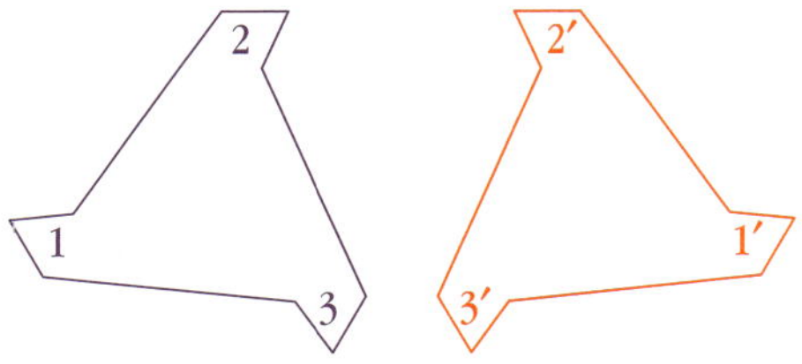

14.

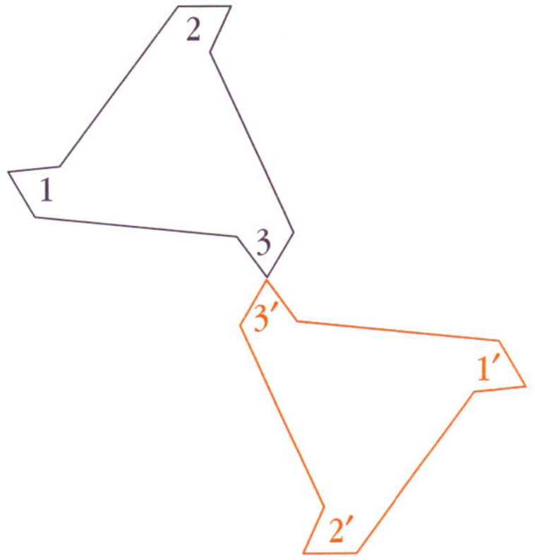

15.

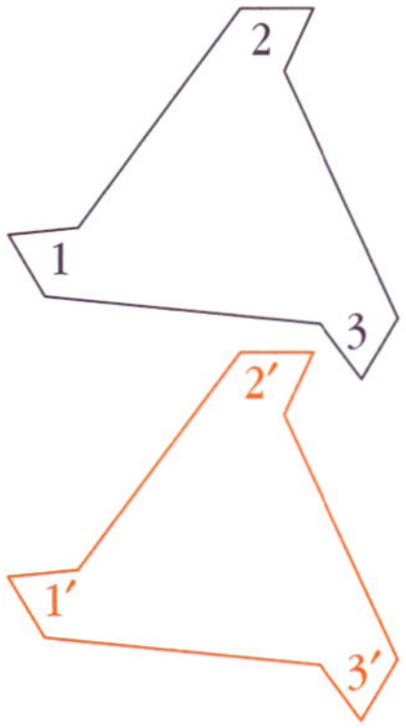

Connections

16. Create a design that has both reflectional symmetry and rotational symmetry. Explain how your design shows both types of symmetry.

17. Create a design that has both reflectional symmetry and translational symmetry. Explain how your design shows both types of symmetry.

18. Create a design that has rotational symmetry, but no reflectional symmetry. Explain how your design fits these constraints.

19. Create a design that has reflectional symmetry but no rotational symmetry. Explain how your design fits these constraints.

20. Create a design that has translational symmetry, but no reflectional symmetry or rotational symmetry. Explain how your design fits these constraints.

Extensions

21. Copy the figures below.

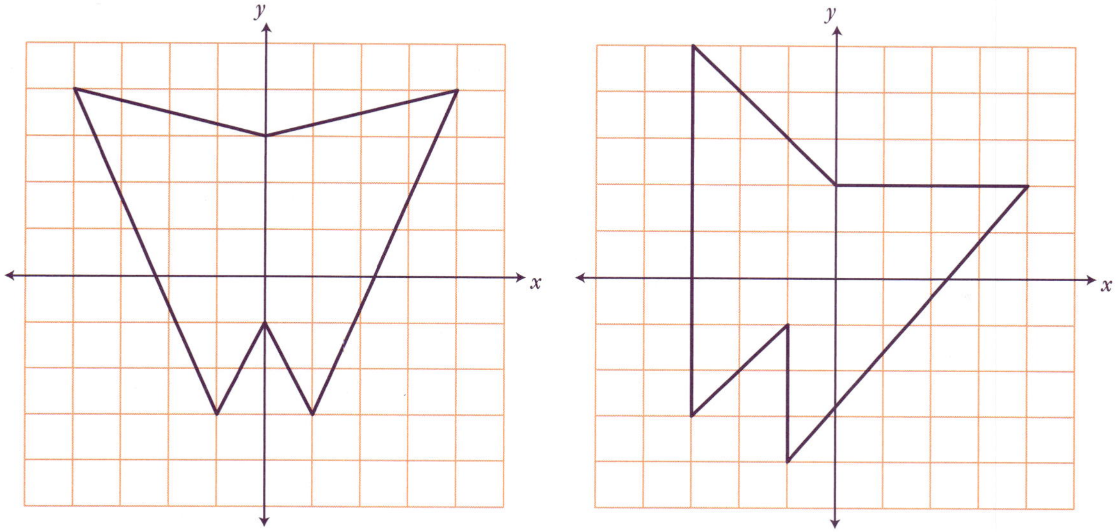

a. Determine whether each polygon has reflectional symmetry about the *y*-axis.

b. Sketch the image of each polygon under a line reflection over the *y*-axis.

c. How does the reflection image of the symmetric figure differ from the reflection image of the nonsymmetric figure?

d. Make a conjecture about whether the difference you observed in part c will occur for *any* pair of polygons in which one polygon has reflectional symmetry over the *y*-axis and the other does not. Test your conjecture on several examples, and see if you can find reasons for the patterns you observe.

22. Copy the figures below.

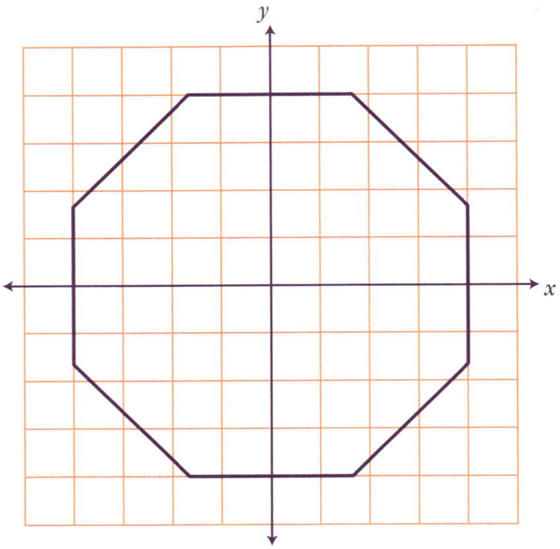

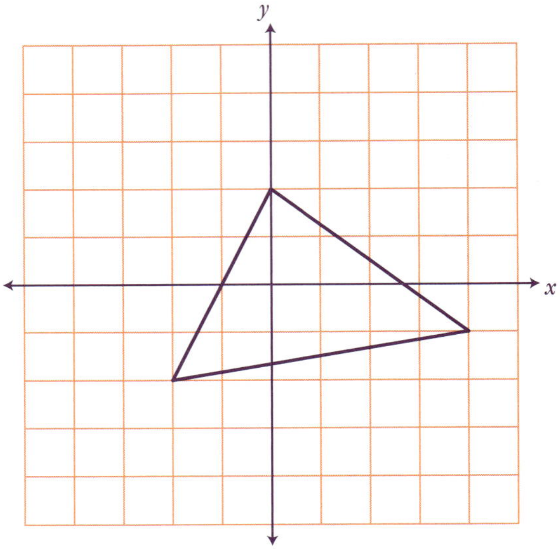

a. Determine whether each polygon has rotational symmetry about the origin.

b. Sketch the image of each polygon under a rotation of 45° about the origin.

c. How does the rotation image of the symmetric figure differ from the rotation image of the nonsymmetric figure?

d. Make a conjecture about whether the difference you observed in part c will occur for any pair of polygons in which one polygon has rotational symmetry about the origin and the other does not. Test your conjecture on several examples, and see if you can find reasons for the patterns you observe.

23. Use the language of line reflections and rotations to explain what it means for figures to have

a. reflectional symmetry.

b. rotational symmetry.

Mathematical Reflections

In this investigation, you explored line reflections, rotations, and translations—the mathematical transformations that create symmetric designs. These questions will help you summarize what you have learned:

1. Describe the relationship between a point and its image under a reflection over a line.
2. Describe the relationship between a point and its image under a rotation of *d* degrees about a point *P*.
3. Describe the relationship between a point and its image under a translation of a given length and direction.
4. What single transformation will produce the same result as reflecting a figure over a line and then reflecting the image over an intersecting line?
5. What single transformation will produce the same result as reflecting a figure over a line and then reflecting the image over a parallel line?

Think about your answers to these questions, discuss your ideas with other students and your teacher, and then write a summary of your findings in your journal.

INVESTIGATION 3

Transforming Coordinates

In this investigation, you will explore transformations of figures drawn on coordinate grids. By looking for patterns in your results, you will be able to write some general algebraic rules for transforming a point (*x*, *y*) under reflections, translations, and rotations.

3.1 Writing Rules for Reflections

The drawing screen in many computer geometry programs is considered to be a coordinate grid. You can create designs by specifying the endpoints of line segments.

The flag below consists of three segments. The commands for creating the flag in a particular geometry program are shown next to the screen. The commands tell the computer to draw segments between the specified endpoints.

```
Draw:
Line [(0,-2), (0,3)]
Line [(0,3), (1,2)]
Line [(1,2), (0,1)]
```

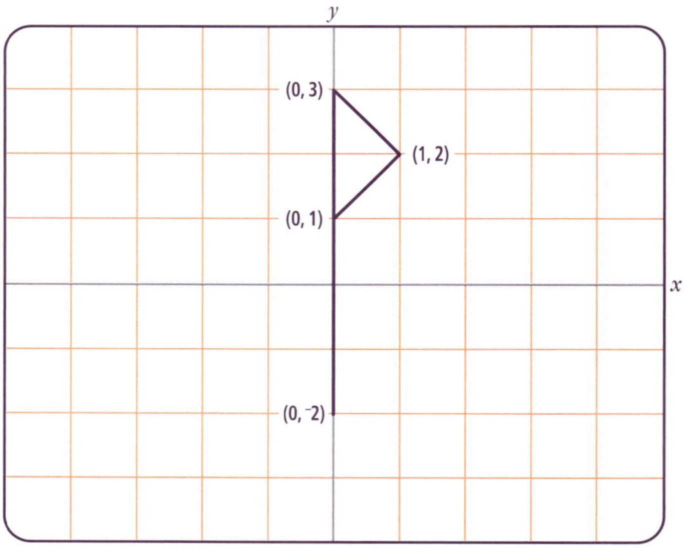

Think about this!

Is there a different set of commands that would create the same flag?

What commands would create a square centered at the origin?

What commands would create a nonsquare rectangle?

Problem 3.1

A. Suppose you want to re-create the flag below using the geometry program that drew the flag on page 42. Copy and complete the commands to create a set of instructions for drawing the flag.

```
Draw:
Line [( , ), ( , )]
Line [( , ), ( , )]
Line [( , ), ( , )]
```

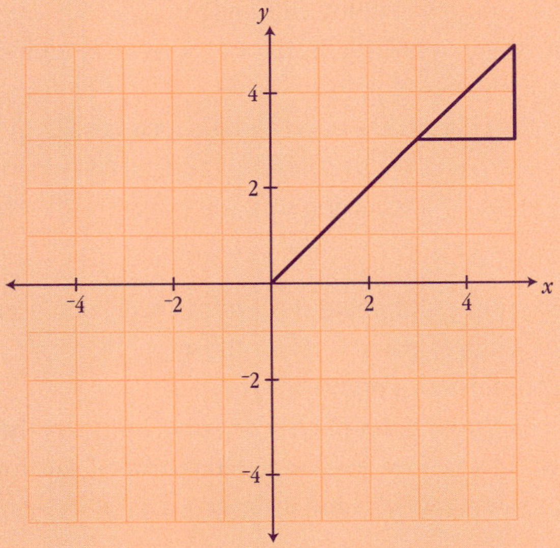

B. Write a set of commands that would draw the image of this flag under a reflection over the y-axis.

C. Write a set of commands that would draw the image of this flag under a reflection over the x-axis.

D. Write a set of commands that would draw the image of this flag under a reflection over the line $y = x$.

Problem 3.1 Follow-Up

The diagram below appears on Labsheet 3.1B. Use this diagram to complete parts 1–4.

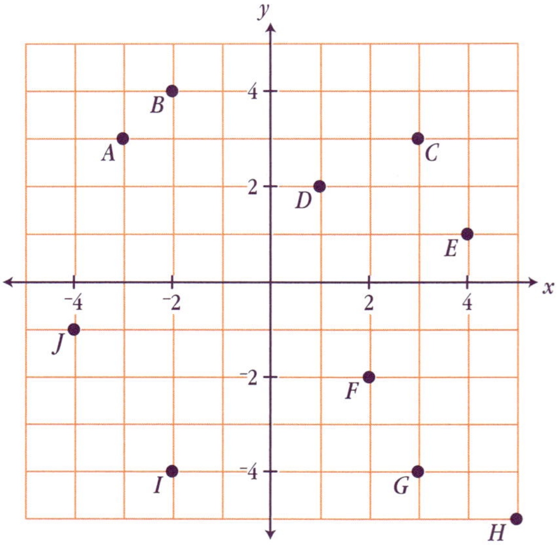

1. List the coordinates of the labeled points.

2. a. Indicate the images of points *A*–*J* under a reflection over the *y*-axis. Use the label *A′* for the image of point *A*, *B′* for the image of *B*, and so on.

   b. List the coordinates of points *A′*–*J′*.

   c. Compare the coordinates of each original point with the coordinates of its image. Use the pattern you see to complete this general rule for finding the image of any point (x, y) under a reflection over the *y*-axis:

$$(x, y) \rightarrow (\quad , \quad)$$

3. a. Indicate the images of points *A*–*J* under a reflection over the *x*-axis. Use the label *A″* for the image of point *A*, *B″* for the image of *B*, and so on.

   b. List the coordinates of points *A″*–*J″*.

   c. Compare the coordinates of each original point with the coordinates of its image. Use the pattern you see to complete this general rule for finding the image of any point (x, y) under a reflection over the *x*-axis:

$$(x, y) \rightarrow (\quad , \quad)$$

4. a. Indicate the images of points *A*–*J* under a reflection over the line $y = x$. Use the label *A‴* for the image of point *A*, *B‴* for the image of *B*, and so on.

   b. List the coordinates of points *A‴*–*J‴*.

   c. Compare the coordinates of each original point with the coordinates of its image. Use the pattern you see to complete this general rule for finding the image of any point (x, y) under a reflection over the line $y = x$:

$$(x, y) \rightarrow (\quad , \quad)$$

3.2 Writing Rules for Translations

The designs below have translational symmetry. In this problem, you will explore the computer commands needed to create these designs.

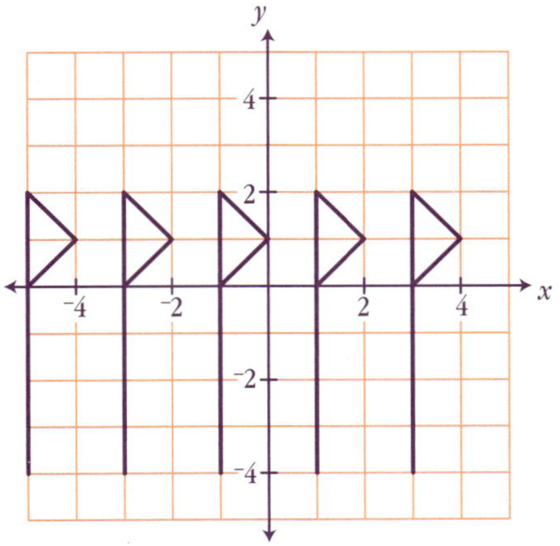

diagram 1

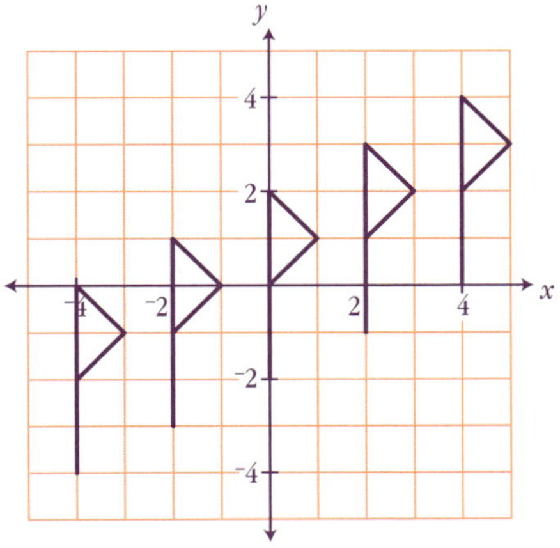

diagram 2

Problem 3.2

A. 1. In diagram 1, the left-most flag can be drawn with these commands:

```
Draw:
Line [(-5,-4), (-5,2)]
Line [(-5,2), (-4,1)]
Line [(-4,1), (-5,0)]
```

These commands draw the vertical segment, then the upper slanted segment, and finally the lower slanted segment. Write sets of commands for drawing the other four flags in diagram 1. Each set of commands should draw the segments in the same order as the commands for the original flag.

2. Compare the commands for the five flags. Describe a pattern that relates the coordinates of each flag to the coordinates of the flag to its *right.*

3. Describe a pattern that relates the coordinates of each flag to the coordinates of the flag to its *left.*

B. 1. Write a set of commands for drawing the left-most flag in diagram 2. Then write comparable instructions for drawing the other four flags.

2. Compare the commands for the five flags. Describe a pattern that relates the coordinates of each flag to the coordinates of the flag to its *right.*

3. Describe a pattern that relates the coordinates of each flag to the coordinates of the flag to its *left.*

Problem 3.2 Follow-Up

In 1–3, refer to the figure below.

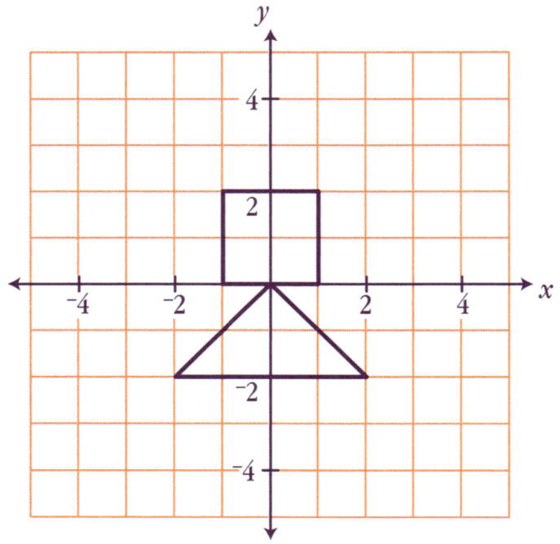

1. Suppose you want to create a design with translational symmetry by sliding this basic figure along the *x*-axis. Consider different designs you could make by using translations of various lengths.
   a. In any design created by translating the figure along the *x*-axis, how are the coordinates of the original figure related to the coordinates of the figure to its right?
   b. How are the coordinates of the second copy to the right of the original related to the coordinates of the first copy to the right? How are the coordinates of the second copy related to the coordinates of the original?
   c. How are the coordinates of copies to the left of the original related to the coordinates of the original?
2. Consider the designs you could make by sliding this basic figure along the *y*-axis.
   a. In any such design, how are the coordinates of the original figure related to the coordinates of the figure directly above it?
   b. How are the coordinates of the second copy above the original related to the coordinates of the copy directly below it? How are the coordinates of the second copy related to the coordinates of the original?
   c. How are the coordinates of copies below the original related to the coordinates of the original?
3. Now consider designs created by sliding the figure along the slanted, or *oblique,* lines $y = x$, $y = {}^{-}x$, and $y = \frac{1}{2}x$. Make sketches of such designs, and examine how the coordinates change from one figure to the next. For each line, tell what happens to a point on the figure as the figure is translated along the line.

4. Look back at the translations you explored in questions 1–3. In each case, think about the rules for finding the image of any point (x, y). How are the rules similar?

5. Which of these rules describe translations? Explain.

a. $(x, y) \rightarrow (x + 2, y - 3)$

b. $(x, y) \rightarrow (2x, y)$

c. $(x, y) \rightarrow (x + 1, 3y)$

d. $(x, y) \rightarrow (x - 2, y + 1)$

3.3 Writing Rules for Rotations

You have explored the rules for transforming a point (x, y) to its image under reflections and translations. Writing rules for rotations is more difficult. In this problem, you will explore a few simple cases.

Problem 3.3

A. Copy and complete the commands below to create a set of instructions for drawing triangle *ABC*.

```
Draw:
Line [( , ), ( , )]
Line [( , ), ( , )]
Line [( , ), ( , )]
```

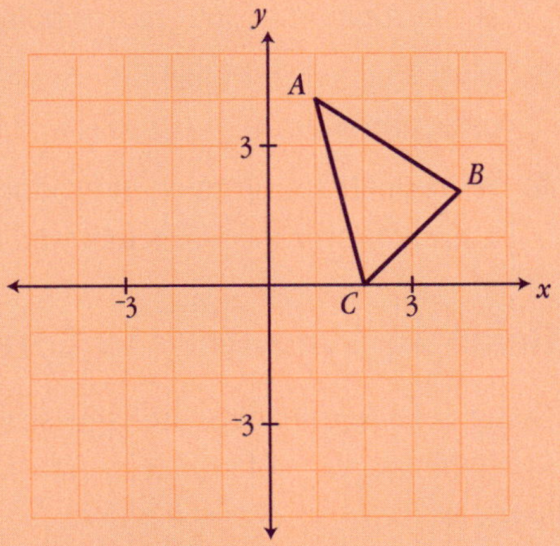

B. Write a set of commands that would draw the image of triangle *ABC* under a 90° rotation about the origin.

C. Write a set of commands that would draw the image of triangle *ABC* under a 180° rotation about the origin.

D. Write a set of commands that would draw the image of triangle *ABC* under a 270° rotation about the origin.

E. Write a set of commands that would draw the image of triangle *ABC* under a 360° rotation about the origin.

Problem 3.3 Follow-Up

1. a. Organize your results from Problem 3.3 as shown below to indicate the images of the vertices under each rotation.

90° rotation	180° rotation	270° rotation	360° rotation
$A(1, 4) \rightarrow (\ ,\ )$ $B(4, 2) \rightarrow (\ ,\ )$ $C(2, 0) \rightarrow (\ ,\ )$	$A(1, 4) \rightarrow (\ ,\ )$ $B(4, 2) \rightarrow (\ ,\ )$ $C(2, 0) \rightarrow (\ ,\ )$	$A(1, 4) \rightarrow (\ ,\ )$ $B(4, 2) \rightarrow (\ ,\ )$ $C(2, 0) \rightarrow (\ ,\ )$	$A(1, 4) \rightarrow (\ ,\ )$ $B(4, 2) \rightarrow (\ ,\ )$ $C(2, 0) \rightarrow (\ ,\ )$

b. Describe what happens to the vertices of triangle *ABC* under each rotation. Be sure to discuss how each rotation affects the coordinates of the points.

2. Complete the following statements:

a. A rotation of 90° moves point (x, y) to point (,).

b. A rotation of 180° moves point (x, y) to point (,).

c. A rotation of 270° moves point (x, y) to point (,).

d. A rotation of 360° moves point (x, y) to point (,).

3. What single transformation produces the same final image of triangle *ABC* as a reflection over the y-axis followed by a reflection over the x-axis? Explain.

4. What single transformation produces the same final image of triangle *ABC* as a reflection over the y-axis followed by a reflection over the line $y = x$? Explain.

3.4 Relating Symmetry to Congruence

Congruent figures have the same size and shape. Congruent figures can also be defined using the language of symmetry transformations: *Two figures are congruent if one is an image of the other under a reflection, a translation, a rotation, or some combination of these transformations.* Put more simply, two figures are congruent if you can flip, slide, or turn one figure so that it fits exactly on the other.

Pentagons *ABCDE* and *PQRST* are congruent. You will look at these pentagons more carefully in the problem.

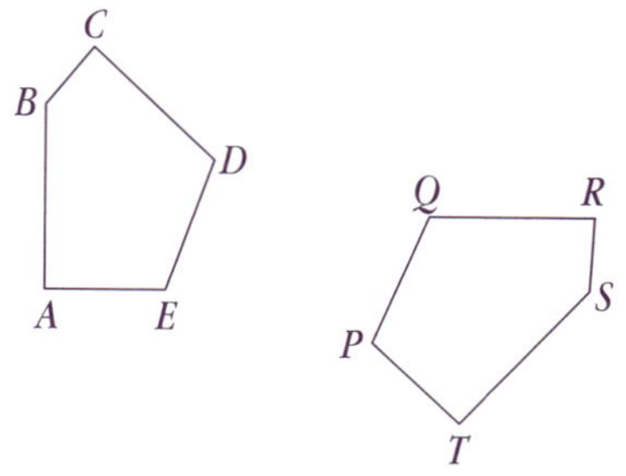

Problem 3.4

Pentagons *ABCDE* and *PQRST* are reproduced on Labsheet 3.4.

A. If you made a copy of one of the pentagons and fit it exactly on the other, which vertices would match?

B. Which pairs of sides in pentagons *ABCDE* and *PQRST* are the same length?

C. Which pairs of angles in pentagons *ABCDE* and *PQRST* are the same size?

D. What combination of reflections, rotations, and translations would move pentagon *ABCDE* to fit exactly on pentagon *PQRST*? Is there more than one possible combination? Make sketches to show your ideas.

Problem 3.4 Follow-Up

1. Drawing a diagonal of a rectangle creates two congruent triangles.

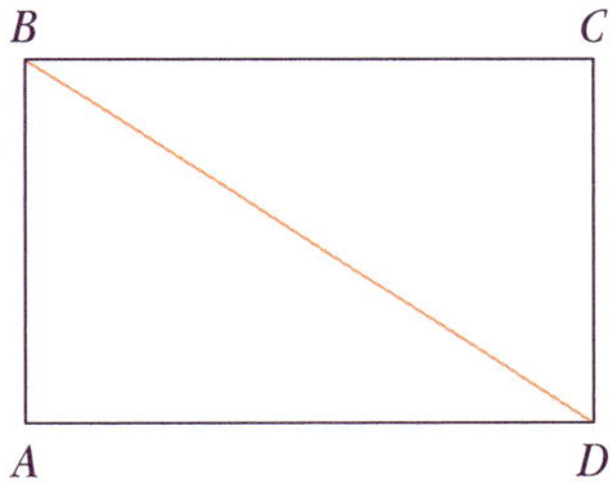

a. If you make a copy of triangle *ABD* and place it exactly on the other triangle, which vertices will match?

b. What single reflection, rotation, or translation would match one of the triangles exactly with the other?

c. Which pairs of sides and angles in the two triangles are congruent?

2. a. How could you determine whether these circles are congruent without making copies of them or performing transformations?

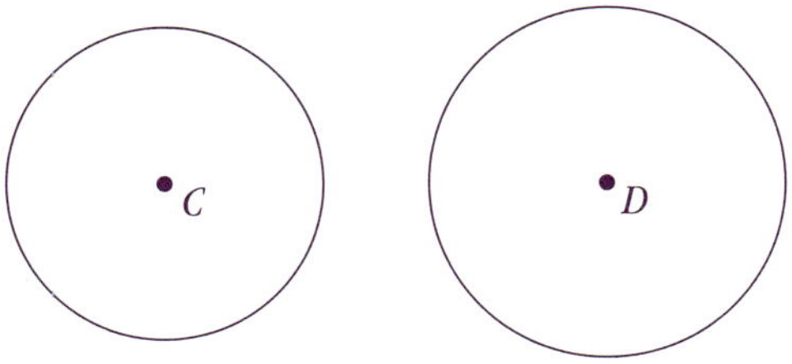

b. What transformations could you perform to move one of the circles onto the other to check for congruence?

As you work on these ACE questions, use your calculator whenever you need it.

Applications

In 1–3, refer to the figures below. These figures are reproduced on Labsheet 3.ACE1.

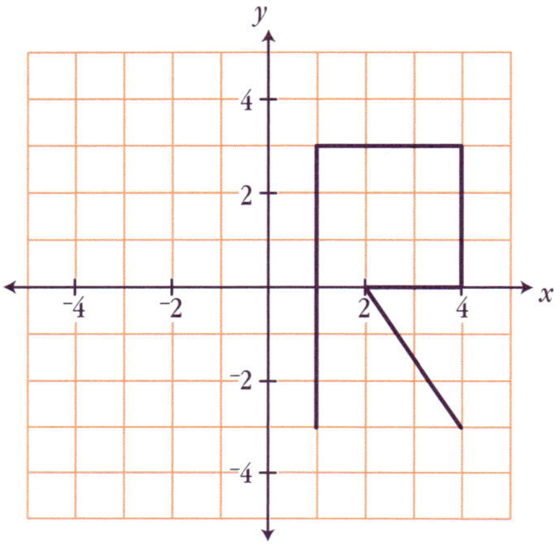

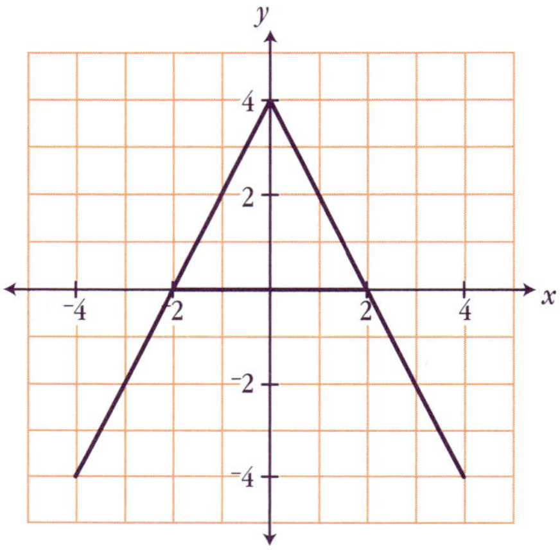

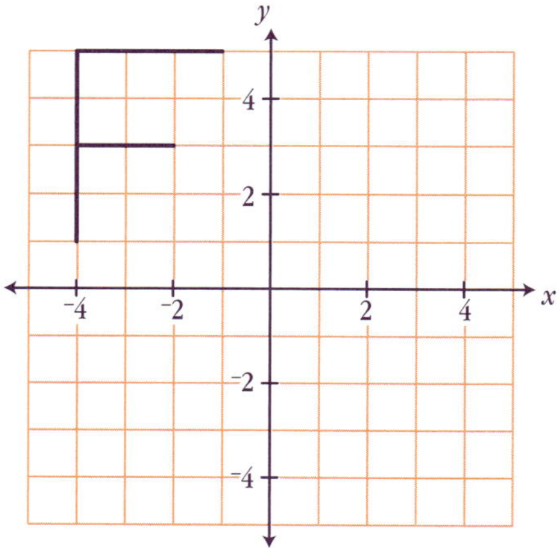

1. a. Write a set of computer commands for drawing the letter R shown.

   b. Write a set of commands for drawing the image of this R under a reflection over the y-axis. Use your instructions to draw the image.

2. a. Write a set of computer commands for drawing the letter A shown.

   b. Write a set of commands for drawing the image of this A under a reflection over the x-axis. Use your instructions to draw the image.

3. a. Write a set of computer commands for drawing the letter F shown.

   b. Write a set of commands for drawing the image of this F under a reflection over the line $y = x$. Use your instructions to draw the image.

4. Draw a figure on a coordinate grid. Perform one transformation on your original figure and a second transformation on its image. Is there a single transformation that will produce the same final result? Explain.

5. Diagonal QS divides the parallelogram into two congruent triangles.

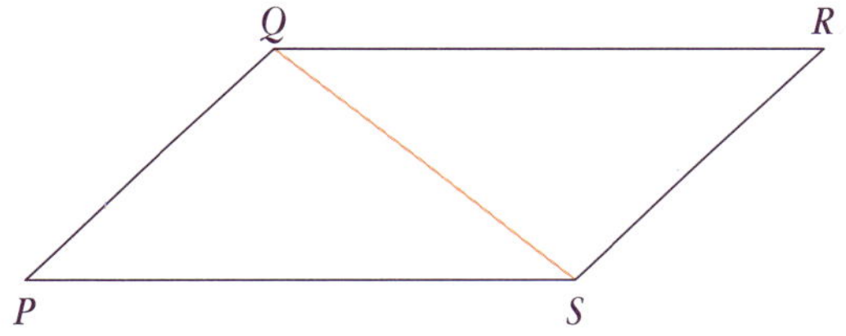

   a. If you make a copy of triangle PQS and place it exactly on the other triangle, which vertices will match?

   b. What single reflection, translation, or rotation would match one of the triangles exactly with the other?

   c. Which pairs of sides and angles in the two triangles are congruent?

In 6–15, refer to the figure below. This figure is reproduced on Labsheet 3.ACE1.

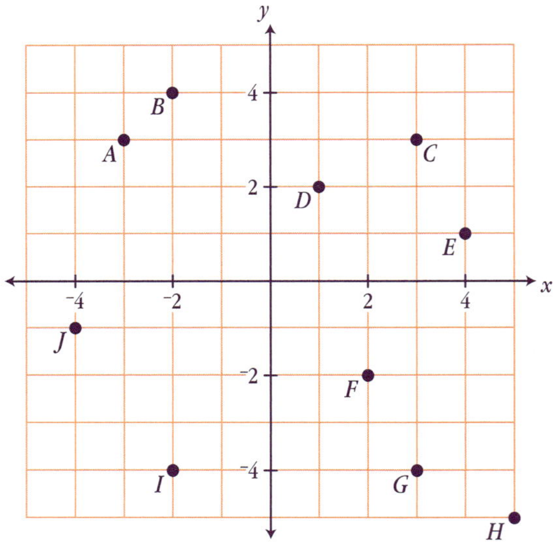

6. What are the coordinates of the image of point *A* under a translation that moves point (1, 2) onto point (2, 4)?

7. What are the coordinates of the image of point *B* under a translation that moves point (1, 2) onto point (3, $^-1$)?

8. What are the coordinates of the image of point *C* under a translation that moves point (1, 2) onto point ($^-2$, $^-3$)?

9. What are the coordinates of the image of point *D* under a reflection over the *y*-axis?

10. What are the coordinates of the image of point *E* under a reflection over the *x*-axis?

11. What are the coordinates of the image of point *F* under a reflection over the line $y = x$?

12. What are the coordinates of the image of point *G* under a 90° rotation about the origin?

13. What are the coordinates of the image of point *H* under a 180° rotation about the origin?

14. What are the coordinates of the image of point *I* under a 270° rotation about the origin?

15. What are the coordinates of the final image of point *J* under a reflection over the *x*-axis followed by a reflection over the *y*-axis?

16. The figure below appears on Labsheet 3.ACE2.

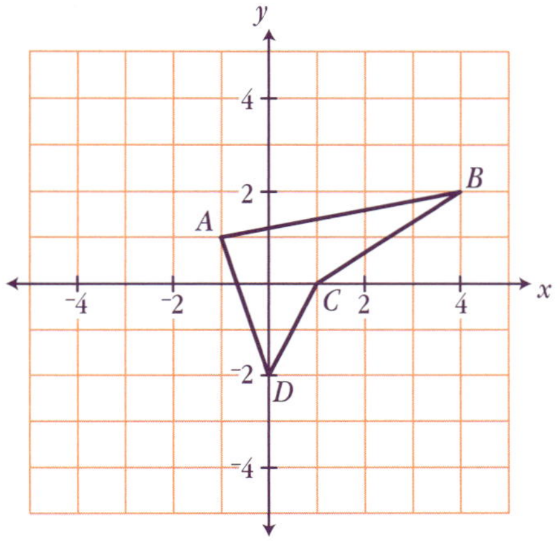

a. Draw the final image that results from rotating polygon *ABCD* 90° about the origin and then reflecting the image over the *x*-axis.

b. Draw the final image that results from reflecting polygon *ABCD* over the *x*-axis and then rotating the image 90° about the origin.

c. Are the final images you found in parts a and b the same? Why or why not?

17. What single transformation is equivalent to a 90° rotation about the origin followed by a 270° rotation about the origin?

18. What single transformation is equivalent to a reflection over the *y*-axis, followed by a reflection over the *x*-axis, followed by another reflection over the *y*-axis?

Connections

In 19–21, describe in detail the symmetries in the design.

19.

20.

21.

22. The diagram below has rotational symmetry.

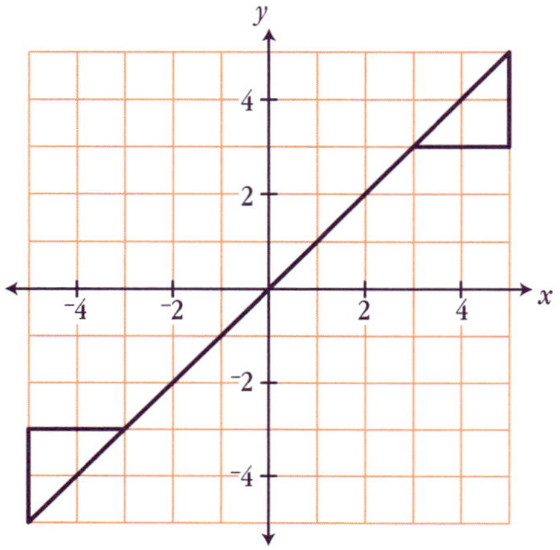

a. What center and angle of rotation will rotate one flag onto the other?

b. Compare the coordinates of key points on one flag with the coordinates of the images of those points on the other flag. Describe the pattern you see.

23. In this diagram, a 90° rotation about the origin will match one flag with another flag.

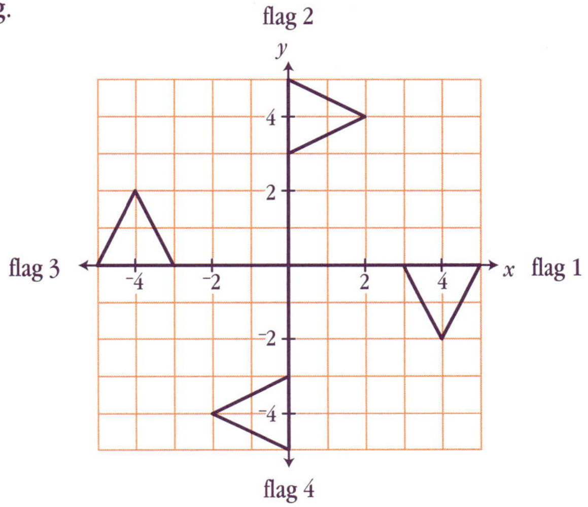

a. Under a 90° rotation about the origin, point (5, 0) on flag 1 is moved to point (0, 5) on flag 2. You can express this by writing $(5, 0) \rightarrow (0, 5)$. Write similar statements to show how the rotation moves each of the key points in flag 1 to a key point in flag 2.

b. Write statements to show how the rotation moves each key point in flag 2 to a key point in flag 3.

c. Write statements to show how the rotation moves each key point in flag 3 to a key point in flag 4.

d. Write statements to show how the rotation moves each key point in flag 4 to a key point in flag 1.

e. Use your results to write a general rule for finding the image of a point (x, y) under a 90° rotation about the origin.

Extensions

24. The figure below is reproduced on Labsheet 3.ACE2. Use symmetry transformations to create a final design that has at least two lines of symmetry. Describe the transformations you used and the order in which you applied them.

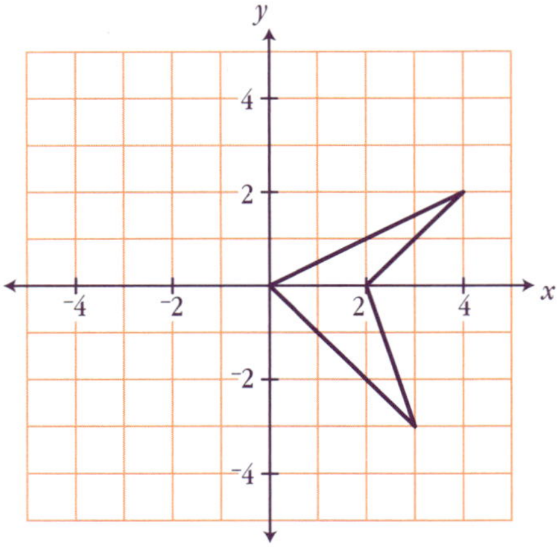

25. The figure below is reproduced on Labsheet 3.ACE2. Use symmetry transformations to create a final design that has rotational symmetry. Describe the transformations you used and the order in which you applied them.

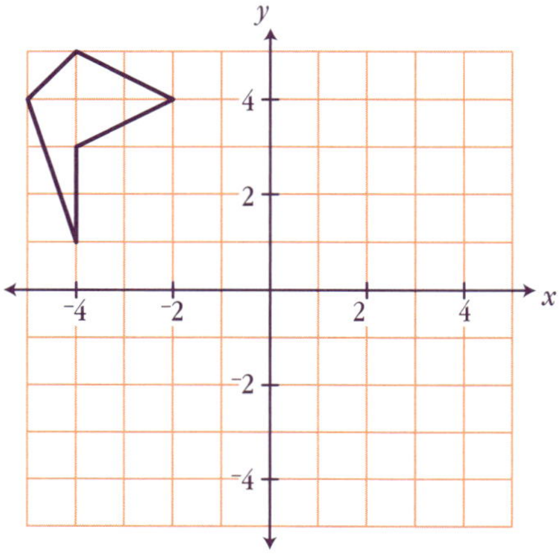

26. The figure below is reproduced on Labsheet 3.ACE2. Use symmetry transformations to create a final design that has both reflectional and rotational symmetry. Describe the transformations you used and the order in which you applied them.

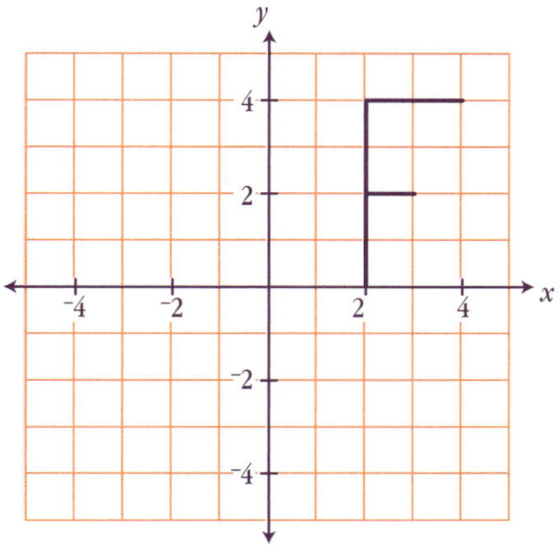

27. Investigate what happens when you rotate a figure 180° about a point and then rotate the image 180° about a different point. Is the combination of the two rotations equivalent to a single transformation? Test several cases, and make a conjecture about the result. You might start your investigation by rotating each polygon below 180° about C_1 and then 180° about C_2. These figures are reproduced on Labsheet 3.ACE3.

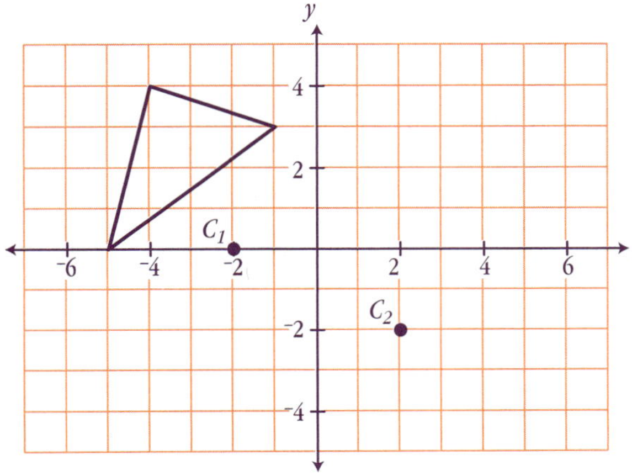

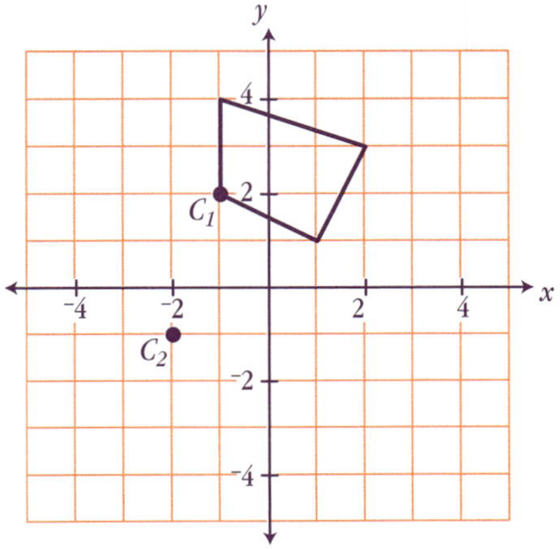

Mathematical Reflections

In this investigation, you looked at transformations of figures drawn on coordinate grids. You found that you could describe some symmetry transformations by telling what happens to a general point (x, y). These questions will help you summarize what you have learned:

1. What is the image of point (x, y) under a reflection over the y-axis?
2. What is the image of point (x, y) under a reflection over the x-axis?
3. What is the image of point (x, y) under a reflection over the line $y = x$?
4. What is the image of point (x, y) under a 90° rotation about the origin?
5. What is the image of point (x, y) under a 180° rotation about the origin?
6. What is the image of point (x, y) under a 270° rotation about the origin?
7. What is the image of point (x, y) under a 360° rotation about the origin?
8. What is the image of point (x, y) under the translation that slides $(1, 2)$ to $(3, {}^-2)$?
9. What is the image of point (x, y) under a translation of 6 units to the left followed by a translation of 2 units down?
10. What does it mean for two shapes to be congruent? How can you determine whether two shapes are congruent?

Think about your answers to these questions, discuss your ideas with other students and your teacher, and then write a summary of your findings in your journal.

INVESTIGATION 4

Symmetry and Algebra

A geometric figure is *symmetric* if a reflection or a rotation of the figure produces an image that matches the original figure exactly. Some figures have several symmetries. For example, an equilateral triangle has three lines of symmetry and can be rotated 120°, 240°, or 360° to exactly match the original figure.

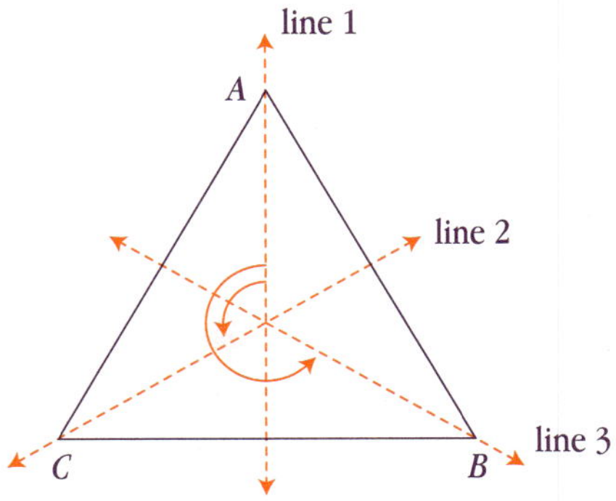

Your teacher will give you a copy of triangle *ABC* and the drawing above. Copy each vertex label onto the back of the triangle.

You can use your triangle as a tool for studying combinations of symmetry transformations. The drawing showing triangle *ABC* and its lines of symmetry will serve as a "frame" to help you keep track of the transformations. To begin, place your triangle in the frame, matching the vertices on your triangle with the vertices on the frame. To model a reflection over line 1 followed by a reflection over line 2, flip your triangle first over line 1 and then over line 2.

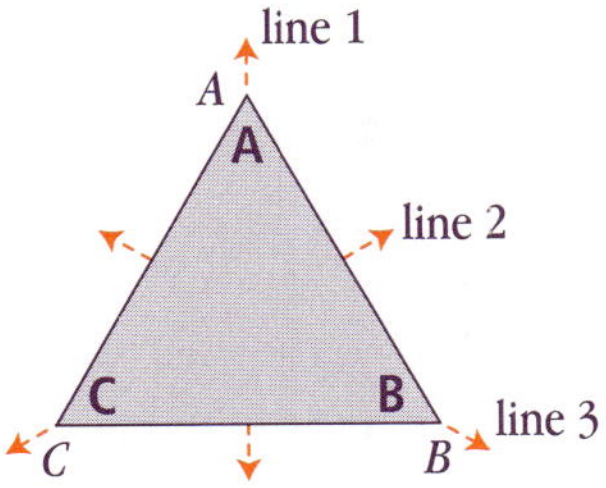

Start.

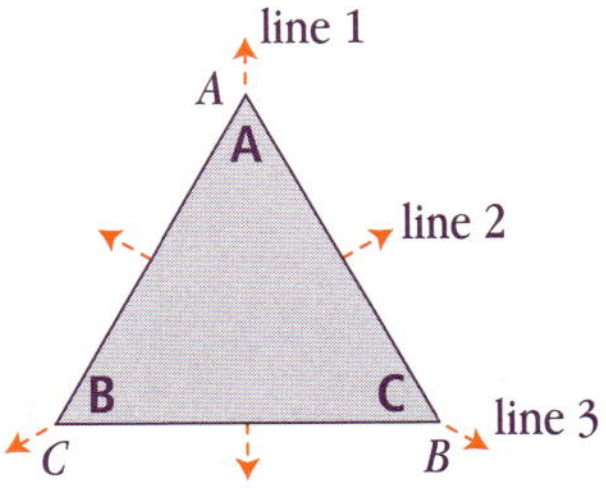

Reflect over line 1.

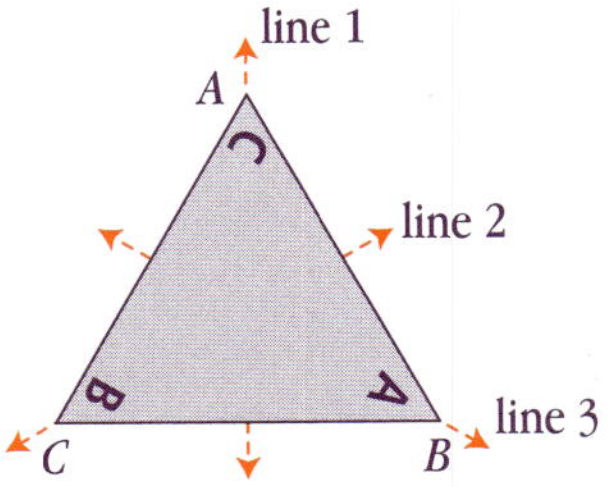

Reflect over line 2.

What single transformation would produce the same result as the combination of the two reflections?

Now use your triangle to find the result of a reflection over line 3 followed by a rotation of 120°. Is there a single transformation that would give the same result?

In this investigation, you will explore combinations of symmetry transformations for equilateral triangles and squares, and you will determine whether the operation of combining transformations satisfies some important algebraic properties.

4.1 Transforming Triangles

The operations of arithmetic—addition, subtraction, multiplication, and division—define ways of putting two numbers together to get a single number. In a similar way, you can think of combining symmetry transformations as an operation that puts two transformations together to produce a single, equivalent transformation.

In this problem, you will explore combinations of symmetry transformations for an equilateral triangle. The notation L_n means a reflection over line *n,* and the notation R_n means a counterclockwise rotation of *n* degrees. The symbol $*$ represents the combining operation. You can read this symbol as "and then." For example, $L_1 * L_2 = R_{240}$ means that reflecting the triangle over line 1 "and then" reflecting it over line 2 is equivalent to rotating the triangle 240°.

Problem 4.1

The operation table below is reproduced on Labsheet 4.1B. Complete the table to show the results of combining symmetry transformations of an equilateral triangle. Each entry should be the result of performing the transformation in the left column followed by the transformation in the top row. The two entries already in the table represent the combinations you explored in the introduction:

$L_1 * L_2 = R_{240}$ $\qquad$ $L_3 * R_{120} = L_2$

$*$	R_{360}	R_{120}	R_{240}	L_1	L_2	L_3
R_{360}						
R_{120}						
R_{240}						
L_1					R_{240}	
L_2						
L_3		L_2				

Note that transformation R_{360}, a 360° rotation, carries every point back to where it started. As you combine transformations, you will discover that many combinations are equivalent to R_{360}.

Problem 4.1 Follow-Up

1. Look carefully at the entries in your table. Describe any interesting patterns in the rows, columns, or blocks of entries. What do these patterns tell you about the results of combining rotations and line reflections?

2. Make an operation table for multiplication of the whole numbers 1, 2, 3, 4, 5, and 6. Compare the patterns in your multiplication table with the patterns in your table of transformation combinations. Describe any interesting similarities and differences you discover.

4.2 Transforming Squares

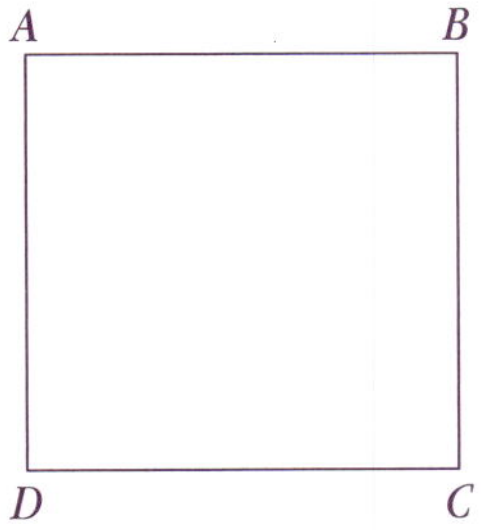

If a polygon has reflectional or rotational symmetry, you can make an operation table to show the results of combining symmetry transformations for that polygon. There are eight symmetry transformations for a square, including a rotation of 360°. In this problem, you will investigate combinations of these symmetry transformations.

Problem 4.2

A. On Labsheet 4.2B, draw all the lines of symmetry and describe all the rotations that produce images that exactly match the original square. Label the lines of symmetry in clockwise order as line 1, line 2, and so on.

B. Cut out a copy of the square, and copy each vertex label onto the back of the square. Use this copy to explore combinations of symmetry transformations. The operation table below is reproduced on Labsheet 4.2B. Complete the table to show the results of combining pairs of transformations. When you enter the column heads, first list the rotations and then the reflections. Use the same order for the row heads.

*	R_{360}							
R_{360}								

Problem 4.2 Follow-Up

1. Compare the patterns in the operation table for the square with the patterns in the operation table for the equilateral triangle. In what ways are the tables similar? In what ways are they different?

2. Make an operation table for multiplication of the whole numbers 1, 2, 3, 4, 5, 6, 7, and 8. Compare the patterns in your multiplication table with the patterns in your table of transformation combinations for the square. Describe any interesting similarities and differences you discover.

4.3 Properties of the Combining Operation

The operations of addition and multiplication satisfy important properties that are useful for reasoning about expressions and equations.

- The order in which numbers are added or multiplied does not affect the result. This is called the commutative property. We say that addition and multiplication are *commutative operations.* In symbols, if a and b are real numbers, then

$$a + b = b + a \quad \text{and} \quad a \times b = b \times a.$$

- Adding 0 to a number has no effect. Multiplying a number by 1 has no effect. In symbols, if a is a real number, then

$$0 + a = a + 0 = a \quad \text{and} \quad 1 \times a = a \times 1 = a.$$

  We call 0 and 1 *identity elements;* 0 is the additive identity, and 1 is the multiplicative identity.

- For any number a, the sum of a and ^{-}a is 0, the additive identity. For any nonzero number a, the product of a and $\frac{1}{a}$ is 1, the multiplicative identity.

$$a + {}^{-}a = {}^{-}a + a = 0 \quad \text{and} \quad a \times \frac{1}{a} = \frac{1}{a} \times a = 1$$

  We call ^{-}a the *additive inverse* of a and $\frac{1}{a}$ the *multiplicative inverse* of a.

In this problem, you will determine whether the operation for combining symmetry transformations for an equilateral triangle satisfies similar properties.

Problem 4.3

Refer to your operation table for combining symmetry transformations for an equilateral triangle.

A. Is $*$ a commutative operation? In other words, does the order in which you combine symmetry transformations make a difference? Justify your answer.

B. Like addition and multiplication, the $*$ operation has an identity element. That is, there is a transformation that has no effect when it is applied before or after another transformation. Tell which transformation is the identity element, and explain how you know.

C. Does each symmetry transformation have an inverse? That is, can you combine each transformation with another transformation, in either order, to get the identity element you found in part B? If so, list each transformation and its inverse.

Problem 4.3 Follow-Up

Refer to your operation table for combining symmetry transformations for a square.

1. Is $*$ a commutative operation for the symmetry transformations for a square?

2. What is the identity element in this situation?

3. Does each symmetry transformation have an inverse? If so, list each transformation and its inverse.

Applications • Connections • Extensions

As you work on these ACE questions, use your calculator whenever you need it.

Applications

1. Rectangle *ABCD* is not a square.

a. Describe all the symmetry transformations for the rectangle.

b. Make a table showing the results of combining pairs of symmetry transformations with the ✳ operation.

c. Is ✳ a commutative operation for this set of symmetry transformations? Explain.

d. What is the identity element in this situation?

e. Match each symmetry transformation with its inverse.

2. Triangle *ABC* is isosceles with congruent sides *AC* and *AB*.

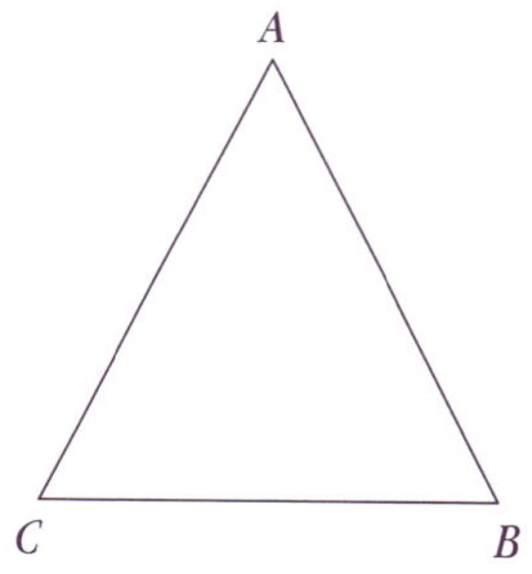

a. Describe all the symmetry transformations for the triangle.

b. Make a table showing the results of combining pairs of symmetry transformations with the ✳ operation.

c. Is ✳ a commutative operation for this set of symmetry transformations? Explain.

d. What is the identity element in this situation?

e. Match each symmetry transformation with its inverse.

3. Study this symmetric design, which is composed of four birds.

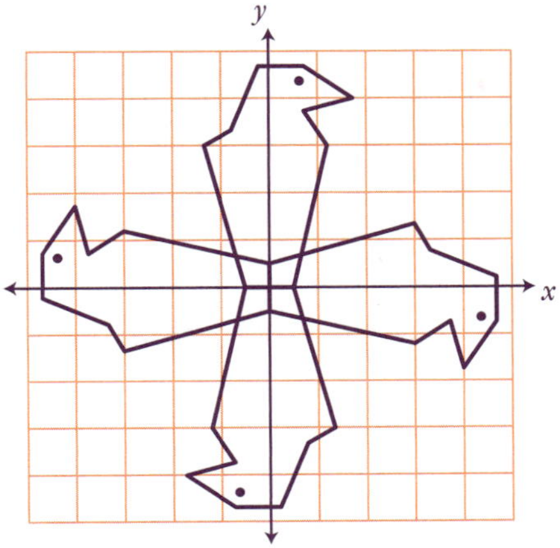

a. Describe all the symmetry transformations for this design.

b. Make a table showing the results of combining pairs of symmetry transformations with the ✳ operation.

c. Is ✳ a commutative operation for this set of symmetry transformations? Explain.

d. What is the identity element in this situation?

e. Match each symmetry transformation with its inverse.

Connections

4. a. What are the additive inverses of 2.3, $^{-}4$, $\frac{2}{3}$, and $-\frac{5}{4}$?

b. What are the multiplicative inverses of 2, 5, 0.4, and $\frac{2}{3}$?

c. Is subtraction of real numbers a commutative operation? Justify your answer.

d. Is division of real numbers a commutative operation? Justify your answer.

5. **a.** Is there an identity element for subtraction of real numbers? Explain.

   b. Is there an identity element for division of real numbers? Explain.

6. Look at the operation tables for combining symmetry transformations for an equilateral triangle, a square, and a rectangle.

   a. What do the patterns in the tables tell you about the result of combining two line reflections?

   b. What do the patterns in the tables tell you about the result of combining two rotations?

   c. What do the patterns in the tables tell you about the result of combining a rotation and a line reflection?

7. **a.** In the equation $x * R_{120} = L_1$, the x represents a symmetry transformation of an equilateral triangle. Use your table from Problem 4.1 to help you solve this equation. Explain how you found your answer. Check your solution by using a paper triangle to perform the transformations.

   b. In the equation $L_3 * x = R_{240}$, the x represents a symmetry transformation of an equilateral triangle. Solve this equation, and explain how you found the solution. Check your solution by using a paper triangle to perform the transformations.

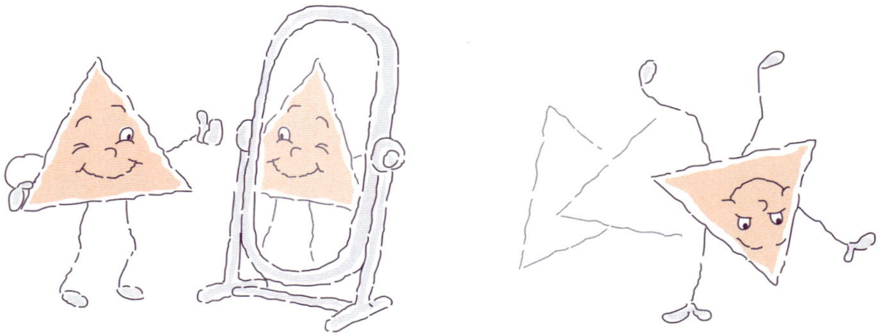

reflecting and rotating triangles

8. a. The figure below appears on Labsheet 4.ACE1. Sketch the image of the flag under the translation $(x, y) \rightarrow (x + 2, y + 3)$. We will call this translation T_1.

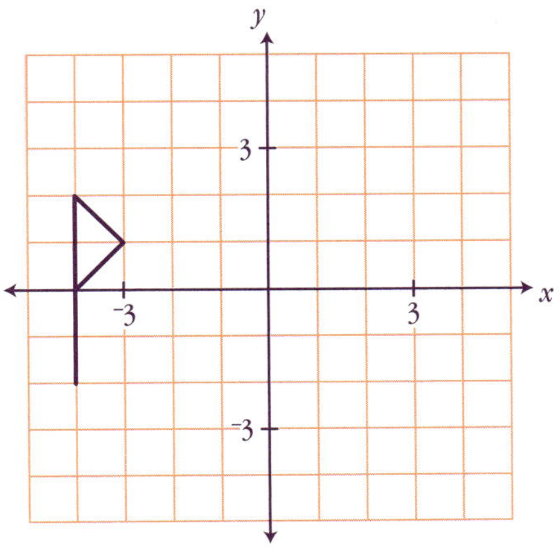

b. Sketch the image of the *original* flag under the translation $(x, y) \rightarrow (x + 4, y - 2)$. We will call this translation T_2.

c. Sketch the image of the original flag under the combination $T_1 * T_2$.

d. Sketch the image of the original flag under the combination $T_2 * T_1$.

9. a. Describe the relationship between pairs of opposite sides and between pairs of opposite angles for parallelogram *ABCD*.

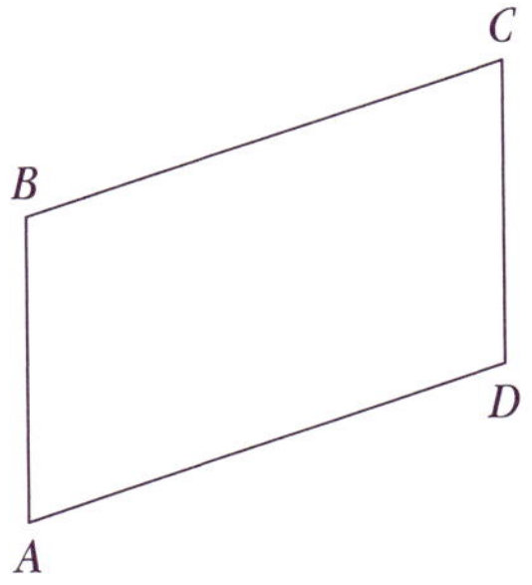

b. Suppose that translation T_2 matches point *A* with point *B*, and translation T_2 matches point *A* with point *D*.

i. Where is the image of point *A* under the combination $T_1 * T_2$?

ii. Where is the image of point *A* under the combination $T_2 * T_1$?

c. What conjecture would you make about commutativity of translations based on your answer to part b?

Extensions

10. Inverses are useful for solving algebraic equations. For example, to solve $x + 5 = 12$, you can add the additive inverse of 5 to both sides of the equation:

$$\begin{aligned} x + 5 &= 12 \\ x + 5 + {}^{-}5 &= 12 + {}^{-}5 \\ x &= 7 \end{aligned}$$

To solve $4x = 36$, you can multiply both sides by the multiplicative inverse of 4:

$$\begin{aligned} 4x &= 36 \\ \tfrac{1}{4}(4x) &= \tfrac{1}{4}(36) \\ x &= 9 \end{aligned}$$

Use a similar strategy to solve these equations involving symmetry transformations of a *square*. Explain the steps in your solution.

a. $x \ast R_{90} = R_{180}$

b. $L_1 \ast x = R_{180}$

c. $R_{270} \ast x = L_1$

11. **a.** Draw a regular pentagon. Describe all the symmetries in the pentagon.

b. Make a table showing the results of combining symmetry transformations with the ∗ operation.

c. Is the ∗ operation commutative for this set of symmetry transformations? Explain.

d. What is the identity element in this situation?

e. Match each symmetry transformation with its inverse.

12. Suppose the symbol ◆ represents the operation of finding the mean. So, for the numbers a and b, $a \blacklozenge b = \frac{a+b}{2}$.

a. Evaluate $12 \blacklozenge 5$, $3 \blacklozenge {}^{-}8$, and $2.5 \blacklozenge 9.7$.

b. Test a few examples to determine whether ◆ is a commutative operation.

c. Does this operation have an identity element?

13. Suppose the numbers from 1 to 7 represent the days of the week: 1 represents Monday, 2 represents Tuesday, and so on.

JANUARY 1997

SUN	MON	TUE	WED	THU	FRI	SAT
			1	2	3	4
5	6	7	8	9	10	11
12	13	14	15	16	17	18
19	20	21	22	23	24	25
26	27	28	29	30	31	

a. What number represents the day 5 days after Tuesday? What number represents the day 6 days after Friday?

b. Suppose the expression $a \blacktriangle b$ means the day b days after day a. For example, $5 \blacktriangle 3$ represents the day 3 days after Friday (day 5). Complete the table below.

▲	1	2	3	4	5	6	7
1	2	3					
2							
3							
4							
5							
6							
7							

c. Is ▲ a commutative operation? Explain.

d. What is the identity element for ▲?

e. Does each number have an inverse under the ▲ operation?

f. January 1, 1996, was a Monday. The year 1996 was a leap year, so it had 366 days. How can you show that January 1, 1997, occurred on a Wednesday?

Mathematical Reflections

In this investigation, you explored combinations of symmetry transformations for geometric shapes, and you determined whether the combining operation satisfies important algebraic properties. These questions will help you summarize what you have learned:

1. How are the patterns in the operation tables for combinations of symmetry transformations similar to the patterns in tables for the arithmetic operation multiplication? How are they different?

2. Explain what the operation tables show about the results of combining
   - **a.** two line reflections.
   - **b.** two rotations.
   - **c.** a rotation and a line reflection.

3. Explain how you could use an operation table to check for
   - **a.** commutativity.
   - **b.** an identity element.
   - **c.** inverse elements.

Think about your answers to these questions, discuss your ideas with other students and your teacher, and then write a summary of your findings in your journal.

The Unit Project

Part 1: Creating Tessellations

Materials: grid paper, isometric dot paper, stiff paper, an angle ruler or protractor, transparent tape, and colored pencils or markers

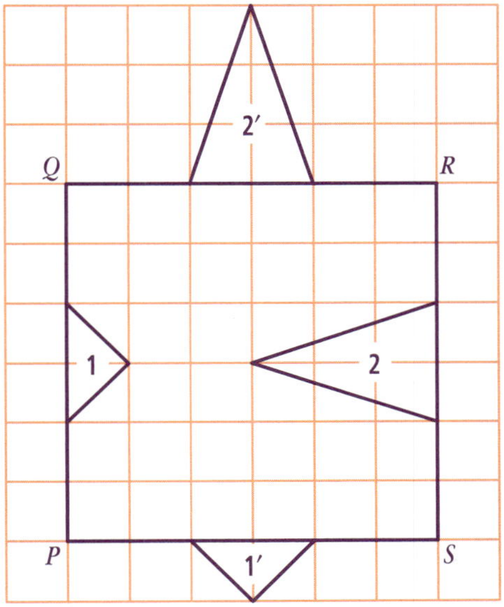

Directions:

- Draw square *PQRS* on grid paper.
- Draw triangle 1 as shown.
- Draw triangle 1′, the image of triangle 1 under a 270° rotation about point *P*.
- Draw triangle 2 as shown.
- Draw triangle 2′, the image of triangle 2 under a 270° rotation about point *R*.

Now you will start with a copy of square *PQRS* and perform the same rotations as before. However, this time you will cut out triangles 1 and 2 and rotate the cut pieces.

- Copy square *PQRS* and triangles 1 and 2 onto a stiff sheet of paper. Cut out square *PQRS*.
- Cut out triangle 1, rotate it 270° about point *P*, and tape it in place.
- Cut out triangle 2, rotate it 270° about point *R*, and tape it in place.

Trace copies of your finished shape to create a tessellation. Recall that a *tessellation* is a design made by fitting together copies of a basic shape without gaps or overlaps. You can decorate the basic shapes to make your tessellation more interesting.

We say that the shape below *tessellates* because it can be used to create a tessellation.

Starting with a square, try to create your own tessellating shape. Cut out pieces from the square, rotate them, and tape them in place. As you work, think about this question: *Will any cutout shape and any rotation turn a square into a shape that tessellates?* When you find a shape that tessellates, trace it several times to make a tessellation. Tape your basic shape to the paper.

Now see if you can create a tessellating shape from a rhombus with angles of 60° and 120°. You may find it easier to make your design on isometric dot paper and then cut out a copy from stiff paper. As you work, think about this question: *Will any cutout shape and any rotation turn a rhombus with 60° and 120° angles into a shape that tessellates?* If you find a shape that tessellates, trace it several times to make a tessellation. Tape your basic shape to the paper. If you were unable to create a shape that tessellates, explain why you think your efforts were unsuccessful.

Part 2: Making a Wreath and a Pinwheel

Origami is the Japanese art of paper folding. In this part of the project, you will make an origami wreath and then transform your wreath into a pinwheel.

Materials: eight paper squares of the same size (four paper squares in each of two colors gives a nice result)

Directions:
The wreath is made by connecting eight folded squares. Follow these instructions to fold each square:

- Fold a paper square to create the creases shown.

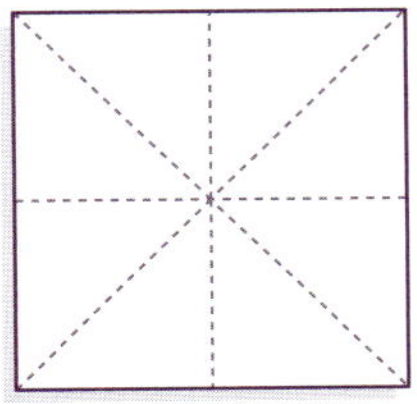

- Fold down the top corners of the square to make a “house,” and then fold the house in half so that the flaps are on the inside.

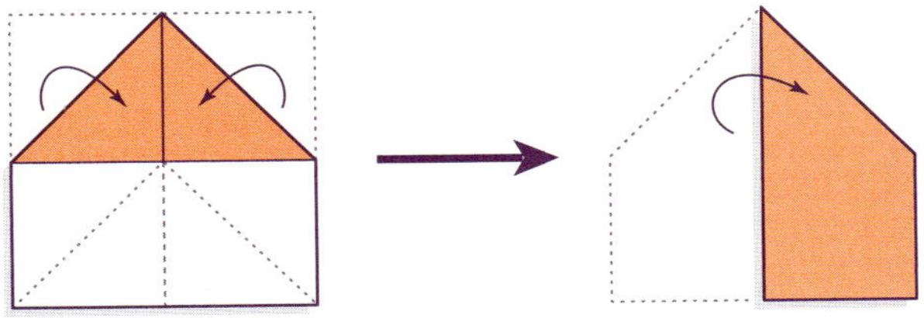

- Hold the "half-house" at its point, and push the bottom corner in along the folds to make a parallelogram.

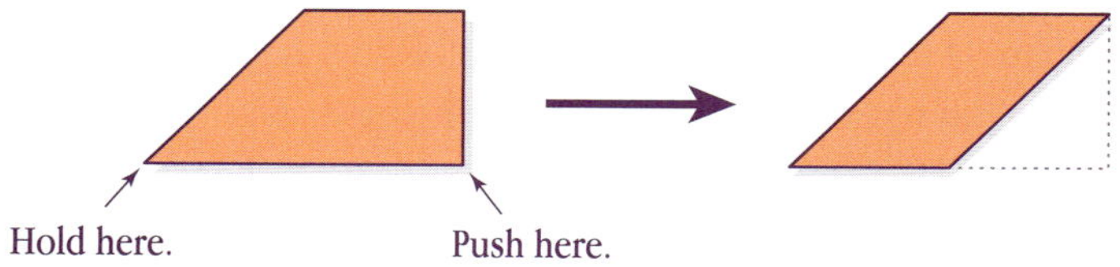

Follow these steps to connect the eight pieces:

- Position two of the folded pieces as shown on the left below. (If you used different colors, use one piece of each color.) Slide the point of the right piece into the fold pocket of the left piece.

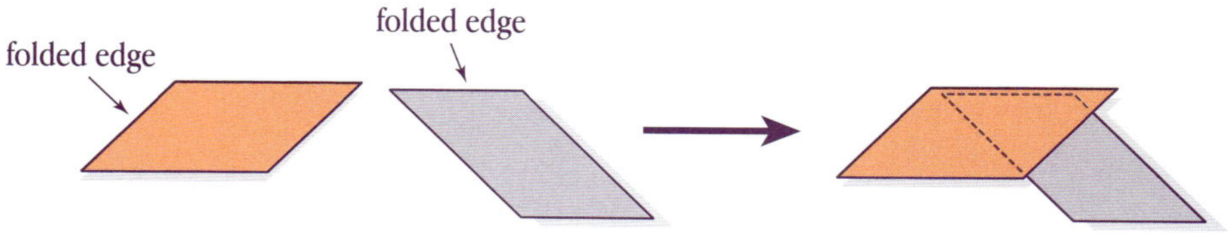

- Fold down the tips that extend over the inserted piece, and tuck them into the valley formed by the folds of the inserted piece.

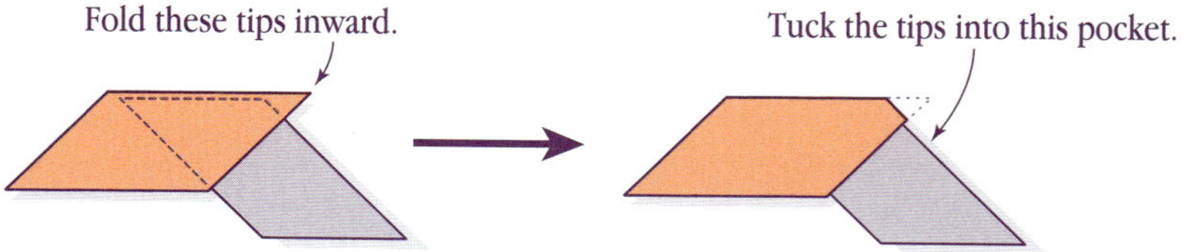

- Follow the steps above to attach the remaining folded pieces.
- Complete the wreath by connecting the last piece to the first piece, being careful to fold each flap over only one folded layer.

- To make a pinwheel, gently slide the sides of the wreath toward the center.

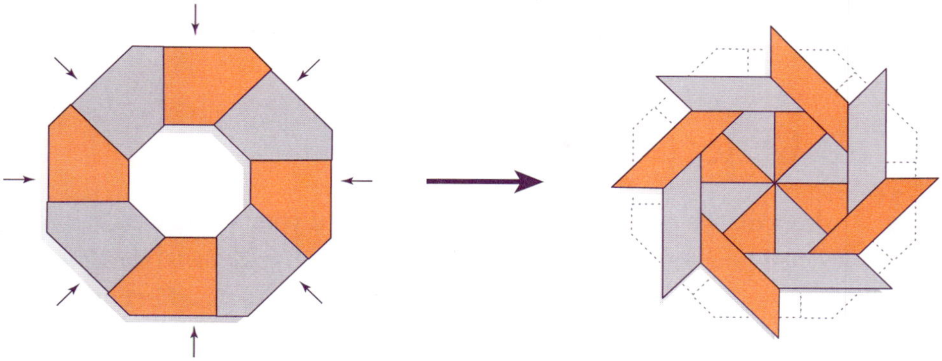

Study the drawings in the instructions for creating the origami wreath and pinwheel, and look for symmetries in the figures created at each stage.

1. Describe the reflectional and rotational symmetries of

a. the square.

b. the "house."

c. the "half-house."

d. the parallelogram.

e. the completed wreath.

f. the pinwheel.

2. Slide your pinwheel back into a wreath shape. If you gently push on a pair of opposite sides of your wreath, you will get a pinwheel with only two "wings." Describe the reflectional and rotational symmetries of this figure.

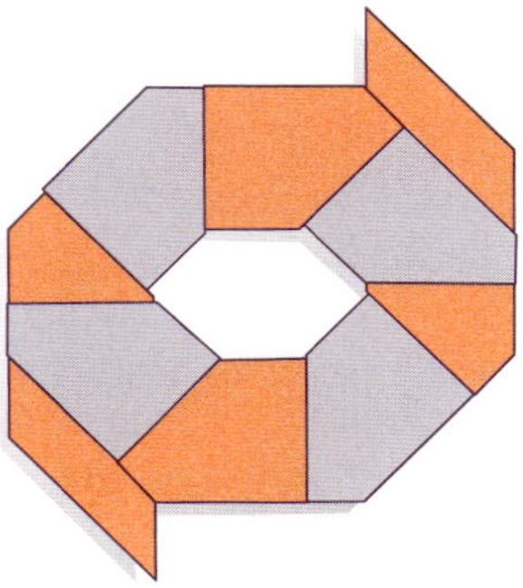

3. Slide your pinwheel back into a wreath shape. Gently push on opposite sides of the pinwheel to produce other shapes. Look at the shape of the center opening. What shapes can you create by pushing on the sides of the wreath?

Looking Back and Looking Ahead

Unit Reflections

Working on the problems of this unit extended your understanding of *symmetry*. You learned how to describe symmetry in terms of *reflections*, *rotations*, and *translations*. You learned how to write rules describing the effect of each *transformation* on points and figures. You discovered the connection between symmetry transformations and *congruence* of geometric figures. By studying the effects of combining reflections and rotations, you discovered ways to connect algebraic and geometric operations.

Using Your Geometric Reasoning—To test your understanding and skill in work with symmetry and transformations, consider the following problems where symmetry arises.

1 *The wallpaper design at the right has been selected for the kitchen.*

a. Describe the different symmetries in the wallpaper pattern, assuming that the design continues in the same way horizontally and vertically.

b. Consider this  element from the wallpaper design. What is the smallest angle through which this figure can be rotated to coincide with the original design?

2 *One of the square tiles for the kitchen floor is shown at the right.*

a. Describe all symmetries of the design on this piece of tile.

b. Identify the smallest basic element from which the rest of this design can be created by transformations of that element. Explain the symmetry transformations that will take the basic element onto all other parts of the design.

3 *The blue living room rug has this design repeated in a regular pattern around its border.*

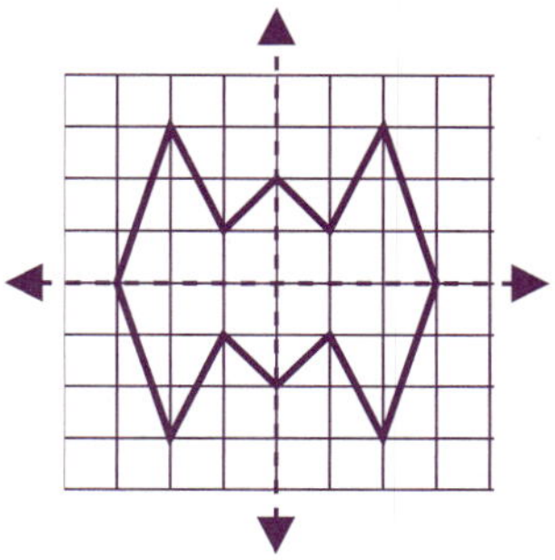

a. Use tracing paper to sketch the design's image after a

i. rotation of 90° counterclockwise about the origin.

ii. reflection over the y-axis.

iii. translation with rule $(x, y) \rightarrow (x, y + 3)$.

b. Sketch the images of the design after these combinations of transformations.

i. Reflection in the y-axis followed by reflection in the x-axis

ii. Rotation of 90° about the origin followed by reflection in the line $y = x$

iii. Reflection in the x-axis followed by reflection in the line $y = 1$

c. Describe the single symmetry transformation equivalent to each combination in part b.

d. Describe a pair of symmetry transformations that commute with each other.

Explaining Your Reasoning—Solving geometric problems requires visual skills to see important patterns. However, you should be able to justify your conclusions.

1. How would you convince someone that a given figure has

a. symmetry in a line? **b.** rotational symmetry? **c.** translational symmetry?

2. What type of symmetry transformation can be expected from the combination of

a. two rotations with a common center point?

b. two line reflections over intersecting lines?

c. two line reflections over parallel lines?

d. two translations?

3. If your friend tells you that subtraction is commutative, how could you convince him that his reasoning is flawed?

4. How are *inverse transformations* like multiplicative and additive inverses of numbers?

The algebraic and geometric ideas and techniques you've used in this unit will be applied and explored in greater depth in future mathematics and science classes and in practical problems about shapes and designs. You'll find them especially valuable in high school geometry and trigonometry.

Glossary

congruent figures Two figures are congruent if one is an image of the other under a translation, a reflection, a rotation, or some combination of these transformations. Put more simply, two figures are congruent if you can slide, flip, or turn one figure so that it fits exactly on the other. The polygons below are congruent.

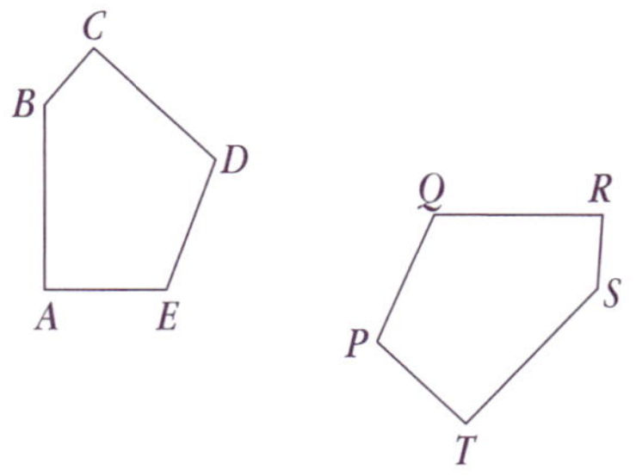

kaleidoscope A tube containing colored beads or pieces of glass and carefully-placed mirrors. When a kaleidoscope is held to the eye and rotated, the viewer sees colorful, symmetric patterns.

line reflection A transformation that matches each point on a figure with its mirror image over a line. Polygon $A'B'C'D'E'$ below is the image of polygon *ABCDE* under a reflection over the line. If you drew a line segment from a point to its image, the segment would be perpendicular to and bisected by the line of reflection.

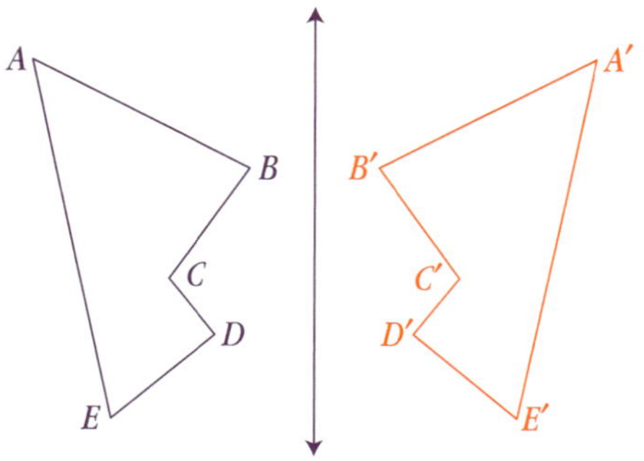

reflectional symmetry A figure or design has reflectional symmetry if you can draw a line that divides the figure into halves that are mirror images. The line that divides the figure into halves is called the *line of symmetry*. The figure below has reflectional symmetry about a vertical line through its center.

rotation A transformation that turns a figure counterclockwise about a point. Polygon *A′B′C′D′* below is the image of polygon *ABCD* under a 60° rotation about point *P*. If you drew a segment from a point on polygon *ABCD* to point *P* and another segment from the point's image to point *P*, the segments would be the same length and they would form a 60° angle.

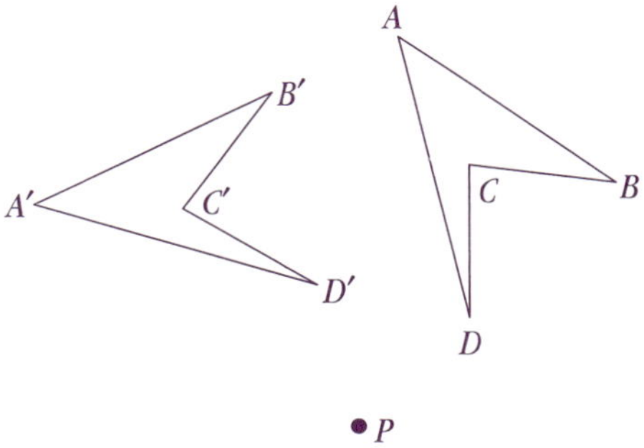

rotational symmetry A figure or design has rotational symmetry if it can be rotated less than a full turn about a point to a position in which it looks the same as the original. The hubcap design below has rotational symmetry with its center as the center of rotation and a 120° angle of rotation. This means that it can be rotated 120°, or any multiple of 120°, about its centerpoint to create an image that matches exactly with the original.

symmetry An object or design has symmetry if part of it is repeated to create a balanced pattern. In this unit, you learned about three types of symmetry. The butterfly below has *reflectional symmetry,* the fan blades have *rotational symmetry,* and the wallpaper design has *translational symmetry.*

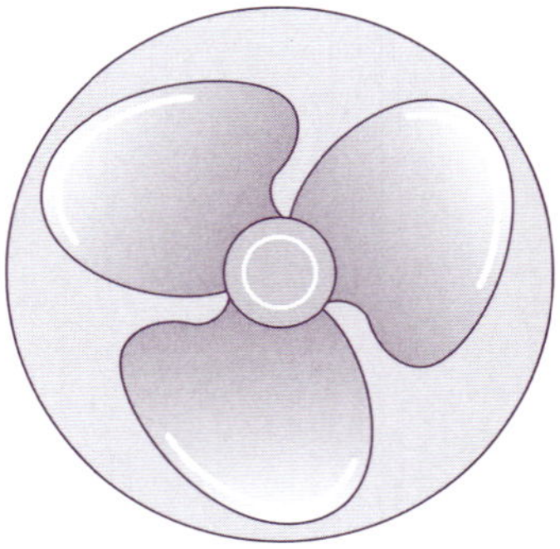

tessellation A design made from copies of a basic design element that cover a surface without gaps or overlaps. Tessellations have translational symmetry. The designs below are tessellations.

transformation A geometric operation that matches each point on a figure with an image point. The transformations you studied in the unit—reflections, rotations, and translations—are symmetry transformations. A symmetry transformation produces an image that is identical in size and shape to the original figure.

translation A transformation that slides each point on a figure to an image point a given distance and direction from the original point. Polygon $A'B'C'D'E'$ below is the image of polygon $ABCDE$ under a translation. If you drew line segments from two points to their respective image points, the segments would be parallel and they would have the same length.

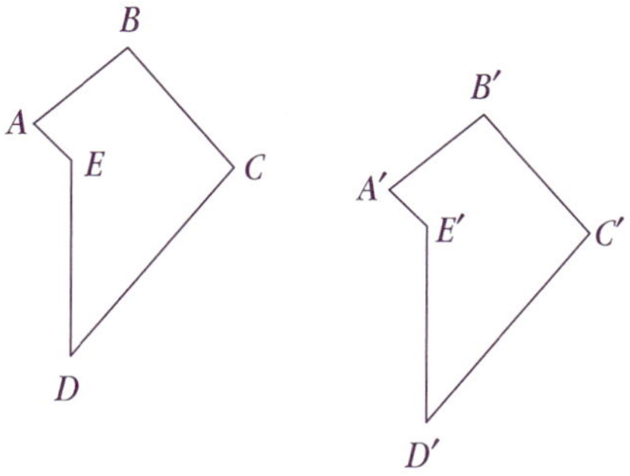

translational symmetry A design has translational symmetry if it can be created by copying and sliding a basic shape in a regular pattern. Translational symmetry is found in wallpaper designs and tessellations. The design below has translational symmetry.

Glosario

caleidoscopio Tubo que contiene cuentas de colores o pedazos de vidrio y espejos estratégicamente ubicados. Cuando alguien mira a través de un caleidoscopio y lo hace girar, puede ver patrones simétricos de gran colorido.

figuras congruentes Dos figuras son congruentes si una es la imagen de la otra sometida a una traslación, una reflexión, una rotación o a alguna combinación de estas transformaciones. Expresado de manera más sencilla, dos figuras son congruentes si puedes deslizar, voltear o rotar una figura para que coincida exactamente con la otra. Los siguientes polígonos son congruentes:

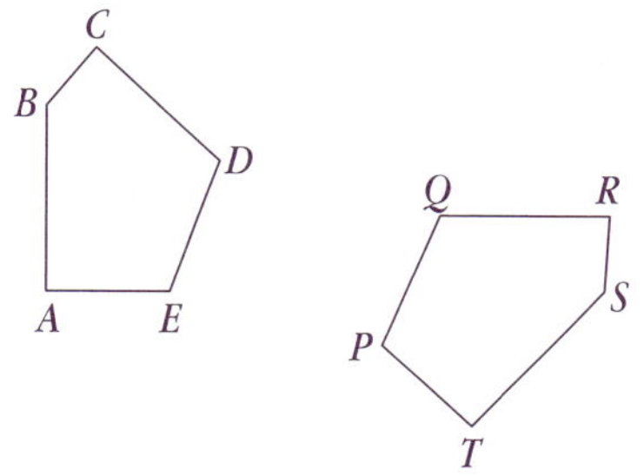

reflexión sobre un eje Una transformación en la que cada punto de una figura coincide con su imagen especular sobre un eje. El polígono *A'B'C'D'E'* es la imagen del polígono *ABCDE* sometido a una reflexión sobre un eje. Si dibujaras un segmento de recta desde un punto hasta su imagen, el segmento sería perpendicular al eje de reflexión y estaría bisecado por éste.

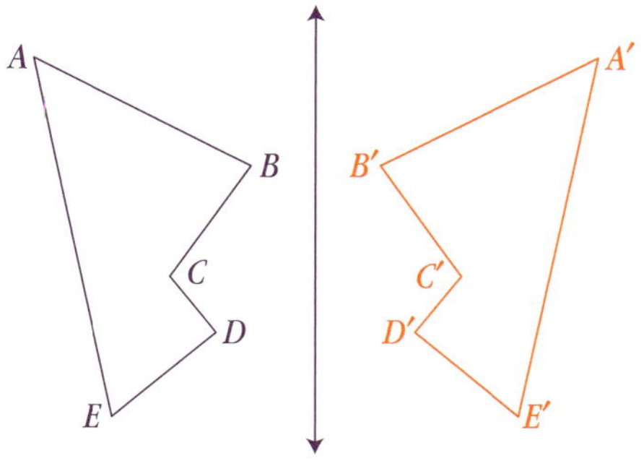

rotación Una transformación por la que una figura gira alrededor de un punto en dirección contraria a las agujas del reloj. El siguiente polígono *A'B'C'D'E'* es la imagen del polígono *ABCD* sometido a una rotación de 60° alrededor el punto *P*. Si dibujaras un segmento desde un punto en el polígono *ABCD* hasta el punto *P* y otro segmento desde la imagen del punto hasta el punto *P*, los segmentos tendrían la misma longitud y formarían un ángulo de 60°.

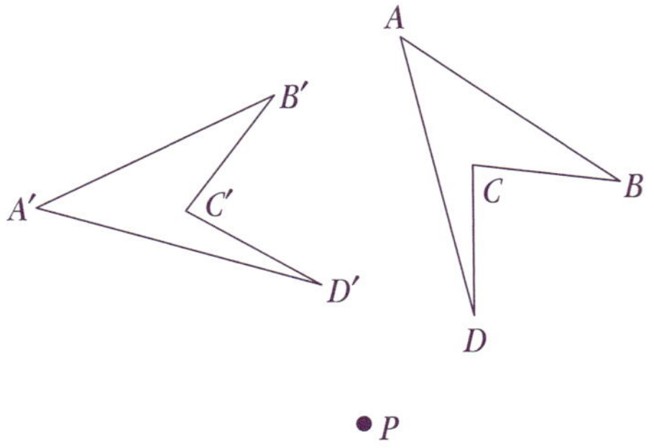

simetría Un objeto o diseño tiene simetría si parte de dicho objeto se repite para crear un patrón equilibrado. En esta unidad, aprendiste tres tipos de simetría. La mariposa que ves a continuación tiene *simetría de reflexión*, las paletas de un ventilador tienen *simetría de rotación* y el diseño del papel para empapelar tiene *simetría de traslación*.

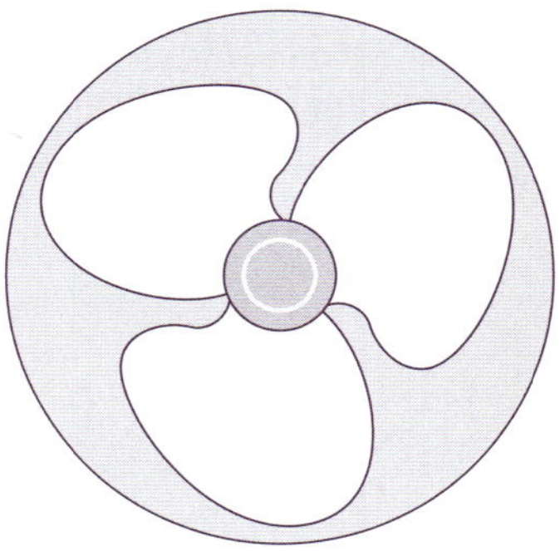

simetría de reflexión Una figura o diseño tiene simetría de reflexión si se puede dibujar una recta que divida la figura en dos mitades que sean imágenes especulares. La recta que divide la figura en dos mitades se llama *eje de simetría*. La siguiente figura tiene simetría de reflexión a ambos lados de una recta vertical que pasa por su centro.

simetría de rotación Una figura o diseño tiene simetría de rotación si se puede rotar casi por completo alrededor de un punto hasta llegar a una posición en la que quede igual al dibujo original. El diseño de la siguiente cubierta tiene simetría de rotación: su centro es el centro de rotación y tiene un ángulo de rotación de 120°. Esto significa que se puede rotar 120°, o cualquier múltiplo de 120°, alrededor de su punto central para crear una imagen que coincida exactamente con la original.

simetría de traslación Un diseño tiene simetría de traslación si puede crearse copiando y deslizando un elemento básico siguiendo un patrón uniforme. La simetría de traslación se encuentra en diseños de papel para empapelar y en teselados. El siguiente diseño tiene simetría de traslación.

teselado Un diseño realizado a partir de copias de un elemento básico de diseño con el que se cubre una superficie sin dejar huecos ni superponer elementos. Los teselados tienen simetría de traslación. El siguiente diseño es un teselado.

transformación Una operación geométrica en la que cada punto de una figura coincide con un punto de su imagen. Las transformaciones que estudiaste en la unidad –reflexiones, rotaciones y traslaciones— son transformaciones de simetría. Una transformación de simetría da como resultado una imagen con el mismo tamaño y la misma forma que la figura original.

traslación Una transformación que desliza cada punto de una figura hacia un punto de su imagen a determinada distancia y dirección del punto original. El polígono *A'B'C'D'E'* que se observa a continuación es la imagen del polígono *ABCDE* sometido a una traslación. Si dibujaras segmentos de recta desde dos puntos hasta los puntos correspondientes en su imagen, los segmentos serían paralelos y tendrían la misma longitud.

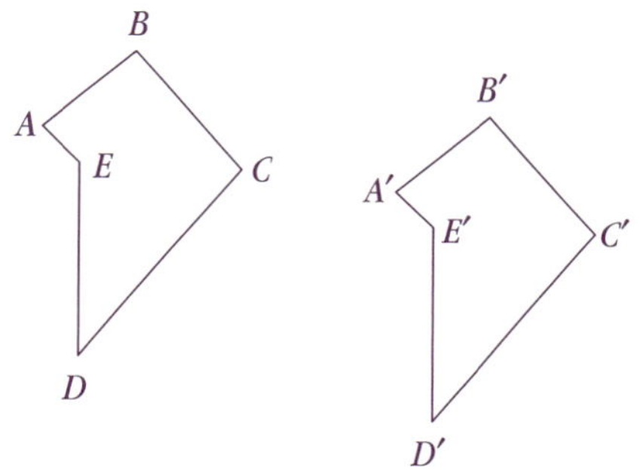

Index

Connected Mathematics™

Samples and Populations

Data and Statistics

Student Edition

Glenda Lappan
James T. Fey
William M. Fitzgerald
Susan N. Friel
Elizabeth Difanis Phillips

PEARSON
Prentice Hall

Glenview, Illinois
Needham, Massachusetts
Upper Saddle River, New Jersey

Samples and Populations

Connected Mathematics™ was developed at Michigan State University with the support of National Science Foundation Grant No. MDR 9150217.

This project was supported, in part,
by the
National Science Foundation
Opinions expressed are those of the authors
and not necessarily those of the Foundation

The Michigan State University authors and administration have agreed that all MSU royalties arising from this publication will be devoted to purposes supported by the Department of Mathematics and the MSU Mathematics Education Enrichment Fund.

Photo Acknowledgements: 5 © Joseph Nettis/Photo Researchers, Inc.; 11 © Bob Daemmrich/Stock, Boston; 20 © Judy Gelles/Stock, Boston; 22 (both photos) Michael Dwyer/Stock, Boston; 24 © Tony Duffy/Allsport; 33 © Rick Lee/Superstock; 45 © Doris DeWitt/Tony Stone Images; 49 © UPI/Corbis-Bettmann; 50 © Stuart Struever/Tony Stone Images; 56 © Sue Ogrocki/Reuters/Corbis-Bettmann; 65 © D. LaBelle/The Image Works

Contents

Samples and Populations

The homecoming committee wants to estimate how many students will attend the homecoming dance, but they don't want to ask every student in the school. How could they select a sample of students to survey? How could they use the results of their survey to predict the number of students who will attend?

A cookie company claims that there are at least 1000 chips in every 1-pound bag of its chocolate chip cookies. How could you test this claim? How do you think the company guarantees this claim?

A radio talk-show host asked her listeners to call in to express their opinions about a local election. Do you think the results of this survey could be used to describe the opinions of all the show's listeners?

The U.S. census attempts to gather information from every household in the United States. Gathering, organizing, and analyzing data from such a large population is expensive and time-consuming. In most studies of large populations, data are gathered from a sample, or portion, of the population. The data from the sample are then used to make predictions or to draw conclusions about the population.

Sampling is an important tool in statistics and data analysis. Understanding how to select samples and how to use them to make predictions will help you when you consider questions like those on the opposite page.

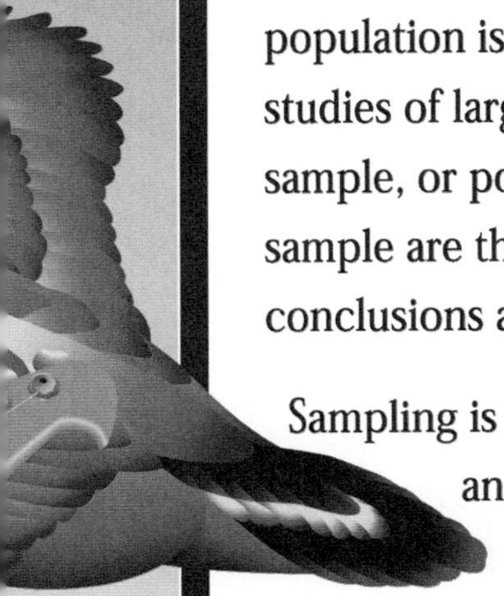

Mathematical Highlights

In *Samples and Populations,* you will explore ways of collecting and analyzing data. This unit will help you to

- Revisit and use the process of statistical investigation to explore problems;
- Compare data using measures of center (mean or median), measures of spread (range or percentiles), and data displays (tables, stem-and-leaf plots, histograms, and box-and-whisker plots);
- Distinguish between samples and populations, compare samples, and use information drawn from samples to draw conclusions about populations;
- Apply concepts from probability to explore the concept of randomness and to select random samples from populations; and
- Explore the representativeness and sample size of random and nonrandom samples to draw conclusions about the characteristics of populations.

As you work on the problems in this unit, make it a habit to ask questions about situations that involve data analysis using samples: *What is the population? What is the sample? What kinds of comparisons and relationships among the data from the sample can I explore? Can I use my results to make predictions or generalizations about the population? Is the sample representative in terms of size and the way in which the data were collected? Was there any bias in the ways the data were collected or analyzed?*

INVESTIGATION 1

Comparing Data Sets

American shoppers have a greater variety of stores and products to choose from than do shoppers anywhere else in the world. With so many choices, it can be difficult to decide which product to purchase. Many people turn to information in consumer surveys and product comparisons to help them make informed decisions.

A recent consumer survey rated 37 varieties of peanut butter. Each brand was assigned a quality rating from 1 to 100 points. A panel of trained tasters made two general statements about quality:

- Peanut butters with higher quality ratings were smooth; had a sweet, nutty flavor; and were not overly dry or sticky.
- Peanut butters with lower quality ratings were not very nutty; had small chunks of peanuts; or had a burnt or slightly rancid taste.

In addition to quality ratings, the article listed the sodium content and the price per 3-tablespoon serving for each brand. Brands were classified according to three attributes: natural or regular, creamy or chunky, and salted or unsalted. The data are presented in the table on the next page. A fourth attribute, name brand or store brand, has been added to the data.

Think about this!

- Who might be interested in the results of this peanut butter study?
- What interesting questions about peanut butter can be answered with these data?
- What interesting questions about peanut butter cannot be answered with these data?

Peanut Butter Comparisons

	Brand	Quality rating	Sodium per serving (mg)	Price per serving	Regular/ natural	Creamy/ chunky	Salted/ unsalted	Name brand/ store brand
1.	Smucker's Natural	71	15	27¢	natural	creamy	unsalted	name
2.	Deaf Smith Arrowhead Mills	69	0	32	natural	creamy	unsalted	name
3.	Adams 100% Natural	60	0	26	natural	creamy	unsalted	name
4.	Adams	60	168	26	natural	creamy	salted	name
5.	Laura Scudder's All Natural	57	165	26	natural	creamy	salted	name
6.	Country Pure Brand (Safeway)	52	225	21	natural	creamy	salted	store
7.	Hollywood Natural	34	15	32	natural	creamy	unsalted	name
8.	Smucker's Natural	89	15	27	natural	chunky	unsalted	name
9.	Adams 100% Natural	69	0	26	natural	chunky	unsalted	name
10.	Deaf Smith Arrowhead Mills	69	0	32	natural	chunky	unsalted	name
11.	Country Pure Brand (Safeway)	67	105	21	natural	chunky	salted	store
12.	Laura Scudder's All Natural	63	165	24	natural	chunky	salted	name
13.	Smucker's Natural	57	188	26	natural	chunky	salted	name
14.	Health Valley 100% Natural	40	3	34	natural	chunky	unsalted	name
15.	Jif	76	220	22	regular	creamy	salted	name
16.	Skippy	60	225	19	regular	creamy	salted	name
17.	Kroger	54	240	14	regular	creamy	salted	store
18.	NuMade (Safeway)	43	187	20	regular	creamy	salted	store
19.	Peter Pan	40	225	21	regular	creamy	salted	name
20.	Peter Pan	35	3	22	regular	creamy	unsalted	name
21.	A & P	34	225	12	regular	creamy	salted	store
22.	Food Club	33	225	17	regular	creamy	salted	store
23.	Pathmark	31	255	9	regular	creamy	salted	store
24.	Lady Lee (Lucky Stores)	23	225	16	regular	creamy	salted	store
25.	Albertsons	23	225	17	regular	creamy	salted	store
26.	Shur Fine (Shurfine Central)	11	225	16	regular	creamy	salted	store
27.	Jif	83	162	23	regular	chunky	salted	name
28.	Skippy	83	211	21	regular	chunky	salted	name
29.	Food Club	54	195	17	regular	chunky	salted	store
30.	Kroger	49	255	14	regular	chunky	salted	store
31.	A & P	46	225	11	regular	chunky	salted	store
32.	Peter Pan	45	180	22	regular	chunky	salted	name
33.	NuMade (Safeway)	40	208	21	regular	chunky	salted	store
34.	Lady Lee (Lucky Stores)	34	225	16	regular	chunky	salted	store
35.	Albertsons	31	225	17	regular	chunky	salted	store
36.	Pathmark	29	210	9	regular	chunky	salted	store
37.	Shur Fine (Shurfine Central)	26	195	16	regular	chunky	salted	store

Sources: "The Nuttiest Peanut Butter." *Consumer Reports* (September 1990): pp. 588–591.
A. J. Rossman, *Workshop Statistics: Student Activity Guide.* Carlisle, Penn.: Dickinson College, 1994, pp. 5–18.

1.1 Comparing Quality Ratings

To help determine which peanut butter is the "best buy," you could make several comparisons. For example, you could compare the quality ratings of the regular brands with the quality ratings of the natural brands, which contain no preservatives. How would you summarize and display the data to help you decide whether natural brands or regular brands have higher quality ratings?

Problem 1.1

Apply some of the data analysis techniques you learned in earlier statistics work to compare the quality ratings for natural brands and regular brands.

In general, do natural brands or regular brands have higher quality ratings? Use the results of your analysis to justify your choice.

Problem 1.1 Follow-Up

1. For the quality ratings of the regular brands, the mean is greater than the median. Why do you think this is true?
2. For the quality ratings of the natural brands, the mean and the median are close in value. Why do you think this is true?

1.2 Using Box-and-Whiskers Plots

Box-and-whiskers plots, or *box plots,* are useful representations of the distribution of values in a data set. The box plot below shows the distribution of quality ratings for the natural brands of peanut butter.

Quality Ratings for Natural Brands

A box plot is constructed from the five-number summary of the data. The **five-number summary** includes the minimum value, maximum value, median, lower quartile, and upper quartile.

You know how to find the minimum value, maximum value, and median in a set of data. The **lower quartile** is the median of the data values below the median. The **upper quartile** is the median of the data values above the median. The diagram below illustrates the five-number summary for the quality ratings of the natural brands of peanut butter.

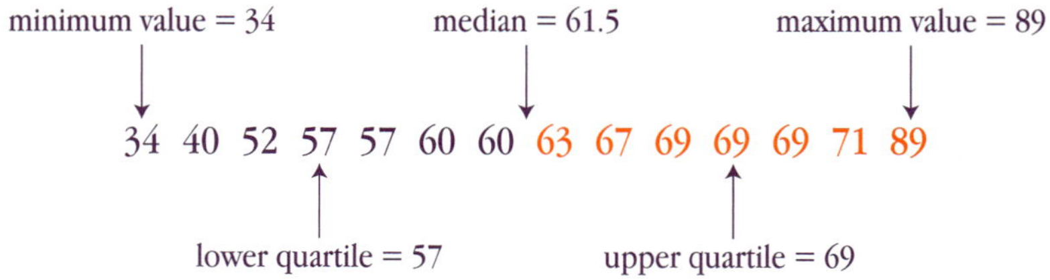

The plot below shows how the numbers in the five-number summary correspond to the features of the box plot.

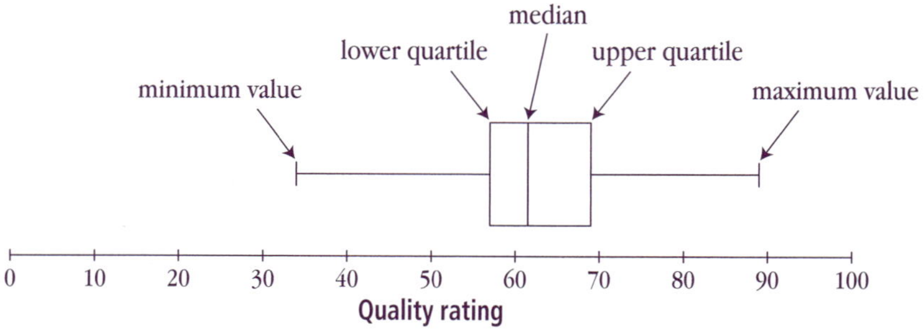

By displaying two or more box plots on the same scale, you can compare distributions. The box plots below allow you to compare the distributions of quality ratings for natural brands and regular brands.

Quality Ratings for Natural and Regular Brands

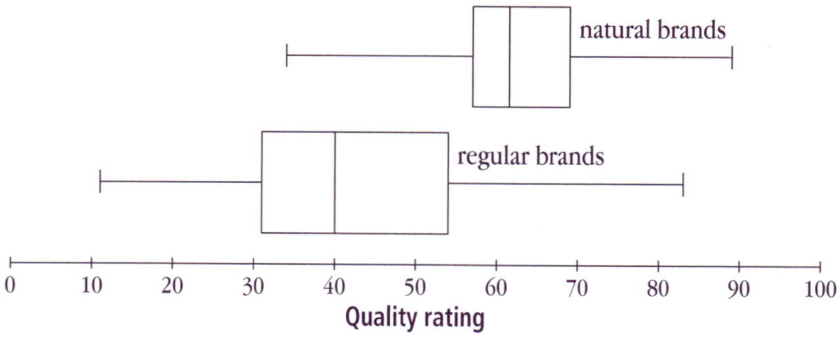

Problem 1.2

A. About what percent of the values in a data set are below the median? About what percent of the values in a data set are above the median?

B. The lower quartile, median, and upper quartile divide a data distribution into four parts. These four parts are called the *first, second, third,* and *fourth quartiles* of the distribution.

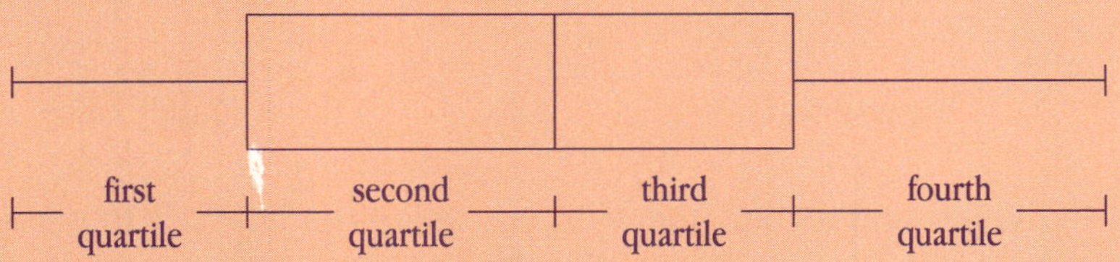

About what percent of the values in a data distribution are in each quartile?

C. Use the box plots of quality ratings for regular and natural brands to help you decide which type of peanut butter—regular or natural—is of higher quality. Explain your reasoning.

■ Problem 1.2 Follow-Up

Values in a data set that are much greater or much less than most of the other values are called *outliers.* To help you decide whether a value is an outlier, find the length of the box in a box plot of the data. The length of the box is the difference between the upper and lower quartiles. This length is called the *interquartile range,* abbreviated IQR. If a value is greater than 1.5 times the IQR added to the upper quartile or less than 1.5 times the IQR subtracted from the lower quartile, it is an outlier.

1. Are there outliers in the quality ratings for the natural brands? Are there outliers in the quality ratings for the regular brands?

2. On a box plot, outliers are sometimes indicated with asterisks (*). Both pairs of box plots below show the distribution of quality ratings for regular and natural brands of peanut butter. In the plots on the right, outliers have been indicated with asterisks.

Quality Ratings for Natural and Regular Brands

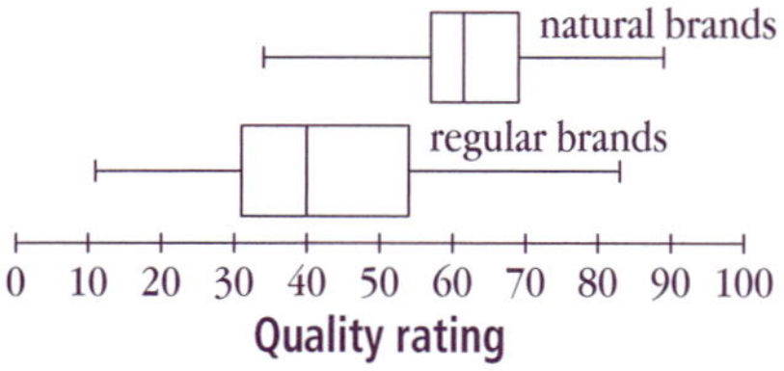

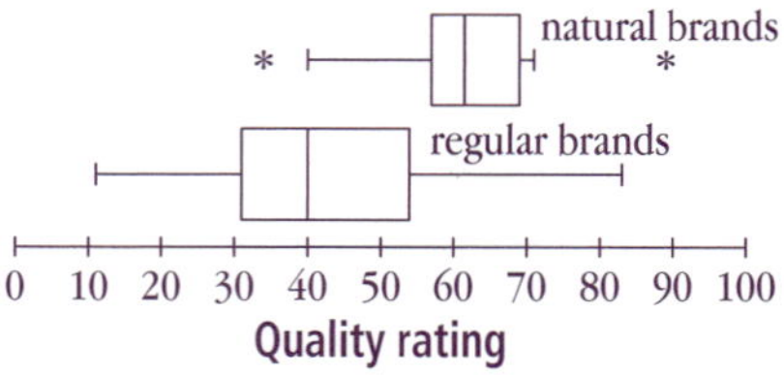

a. In the plots on the left, the whiskers extend from the box to the minimum and maximum values. What values do the whiskers in the plots on the right extend to?

b. Describe how you would construct a box plot if you wanted to show the outliers in a set of data.

1.3 Comparing Prices

Many people consider *both* quality and price when deciding which products or brands to buy. The box plots below show the distributions of per-serving prices for natural and regular brands of peanut butter.

Peanut Butter Prices

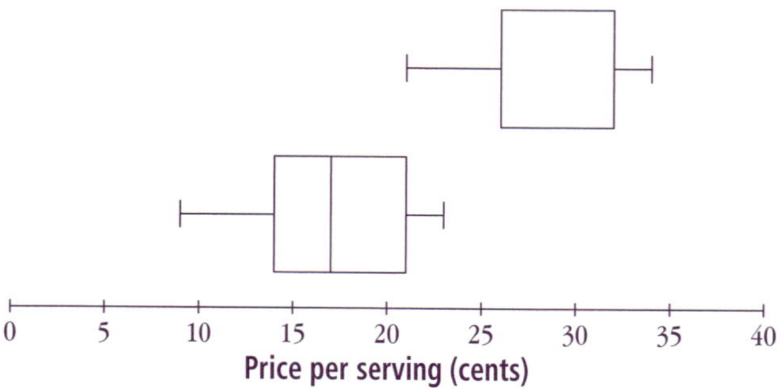

Problem 1.3

In the peanut butter data on page 6, refer to the column giving price per serving.

A. Calculate the five-number summary for the prices of the natural brands.

B. Calculate the five-number summary for the prices of the regular brands.

C. Compare the five-number summaries you found in parts A and B with the box plots shown on the previous page. Decide which plot shows the distribution of prices for the natural brands and which plot shows the distribution of prices for the regular brands. Explain how the numbers in the five-number summaries are shown by various features of the plots.

D. How do the prices of the natural brands compare with the prices of the regular brands? Explain how you can make this comparison by using the box plots.

E. If *price* were the only factor a buyer considered, would natural peanut butter or regular peanut butter be a better choice? If *quality* were the only factor a buyer considered, would natural peanut butter or regular peanut butter be a better choice? Explain your reasoning.

Problem 1.3 Follow-Up

1. About what percent of the data are in the box of a box plot? That is, what percent are between the upper and lower quartiles?

2. About what percent of the data are in the interval from the minimum value to the upper quartile?

3. About what percent of the data are in the interval from the lower quartile to the maximum value?

1.4 Making a Quality Choice

The 37 brands of peanut butter listed on page 6 are classified according to four attributes: natural or regular, creamy or chunky, salted or unsalted, and name brand or store brand. In Problems 1.1 and 1.2, you compared the quality ratings of regular brands with the quality ratings of natural brands. You found that natural brands are a good choice based on their quality ratings. In this problem, you will compare the quality ratings for the other three attributes.

Problem 1.4

Justify your answers to the questions below with statistics and box plots.

A. Compare the quality ratings of the creamy brands with the quality ratings of the chunky brands. Based on quality, are creamy brands or chunky brands a better choice?

B. Compare the quality ratings of the salted brands with the quality ratings of the unsalted brands. Based on quality, are salted brands or unsalted brands a better choice?

C. Compare the quality ratings of the name brands with the quality ratings of the store brands. Based on quality, are name brands or store brands a better choice?

Problem 1.4 Follow-Up

1. List the four attributes—natural or regular, creamy or chunky, salted or unsalted, and name brand or store brand—you would recommend to someone who wants to choose a peanut butter based on quality ratings.

2. Can you find at least one brand of peanut butter in the list that has all the attributes you recommend?

1.5 Comparing Quality and Price

In previous problems, you explored the quality and price data for natural and regular peanut butters. You may have wondered how the price of a brand of peanut butter is related to its quality. What connection would you expect between price and quality for any product?

To explore the relationship between two variables, you can make a coordinate graph, or **scatter plot**. The scatter plot below shows the (quality rating, price) data for all 37 brands of peanut butter.

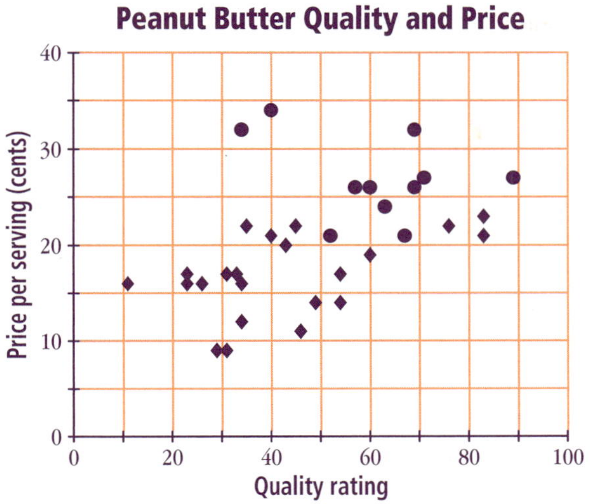

Problem 1.5

For these questions, refer to the quality ratings and per-serving prices in the table of peanut butter data on page 6.

A. In the graph above, which plot symbol, • or ♦, represents data for natural peanut butter? Which represents data for regular peanut butter?

B. Is there an overall relationship between quality and price? Explain.

C. Do any (quality rating, price) data pairs appear to be unusual? Explain your reasoning.

D. In Problems 1.2 and 1.3, you used box plots to compare quality ratings and prices of natural and regular peanut butters.

1. How can you use the scatter plot to compare the quality ratings of the natural brands with the quality ratings of the regular brands?
2. How can you use the scatter plot to compare the prices of the natural brands with the prices of the regular brands?

Problem 1.5 Follow-Up

Some people are concerned about the sodium content of the foods they eat. People with heart and blood-pressure problems are often put on low-sodium diets. Notice in the table on page 6 how the unsalted brands contain very little sodium compared to the salted brands. This is because table salt contains sodium.

1. Make a scatter plot of the (quality rating, sodium) data for all 37 brands of peanut butter. Use different symbols for salted brands and unsalted brands.

2. Does there appear to be an overall relationship between sodium content and quality rating? Explain.

3. Look back at the box plots you made of the quality ratings for the salted brands and of the quality ratings for the unsalted brands in part B of Problem 1.4. Is there a connection between quality rating and the salt content of peanut butter? Explain your thinking.

4. In questions 1–3, you looked for a relationship between quality rating and sodium content or added salt. Compare your conclusions about this relationship based on the scatter plot with your conclusions based on the box plots. What are the strengths and weaknesses of each type of data display?

As you work on these ACE questions, use your calculator whenever you need it.

Applications

1. Refer to the peanut butter data on page 6.

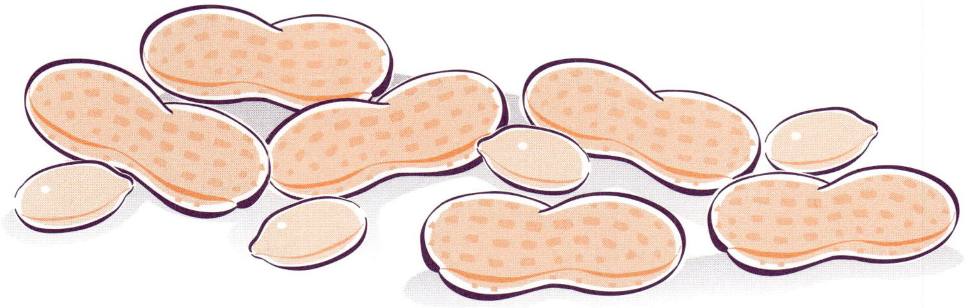

a. In Problem 1.3, you compared the prices of natural brands with the prices of regular brands. Based on price, are natural brands or regular brands a better choice?

b. Based on price, are creamy brands or chunky brands a better choice? Justify your answer with statistics and graphs.

c. Based on price, are salted brands or unsalted brands a better choice? Justify your answer with statistics and graphs.

d. Based on price, are name brands or store brands a better choice? Justify your answer with statistics and graphs.

e. List the four attributes—natural or regular, creamy or chunky, salted or unsalted, and name brand or store brand—you would recommend to someone who wants to choose a peanut butter based on price.

f. Can you find at least one brand of peanut butter that has all the attributes you recommend?

2. The scatter plot below shows (quality rating, sodium) data for the 37 brands of peanut butter listed on page 6.

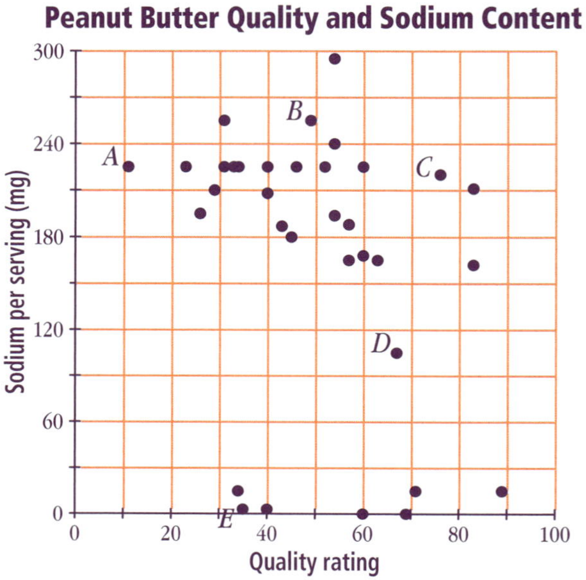

a. Compare the values in the table with the scatter plot. Why are some points located on or very near the horizontal axis?

b. Give the approximate coordinates of each labeled point. Explain what the coordinates tell you about the brand represented by the point.

3. The table on the next page gives the engine type, body length, and wingspan of several airplanes flown by major airlines.

a. Based on body length, how do propeller planes compare to jet planes? Justify your answers with statistics and graphs.

b. Based on wingspan, how do propeller planes compare with jet planes? Justify your answers with statistics and graphs.

4. Make a scatter plot of the (wingspan, body length) data given in the table on page 17. Describe the overall relationship between these two variables.

Airplane Data

Plane	Engine type	Body length (m)	Wingspan (m)
Boeing 707	jet	46.6	44.4
Boeing 747	jet	70.7	59.6
Ilyushin IL-86	jet	59.5	48.1
McDonnell Douglas DC-8	jet	57.1	45.2
Antonov An-124	jet	69.1	73.3
British Aerospace 146	jet	28.6	26.3
Lockheed C-5 Galaxy	jet	75.5	67.9
Antonov An-225	jet	84.0	88.4
Airbus A300	jet	54.1	44.9
Airbus A310	jet	46.0	43.9
Airbus A320	jet	37.5	33.9
Boeing 737	jet	33.4	28.9
Boeing 757	jet	47.3	38.1
Boeing 767	jet	48.5	47.6
Lockheed Tristar L-1011	jet	54.2	47.3
McDonnell Douglas DC-10	jet	55.5	50.4
Aero/Boeing Spacelines Guppy	propeller	43.8	47.6
Douglas DC-4 C-54 Skymaster	propeller	28.6	35.8
Douglas DC-6	propeller	32.2	35.8
Lockheed L-188 Electra	propeller	31.8	30.2
Vickers Viscount	propeller	26.1	28.6
Antonov An-12	propeller	33.1	38.0
de Havilland DHC Dash-7	propeller	24.5	28.4
Lockheed C-130 Hercules/L-100	propeller	34.4	40.4
British Aerospace 748/ATP	propeller	26.0	30.6
Convair 240	propeller	24.1	32.1
Curtiss C-46 Commando	propeller	23.3	32.9
Douglas DC-3	propeller	19.7	29.0
Grumman Gulfstream I/I-C	propeller	19.4	23.9
Ilyushin IL-14	propeller	22.3	31.7
Martin 4-0-4	propeller	22.8	28.4
Saab 340	propeller	19.7	21.4

Source: William Berk and Frank Berk. *Airport Airplanes.* Plymouth, Mich.: Plymouth Press, 1993.

Connections

5. The graphs below compare prices (in U.S. dollars) of 2-liter bottles of soft drink in cities around the world. The titles and the axis labels are missing.

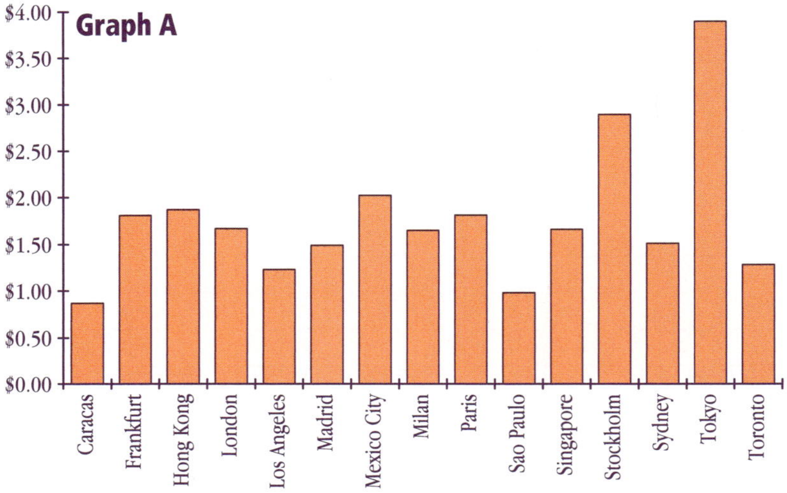

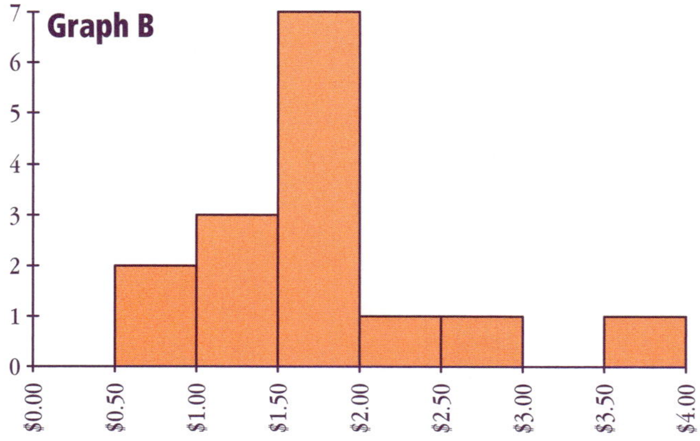

Source: Runzheimer International, Rochester, Wis., as reported in *Consumer Digest* (December, 1994): p. 8.

a. Which graph could you use to identify the cities with the highest and lowest soft-drink prices? Give the names of these cities and the prices.

b. Which graph could you use to find the typical price of a 2-liter bottle of soft drink for all the cities? What is the typical price? Explain how you found your answer.

c. What title and axis labels would be appropriate for each graph?

d. If you were given only graph A, would you have enough information to make graph B? Explain your reasoning.

e. If you were given only graph B, would you have enough information to make graph A? Explain your reasoning.

6. Two students were comparing snack-size boxes of two brands of raisins, TastiSnak and Nature's Best. The brands sell for the same price. Tim said that TastiSnak raisins are a better deal because there are more raisins in each box. Kadisha disagreed. She said that since a box of either brand contains half an ounce, the brands give you the same amount for your money.

To test these claims, the students determined the actual number of raisins and the mass in grams for 50 boxes of each brand. The results are shown in the box plots below. Based on the mass and the number of raisins, which brand is a better deal? Explain how you used the graphs to determine your answer.

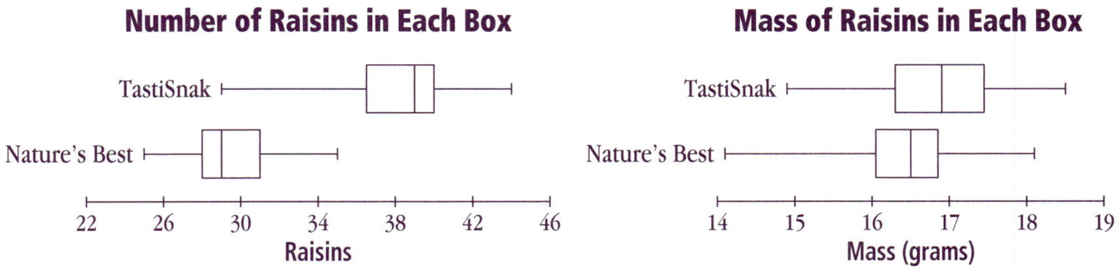

7. The sum of the values in a particular set of data is 250, and the mean is 25.

   a. Create a data set that fits this description.

   b. Do you think other students in your class created the same data set you did? Explain.

   c. Must the median of the data set be close in value to the mean? Explain.

Extensions

8. In many sports, the length of a game or match is determined by a time clock. In baseball, however, a game ends when nine innings have been completed and one team is ahead. If the teams are tied after nine innings, extra innings are played until one team is ahead. The graph below displays data about the duration of professional baseball games (in minutes). The title and the axis labels are missing.

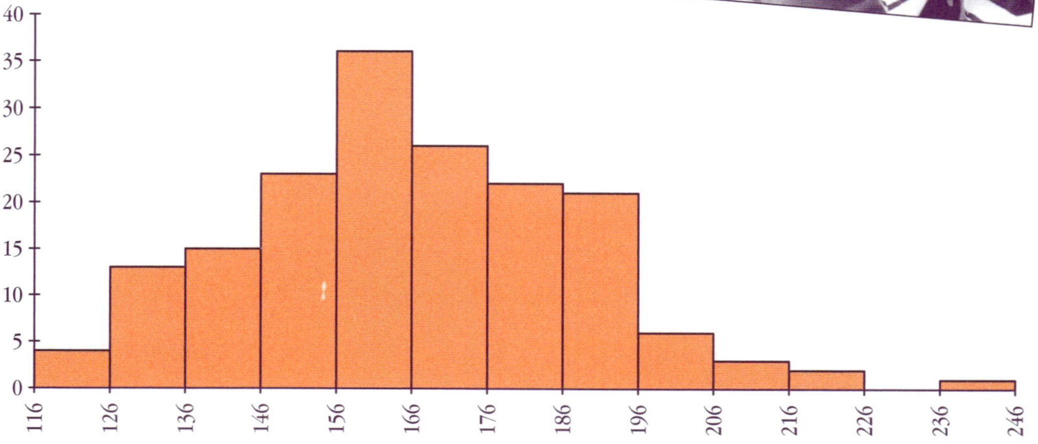

Source: *Student Poster Projects: Winners of the American Statistics Poster Competition, 1991–1992.* Palo Alto, Calif.: Dale Seymour Publications, 1994, p. 20.

a. What title and axis labels are appropriate for this graph?

b. What does the shape of the graph tell you about the length of a typical baseball game?

c. About how many games are represented in the graph?

d. Estimate the lower quartile, the median, and the upper quartile for these data. What do these numbers tell you about the length of a typical baseball game?

9. The scatter plot below shows (body length, wingspan) data for jet and propeller planes. The plot shows that, in general, greater body lengths are associated with greater wingspans. It's often useful to model such a trend with a linear graph and an equation.

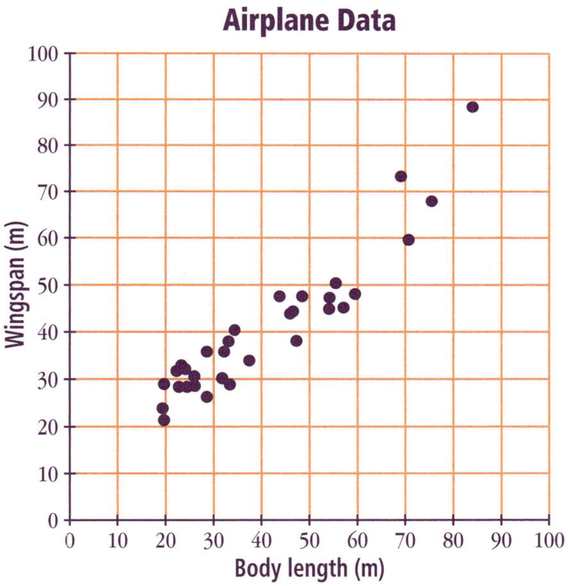

a. The line that passes through (0, 0) and (100, 100) is a good model for this data. Draw this line on the (body length, wingspan) scatter plot on Labsheet 1.ACE.

b. Write an equation for the line.

c. What are the slope and the y-intercept of the line? What does the slope tell you about the relationship between body length and wingspan?

d. What can you conclude about the wingspan and body length of an airplane that is represented by a point *above* the line?

e. What can you conclude about the wingspan and body length of an airplane that is represented by a point *below* the line?

f. What can you conclude about the wingspan and body length of an airplane that is represented by a point *on* the line?

Mathematical Reflections

In this investigation, you reviewed your knowledge of statistics and data displays. You learned how to use the five-number summary of a data set to make a box plot. And, you used box plots to compare data distributions. These questions will help you summarize what you have learned:

1. Describe how you would construct a box plot for a set of data.
2. **a.** What is true about the values in a data set if the mean is *greater than* the median?

   b. What is true about the values in a data set if the mean is *close in value* to the median?

   c. What is true about the values in a data set if the mean is *less than* the median?
3. How can you use box plots to compare two or more data sets?
4. **a.** In what types of situations is a scatter plot useful?

   b. Describe how you would construct a scatter plot.

Think about your answers to these questions, discuss your ideas with other students and your teacher, and then write a summary of your findings in your journal.

INVESTIGATION 2

Conducting Surveys

If you wanted to gather information about students in your class—such as their preferences for food, television programs, music, or sports—it would be fairly easy to conduct an accurate survey. But what might you do if you wanted information about all the students in your school, or all the people in your city, your state, or the entire country?

Some recent reports made these claims:

- Americans spend 44% of their food budget on meals prepared away from home.
- Of all restaurant orders, 49% are for off-premises consumption.
- More than 2 million American youths, most of them girls, participate in competitive gymnastics.
- On Tuesday, July 30, 1996, more than 45 million American households watched evening broadcasts of the Atlanta Olympic Games.

Think about this!

How could the people who reported these data know about the eating, sports, and television-viewing activities of all 260 million Americans?

You can study a large **population** by collecting data from a small part, or **sample,** of that population. You can then *make predictions* or *draw conclusions* about the entire population based on data from the sample. The challenge in such studies is to find a sample that accurately represents the population. Such a sample is called a **representative sample**.

2.1 Asking About Honesty

Newspapers, magazines, and radio and television programs conduct surveys on a variety of subjects. Such surveys often ask readers or listeners to call in to express their views. A magazine with a national circulation asked its readers to phone in their answer to five questions about honesty.

How Honest Is America?

A. If you found someone else's wallet on the street, would you
  1. try to return it to the owner?
  2. return it, but keep the money?
  3. keep the wallet and the money?

B. If a cashier mistakenly gave you $10 extra in change, would you
  1. tell the cashier about the error?
  2. say nothing and keep the cash?

C. Would you cheat on an exam if you were sure you wouldn't get caught?
  1. yes
  2. no

D. If you found someone else's telephone calling card, would you use it?
  1. yes
  2. no

E. Do you feel that you are an honest person in most situations?
  1. yes
  2. no

Call 1-900-555-8281, and enter your answers by pressing the appropriate number keys.

Problem 2.1

A. A *sampling plan* is a strategy for choosing a sample from a population. What is the sampling plan for this survey? What are the population and the sample for this survey?

B. Suppose 5280 people answered the survey, and 4224 of them pressed 2 for question C. What percent of the callers said they would not cheat on an exam?

C. Of the 5280 callers, 1584 pressed 1 for question D. What percent of the callers said they would not use someone else's calling card?

D. The U.S. population is about 260 million. Based on the results of this survey, how many people in the United States would not cheat on an exam? How many would not use someone else's calling card?

E. List some reasons why predictions about all Americans based on this survey might be inaccurate.

Problem 2.1 Follow-Up

1. The magazine conducting the survey assumes a person is honest if he or she reports honest behavior for all five questions. Suppose that, according to these criteria, 3507 people out of the 5280 who responded are honest. Based on these results, what percent of the U.S. population would you predict is honest?

2. Write two questions that could be used to gather additional information about honest behavior.

3. How could you revise the sampling plan for this survey so you would be more confident that the results would predict the percent of the U.S population that is honest?

2.2 Selecting a Sample

The results of the telephone survey in Problem 2.1 were used to make predictions about the U.S. population. Making accurate predictions about a population based on the results of a survey can be complicated, even when you are interested in a relatively small population.

Suppose you are doing a research project on the lives of students at your school and would like to answer these questions:

- How many hours of sleep do students get each night?
- How many students eat breakfast in the morning?
- How many hours of television do students watch in a week?
- How many soft drinks do students consume in a day?
- How many students wear braces on their teeth?

If your school has a large student population, it might be difficult to gather and analyze information from every student. How could you select a sample of your school population to survey?

Problem 2.2

Ms. Baker's class wants to find out how many students in their school wear braces on their teeth. The class divides into four groups. Each group devises a plan for sampling the school population.

- Each member of group 1 will survey the students who ride on his or her school bus.
- Group 2 will survey every fourth person in the cafeteria line.
- Group 3 will read a notice on the school's morning announcements asking for volunteers for their survey.
- Group 4 will randomly select 30 students for their survey from a list of three-digit student ID numbers. They will roll a 10-sided number cube three times to generate each number.

A. What are the advantages and disadvantages of each sampling plan?

B. Which plan do you think would most accurately predict the number of students in the school who wear braces? That is, which plan do you think will give the most *representative* sample? Explain your answer.

■ Problem 2.2 Follow-Up

The plans developed by the groups in Ms. Baker's class are examples of common sampling methods.

1. Group 1's plan is an example of **convenience sampling.** What do you think convenience sampling is? Describe another plan that would use convenience sampling.
2. Group 2's plan is an example of **systematic sampling.** What do you think systematic sampling is? Describe another plan that would use systematic sampling.

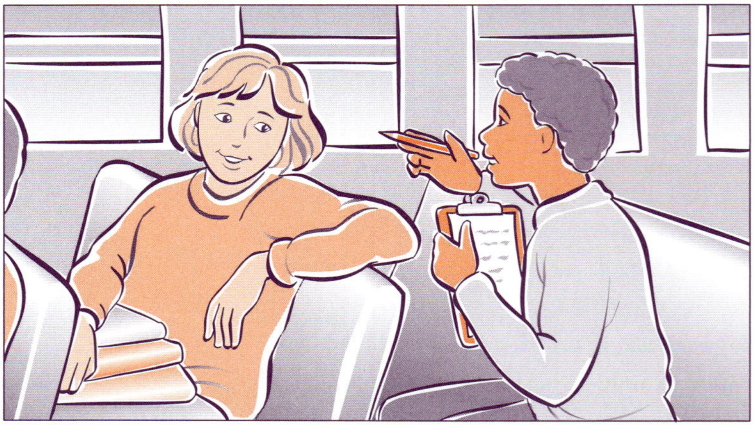

3. Group 3's plan is an example of **voluntary-response sampling.** What do you think voluntary-response sampling is? Describe another plan that would use voluntary-response sampling.
4. Group 4's plan is an example of **random sampling.** What do you think random sampling is? Describe another plan that would use random sampling.
5. When using sampling methods to study a large population, it is important to choose samples that are representative of the population. Samples that give misleading impressions are called **biased samples.** Which groups in Problem 2.2 are likely to get a biased sample? Explain your answers.
6. Which sampling method was used in Problem 2.1?

2.3 Asking the Right Questions

You have seen that when conducting a survey, it is important to select a representative sample. You must also be careful about how you ask your questions.

When you write a survey, you need to think about whether each question should be an open question or a closed question.

An *open question* asks a person to write a response. Here are two examples of open questions:

What is your age?

After high school, what do you plan to do?

The first question has predictable responses that should be easy to organize and analyze. Although answers to the second question are less predictable, the question gives the person the freedom to answer in any way he or she chooses.

A *closed question* provides a person with a set of choices. Here, the two questions above are restated as closed questions:

What is your age?

______ under 12	______ 12	______ 13	______ 14
______ 15	______ 16	______ 17	______ over 17

After high school, which of the following do you plan to do?

______ attend a two-year college	______ join the service
______ attend a four-year college	______ get a full-time job
______ attend a trade or vocational school	______ other

The answers to closed questions are generally easier to organize and analyze than the answers to open questions, but closed questions limit the possible responses.

When you critique a survey you have written, you should ask yourself several things:

- Are the questions clearly stated?
- Can any of the questions be misinterpreted?
- Have I provided good, reasonable choices for the closed questions in my survey?
- What types of answers can I expect to the open questions?
- Will I be able to organize and analyze the data I collect?

Problem 2.3

In this problem, you will work with a partner to design a survey to gather information about middle school and high school students and their plans for the future. Your survey should include questions about characteristics of the students, such as age, gender, and favorite school subject. Your survey should also gather information about what students plan to do after graduation from high school. For example, your survey might include questions about the following topics:

- Students' plans for college or a job immediately after high school
- The types of careers students would like to pursue
- The places students would like to live

A. Work with a partner to develop a first draft of a survey. Exchange surveys with another pair of students, and critique each other's survey.

B. Prepare a final version of your survey.

C. Write a paragraph describing a sampling plan you could use to survey students in your school.

Problem 2.3 Follow-Up

1. At Hilltop Middle School, there are 200 sixth graders, 200 seventh graders, and 200 eighth graders. If you gave your survey to one class of 25 students in each grade, could you use the results to make predictions about all the students in the school? Explain your reasoning.

2. At Valleyview Middle School, there are 250 sixth graders, 250 seventh graders, and 250 eighth graders. About 60% of the students at each grade level are girls. How could you select a random sample of students in the school so that 60% of the students in your sample are girls and 40% are boys?

Applications • Connections • Extensions

As you work on these ACE questions, use your calculator whenever you need it.

Applications

There are 350 students in Banneker Middle School. Mr. Abosch's math class wants to find out how many hours of homework a typical student in the school did last week. Several students in the class devised plans for selecting a sample of students to survey. In 1–4, tell whether you think the plan would give a representative sample, and explain your answer.

1. Anna suggested surveying every third student on each homeroom class list.

2. Kwang-Hee suggested putting 320 white beans and 30 red beans in a bag and asking each student to draw a bean as he or she enters the auditorium for tomorrow's assembly. The 30 students who draw red beans will be surveyed.

3. Ushio suggested that each student in Mr. Abosch's class survey everyone in his or her English class.

4. Kirby suggested putting surveys on a table at the entrance to the school and asking students to return completed questionnaires at the end of the day.

In 5–8, describe the population being studied and the sampling method being used.

5. A magazine for teenagers asks its readers to write in with information about how they solve personal problems.

6. To find out how much time middle school students spend on the telephone each day, members of an eighth grade class kept a record for a week of the amount of time they spent on the phone each day.

7. To estimate the number of soft drinks consumed by middle school students each day, Ms. Darnell's class obtains a list of students in the school and writes each name on a card. They put the cards in a box and select the names of 40 students to survey.

8. A television news report said that 80% of adults in the United States support the right of school authorities to open student lockers to search for drugs, alcohol, and weapons. The editors of the school paper want to find out how students in their school feel about this issue. They select 26 students for their survey—one whose name begins with A, one whose name begins with B, one whose name begins with C, and so on.

9. Choose one of the issues in questions 5–8. Write a survey question you could ask about the issue, and explain how you could analyze and report the results you collect.

Connections

10. Students at Banneker Middle School were asked how much time they spent doing homework last Monday night. The results are shown in this back-to-back stem-and-leaf plot.

Minutes Spent on Monday-Night Homework

Grade 6		Grade 8
0 0 0 0 0 0	0	0
5 5 5 5 5 5	1	0 5 5
5 0 0	2	0 0 0 5 5 5 5
5 5 5	3	0 0 0 0 5 5 5
5 5 0	4	0 0 0 5 5 5
0 0	5	0 5
	6	0 5 5
0	7	5
5	8	0

a. Find the median homework time for each grade.

b. For each grade, describe the overall distribution of homework times. How do the homework times for sixth graders compare with the homework times for eighth graders? Explain your reasoning.

c. Could these data be used to describe what is typical of all school nights in each of the two grades? Explain your reasoning.

11. Samples of adults and eighth grade students were asked how much time they spend on the telephone each evening. The results are displayed in the box plots below.

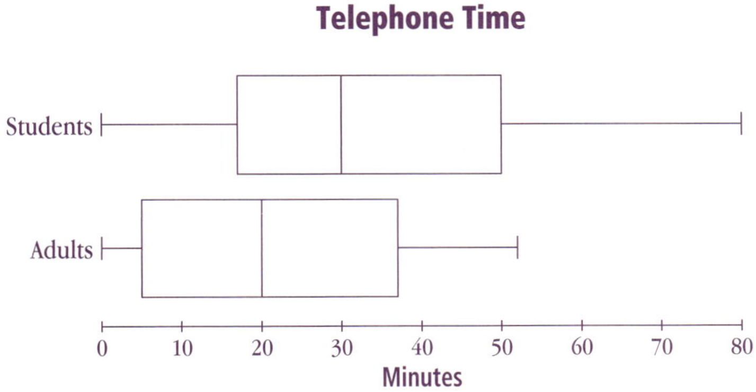

a. What are the median, lower quartile, upper quartile, and range of the telephone times for the students?

b. What are the median, lower quartile, upper quartile, and range of the telephone times for the adults?

c. Describe the similarities and differences between the distribution of telephone times for adults and the distribution of telephone times for students.

12. There are 350 students in Banneker Middle School. Ms. Cabral's class wants to research how many students attended camp last summer. They survey two random samples of students. Here are the results:

Sample 1: 8 of 25 attended camp

Sample 2: 7 of 28 attended camp

a. Based on the results from sample 1, how many students in the school would you predict attended camp?

b. Based on the results from sample 2, how many students in the school would you predict attended camp?

c. Lawrence, one of Ms. Cabral's students, was confused by the results of the study. He said, "We were careful to choose our samples randomly. Why did the two samples give us different predictions?" How would you answer Lawrence's question?

13. A local television station wanted to find out how the people in the broadcast area felt about women serving in combat roles in the military. During its evening news broadcast, the station asked viewers to call in with their opinions about this question:

Should women be allowed to have combat roles in the military?

a. What possible biases could there be in the results of this opinion poll?

b. Why do you think the media conduct such polls, even though they know the results are biased?

Extensions

14. Television stations, radio stations, and newspapers often predict the winners of important elections long before the votes are counted. They make these predictions based on polls.

a. What factors might cause a preelection poll to be inaccurate?

b. Political parties often conduct their own preelection polls to find out what voters think about their campaign and their candidates. How might a political party bias such a poll?

c. Find out how a local television station, radio station, or newspaper takes preelection polls. Do you think the method they use is sensible?

15. In times of war, our government has set up a selective-service, or draft, system to identify young men who will be called into military service. For reasons of fairness, the selective-service system must make every effort to be sure that everyone eligible for the draft has the same chance of being selected. What do you think would be a fair system for selecting people to be drafted?

Mathematical Reflections

In this investigation, you learned about several sampling techniques, and you practiced writing effective survey questions. These questions will help you summarize what you have learned:

1. Why are data often collected from a sample rather than from an entire population?
2. Describe several methods for selecting a sample from a population. Discuss the advantages and disadvantages of each method.
3. **a.** What does it mean for a sample to be *representative* of a population?

   b. In what ways might a sample *not* be representative of a population?

Think about your answers to these questions, discuss your ideas with other students and your teacher, and then write a summary of your findings in your journal.

INVESTIGATION 3

Random Samples

What is the best way to choose a sample from a large population? In most situations, statisticians agree that it is preferable to use a procedure that gives each member of the population the same chance of being chosen. Sampling plans with this property are called *random sampling plans.* Samples chosen with a random sampling plan are called *random samples.*

3.1 Choosing Randomly

This problem will help you think about what it means to use a random sampling plan. Keep in mind that for a sampling plan to be random, all members of the population must have an equally likely chance of being selected.

Problem 3.1

Imagine that you have two tickets to a sold-out rock concert, and your six best friends all want to go with you. To choose a friend to attend the concert, you want to use a strategy that gives each friend an equally likely chance of being selected. Which of the three strategies below would accomplish this? Explain your reasoning.

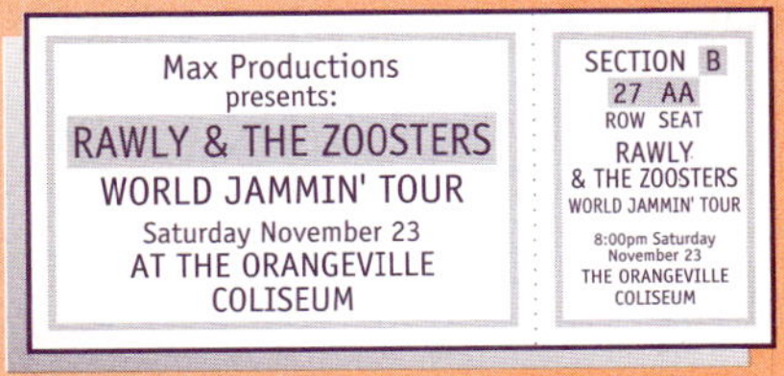

Strategy 1: The first person who calls you on the phone tonight gets to go with you.

Strategy 2: You assign each friend a different whole number from 1 to 6. Then, you roll a six-sided number cube. The number that is rolled determines who attends the concert.

Strategy 3: You tell each friend to meet you by the rear door right after school. You toss a coin to choose between the first two friends who arrive.

Problem 3.1 Follow-Up

Describe another strategy you could use that would give each of your friends an equally likely chance of being selected.

3.2 Selecting a Random Sample

The table on the next page contains data for 100 eighth graders at Clinton Middle School. The data were collected on a Monday. They include the number of hours of sleep each student got the previous night and the number of movies, including television movies and videos, each student watched the previous week.

You could describe these data by calculating five-number summaries or means, and you could display the distribution of the data by making stem plots, histograms, or box plots. However, doing calculations and making graphs for the entire data set would require a lot of work.

Think about this!

Instead of working with the entire data set, you can select a random sample of students. You can look for patterns in the data for the sample and then use your findings to make predictions about the population.

- What methods might you use to select a random sample of students?
- How many students would you need in your sample in order to make accurate estimates of the typical number of hours of sleep and the typical number of movies watched for the entire population of 100 students?

One way to select a random sample of students is to use two spinners like these:

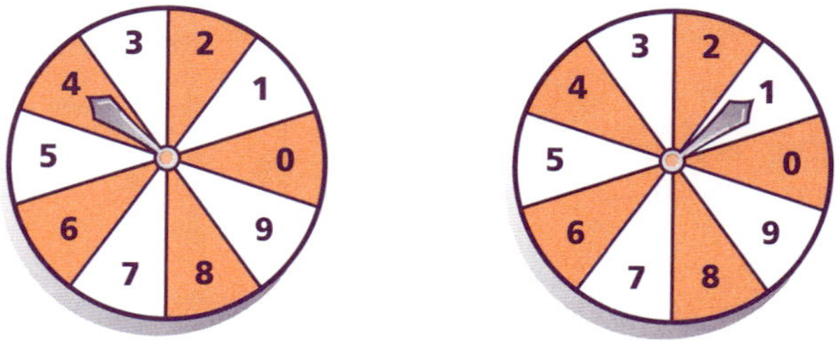

You can use the spinners to generate random pairs of digits that correspond to the two-digit student numbers. What two-digit numbers can you generate with these spinners? How can you make sure that student 100 has an equally likely chance of being included in your sample?

There are many other ways to select a random sample of students. For example, you can roll two 10-sided number cubes, or you can generate random numbers with your calculator.

Grade 8 Database

Student number	Gender	Sleep (hours)	Movies
01	boy	11.5	14
02	boy	2.0	8
03	girl	7.7	3
04	boy	9.3	1
05	boy	7.1	16
06	boy	7.5	1
07	boy	8.0	4
08	girl	7.8	1
09	girl	8.0	13
10	girl	8.0	15
11	boy	9.0	1
12	boy	9.2	10
13	boy	8.5	5
14	girl	6.0	15
15	boy	6.5	10
16	boy	8.3	2
17	girl	7.4	2
18	boy	11.2	3
19	girl	7.3	1
20	boy	8.0	0
21	girl	7.8	1
22	girl	7.8	1
23	boy	9.2	2
24	girl	7.5	0
25	boy	8.8	1
26	girl	8.5	0
27	girl	9.0	0
28	girl	8.5	0
29	boy	8.2	2
30	girl	7.8	2
31	girl	8.0	2
32	girl	7.3	8
33	boy	6.0	5
34	girl	7.5	5
35	boy	6.5	5
36	boy	9.3	1
37	girl	8.2	3
38	boy	7.3	3
39	girl	7.4	6
40	girl	8.5	7
41	boy	5.5	17
42	boy	6.5	3
43	boy	7.0	5
44	girl	8.5	2
45	girl	9.3	4
46	girl	8.0	15
47	boy	8.5	10
48	girl	6.2	11
49	girl	11.8	10
50	girl	9.0	4

Student number	Gender	Sleep (hours)	Movies
51	boy	5.0	4
52	boy	6.5	5
53	girl	8.5	2
54	boy	9.1	15
55	girl	7.5	2
56	girl	8.5	1
57	girl	8.0	2
58	girl	7.0	7
59	girl	8.4	10
60	girl	9.5	1
61	girl	7.3	5
62	girl	7.3	4
63	boy	8.5	3
64	boy	9.0	3
65	boy	9.0	4
66	girl	7.3	5
67	girl	5.7	0
68	girl	5.5	0
69	boy	10.5	7
70	girl	7.5	1
71	boy	7.8	0
72	girl	7.3	1
73	boy	9.3	2
74	boy	9.0	1
75	boy	8.7	1
76	boy	8.5	3
77	girl	9.0	1
78	boy	8.0	1
79	boy	8.0	4
80	boy	6.5	0
81	boy	8.0	0
82	girl	9.0	8
83	girl	8.0	0
84	boy	7.0	0
85	boy	9.0	6
86	boy	7.3	0
87	girl	9.0	3
88	girl	7.5	5
89	boy	8.0	0
90	girl	7.5	6
91	boy	8.0	4
92	boy	9.0	4
93	boy	7.0	0
94	boy	8.0	3
95	boy	8.3	3
96	boy	8.3	14
97	girl	7.8	5
98	girl	8.5	1
99	girl	8.3	3
100	boy	7.5	2

Problem 3.2

In this problem, each member of your group will select a random sample of students and calculate the five-number summary for the movie data. Use spinners, 10-sided number cubes, a graphing calculator, or some other method to select your sample.

A. Select a random sample of 25 students. For each student in your sample, record the number of movies watched. (Each sample should contain 25 *different* students, so if you select a student who is already in the sample, select another.)

B. Calculate the five-number summary for the movie data for your sample.

C. With your group, make box plots of the movie data for your group's samples on Labsheet 3.2.

D. What can you conclude about the movie-viewing behavior of the population of 100 students based on the patterns in the samples selected by your group? Explain how you used the data from your samples to arrive at your conclusions.

E. Compare your findings with those of other groups in your class. Describe the similarities and differences you find.

Problem 3.2 Follow-Up

1. Select a random sample of 25 students, and record the number of hours of sleep for each student. Calculate the five-number summary for these sleep data, and make a box plot of the distribution. Use your findings to estimate the typical hours of sleep for the population of 100 students. Compare your box plot and estimate with those of the other members of your group, and describe the similarities and differences.

2. The data on page 39 were collected by conducting a survey. The students who wrote the survey considered two possible questions for finding the number of movies watched.

- How many movies and videos did you watch last week?
- How many movies did you watch at a theater, on television, or on video last week? Include all movies and videos you watched from last Monday through this Sunday.

a. Which question do you think is better? Why?

b. Can you write a better question? If so, write one, and explain why you think your question is better.

3.3 Choosing a Sample Size

In Problem 3.2, you selected random samples of 25 students to estimate the sleep and movie-viewing habits of all 100 students. You might wonder whether you could make good estimates with less work by selecting smaller samples.

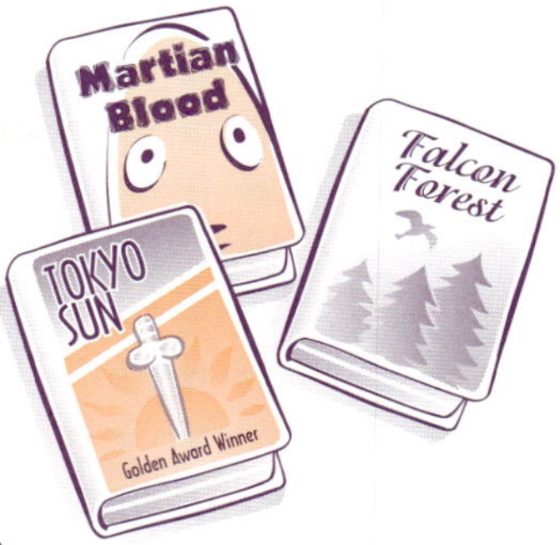

If you took the time to analyze the movie data for all 100 students, you would find that the median number of movies and videos watched is 3. Do you think you could make a good estimate of this figure by analyzing samples of 5 or 10 students?

Problem 3.3

In this problem, you will explore how the size of a sample affects the accuracy of statistical estimates.

A. In Problem 3.2, you calculated five-number summaries for the movie data for random samples of 25 students. Work with your class to make a line plot of the medians found by all groups. Compare these results with the median for the population of 100 students.

B. 1. Select three random samples of 5 students, and find the median movie value for each sample. Compare the medians for your samples with the population median.

2. Compare the medians for your samples with the medians found by other members of your group. Describe the similarities or differences you find.

3. Record the medians found by your group on the board. When all groups have recorded their medians, make a line plot of the medians.

C. 1. Select three random samples of 10 students, and find the median movie value for each sample. Compare the medians for your samples with the population median.

2. Compare the medians for your samples with the medians found by other members of your group. Describe the similarities or differences you find.

3. Record the medians found by your group on the board. When all groups have recorded their medians, make a line plot of the medians.

D. Compare the distribution of medians for samples of size 5, 10, and 25. Write a paragraph describing how the median estimates for samples of different sizes compare with the actual population median.

Problem 3.3 Follow-Up

1. With your class, use the sleep data to explore the relationship between sample size and the accuracy of median estimates. The median sleep value for the population of 100 students is 8 hours.

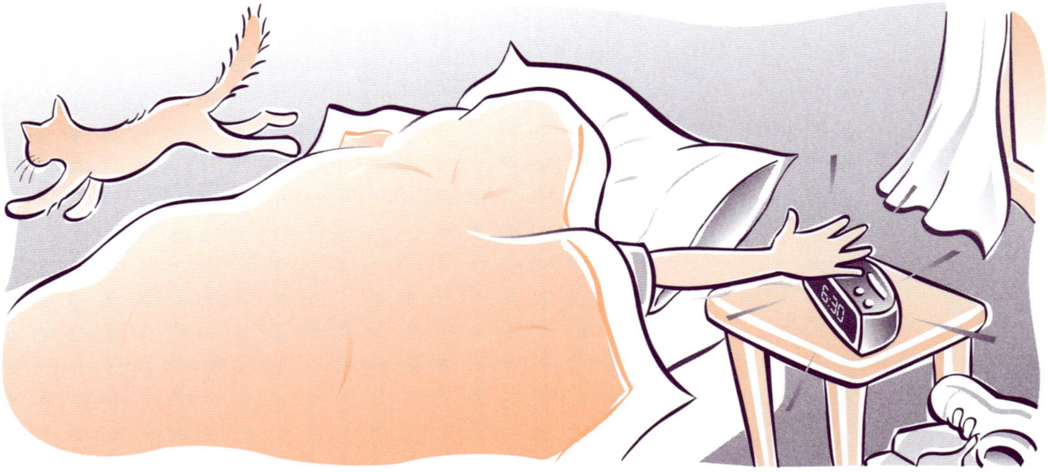

a. In Problem 3.2 Follow-Up, you calculated the median sleep value for random samples of 25 students. Work with your class to make a line plot of the medians found by all the students in your class. Compare these results with the median for the population.

b. Select a random sample of 5 students and a random sample of 10 students. Find the median sleep value for each sample.

c. Work with your class to make a line plot of the medians for the samples of 5 students and a line plot for the samples of 10 students.

d. Compare the distribution of medians for samples of size 5, 10, and 25. How do the median estimates for samples of different sizes compare with the median for the population?

2. If each student in your class chose a sample of 50 students and found the median sleep value, what would you expect the line plot of the medians to look like? Explain your reasoning.

As you work on these ACE questions, use your calculator whenever you need it.

Applications

1. a. Refer to the data on page 39. Select three random samples from the population of 100 students: one sample of 5 students, one sample of 10 students, and one sample of 25 students. Record the sleep values for the students in each sample.

b. Calculate the mean sleep value for each sample.

c. Your teacher will display axes for three line plots: one for means for samples of size 5, one for means for samples of size 10, and one for means for samples of size 25. Add your data to the line plots.

d. The mean sleep value for the population is 7.96 hours. Compare this value with the estimates shown in the three line plots. Write a paragraph describing how the mean estimates for samples of different sizes compare with the mean for the population.

2. a. Refer to the data on page 39. Select three random samples from the population of 100 students: one sample of 5 students, one sample of 10 students, and one sample of 25 students. Record the movie values for the students in each sample.

b. Calculate the mean movie value for each sample.

c. Your teacher will display axes for three line plots: one for means for samples of size 5, one for means for samples of size 10, and one for means for samples of size 25. Add your data to the line plots.

d. The mean movie value for the population is 4.22. Compare this value with the estimates shown in the three line plots. Write a paragraph describing how the mean estimates for samples of different sizes compare with the mean for the population.

In 3–6, use this information: Manufacturers often conduct quality-control tests to ensure that their products perform well and are safe. Depending on the type of item and the quantity produced, a manufacturer may test every item or select samples to test. For each situation described below, imagine that you are the quality-control manager for the company. Describe the testing program that you would recommend, and justify your recommendation.

3. Happy Bug Toys produces 5000 video-game systems each day.

4. The Spartan Music company manufactures a total of about 200,000 compact discs for 100 recording artists each day.

5. Fourth of July Fireworks, Incorporated, produces rockets used in fireworks displays. In the spring and early summer, they produce more than 1500 rockets each day.

6. The Clear Spring bottling company produces 25,000 bottles of spring water each day.

Connections

7. Consider the following data set: 20, 22, 23, 23, 24, 24, 25.

a. Find the mean and the range of the values.

b. Add three values to the data set so that the mean of the new data set is greater than the mean of the original data set. What is the range of the new data set?

c. Add three values to the original data set so that the mean of the new data set is less than the mean of the original data set. What is the range of the new data set?

d. Look at the ranges for the original data set and the data sets you created in parts b and c. How do the ranges compare? Why do you think this is so?

8. A geyser is a spring from which columns of boiling water and steam erupt. The data displayed in the graph below were collected for the Grand Geyser in Yellowstone National Park. Each point represents the height of an eruption and the time since the previous eruption.

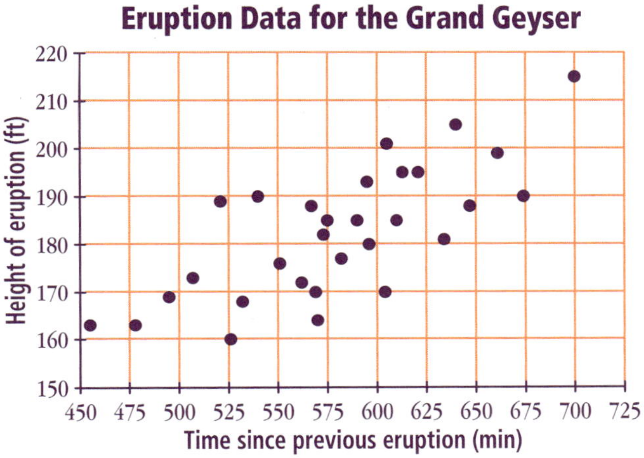

a. Describe the overall relationship between the height of an eruption and the time since the previous eruption.

b. The data above were collected for one particular geyser. What additional information would you need to decide whether the relationship you described in part a is true for most geysers?

9. **a.** Suppose that instead of choosing random samples of 25 students from the population of 100 students, you selected the first 25 students for the first sample, the next 25 students for the second sample, and so on. How might this sampling procedure bias the statistical results?

b. Suppose you had chosen your samples systematically, by choosing students 1, 5, 9, 13, 17, 21, 25, . . . for the first sample; students 2, 6, 10, 14, 18, 22, 26, . . . for the second sample; students 3, 7, 11, 15, 19, 23, 27, . . . for the third sample; and so on. How might this sampling procedure bias the statistical results?

Extensions

10. Polls conducted prior to presidential elections commonly use samples of about 1000 eligible voters.

a. There are about 190 million eligible voters in the United States. What percent of eligible voters are in a sample of 1000?

b. How do you think this small sample is chosen so that the results will predict the winner with reasonable accuracy?

11. M&M's® candies are coated in six colors: green, yellow, orange, blue, brown, and red. The company produces a fixed percent of each color, but the percents are not equal. The table on the next page shows the distribution of colors in 100 bags of plain M&M's candies.

a. From the table, select random samples of 5, 15, and 25 bags, and use the samples to estimate the percent of red candies in a typical bag of M&M's.

b. Calculate the percent of red M&M's in all 100 bags. Which sample from part a produced a percent estimate closest to the overall percent? Why do you think that sample gave the closest estimate?

Data from 100 Bags of Plain M&M's Candies

Bag	Green	Yellow	Orange	Blue	Brown	Red	Total
1	3	10	9	5	10	18	55
2	5	12	4	6	19	11	57
3	7	10	9	4	16	12	58
4	4	14	2	1	14	19	56
5	12	7	8	7	14	13	61
6	10	9	6	5	15	8	55
7	11	11	6	6	12	12	58
8	8	15	5	3	16	10	57
9	2	11	4	4	24	12	57
10	5	7	4	1	26	13	56
11	6	13	4	4	15	18	60
12	5	8	4	2	23	16	58
13	9	13	4	4	14	11	55
14	9	10	5	5	14	14	57
15	5	19	5	2	13	14	58
16	3	15	5	2	19	11	55
17	3	10	4	3	23	14	57
18	6	7	5	5	15	22	60
19	5	7	3	4	21	14	54
20	8	7	8	2	20	16	61
21	10	11	7	7	8	14	57
22	7	10	3	5	20	12	57
23	3	8	6	3	25	10	55
24	6	11	9	3	10	17	56
25	10	12	1	2	15	17	57
26	4	12	4	7	14	16	57
27	6	9	6	7	15	13	56
28	5	11	6	7	17	7	53
29	1	10	6	5	22	14	58
30	10	4	8	0	26	9	57
31	4	14	6	4	18	12	58
32	6	18	2	4	19	14	58
33	6	7	8	4	20	11	56
34	12	11	6	4	11	11	55
35	5	10	6	2	12	16	51
36	8	9	4	4	16	17	58
37	2	12	2	6	11	21	54
38	5	7	3	4	21	19	59
39	8	7	8	2	20	16	61
40	10	11	7	7	8	14	57
41	7	10	3	5	20	12	57
42	3	8	6	3	23	10	50
43	6	11	9	3	10	17	56
44	10	12	1	2	15	17	57
45	5	13	2	4	22	11	57
46	6	10	9	5	14	13	57
47	6	16	7	3	16	9	57
48	6	10	4	5	23	10	58
49	10	7	2	6	19	9	53
50	4	12	8	6	10	15	55

Bag	Green	Yellow	Orange	Blue	Brown	Red	Total
51	9	9	6	6	17	10	57
52	4	13	4	6	17	13	57
53	6	12	3	8	13	12	54
54	11	8	8	12	9	8	56
55	1	16	7	3	22	10	59
56	6	11	6	4	19	11	57
57	7	7	7	3	10	21	55
58	7	2	8	10	15	13	55
59	6	10	6	7	12	15	56
60	6	16	7	3	16	9	57
61	6	10	4	5	23	10	58
62	10	7	2	6	19	9	53
63	4	12	8	6	10	15	55
64	9	12	8	6	8	15	58
65	10	6	5	4	12	16	53
66	4	11	3	2	21	15	56
67	6	15	4	8	10	10	53
68	6	8	7	1	19	14	55
69	6	8	8	6	10	16	54
70	9	11	7	4	15	10	56
71	6	9	8	2	19	14	58
72	3	10	9	5	10	18	55
73	5	12	4	6	19	11	57
74	7	10	9	4	16	12	58
75	4	14	2	1	16	19	56
76	1	8	10	1	22	14	56
77	5	15	4	9	11	11	57
78	3	11	6	3	24	10	57
79	10	9	4	1	23	10	57
80	5	10	7	1	21	13	57
81	6	14	7	7	14	5	53
82	9	11	2	6	13	16	57
83	7	7	9	0	13	20	56
84	8	10	4	5	13	10	50
85	4	11	2	1	24	15	57
86	4	12	6	3	21	12	58
87	5	8	7	4	20	13	57
88	7	11	7	7	13	10	55
89	9	11	4	2	12	18	56
90	4	15	8	4	16	10	57
91	7	11	6	4	18	11	58
92	5	8	8	3	20	12	56
93	7	3	2	6	26	11	55
94	9	6	3	1	28	12	59
95	12	11	9	2	18	5	58
96	9	11	3	3	17	12	55
97	5	12	6	5	17	13	58
98	4	11	9	3	21	10	58
99	11	12	5	3	17	9	57
100	6	16	6	6	16	4	54

Mathematical Reflections

In this investigation, you made predictions about a population by examining data for random samples. These questions will help you summarize what you have learned:

1. How are random samples different from convenience, voluntary-response, and systematic samples?
2. Why is random sampling preferable to convenience, voluntary-response, and systematic sampling?
3. Describe three methods for selecting a random sample from a given population. What are the advantages and disadvantages of each method?
4. If several random samples are selected from the same population, what similarities and differences would you expect to find in the medians, means, ranges, and quartiles of the samples?
5. How does the size of a sample affect its accuracy in estimating statistics for a large population?

Think about your answers to these questions, discuss your ideas with other students and your teacher, and then write a summary of your findings in your journal.

INVESTIGATION 4

Solving Real-World Problems

In this investigation, you will apply what you have learned about statistics to two real-world problems.

4.1 Solving an Archaeological Mystery

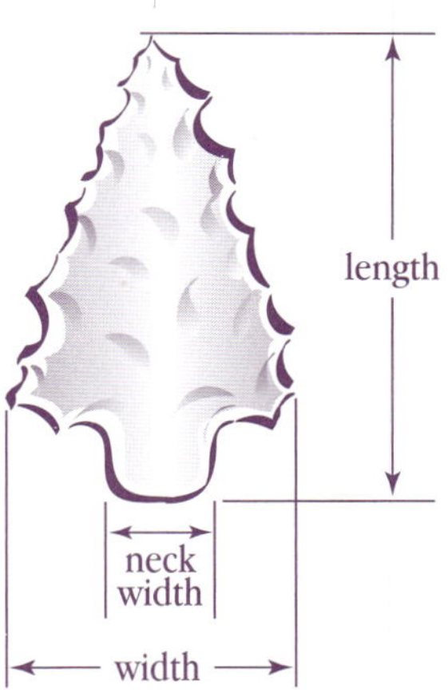

Archaeologists study past civilizations by excavating ancient settlements and examining the artifacts of the people who lived there. On digs in southeastern Montana and north-central Wyoming, archaeologists discovered the remains of two Native American settlements. They unearthed a number of arrowheads at both sites. The tables on the next page list the length, width, and neck width for each arrowhead that was found. All measurements are in millimeters.*

*Source: George C. Knight and James D. Keyser. "A Mathematical Technique for Dating Projectile Points Common to the Northwestern Plains." *Plains Anthropologist 28,* no. 101 (1983): pp. 199–207.

Arrowheads from Two New Sites

Site I: 15 arrowheads		
Length	Width	Neck width
62	26	14
31	32	16
40	25	16
63	29	18
37	23	11
24	19	8
29	22	12
38	22	12
29	19	11
45	22	11
27	19	10
31	16	12
38	26	14
45	28	15
55	22	13

Site II: 37 arrowheads					
Length	Width	Neck width	Length	Width	Neck width
16	13	7	15	11	7
13	10	6	25	13	7
22	14	10	43	14	9
19	12	8	22	13	8
24	11	8	24	13	8
20	12	7	21	11	7
26	15	11	28	11	6
19	13	9	16	12	8
25	15	10	24	14	10
17	15	9	25	24	7
22	13	9	28	13	9
22	13	9	20	12	9
27	14	8	18	12	10
23	14	9	32	12	8
26	14	10	24	13	8
24	15	9	23	15	9
25	13	7	24	12	7
26	14	11	24	15	8
42	16	11			

The archaeologists hoped to use the arrowhead data to estimate the time period during which each site was inhabited. To help them, they used arrowhead data from four other settlement sites. The archaeologists knew that two of the sites—Laddie Creek/Dead Indian Creek and Kobold/Buffalo Creek—were settled between 4000 B.C. and A.D. 500, and that the other two sites—Big Goose Creek and Wortham Shelter—were settled between A.D. 500 and A.D. 1600. The arrowhead data for these four sites are given on the next page.

Think about this!

How could you use these data to help you guess the settlement periods for the new sites?

Arrowheads from Four Old Sites

Big Goose Creek 52 Arrowheads		
Length	Width	Neck width
30	14	8
21	11	7
24	14	9
18	13	8
30	15	11
27	13	9
39	18	12
33	13	7
22	13	10
26	11	8
23	13	8
20	11	6
21	12	7
26	14	9
16	13	9
30	14	8
23	14	9
34	15	9
27	13	9
22	13	8
30	11	7
22	12	9
27	14	9
18	12	7
33	15	9
28	15	9
25	13	7
24	14	11
31	12	8
30	14	9
35	14	10
25	14	8
26	12	12
30	13	8
19	11	8
40	14	8
29	15	8
20	12	8
17	13	8
25	13	8
16	14	10
17	13	10
23	13	9
18	15	11
27	17	13
28	13	7
28	10	5
26	16	10
21	12	9
18	12	8
18	13	7
27	14	9

Wortham Shelter 45 Arrowheads		
Length	Width	Neck width
22	14	8
42	18	7
28	14	10
31	13	10
25	15	12
20	13	8
20	14	10
25	15	10
19	12	9
28	13	11
29	13	10
29	14	9
18	11	8
27	15	11
32	15	10
24	13	10
31	14	11
26	13	10
19	14	10
30	14	11
25	14	10
31	16	12
31	14	10
24	12	9
28	16	12
35	18	14
22	12	9
23	14	11
23	15	11
27	14	10
30	16	9
31	17	12
19	14	10
26	15	12
23	13	11
27	14	8
25	14	8
19	16	14
29	14	9
26	13	9
25	15	10
29	17	12
20	15	11
32	14	7
30	17	11

Laddie Creek/Dead Indian Creek: 18 Arrowheads		
Length	Width	Neck width
29	20	13
25	18	13
32	16	10
52	21	16
29	14	11
35	20	15
27	20	14
37	17	13
44	18	13
38	17	14
27	20	13
39	18	15
41	15	11
30	23	13
40	18	11
32	19	10
31	18	11
42	22	12

Kubold/Buffalo Creek 52 Arrowheads		
Length	Width	Neck width
80	25	11
38	24	15
39	21	14
50	23	15
42	22	14
37	21	11
32	23	18
44	20	11
40	20	12
40	20	13
56	19	12
52	17	12
46	23	14
32	22	17
35	22	14
46	20	14
38	18	9
40	21	12
46	17	13
44	20	12
40	19	15
30	19	15
31	17	12
31	16	13
32	20	13
41	21	13
25	18	15
49	20	14
35	19	11
42	22	15
44	25	14
47	19	13
47	22	13
45	22	13
54	24	13
56	21	15
37	18	12
51	18	10
71	24	13
45	20	13
52	24	16
67	21	13
47	20	12
50	23	16
56	25	13
50	21	13
52	22	15
57	22	15
61	19	12
66	20	15
64	21	13
30	17	12

Problem 4.1

The archaeologists hypothesized that Native Americans inhabiting the same area of the country during the same time period would have fashioned similar tools.

A. Use what you know about statistics and data representations to compare the lengths of the arrowheads discovered at the new sites with the lengths of the arrowheads from the known sites. Based on your comparisons, during which time period—4000 B.C. to A.D. 500 or A.D. 500 to A.D. 1600—do you think site I was settled? During which time period do you think site II was settled? Explain how your statistics and graphs support your answers.

B. Compare the widths of the arrowheads discovered at the new sites with the widths of the arrowheads from the known sites. Do your findings support your answers from part A? Explain.

C. If the archaeologists had collected only a few arrowheads from each new site, might they have reached a different conclusion? Explain your answer.

Problem 4.1 Follow-Up

1. Select a random sample of 15 arrowheads from each of the six sites. For each arrowhead, find the ratio of length to width. Express each ratio as a decimal rounded to the hundredths place.
2. Compare the length-to-width ratios for the various sites. Do the ratios help you match the new sites with the sites whose settlement time is known? Explain your answer.

4.2 Simulating Cookies

Jeff and Ted operate the Custom Cookie Counter in Durham Mall. Their advertising slogan is "Five giant chips in every cookie!" One day, a customer complained that she found only three chips in her cookie. Jeff said the customer must have miscounted because he mixes 60 chips into every batch of a dozen cookies. Jeff and Ted examined a batch of cookies that were fresh from the oven. The drawing on the right shows what they found.

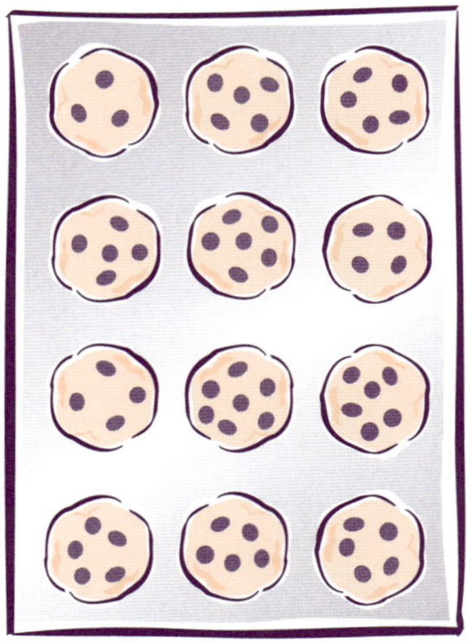

Think about this!

What is wrong with Jeff's reasoning about how many chips to add to each batch of cookie dough? What advice would you give to Jeff and Ted to help them solve their quality-control problem?

Ted had an idea about how to use random sampling to determine how many chips they should add to each batch of dough in order to be fairly confident that every cookie will contain at least five chips. He explained his idea to Jeff:

"Think about a batch of dough as 12 cookies packed in a bowl. As chips are added to the dough, each chip lands in one of the cookies. There is an equally likely chance that a chip will land in any one of the 12 cookies. We need to add chips to the dough until every cookie contains at least five chips."

"We can simulate adding the chips by generating random integers from 1 to 12. Generating a 1 is equivalent to adding a chip to cookie 1, generating a 2 is equivalent to adding a chip to cookie 2, and so on. We can keep a tally of where the chips land and stop when each 'cookie' contains at least five 'chips.' The total number of random integers we generated will be an estimate of the number of chips we need to add to each batch to be fairly confident that each cookie will contain at least five chips."

Problem 4.2

Study Ted's plan for simulating the cookie mixing until it makes sense to you.

A. Conduct the simulation Ted describes. You might use a chart like this to tally the number of chips in each cookie.

cookie 1 ______________________
cookie 2 ______________________
cookie 3 ______________________
cookie 4 ______________________
cookie 5 ______________________
cookie 6 ______________________
cookie 7 ______________________
cookie 8 ______________________
cookie 9 ______________________
cookie 10 ______________________
cookie 11 ______________________
cookie 12 ______________________

Generate random numbers until each cookie contains at least five chips. When you are finished, find the total number of chips in the entire batch.

B. Your teacher will display the stem values for a stem plot. Add your number-of-chips data to the plot.

C. Jeff and Ted want to be quite certain there will be at least five chips in each cookie, but they don't want to waste money by mixing in too many chocolate chips. Based on your class data, how many chips would you advise Jeff and Ted to use in each batch? Explain how you determined your answer.

Problem 4.2 Follow-Up

1. What other methods might Jeff and Ted use to be fairly confident that each cookie they sell contains at least five chips?

2. As Jeff and Ted's business becomes more successful, they decide it would be more efficient to make cookies in batches of four dozen. How many chips should they add to each batch to be confident that each cookie has at least five chips?

3. How many chips would Jeff and Ted have to put in a batch of 12 cookies to be *absolutely certain* no cookie will have fewer than five chips?

Applications • Connections • Extensions

As you work on these ACE questions, use your calculator whenever you need it.

Applications

1. The arrowhead data on pages 50 and 51 include the neck width of each arrowhead found in the six archaeological sites.

a. Calculate five-number summaries of the neck width for each site's arrowhead data. Based on these statistics, what conclusions can you draw about the time periods in which the new sites were settled?

b. On the same scale, make box plots of the neck-width data for all the sites. Explain how the relationships among the plots illustrate your conclusions from part a.

2. Oatmeal-raisin cookies are the most popular cookie at Jeff and Ted's Custom Cookie Counter. Jeff and Ted bake these cookies in batches of four dozen. They pour a box of raisins into each batch.

a. How could you use a sample of the cookies to estimate the number of raisins in a box?

b. If there are 1000 raisins in a box, how many raisins would you expect to find in a typical cookie?

3. Keisha opened a bag containing 60 chocolate chip cookies. She selected a sample of 20 cookies and counted the chips in each cookie.

Cookie	Chips
1	6
2	8
3	8
4	11
5	7
6	6
7	6
8	7
9	11
10	7

Cookie	Chips
11	8
12	7
13	9
14	9
15	8
16	6
17	8
18	10
19	10
20	8

Use the data from Keisha's sample to estimate the number of chips in the bag. Explain your answer.

4. The tables on page 57 list age and height data for the 1995 rosters of two professional basketball teams, the Houston Rockets and the Chicago Bulls.

a. Do the players on one team seem older than the players on the other team, or are they about the same age? Use statistics and graphs to support your answer.

b. Do the players on one team seem taller than the players on the other team, or are they about the same height? Use statistics and graphs to support your answer.

c. Based on the data for these two teams, what estimates could you make for the age and height distributions of a typical NBA team? What cautions would you suggest in making generalizations from the given data?

Houston Rockets

Player	Age	Height (cm)
Breaux	25	198
Brown	27	200
Cassell	26	188
Chilcutt	27	208
Drexler	33	198
Elie	32	193
Herrera	29	203
Horry	25	205
Jones	38	203
Maxwell	30	190
Murray	24	198
Olajuwon	32	210
Smith	30	188
Tabak	25	210

Chicago Bulls

Player	Age	Height (cm)
Armstrong	28	185
Blount	26	205
Buechler	27	195
Harper	31	195
Jordan	33	198
Kerr	30	188
Krystakowiak	31	203
Kukoc	27	208
Longley	26	215
Myers	32	195
Perdue	30	210
Pippen	30	198
Simpkins	23	205
Wennington	32	210

Connections

5. The U.S. Department of Transportation provides money to help states build new highways. However, there are strings attached. For example, if states fail to enforce the speed limits on interstate highways, they could lose their federal funding. To monitor driving speeds, states set up radar checkpoints to measure the speeds of samples of drivers.

a. Suppose you wanted to show that drivers in your state generally obey speed limits. Where and when would you set up radar checkpoints?

b. Suppose you wanted to show that drivers in your state often exceed speed limits. Where and when would you set up radar checkpoints?

6. Graphs are often used to support statistical arguments. However, sometimes graphs can be misleading. The graphs below all display the same data about the increase in newspaper recycling.

a. Which graph do you think gives the most honest picture of the data pattern? Why?

b. Why are the other graphs misleading?

Percent of Newspapers Recycled, 1980–1991

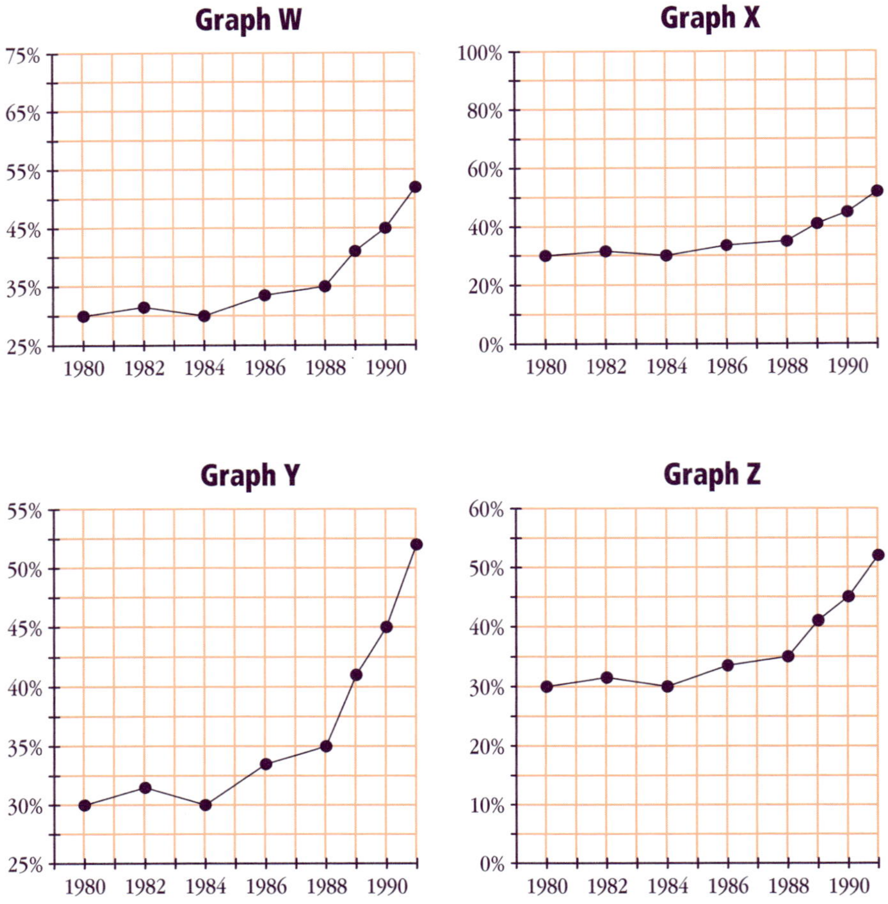

Even if you never have a job that requires you to design or analyze surveys, you will hear and read about surveys that interest you or that affect your daily life. When you are dealing with a survey, it is a good idea to ask yourself these questions:

- What was the goal of this survey?
- What was the population being studied?
- How was the sample chosen?
- How have the data been analyzed and reported?
- Do the data seem to support the conclusions?

In 7–11, use these and other relevant questions to analyze the survey.

7. In designing a television remote-control device, representatives for a manufacturer called 1000 households with television sets. They found that remote-control users sit an average of 3 meters from their television sets. Based on these findings, the manufacturer designed the remote control to work well at distances of 2.5 meters to 3.5 meters from a television set.

8. A lightbulb manufacturer wanted to know the "defect rate" for its product. One morning, the quality-control manager took 10 boxes of 50 lightbulbs from the assembly line and tried them in test sockets. All but 5 bulbs worked, so the manager concluded that production quality was acceptable.

9. A nutritionist wanted to estimate what percent of the calories in a typical U.S. teenager's diet were from fat. She asked health teachers in Dallas, Texas, to have their students keep logs of what they ate on one school day. The nutritionist analyzed the students' logs and found that the median intake was 500 fat calories per day, which is the recommended daily allowance. She concluded that calories from fat are not a problem in the diets of teenagers.

10. The Nabisco Company claims that there are over 1000 chocolate chips in a one-pound bag of ChipsAhoy!® cookies. A skeptical consumer asked how the company knew this was true. A spokesperson said that the company chose a sample of bags of cookies, soaked each bag in cold water to remove all the cookie dough, and weighed the chips that remained. In each case, the chips weighed more than a bag of 1000 chocolate chips.

11. In the cafeteria line, a student wrinkled his nose when he saw that salami-and-cheese subs were being served for lunch. When the cook asked what he would prefer, he replied, "I like bologna better." The cook asked the next ten students in line if they preferred bologna to salami. Seven students said yes, so she decided that in the future she would serve bologna subs instead of salami subs.

Extensions

12. Plain M&M's® candies are produced in the following percents.

Color	Percent in plain M&M's
brown	30%
yellow	20%
red	20%
orange	10%
green	10%
blue	10%

Suppose you are setting a table for a holiday party. You are placing small cups of M&M's candies at each place setting. Each cup contains 50 candies poured from a large bag of plain M&M's candies.

a. How many candies of each color would you expect to be in a typical cup?

b. How would you expect the number of candies of each color to vary across the samples?

c. You can simulate filling the cups with M&M's candies by generating random integers from 1 to 10. Which numbers would you let represent each color? How many random numbers would you need to generate to simulate filling one cup?

d. Carry out the simulation described in part c three times. Compare the distributions of colors in your simulated samples with the expected distribution from part a.

e. If you selected a random sample of 1000 candies from a large bag of plain M&M's candies, how closely would you expect the percent of each color in your sample to match the percents given in the table?

13. If you select five students at random from your class, what is the probability that at least two will have the same birth month? You can use a simulation to help you answer this question.

a. Design a simulation to model this situation. Tell which month each simulation outcome represents.

b. Use your birth-month simulation to produce at least 25 samples of five people. Use your results to estimate the probability that at least two people in a group of five will have the same birth month.

c. Explain how you could revise your simulation to explore this question: What are the chances that at least two students in a class of 25 have the same birthday?

Mathematical Reflections

In this investigation, you applied your knowledge of statistics and data displays to two real-world problems. These questions will help you summarize what you have learned:

1. How can you use descriptive statistics such as the median, mean, range, and quartiles to compare samples and to draw conclusions about the populations from which they were selected?
2. In what ways can you expect the distribution of data values for a sample to be similar to and different from the distribution of data values for the entire population?
3. What rule of thumb can you use in thinking about the role of sample size in making accurate estimates of population properties?

Think about your answers to these questions, discuss your ideas with other students and your teacher, and then write a summary of your findings in your journal.

The Unit Project

Part 1: Safe Water and Life Expectancy

In most areas in the United States, tap water is safe to drink and purified drinking water is sold in grocery stores. In many countries, however, people do not have access to safe drinking water. In this project, you will explore the relationship between life expectancy and access to safe water.

Use the data in the table below and your knowledge of statistics and data representations to prepare a report that summarizes the relationship between life expectancy and access to safe drinking water.

Country	Region	Life expectancy (years)	Percent of people with access to safe water
Oman	Near East/South Asia	49	52
Yemen, Arab Republic	Near East/South Asia	43	4
Yemen	Near East/South Asia	46	37
Afghanistan	Near East/South Asia	37	10
Bangladesh	Near East/South Asia	48	68
Kampuchea	Near East/South Asia	39	45
Laos	Far East/Pacific	43	48
Nepal	Near East/South Asia	45	11
Angola	Africa	42	17
Central African Republic	Africa	43	18
Chad	Africa	43	26
Congo	Africa	43	26
Ethiopia	Africa	46	13
Guinea	Africa	43	10
Ivory Coast	Africa	47	14
Madagascar	Africa	48	26
Malawi	Africa	44	44
Mali	Africa	45	23
Mauritania	Africa	44	17
Mozambique	Africa	49	7

Country	Region	Life expectancy (years)	Percent of people with access to safe water
Niger	Africa	45	49
Nigeria	Africa	49	28
Rwanda	Africa	46	38
Senegal	Africa	44	35
Sierra Leone	Africa	47	9
Somalia	Africa	39	38
Sudan	Africa	47	46
Togo	Africa	48	11
Uganda	Africa	48	16
Upper Volta	Africa	44	14
Canada	Western Hemisphere	75	99
United States	Western Hemisphere	75	99
Argentina	Western Hemisphere	71	60
Costa Rica	Western Hemisphere	73	81
Cuba	Western Hemisphere	73	62
Jamaica	Western Hemisphere	71	82
Panama	Western Hemisphere	71	83
Trinidad and Tobago	Western Hemisphere	72	89
Uruguay	Western Hemisphere	71	78
Belgium	Western Europe	73	89
Denmark	Western Europe	75	99
France	Western Europe	76	97
Western Germany	Western Europe	73	99
Greece	Near East/South Asia	74	97
Italy	Western Europe	74	86
The Netherlands	Western Europe	76	97
Norway	Western Europe	76	98
Portugal	Western Europe	72	92
United Kingdom	Western Europe	74	99
Czechoslovakia	Eastern Europe	72	78
East Germany	Eastern Europe	73	82
Hungary	Eastern Europe	71	44
Poland	Eastern Europe	73	55
Austria	Eastern Europe	73	88
Finland	Western Europe	75	84
Ireland	Western Europe	73	73
Spain	Western Europe	74	78
Sweden	Western Europe	77	99
Switzerland	Western Europe	76	96
Yugoslavia	Western Europe	71	58
Israel	Near East/South Asia	73	99
Japan	Far East/Pacific	77	98
Singapore	Far East/Pacific	72	100
Australia	Far East/Pacific	74	97
New Zealand	Far East/Pacific	74	93

Source: David Nelson, Geroge Gheverghese Joseph, and Julian Williams. *Multicultural Mathematics.* New York: Oxford University Press, 1993, pp. 178 and 179.

Part 2: Estimating Populations

The three drawings below represent fields of Canadian geese. Each dot represents one goose. A 10-by-10 grid has been placed over each drawing. Use what you know about random samples and data analysis to estimate the total number of geese in each field without counting all the geese. Prepare a report describing your methods and your findings.

Field A

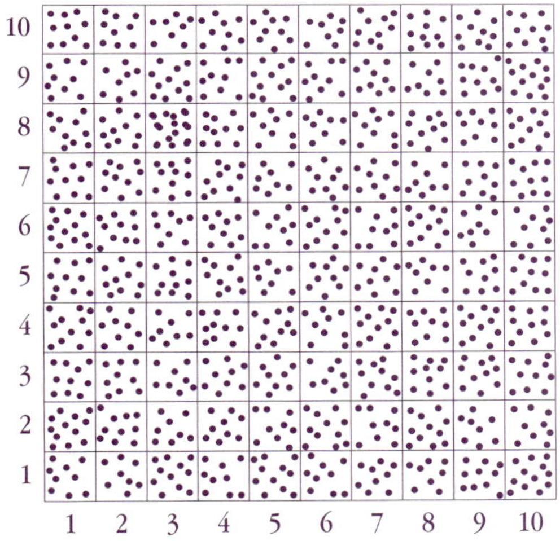

Field B

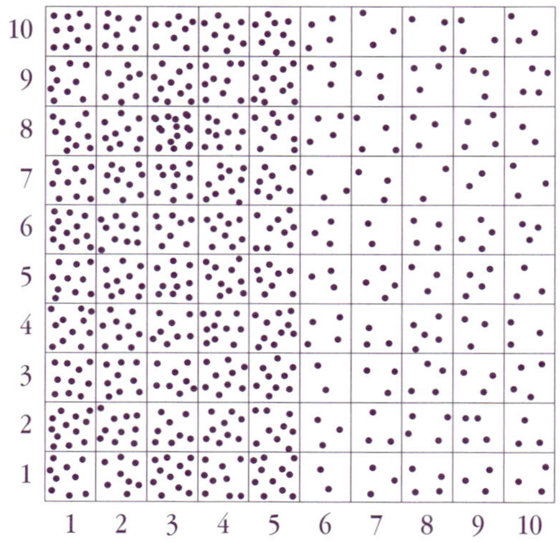

Field C

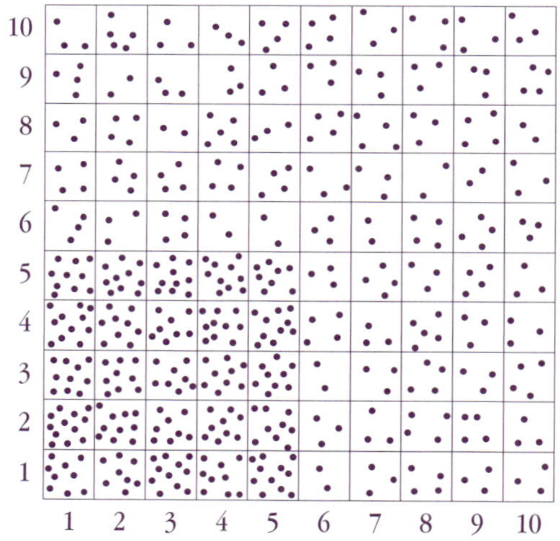

Looking Back and Looking Ahead

Unit Reflections

Working on the problems of this unit, you learned how to collect, organize, and display sample data. You learned how to *choose samples* and how to *compare samples* in order to *draw conclusions about populations* from which the samples were taken.

Using Statistical Reasoning—To test your understanding and skill in use of samples to describe populations, consider the following problems that arose when students in Elizabeth City Middle School were talking about nutrition in health class. One student objected to a cereal marketing strategy. She claimed that stores try to promote sales of cereals with high sugar content by placing them where young children will see them on the supermarket shelves.

1 *To test her claim, the class collected data on sugar content in grams per serving, calories per serving, and shelf placement—top, middle, bottom—for 77 different cereals. For example, they found Oaters on the top shelf with 110 calories and 1 gram of sugar per serving, Crunchy Critters on the middle shelf with 120 calories and 12 grams of sugar per serving, and Fancy Flakes on the bottom shelf with 140 calories and 14 grams of sugar per serving.*
The sugar content data for all 77 cereals are shown in the following calculator box plots.

Shelf Location and Sugar Content

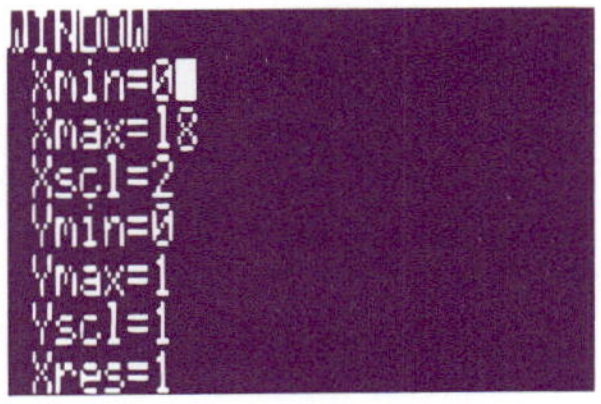

Top shelf, n = 20

Middle shelf, n = 24

Bottom shelf, n = 33

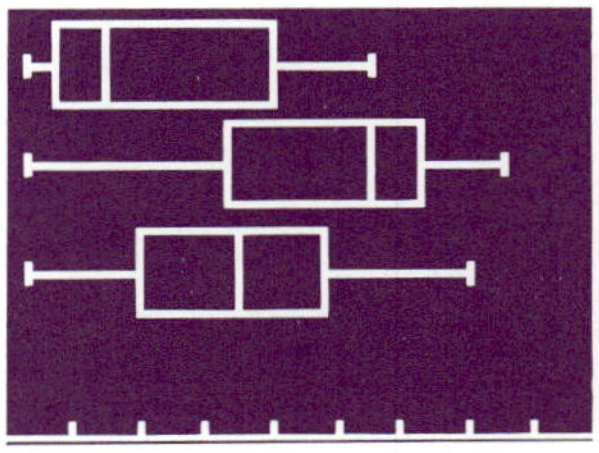

a. What is the range of sugar content in cereals on

i. the top shelf? **ii.** the middle shelf? **iii.** the bottom shelf?

b. Estimate the median grams of sugar in boxes of cereal found on the

i. top shelf. **ii.** middle shelf. **iii.** bottom shelf.

c. Use the data given for cereals found on the top and bottom shelves.

i. How many of the 20 top-shelf cereals are in the top quartile?

ii. What percent of the 33 bottom-shelf cereals are in the two middle quartiles?

2 *The students wanted to look at the cereal sugar-content and shelf-placement data to test claims that cereal companies put their products where they will catch the eyes of likely customers.*

a. Do you notice a pattern relating sugar content and shelf placement for cereals?

b. The samples for top shelf, middle shelf, and bottom shelf have different numbers of cereals. Can you still compare the data?

c. If you took a sample of cereals from a supermarket near you, what do you think you would find out about the sugar content in cereals on the different shelves?

3 *Jerome decided to make a scatter plot of the cereal data to see if there is any relationship between grams of sugar and calories in the cereal. He did not want to enter the data from 77 boxes of cereal. He wanted to choose a sample of about 25 boxes of cereal. He listed three ways he might do this.*

1. Organize the 77 cereals so they are listed in alphabetical order in one list. Choose every third cereal from this list to include in the sample.
2. Organize the cereals on each shelf in alphabetical order and choose the first 8 cereals from each of the three lists.
3. Number the entries in the alphabetical list of 77 cereals. Use two spinners (numbered 0 to 9) to produce two-digit numbers. Pick the first 25 cereal entries that match the numbers produced on the spinners.

a. Which method is an example of *convenience sampling*?

b. Which method is an example of *random sampling*?

c. Which method is an example of a *systematic sampling*?

d. Which method would you recommend?

4 *There are 600 students in Elizabeth City Middle School. Fifty students were selected at random to participate in a survey. They were asked the following two questions.*

1. *Using a scale of 1 to 5, how often did you eat cereal for breakfast on school days last week? (14 students responded with either a 4 or a 5.)*

2. *When you eat cereal, do you prefer unsweetened or sweetened brands? (32 students responded with a preference for sweetened cereal.)*

If all 600 students responded to both questions,

a. How many students would you expect to answer the first question with either a 4 or a 5?

b. How many students would you expect to answer the second question with a preference for presweetened cereal?

Explaining Your Reasoning—When you compare data sets, read graphs, choose samples, and use samples to make predictions about populations, you should be able to justify your procedures and conclusions.

1. In what types of situations are *box plots* useful tools?

2. In what types of situations are *scatter plots* useful tools?

3. When does it make sense to use data from a sample to study a population?

4. What does it mean when we say that a sample is *representative* of a population?

5. Describe three kinds of sampling methods that might *not* result in a representative sample.

6. Rules of thumb are guidelines for thinking about some topic. One rule of thumb about sampling is that it is wise to use a random sample whenever possible. What rule of thumb would you suggest about the size a sample needs to be in order to be used to make estimates about the population?

Statistical ideas and techniques for collecting and displaying data and drawing conclusions are used in nearly every branch of science, business, and government work. You'll extend and use your statistical understanding and skills in future studies, work, and reasoning about important questions faced by all people.

Glossary

biased sample A sample that does not accurately represent the population. Biased samples can give misleading results. If you wanted to predict how many students in your school recycle their soda cans, surveying only the ecology club would give you a biased sample.

box-and-whiskers plot (or box plot) A display that shows the distribution of values in a data set. A box plot is constructed from the five-number summary of the data. The box plot below shows the distribution of quality ratings for natural brands of peanut butter.

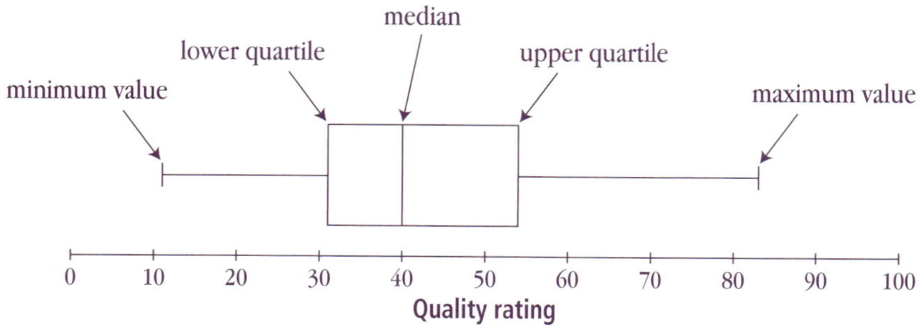

convenience sample A sample that is selected because it is convenient. If you survey everyone on your soccer team who attends tonight's practice, you are surveying a convenience sample.

distribution The arrangement of values in a data set.

five-number summary The minimum value, lower quartile, median, upper quartile, and maximum value for a data set. These five values give a summary of the shape of a distribution. The five-number summary for the quality ratings for regular brands of peanut butter is as follows:

minimum value = 11
lower quartile = 31
median = 40
upper quartile = 54
maximum value = 83

histogram A display that shows the distribution of continuous data. The range of data values, divided into intervals, is displayed on the horizontal axis. The height of the bar over each interval indicates the number of data values in that interval. The histogram below shows quality ratings for regular brands of peanut butter. The height of the bar over the interval from 20 to 30 is 4. This indicates that four brands of peanut butter have quality ratings between 20 and 30.

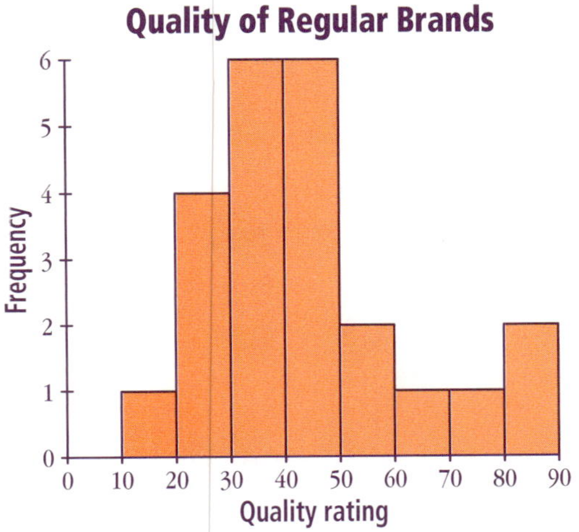

population The entire collection of people or objects you are studying.

random sample A sample chosen in a way that gives every member of a population an equally likely chance of being selected.

representative sample A sample that accurately represents a population.

sample A group of people or objects selected from a population. You can study a large population by collecting data from a sample. You can make predictions or draw conclusions about the entire population based on data from the sample.

scatter plot A graph used to explore the relationship between two variables. The graph below is a scatter plot of (length, wingspan) data for several airplanes. Each point represents the length and wingspan for one airplane.

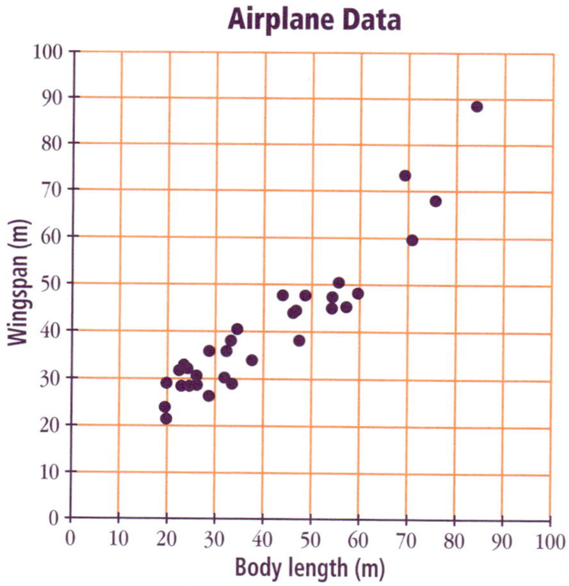

stem-and-leaf plot (or stem plot) A display that shows the distribution of values in a data set. Unlike a box plot or a histogram, a stem plot allows you to see the individual values in the data set. The stem plot below shows the distribution of quality ratings for regular brands of peanut butter. In this plot, the *stems* are a vertical list of the tens digits of the ratings. Attached to each stem are the corresponding *leaves,* in this case the ones digits. The leaves 3, 3, 6, and 9 next to the stem 2 indicate that the data set includes the values 23, 23, 26, and 29.

Quality Ratings of Regular Brands

0	
1	1
2	3 3 6 9
3	1 1 3 4 4 5
4	0 0 3 5 6 9
5	4 4
6	0
7	6
8	3 3
9	

Key

2 | 6 means 26.

systematic sample A sample selected in a methodical way. If you survey every tenth person on an alphabetical list of names, you are surveying a systematic sample.

voluntary-response sample A sample that selects itself. If you put an ad in the school paper asking for volunteers to take a survey, the students who respond will be a voluntary-response sample.

Glosario

distribución La disposición de valores en un conjunto de datos.

gráfica de dispersión Una gráfica usada para explorar la relación entre dos variables. La siguiente es una gráfica de dispersión de datos (longitud, envergadura) para varios aviones. Cada punto representa la longitud y la envergadura de un avión.

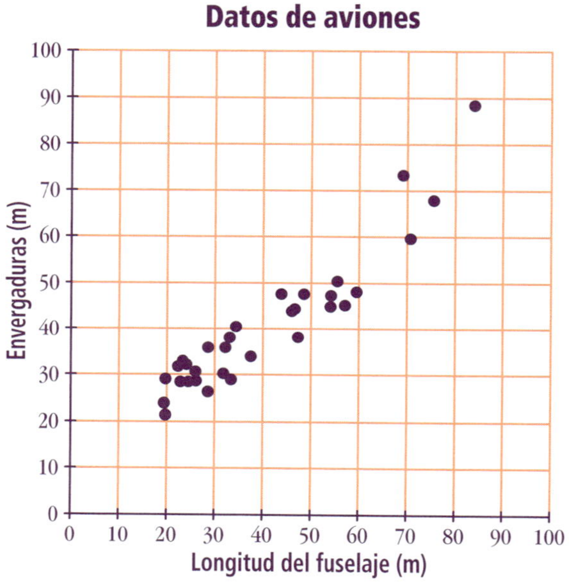

gráfica de frecuencias acumuladas Una representación que muestra la distribución de valores de un conjunto de datos. Una gráfica de frecuencias se construye con el resumen de cinco números del conjunto de datos. La gráfica de frecuencias siguiente representa la distribución de las calificaciones según la calidad de distintas marcas de mantequillas de maní natural.

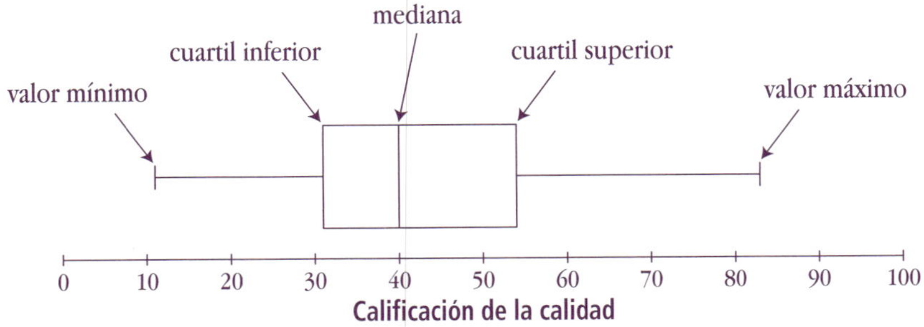

histograma Una representación que muestra la distribución de datos continuos. La gama de valores de los datos, dividida en intervalos, se representa en el eje horizontal. La altura de la barra sobre cada intervalo indica el número de valores de datos de ese intervalo. El siguiente histograma representa la calificación por calidad de las marcas de mantequilla de maní común. La altura de la barra sobre el intervalo de 20 a 30 es 4. Esto indica que hay 4 marcas de mantequilla de maní que tienen una calificación entre 20 y 30.

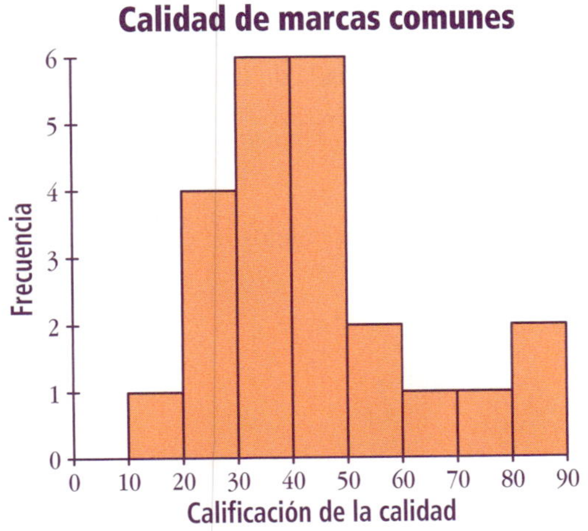

muestra Un grupo de persona u objetos seleccionados de una población. Puedes estudiar una población grande juntando datos de una muestra. Puedes hacer predicciones o sacar conclusiones sobre la población entera basándote en los datos de la muestra.

muestra aleatoria Una muestra elegida de una manera que permite que cada miembro de la población tenga la misma posibilidad de ser elegido.

muestra de conveniencia Una muestra seleccionada porque es conveniente. Si entrevistaras a todos los componentes de tu equipo de fútbol que asistan a la práctica esta noche, estarás encuestando una muestra de conveniencia.

muestra de respuestas voluntarias Una muestra que se selecciona a sí misma. Si pones un anuncio en el periódico escolar pidiendo voluntarios para participar en una encuesta, los estudiantes que respondan serán una muestra de respuestas voluntarias.

muestra representativa Una muestra que representa una población con exactitud.

muestra sesgada Una muestra que no representa con exactitud la población. Las muestras sesgadas pueden dar resultados erróneos. Si quisieras predecir cuántos estudiantes de tu escuela reciclan sus latas de refrescos, llevar a cabo una encuesta solamente en el club de ecología daría una muestra sesgada.

muestra sistemática Una muestra seleccionada de una manera metódica. Si entrevistaras a cada décima persona en una lista de nombres ordenados por orden alfabético, estarías encuestando una muestra sistemática.

población Un conjunto entero de persona u objetos en estudio.

resumen de cinco números El valor mínimo, el cuartil inferior, la mediana, el cuartil superior y el valor máximo de un conjunto de datos. Estos cinco valores dan un resumen de la forma de una distribución. El resumen de cinco números para la calificación según la calidad de las marcas de mantequilla de maní común es el siguiente:

valor mínimo = 11
cuartil inferior = 31
mediana = 40
cuartil superior = 54
valor máximo = 83

tabla arborescente Una representación que muestra la distribución de valores en un conjunto de datos. A diferencia de una gráfica de frecuencias acumuladas o un histograma, una tabla arborescente permite que veas los valores individuales de un conjunto de datos. La tabla arborescente siguiente representa la distribución de la calificación según la calidad de las marcas de mantequilla de maní común. En esta tabla, los tallos son una lista vertical de los dígitos de las decenas de las calificaciones. Añadidas a cada tallo están las hojas correspondientes, en este caso, los dígitos de las unidades. Las hojas 3, 3, 6 y 9 al lado del tallo 2 indican que el conjunto de datos incluye los valores 23, 23, 26 y 29.

Calificación por calidad de las marcas comunes

0	
1	1
2	3 3 6 9
3	1 1 3 4 4 5
4	0 0 3 5 6 9
5	4 4
6	0
7	6
8	3 3
9	

Clave
2 | 6 significa 26.

Index

Connected Mathematics™

Clever Counting

Combinatorics

Student Edition

Glenda Lappan
James T. Fey
William M. Fitzgerald
Susan N. Friel
Elizabeth Difanis Phillips

PEARSON
Prentice Hall

Glenview, Illinois
Needham, Massachusetts
Upper Saddle River, New Jersey

Clever Counting

Connected Mathematics™ was developed at Michigan State University with the support of National Science Foundation Grant No. MDR 9150217.

This project was supported, in part,
by the
National Science Foundation
Opinions expressed are those of the authors
and not necessarily those of the Foundation

The Michigan State University authors and administration have agreed that all MSU royalties arising from this publication will be devoted to purposes supported by the Department of Mathematics and the MSU Mathematics Education Enrichment Fund.

Photo Acknowledgements: 12 © Michael J. Olonlewski/The Image Works; 13 © Ann and Myron Sutton/FPG International; 22 © Geoffrey Apple; 34 © Miro Vintoniv/Stock, Boston; 38 © Nick Dolding/Tony Stone Images

Contents

Clever Counting

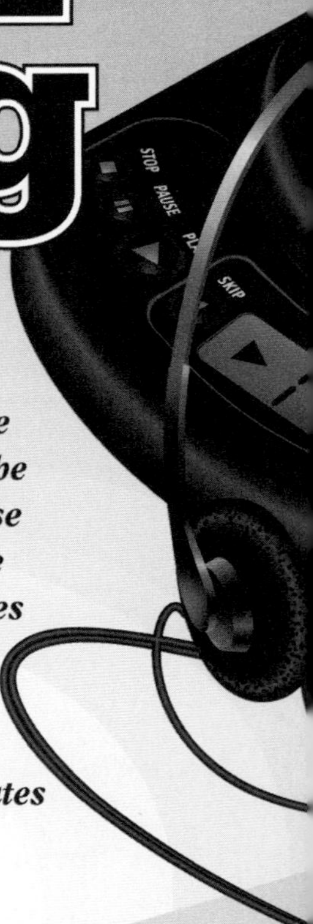

A locker at a storage warehouse was robbed. The police suspect that the thief tried possible lock combinations until the lock opened. A lock combination consists of three numbers from 0 to 39, with no repeated numbers. How many combinations are possible?

A witness saw a white van speed away from the scene of a crime. He said the van had in-state license plates starting with the letters MTU. License plates in the state where the robbery took place contain three letters followed by three numbers. How many possible plates start with MTU?

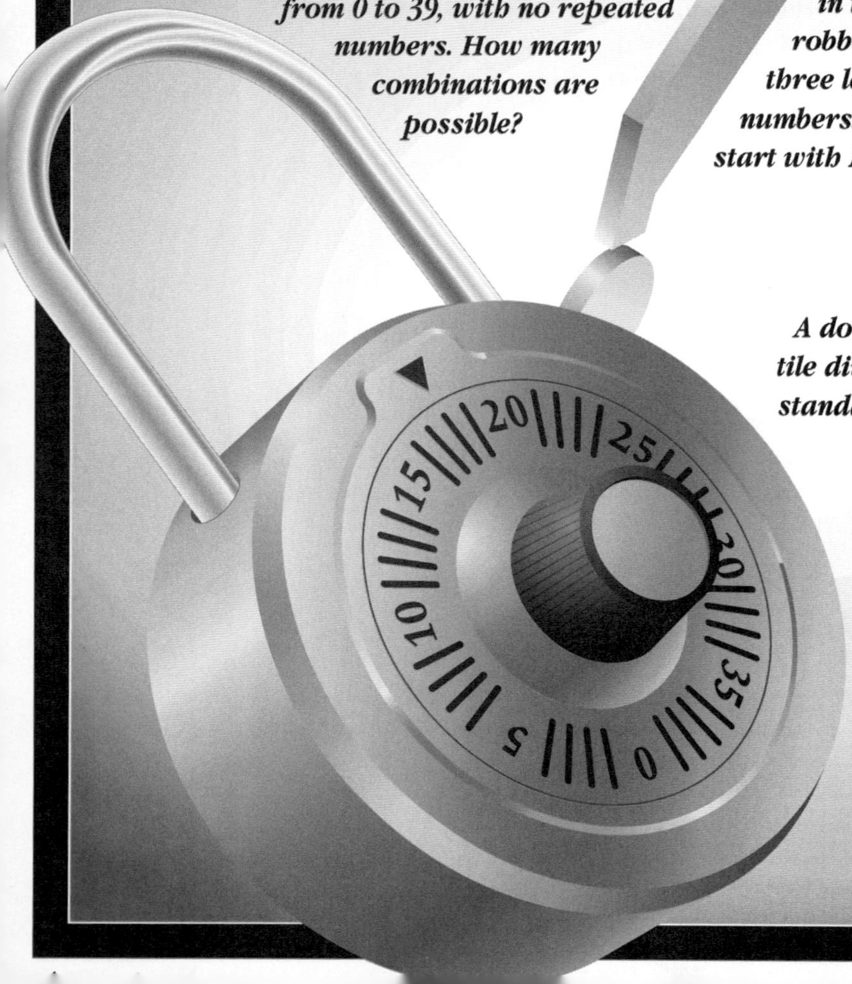

A domino is a rectangular tile divided into halves. On a standard double-six domino, each half contains from 0 to 6 dots, called pips. A complete set of dominoes contains one domino for each possible combination of halves. How many dominoes are in a complete set?

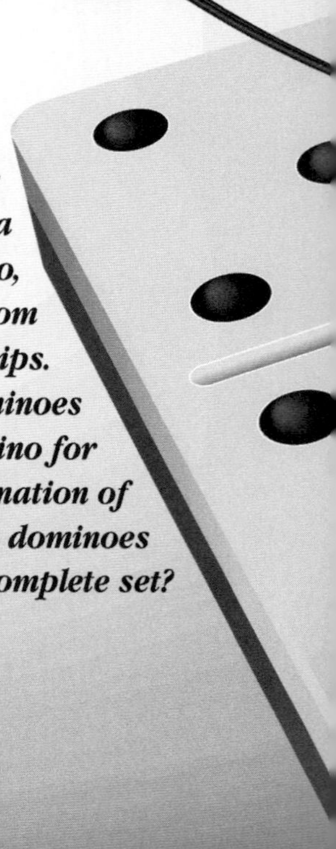

All the problems on the opposite page involve counting. To solve these problems, you could make organized lists or counting trees to help you find all the possiblities. However, these methods would be time-consuming and tedious. In this unit, you will investigate a robbery. As you explore the evidence involved in the case, you will develop mathematical strategies for solving complex counting problems.

Mathematical Highlights

In *Clever Counting* you will explore some basic techniques for counting the possible outcomes of complex processes. The unit should help you to

- Recognize situations in which fundamental counting techniques apply;
- Construct organized lists and diagrams that display the outcomes of processes in systematic and easily-counted ways;
- Analyze and count paths through networks; and
- Use counting techniques to solve problems.

As you work on the problems of this unit, make it a habit to ask questions about problem situations that involve multi-step processes: *Is this a situation in which actions must take place in distinct stages to produce an outcome, with several options at each stage of the process? How many options are there at each stage? Does order of actions and choices make a difference? How could the possibilities be displayed and counted with a tree diagram, a network, or a systematic list?*

INVESTIGATION 1

Counting Possibilities

Rodney's Radical Sounds sells radios, tape decks, and compact disc players at discount prices. There is very little room in the store to keep merchandise that is not on display, so Rodney rents a storage locker at the nearby Fail-Safe storage warehouse.

One afternoon, Rodney went to his locker and discovered that a box of expensive compact disc players was missing. He called the police, and Detective Ima Curious came to investigate.

During her initial investigation, Detective Curious gathered the following information:

- There were no signs of forced entry, and the only fingerprints on the locker were Rodney's.
- Rodney had visited his locker at noon the day before, and nothing was missing.
- The warehouse manager is on duty from 9 A.M. to 6 P.M. every day.

- Some of the lockers at Fail-Safe have push-button locks; others have combination locks. The manager keeps a list of all the combinations hidden in his office.
- The night security guard was on duty from 9 P.M. to 6 A.M. The manager suspects that the guard committed the robbery. He thinks the guard tried various combinations until the lock opened.
- The security guard said that, although she makes frequent rounds of the warehouse to inspect the locks and doors, she does not pass every locker on every trip through the warehouse.
- The security guard admitted that she was visited by a friend from 9:30 P.M. until about 11:30 P.M. She and her friend played dominoes for about an hour. After the friend left, the guard conducted a half-hour check of the warehouse.
- The guard's friend said that as he was leaving the warehouse, a van raced out of the parking lot with its lights off. He thought this was odd, so he tried to read the license plate. He could see that it was an in-state plate and contained the letters MTU, in that order. As the van passed under a street light, the friend caught a glimpse of the driver. He is certain the driver was a man.

Think about this!

Based on this information, whom, if anyone, do you suspect of committing the robbery? What questions would you like to ask Rodney, the manager, the night guard, the guard's friend, or the detective?

1.1 Making Faces

Detective Curious asked the guard's friend to work with a police artist to create a sketch of the man driving the van. To make an accurate sketch, the artist gave the witness choices for several facial features. For example, she asked, "What did his nose look like? Was it hooked? Long and straight? Turned up? Broken?"

Problem 1.1

Here are the choices the artist gave the witness:

Hair	**Eyes**	**Nose**
bushy	staring	hooked
bald	beady	long and straight
	droopy	turned up
	wide open	broken

A. How many facial descriptions can you make by choosing one attribute for each feature?

B. The witness said he remembered something distinctive about the driver's mouth. The artist suggested these possibilities:

Mouth
thin and mean
toothless
sinister grin

If you consider the hair, eyes, nose, and mouth, how many facial descriptions can you make by choosing one attribute for each feature?

Problem 1.1 Follow-Up

1. Of all the facial descriptions you found in part B, how many include droopy eyes?

2. Of all the facial descriptions you found in part B, how many include a bald head and a thin, mean mouth?

1.2 Checking Plate Numbers

The witness claimed that he saw the license plate of the van. He said that it was an in-state plate containing the letter sequence MTU. In the state in which the robbery took place, license plates contain three letters followed by three numbers. How might this information help the detective solve her case?

Problem 1.2

Detective Curious wants to run each possible plate number through the computer to find out whether the registered owner has a criminal record. It takes about 20 seconds to check each plate number. How many possible plates start with MTU? Do you think this is a reasonable number of plates for the detective to check?

Problem 1.2 Follow-Up

1. When the detective questioned him a second time, the witness said he was really only sure that the first two letters of the plate were MT. How many possible license plates start with MT? How does this compare to the number of possible plates that start with MTU?

2. In a neighboring state, license plates have four letters followed by two numbers. Is the number of possible plates for this state greater than, less than, or equal to the number of possible plates for the state in which the crime took place? Explain your answer.

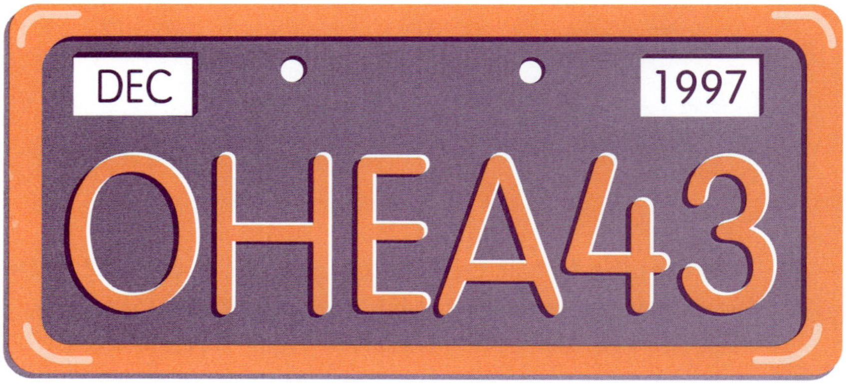

Applications • Connections • Extensions

As you work on these ACE questions, use your calculator whenever you need it.

Applications

1. Makoto is getting dressed for school. The counting tree below shows his choices for shoes, pants, and shirts.

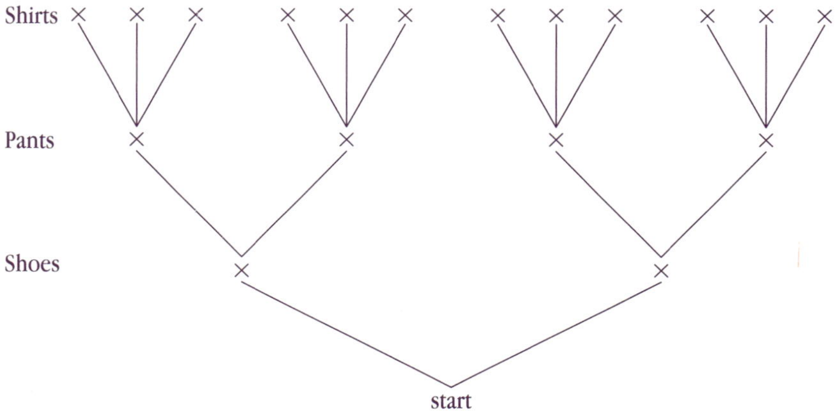

a. How many pairs of shoes does Makoto have to choose from?

b. How many pairs of pants does he have to choose from?

c. How many shirts does he have to choose from?

d. How many different combinations of shoes, pants, and a shirt can Makoto put together from these choices?

e. How can you find the answer to part d without counting each path in the diagram?

2. Ms. Suárez is choosy about what she eats. When she buys lunch in the company cafeteria, she considers only these options:

Main course	**Drink**	**Dessert**
salad	milk	fruit
pizza	orange juice	frozen yogurt
turkey sandwich		pie
		pudding

  a. List four lunches Ms. Suárez might purchase. Each lunch should consist of one main course, one drink, and one dessert.

  b. Copy and complete this tree diagram to show all the lunches Ms. Suárez might purchase.

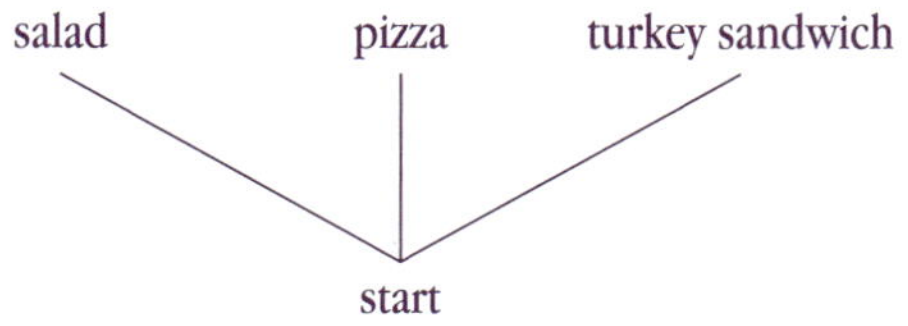

  c. How many days can Ms. Suárez buy lunch in the cafeteria without having the same lunch twice?

3. At the meeting of the Future Teachers of America, ice cream cones were served. There were two kinds of cones, five flavors of ice cream, and three types of sprinkles. Each member chose one cone, one ice cream flavor, and one type of sprinkles. How many combinations were possible? Show your work.

4. Look back at the lists of hair, eyes, nose, and mouth attributes in Problem 1.1. The witness told the artist that he was sure the driver of the van was not bald. He was also certain that the driver did not have droopy eyes, a broken nose, or a sinister grin. If you eliminate these choices from the lists of attributes, how many descriptions can you make from the choices that remain?

5. In a particular counting tree, four branches extend from the starting point. At the second level, five branches extend from each branch from the previous level. At the third level, three branches extend from each branch from the previous level. How many paths through the branches of the tree are possible?

6. License plates in the state where the locker robbery took place contain three letters followed by three numbers. In Problem 1.2, you found that this scheme provides enough plates for over 17 million cars. In states with small populations, such as Alaska, North Dakota, Wyoming, and Vermont, fewer than 1 million cars are registered.

   a. Suppose you are in charge of developing a license-plate scheme for a state with a million registered cars. Describe a scheme that would provide enough plates for all the cars and require the fewest characters.

   b. Can you think of another acceptable scheme that would use the same number of characters as the scheme you described in part a? Explain.

7. If a state's motorcycle plates contain four letters, such as ABCD or MIKE, how many plates are possible?

8. If a state's license plates contain three numbers followed by four letters, such as 543 JOHE or 112 BETY, how many plates are possible?

Connections

9. Suppose the witness remembers the three letters and the first two numbers of the van's license plate and guesses the last number. What is the probability that his guess will be correct? Explain your answer.

10. Suppose the witness recalls that the driver had bushy hair and beady eyes and guesses what his nose looked like. Can you determine the probability that his guess will be correct? Explain your answer.

11. U.S. postal zip codes have two forms. The short form is a five-digit number, such as 54494. The longer form, called zip+4, has 9 digits, such as 48824-1027.

a. What is the short form for your zip code?

b. How many short-form zip codes are possible?

c. How many zip+4 zip codes are possible?

d. The U.S. population is about 260 million people. How does the number of possible zip+4 codes compare with the number of people in the United States?

12. **a.** Suppose it takes 3 seconds to manufacture a license plate. How much time would it take to manufacture every possible plate with three letters followed by three numbers? Assume the plates are made one at a time on a continuous production line. Express your answer in each of these units:

i. seconds **ii.** minutes **iii.** hours

iv. days **v.** weeks **vi.** years

b. Make a table and a graph to show how the manufacturing time in hours varies with the number of license plates produced.

c. Write an equation that shows how the manufacturing time relates to the number of license plates produced. Explain what each part of your equation means in terms of the situation.

13. If you held the letter U up to a mirror, its reflection would also be a U.

a. List all the capital letters with this reflection property.

b. The reflection of UTM in a mirror would be MTU. How many three-letter combinations have reflections that are also three-letter combinations?

Extensions

14. In the Clue® board game, players try to solve a murder mystery. To win, a player must identify the murderer, the murder weapon, and the room in which the murder was committed. Amadi claims that there are 118 possible solutions to the game. His sister Ayana, who has never played the game, says she can't believe this is true. Why does she say this?

In 15–18, use a current almanac to help you answer the question.

15. In Texas, license plates have four letters followed by three numbers. What is the ratio of the number of possible plates to the state's population?

16. In Michigan, license plates have three letters followed by three numbers or three numbers followed by three letters. What is the ratio of the number of possible plates to the state's population?

17. In Alaska, license plates have three letters followed by three numbers. What is the ratio of the number of possible plates to the state's population?

18. In Utah, license plates have three letters followed by three numbers. What is the ratio of the number of possible plates to the state's population?

19. **a.** Suppose a country's postal codes consist of two characters. A code may have two letters, two numbers, or a letter and a number. How many two-character codes are possible? Consider A3 to be different from 3A.

b. Suppose a country's postal codes consist of three characters. A code may have three letters, three numbers, or a combination of letters and numbers. How many three-character codes are possible?

c. Suppose a country's postal codes have six characters that are a mixture of letters and numbers, such as CB2 1QA, 3B2 A3H, and V6J 1Z8. How many six-character codes are possible?

Mathematical Reflections

In this investigation, you developed strategies for counting in situations in which there are many possibilities. These questions will help you summarize what you have learned:

1. Suppose you are given a list of options in each of several categories. You are to choose one option from each category. Describe how you could make a counting tree to help you find all the possible combinations of options. Use an example if it helps you to explain your thinking.

2. Suppose you must choose one option from each of three categories. The first category has two options, the second has three options, and the third has three options. Describe how you could list all the possible combinations without using a counting tree. Use an example if it helps you to explain your thinking.

3. In counting situations in which there are many possibilities, making a counting tree or a list can be time-consuming and cumbersome. In these cases, you can do calculations to find the number of possibilities. Look back at your work in this investigation. Find an example of a counting problem you solved by doing calculations. Describe the problem, and explain the strategy you used to find your answer.

Think about your answers to these questions, discuss your ideas with other students and your teacher, and then write a summary of your findings in your journal.

Imagine that you are writing a mystery story about a detective's investigation of a crime. What type of crime would you write about? Describe some of the characters you might include. What situations could you include in your story that would require the detective to count possibilities? You will continue to brainstorm about your story at the end of each investigation.

INVESTIGATION 2

Opening Locks

The manager of Fail-Safe suspects that the security guard stole Rodney's CD players. He suggested to Detective Curious that the guard had tried different combinations until the lock opened. The detective wondered how long it would take to try every possible combination.

2.1 Pushing Buttons

Some of the lockers at Fail-Safe have push-button locks that consist of five lettered buttons.

To open a push-button lock, the letters must be pressed in the correct sequence.

Problem 2.1

A lock sequence may have two, three, four, or five letters. A letter may not occur more than once in a sequence.

A. How many two-letter sequences are possible?

B. How many three-letter sequences are possible?

C. How many four-letter sequences are possible?

D. How many five-letter sequences are possible?

E. The security guard would not have known whether the sequence that would open Rodney's lock consisted of two, three, four, or five letters. How many possible lock sequences might she have had to try?

Problem 2.1 Follow-Up

1. How long do you think it would take to try every possible lock sequence? Explain how you made your estimate.
2. Based on your work, do you think it is likely that someone opened Rodney's lock by trying all the possible lock sequences? Explain.
3. Does your answer to question 2 make you suspicious of anyone who was near the crime scene? Explain.

2.2 Dialing Combinations

The detective was trying to make her case based on the push-button lock data when she discovered that Rodney's locker has a *combination* lock!

The combination locks at Fail-Safe have combinations consisting of three numbers from 0 to 39 in a given order, such as 15-5-33 and 7-11-21. Do you think it would have been possible for someone to try every possible combination?

Problem 2.2

A. How many possible combinations are there for Rodney's lock? Assume that a number may not appear more than once in a combination.

B. How long do you think it would take someone to try all the possible combinations? Explain how you made your estimate.

Problem 2.2 Follow-Up

1. The detective started to list the possible lock combinations, but she soon became tired.

She then tried to make a counting tree, but she found it very tedious to draw. As she studied the patterns in her work, she had an idea:

"I can determine how many choices I have for each position in the combination. Then I can multiply those numbers together to predict the total number of possibilities!"

Do you think the detective's idea is reasonable? Why or why not?

2. For some locks, a combination may have the same number in the first and last positions but not in adjacent positions. This means that 3-1-3 is allowed, but 3-3-1 is not. If such combinations were allowed for the locks at Fail-Safe, how would the number of possible combinations for Rodney's lock change?

3. If you were in charge of security at Fail-Safe, would you recommend push-button locks or combination locks? Explain.

4. Does your work on this problem make you suspicious of anyone who was near the crime scene? Explain.

2.3 Increasing Security

In Problem 2.2, you found the number of possible combinations for a lock with 40 marks, representing the numbers from 0 to 39. Some combination locks have more or fewer than 40 marks. In this problem, you will explore the relationship between the number of marks on a lock and the number of possible combinations.

Problem 2.3

When the owner of Fail-Safe learned about the robbery, he told the manager to replace all the locks with more secure locks. However, he made it clear that he did not want to spend a lot of money. The manager did some research and found that combination locks with more marks are more expensive than locks with fewer marks. He wanted to convince the owner that the increased security provided by locks with more marks was worth the extra investment.

A. Make a table showing the number of possible combinations for locks with from 3 to 10 marks. Consider only three-number combinations with no repeated numbers. For example, to complete the row for 3 marks, consider all possible combinations of the numbers 0, 1, and 2.

Number of marks	Number of combinations
3	
4	
5	
6	
7	
8	
9	
10	

B. Use the pattern in your table to write an equation for the relationship between the number of marks, m, and the number of combinations, C.

C. Sketch a graph of your equation for m values from 3 to 10.

D. How could the manager use your graph to convince the owner to buy locks with more marks?

Problem 2.3 Follow-Up

1. Use your equation to find the number of possible combinations for Rodney's lock.

2. How does your answer to question 1 compare with the answer you would find by using the detective's strategy from Problem 2.2 Follow-Up?

3. **a.** If a lock has 40 marks and a combination consists of two numbers without repeats, how many combinations are possible? Explain your answer.

b. If a lock has 40 marks and a combination consists of four numbers without repeats, how many combinations are possible? Explain your answer.

c. If a lock has 20 marks and a combination consists of four numbers without repeats, how many combinations are possible? Explain your answer.

4. **a.** Suppose a combination consists of two numbers without repeats. Write an equation for the relationship between the number of marks, m, and the number of combinations, C.

b. Suppose a combination consists of four numbers without repeats. Write an equation for the relationship between the number of marks, m, and the number of combinations, C.

Applications • Connections • Extensions

As you work on these ACE questions, use your calculator whenever you need it.

Applications

1. Tina's new car has a push-button lock. The car is locked, and Tina has forgotten the lock sequence. She is trying to open the lock by testing each possible sequence. It takes her 5 seconds to test each sequence. The manufacturer says that there are 100,000 possible sequences.

a. If Tina has to test every possible sequence, how many seconds will it take her to open the car door?

b. Express your answer to part a in minutes, in hours, and in days.

c. Make a table and a graph of the relationship between number of minutes and number of combinations tested.

d. How could lock designers protect owners against people who might try to break into cars by trying possible lock sequences?

2. To play the Take-3 lottery game, players must choose three numbers from 0 to 30 in a particular order. The same number may appear more than once in a selection. The order of the numbers is considered, so 3-2-4 is different from 4-3-2. If a player's selection matches the winning selection, the player wins the grand prize.

a. How many possible selections begin with 0-0?

b. How many possible selections begin with 0-1?

c. How many possible selections begin with 0-2?

d. How many possible selections begin with 0-3?

e. How many possible selections begin with 0?

f. What is the total number of possible selections?

g. Freija says that if she purchases a Take-3 lottery ticket every day for a year, she is guaranteed to win at least once. Do you agree? Explain.

h. If you could write one selection every 2 seconds, how long would it take you to list all the possibilities? Express your answer in seconds, in minutes, in hours, in days, and in weeks.

3. The Guess-and-Win lottery game requires players to choose three *different* numbers from 0 to 30. The order of the numbers matters, so 3-2-4 is different from 4-3-2.

a. How many possible selections begin with 0-1?

b. How many possible selections begin with 0-2?

c. How many possible selections begin with 0-3?

d. How many possible selections begin with 0?

e. How many possible selections begin with 1?

f. What is the total number of possible selections?

4. Which of the following has the greatest number of possible combinations? Explain how you arrived at your answer.

i. a lock with 10 numbers for which a combination consists of 3 numbers with repeated numbers allowed

ii. a lock with 5 numbers for which a combination consists of 5 numbers with repeated numbers allowed

iii. a lock with 5 numbers for which a combination consists of 5 numbers with repeated numbers *not* allowed

5. Some bicycle locks are composed of several numbered wheels. To open the lock, you line up the correct sequence of numbers with the arrow.

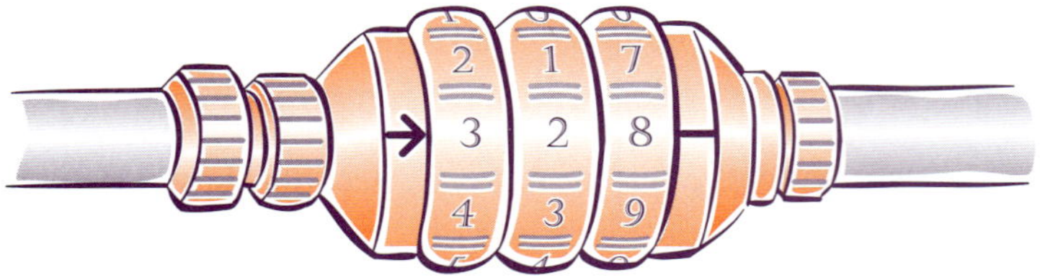

Suppose a bicycle lock has three wheels with the numbers from 0 to 9 on each wheel.

a. List five possible combinations for this lock.

b. How many possible combinations are there? Explain how you found your answer.

6. Suppose a bicycle lock has five wheels with the numbers from 0 to 9 on each wheel. To open the lock, you line up the correct sequence of numbers with the arrow.

a. List five possible combinations for this lock.

b. How many possible combinations are there? Explain how you found your answer.

7. Suppose a lock has three wheels with the numbers from 0 to 4 on each wheel. To open the lock, you line up the correct sequence of numbers with the arrow.

   a. List five possible combinations for this lock.

   b. How many possible combinations are there? Explain how you found your answer.

Connections

8. Sammy looks in his closet and sees four shirts, three pairs of jeans, high-top tennis shoes, running shoes, and three caps. He wants to wear a shirt, a pair of jeans, shoes, and a cap. How many different outfits can he make?

9. Winona and her friends walk to the pizza parlor for dinner. They decide to order the special, a cheese pizza with one topping and a choice of crust. The choices for toppings are onions, mushrooms, green peppers, olives, pepperoni, ham, and sausage. The choices for crust are garlic, sesame seed, whole wheat, and extra crispy. How many different pizzas are possible?

10. A lock has five buttons, labeled A, B, C, D, and E. A combination consists of five letters pressed in a particular order. A letter may be repeated. Some possible combinations are A-B-A-A-E and D-D-D-D-D. How many combinations are possible?

11. a. How many different eight-letter "words" can you make by rearranging the letters in the word COMPUTER? In this situation, a "word" is any combination that includes each letter in COMPUTER exactly once. Two possible words are TRPOCMEU and ETOUMPCR.

   b. Which lock problem does this resemble? Explain.

12. Randy is helping his little sisters develop a secret code for their club. The girls want their code words to be made up of combinations of 0s and 1s, and they want to make a list of messages that correspond to the code words. For example, 01 might mean "meet me after school," and 010 might mean "bring your bike."

a. **i.** How many two-digit code words are possible?

ii. How many three-digit code words are possible?

iii. How many four-digit code words are possible?

iv. How many *n*-digit code words are possible?

b. Make a table and a graph and write an equation to show the relationship between the length of a code word and the number of possible code words. What kind of relationship does your graph reveal?

Extensions

13. a. Find the number of possible combinations for each lock described, and tell how the two numbers compare.

i. a bicycle lock composed of five wheels with ten numbers on each wheel

ii. a bicycle lock composed of ten wheels with five numbers on each wheel

b. Find the number of possible combinations for each lock described, and tell how the two numbers compare.

i. a bicycle lock composed of five wheels with *n* numbers on each wheel

ii. a bicycle lock composed of *n* wheels with five numbers on each wheel

14. In the Take-Your-Chances lottery game, players choose three numbers from 0 to 30 in a particular order. A number may appear more than once in a selection. To win the grand prize, a player must have selected the winning numbers in the correct order. A player wins a smaller prize if he or she has selected the winning numbers but in an incorrect order.

a. Suppose this week's winning selection is 8-13-21. List all the selections for which a prize will be awarded.

b. Suppose this week's winning selection is 9-18-27. List all the selections for which a prize will be awarded.

c. If a player makes one selection for next week's game, what is the probability that he or she will win the grand prize? What is the probability that he or she will win a smaller prize?

d. Let a, b, and c represent any three numbers. In how many different orders can a, b, and c be written?

Did you know?

You can use the *factorial* function on your calculator to help you solve problems about combinations. The factorial symbol is an exclamation point. When an exclamation point appears after a whole number, it means "multiply all the whole numbers up to and including this number." For example, 6! represents $1 \times 2 \times 3 \times 4 \times 5 \times 6$.

The number of possible four-number combinations with no repeats that you can make from four numbers is $4 \times 3 \times 2 \times 1$. You can evaluate this by entering 4! on your calculator. What problem can you solve by entering 5! on your calculator?

Mathematical Reflections

In this investigation, you learned strategies for finding the number of possible combinations for push-button locks and combination locks. These questions will help you summarize what you have learned:

1. Suppose a lock has five numbers. How many three-number combinations are possible if repeated numbers are not allowed?
2. Suppose a lock has n numbers. How many three-number combinations are possible if repeated numbers are not allowed? Assume $n \geq 3$.
3. Suppose a lock has n numbers. How many r-number combinations are possible if repeated numbers are not allowed? Assume $n \geq r$.
4. Compare the strategies you used to find the number of possible sequences for push-button locks with the strategies you used to find the number of combinations for combination locks. Consider two types of combination locks:
    - locks for which combinations with repeated numbers are not allowed
    - locks for which the first and third numbers of the combination may be the same

Think about your answers to these questions, discuss your ideas with other students and your teacher, and then write a summary of your findings in your journal.

What situations might you include in your mystery story that would require the detective to estimate how long it would take to do or make something?

INVESTIGATION 3

Networks

Detective Curious decided to investigate the possibility that someone broke into the warehouse while the night guard was on duty. The guard told the detective that, although she makes frequent rounds of the warehouse to inspect the locks and doors, she does not pass every locker on every trip through the warehouse. The detective thought the thief may have hidden in Rodney's locker during the guard's rounds. If the guard did not pass Rodney's locker, she would not have noticed that the lock had been opened.

3.1 Making Rounds

The floor plan of the Fail-Safe storage warehouse is shown below. The left section contains rows of small lockers, and the right section contains rows of large lockers. During each of her inspection rounds, the guard starts at checkpoint A and walks down an aisle of small lockers to checkpoint B. From there, she walks down an aisle of large lockers to checkpoint C. One possible path is shown in the diagram.

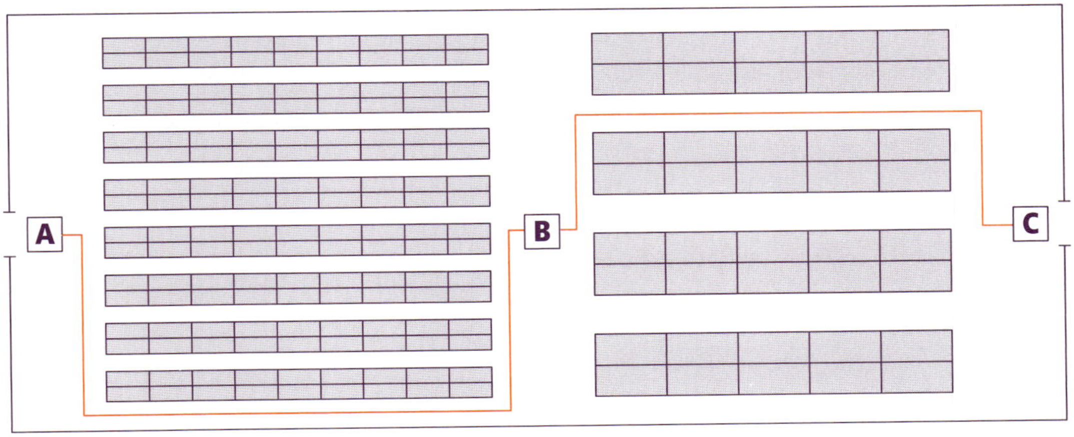

Problem 3.1

A. How many paths are there from A to B? How many paths are there from B to C?

B. How many paths are there from A to C through B? Explain your reasoning.

C. If Rodney has a small locker, how many of the paths from A to C pass by his locker?

D. If Rodney has a large locker, how many of the paths from A to C pass by his locker?

E. If Rodney has a small locker, what is the probability that the guard will *not* pass his locker on one of her rounds?

F. If Rodney has a large locker, what is the probability that the guard will *not* pass his locker on one of her rounds?

Problem 3.1 Follow-Up

1. Suppose the warehouse were laid out so that there were 15 paths from A to B and 12 paths from B to C. How would your answers to parts B–F of Problem 3.1 change?
2. Compare the method you used to count paths through the warehouse with the methods you used in previous investigations to count facial descriptions, license plates, and lock combinations.

3.2 Networking

The diagram below is a model of the floor plan of the warehouse. A diagram like this is called a **network**. A network is made up of *nodes* and *edges*. In the network below, the nodes A, B, and C represent the warehouse checkpoints, and the edges connecting the nodes represent aisles between the rows of lockers. A *path* from node A to node C consists of an edge from node A to node B followed by an edge from node B to node C.

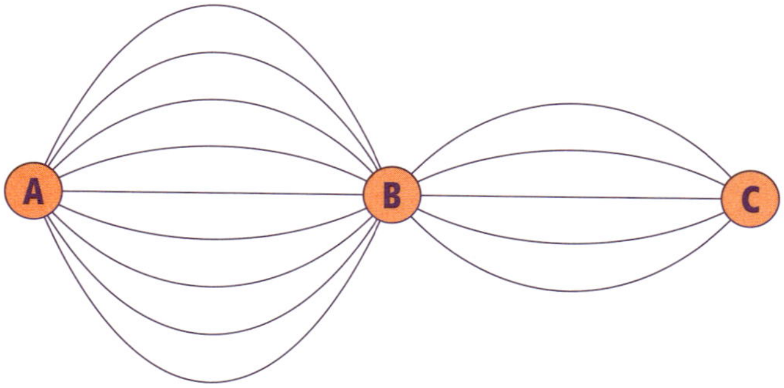

This network models the warehouse floor plan because it contains all the important information in a simplified form.

Problem 3.2

A. In this network, a single edge connects node A to node B, and 8 edges connect node B to node C. How many paths are there from node A to node C that pass through node B?

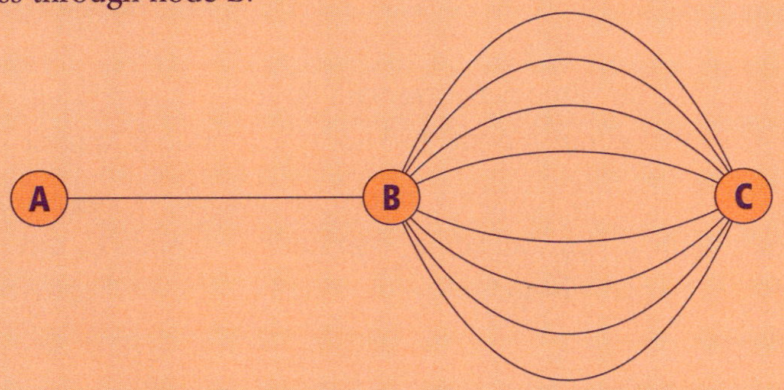

B. In this network, 2 edges connect node A to node B, and 5 edges connect node B to node C. How many paths are there from node A to node C that pass through node B?

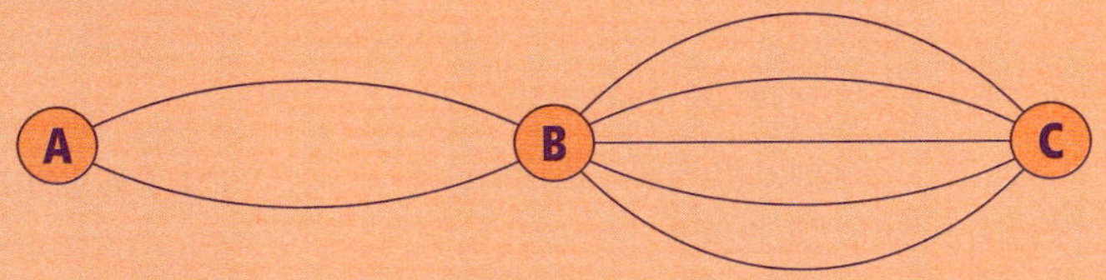

C. In another network, 25 edges connect node A to node B, and 32 edges connect node B to node C. How many paths are there from node A to node C that pass through node B? Explain your reasoning.

Problem 3.2 Follow-Up

1. For each network in Problem 3.2, find the number of different *round trips* from node A to node C and back to node A.
2. For parts A and B of Problem 3.2, describe how adding another edge connecting nodes A and B would change the number of round trips.

3.3 Designing Networks

You have found the number of paths through several networks. In this problem, you will design networks that satisfy given constraints.

Problem 3.3

A. **1.** Design at least three networks with nodes A, B, and C and 12 edges. Each edge should connect node A to node B or node B to node C.

2. For each network you drew, record the number of edges from node A to node B, the number of edges from node B to node C, and the total number of paths from node A to node C. Look for a pattern in your results.

3. Use your findings from part 2 to help you draw the network with the maximum number of paths from node A to node C. Explain how you know that your network has the maximum number of paths.

B. Design a network with nodes A, B, C, and D and 12 edges that has the maximum number of paths from node A to node D through nodes B and C. How did you decide how to distribute the 12 edges?

C. Suppose you are given a specific number of nodes and a specific number of edges. How can you design a network with the maximum number of paths from the first node to the last node?

D. Describe how the numbers of edges between consecutive pairs of nodes are related to the total number of paths in a network.

Problem 3.3 Follow-Up

1. In the network below, how many paths are there from node A to node F?

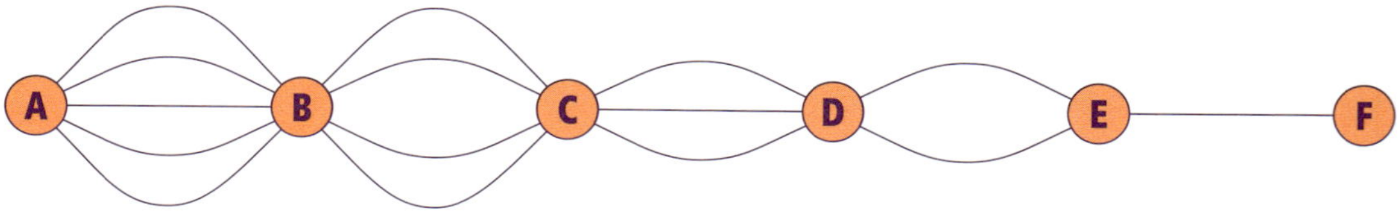

2. In the network below, the number on each edge represents the time, in seconds, it takes to travel along that edge. Which path from node A to node F will take the least amount of time to travel? Explain your answer.

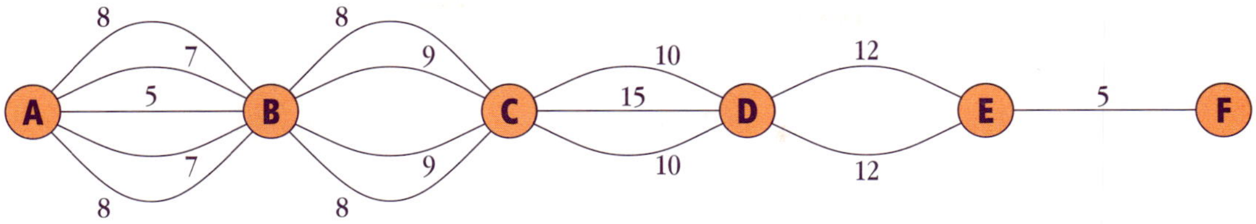

Applications • Connections • Extensions

As you work on these ACE questions, use your calculator whenever you need it.

Applications

1. **a.** In the diagram below, how many paths are there from A to D?

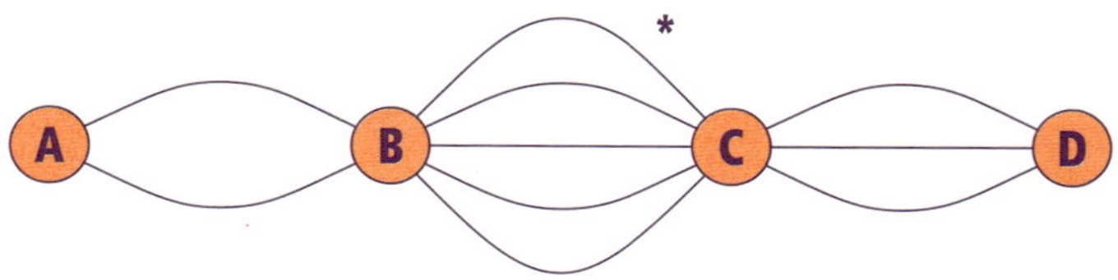

b. How many paths from A to D pass the location represented by the asterisk?

2. Design a network with 3 nodes, 11 edges, and the maximum number of paths from the first node to the last node.

3. Design a network with nodes A, B, and C and exactly 12 paths from node A to node C that pass through node B.

4. Design a network with nodes A, B, and C and exactly 11 paths from node A to node C that pass through node B.

5. If possible, design a network with nodes A, B, C, and D and exactly 6 paths from node A to node D that pass through nodes B and C. If you think this cannot be done, explain why.

6. If possible, design a network with nodes A, B, C, and D and exactly 5 paths from node A to node D that pass through nodes B and C. If you think this cannot be done, explain why.

Connections

7. Shelly wants to build a rectangular pen for her dog Sam. She has 24 meters of fencing.

a. Draw and label some rectangles that Shelly could form with the fencing.

b. What are the dimensions of the rectangle that would give Sam the greatest area in which to run?

c. How is this problem similar to part A of Problem 3.3?

8. In question 7, you explored rectangles that could be constructed from 24 meters of fencing.

a. Write an equation for the relationship between the length of one side of the rectangle and the area enclosed by the fencing.

b. Make a graph of the relationship between the length of one side of the rectangle and the area enclosed by the fencing.

c. What type of relationship do your graph and table represent? Explain how you know.

Extensions

9. The diagram below represents a grid of city streets. Officer Hansel is at point A when he gets a call about a crime in progress at point B.

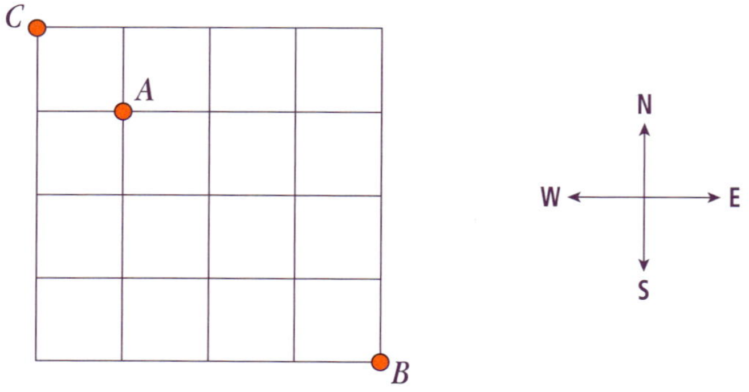

a. List five different shortest routes that Officer Hansel could take to the crime scene. Describe each route with a string of letters specifying one-block moves. For example, Officer Hansel could go east, then south, then south, then east, then south, and then east. You would indicate this by writing ESSESE.

b. How many different shortest routes are there? Explain.

c. Officer Valdez is at point C. How many different shortest routes could she take to the crime scene?

10. The diagram on the next page shows the routes a professor who lives in Detroit, Michigan, could take to the University of Windsor in Ontario, Canada.

a. Draw a simple network with nodes and edges to model this situation.

b. Use your network to find the number of possible routes from the professor's home to the university.

c. How many different routes could the professor take from the university to her home?

d. How many different round-trip routes could the professor make between her home and the university?

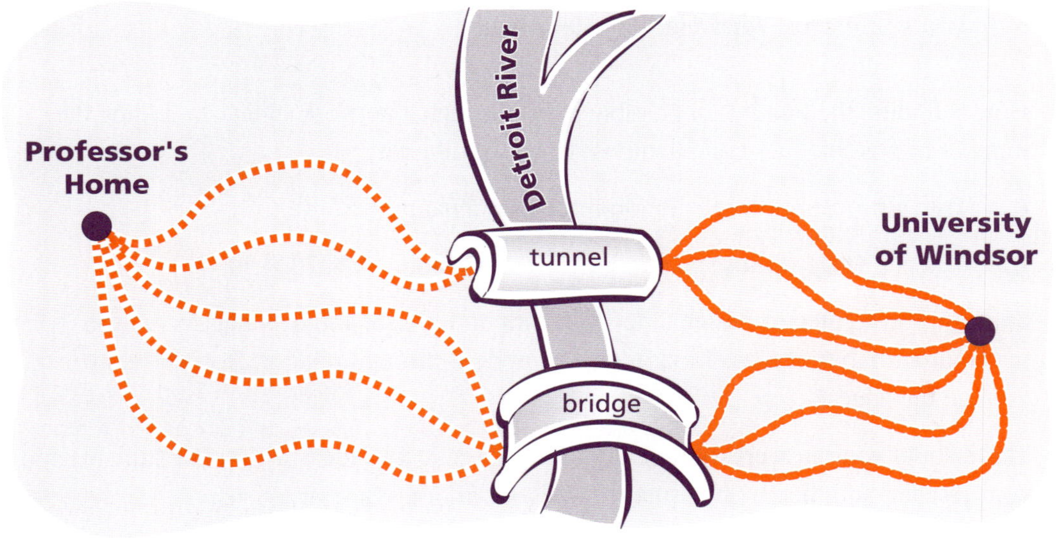

Mathematical Reflections

In this investigation, you explored the number of paths through given networks, and you designed networks that satisfied given conditions. These questions will help you summarize what you have learned:

1. How is finding the number of possible paths through a network similar to finding the number of possible lock combinations? How is it different?

2. **a.** Write a problem whose solution involves evaluating $5 \times 4 \times 3$.

   b. Write a problem whose solution involves evaluating $20 \times 20 \times 20$.

3. Suppose you wanted to design a network with nodes A, B, and C; n edges; and the maximum number of paths from node A to node C through node B. How should you arrange the edges?

Think about your answers to these questions, discuss your ideas with other students and your teacher, and then write a summary of your findings in your journal.

In your mystery story, what situation might you include that would require the detective to find the number of paths through a network?

INVESTIGATION 4

Deciding Whether Order Is Important

Detective Curious considered the possibility that the locker robbery may have taken place while the security guard and her friend were playing dominoes. She reasoned that they may have been so involved in their game that they would not have noticed a disturbance among the lockers.

4.1 Playing Dominoes

A domino is a rectangular tile divided into halves. On a standard *double-six* domino, each half contains from 0 to 6 dots, called *pips*. A complete set of dominoes contains one domino for each possible combination of halves.

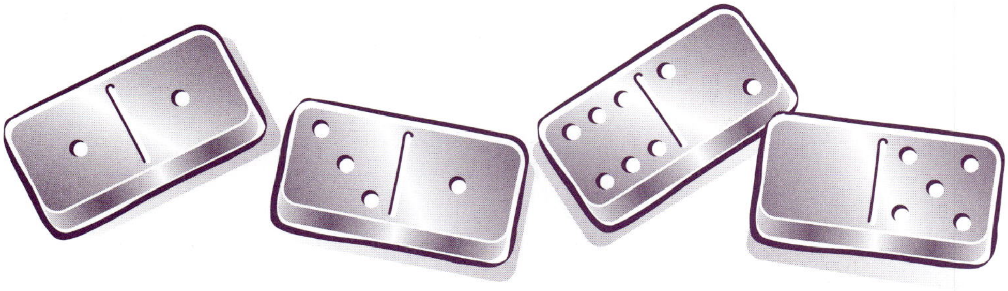

Problem 4.1

A. How many different dominoes are in a complete set?

B. The vending machines at Fail-Safe offer seven types of sandwiches and seven different drinks. The security guard wants to buy one sandwich and one drink. From how many combinations can she choose?

C. The security guard in a nearby storage warehouse can follow seven routes from checkpoint A to checkpoint B and seven routes from checkpoint B to checkpoint C. How many routes can he follow from checkpoint A to checkpoint C through checkpoint B?

D. Parts A–C each involve finding the number of ways to fill two positions when there are seven choices for each position. Compare the strategies you used to answer each part. How are the strategies similar? How are they different?

Problem 4.1 Follow-Up

1. a. Is it possible to arrange *all* the different dominoes in a chain so that adjacent halves match and the domino half that starts the chain matches the domino half that ends the chain? If it is possible to make such a chain, give an example of a chain that works.

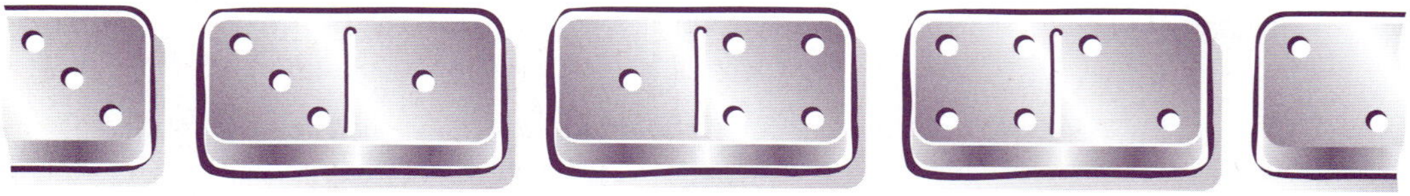

b. Is there more than one way to make such a domino chain? Explain.

2. How many pips are in a set of double-six dominoes?

4.2 Choosing Locks

When you first tried to find the number of dominoes in a set, you may have counted some dominoes twice. If you used number pairs to represent the dominoes, you may have counted both 1–2 and 2–1. Because 1–2 and 2–1 represent the same domino, you need to count only one of the pairs. In counting situations like this, *order is not important*.

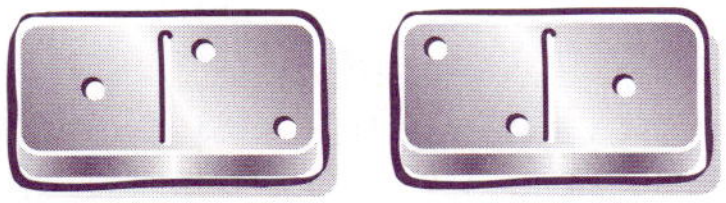

1–2 and 2–1 represent the same domino.

When you consider possible zip codes, however, 94601 *is* different from 19460. In this situation, *order is important*.

94601 and 19460 are zip codes for different cities

As you work on this problem and the follow-up questions, think carefully about whether the order of the choices is important.

Problem 4.2

After reviewing all he had learned about locks, the manager of Fail-Safe narrowed his choices to six models: the ACME CrimeStopper, the BurgleProof 2000, the Citadel, the Deterrent, the EverSafe, and the Fortress. He planned to bring samples of the locks to a meeting of Fail-Safe customers. Just before the meeting, he decided that offering so many choices would just confuse the customers. He chose two of the locks to bring to the meeting.

A. There are several ways the manager could have chosen the two locks. For example, he could have chosen the ACME CrimeStopper and the EverSafe. In how many different ways could the manager have chosen the two locks? Prove your answer is correct by listing all the possible pairs of locks.

B. If the manager had taken three locks to the meeting, in how many different ways could he have chosen them? Prove your answer is correct by listing all the possible sets of three locks.

C. How is finding the number of different ways the manager could have chosen the locks similar to and different from finding the number of lock combinations in Investigation 2?

Problem 4.2 Follow-Up

1. Six students are competing in the 100-meter dash. How many different arrangements of first-place, second-place, and third-place finishers are there?

2. How is question 1 similar to part B of Problem 4.2? How is it different?

Applications • Connections • Extensions

As you work on these ACE questions, use your calculator whenever you need it.

Applications

1. Suppose a special type of dominoes has from 0 to 8 pips on each half. How many different dominoes would be in a complete set?

2. Anya is forming a chain of double-six dominoes like the one described in Problem 4.1 Follow-Up. She started with the domino shown below. Now she must select a domino to connect to either side of this one. How many dominoes does she have to choose from? Remember, adjacent domino halves must match.

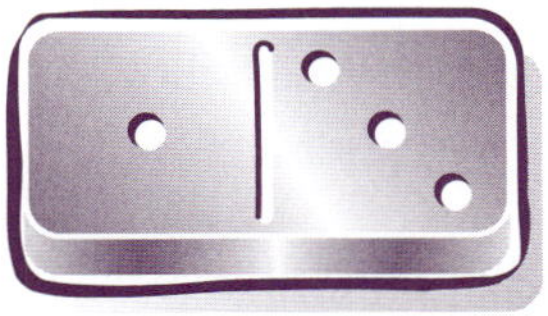

3. **a.** In how many different ways can two locks be chosen from a set of four locks?

b. In how many different ways can two locks be chosen from a set of five locks?

c. In how many different ways can two locks be chosen from a set of seven locks?

d. Look at your answers to parts a–c and Problem 4.2. Describe a pattern you could use to predict the number of different ways two locks can be chosen from a set of *n* locks.

Connections

4. Kyle just bought a new car. His friends Alexis, Bob, Carlos, Emile, and Frankie all want to ride with him to the football game, but he can take only three people with him.

a. Kyle decides to choose three friends by randomly drawing names. He writes the five names on slips of paper and puts them in his cap. In how many ways can he choose three of the five friends?

b. What is the probability that he will choose Alexis, Carlos, and Emile?

5. a. Al, Betty, and Conrado meet and shake hands. If each person shakes hands with everyone else, how many handshakes take place? Explain.

b. Al, Betty, Conrado, and Ezra meet and shake hands. If each person shakes hands with everyone else, how many handshakes take place? Explain.

c. Twenty people meet and shake hands. If each person shakes hands with everyone else, how many handshakes take place? Explain.

d. How is finding the number of handshakes exchanged among a group of people similar to finding the number of different dominoes in a set? How is it different?

e. How is finding the number of handshakes exchanged among a group of people similar to finding the number of two-number lock combinations? How is it different?

6. a. Before the championship match, the four members of the East High quiz-bowl team exchanged handshakes with the four members of the West High team. Each member of one team shook hands with each member of the other team. How many handshakes took place?

b. The seven members of the North High debate team shook hands with the seven members of the South High team. Each member of one team shook hands with each member of the other team. How many handshakes took place?

c. The nine members of the Miller Middle School swim team exchanged high fives with one another after Tuesday's meet. How many high fives took place?

d. Which of the problems in parts a–c is most similar to finding the number of different dominoes in a set? Explain your answer.

e. Which of the problems in parts a–c is most similar to finding the number of two-number combinations for a push-button lock with repeats allowed? Explain your answer.

7. Donae made a chart to help her find the number of different dominoes in a set.

	0	1	2	3	4	5	6
0	(0, 0)	(0, 1)	(0, 2)	(0, 3)	(0, 4)	(0, 5)	(0, 6)
1	(1, 0)	(1, 1)	(1, 2)	(1, 3)	(1, 4)	(1, 5)	(1, 6)
2	(2, 0)	(2, 1)	(2, 2)	(2, 3)	(2, 4)	(2, 5)	(2, 6)
3	(3, 0)	(3, 1)	(3, 2)	(3, 3)	(3, 4)	(3, 5)	(3, 6)
4	(4, 0)	(4, 1)	(4, 2)	(4, 3)	(4, 4)	(4, 5)	(4, 6)
5	(5, 0)	(5, 1)	(5, 2)	(5, 3)	(5, 4)	(5, 5)	(5, 6)
6	(6, 0)	(6, 1)	(6, 2)	(6, 3)	(6, 4)	(6, 5)	(6, 6)

a. What do the number pairs on the diagonal represent?

b. Do (2, 3) and (3, 2) represent the same domino or different dominoes?

c. How are the dominoes represented by pairs *above* the diagonal related to the dominoes represented by pairs *below* the diagonal?

d. Explain how you could use the chart to find the number of different dominoes in a set.

e. Write a general equation for the number of different dominoes, d, in a set if each domino has from 0 to n pips on each half.

8. The chart in question 7 can also represent the number of handshakes exchanged among a group of seven people. Use this interpretation of the chart to answer parts a–d.

a. What do the number pairs on the diagonal represent?

b. What do the pairs (2, 3) and (3, 2) represent?

c. How many different handshakes are represented in the chart? Explain.

d. Write a general equation for the number of handshakes, h, exchanged among n people.

9. Kari drew this diagram to help her visualize the problem of counting the dominoes in a set of double-six dominoes. The diagram leads to a general equation for the number of different dominoes, d, in a set if each domino has from 0 to n pips on each half.

Diagram

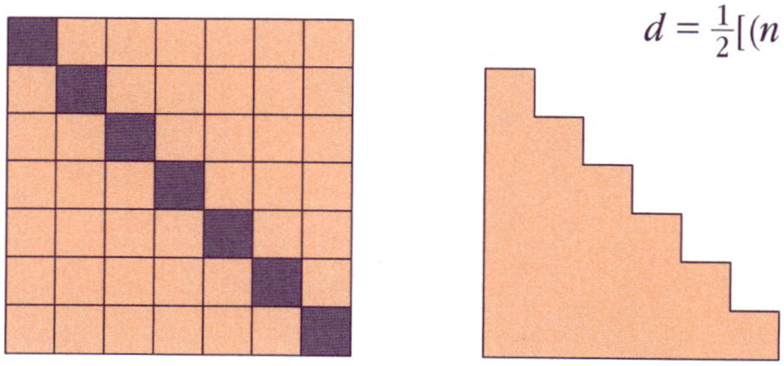

General Equation

$$d = \frac{1}{2}[(n + 1)^2 - (n + 1)] + n + 1$$

a. How might Kari have been thinking about the problem?

b. Explain how her diagram leads to the general equation.

c. Describe the shape of the graph of the general equation.

Extensions

In 10–14, use the following information: The tiles in the Tri-Ominoes® game are shaped like triangles. Each corner of a tile contains the number 0, 1, 2, 3, 4, or 5. A Tri-Ominoes game contains a tile for every combination of three numbers.

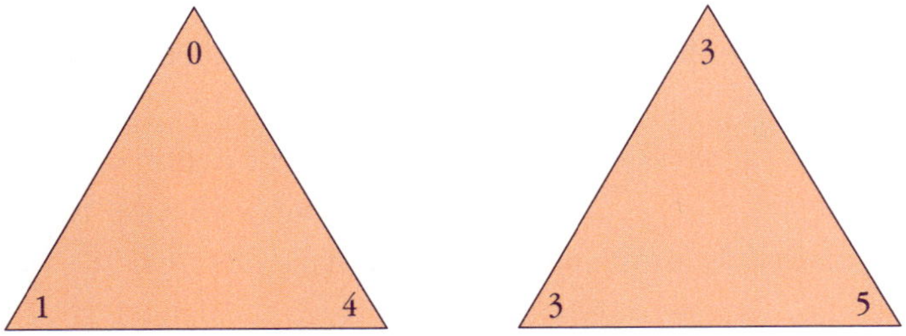

10. How many tiles contain exactly two 1s? Explain how you found your answer.

11. How many tiles contain exactly one 1? Explain how you found your answer.

12. How many tiles contain at least one 1? Explain how you found your answer.

13. How many tiles contain at least one 2? Explain how you found your answer.

14. Find the error in this argument: There are 21 Tri-Ominoes tiles that contain 1s. There must also be 21 tiles that contain 0s, 21 tiles that contain 2s, 21 tiles that contain 3s, and so on. So, the total number of tiles must be 6×21, or 126.

Mathematical Reflections

In this investigation, you found the number of dominoes in a set and the number of ways a given number of locks can be chosen from a set of six locks. You discovered that in these counting situations, order is not important. These questions will help you summarize what you have learned:

1. **a.** In some counting situations, order is important. For example, when counting possible lock combinations, 2-3-4 is different from 3-4-2. Give two more examples of counting situations in which order is important.

   b. Explain why order is important in your examples.

2. **a.** In some counting situations, order is not important. For example, when counting combinations of pizza toppings, a mushroom-and-onion pizza is the same as an onion-and-mushroom pizza. Give two more examples of counting situations in which order is not important.

   b. Explain why order is not important in your examples.

Think about your answers to these questions, discuss your ideas with other students and your teacher, and then write a summary of your findings in your journal.

In your mystery story, what counting situations might your detective encounter in which order is not important?

INVESTIGATION 5

Wrapping Things Up

In the previous investigations, you learned techniques for solving counting problems. In this investigation, you will use what you have learned to help Detective Curious investigate a second robbery.

5.1 Catching a Bicycle Thief

Detective Curious was narrowing in on a suspect when another robbery took place at Fail-Safe. The detective was called to the scene on the morning the second burglary was discovered. During her investigation, she gathered the following information:

- Three mountain bikes were stolen from a locker rented by Bagged Bikes, Inc. The locker has a push-button lock with five buttons.
- The warehouse manager suspects that the night security guard committed the crime. The guard was on duty alone for several hours the night of the robbery. The guard claims she is innocent.
- There is an emergency exit at the end of the aisle in which Bagged Bikes' locker is located. The detective discovered tape over the latch of the exit, which prevented the door from closing properly.
- When the detective went to the manager's home to question him, she noticed a new mountain bike just inside his apartment door. The bike was the same model as one of the stolen bikes. The manager pointed out that mountain bikes are very popular and that many people own them.

- When the owner of Bagged Bikes checked the serial numbers for the stolen bikes, she found that the records had been smudged. She knew that each serial number consisted of three letters followed by six numbers, but she could read only the first two letters and the last four numbers of each.

Model	Serial number
Rocky Road	UM[illegible]3245
Trail Blazer	UM[illegible]4397
Rugged Rider	UM[illegible]7711

Problem 5.1

You know as much as the detective does about counting combinations and calculating probabilities. Imagine that the detective asks you to help her with the case.

A. Which pieces of evidence would you investigate further? How would you proceed with your investigation?

B. What questions would you ask the security guard, the manager, or someone else involved in the case?

C. Does the evidence from the second robbery clear any of the suspects? Who are your suspects now? Why?

Problem 5.1 Follow-Up

1. a. One of the smudged serial numbers was UM _ _ _ 7711. The first blank represents a letter, and the other two blanks represent numbers. In how many ways can this serial number be completed?

b. The bike at the manager's home had the serial number UMZ567711. Based on your findings from part a, can you draw any conclusions about the manager's guilt or innocence? Explain.

2. a. Assume that all mountain bikes have serial numbers with three letters followed by six numbers. How many possible combinations are there for the first two letters and the last four numbers of the serial number for a mountain bike?

b. What are the chances that the serial number on the manager's bike would contain the sequence UM_ _ _ 7711?

c. Based on your findings, can you draw any conclusions about the manager's guilt or innocence? Explain.

Applications • Connections • Extensions

As you work on these ACE questions, use your calculator whenever you need it.

Applications

1. Detective Curious took her team of detectives out for ice cream. The ice cream shop offers 12 flavors of ice cream.

A single scoop of ice cream costs \$1.25, and two scoops cost \$1.75. A cup or a sugar cone is included in the price of the ice cream; a waffle cone is 25¢ extra.

a. How many different one-scoop orders are possible?

b. How many different \$2 orders are possible?

c. How many different \$1.75 orders are possible?

In 2–6, use this information: To keep data on computer networks secure, many computer systems require users to enter a password.

2. If a computer system accepts only three-digit passwords, such as 314 or 007, how many passwords are possible?

3. If a computer system accepts only passwords consisting of one letter followed by three numbers, such as Z300 and E271, how many passwords are possible?

4. If a computer system accepts only two-letter passwords, such as AZ and CC, how many passwords are possible?

5. If a computer system accepts only passwords consisting of two letters followed by three numbers, such as AB123 and LP333, how many passwords are possible?

6. The computer system at Jamie's school accepts only six-character passwords. A password may be all letters, all numbers, or a combination of numbers and letters. For example, A23BC7 and JTFEY1 are possible passwords. Jamie forgot his password and is attempting to log onto the system by guessing six-character sequences. How many such combinations are possible?

Connections

7. Akili, Beatrice, Consuelo, and David eat lunch together every day.

a. Use the letters A, B, C, and D to represent the students. List all the possible orders in which the four students could stand in the lunch line.

b. Make a counting tree for finding all the possible orders in which the four students could stand in the lunch line. How many paths are there through the branches of your tree?

c. If Elena joined the students for lunch, in how many possible orders could the five students stand in line?

8. When counting two-choice combinations, it often helps to make a chart like the one below. Detective Curious made this chart to help her assign tasks to her detectives. The names of the detectives are listed across the top of the chart, and the tasks are listed along the side. Each box in the chart represents a possible assignment. The mark indicates that Clouseau has been assigned the task of gathering descriptions.

	Clouseau	Hercule	Jane	Sherlock	Jessica
determining lock combinations					
investigating license plates					
conducting interviews					
gathering descriptions	✓				
researching phone numbers					

a. In how many ways can Detective Curious make the assignments if each detective is to have a different task?

b. What other method could you use to count the possible ways to assign the tasks?

c. Would this type of chart be useful for counting the number of different faces a police artist could draw by combining eye, nose, hair, and mouth attributes? Explain.

d. Would this type of chart be useful for counting the number of possible three-number lock combinations? Explain.

9. Mr. Saari makes a chart each semester for recording grades. He writes student names down the left column of the chart, and lists assignments, tests, quizzes, and projects along the top.

	Q1	Q2	Test 1	Proj 1
L. Alavosus	18	24	85	93
D. Alvarez	23	21	81	100
N. Chan	21	15	92	89

a. Next semester, Mr. Saari plans to give 5 quizzes, 3 tests, 10 homework assignments, and 3 projects. How many columns will he need to record all the scores?

b. If Mr. Saari has 28 students, how many score boxes will be filled at the end of the semester? Assume he will record a 0 for any missed or incomplete assignment, quiz, test, or project.

c. **i.** If Mr. Saari has 35 students, how many score boxes will be filled at the end of the semester?

ii. Would adding one student or adding one test cause the greater increase in the number of score boxes filled?

10. Write a problem that could be answered by using this counting tree. Copy the counting tree, and label it to represent the solution to your problem.

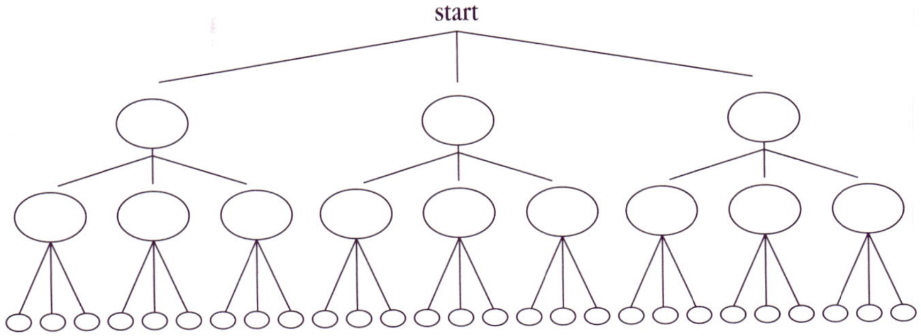

11. Write a problem that could be answered by using this counting tree. Copy the counting tree, and label it to represent the solution to your problem.

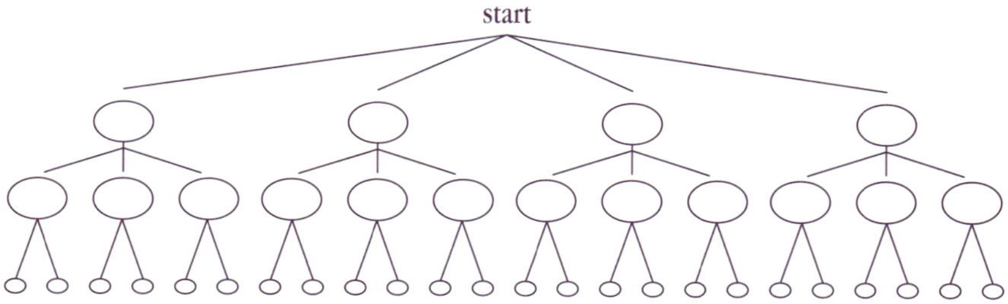

Extensions

In 12–16, use this information: In North America, a telephone number consists of a three-digit *area code,* followed by a three-digit *prefix,* followed by four more digits. For example, the telephone number of the White House in Washington, D.C., is (202) 456-1111.

(202) 456-1111

area code prefix

The first digit of an area code and the first digit of a prefix must be greater than or equal to 2.

12. How many telephone numbers with an area code of 500 are possible?

13. Toll-free telephone numbers have an area code of 800 or 888. How many toll-free telephone numbers are possible?

14. How many telephone numbers with the same area code and prefix as your telephone number are possible?

15. How many different U.S. telephone numbers are possible?

16. Telephone numbers mentioned in television shows and movies have the prefix 555. No actual phone numbers have this prefix. If you exclude phone numbers with the prefix 555, how many different U.S. phone numbers are possible?

Did you know?

As people within a particular area code add telephone lines for computer modems, fax machines, and cellular phones, more and more telephone numbers are needed. When all the possible numbers for an area code are taken, a new area code must be instituted. Until recently, all area codes started with digits from 2 to 9 and had 0 or 1 as the second digit. Now area codes can be any three-digit combination with a first digit greater than or equal to 2 except 411, 611, and 911.

17. A traveling salesman is trying to plan the least expensive route for visiting his customers. He needs to stop in ten cities on his trip. He can visit the cities in any order, but he doesn't want to visit the same city twice. He decides to list the cities in every possible order and then check the travel costs for each possibility.

a. Do you think the salesman's plan of figuring out the cost for each possibility is a good one? Explain.

b. Do you think a counting tree would help the salesman with his plan? Explain.

Mathematical Reflections

In this unit, you learned techniques for counting the number of ways a group of choices can be made or a set of positions can be filled. These questions will help you summarize what you have learned:

1. Identify the choices or positions involved in each counting problem.

   a. finding the number of faces the police artist could draw (Problem 1.1)

   b. finding the number of license plates with three letters followed by three numbers (Problem 1.2)

   c. finding the number of three-number lock combinations (Problem 2.2)

   d. finding the number of paths through a network (Problem 3.2)

   e. finding the number of dominoes in a set (Problem 4.1)

2. State a rule or rules for finding the number of ways a group of choices could be made or a set of positions could be filled.

3. Explain how you can find the number of possibilities represented by a counting tree without counting the last set of branches.

4. A particular counting problem involves making three choices in order. There are a options for the first choice, b options for the second choice, and c options for the third choice. Explain how you would find the number of possible combinations of options.

Think about your answers to these questions, discuss your ideas with other students and your teacher, and then write a summary of your findings in your journal.

Describe how the detective in your story might use charts, graphs, or counting trees to explain his or her solution.

The Unit Project

Complete one of the projects described below.

Project 1: Writing a Detective Story

Throughout this unit, you have been recording ideas for a mystery story. Use your ideas to write a story about a detective's investigation of a crime. Your story should include some of the following:

- a cast of suspicious characters
- a detective with mathematical ability and an assistant who always needs explanations
- a lock combination
- a getaway vehicle
- different getaway routes
- a partially legible telephone number found at the scene of the crime

Your story must show the detective doing the following:

- counting combinations
- figuring out how long it would take to make, do, or check something
- using probability to show what is likely or unlikely to have happened
- using charts, graphs, or counting trees to explain his or her solution

Project 2: Making Trains

In this project, you will make "trains" by joining "cars" of different lengths. A "car" is a rectangular strip of paper; a "train" is one car or two or more cars placed end-to-end. You will find the cars on Labsheet UP. Each car is labeled with a number that indicates its length in centimeters.

For each different car, find every possible train you can make with the same length as that car. Consider trains made from the same cars, but in a different order, to be different. This means that a 1-car followed by a 2-car is different from a 2-car followed by a 1-car. The drawing below shows the four trains that can be made with the same length as a 3-car.

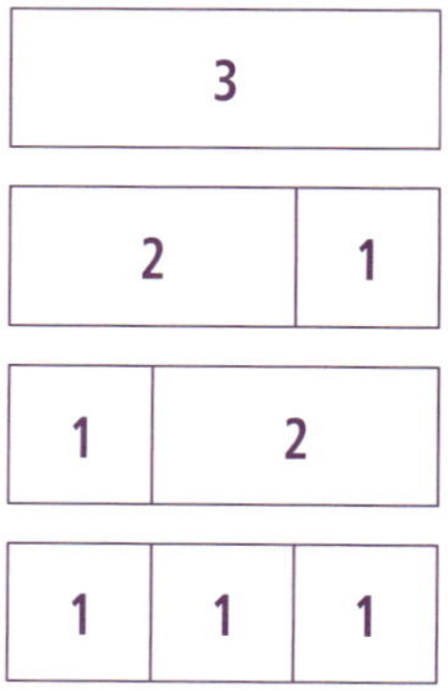

For each different car on the labsheet, record the length of the car and the number of trains with the same length as that car. Look for a pattern in your results. Write an equation for the relationship between the length of a car, *L,* and the number of trains with that length, *N.* Compare the pattern of change and the equation for this situation with the patterns and equations for other situations you have studied in this unit.

Write a paper two or three pages in length summarizing your findings.

Looking Back and Looking Ahead

Unit Reflections

Working on the problems of this unit, you have learned strategies for counting the possibilities in complex situations. You learned how to recognize problems where *counting* techniques apply and how to use diagrams and tables to find patterns in counting tasks. You learned how to analyze and count paths through networks. Most important of all, you learned how to apply thinking and reasoning skills in problem situations and how to provide persuasive arguments to support your proposed solutions.

Using Combinatorial Reasoning—To test your understanding and skill in work with counting techniques, consider the following questions about activity in a Summer Creative Arts Camp.

1. *Pat visited the camp's library and decided to select one book by each of these authors:*

   J.K. Rowling books: Harry Potter and the Sorcerer's Stone, Harry Potter and the Prisoner of Azkaban, Harry Potter and the Chamber of Secrets, *and* Harry Potter and the Goblet of Fire;

   Charles Dickens books: Great Expectations, Oliver Twist, *and* David Copperfield;

   Mildred Taylor books: Let the Circle Be Unbroken *and* Roll of Thunder, Hear My Cry.

   a. How many different sets of books could Pat choose? Draw a counting tree that shows the selection possibilities.

   b. How many sets of books are possible if Pat chooses to read *Harry Potter and the Chamber of Secrets* as the J.K. Rowling selection?

   c. Suppose Pat chooses *Prisoner of Azkaban, Oliver Twist, and Let the Circle Be Unbroken.* In how many orders could Pat read the books, if he chose to read them one at a time?

2. *Each book in the Summer Creative Arts Camp library is coded using a pattern with groups of letters and digits like "XAN-MP-18." The first three letters identify the author. The next two letters identify the title. The last two digits identify the copy number.*

a. How many author codes are available?

b. How many title codes are available for each author?

c. How many copy codes are available for each author-title combination?

d. How many book codes are available for the library?

3 *The Creative Arts Camp is held at a university in Pat's hometown. Pat travels by bike to the library and then takes a bus to the university. There are three bike paths from Pat's home to the library and two public buses that travel from the library to the university.*

a. How many different routes can Pat take from home to the university? How many from the university to Pat's home?

b. During the second week of the program, Pat learned that the university has its own shuttle that carries passengers from the library to the university with no stops in between. How many routes are available from Pat's home to the university if that shuttle is used?

4 *The Summer Creative Arts Camp offers classes in drama, music, creative writing, reading, photography, and painting. There are four class periods each day.*

a. How many different class schedules are possible for the campers if no subject is taken more than once in a day?

b. If all students take reading as their first class, how many class schedules are possible?

5 *At the end of the summer camp, students submit their work for judging by the camp teachers. Prizes are awarded for first, second, and third place in each of the six subject areas. There are 60 students attending the camp, and 10 are from Pat's school.*

a. In how many ways could students from Pat's school win all three prizes in drama?

b. In how many ways could the top two prizes in photography be awarded to students who are *not* from Pat's school?

c. If one student is randomly selected to win a book signed by his or her favorite contemporary author, what is the probability that the lucky student will be from Pat's school? What is the probability that the lucky student will *not* be from Pat's school?

Explaining Your Reasoning—To solve the problems about activities at the Summer Creative Arts Camp, you needed to use counting strategies. When you use such mathematical calculations to solve a problem or make a decision, it is important to be able to justify each step in your reasoning.

1. What general counting idea is needed to answer questions such as those in Problems 1–5, without simply listing all possibilities? How could you use a diagram to persuade someone that the counting idea is correct?

2. How is the general counting technique adjusted for questions where

a. the order of action or selection matters or doesn't matter?

b. repeats are not allowed?

The counting ideas and techniques used in this unit will be applied and extended in future mathematics classes and in other work on problems of science and mathematics, especially those that involve probability. Clever counting will often help you figure out the number of possible actions in a situation that at first may seem very complex.

Glossary

counting tree A diagram that shows all the possible ways a set of choices—each with one or more options—can be made. The counting tree below shows the possible three-number lock sequences for a push-button lock with three buttons—labeled 1, 2, and 3—if repeated numbers are not allowed.

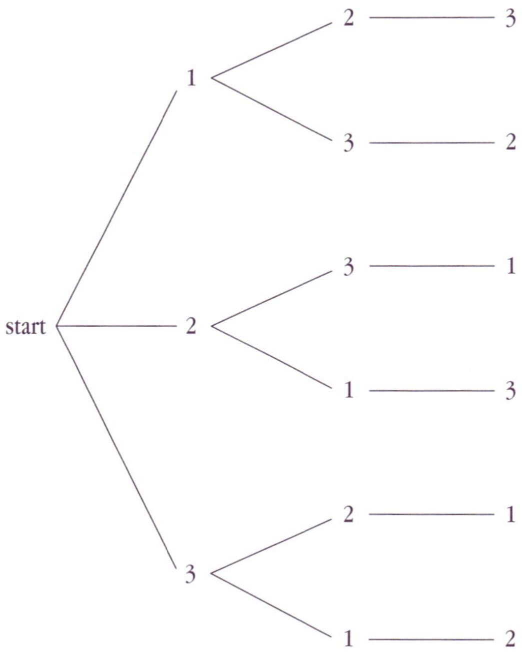

network A collection of points, or nodes, connected by edges. The network on the left has two nodes and three edges. The network on the right has four nodes and five edges. In this unit, you found the number of paths through a network. For example, in the network on the right, there are four paths from node A to node D.

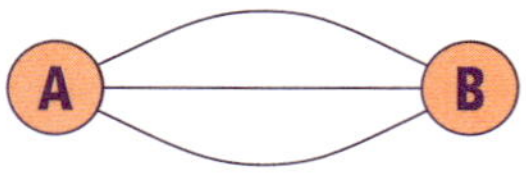

Glosario

diagrama de árbol Un diagrama que muestra todas las formas posibles en que se puede hacer un conjunto de selecciones (cada una con una o más opciones). El siguiente diagrama de árbol muestra las secuencias posibles de combinaciones de tres números para una cerradura de tres botones (con los números 1, 2 y 3) en donde no se pueden repetir los números.

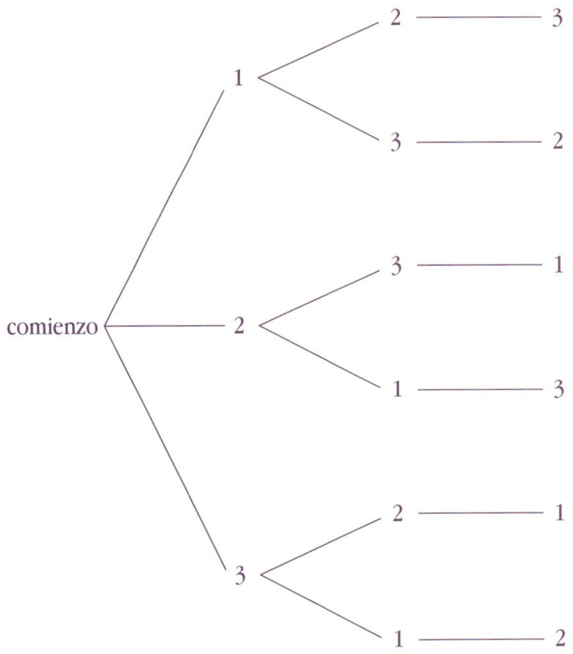

red Un conjunto de puntos, o nodos, unidos por bordes. La red de la izquierda tiene dos nodos y tres bordes. La red de la derecha tiene cuatro nodos y cinco bordes. En esta unidad hallaste el número de caminos a través de una red. En la red de la derecha, por ejemplo, hay cuatro caminos desde el nodo A hasta el nodo D.

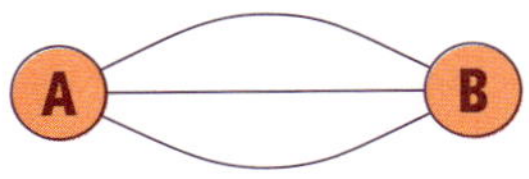

Index